Trade and Employment
in Developing Countries

1   Individual Studies

Trade and Employment in Developing Countries

National Bureau of Economic Research

Trade and Employment in Developing Countries

1 Individual Studies

Edited by **Anne O. Krueger, Hal B. Lary, Terry Monson, and Narongchai Akrasanee**

The University of Chicago Press

Chicago and London

ANNE O. KRUEGER is director of this study and professor of economics at the University of Minnesota. She was joint director of the NBER study *Foreign Trade Regimes and Economic Development*; author of the NBER volumes *Turkey* and *Liberalization Attempts and Consequences*; and author of *The Benefits and Costs of Import Substitution in India*. HAL B. LARY is recently retired as vice-president for research of the NBER and is the author of *Imports of Manufactures from Less Developed Countries*. TERRY MONSON is professor of economics at the School of Business, Michigan Technological University. NARONGCHAI AKRASANEE is director of the Asian and Pacific Development Institute, Bangkok.

The University of Chicago Press, Chicago 60637
The University of Chicago Press, Ltd., London

HD
5852
,T7
vol. I

Library of Congress Cataloging in Publication Data
Main entry under title:

Trade and employment in developing countries.

"[Results] from the research project sponsored by the National Bureau of Economic Research on alternate trade strategies and employment."
  Includes index.
  CONTENTS: v. 1. Individual studies.
  1. Underdeveloped areas—Foreign trade and employment—Case studies. I. Krueger, Anne O. II. National Bureau of Economic Research.
  HD5852.T7   331.12'09172'4   80–15826
  ISBN 0-226-45492-4 (v. 1)

Dec. 85

Relation of the Directors to the
Work and Publications of the
National Bureau of Economic Research

1. The object of the National Bureau of Economic Research is to ascertain and to present to the public important economic facts and their interpretation in a scientific and impartial manner. The Board of Directors is charged with the responsibility of ensuring that the work of the National Bureau is carried on in strict conformity with this object.

2. The President of the National Bureau shall submit to the Board of Directors, or to its Executive Committee, for their formal adoption all specific proposals for research to be instituted.

3. No research report shall be published by the National Bureau until the President has sent each member of the Board a notice that a manuscript is recommended for publication and that in the President's opinion it is suitable for publication in accordance with the principles of the National Bureau. Such notification will include an abstract or summary of the manuscript's content and a response form for use by those Directors who desire a copy of the manuscript for review. Each manuscript shall contain a summary drawing attention to the nature and treatment of the problem studied, the character of the data and their utilization in the report, and the main conclusions reached.

4. For each manuscript so submitted, a special committee of the Directors (including Directors Emeriti) shall be appointed by majority agreement of the President and Vice Presidents (or by the Executive Committee in case of inability to decide on the part of the President and Vice Presidents), consisting of three Directors selected as nearly as may be one from each general division of the Board. The names of the special manuscript committee shall be stated to each Director when notice of the proposed publication is submitted to him. It shall be the duty of each member of the special manuscript committee to read the manuscript. If each member of the manuscript committee signifies his approval within thirty days of the transmittal of the manuscript, the report may be published. If at the end of that period any member of the manuscript committee withholds his approval, the President shall then notify each member of the Board, requesting approval or disapproval of publication, and thirty days additional shall be granted for this purpose. The manuscript shall then not be published unless at least a majority of the entire Board who shall have voted on the proposal within the time fixed for the receipt of votes shall have approved.

5. No manuscript may be published, though approved by each member of the special manuscript committee, until forty-five days have elapsed from the transmittal of the report in manuscript form. The interval is allowed for the receipt of any memorandum of dissent or reservation, together with a brief statement of his reasons, that any member may wish to express; and such memorandum of dissent or reservation shall be published with the manuscript if he so desires. Publication does not, however, imply that each member of the Board has read the manuscript, or that either members of the Board in general or the special committee have passed on its validity in every detail.

6. Publications of the National Bureau issued for informational purposes concerning the work of the Bureau and its staff, or issued to inform the public of activities of Bureau staff, and volumes issued as a result of various conferences involving the National Bureau shall contain a specific disclaimer noting that such publication has not passed through the normal review procedures required in this resolution. The Executive Committee of the Board is charged with review of all such publications from time to time to ensure that they do not take on the character of formal research reports of the National Bureau, requiring formal Board approval.

7. Unless otherwise determined by the Board or exempted by the terms of paragraph 6, a copy of this resolution shall be printed in each National Bureau publication.

(Resolution adopted October 25, 1926, as revised through September 30, 1974)

Contents

Editors' Preface

This is the first of three volumes emanating from the research project on alternative trade strategies and employment sponsored by the National Bureau of Economic Research. The basic question underlying the entire project has been, What links are there, if any, between a developing country's policies toward international trade and its ability to create enough jobs to employ its population? The question has many aspects, including as it does both policies concerning the trade and payments regime and also policies concerning domestic labor and capital markets.

A brief description of the history of the project and its organization is given in the introductory chapter. A first phase focused upon delineating research methods and concepts that could be used in the project. The second phase then entailed research on individual countries and their experience with trade strategies and employment in light of the methods and concepts that had been developed. A final phase entails an analysis of the findings that emerge from the entire project.

This volume presents the results of ten individual country studies that were undertaken in the context of a common framework of analysis (although flexible, given the different situations encountered with regard to policies and data).

Two subsequent volumes will deal with research findings, focusing upon supply response and factor substitution, and provide a synthesis of the project results. The countries covered in the project and in this volume are: Brazil, Chile, Colombia, Indonesia, the Ivory Coast, Pakistan, South Korea, Thailand, Tunisia, and Uruguay. Each author (or authors) was already knowledgeable about the circumstances of his particular country, and also about prior research and data availability, before the start of the project. Each was invited to undertake a study of the trade strategies–employment relationship in his country in the context of the project. The editors believe NBER was fortunate in persuading such a highly qualified and competent group of authors to undertake the studies of the individual countries.

The United States Agency for International Development provided the major source of financing for the project. In addition, individual authors received support for their research from institutions in their home countries.

The country authors have contributed to the intellectual development of the entire project. In addition, researchers focusing upon particular aspects of the relationship between trade strategies and employment, whose papers will appear in the second volume, contributed greatly to the overall development of the project. We are indebted to Jere R. Behrman, James M. Henderson, Robert Lipsey, and T. Paul Schultz for their many valuable contributions, both in working parties of project participants and in commenting upon individual country studies.

Constantine Michalopoulos, Keith Jay, and Peter Allgeier of the United States Agency for International Development contributed valuable suggestions and comments at various stages of the research. Larry E. Westphal read and made extensive comments upon the entire manuscript once it was assembled. The manuscript is vastly improved thanks to his painstaking work.

Delma Burns, with the assistance first of Marlyn Hilario and then of Dennis Graves, was invaluable in typing the manuscript, assembling authors' corrections and comments, and generally coordinating the flow of information between the country authors and the editors. To all these individuals, we are grateful.

> Anne O. Krueger, Hal B. Lary, Terry Monson,
> and Narongchai Akrasanee

1   The Framework of the Country Studies

Anne O. Krueger

This is the first of three planned volumes from the National Bureau of Economic Research project on alternative trade strategies and employment. It presents the major results from ten studies of individual countries' experience with their trade and payments strategy—in particular, the degree of emphasis on export promotion relative to import substitution—and the implications alternative strategies have for employment.

The country studies were undertaken within a common framework. We hope that the comparability among them (though still imperfect owing to data limitations and differences in experience) will add a dimension of interest to the studies. Nonetheless, each country's experience is of interest in its own right. The country findings are designed to "stand alone" in the sense of being self-contained analyses of value for understanding the individual economy.

Two subsequent volumes will explore some of the findings that emerge from systematic evaluation of the experience of the individual countries. The second volume will contain a series of essays on particular aspects of the relationship between trade strategy and employment, while the third will provide an overall analysis of the relationship and of the results of the individual studies viewed all together. The reader interested in a full discussion of the underlying theory or in an interpretation of the comparative results across countries is referred to those volumes.

This chapter will provide background information about the common framework within which the country studies were undertaken, including a few particulars about the history of the project, a sketch of the underlying theory upon which empirical analysis was based, and a definition of the concepts used by all the country authors in carrying out their

Anne O. Krueger is associated with the University of Minnesota.

analyses. The purpose is not to provide an extensive review of the theory, but rather to enable this volume to be utilized independently, while avoiding the need for each author to repeat the underlying theory, definitions, and concepts necessary for a statement and interpretation of his results.

1.1 The Project

During the late 1960s and early 1970s, disillusionment with the import substitution strategy and its results was increasing. Contributing to this trend were both the results of research on the effects of the strategy[1] and the remarkable increases in growth rates experienced by some of the countries that had shifted to an export promotion strategy. Simultaneously with that disillusionment, however, came a fundamental questioning of the adequacy of economic growth itself as an objective. Many observers began doubting the degree to which economic growth had resulted in increased employment opportunities and higher living standards for the majority within the developing countries.

A natural question, but one that was not addressed, was the extent to which the unfavorable results with respect to employment and income distribution had themselves originated from the policies adopted to encourage import substitution. Failure to investigate this possible linkage was all the more surprising in light of the implications of the fundamental Heckscher-Ohlin-Samuelson (HOS) model of international trade so widely used in international economics, and the questions that had earlier been raised by Wassily Leontief (1968) in his famous Leontief paradox. For, if the HOS model were valid, and if developing countries were labor-abundant, their failure to encourage export growth would naturally and directly affect the demand for labor. However, findings from empirical studies for a variety of countries following Leontief were not sufficiently uniform and comprehensive to permit any conclusions, and considerable doubt remained about the validity of the HOS predictions.[2]

Moreover, early evidence from two countries—Brazil and Colombia—that had switched trade strategies suggested that emerging exports might be capital-intensive. Noteworthy in particular was Diaz's conclusion regarding Colombia that "it would be a mistake to assume that all these [nontraditional] exports are made up of labor-intensive commodities."[3]

The NBER project on alternative trade strategies and employment was designed to analyze the implications for labor markets of alternative trade strategies and also to examine the effect of different institutional arrangements in labor markets on factor proportions in trade. It was felt that if studies were undertaken for a number of developing countries within a common framework, the results would provide considerable insight into the links between trade strategy choices and the development of employment opportunities.

1.1.1   Project Participants and Procedures

From the outset it was recognized that the project would necessarily entail several phases. The first phase was to provide a formal statement of the empirical implications of a multicountry, multicommodity model of international trade. This was done in Krueger (1977).

The next step was to identify economists knowledgeable about individual countries who would be interested and willing to undertake studies and to develop, in cooperation with those economists, a set of concepts, definitions, and research goals. This was done partly through correspondence, with the aid of a draft working paper, and was completed after a conference of project participants during which the various concepts and definitions discussed in the draft were amended and agreed upon.[4]

The countries, country authors, and their affiliations are as follows.[5]

Brazil: José L. Carvalho and Cláudio L. S. Haddad, Fundação Getúlio Vargas, Rio de Janeiro.

Chile: Vittorio Corbo, International Institute of Quantitative Economics, Montreal; and Patricio Meller, Corporacion de Investigaciones Economicas para Latinamerica, Santiago.

Colombia: Francisco E. Thoumi, Inter-American Development Bank.

Indonesia: Mark M. Pitt, University of Minnesota.

Ivory Coast: Terry Monson, Michigan Technological University.

Pakistan: Stephen Guisinger, University of Texas at Dallas.

South Korea: Wontack Hong, then of the Korean Development Institute, now of Seoul University.

Thailand: Narongchai Akrasanee, Thammasat University, Bangkok.

Tunisia: Mustapha K. Nabli, Faculté de Droit des Sciences Politiques et Economiques, Tunis.

Uruguay: Alberto Bension and Jorge Caumont, Universidad de la Republica, Montevideo.

The NBER was extremely fortunate in that a group of economists had been planning to undertake research on an almost identical topic under the auspices of the Center for Asian Manpower Studies. Three of them— Narongchai Akrasanee of Thammasat University, Wontack Hong, then of the Korean Development Institute, and Kuo-Shu Liang, deputy governor of the Bank of Taiwan—attended the first working party, and Akrasanee and Hong participated throughout the project and are contributors to this volume.

As arrangements were being made for the country studies, it was recognized that problems were likely to arise in particular fields—such as labor markets and the nature of substitution possibilities—while some research along cross-country lines would complement the work of the country authors. Jere Behrman, University of Pennsylvania, agreed to work on production functions and substitution possibilities; James M. Henderson, University of Minnesota, developed optimizing trade models for the individual countries; Robert Lipsey, Queens College and National Bureau of Economic Research, analyzed factor substitution by multinational corporations; and T. Paul Schultz, Yale University, focused on income distribution implications of the structure of effective protection and on labor markets. These individuals participated in the working parties and have been valuable consultants to some of the country authors when particular issues in their areas of competence have arisen. The results of their research, along with papers on special topics emanating from some of the country studies, will be found in the second volume of this series.

After the first working party, held in December 1975, individual country analysts began carrying out their own research plans, amending the uniform procedures as necessary in light of their countries' particular circumstances and data availability. At the midpoint in the research a second working party was held, in September 1976, at which authors presented preliminary results, discussed common problems, and raised new questions. Finally, research on the country studies has been completed and the major findings are presented in this volume. Not all results from each study are given here, however, because of limitations of space. In many instances the research findings are sufficiently rich so that monographs have resulted that will be separately published.

Coverage of Country Studies

Among other differences between countries, the amount of prior research available has been a significant determinant of the emphasis of the research undertaken by individual authors. Some countries, such as Chile, have been subject to numerous earlier investigations, so that a data base, as well as an analysis of the trade regime itself, was already at hand. In those cases, the authors were able to delve extensively into particular aspects of the relation between trade strategy and employment, including such areas as substitution possibilities and the extent of factor market imperfections. For other countries, little prior research had been done on even the most basic of topics, and the authors had to concentrate their efforts there. Such was the case with Indonesia, where no prior estimates existed of effective rates of protection for different industries, and with Uruguay, where data had to be obtained from individual records.

In addition to differences in the amount of prior research and in data availability, countries have differed significantly both in their choice of trade strategy and in underlying factor market conditions. These factors, too, have influenced the focus of individual country authors' efforts in analyzing their countries' experience.

Although individual differences would significantly influence the thrust of research efforts, country authors nonetheless examined and analyzed a common range of questions. They were asked to identify a particular period for which the necessary data were available, to trace the major characteristics of the trade and payments regime for that period that were likely to influence the commodity composition of trade and the factor proportions in traded goods industries, and to gather data on employment per unit of value added in different industries. From these data, estimates were made of the net factor content of trade and of labor utilization for different commodity aggregates. Most authors were able to provide some indicators of the skill content, as well as the input of labor units, in traded goods industries. Some traced the evolution of the commodity composition of trade, and the change in factor proportions, over time, linking those changes to alterations in the trade and payments regime itself. Finally, when previous research enabled country authors to obtain these estimates without time-consuming data collection, they examined factor markets to estimate the degree to which incentives in those markets affected factor proportions utilized in traded goods industries.

That, then, is the background of the country studies in this volume. All country authors commented upon project working papers, which contained much the same substance as the content in the next two sections. Throughout this volume, all instances where concepts and definitions do not accord with those given in this chapter are explicitly noted.

1.2   The Trade Strategies–Employment Relationship

1.2.1   Import Substitution and Export Promotion

One of the early lessons emerging from developing countries' experience in trying to raise their growth rates and standards of living was that there is an extremely close interconnection between the domestic pattern of industrial development and the nature of the trade and payments regime. It is widely recognized that successful growth will inevitably be accompanied by a more rapid rate of increase of nonagricultural than of agricultural employment. Growth of the nonagricultural sector can come about in two ways: new industries can arise whose output is to be sold on the domestic market, replacing imports; and new industries can be developed whose output is expected in large part to sell on the international market.

The first of these alternatives, import substitution, basically relies upon the fact that an industry can achieve an above-average growth rate if, in addition to increasing output to satisfy the growth of demand associated with rising incomes, increases in domestic output can substitute for imports. The second alternative, export promotion, depends upon the international market to absorb higher rates of growth of output in particular sectors than could be sold domestically without depressing price unduly. The first inevitably entails trade interventions to protect the domestic market, while the second involves an open trade policy.

Economic theory, of course, suggests that *both* strategies should be pursued—each to the point where the last unit of domestic resources devoted to it yields the same return in terms of foreign exchange earned or saved. An optimal export promotion strategy would not imply that new industries would develop to sell exclusively abroad without any domestic sales, or that no import substitution industries would start up; nor does import substitution imply that no new products would be produced for export. It is the degree of emphasis on each that is in question. Further, there can be degrees of "bias" of either strategy: some countries, such as Chile, have relied almost exclusively upon import substitution, providing extreme incentives for producing and selling in the domestic market and failing to encourage—perhaps even implicitly taxing —development of exports. Others, such as Pakistan, have tended to encourage development of production for the domestic market, but incentives have been more moderate, some encouragement to exports has been given, and the result has been a less extreme orientation of new production to the domestic market. Likewise, some countries, most notably (among those included in the project) South Korea since 1960, have provided virtually no across-the-board incentives for import substituting industries, while heavily encouraging all lines of export activity; others, such as Colombia since 1967, have leaned somewhat in the direction of favoring export growth but have kept incentives sufficiently moderate so that the overall bias toward exports of the system has not been very great.[6]

Nonetheless, policymakers have generally regarded import substitution and export promotion as alternatives. In addition, experience has indicated that there is a tendency for the choice between the two strategies to be self-reinforcing. Once import substitution is adopted as a development strategy, there are built-in tendencies discouraging the growth of exports and thereby leading to the adoption of policies to correct balance of payments deficits that further encourage import substitution and discourage exports. These include such phenomena as the higher price domestic firms must pay for inputs produced domestically, which reduces their international competitiveness; the lure of resources toward the lucrative and protected domestic market, which automatically reduces export growth; and the built-in requirements for capital goods, raw materials, and intermediate goods associated with many import substituting industries, which in turn lead to rapid growth of demand for imports and resulting quantitative restrictions upon imports, raising their price in the domestic market. These phenomena usually result in a tendency, once import substitution is adopted as a strategy, for increasing overvaluation of the exchange rate, which in turn intensifies the emphasis on import substitution as exports are further discouraged. An export promotion strategy also seems to entail tendencies that are self-reinforcing: rapid growth of exports leads to availability of foreign exchange, thereby mitigating the need for barriers to imports; exporters' needs for imported inputs prevent the erection of any elaborate structure to attempt to contain imports; an export promotion strategy mandates the maintenance of a realistic exchange rate, which itself encourages export performance and contains the demand for imports.

It is not the purpose here, or subsequently in the country chapters, to analyze the alternative trade strategies in all their ramifications. Rather, the central question is the relationship between those strategies and employment.

1.2.2 Employment

The level of employment is determined by the demand for, and the supply of, labor. That much said, however, arguments can rage as to the next step of the analysis: Do the demand and supply curves for labor depend upon the microeconomic properties of production and cost functions, or are they instead the result of macroeconomic variables? Is the level of employment determined within some sort of Keynesian or neo-Keynesian framework so that it is really the outcome of macroeconomic policy? Or is the world really neoclassical, so that the level of employment is determined by demographic variables, with the real wage being determined by the supply and demand curves for labor?

Answers to these questions range widely over all fields of economics, and there was no basis for believing that the NBER project could make a significant contribution to them. For purposes of the project, authors were essentially asked to assume a perfectly elastic supply curve of labor and to examine the basic question, How does the choice of trade strategy, abstracting from its effect on the overall rate of economic growth, affect employment?[7] This way of posing the question is tantamount to analyzing the extent to which alternative trade strategies shift the demand curve for labor to the right or the left. It avoids attempting to analyze the determinants of the extent to which any change in the demand curve for labor will be divided between changes in the real wage and changes in employment.

There were several reasons for this procedure. First, there is the fact, already mentioned, that too many unresolved questions surround the operation of labor markets to permit a satisfactory sorting of any shift into the price and quantity responses. In addition, it is widely recognized that population growth is rapid in most developing countries and that the rate of growth of the labor force will be sizable for the next several decades regardless of the degree of success in reducing birthrates. For that reason, the supply curve of labor will be shifting outward (usually at a more rapid rate than the rate of population growth, owing to a changing age composition of the population), and it can be argued that an outward shift in the demand for labor of comparable proportions will be necessary simply to increase employment at a constant real wage, with a constant *rate* of unemployment. Finally, employment in tradable goods industries is usually a relatively small fraction of total employment. To the extent that this is so, the supply of labor to those industries may be perfectly elastic within the relevant range.

To be sure, the response to an outward shift in the demand for labor depends on a wide variety of conditions, including the conditions of wage determination in the labor market. Although authors were not asked to investigate the determinants of the extent to which outward shifts in the demand for labor are reflected in real wage (as compared with employment) increases, they were asked to investigate, where data and time permitted, the functioning of factor markets to attempt to ascertain the extent of factor-market imperfections and their possible effect on employment and factor proportions in traded goods industries. That topic is further discussed below.

Inevitably, any investigation of labor market conditions confronts the problem of defining homogeneous units of labor. Indeed, the general belief is that developing countries have a relative abundance of unskilled labor and a relative scarcity of skilled labor. The difficulty arises in estimating the skill attributes of the labor force well enough to have measured differences in "efficiency" of different categories of labor. Authors were asked, wherever possible, to attempt to analyze the composition of employment within industries, and general guidelines were agreed upon. Nonetheless, it was recognized that each author would be confronted with different data sets and different labor market circumstances; consequently, no attempt was made to achieve uniformity in the definitions of skill categories across countries. Thus, each author who was able to obtain any data shedding light on the skill composition of the labor force was to use his own judgment as to the reliability of the data. The country chapters therefore contain the authors' analyses of the skill composition of different industries as far as data permit, but definitions of skills are not comparable across countries.[8]

1.2.3   Links between Trade Strategies and Employment

There are several levels at which the trade regime can interact with employment and its rate of growth:

1. One strategy might result in a higher rate of growth of the overall economy owing to superior resource allocation, and faster growth would presumably entail more employment growth.

2. Different trade strategies imply different compositions of output at each point in time. Under an export promotion strategy, export industries grow faster, as do import industries under import substitution. If employment per unit of output and value added is greater in one set of industries than in the other, then employment growth will be faster, on this account, under the strategy that lets the labor-intensive industries grow relatively faster.

3. Alternative trade policies could influence the choice of technique and the capital-labor ratio in all industries, as, for example, through implicit subsidization of capital goods imports. If such policies lead to greater capital intensity and fewer jobs per unit of output in all lines of economic activity, then employment opportunities will grow more slowly, while there is continued capital deepening.

Not all three classes of effects need to be in the same direction. It is possible, in particular, that the first effect—a higher rate of growth of employment owing to faster output growth—might go in one direction, while the second or third effect could go in the other. It was decided early in the project, however, that the first issue must of necessity remain outside the scope of the study, because to investigate it would require rehashing all the issues involved in the analysis of the merits of export promotion versus import substitution.

The objective of the present research project has been to come to grips with the second and third of the three levels defined above. Regarding the second, there are three possibilities:

1. The amount of employment generated is relatively independent of the trade strategy.

2. Export promotion generates significantly more employment growth than does an import substitution strategy.

3. An export promotion strategy is unlikely to entail significantly more employment growth than an import substitution strategy and may in fact conflict with efforts to expand employment.

The first possibility—that trade strategy does not affect employment very much—might be the correct one in several circumstances. First, one might be able to establish the direction of difference in labor intensity of production but find that the difference, if any, was sufficiently small that, within the conceivable range of relative growth rates, the effects on employment would be negligible. Second, one might find that a particular policy not really essential to the trade strategy adopted had adverse effects on employment, and that the same trade strategy could be carried out under a different set of policies without adverse employment effects. This could happen if export promotion policies were to encourage capital-intensive industries. Finally, it might be that the influences determining the composition of exporting and import substituting industries are independent of factor intensities, and that different relative rates of growth of the two groups of industries would not necessarily affect the rate of growth of employment.

The second possibility—that export industries require more labor per unit of capital and per unit of output—is the forecast that would arise from a straightforward interpretation of the two-factor HOS model of trade. Developing countries would presumably have their comparative advantage, at least in the early stages of growth, in exporting labor-intensive commodities and importing goods with relatively higher capital (and perhaps skilled labor) requirements. The country studies tend to substantiate this possibility and also shed some light on the magnitude of the potential for creating employment through an export promotion strategy.

Finally, as I mentioned above, there were some who argued when this project began that there is a possibility that import competing industries are the more labor-intensive ones, and that export promotion and employment growth might be conflicting objectives. Several reasons were given. One view was that developed countries themselves had erected—or would erect if export promotion strategies were seriously adopted—such high barriers to imports of labor-intensive goods that the developing countries could compete only in capital-intensive industries. Another basis for the argument was early experience, mentioned above, suggesting that the exports of Colombia and Brazil under their export promotion policies were capital-intensive. Yet others claimed that most of the exports of manufactured goods originating in developing countries were produced by branches and subsidiaries of multinational corporations that, it was alleged, used the capital-intensive technology of the home country. Although there are examples of each of these circumstances among the country results, they tend to be the exception rather than the rule.

Influences of the trade regime on choice of technique, and influences of the factor market on commodity composition of trade, can be equally important. The underpricing of capital-goods imports may encourage the use of overly capital-intensive techniques for those fortunate enough to be permitted to import at overvalued exchange rates. High and enforced minimum wage rates may prevent the development of otherwise profitable labor-intensive export industries. Extending subsidized credit to exporters may induce them to use more capital-intensive techniques than would otherwise be optimal.

All these influences can operate separately or together on the factor proportions in exportable and import competing industries. It is entirely possible that interactions between the domestic factor market and the trade regime are more important than differences between exportable and import competing industries in their factor proportions. Little is known about the direction or magnitude of these effects.

These are the basic questions addressed by the authors of the chapters that follow. As will be seen, there is enough evidence to conclude that trade strategies are important in affecting employment and that significant potential exists for expanding employment opportunities both by appropriate choice of strategy and by selection of incentives that do not discourage employment.

1.2.4 Market Imperfections

It has long been recognized that a nonoptimal trade strategy will result in commodity market distortions—in the form of import duties, quotas protecting domestic industries and allocating scarce foreign exchange, and export subsidies—that in turn can affect the commodity composition of trade and of domestic production. Any effort to analyze the relationship between trade strategies and employment must therefore take into account the commodity market distortions imposed by the trade regime and their interaction, if any, with other market distortions in the system. A significant question is the nature of the relationship between such commodity market interactions in particular industries and the factor intensity of those industries. A useful measure for characterizing the net effects of commodity distortions induced by the trade strategy on individual sectors and industries is the effective rates of protection (defined in section 1.3 below) for those industries. Country authors have analyzed the relationship between the height of protection (as reflected in effective rates of protection and other measures) for individual industries and the labor intensity of those industries. It is of interest that, although there are marked differences in individual cases, most authors found that industries subject to higher rates of protection were generally less labor-using than those subject to low rates of protection.

In recent years it has also been recognized that the trade regime and domestic policies affect the functioning of factor markets and can influence not only the commodity composition of production of tradable goods but also the choice of techniques within individual industries. A simple example relates to the practice, followed in many countries adopting an import substitution strategy, of permitting currency overvaluation and then failing to impose compensating duties and surcharges on imported capital goods and relying instead on quantitative restrictions. Depending on policies used in allocating capital goods import licenses, such a practice may entail the implicit subsidization of the use of capital for those who get licenses. If, simultaneously, there is credit rationing, firms fortunate enough to receive loans and import licenses may face a very low cost of capital. This encourages the use of capital-intensive techniques within industries and makes the profitability of capital-intensive industries greater than it would otherwise be. In such circumstances, one can well imagine a country with abundant unskilled labor nonetheless exporting a commodity using capital intensively, while failing to export labor-intensive commodities.

Similar phenomena can exist in labor markets. The structure of protection may affect the relative price of wage goods. There are many cases in which economists have believed that domestic phenomena, including government legislation and trade union agreements, have influenced the real wage. The Harris-Todaro model (Harris and Todaro 1970) is one such labor market representation. In that model an artificially high urban wage induces migration from the countryside and urban unemployment. If such a representation were valid, increasing the number of employment opportunities could even increase unemployment. To be sure, wage differences can reflect differences in "human capital" and living costs as well as factor market imperfections. Obviously, skilled and experienced workers will receive a higher wage than unskilled workers in a competitive environment, so that a major problem for analyzing the functioning of labor markets is to ascertain the reasons for differences in wages among groups of workers.

The problem is therefore not simple. Before the extent of "distortions" in factor proportions in traded goods industries can be assessed, one must evaluate the private costs of capital and the determinants of wage differences, sorting the latter into their "efficiency" component and their "distortion" component. Given our limited understanding of labor markets in developing countries and the scarcity of reliable data, it was too much to hope that country authors could reach definitive judgments on these matters. Nonetheless, many were able to analyze some aspects of the functioning of labor and capital markets. Their results are of great interest for the light they shed on the functioning of those markets and the determinants of employment. In general, authors found considerable evidence that market imperfections induced the choice of techniques that were more capital-intensive than was optimal. But there is little evidence that these distortions resulted in export of the "wrong" commodities. This is important because if the observed factor intensity of trade is the outcome of distorted factor markets, one cannot infer causation running directly from the trade strategy to factor utilization: some market imperfections, such as government-enforced minimum wage legislation, may themselves directly affect, if not determine, employment. If such were the case, one could not infer that the prevailing commodity composition of trade reflected comparative advantage. It is of great interest, therefore, that no country author found factor market distortions strong enough to have reversed the commodity composition of trade between capital-intensive and labor-intensive goods. Many of their results are highly suggestive for further research into the employment problem in developing countries.[9]

1.3 Definition of Concepts Used through the Project

1.3.1 Trade Categories, Sectors, Industries, and Commodities

In analyzing the relationship between trade and employment, one naturally wants to associate different structures of production and trade with alternative strategies.[10] In theory, there are homogeneous and readily identifiable commodities, each produced within a single industry, and output is either imported or exported, but never both. The problems of deciding which commodity belongs to which trade category and of associating commodities with industries never arise.

For empirical work the situation is vastly different. Trade data are presented by commodities: at even the most detailed level, there are often two-way flows in most categories.[11] To complicate matters, production and employment statistics are of necessity collected according to industry rather than according to commodity. Even at the level of the individual firm, more than one output may be produced, and the problem is intensified at any level of aggregation. To confound issues still further, any nationwide set of production accounts, such as is found in input-output statistics, must be at some level of aggregation as industries are allocated to sectors.

Taking trade statistics by commodity and classifying them in a meaningful way with sectoral statistics originating from an industrial classification is a difficult and time-consuming job. For the project, all authors agreed upon a common terminology and set of concepts that it was desirable to use in reconciling trade and production statistics. Because of differences in data availability and in individual countries, however, it was not possible to agree upon a common criterion for deciding levels of aggregation, weighting systems, or classification. This was left to the judgment of each author, and the choices made are clearly indicated in each country study.

In this section I will set forth the trade categories used, then discuss some of the fairly general problems that authors faced in aggregation and in reconciliation of trade and production data. Thereafter, I will discuss measures used to characterize the dimensions of employment and of the trade regime.

1.3.2   Trade Categories

The first task is selecting and defining the relevant trade categories into which to allocate the various commodities or sectors.[12] One must start by identifying the main categories of interest for the analysis. An empirical criterion is then needed for allocating various commodities and sectors to the relevant categories.

For this project, several categorizations were deemed useful. At the broadest level, it obviously made sense to define a class of tradable commodities viewed as importables and exportables and to regard other activities—that is, those with transport costs sufficiently high so that they are not tradable within the relevant range—as home goods (or nontradables).[13] Among tradables, importables and exportables were natural divisions, referring to commodities and activities for which there would be observed flows of commodities under an efficient allocation of resources within a "reasonable" variation of prices.

Among importable commodities, a three-way classification appeared to make most sense. The importables for which no domestic substitutes exist within the relevant price range are referred to as noncompeting imports. To the extent that domestic production is reported within such a sector, it presumably is due to aggregation and reflects the output of a subsector of the category.[14] The other types of importables are those for which there is competitive domestic production and those that can be produced domestically only under the protection afforded by the trade and payments regime. The three types of importables, then, are noncompeting imports, "naturally" competitive import-competing goods, and protected import-competing goods.[15] The criterion for assigning sectors to these categories and to exportables and home goods is given below.

For both importable and exportable categories, a further breakdown is essential. That has to do with the nature of the activity involved. In particular, there is a great deal of evidence that the behavior of tradable commodities that depend upon the local availability of natural resources for their production may be quite different, both in its determinants and in the likely supply response to altered prices, from the behavior of the tradable commodities for which location is not contingent upon direct access to the source of the raw material.

It was therefore decided that the categorization, within exportables and importables, would be (1) natural resource based goods and activities divided into agricultural, mineral, and other (including processing manufacturing industries); and (2) HOS goods.

Natural resource based (NRB) activities are those whose profitability depends basically upon the existence of some resource deriving a rent, such as land and mineral resources. While a change in the relative price of capital and labor might induce both substitution between these factors and perhaps also a change in the extensive margin of exploitation of minerals or cultivation of land, the industry's existence or absence, and hence the country's comparative advantage, is primarily the result of the presence of the natural resource whose exploitation is economic.

By contrast, HOS goods are defined as those whose production location is not determined by the location of the resource to which rent accrues. For HOS sectors, profitability (and hence location) is primarily a function of the relative prices of labor (of various grades of skills) and capital goods and their services.

All country authors treated primary commodities as NRB. The chief difficulty lay in categorizing manufacturing activities. In theory, if the primary commodity cannot economically be traded without processing, the processing activity is NRB. If the primary commodity can be traded economically, then processing it is an HOS activity. In practice, however, there is always an element of doubt for some activities, and country authors were asked to use their judgment. In many instances the decision was to present figures in two ways. For the Ivory Coast, for example, there is a petroleum-refining facility that provides oil for the Ivory Coast and several neighboring countries. Its categorization is doubtful, and Monson provided totals both with and without it. In other instances authors have treated all manufacturing as HOS, but then subdivided HOS industries into those that are primary commodity based and those that are not.

There are several reasons for selecting these categorizations. First, it seems clear that the determinants of comparative advantage in such commodities as oil (e.g., Indonesia) and coffee (Brazil, Colombia) are the availability of the raw material and hence of the underlying natural resource—the mineral or the right kind of land. While factor proportions are of interest in those industries, they are open to somewhat different interpretations than are factor proportions in the HOS goods, discussed below. It can be plausibly argued that many, though not all, NRB sectors will be exportable or importable independent of the trade strategy. In other words there is a basis for believing that many NRB commodities are intramarginal, because the natural resource itself is earning rents. This leads immediately to the second reason. That is, while one may wish to examine the "net factor content of trade" to determine the extent to which the demand for factors of production has shifted upward or downward in the aggregate, consideration of alternative trade strategies and their employment implications should legitimately be focused more directly on the factor requirements for a marginal expansion of trade. It can plausibly be argued that a switch in trade policy will not result in proportionate expansion of existing exporting industries. Rather, it is likely (and is verified by the experience of such countries as Korea) that a switch in strategy will entail the disproportionately large expansion of manufactured exports, especially in the HOS industries.

The decision to categorize industries and activities according to the NRB-HOS dichotomy was based essentially on the two reasons already given. Country authors' results, however, indicate that there was a third, practical reason for so doing. That is, the labor per unit of value added or of output is so much higher in the agricultural sectors than in the manufacturing sectors of the developing countries that agricultural exports always appear labor-intensive. The labor requirements per unit of output, as calculated from an input-output table or census of agriculture, are so much greater than those in other sectors of the economy that they completely dominate the estimate of the total labor requirements for different commodity categories. It is arguable, moreover, that a significant part of the labor input record in the agricultural sector may reflect an average, not a marginal, figure. Those who contend that there is "disguised unemployment" in agriculture would adhere to that view. Whether there is or not, it makes sense to estimate labor coefficients for primary and other activities separately.

A final categorization of sector, usually within the categories indicated above, was between those where trade was predominantly either with other developing countries or with developed countries.[16] For some countries, such as Indonesia and Tunisia, trade was so overwhelmingly with developed countries that the categorization according to type of trading partner had little meaning. For other countries, such as Brazil, Chile, and Uruguay, where a significant fraction of HOS trade was within a regional preferential trading arrangement, analysis of the difference in factor proportions as a function of the direction of trade proved more meaningful.

As I have already indicated, it was left to the authors' judgment to determine whether an activity was NRB or HOS, and the allocation according to trade destinations or origins was straightforward when the data were available. The major procedural question pertained to the allocation of activities among the categories of tradables. It was clear that judgment would have to be used. Especially for countries where quantitative restrictions and very high tariff levels distort the pattern of trade significantly from what would be observed under an efficient allocation of resources, authors had to allocate activities to tradable categories based upon their detailed knowledge of the situation. In Pakistan, for example, import substitution proceeded so far in most consumer goods lines that imports virtually ceased. Nonetheless, Guisinger treated these industries as tradables based upon his knowledge of the regime.

There were other reasons why no single criterion could be used for all countries. Of particular importance was the fact that the degree of aggregation of the available statistics varied widely. For countries with more disaggregated statistics, cross-flows—that is, observed exports and imports within the same sector—were likely to be less of a problem than for countries with a more highly aggregated data base. Nonetheless, it was deemed useful to ask authors to compute a common statistic, and then to choose their cutoff points around it and defend departures from it in line with their individual country's experience.

It was decided that assignment of sectors, at the feasible level of disaggregation, should be based upon a "T" statistic, defined as:

$$(1) \qquad T_i = \frac{C_i - P_i}{C_i},$$

where $C_i =$ domestic utilization and $P_i =$ domestic production. Each commodity or sector is classified as exportable if $T_i < X_0$; import competing if $X_0 \leq T_i < X_1$; and noncompeting if $X_1 \leq T_i \leq X_2$; where X_is were chosen as cutoff points. Each country author determined the appropriate X_0 and X_1 for his country. If X_0 were set at zero, for example, a negative T_i would mean the commodity or sector was classified as an exportable. Because of the possibility that domestic production might represent a nonhomogeneous product group, it was often best to let X_1 assume a value somewhere between 0.5 and 0.99, depending on the degree of disaggregation at which the analysis was conducted. When there is little or no domestic production, the ith commodity can be regarded as a noncompeting import, and the upper limit X_2 would necessarily be 1.

As I already mentioned, calculation of the T_is was a starting point. That some import regimes contain import prohibitions led to some modifications of the rules. Likewise, some authors identified commodities for which domestic production equaled domestic demand but that would be exported at a realistic exchange rate, and they modified their procedures accordingly. In effect, authors were asked to use their judgment on what the T statistic would be under an efficient allocation of resources.

1.3.3 Aggregation and Weights

Reconciling trade and production statistics is an onerous job. In general, most of the decisions made by country authors were forced upon them by the nature of the data available, and there was not much scope for judgment. Authors did, whenever possible, attempt to avoid aggregation whenever there would be sizable imports and exports within a given sector, or whenever the factor proportions utilized were significantly different among otherwise similar categories.

The major area where choices arose was in the construction of statistics characterizing the employment coefficients associated with various categories of tradable activities. There is no one correct basket of goods. The choice depends on the question being asked. Consider, for example, the straightforward question, At existing factor proportions, what would be the shift in the demand for labor associated with a marginal increase of $1 million in exports contrasted with an increase of $1 million of import substitutes? Even once sectors are identified with appropriate categories of tradables, there is a question as to the appropriate set of weights to be used in aggregation.

To estimate empirically the likely content of a $1 million basket of exports, the most reasonable approximation for weights might be either the observed basket of exports or the observed composition of manufactured exports only.[17] The choice would depend on one's judgment about the feasibility of expanding traditional exports both in production and in sales abroad. Thus one would probably apply trade weights to some subset of exports to the coefficients of different exportables to attempt to answer the question of the net employment effect of expanding exports.

On the import side the choices are different. The relevant unit is probably not the entire vector of imports, since there are some commodities that cannot be domestically produced. It may be that one should use consumption weights for commodities that are domestically produced but importable (import competing), or it might be that trade weights for that same category of goods were a better indicator of the likely direction of trade expansion.

There is no entirely satisfactory answer on a priori grounds to the choice of trade weights, production weights, or consumption weights. In fact, some authors were constrained in their choices by data availability. In instances where authors could experiment with alternative sets of weights, such as in Chile and the Ivory Coast, the weights used did not appear to affect the results significantly, once categories of tradables were selected. On a priori grounds, therefore, one might anticipate that results would differ significantly depending upon the choice of weights. In practice, however, that does not appear to be a significant problem in interpretation of country authors' results.

1.3.4   Characterizing Trade Regimes

All country authors have analyzed the trade regime in their country as it influenced the commodity composition of trade, thereby affecting factor proportions. Each author has evaluated the degree to which the regime was oriented toward export promotion or toward import substitution and the effect of the regime on the choice of techniques in various industries.

To do this, authors first had to obtain estimates of effective exchange rates (EERs) for various categories of goods. Next they needed to derive estimates of the relationship of domestic value added to international value added per unit of output. To do this they generally obtained estimates of effective rates of protection.

Exchange Rates

In many developing countries, the nominal or official exchange rate bears little relation either to the costs of foreign exchange paid by buyers or to the receipts of exporters. Some trade regimes are restrictive enough so that the prevailing exchange rate, even after adjustment for tariffs and surcharges, bears little relation to a realistic one that might prevail under an efficient allocation of resources.

All country authors were asked to provide estimates of effective exchange rates (EERs) for different categories of transactions—those exchange rates being defined as the amount of local currency actually received or paid per unit of foreign exchange. The distinction was further drawn on the import side between EERs, on the one hand, and premium-inclusive EERs on the other. These latter represent the exchange rate that would have to prevail for individual commodity categories in order for the domestic price to equal the international price in a competitive market. Since quantitative restrictions (QRs) as well as tariffs influence the protection given to domestic producers, these rates are the ones theoretically correct to measure the incentives to produce import substitutes and are therefore relevant for determining the degree to which the pattern of production is influenced by the trade regime.

Because countries have widely different inflation rates, it also is useful to distinguish between EERs, which refer to actual currency values at given points of time, and price level deflated EERs (PLD-EERs), which are the actual EERs deflated by the most relevant price index (home goods, if available). Until the early 1970s, the world inflation rate was extremely slow, and the dollar index of the prices of internationally traded goods moved hardly at all. Therefore it was usually permissible to compute PLD-EERs and to use them to interpret the behavior of the "real" exchange rate. Since the early 1970s, however, world prices have been rising rapidly enough so that a constant PLD-EER would imply an increasingly competitive currency on world markets. For that reason it has become necessary to take into account not only the behavior of the prices in the country under scrutiny but also that of the prices of its major trading partners. To do that, one must deflate (i.e., multiply) the EERs by the ratio of an index of prices in other countries to the domestic price index. Such a construct, the purchasing power parity effective exchange rate (**PPP-PLD-EER**) is perhaps the most appropriate measure of the behavior of a currency and trade regime over time. To be sure, this is not intended to imply that **PPP-PLD-EERs** should remain constant over time. When the discovery of new mineral deposits or a tremendous increase in the price of an exportable, such as coffee or oil, significantly alters a country's situation vis-à-vis the rest of the world, a change in the **PPP-PLD-EER** may well be called for. But when changes are brought about by differentials in inflation rates, there is no presumption that those differentials reflect changes in the underlying international situation. In those cases, **PPP-PLD-EER** calculations provide a first approximation of the effect of the trade and exchange regime on the domestic producers of exportables and import competing products.

Effective Rates of Protection and Domestic Resource Costs

In addition to estimating EERs, country authors were asked to obtain estimates of effective rates of protection (ERPs) (including the value of nontariff barriers) for the same commodity or sector classification that they used for estimates of labor coefficients. In some cases, such as Chile, estimates were readily at hand from earlier research. In others, such as Indonesia and Uruguay, providing estimates of ERPs is a significant contribution to knowledge.

The basic data required are domestic and international prices. In instances where tariffs (and other charges translatable into tariff equivalents) are the only form of protection, it is relatively simple to compute the statistic

$$(2) \qquad ERP_j = \frac{t_j - \Sigma_i \, a_{ji} \, t_i}{1 - \Sigma_i \, a_{ji}},$$

where t_j is the tariff on the jth commodity, a_{ji} is the input of i per unit of output of j, and where all international prices are normalized at unity.[18] In effect, the numerator reflects the excess of domestic value added over international value added and the denominator represents international value added; that is, value added measured at international prices. An ERP, therefore, is the proportionate protection provided to a value-adding activity.

When data on tariffs were available (and tariffs were the only barrier to trade) a first problem was to ascertain whether the rates were binding or whether there was water in the tariff. A number of authors, notably Bension and Caumont for Uruguay, concluded that domestic prices were considerably below the c.i.f.-plus-tariff price and adjusted their estimates accordingly. Once that was done, the only task was to compute the ERPs for individual commodities and then to transform them to sectoral estimates in conjunction with the input-output table.[19] In most countries, however, tariffs do not constitute the only form of protection, and a major problem is to determine the tariff equivalent of quotas and other protective devices. Obtaining direct price comparisons is the most satisfactory means of surmounting that difficulty, but it is extremely time-consuming if no prior study is available. In cases where prior studies are not available, authors have supplemented tariff data with attempts to estimate the probable effect of quantitative restrictions on different commodity classes.

Protection does two things: it can provide cover for the difference between domestic and foreign costs of production, and it can permit domestic producers to enjoy a monopoly position they would otherwise not have. Measures of effective protection can therefore be interpreted as a measure of the change in incentives caused by the trade regime from those that would occur under free trade. To estimate the additional costs of production resulting from protection, a measure eliminating the monopoly element and also adjusting for divergences between market and shadow prices,[20] is needed. The domestic resource cost (DRC) measure has been used for this purpose, especially in contexts where there is reason to believe that significant distortions occur both in factor prices and in monopoly positions of individual industries. Some country authors have used DRCs in their studies as an indicator of the costs of trade regime and of potential expansion of alternative activities. DRCs are computed by taking the data necessary for ERP computations and altering the estimates of the costs of inputs to adjust for differentials between market prices and those believed to reflect opportunity costs better.

IVA and DVA

An ERP estimate is basically an estimate of the percentage by which domestic value added (DVA) in a particular industry or activity exceeds value added measured at international prices (IVA) in the same activity. Both DVA and IVA are important, but for different purposes: domestic value added (unless there are large differences between market and shadow prices) is probably the appropriate concept for examining the domestic marginal rate of transformation between activities, while international value added is more appropriate for examining opportunities for transformation through trade. Authors initially obtained data on labor (in various units—man-years, wage bills, etc.) in different activities from what were, in their judgment, the best sources available. In all cases, a major task was to transform data on labor utilization, usually derived from production data, into units conformable with the trade data. These data were generally expressed in terms of units of labor per unit of DVA. In most instances, once ERPs were available, authors were able to transform these data into units of labor per unit of IVA in a straight-forward manner.

It seems clear that any measurement of the labor utilization should be done per unit of value added, rather than per unit of output. The reason for this is that different industries have very different ratios of intermediate inputs to outputs: if labor per unit of output was calculated, it is likely that industries with low ratios of purchased inputs to outputs would show high labor coefficients.

1.3.5 Labor Coefficients

In addition to the problem of defining and estimating skills, there are three problems pertaining to the estimation of labor coefficients: (1) even though it is recognized that it should be labor per unit of value added, there is a question of the appropriate value-added concept; (2) there is a question of the choice of units with which to measure labor; and (3) there is a question of how to obtain meaningful coefficients for sectors where imports are classified as not competing with domestic production.

With regard to the relevant unit of value added, it was decided at the outset that two distinct sets of labor data should be obtained if at all possible. On one hand, there should be an estimate of the "direct" labor utilized in the production of one unit of domestic currency's worth of value added. On the other hand, an estimate should also be made of the direct labor requirements per unit of value added *plus* the requirements of labor in the production of home goods for use in tradable goods production. This latter concept is perhaps more relevant for examining the effect of a change in trade strategy: if trade policies were altered in a manner that increased value added in imports and exports by an equal amount, it seems clear that the expansion of exportable production would require not only factors of production directly, but also home goods such as construction, electricity, finance, and domestic transport. Home goods production itself requires factor inputs and purchased inputs, some of which are themselves home goods. The term "direct requirements of labor plus indirect requirements in home goods" is designed to capture this total expansion, and it is this concept that was set out in the guidelines for the project.[21]

Given the ambiguity of words when it comes to such concepts, it may be useful to express algebraically what is being measured. The direct labor requirement per unit of DVA in the jth activity, L^d_j, can be computed from data on total employment in j, E_j (measured in the most appropriate unit available, being sure that units are comparable in different activities), the domestic value of output, V_j, and the domestic value of purchased inputs, M_j, as

$$(3) \qquad L^d_j = \frac{E_j}{V_j - M_j} .$$

Indirect labor requirements in home goods per unit of output of the jth tradable are $a_{hj} \cdot \dfrac{E_h}{V_h}$, where a_{hj} is the input of home goods per unit of traded goods output. Value added per unit of output of home goods is $(V_h - M_h)/V_h$, so that value added in home goods per unit of output of tradables is that times a_{hj}.

Labor used directly and indirectly in home goods per unit of value added directly in traded goods and directly and indirectly in home goods is therefore

$$(4) \qquad L^i_j = \frac{a_{hj}(E_h/V_h) \cdot V_j}{V_j - M_j + a_{hj}[(V_h - M_h)/V_h]}.$$

Total requirements of labor directly in the jth tradable plus indirect requirements in home goods, L^t_j, per unit of value added directly in tradable and indirectly in home goods used in tradables is therefore

$$(5) \qquad L^t_j = \frac{E_j + (a_{hj} E_h/V_h) \cdot V_j}{V_j - M_j + a_{hj}[(V_h - M_h)/V_h]}.$$

Of course, if home goods themselves require inputs of other home goods, a_{hj} should be interpreted as including such further indirect use of home goods per unit of tradable, and $a_{hj} (V_h - M_h)$ should be domestic value added in indirect plus "indirect-indirect" use of home goods. It should be noted that both numerator and denominator increase when the measurement of labor requirements per unit of value added goes from direct requirements only to direct-plus-indirect and on to indirect-indirect requirements.

The choice of the unit with which to measure labor utilization, which is closely related to the problem of measuring skills, was left to the individual authors. Ideally, one would like to measure man-hours of homogeneous labor categories, because years, months, or even man-weeks can obscure considerable variation in hours worked, seasonality of the industry, and so on. However, data limitations made this ideal unattainable in most of the country studies, and the practical choice was between a physical unit such as man-years and a value unit such as the wage bill. When a unit such as man-years closely reflects workers of like skill (or workers in different industries employing the same mix of skills), use of the physical measure is preferable. When, however, few data are available on skill and there is reason to believe that the proportions in which skilled and unskilled labor are used differ significantly across industries, a value unit can be preferable, especially if it is believed that the labor market functions with few imperfections between the industries across which comparison is made. Using the wage bill as the unit of observation is equivalent to assuming that more highly skilled workers are perfect substitutes for unskilled workers, but more efficient in proportion with the wage difference. The use of a physical unit such as man-years uncorrected for skill differentials is equivalent to assuming perfect substitutability of all workers at a one-to-one ratio. The truth probably lies somewhere in between, and it was left to individual country authors to determine what measure, in their judgment, best reflected labor utilization rates. The best solution, of course, was to obtain data separately for different skill categories. As can be seen in the individual studies, authors met with varying degrees of success in obtaining such data, but in no case was it possible to achieve an ideal data set.

There was little question of how to obtain estimates of the labor coefficients for exportable sectors and for sectors where domestic production was competitive with imports. To be sure, authors had to use judgment in aggregation, but once that decision was made the computation was straightforward.[22] However, it is readily apparent that estimating the potential factor intensity of sectors where domestic demand is now met by imports is of great importance in estimating the employment implications of import substitution. Moreover, insofar as the imports are truly noncompeting, whatever production is reported domestically for ostensibly similar goods is usually the result of aggregation and reflects factor proportions in an industry not representative of what would happen with development of the import substitution industry.

The recommended procedure in such cases was to obtain an estimate of factor proportions in the corresponding industry in another country along with factor proportions in an industry producing in both that country and the country under study. The ratio of the labor inputs in the two industries in the foreign country was then computed and applied to the labor input in the common industry in the home country to estimate the potential labor requirement in the hypothetical industry. Algebraically, L^d_i, the computed labor coefficient for the ith industry in the home country, was derived from

$$(6) \qquad \frac{L^d_i}{L^d_j} = \frac{L^o_i}{L^o_j},$$

where d is the home country, o is the other country, the ith industry operates in o but not in d, and the jth industry operates in both countries.

This procedure is tantamount to assuming that the industries have the same elasticity of substitution in both countries and that observed differences in coefficients reflect substitution in response to changes in relative factor prices.

1.3.6   Measures of Capital Services

Although there are significant problems in measuring the labor input into a particular activity in an economically meaningful way, those problems are not as serious as the problems associated with attempting to estimate the input of capital services. For the latter, problems of aggregation are significant, and valuation is affected by bookkeeping practices, inflation rates, and tax laws. In addition, rates of utilization of machinery differ widely and present conceptual as well as empirical problems.

Since emphasis in the present study was on the relationship between trade strategies and employment, attempts at estimating capital inputs were not of primary concern for analysis. Nonetheless, there are a number of questions for which such estimates provide valuable information, and country authors were urged to present them whenever they were available and meaningful. In some instances, physical measures, such as electricity used per unit of value added or horsepower of installed capacity, were utilized in addition to a value measure. Given the theoretical difficulties known to surround any measure of capital services, it is reassuring that, for those countries where several proxy measures could be presented, the results did not appear to be sensitive to the choice of unit.

1.4 Conclusion

This is not the place to attempt to synthesize the results of the individual studies; they are of great interest in their own right and the findings and methodology used in each merit scrutiny.

What should be evident is that, despite severe data limitations, each country author has been able to derive meaningful results that appear fairly robust. While care will be needed in drawing conclusions, it is already clear that, given reasonably open markets abroad, export oriented policies have been more favorable in some cases, or could have been in others, than import substitution policies in expanding employment in developing countries. Many of the authors have devised methods for estimating the total employment effect of trade strategy choices and domestic factor market distortions. Their estimates are indicative of the importance of the topic and of the need for a great deal of additional research.

Given the data limitations confronted by the country authors, it is surprising how much they could accomplish with the information at hand. It is perhaps not surprising, however, that little had been done earlier on the trade-employment relation. The results testify to the importance of the topic and the need for better data. In this regard it is clear that much must be done to provide closer comparability between trade, production, and input-output statistics. There are few countries for which these data are currently available on a common basis, and the task of reconciling them has consumed enormous time and energy in the project. In a world where trade flows are assuming increased importance, I hope that reconciliation of these data with domestic production data will assume high priority.

The results of the individual studies that follow represent a significant step forward in our understanding of the relationship between trade strategies and employment. To say that further research is called for is only to conclude that the contribution to knowledge from investigation of the topic is significant.

Notes

1. See, in particular, Little, Scitovsky, and Scott (1970); Bhagwati (1978); and Krueger (1978).

2. For a recent summary of the Leontief paradox literature and findings, see Baldwin (1971, 1979) and Branson and Monoyios (1977).

3. Diaz-Alejandro (1976, p. 45).

4. The working paper is available upon request from the NBER. The chief concepts and definitions emerging from it are, however, given in section 1.3 of this chapter.

5. Studies of India and Kenya were also undertaken but could not be completed in time for inclusion in this volume.

6. For further discussion of these issues, see Krueger (1978).

7. An alternative interpretation would be that authors were asked to investigate the horizontal shift in the demand-for-labor function associated with an alternation in trade strategy.

8. Even if it were, there would be no assurance that labor in a particular skill category was the same in one country as in another.

9. These results will be assessed in the third volume of this series. See also the contribution by T. Paul Schultz in the forthcoming second volume.

10. The concepts used in this project are consistent with those used in the earlier NBER project, Exchange Control, Liberalization, and Economic Development. See Krueger (1978, chap. 5 and Appendix A).

11. The problem of two-way flows has vexed analysts for years. There are important questions about why such flows should exist. On one hand, they might reflect aggregation, and on the other hand it is conceivable that they are the outcome of spatial separation, such as when western Canada exports oil to the western part of the United States and eastern Canada imports oil from the eastern part of the United States. Recently, however, additional attention has been given to the phenomenon, and there have been extensive investigations of the phenomenon of intraindustry trade. Grubel and Lloyd (1975) have investigated this subject in detail and conclude that much of it represents efficient location of production within industries.

12. The question is closely related, but not identical, to the problem of choosing appropriate weights, which is discussed below.

13. The term "nontraded" is to be avoided, since it is ambiguous in trade regimes in which quantitative restrictions are used. Some goods, although tradable, are nontraded because of prohibitions against their import (or, rarely, export). For

purposes of analyzing the trade regime, these goods are quite distinct from home goods.

14. For example, in many developing countries one observes the sector "transportation equipment" as being very labor-intensive. This is usually because repairs dominate the economic activity in that sector.

15. Language becomes awkward when referring to the production counterparts of the import categories. "Import-competing" production of both types makes sense, but "noncompeting" production is ambiguous. Throughout this volume, an effort has been made to refer to production of noncompeting importables as a means of avoiding ambiguity.

16. For the rationale behind the DC-LDC categorization, see Krueger (1977).

17. Even here, there would remain a question whether the $1 million basket was to be measured in terms of output or of value added in export industries. This problem is discussed below.

18. The formula should be computed at the prices and input-output relationships that would prevail under free trade. In fact, all authors used actually observed domestic coefficients for each alternative. When there are no substitution possibilities between the intermediate inputs and other factors, this procedure is unbiased.

19. Country authors were asked to follow Corden (1971) in their treatment of home goods.

20. Shadow prices themselves can have a number of interpretations. There is an opportunity cost that would occur under an efficient allocation of resources. It might be quite different than the opportunity costs for a marginal change from a given, nonoptimal allocation of resources.

21. It can also be argued that, under import substitution, the relevant labor requirement for expansion of any sector is the direct plus *total* indirect requirement. Many authors computed those data, and the numbers are sometimes presented in the country studies. However, even for that purpose there is a question whether the total indirect requirements reflect an efficient use of resources, even under import substitution.

22. It is possible that exports and domestic sales are different qualities or sell at different prices. Authors were asked to evaluate the severity of the problem for their countries, but in all cases except Uruguay the data did not permit them to pursue the question.

References

Baldwin, Robert E. 1971. Determinants of the commodity structure of U.S. trade. *American Economic Review* 61 (March): 126–46.

———. 1979. Foreign trade and U.S. research and development: Further evidence." *Review of Economics and Statistics* 61 (February): 40–48.

Bhagwati, Jagdish. 1978. *Foreign trade regimes and economic development: Anatomy and consequences of exchange control regimes.* Cambridge, Mass.: Ballinger Press for NBER.

Branson, William H., and Monoyios, W. 1977. Factor inputs in U.S. trade. *Journal of International Economics* 7 (May): 111–31.

Corden, Warner M. 1971. *The theory of protection.* Oxford: Clarendon Press.

Diaz-Alejandro, Carlos. 1976. *Foreign trade regimes and economic development: Colombia.* New York: Columbia University Press for NBER.

Grubel, Herbert, and Lloyd, Peter J. 1975. *Intra-industry trade.* New York: Halsted Press.

Harris, John R., and Todaro, Michael P. 1970. Migration, unemployment and development: A two-sector analysis. *American Economic Review,* 60 (March): 126–42.

Hirsch, Seev. 1974. Hypotheses regarding trade between developing and industrial countries. In *The international division of labour,* ed. Herbert Giersch. Tubingen: J. C. B. Mohr.

Krueger, Anne O. 1977. *Growth, factor market distortions and patterns of trade among many countries.* Princeton Studies in International Finance, no. 40. Princeton: Princeton University Press.

————. 1978. *Foreign trade regimes and economic development: Liberalization attempts and consequences.* Cambridge, Mass.: Ballinger Press for NBER.

Leontief, Wassily. 1968. Domestic production and foreign trade: The American capital position reexamined. In *A.E.A. readings in international economics,* ed. Richard E. Caves and Harry G. Johnson. Homewood, Ill.: Richard D. Irwin.

Little, I. M. D.; Scitovsky, Tibor; and Scott, Maurice. 1970. *Industry and trade in some developing countries: A comparative study.* New York: Oxford University Press.

Vanek, Jaroslav. 1963. *The natural resource content of United States foreign trade, 1870–1955.* Cambridge, Mass.: Harvard University Press.

2 Foreign Trade Strategies and Employment in Brazil

José L. Carvalho and
Cláudio L. S. Haddad

2.1 Introduction

Brazil, along with Korea, is one of the countries included in this volume that has had experience with both import substitution and export promotion policies. Import substitution policies were followed until 1965; by 1968 policies were reversed to promote exports. The export promotion policies have been successful in many respects. For example, in the last ten years of the import substitution phase, the average annual growth rates of GDP, industrial output, and manufacturing employment were roughly 5, 6, and 2 percent respectively. After export promotion policies were introduced these rates increased dramatically. In the period 1966–75 they averaged 9, 11, and 10 percent. The manufacturing sector responded enthusiastically to the new policies. Its share in GDP rose from about 25 to 30 percent from 1966 to 1974 while the share of manufacturing exports in total exports increased from about 6 to 16 percent in the same period. From 1964 to 1974 Brazil's manufactured exports increased eighteenfold in dollar terms, or at an average annual rate of 33 percent.

José L. Carvalho and Cláudio L. S. Haddad are associated with the Escola de Pós-Graduação em Economics, Fundação Getúlio Vargas.

During the time we worked on this project, we benefited from the working parties organized by NBER and from discussions in the economic research seminar at the Graduate School of Economics (EPGE) of Getúlio Vargas Foundation (FGV), where this study was presented in fragmented form.

Although we are sure to omit names, we would like to thank Anne O. Krueger for her comments and guidance throughout the entire work; Hal Lary for his meticulous comments and editing suggestions; Arnold C. Harberger for the time he spent reading and editing parts of this work and for discussing it with us during his short, but very helpful, visits to EPGE during these past two years; Hugo Barros de Castro Faria for his assistance and for sharing with us his large experi-

Thus Brazil is a particularly appropriate case study of the relation between trade strategies and employment. Such a study is important in its own right, but, more important, it is suggestive of the potentials of export promotion and the pitfalls of import substitution policies.

Our purpose then is to analyze the employment implications of Brazil's trade policies. We are fortunate that we have data covering both phases of its trade regime and can estimate labor requirements for 1959, 1970, and 1971. It should be noted at the outset, though, that our labor requirements are not strictly comparable with those of other countries discussed in this volume. Namely, our indirect labor requirements include all manufacturing and mining industries (but not agriculture and services), whereas those for most other countries pertain to home goods, as was described in the introductory chapter. Data problems necessitated this treatment. Its implications are dealt with in more detail in section 2.3 below.

2.2   A Summary of Brazilian Economic Development

2.2.1   Growth: An Overview

Brazil is a large, prosperous, and populous developing country that has historically had relatively high rates of growth.[1] Its total area of 3,286,470 square miles makes it larger than the United States, including Alaska. Its income per capita of about U.S. $1,400 (1977) places it in the middle-income category used by the World Bank. Its population of 110 million (1976) makes it the third most populous (not centrally planned) LDC (behind India and Indonesia).

The Brazilian economy has had relatively high growth rates for nearly half a century. From 1911 to 1947 industrial production in Brazil grew at an annual average of 6.5 percent while the population was growing at 2.1 percent a year (Haddad 1974).[2] For that period a per capita indus-

ence with Brazilian trade data; Carlos Alexandre Tardin Costa for his assistance on computer programming; Nerine Mirian Leinemann, Sonia Teresa Terra Figueiredo, José Maria Cardoso Vasconcellos Filho, and Luiza Riberio Fernandes Braga for their efficient and careful work as research assistants; Raimunda Georgina Ribeiro de Mattos, Marília A. Resende, Araci Benites dos Santos Pugliese, and Maria Stela Pereira do Nascimento for typing several versions of horrible manuscripts.

We would like also to acknowledge the infrastructure support provided by EPGE.

Finally, we would like to thank the Ministry of Finance, which, under a special contract with FGV/EPGE, provided most of the funds for this research. Financial support was also obtained from NBER, in the early stages of this work, through funds provided by the United States Agency for International Development.

As usual, the persons or institutions mentioned above are not responsible for remaining errors or for the interpretations and conclusions expressed here.

trial growth rate of about 4.4 percent a year is very impressive by international standards. After World War II, the rate of economic growth accelerated. Brazilian real GDP grew at an annual average rate of 7.1 percent; industrial output increased faster than agriculture (as is shown in table 2.1), so that the share of industry in GDP was nearly 40 percent in 1975 as opposed to 26 percent in 1949 (see table 2.2). Manufacturing makes up about 75 percent of output of the broad industrial category that also includes mining, public utilities, and construction. Manufacturing output alone increased its share of GDP from 20 to 30 percent in the period 1949–75.

2.2.2   Trade and the Brazilian Economy

Pattern and Composition of Trade

Trade has been important for Brazil, even during the import substitution trade regime. Imports and exports in the late 1950s and early 1960s each were about 8 percent of GDP. In more recent years, their combined total has been about 25 percent. About 65 percent of current exports consist of natural-resource-based (NRB) goods, of which coffee, soybeans, and iron ore are most important. However, the share of NRB goods in total exports has fallen dramatically (in 1960, it was 97 percent). As mentioned above, manufactured exports increased rapidly after export promotion began. Major manufactured exports include leather products, chemicals, textiles, clothing, and food products (see appendix tables 2.A.1 to 2.A.3). In 1976 merchandise exports totaled slightly more than U.S. $10 billion, of which manufactured exports were nearly U.S. $3 billion. Brazil's major imports are machinery and equipment with a high technological content (about 25 percent of total imports), oil (another 25 percent), nonferrous metals, coal, and wheat. Brazil produces most of the consumer durables consumed domestically. Consumer goods made up about 13 percent of total imports in the early 1970s. However, this represented a doubling of the 6 to 7 percent share of consumer goods in total imports in the late 1950s and early 1960s, when the import substitution policy was most severe.

Brazil has succeeded in diversifying the destinations of its exports, though not the sources of its imports. About 60 percent of total exports went to developed nations in 1976 compared with 80 percent in 1960. For manufactured exports, the share of developed nations fell from about 90 to 70 percent in the same period. The developed nations' share in Brazil's imports has remained fairly stable at about 75 percent in the past two decades. Major trading partners among developed countries include the United States, Germany, Japan, and the Netherlands. Among LDCs, major trading partners include fellow Latin American Free Trade Area (LAFTA) members, Argentina, Chile, Venezuela, and Mexico.

Table 2.1   Rates of Growth of Gross Domestic
                 Product in Brazil, 1951–74: Total,
                 Agriculture, and Industry (Annual
                 Percentage Change)

Years	Total GDP	Agriculture[a]	Industry[b]
1951	6.0	0.7	6.4
1952	8.7	9.1	5.0
1953	2.5	0.2	8.7
1954	10.1	7.9	8.7
1955	6.9	7.7	10.6
1956	3.2	−2.4	6.9
1957	8.1	9.3	5.7
1958	7.7	2.0	16.2
1959	5.6	5.3	11.9
1960	9.7	4.9	5.4
1961	10.3	7.6	15.0
1962	5.3	5.5	7.8
1963	1.5	1.0	0.2
1964	2.9	1.3	5.2
1965	2.7	13.8	−4.7
1966	5.1	−3.2	11.7
1967	4.8	5.7	3.0
1968	9.3	1.4	15.5
1969	9.0	6.0	10.8
1970	9.5	5.6	11.1
1971	11.1	11.4	11.2
1972	10.4	4.5	13.8
1973	11.4	3.5	15.0
1974	9.5	8.5	8.2
Average Annual Rate			
1952–73	7.1	4.9	8.9
1952–58	6.7	4.8	8.8
1959–64	5.9	4.3	7.6
1965–73	8.1	5.4	9.7
1968–73	10.1	5.4	12.9

Source: Fundação Getúlio Vargas, *Conjuntura Economica*, various issues. A new set of estimates for the national accounts was recently published by FGV (*Conjuntura Economica* 31 [July 1977]), but the revision was performed from 1965 on. Here we present the previous estimates.

[a]Agriculture includes fishing and forestry. The share of agriculture in GDP fell from 26.1 percent in 1953 to 14.8 percent in 1973.

[b]Industry includes, in addition to manufacturing, mining, construction, and utilities. The share of industry rose from 23.7 percent of GDP in 1953 to 31.8 percent in 1973.

Table 2.2   **Sectoral Distribution of Total Income at Factor Cost, Selected Years (Percentage)**

Year	Agri- culture	Services	Industry Total	Mining	Manu- factures	Public Utilities	Con- struction
					Industry		
1949	24.9	49.1	26.0	0.5	20.0	1.1	4.3
1959	19.2	48.2	32.6	0.5	25.0	1.4	5.6
1965	15.9	51.6	32.5	0.8	24.8	1.7	5.3
1970	10.2	53.5	36.3	0.8	27.4	2.1	6.0
1975	10.5	50.0	39.4	1.4	30.2	2.2	5.7

Source: Total income from Fundação Getúlio Vargas, *Conjuntura Economica* 31 (July 1977):95; industry income, ibid., p. 97.

Balance of Payments

Brazil has almost continuously run deficits in its current account, often because of deficits in its service account (see table 2.3). Long-term capital inflows often do not counteract the current account deficit, although they are generally fairly large (in recent years being about one-half the value of exports). Direct investment inflows make up about one-third of long-term capital inflows in a normal year. To finance balance of payments deficits, Brazil has used currency swaps and deferred import payments as well as its foreign exchanges reserves.

The Trade Regime

Brazil followed an import substitution strategy from 1945 to 1964, then reversed direction and by 1968 was vigorously promoting exports.[3]

Table 2.3   **Balance of Payments Indicators, Selected Years (Millions of U.S. Dollars)**

Indicator	1947	1952	1959	1964	1970	1975
Merchandise exports	1,157	1,416	1,282	1,430	2,739	8,493
Merchandise imports	1,027	1,702	1,210	1,294	2,507	12,042
Merchandise balance (net)	130	−288	72	344	232	−3,549
Other current account	−299	−424	−404	−263	−402	−3,540
Current account balance	−169	−710	−332	81	−561	−6,999
Long- and medium-term capital inflows	27	96	270	167	723	4,935
Balance on current account + capital account + net errors	−195	−615	− 73	55	563	−1,061
Change in reserves	−113	− 51	25	− 60	563	−1,062

Source: International Monetary Fund, *International Financial Statistics*, (various years).

The import substitution phase can be further divided into four periods with varying degrees of restrictiveness (1946–53, 1953–57, 1957–60, 1961–64).

The early phase of the import substitution period (1946–53) was characterized by a highly overvalued exchange rate. After World War II, there was a tremendous surge in imports as war restrictions were lifted. Even a large increase in coffee prices was not sufficient to equilibrate the current account. Rather than devalue the cruzeiro, the government instituted an import licensing system. A continuing fall in the real exchange rate (see table 2.4), coupled with expansionary domestic policies (which raised the rate of inflation—see table 2.5) and a stabilization of coffee prices, led to a trade deficit of nearly U.S. $300 million in 1952 and an overall deficit of U.S. $615 million. This deficit led to the adoption of a multiple exchange rate system in 1953.

Under this system, foreign exchange available for imports was divided into five categories and auctioned off. In general the exchange rate system and other incentives laid a basis for import substitution of finished consumer goods and food products. The most-preferred import category was chemicals and capital equipment. Its nominal exchange rate was usually one-third that for the least-favored finished consumer goods import category. On the other hand, exports were clearly discouraged, with the noncoffee rate being well below all import rates.

In 1957 the auction system was modified. The number of import categories was reduced to three, but in general rates for the most-preferred imports were again about one-third of those for the least-preferred imports. At this time a system of ad valorem tariffs was introduced. It too was cascaded; nominal rates varied from 60 to 150 percent for products available from domestic sources and from 0 to 10 percent for products not produced domestically. In addition, the Law of Similars was activated. This law prohibited imports of products available from domestic sources. However, Fishlow (1975, p. 29) concluded that the Law of Similars did not impose significant quantitative restrictions on imports, probably because it was redundant, given all the other import restrictions.

The end of the import substitution phase (1961–64) was a difficult one for the Brazilian economy. The "industrialization at any cost" program of the late 1950s coupled with ambitious government projects generated large budget deficits that were mainly financed through increases in the money supply. (The money supply increased by nearly 500 percent from 1961 to 1964.) Inflation worsened (see table 2.5); at their worst in 1964–65, prices were rising at an annual rate exceeding 80 percent.

In 1961 the multiple rate system was eliminated, the currency was devalued by 40 percent (followed by devaluations of close to 50 percent in 1962 and 1963 and more than 100 percent in 1964). But these devaluations did little more than counteract inflation. Finally, in 1964, after a military takeover, policies were abruptly changed.

Table 2.4   Nominal and Real Exchange Rates, 1946–74

Year	Nominal Export Rate[a] (Old Cruzeiros/ U.S. Dollars)	Real Export Rate Index (1951 = 100)
1946	19.6	108.8
1947	18.7	116.4
1948	18.7	117.3
1949	18.7	107.3
1950	18.7	108.8
1951	18.7	100.0
1952	18.7	86.4
1953	28.4	n.a.
1954	36.3	n.a.
1955	43.0	100.7
1956	50.0	109.6
1957	53.0	77.3
1958	65.4	117.1
1959	114.0	143.2
1960	160.0	152.6
1961	268.0	182.0
1962	390.0	176.3
1963	575.0	148.1
1964	1,284.0	181.8
1965	1,900.0	178.3
1966	2,220.0	152.5
1967	2,660.0	145.3
1968	3,390.0	154.0
1969	4,070.0	161.6
1970	4,590.0	158.2
1971	5,290.0	154.7
1972	5,930.0	154.0
1973	6,130.0	156.0
1974	6,790.0	159.4

Source: Fishlow (1975) for nominal rates; real rates are the product of nominal rates multiplied by the ratio of United States wholesale prices to Brazilian wholesale prices. See Carvalho and Haddad (1978, chap. 2) for details. This has been called the purchasing power parity adjusted nominal exchange rate (PPP-NER) (see chap. 1 of this volume).

[a]For noncoffee exports during years of multiple exchange rates.

In summary, the import substitution phase was characterized by increasingly severe restrictions on imports. The major policy instrument was a cascaded multiple exchange rate system favoring domestic pro-

Table 2.5   Inflation Rates in Brazil, 1951–74 (Annual Percentage Change)

Years	General Price Index[a] (1)	Wholesale Price Index[a] (2)	Consumer Price Index[b] (3)	Implicit Price Deflator (4)
1951	16.5	17.4	10.8	12.0
1952	11.8	9.4	20.4	13.2
1953	14.8	25.0	17.6	15.3
1954	27.0	22.3	25.6	21.4
1955	16.4	15.9	18.9	16.8
1956	19.9	26.2	21.8	23.2
1957	14.2	3.8	13.4	13.2
1958	13.0	35.1	17.3	11.1
1959	37.8	36.0	51.9	29.2
1960	29.2	34.5	23.8	26.3
1961	37.0	53.2	42.9	33.3
1962	51.6	45.5	55.8	54.8
1963	75.4	83.2	80.2	78.0
1964	90.5	84.5	86.6	87.8
1965	56.8	31.4	45.5	55.4
1966	38.0	42.1	41.2	38.8
1967	28.3	21.2	24.1	27.1
1968	24.2	24.8	24.5	27.8
1969	20.8	18.7	24.3	22.3
1970	19.8	18.7	20.9	19.8
1971	20.4	21.3	18.1	20.4
1972	17.0	16.1	14.0	17.0
1973	15.1	15.0	13.7	15.5
1974	28.7	35.2	33.7	34.0
	Annual Average Rate			
1952–73	30.9	31.1	32.9	30.4
1952–58	16.7	19.7	19.3	16.3
1959–64	53.6	56.2	56.9	51.6
1965–73	26.7	23.3	25.1	27.1
1968–73	19.6	19.2	19.3	20.5

Source: Fundação Getúlio Vargas, Conjuntura Economica (various issues).
Note: The changes in cols. 1 and 4 are measured from annual averages, those in cols. 2 and 3 from December to December.
[a]The general price index is a weighted average of the wholesale price index (0.6), consumer price index (0.3), and construction cost index (0.1).
[b]Consumer price index in Rio de Janeiro City.

duction of finished consumer goods. Exports were discouraged at the same time, since the export rate was always below the import rate.

After 1964, exchange premiums and advance deposits were eliminated or reduced, tariffs were lowered (1967), and a crawling-peg system was adopted (1968). More important, specific incentives, such as rebates of domestic taxes and direct subsidies in some cases, were introduced to encourage exports. The effects of these changes are evident in the growth rates of manufacturing output, employment, and exports presented earlier. The major export promotion instruments will be analyzed in greater detail in section 2.3.

2.2.3   The Structure of the Manufacturing Sector

The export promotion strategy of the late 1960s transformed Brazil's manufacturing sector. The size of the manufacturing sector grew relative to other economic activities, and manufactured exports that formed less than 1 percent of the value of manufactured output rose to more than 3 percent in 1970. The structure of manufacturing activity also changed. Notable have been increases in the relative share of basic industries such as iron and steel, machinery, and transportation equipment. Their share in manufacturing output and employment rose from 29 to 35 percent and from 30 to 37 percent respectively from 1959–70 (see table 2.6). In 1959, exports of these industries formed less than 3 percent of manufactured exports, in 1970 their combined share was more than 40 percent. On the other hand, there have been decreases in the relative shares in output of textiles and clothing and food products. Most other activities have experienced no changes in their relative roles.

2.2.4   The Labor Market

Brazil's population and labor force growth rates are high, even in contrast with those of most other developing countries. The population growth rate has remained stable at 2.9 percent, both during the 1960s and for the five-year interval from 1970 to 1975. This rate was almost exactly equal to the growth rate of the labor force over the same period, although the urban population rose considerably more rapidly, at a rate of 5 percent per annum in the 1960s and at 4.5 percent from 1970 to 1975. Nonetheless, the fraction of the labor force engaged in agriculture remains high and was still 46 percent in 1975. Thus Brazil's urban labor force will grow rapidly for years to come, as urban in-migration and the rapidly growing population both contribute to its increase.

Brazil's experience with employment and real wage rates has been marked by as sharp a contrast as have her trade policies. Tables 2.7 and 2.8 give the data on wages, employment, and changes in employment and output. From the late 1950s until the late 1960s, manufacturing

Table 2.6   **The Structure of Employment, Production, and Trade in the Brazilian Manufacturing Sector, 1959 and 1970**

Manufacturing Sector	% of Total Mfg. Employment		% of Total Mfg. Production		% of Total Mfg. Exports		% of Total Mfg. Imports	
	1959	1970	1959	1970	1959	1970	1959	1970
Nonmetallic minerals	9	8	4	4	*	2	1	1
Metal products	11	11	11	12	*	21	13	9
Machinery	3	7	3	5	1	11	22	11
Electrical equipment	3	5	4	5	*	3	6	5
Transportation equipment	4	6	7	9	1	4	21	7
Wood products	5	5	2	2	2	5	*	*
Furniture	4	4	2	2	*	*	*	*
Paper products	3	3	3	3	*	1	5	1
Rubber products	1	3	3	2	*	1	*	*
Leather and hides	1	1	1	1	4	3	*	*
Chemicals	4	1	10	12	35	20	25	12
Pharmaceuticals	1	4	2	3	*	1	1	1
Perfumery	1	1	2	2	3	2	*	*
Plastics	1	2	1	2	*	*	*	*
Textiles	21	15	13	10	2	6	*	1
Clothing and footwear	6	7	3	3	*	2	*	*
Food	14	13	21	19	50	15	3	2
Beverages	2	2	2	2	*	*	*	*
Tobacco	1	1	1	1	*	*	*	*
Printing and publishing	3	3	2	2	*	*	*	*
Miscellaneous	2	2	1	1	*	1	2	2

Source: Carvalho and Haddad (1978).
*Less than 0.5%; values may not add to 100 because of rounding.

employment growth was very slow: an index of manufacturing employment, with 1970 equal to 100, stood at 60.3 in 1955 and at 73.1 in 1965, indicating a growth rate of less than 2 percent per annum over that decade. Growth was slow despite the rapid growth of manufacturing output, which averaged 9.1 percent annually in the 1950s, 3.7 percent annually between 1960 and 1965, and 10.3 percent annually from 1965 to 1970. From 1965 to 1968, manufacturing employment rose only marginally faster, but thereafter growth was considerably more rapid: from 78.6 in 1968, the index of manufacturing employment rose to 100 in 1970 and 133.7 in 1975.

In 1959–70, manufacturing real output and manufacturing employment grew by 105 and 51 percent respectively, implying an average manufacturing employment-output elasticity of about 0.5 (see table 2.8). No pattern in elasticities is discernible between faster- and slower-growing industries. Output of eleven industries grew more than 105 percent over the period. Of those eleven, six had employment-output elasticities above the average; five had lower employment elasticities. The ten slower-growing industries were evenly split between those with above- and below-average employment elasticities.

Parallel with the increase in employment growth after the export promotion strategy was introduced, there was a marked change in regulations governing employment in Brazil. In earlier years there had been a fairly high minimum wage (see table 2.7) that affected a significant fraction of the urban labor force. In the 1960s, however, the nominal minimum wage was not increased in pace with the price level, so that the real minimum wage fell, until it was constant in the late 1960s at a significantly lower level than earlier. As will be seen below in section 2.4, the fraction of the labor force covered by the minimum wage fell con-

Table 2.7   **Labor Market Conditions in Brazil, 1955–74**

Year	Population (Millions) (1)	Manufacturing Employment (1970 = 100) (2)	Real Wage in Manufacturing (1963 = 100) (3)	Real Minimum Wage, Rio de Janeiro (1974 Cruzeiros) (4)
1955	60.2	60.3	91.1	629
1956	62.0	60.0	98.2	657
1957	63.1	56.2	105.6	—
1958	65.8	60.8	106.2	—
1959	67.8	66.1	99.2	701
1960	69.8	n.a.	n.a.	658
1961	71.8	64.0	104.6	666
1962	73.9	73.8	100.0	—
1963	76.0	73.4	114.2	608
1964	78.2	77.4	116.8	581
1965	80.5	73.1	118.2	480
1966	82.8	72.7	118.4	440
1967	85.2	73.2	121.6	406
1968	87.6	78.6	126.9	416
1969	90.2	78.5	139.1	394
1970	92.8	100.0	139.1	385
1971	95.4	88.7	150.8	382
1972	98.2	95.1	153.4	388
1973	101.0	125.4	155.0	397
1974	n.a.	133.7	162.8	377

Sources: Col. 1: Fundação Getúlio Vargas, *Conjuntura Economica*, 1973; cols. 2 and 4: Carvalho and Haddad (1978).

Table 2.8   Percentage Increases in Real Output and Employment and Employment-Output Elasticities, 1959–70

Manufacturing Sector	Percentage Changes		Employment Output Elasticity
	Employment	Real Output[a]	
Nonmetallic minerals	30	89	.34
Metal products	52	133	.39
Machinery	211	292	.72
Electrical equipment	121	249	.48
Transportation equipment	119	136	.88
Wood products	48	89	.54
Furniture	54	107	.50
Paper products	66	60	1.11
Rubber products	80	31	2.62
Leather and hides	9	24	.35
Chemicals	47	138	.34
Pharmaceuticals	56	289	.19
Perfumery	44	86	.51
Plastics	385	379	1.02
Textiles	5	29	.18
Clothing and footwear	69	115	.60
Food	38	87	.44
Beverages	37	60	.62
Tobacco	15	67	.23
Printing and publishing	62	123	.50
Miscellaneous	66	150	.44
Total	51	105	.49

Source: Calculated from data in Carvalho and Haddad (1978).
[a]Real output obtained by deflating nominal values by the wholesale price index.

siderably in the face of this decline and constancy. It therefore seems evident that the considerably more rapid rate of expansion of employment in the manufacturing sector occurred at the same time when the minimum wage was becoming less restrictive. This is not to state, however, that there were no remaining labor market distortions in Brazil. On the contrary, there were a social security tax (which amounted to 20–30 percent of direct wage payments by the late 1960s), fairly severe restrictions on wages to be paid for second- and third-shift workers, and a fairly strict set of conditions under which employees could be laid off or dismissed from their jobs. Moreover, funds were available for the purchase of capital goods, which tended to induce the choice of more capital-intensive techniques than might otherwise have been chosen. The effects of these factors upon employment and the consequences of trade strategy for it are covered later in this chapter.

2.3 The Brazilian Trade Regime

This section has the dual purpose of presenting estimates of effective rates of protection covering the period 1958 to 1967 and determining the extent of subsidization of given exports in the export promotion phase.

2.3.1 Effective Protection Estimates

There are three major effective protection studies for Brazil: Bergsmann (1970, 1975) and Fishlow (1975). We have reproduced Fishlow's estimates only in table 2.9 below. These are based upon price comparisons and use the so-called Balassa method. They thus correct for redundancy in activities where there are few if any imports. Fishlow observed that domestic prices were typically lower than those implied by the tariff plus the premium implied by other trade restrictions. This was especially true for the highly protected consumer nondurables and durables but less so for intermediate and capital goods (Fishlow 1975, pp. 48–50). The estimates given below are not grouped according to trade category (exportable, importable, etc.) as suggested in chatper 1 because there were so few manufactured exports in the late 1950s and early 1960s and because the high degree of aggregation of each activity meant that both imports and exports could be significant within a category. Interpretation of ERPs would be difficult in such a case.[4] This point is further discussed in section 2.4.

Several points are illustrated in table 2.9. First, observe the sharp increase in protection from 1958 to 1963. Rates went up in all activities; the general average more than doubled, while that for manufactures rose by 75 percent. Then, after the inauguration of the export promotion policy, protection fell precipitously. In 1967 protection given the manufacturing sector was approximately 50 percent less than it was in 1958. However, manufacturing ERPs were still high despite the reduction, and the range was wide (8 percent for printing and publishing to 182 percent for rubber products).

The "cascaded" nature of protection is well reflected in the averages for consumer, intermediate, and capital goods. Until 1966 there was a clear distinction among the groups, rates being very high for consumer goods and much lower for intermediate and capital goods. In 1966 and 1967 the rates for capital goods were higher than those for intermediate goods, although this may be because some consumer durables were included in the "capital goods" group. The cascade effect is reinforced when one notes that raw materials and agricultural products were imported with zero or very low tariffs.

The cascade structure was reduced in relative terms after 1963. In 1958 the average rate for consumer goods was almost five times that for capital goods; by 1963 this ratio was reduced to about three, and by 1967 to either two or 1.25, depending upon the choice of estimate. Since one of the main causes of distortions from protection comes from variation among the rates, we can infer from table 2.9 that the tariff

Table 2.9   Effective Rates of Protection in Brazil (Percentage)

Sector	1958[a]	1963[a]	1966[a]	1967[a]	1967[b]
Primary vegetable products	−47	−15	−13	−14	−14
Primary animal products	24	12	16	18	—
Mining	− 5	34	24	13	9
Manufacturing (average)[d]	106	184	108 (106)	63 (61)	48
Nonmetallic minerals	73	103	72	45	48
Metal products	61	124	63	35	33
Machinery	22	68	30	32	31
Electrical equipment	83	169	112	67	57
Transportation equipment	82	147	103	64	81
Wood products	138 (105)	176 (169)	120 (112)	81 (72)	44
Furniture	221	367	251	90	92
Paper products	86	169	91	43	42
Rubber products	139 (114)	221 (215)	158 (152)	126 (119)	182
Leather and hides	248	405	174	127	84
Chemicals	56	146	56	29	20
Pharmaceuticals	17	60	1	10	10
Perfumery	279	453	281	121	70
Plastics	281	489	332	133	117
Textiles	239 (210)	298 (291)	232 (224)	162 (154)	88
Clothing	264	481	321	107	154
Food	502 (387)	687 (652)	423 (394)	252 (218)	71
Beverages	171	243	183	104	76
Tobacco	273 (252)	469 (464)	299 (293)	114 (108)	79
Printing and publishing	139	305	142	4	8
Miscellaneous	88	175	95	47	45
General average, all sectors[d]	30 (26)	75 (74)	44 (43)	24 (23)	14
Manufacturing industry by economic groups[d]					
Consumer goods	242 (211)	360 (352)	230 (222)	122 (113)	66
Intermediate goods	65 (63)	131 (130)	68 (67)	40 (40)	39
Capital goods[c]	53	113	69	56	52

Source: Fishlow (1975, p. 58a).

[a]Computed with input-output coefficients from the 1959 matrix deflated by 1959 tariffs. The numbers in parentheses were obtained under the hypothesis that the agricultural inputs were not taxed.

[b]Computed with input-output coefficients from the 1971 matrix deflated by 1967 tariffs. All totals and subtotals were weighted by the structure of value added in 1959 adjusted for tariffs, with vegetable products assumed to have zero taxes.

[c]Includes some consumer durables.

[d]Averages are weighted by 1959 value added.

structure became much less distorted after 1966. Not only was the average level of protection substantially reduced, but the tariff structure also became much more homogeneous.

2.3.2 Price Differentials between Domestic and Foreign Markets

Brazil's export promotion strategy was based on three main instruments: the import liberalization measures of 1966 and 1967, the minidevaluation (crawling-peg) policy, and fiscal incentives. Here we analyze and quantify the fiscal instruments used to stimulate exports. These fiscal incentives are tax exemptions, subsidies, and various other benefits of a more general nature.[5] We will show that these instruments allow domestic producers to sell in world markets at prices some 40 percent below what they would receive in domestic markets. The most important fiscal incentives are related to two Brazilian taxes:` the IPI (tax on industrialized products) and the ICM (tax on the turnover of merchandise).[6] The IPI is a federal tax applied to all industrial products. The IPI tax rates vary among products according to their "essentiality." Thus cigarettes, alcoholic beverages, and cars are, on average, heavily taxed, while foodstuffs are subject to the lowest rate. The ICM is a state tax applied to all traded products. A single rate applies within each state, although it varies from state to state.[7]

Tax exemptions for exports include both (*a*) rebates of IPI tax by Law 4502 (1964) and regulated by Decree-Law 6514 (1967); and (*b*) a drawback of ICM tax on manufactured products (constitution of 1967 and Decree-Law 406 [1968]). Pressed by the federal government, some states have extended the rebates to primary products exported as well.

Subsidies to encourage exports include a tax credit premium and low interest rates on loans related to export activities. IPI tax credits are given up to the limit of 15 percent of value added. In some cases, depending on the state, a similar tax credit is given for the ICM tax. When given, the ICM credit rate is equal to the IPI rate up to the limit of 13 percent of value added. These tax credits are granted against exports of manufactures and can be used to pay other IPI or ICM debts. Eventually, any positive balance remaining in favor of the firm can be paid in cruzeiros by the government (federal or state). If the drawback of tariffs on imported inputs is used, tax credits are applied to the exporting price net of the imported inputs. The firm has the option of deciding to take the drawback or applying these tax subsidies to the full exporting price.

Credit incentives take the form of subsidized interest rates for loans linked to exporting activities. Some industries benefit from existing programs under which loans are awarded under very special conditions. The principal source of subsidy to the exporting sector via credit was

Resolucão 71 (1967) of the Central Bank.[8] Under Resolucão 71, commercial banks that operate with foreign currencies can obtain resources from the discount window at low rates (4 percent a year) as long as they are lending to the export sector. The exporting firm obtains from CACEX[9] a certificate that the firm will export (Certificado de Habilitacão). With this certificate the firm can borrow up to 80 percent of the export value for 120 days at an interest rate of 8 percent a year. Credit can be obtained under these same conditions based on previous exports for which no borrowing was undertaken earlier.

In Appendix B, we have derived expressions that incorporate the effects of these fiscal incentives upon exporters' prices in the domestic market and the world market. Table 2.10 summarizes results under four sets of assumptions concerning tax rates and credits and subsidized credit. The top half of table 2.10 gives these assumed values for the various elements of the expressions in Appendix B. The differences

Table 2.10   Subsidies to Exports of Industrial Goods in Brazil under Different Hypotheses

	Cases			
Parameters	1	2	3	4
ICM tax rate applied to the internal supply price	0.13	0.13	0.13	0.13
IPI tax rate applied to the internal supply price	0.08	0.10	0.10	0.15
Income tax rate	0.225	0.225	0.225	0.225
Tariff rate on imported inputs	0.25	0.25	0.25	0.25
Market interest rate minus interest rate given on loans to export activities	0.08	0.08	0.08	0.14
ICM tax premium	0.08	0.10	0.10	0.13
IPI tax premium	0.08	0.10	0.10	0.15
Sum of ICM and IPI tax premiums	0.16	0.20	0.20	0.28
Profits per unit of output as a fraction of the foreign price	0.10	0.10	0.10	0.16
Imported input content	0.20	0.20	0.30	0.20
Loans to export activities per unit of output (as a fraction of the foreign price)	0.50	0.50	0.50	0.65
Ratio, world to domestic price	0.6331	0.6057	0.6026	0.5047
Ratio, simplified version[a] world to domestic price	0.6944	0.6591	0.6591	0.5910
Ratio, world to internal supply price[b]	0.6837	0.6662	0.6629	0.5804
Subsidy as a percentage of the internal supply price	14.63	16.30	14.71	28.95

[a]The simplified version (see eq. A6, App. B) includes only the effects of ICM and IPI tax credits and rebates.

[b]The internal supply price does not include the IPI but includes the ICM on inputs.

among the cases are: case 2 has a higher IPI tax rate (10 percent) than case 1; case 3 has a higher imported input content (30 percent) than case 2; case 4 has the same imported input content as cases 1 and 2 but has a greater amount of special program loans than cases 1–3; case 4 also has a higher IPI tax rate, obtains a higher credit subsidy, and has higher ICM and IPI tax credits than cases 1–3.

Reasons for the choice of values in each case are as follows: (1) the 13 percent ICM tax rate is the current rate; (2) the 8–15 percent rates are the typical range for the IPI tax; (3) the legal income tax rate is 30 percent, but a deduction of 25 percent (of the 30 percent, or 7.5 percent) is allowed if firms engage in special export programs; (4) the interest rate differential is arbitrarily assumed to be 8 or 14 percent; and (5) other values are arbitrary choices.

Under the various assumptions, exporters can sell in world markets at prices about 50 to 60 percent of those in domestic markets. The subsidy is in the range of 15 to 30 percent of the internal supply price.[10] It must be emphasized here that these subsidies apply mainly to exports of industrial goods. Most of the exports of agricultural goods are still taxed. Occasionally the taxation is direct either in terms of tariffs or in terms of export quotas. In other cases it is indirect, since no rebate of ICM paid is granted to exports in a number of important cases like coffee and soybeans.

2.3.3 Summary

Levels of protection on domestic production fell markedly and became more homogeneous after the introduction of the export promotion strategy in the mid-1960s. In 1967 average ERPs on manufactures were in the neighborhood of 50 percent while average ERPs on consumer goods were some 50 to 100 percent higher than those for intermediate and capital goods. In the import substitution phase, ERPs on consumer goods were approximately four times those on capital and intermediate goods. As in most LDCs, manufacturing activity is more protected than NRB production. In Brazil, nonanimal primary products faced negative effective protection.

The export promotion strategy has used tax exemptions and subsidies and preferential credit facilities to encourage manufactured exports. The total subsidy from these measures was found to range from 15 to 30 percent under various assumptions about the extent of the various individual subsidy elements.

2.4   Trade and Employment in Brazil

In this section we calculate the labor content of Brazilian tradable activities. Our focus is limited to manufacturing activities mainly to avoid problems stemming from the availability of natural resources. Given Brazil's factor endowment, our a priori expectations are that Brazil's manufactured exports will be more labor-intensive than her import-competing manufactures. Furthermore, if human capital and physical capital are complementary factors of production, then manufactured exports will be relatively less skill-intensive than Brazilian import substitutes. Labor intensities will be examined first, and skill intensities will be analyzed later in the section.

2.4.1   Labor Requirements

Total direct and indirect labor requirements used in producing exportables and importables can be estimated from the input-output matrixes available for Brazilian economy for the years 1959, 1970, and 1971.[11] In principle, labor requirements should be computed per unit of value added in any given sector. The input-output matrixes presented input coefficients with respect to value of production, however, and so we first computed labor requirements on this basis, then derived estimates per unit of value added more indirectly.

The matrixes for 1959 and 1971 were aggregated into twenty-five sectors, of which twenty-one were manufacturing activities and the others were mining, construction, agriculture, and services. The 1970 matrix was more highly disaggregated than those for 1959 and 1971 but covered only mining and manufacturing sectors. The matrix contained fifty-eight activities, of which two were mining and fifty-six were manufacturing activities. We first present our labor estimates derived from the relatively aggregative 1959 and 1971 I-0 (input-output) tables, then give results computed from the more detailed 1970 table. It should be noted that the 1959 and 1971 estimates relate to all exports and all imports of manufactures. That is, we do not classify activities as importables and exportables, then calculate weighted averages of labor coefficients of activities in each category. Rather, we calculate labor coefficients for exportables and importables using exports and imports in all categories as weights. The reason for this procedure is the high degree of aggregation in these tables. In many cases there were significant exports and imports in each activity (see appendix tables 2.A.1 and 2.A.2). This made interpretation of trade categories ambiguous. However, the 1970 I-0 table was disaggregated to the extent that categorization of activities was possible. In that case we present estimates of labor requirements corresponding more closely to the trade categories defined by the T statistic outlined in the chapter 1 of this volume.

Estimates for 1959 and 1971

To obtain direct and indirect labor requirements per unit of exports and of import substitutes, we used the following procedure. First we derived trade weights from the percentage distribution of 1959 and 1971 exports and imports among the twenty-one manufacturing sectors. Next we computed direct labor inputs, in man-years, per million cruzeiros of value of production for each manufacturing activity. These coefficients were derived from the 1960 and 1970 censuses. The census of 1960 gave values for 1959 expressed in prices of that year. The 1970 census values were assumed to be valid for 1971 once they were adjusted to 1970 prices. After computing direct labor requirements for each sector per unit of value of production, we next derived indirect requirements. This was done by applying the direct labor coefficients for 1959 and 1970 to the commodity inputs (both direct and indirect) from each of the twenty-one sectors into each other sector, as given by the input-output matrixes for 1959 and 1971. The procedure just outlined gave labor requirements, direct and indirect separately, for 1959 in terms of value of production at prices of that year and for 1971 in terms of value of production at 1970 prices. The coefficients for 1959 were deflated by the increase in prices between that year and 1970 to allow a meaningful comparison of the two vectors as given in tables 2.11 and 2.12.

The vectors of labor requirements per unit of value added, also shown in tables 2.11 and 2.12, were computed as follows. First we calculated value added by deducting transportation, advertising, and other expenses not related to payments to labor or capital from the value of "industrial transformation" (defined as the value of production minus the value of intermediate products). Second, we computed direct labor requirements per unit of value added (increasing the ratio of labor to value of production by the ratio of the latter to value added). We then computed indirect labor per unit of value added in each sector, such indirect labor being the sum of direct and indirect labor incorporated in inputs from all other sectors. Finally we added the direct and indirect labor requirements to obtain the ratio of total labor to value added for each of the twenty-one manufacturing activities.[12] In contrast to the method outlined in chapter 1, this procedure relates direct and indirect labor requirements to direct value added rather than to direct plus indirect value added. That is the reason for the differences between direct and total (direct plus indirect) labor coefficients given in tables 2.11 and 2.12.[13]

The results given in tables 2.11 and 2.12 indicate the wide range of labor requirements in manufacturing. In 1959 the most labor-using industry (in terms of value-added measures) was clothing. Other labor-intensive industries were wood products, furniture, nonmetallic minerals, textiles, publishing, and leather. The same pattern occurred in 1971, with clothing being the second most labor-using industry behind wood products. The other labor-intensive industries in 1959 generally remained labor-intensive in 1971.

Table 2.11   Direct and Indirect Labor Requirements in Manufacturing, 1959 (Man-Years per One Million 1970 Cruzeiros of Value of Production or of Value Added)

Manufacturing Sector	Value of Production			Value Added		
	Direct	Indirect	Total	Direct	Indirect	Total
Nonmetallic minerals	46.17	12.12	58.29	144.60	30.03	174.64
Metal products	31.36	22.57	53.93	87.58	58.71	146.30
Machinery	41.30	23.31	64.61	102.63	62.53	165.16
Electrical equipment	27.58	28.05	55.63	85.17	76.30	161.47
Transportation equipment	22.84	24.21	47.05	72.34	67.40	139.75
Wood products	62.89	14.31	77.20	157.23	36.31	193.55
Furniture	65.33	28.47	93.80	159.53	74.64	234.18
Paper products	26.06	22.57	48.63	87.63	70.20	157.83
Rubber products	15.64	12.05	27.69	39.22	33.23	72.45
Leather and hides	43.27	17.12	60.39	129.40	47.87	177.28
Chemicals	16.16	23.47	39.63	47.15	49.23	96.39
Pharmaceuticals	26.26	13.03	39.29	80.46	32.80	113.26
Perfumery	18.13	17.97	36.10	72.39	44.63	117.02
Plastics	27.09	19.38	46.47	68.83	50.51	119.34
Textiles	49.57	22.80	72.37	150.34	65.82	216.16
Clothing and footwear	54.38	57.03	111.41	155.57	156.38	311.96
Food	20.87	6.58	27.45	99.05	22.48	121.53
Beverages	35.09	8.98	44.07	95.88	29.43	125.31
Tobacco	22.35	3.82	26.17	52.18	10.98	63.16
Printing and publishing	50.25	19.72	69.98	120.69	60.85	181.54
Miscellaneous	55.47	15.69	71.16	126.18	41.79	167.98

Source: Census of 1960 and input-output matrix for 1959. The relative price level used for 1959 over 1970 is 0.02235.

Before going further we need to mention two qualifications, rather opposite in nature, with respect to the methods employed in computing indirect labor requirements. One is that, because of limitations imposed by the available input-output matrixes, the estimates refer only to employment in manufacturing and mining. The omission of indirect employment in agriculture results in an understatement of total employment generated by manufacturing and by exports in particular.[14] This omission is not necessarily bad, since agriculture is an NRB tradable category that should have been omitted if we were able to calculate indirect employment following the procedure outlined in chapter 1. The second qualification is that the procedure we have followed in estimating indirect labor inputs implicitly assumes that all industrial inputs are, or can be, domestically supplied.[15] Indeed, the assumption is that all inputs are nontradables (like "home goods" as specified in the introductory chapter of this volume for purposes of estimating indirect inputs). This qualification biases our direct plus indirect estimates upward. The net effect of these qualifications is that the employment coefficients reported here may be too low or too high, depending on the relative weight assigned to these two qualifications.

Having determined the vectors of total labor requirements across manufacturing, the next step was to apply them to the vectors of exports and imports for 1959 and 1971 (see appendix tables 2.A.1 and 2.A.2), to obtain average labor coefficients generated by an increase of one million cruzeiros of exportables or importables.[16] We used both value added and value of production in these calculations. Both are reported in tables 2.13 and 2.14.

In 1959 importable manufactures were more labor-intensive than exportables. On the other hand, the reverse is true in 1971. The 1959 relationship reflects the fact that exports of manufactured goods in 1959

Table 2.12   **Direct and Indirect Labor Requirements in Manufacturing, 1971 (Man-Years per One Million 1970 Cruzeiros of Value of Production or of Value Added)**

Manufacturing Sector	Value of Production			Value Added		
	Direct[a]	Indirect	Total	Direct[a]	Indirect	Total
Nonmetallic minerals	48.73	11.08	59.81	88.65	21.51	110.16
Metal products	18.37	11.29	29.66	49.15	29.04	78.19
Machinery	27.18	12.15	39.33	53.82	28.13	81.95
Electrical equipment	21.06	12.03	33.09	45.06	28.48	73.54
Transportation equipment	16.58	14.96	31.54	41.11	35.07	76.18
Wood products	51.07	30.37	81.44	120.64	72.15	192.79
Furniture	50.67	16.78	67.45	105.78	40.67	146.45
Paper products	23.54	10.07	33.61	58.26	24.85	83.11
Rubber products	16.61	8.14	24.75	34.41	19.52	53.93
Leather and hides	34.37	20.30	54.67	88.32	50.93	139.25
Chemicals	8.22	6.47	14.69	21.88	15.75	37.63
Pharmaceuticals	12.33	6.92	19.25	18.90	14.71	33.61
Perfumery	11.86	9.44	21.30	26.26	22.84	49.10
Plastics	22.11	8.51	30.62	46.89	20.69	67.58
Textiles	31.67	13.91	45.58	77.38	34.24	111.62
Clothing and footwear	41.82	30.54	72.36	102.20	74.97	177.17
Food	15.82	10.92	26.74	61.24	32.71	93.95
Beverages	26.70	9.08	35.78	58.19	21.26	79.45
Tobacco	13.01	1.79	14.80	22.06	4.04	26.10
Printing and publishing	33.06	10.83	43.89	55.87	23.98	79.85
Miscellaneous	33.83	10.62	44.45	62.52	23.95	86.47

Source: Census of 1970 and input-output matrix for 1971; see text for computations.

[a]Taken as equal to the direct requirements for 1970 from the census.

Table 2.13   Total Labor Requirements in Manufacturing, 1959 and 1971
(Man-Years per One Million 1970 Cruzeiros Increase in Value
of Production or in Value Added)

Source of Increase in Demand[a]	Value of Production		Value Added	
	1959[b]	1971	1959[b]	1971
Import substitution	50	31	128	71
Exports	36	37	115	87

Source: See text.
[a]Computed from the overall composition of value added or value of production in manufacturing for 1959 and 1970.
[b]To obtain values in current cruzeiros, divide figures for labor requirements by 0.02235.

Table 2.14   Total Labor Requirements in Manufacturing Exports by
Destination, 1959, 1970, and 1972 (Man-Years per One Million
1970 Cruzeiros Increase in Value of Production or in Value
Added of Exports)

Export Destination	Value of Production			Value Added		
	1959	1970	1972	1959	1970	1972
United States and Canada	38	34	42	115	94	106
European Economic Community	32	33	43	114	85	112
Latin American Free Trade Area	53	34	34	141	79	78
Other developing countries	42	29	25	133	72	62

Source: See text. For data on exports, see Carvalho and Haddad (1978, appendix table A.13).
Note: For 1959 the direct plus indirect labor requirement vector was obtained from the input-output table of 1959; for 1970 and 1972 this vector was based on the matrix of 1971. Results for 1959 and 1972 have been converted to 1970 prices.

were not only small in value but also heavily weighted by food and chemical products (the latter consisting mainly of raw vegetable oils). Since the labor/output ratios for both of these sectors are likely to be seriously understated because of the omission of (indirect) agricultural labor input, it is not surprising to find a low ratio of labor absorption in 1959. It is also possible that the 1959 system of incentives distorted production to the extent that it reversed the pattern of labor requirements from what one might expect in the absence of commodity market distortions. The relative difference between import substitutes and exports is narrowed, though, when we consider labor in relation to value added instead of value of production. As the weights change from value of production to value added, exports become proportionately more weighted with labor-intensive industries while imports become proportionately more capital-intensive.

The results for 1971 match our expectations. Exports were labor-intensive relative to import-competing industries, with labor coefficients being about 20 percent higher in exports when value-of-production weights were used and 23 percent higher when value-added weights were used.

Next we proceeded to estimate exportable labor requirements by destination of exports. Four destinations were used: the United States and Canada; the European Economic Community (EEC);[17] other Latin American countries (LAFTA);[18] and other developing countries.

Estimates were made for 1959, 1970, and 1972 trade patterns, using the census data and the input-output matrixes for 1959 and 1971. The results are shown in table 2.14.

Given Brazil's factor endowments, we expected that exports to developed countries would have larger labor requirements than those for LDC trade. Again, the 1959 estimates do not meet these expectations, probably because, as we mentioned before, exports of manufactures in that year still consisted mainly of food and vegetable oils. However, the results for 1970 and 1972 are fairly robust; the pattern of labor requirements meets our expectations except that exports to LAFTA in 1970 were as labor-intensive per unit of value of production as those to the United States and EEC. It is possible that the preferences accorded manufactures in LAFTA countries may have affected these estimates. LAFTA countries have lower, and in some cases zero, duties on Brazilian exports. Thus Brazil may be able to export more labor-intensive production within LAFTA. When we use value-added weights, the anomaly with respect to 1970 LAFTA exports disappears and the ranking by country grouping for 1970 and 1972 is consistent with Brazil's factor endowment, but the 1959 estimates remained inverted.

Estimates for 1970 and 1967–74

The 1970 Instituto Brasilero de Geografia e Estatistica (IBGE) matrix is much more disaggregated than the earlier ones but covers only mining and manufacturing activities. Therefore the problems concerning the linkages with the other sectors of the economy still remain.[19] The matrix consists of fifty-eight sectors, two in mining and fifty-six in manufacturing activities. This disaggregation, corresponding roughly to a three-digit classification, is a substantial improvement over the twenty-one manufacturing activities in the other I-0 tables.[20]

The IBGE matrix also included a vector of total (direct and indirect) labor requirements (production workers only) per value of production (again *industrial* employment only) for the same fifty-eight sectors.

Therefore our task was simply to classify 1970 imports and exports into the same categories as the matrix. (Imports and exports are presented in a disaggregated form in appendix table 2.A.3.) We should note two points. First, the classification was made from the dollar and not the cruzeiro value of imports and exports as was done previously, since the four-digit classification was available only in dollars. Second, in a few cases the classification was somewhat arbitrary, since we did not know the exact nature of the products included either in the matrix sectors or in the trade categories.

We then repeated the exercise described above to obtain labor requirements in terms of value of production and value added. These total labor requirements are (in man-years per million cruzeiros of exports or import substitutes):

	Value-of-Production Basis	Value-Added Basis
Exports of manufactures	23.3	39.3
Import substitutes	24.4	36.0

The values are lower than those for 1971 given in table 2.11 because these estimates refer to production workers only. Those of table 2.11 include all employees. Observe that the previously obtained higher labor requirement for exports disappears when computed on a value-of-production basis and is greatly reduced when computed on a value-added basis. We tried to determine whether this difference stems from differences in the input-output coefficients for 1970 and 1971 or changes in the composition of the trade flows from one year to the next. To do so, we aggregated the labor requirements of the IBGE 1970 matrix.[21] (The Spearman correlation coefficients among the labor/output vectors for the two matrixes were 0.99 for the direct and 0.97 for the total requirements.) Next we calculated labor requirements annually for the period 1967–74 by applying the IBGE matrix to trade flows in each year. The results, in table 2.15, suggest two conclusions. First, the larger exportable labor requirements (per unit of value of production) re-emerge in the results for 1970, but the change is so small as to suggest that the difference in level of aggregation does not make a great deal of difference in the results. Second, and more interesting, the composition of Brazil's exports has shifted in a more labor-intensive direction as export promotion efforts progressed after 1967. This observation also can be extended back to 1959, since it corresponds with the earlier observed increase in labor requirements in exportables between that year and 1971. Thus, the difference in calculated labor requirements appears to be much more the consequence of changes in the composition of trade flows than of changes in coefficients.

Table 2.15		Total Requirements of Production Workers in Manufacturing, 1967–74 (Man-Years per One Million 1970 Cruzeiros Increase in Value of Production)	
Years	Import Substitution[a] (1)	Exports[a] (2)	(2)/(1) (3)
1967	22	22	1.00
1968	23	22	.96
1969	23	20	.87
1970	23	24	1.04
1971	23	26	1.13
1972	24	28	1.17
1973	23	29	1.26
1974	22	28	1.27

Source: Labor requirements in man-years from IBGE input-output matrix. For details on computations, see text.
Note: Takes into account only the industrial sector.
[a]Computed from the composition of imports and exports of manufactures in each year.

2.4.2   Labor Requirements by Major Trade Categories

Thus far we have derived our labor coefficients using total exports and total imports of manufactures regardless of their source. Now we wish to compute labor coefficients for trade categories corresponding more closely to those outlined in the introductory chapter of this volume. To do so, we classified activities into exportables, importables, or noncompeting production on the basis of the share of net imports (imports minus exports) in total consumption (production plus imports minus exports). Calling that statistic T, manufactures were categorized:

(a)   as non-import-competing activities if T was greater than 0.75;
(b)   as importable activities if T fell between 0.05 and 0.75;
(c)   as marginal trade activities if T fell between ± 0.05; and
(d)   as exportable activities if T was less than -0.05.

The above criteria were modified in some cases by a judgment of the nature of the product. For instance, glass, automobiles and parts, rubber, and plastics would be classified as marginal trade items following these criteria. However they are clearly import-competing products and are so treated here.

Using this procedure, there were thirty-six importable, twelve marginal, and eight exportable activities in the fifty-six-activity 1970 IBGE matrix. Since the statistic T is always below 0.6 at our level of aggregation, no activity was classified as noncompeting. Of the exportables, five were further classified as processed natural-resource-based (NRB) and three as Heckscher-Ohlin-Samuelson (HOS) goods. The processed NRB exportables are wood products, leather and hides, raw vegetable oils, spun and woven natural fibers, and sugar. The HOS exportables are iron and steel, footwear, and other foodstuffs (see appendix table 2.A.3 for a complete listing of all activities and trade flows for each activity).

Weighted average labor requirements for each category are shown in two ways in table 2.16; one gives the direct labor content per unit of production or value added, and the other includes indirect labor (in the numerator) and indirect output or value added (in the denominator) of supplying manufacturing industries. Note that, as we mentioned earlier, these estimates use the procedure outlined in chapter 1 of this volume; those of tables 2.11 to 2.15 do not. These results are similar to those presented earlier. Manufactures classified as HOS exportables had significantly higher labor requirements than import competing manufactures irrespective of the measure (direct or direct plus indirect) or the weight (value added or value of production) used.

2.4.3 Skill Intensities of Brazilian Imports and Exports

In sections 2.3.1 and 2.3.2 we determined that Brazilian exports have higher labor requirements than Brazilian imports. It is important to extend this analysis further to make inferences of labor requirements, according to the skill content of the work force. That is the purpose of this section. Skill contents have been generally estimated with an arbitrary

Table 2.16   **Labor Requirements by Trade Categories, 1970 (Man-Years per One Million Cruzeiros of Value of Production or Value Added)**

Trade Category[a]	Direct Requirements per Unit		Direct Plus Indirect Requirements per Unit	
	Value of Production	Direct Value Added	Value of Production	Direct Plus Indirect Value Added
Import competing products	16.0	31.4	22.8	30.9
Exportables	22.3	63.9	30.2	57.8
NRB goods	24.9	63.4	32.1	61.0
HOS goods	18.0	65.1	27.1	51.1
Marginal trade items	18.2	46.8	24.4	45.7

Source: See text.

Note: Weighted by the composition of the value of production in each category for 1970. Estimates cover production workers only.

[a]Defined using the statistic T with some adjustments.

weighting of the number of persons employed in each skill category.[22] An alternative method is to compute an index based on wages. However, this measure includes other factors besides skills that do not pertain just to the "quality" of the labor force. We propose to use a variation of the wage index to approximate labor skills.

Previous work by Senna (1975) simplified our task. Using data for 1970 from the Two-thirds Law,[23] he developed a model similar to that of Mincer (1974) to explain the differences in the effects of schooling and job experience on the labor earnings. This model is given by the equation:

(1) $$ln\, W_i = \alpha + \beta_1 S_i + \beta_2 J_i + \beta_3 J_i{}^2 + u_i,$$

where

> $ln\, W_i =$ logarithm of wages and salaries of worker i;
> $S_i =$ schooling, measured by the number of full years of formal school attendance, for worker i;
> $J_i =$ job experience, measured by the number of years in the labor force, for worker i;
> $u_i =$ residual due to other effects.

We propose to use the estimated wage $(\hat{l}n\, W_i)$ implied by Senna's model to construct an index of labor skill. The advantage of using $\hat{l}n\, W_i$ rather than actual wages $(ln\, W_i)$ is that we are certain to capture the human capital content of the labor earnings. Thus, occasional quasi-rents or other distortions generated by transitory events will be left out of $\hat{l}n\, W_i$ (but not of $ln\, W_i$). That is, under the hypotheses associated with equation (1), $\hat{l}n\, W_i$ reflects only skill contents of the labor force.[24] We first computed the implied $\hat{l}n\, W_i$ for each worker, then calculated the average of $\hat{l}n\, W_i$ for each activity. The index was constructed from the anti-ln of the averages using as base the anti-ln of the overall weighted average of $\hat{l}n\, W_i$—that is, the estimated overall average. The results are presented in table 2.17.

To determine the total average skill intensities, we proceeded to calculate the production requirements for an increase of one million cruzeiros of final demand from exportables or importables for 1959[25] and 1971.

Next we constructed a weighted average of the direct and direct-indirect skill indexes for exportables and importables using as weights the production requirements in each industry divided by the total production requirements. The results are presented in table 2.18. For 1971 we also present figures in parentheses computed directly from average wages.

Observe first (in table 2.17) the wide range of skill index values (89.4 to 165.4). However, most (17) activities had skill index values

Table 2.17   Skill Content Indexes for Selected Sectors, 1970

Sector	Sample Size	Model Adjusted for Brazil	
		Estimated Average Wage[a]	Index of Skill (3.684 = 100)
Vegetable extraction	561	3.66	99.4
Mining	1,057	3.49	94.7
Food	2,384	3.59	97.5
Beverages	682	3.83	103.9
Tobacco	156	4.11	111.5
Textiles	1,670	3.71	100.7
Clothing and footwear	861	3.64	98.8
Wood products	1,167	3.33	90.3
Furniture	1,055	3.44	93.3
Paper products	690	3.57	96.9
Printing and publishing	870	4.08	110.7
Leather products	558	3.61	98.1
Rubber products	773	3.78	102.5
Chemicals	872	4.54	123.1
Oil and derivatives	275	6.09	165.4
Plastics	433	3.84	104.3
Nonmetallic minerals	1,498	3.40	92.4
Metal products	1,139	3.99	108.4
Machinery	4,663	3.90	105.9
Transportation equipment	1,753	3.99	108.2
Construction	5,125	3.29	89.4
Electricity generation	427	4.64	125.9
Miscellaneous	1,099	3.50	95.1

[a]Anti-$ln \left[\dfrac{\hat{l}n\ W_i}{n} \right]$.

within ±10 percent of the average for manufacturing. When skill content indexes were calculated for exportables and importables (table 2.18), we note that importables were more skill-intensive than exportables in both 1959 and 1971, with the difference being more marked for 1959, at least with regard to direct skill requirements. For 1971 the use of average wages as a proxy for skill content (see values in parentheses) also indicates that Brazilian imports are more skill-intensive than Brazilian exports. The inclusion of indirect requirements makes skill content differences larger in 1959 but smaller in 1971. In fact, in 1974 there is no difference between the direct plus indirect skill contents of exportables and importables. Our findings are broadly consistent with the HOS model of factor proportions, since the average skill content of the Brazilian work force is certainly lower than those of Brazil's major trading partners.[26]

2.4.4 Summary

In this section we have presented estimates of total labor requirements and the skill contents of Brazilian exportable and importable production. These estimates indicate first that Brazil's exportable production has become more labor-intensive since 1959. Second, estimated total labor coefficients are consistent with the expectations of the HOS model—namely, Brazil's exportables had higher labor requirements than her importables (in 1970–71), regardless of the weight (value of production or value added) or the labor requirement measure (direct or direct plus indirect) used. Third, estimated exportable labor requirements by destination of exports (DC or LDC) are also consistent with the HOS model, with export to developed nations having higher labor requirements than exports to developing nations. Finally, the skill content estimates suggest a complementarity between human and physical capital. Brazil's production of importables requires less labor (and presumably more capital) but more skill than her production of exportables.

Table 2.18 **Index of Average Skill Content of Brazilian Imports and Exports for 1959 and 1971**

| | Average Skill Content Indexes | |
Indexes	Direct Labor Requirements	Direct and Indirect Labor Requirements
1959		
Imports	100.3	168.4
Exports	95.7	130.6
1971		
Imports	111.9	174.4
	(130)	(199)
Exports	109.5	174.9
	(120)	(187)

Source: See text and table 2.17 for construction of index. (The base is the average direct skill requirements for each year.)
Note: The values in parentheses are the corresponding indexes based on average wages.

2.5   Factor Market Distortions and Factor Use: Trade and Employment Revisited

In this section we will describe the main factor market distortions and their possible effects on factor use.

2.5.1   The Labor Market

There are many phenomena that may cause labor market distortions in Brazil. We will concentrate our attention here upon the possible distortions generated by the minimum wage and the social security legislation which in our judgment are potentially the most important causes of labor market distortions.[27]

From the technical point of view, effective minimum wage legislation burdens less-skilled workers by limiting their employment and inducing people to hire better-qualified workers at the minimum wage level. Despite the lack of data to quantify the effects of minimum wage legislation, we do not think that minimum wage legislation has created significant distortions.

To support our argument, we calculated the distribution of industrial workers by wage levels where various wage levels were defined as fractions of the highest minimum wage in Brazil. (Unfortunately this information was not consistently available over time; the ratio of median wage to minimum wage was also used; see Carvalho and Haddad 1978, chap. 5.) Our calculations indicate that most workers earn more than the minimum, so that it may be inferred that the minimum wage was not effective. The main reason the minimum wage was not effective was inflation. The nominal minimum wage was often kept constant in the presence of inflation, so that, except in years when changes in the nominal minimum wage occurred, the number of workers earning more than the minimum wage increased. This has been especially true in recent years. For example, there was a substantial increase in the percentage of workers earning more than 3.7 times the minimum wage in 1972. In fact, almost 44 percent of total workers belonged to that group in 1972, compared to just 14 percent in 1968.

Since the minimum wage was kept fairly constant in real terms from 1968 to 1972, and since more workers have been earning more than the minimum wage, we can infer that the average real wage increased substantially during that period. In fact from 1968 to 1972 the average wage in manufacturing increased by about 21 percent in real terms.

Another potential cause of labor market distortions is the social security program that was introduced in 1945. According to Bacha, Mata, and Modenesi (1972), social security taxation was 7.9 percent of wages in 1945. Since then it has increased gradually to a rate of 43.9 percent in 1971. Since 1971, other labor legislation has been enacted introducing some other taxes. Generally these have had a small effect on the labor market.[28]

The legal social security rates are the same for all manufacturing sectors. However, firms may actually be subject to a lower rate for a variety of reasons (for details, see Bacha, Mata, and Modenesi 1972, Appendix A-3). For example, the Instituto Nacional do Previdencia Social (INPS) portion of the contribution[29] applies up to the limit of twenty times the minimum wage in Rio de Janeiro. This implies discrimination against unskilled labor in that city. We can draw inferences about the effect of social security legislation by computing the effective tax paid by each industry. This was possible only for the census years. Thus, for 1970 we computed the tax rate on labor by dividing social security payments by total payments to labor. In this way we have the effective proportional tax rate imposed on labor in each industrial activity at a two-digit level of disaggregation. These effective rates ranged from 22.85 percent to 29.72 percent in 1970. The average was 27.13 percent. Thus, there was a 30 percent difference between the lowest and highest rates. This difference certainly affected labor utilization in Brazil. The results will be used in section 2.5.3, where we attempt to quantify the effects of factor market distortions.

2.5.2   The Capital Market

As in other developing countries, capital markets were fragmented and highly distorted in Brazil until 1964. After 1964 many institutional changes, the most important one being the creation of "monetary correction," produced a sharp rise in financial intermediation. New financial assets and institutions were created, and by now it can be said that capital markets in Brazil are very developed and sophisticated when compared with those in other LDCs.

Since we are interested in the distortions in the use of capital, we will ignore incentives affecting savings and concentrate on those affecting investment. The potential distortions come from two sources: artificially low prices of capital goods, especially machinery and equipment, and subsidies in the form of credit at below market rates.

The Behavior of Prices of Capital Goods

The main distortion in the prices of capital goods is due to tariff differentials between capital goods and consumer goods. As we mentioned in section 2.3, nominal rates for capital goods imports have traditionally been lower than those for consumer goods. Also, recall that the allocation of foreign exchange from 1950 to 1957 tended to favor imports of raw materials and capital equipment.

It is also relevant to observe that, over the period 1955 to 1974, prices of capital goods in Brazil have risen less rapidly than in general. In the same period, real wages increased dramatically. Our calculations indicate that over these twenty years, the prices of imported capital goods inclusive of tariffs have risen less than half as much as wholesale prices in Brazil, while real wages in manufacturing rose by 80 percent in the same period (Carvalho and Haddad 1978, chap. 5). Thus nominal wages rose faster and the price of capital goods rose at a lower rate than inflation. Capital utilization ought to have been encouraged.

Distortions in the Credit Market

Until 1964, credit possibilities were limited principally to short-term loans to finance working capital made by the commercial banking system. Government credit policies were executed until 1952 through the Banco do Brasil, which acted as the central bank and revenue agent of the government. It also lent, at subsidized interest rates, to some favored sectors of the economy. After the creation of Banco Nacional de Desenvolvimento Econômico (BNDE), many of the lending activities of Banco do Brasil were transferred to it. From 1955 to 1963, all the credit operations of the BNDE were carried through the Fund for Economic Re-Equipment (FRE). The lion's share of the loans during 1955–57 went to public utilities. In this initial period the credit operations of the BNDE were limited in scope.

The conditions of the BNDE loans vary. The interest rate on the FRE (terms up to twenty years) ranged from 4 to 12 percent, depending on the sector that received the loan, plus monetary correction. The BNDE also has other lending facilities, such as FINAME (Special Fund Agency for Industrial Financing), FIPEME (Financing of Small and Medium Enterprises), FUNGIRO (Special Fund for the Financing of Working Capital), and FRMI (Fund for Industrial Modernization and Reorganization).

In all its operations, the real rate of interest on the BNDE loans was generally low (below 5 percent). Since some studies place the real private rate of return on capital in Brazil in the period 1954–67 at about 12 percent per year (see, e.g., Langoni 1973, p. 29), and since the minimum real rate on savings in Brazil during 1965–75 equaled 6 percent,[30] the market rate of interest charged on loans may be put at 10 percent plus full monetary correction.[31] We can then compute the implicit subsidy on the BNDE loans under several assumptions concerning terms and loan rates. The subsidy rate is the difference between the value of the loan and the present value of the implicit flow of payments on the loan, discounted at a real interest rate of 10 percent.

We assumed repayments in equal installments of $i/2$ percent each half-year, where i is the interest rate. This procedure tends to underestimate the subsidy. The results obtained were not sensitive to the assumptions concerning payments conditions, but the implicit subsidy rate varied substantially according to the interest rate and its term. For the period 1965–74, we estimated an implicit subsidy in BNDE loans varying from 10 percent to 50 percent of the value of the loan. On the average, we believe that this subsidy would be about 20 percent, which corresponds to a ten-year loan at a 4 percent real interest rate or to a six-year loan at a 2 percent real interest rate. Since the BNDE system financed about 60 to 70 percent of the cost of capital goods of the loan recipients during 1965–74, we can conclude, assuming that the remaining funds were obtained at market rates, that there was an average implicit subsidy of about 12 percent in the acquisition of capital goods partly financed by BNDE.

Although the BNDE loans are the most important among subsidized loans, they still constitute a very limited part of industrial loans. As table 2.19 shows, the average share of BNDE loans in total investment during 1967–69 was only 17 percent. With the exception of metal products, all groups of industries received less than 15 percent. Consequently, the average industrywide implicit subsidy rate was only 3.4 percent. In fact, for most industries the rates were less than 3 percent (table 2.19).

2.5.3   The Effect of Factor Market Distortions

During the import substitution process in Brazil, the technology used in production was similar to that of the countries exporting capital goods to Brazil; very few capital goods were produced locally. Thus, during that period, the nature of imported technology and the relative factor-price ratio tended to favor the use of capital over labor.

We have developed a model (presented in detail in Appendix C), that relates the effects of factor market distortions on factor utilization. The

Table 2.19   **Average Share of BNDE Loans in Total Investment and Implicit Subsidy, 1967–69 (Percentage)**

Sector	Average Share	Implicit Subsidy
Nonmetallic minerals	12	2.4
Metal products	55	11.0
Machinery and electric equipment	12	2.4
Transportation equipment	14	2.8
Chemicals[a]	10	2.0
Textiles[b]	8	1.6
Other[c]	8	1.6
Total manufacturing	17	3.4

Source: See text.

[a]Includes chemicals, perfumery, pharmaceuticals, and plastics.

[b]Includes textiles, clothing, and footwear.

[c]Includes food, beverages, tobacco, wood, furniture, paper, leather, publishing, rubber, and miscellaneous.

two distortions analyzed by the model are social security payments and subsidies to capital from BNDE loans only, both of which were described above.

The model can be reduced to a system of equations from which labor coefficients can be derived, given values for elasticities of substitution of capital for labor and elasticities of factor supply in each industry. (These are denoted as σ, ϵ_κ, and ϵ_ℓ in the discussion that follows.) Estimates of elasticities of substitution for the twenty-one industrial activities were available from Macedo (1974); no information on supply elasticities (ϵ_κ and ϵ_ℓ) was available, so the model was solved for the following three assumptions: (1) infinite labor and capital supply elasticities; (2) both labor and capital supply elasticities equal to unity; and (3) a capital supply elasticity of two, a labor supply elasticity of one.

Consider first the case of infinite supply elasticities. For this case we calculated percentage changes in employment in each activity resulting from each distortion, then applied those percentage changes to the direct labor requirements (per unit of value of production) actually observed in 1970. This gives us an estimate of what labor absorption would have been in 1970 had either the social security tax or the BNDE subsidy (or both) been eliminated. Our results are shown in table 2.20; the first four columns give the effects on direct coefficients; the last four give the effects upon total labor coefficients. Columns 2 and 6 give the new labor coefficient had the social security tax been eliminated; columns 3 and 7 give the effects of eliminating the subsidy to capital; and columns 4 and 8 give the effects of both policies.

A comparison of the nondistorted labor coefficients with the actually observed labor requirements indicates that the social security legislation had a much more significant effect on direct labor absorption than did the BNDE subsidy. This is true for both direct and total labor requirements. Actually, the effect of social security legislation on the labor/output ratio would be, on the average, 18 percent if no subsidy was given to capital. This follows from the fact that, on average, the elasticity of substitution is about one, the share of labor in value added is about 35 percent, and the share of social security in the wage bill is about 27 percent ($1 \times 0.65 \times 0.27 = 0.18$). By the same token, the effect of the subsidy to capital (if wages are unchanged) on labor output ratio would be, on the aggregate, about 2 percent ($1 \times 0.65 \times 0.034$).

Now consider the case where factor supplies are not perfectly elastic.[32] In table 2.21 we present percentage changes in capital and labor utilization and the degree of factor market distortions (as a percentage of market prices of capital and labor) under the two sets of supply elasticity assumptions outlined above. In table 2.22 we have recomputed the new vector of total labor requirements when both distortions are removed.

Table 2.20 Direct and Total Labor Requirements Produced by Policy Changes, 1970 (Man-Years per One Million 1970 Cruzeiros of Value of Production)

	Direct				Total			
Sectors	Actual in 1970 (1)	From Change in Social Security (2)	From Elimination of Subsidies to Capital (3)	From Both Policies (4)	Actual in 1970 (5)	From Change in Social Security (6)	From Elimination of Subsidies to Capital (7)	From Both Policies (8)
Nonmetallic minerals	48.73	54.57	49.30	55.14	67.46	75.54	68.24	76.32
Metal products	18.37	20.79	19.39	21.81	29.10	32.93	30.71	34.54
Machinery	27.18	30.64	27.53	30.99	42.27	47.65	42.81	48.19
Electrical equipment	21.06	23.97	21.35	24.26	33.50	38.12	33.96	38.58
Transportation equipment	16.58	19.25	16.89	19.56	28.80	33.43	29.34	33.97
Wood products	51.07	57.62	51.57	58.12	89.64	101.14	90.52	102.02
Furniture	50.67	55.61	51.02	55.96	81.62	89.58	82.19	90.15
Paper products	23.54	26.66	23.75	26.87	35.01	39.65	35.32	39.96
Rubber products	16.61	19.66	16.83	19.88	25.24	29.88	25.58	30.22
Leather products	24.37	38.29	34.64	38.56	61.75	68.79	62.23	69.27
Chemicals	8.22	9.22	8.31	9.31	11.97	13.43	12.10	13.56
Pharmaceuticals	12.33	15.19	12.58	15.44	16.72	20.60	17.06	20.94
Perfumery	11.86	13.92	12.04	14.10	18.38	21.57	18.66	21.85
Plastics	12.11	14.53	12.32	14.74	18.67	22.40	18.99	22.72
Textiles	31.67	34.99	31.89	35.21	52.70	58.22	53.06	58.58
Clothing and footwear	41.82	47.34	42.24	47.76	89.89	101.76	90.79	102.66
Food	15.82	18.58	15.99	18.75	26.54	31.18	26.83	31.47
Beverages	26.70	31.69	27.05	32.04	36.48	43.30	36.96	43.78
Tobacco	13.01	16.76	13.29	17.04	14.42	18.58	14.74	18.90
Printing and publishing	33.06	36.68	33.36	36.98	48.50	53.81	48.94	54.25
Miscellaneous	33.83	37.56	34.10	37.83	48.55	53.91	48.94	54.30

This was accomplished by increasing the direct labor requirements by the percentages[33] from table 2.21 and applying the new vectors to the matrix $(I-A)^{-1}$.

The existence of an implicit subsidy to capital due to BNDE credits plus a tax on labor would have produced an increase of 5.1 percent in the price received by capital owners and a drop of 9.4 percent in the price received by the workers in the industrial sector compared with the undistorted situation (with unitary supply elasticities). As we would expect, when we increase the value of the elasticity of supply of capital, both the fall in the wage paid and the increase in the rental price of capital are reduced. Accordingly, the effects on the use of factors are less pronounced. With unitary supply elasticities, labor requirements are reduced by 5.35 to 22.91 percent while capital utilization is increased by 2.68 to 7.30 percent. As the capital supply elasticity increases to two, the effects of distortions upon both capital and labor utilization become less pronounced but are still significant.

2.5.4   The Effects of Distortions on Trade and Employment

With the new nondistorted total labor requirements, we can calculate new labor requirements for exportables and importables by multiplying the vectors of sectoral shares of exports and of importables in manufacturing by the new total labor requirements. Two sets of results, computed with 1971 data, are shown in table 2.23. The first set assumes perfectly elastic factor supplies and uses the total labor requirements of table 2.20. The second set assumes the same factor elasticities used in constructing tables 2.21 and 2.22 and uses total labor requirements of table 2.12. The first set contains three estimates: (1) elimination of the social security tax; (2) elimination of the subsidies to capital implicit in the loans from the BNDE; and (3) policies 1 and 2 taken simultaneously. The second set of results considers only the simultaneous elimination of both distortions.

For the perfectly elastic factor supply case, eliminating the capital subsidy would affect the total labor requirements only marginally. The

---

Notes to Table 2.20: Col. 1 is from table 2.12. Col. 5 differs slightly from total column in table 2.12 because of differences in refinement of calculations. Cols. 2 and 6 are estimates of requirements that would follow from removal of tax on labor implicit in social security legislation. Cols. 3 and 7 are estimates of requirements that would follow from elimination of subsidy to capital from BNDE. Cols. 4 and 8 are equal to (2) + (3) − (1), and (6) + (7) − (5), respectively.

Notes to Table 2.21: [a]Macedo (1974). The elasticity of substitution for miscellaneous was taken as the industrial average.
[b]Table 2.14 above, taken as proportion of the supply price. The aggregated values were considered constant for each subsector involved in the aggregation.
[c]Industrial census of 1970. Taken as proportion of the supply price. For more details see Carvalho and Haddad (1978, Chap. 5).

Table 2.21   Effects of Factor Price Distortions with Supplies Not Perfectly Elastic, 1970

	If $\varepsilon_\kappa = 1.0$ and $\varepsilon_\ell = 1.0$		If $\varepsilon_\kappa = 2.0$ and $\varepsilon_\ell = 1.0$			Capital Market Distortions as a Percentage of the Market Rental Value of Capital[b]	Labor Market Distortions as a Percentage of the Market Wage[c]
	% Δ in capital (1)	% Δ in labor (2)	% Δ in capital (3)	% Δ in labor (4)	σ_i^a (5)	(6)	(7)
Nonmetallic minerals	4.36	− 7.43	3.67	− 6.27	81	2.4	26.6
Metal products	7.43	−13.36	6.75	−12.13	84	11.0	28.2
Machinery	7.66	− 7.94	6.46	− 6.69	108	2.4	26.5
Electrical equipment	5.68	− 8.90	4.84	− 7.58	5	2.4	27.4
Transportation equipment	7.78	−11.37	6.73	− 9.85	113	2.8	28.6
Wood products	4.70	− 6.87	3.76	− 5.49	102	1.6	24.2
Furniture	4.26	− 5.09	3.42	− 4.09	81	1.6	24.4
Paper products	5.54	− 7.99	4.64	− 6.69	97	1.6	26.8
Rubber products	4.54	−11.76	3.80	− 9.85	116	1.6	26.9
Leather products	4.29	− 6.58	3.55	− 5.45	82	1.6	26.1
Chemicals	2.39	− 7.30	2.00	− 6.10	70	2.0	26.3
Pharmaceuticals	4.48	−17.03	3.84	−14.62	134	2.0	28.5
Perfumery	2.68	−11.60	2.28	− 9.88	93	2.0	27.8
Plastics	6.13	−14.18	5.27	−12.20	125	2.0	28.7
Textiles	4.17	− 6.30	3.53	− 5.34	70	1.6	27.8
Clothing and footwear	5.21	− 7.33	4.22	− 5.94	105	1.6	24.8
Food	4.09	−11.89	3.53	−10.27	96	1.6	29.5
Beverages	7.30	−12.67	6.25	−10.85	126	1.6	28.7
Tobacco	5.06	−22.91	4.37	−19.82	166	1.6	29.7
Printing and publishing	5.00	− 5.35	3.86	− 4.12	104	1.6	22.8
Miscellaneous	4.05	− 6.12	3.31	− 5.01	81[a]	1.6	25.4
% Δ in market rental value of capital	5.09		2.18				
% Δ in market wage		−9.36		−8.01			

Table 2.22   Total Labor Requirements in Industry Produced by Policy Changes with Factor Supplies Not Perfectly Elastic, 1970 (in Man-Years)

Sectors	Actual in 1970 (1)	$\varepsilon_\kappa = 1$ $\varepsilon_\ell = 1$ (2)	$\varepsilon_\kappa = 2$ $\varepsilon_\ell = 1$ (3)
Nonmetallic minerals	67.46	72.12	71.44
Metal products	29.10	32.52	32.25
Machinery	42.27	45.38	44.91
Electrical equipment	33.50	36.23	35.85
Transportation equipment	28.80	31.73	31.38
Wood products	89.64	95.40	94.31
Furniture	81.62	85.57	84.83
Paper products	35.01	37.59	37.21
Rubber products	25.24	27.90	27.51
Leather products	61.75	65.56	64.94
Chemicals	11.97	12.79	12.66
Pharmaceuticals	16.72	19.15	18.85
Perfumery	18.38	20.28	20.04
Plastics	18.67	20.98	20.70
Textiles	52.70	55.82	55.38
Clothing and footwear	89.89	96.04	94.94
Food	26.54	29.36	29.01
Beverages	36.48	40.58	40.05
Tobacco	14.42	17.12	16.81
Printing and publishing	48.50	50.96	50.42
Miscellaneous	48.55	51.35	50.86

Source: See text and table 2.21.

Note: Changes are the elimination of the tax on labor implicit in the social security legislation and the elimination of subsidies to capital.

absorption of labor in importables would increase by about 2 percent (from 30.9 to 31.5); in exportables the increase would be about 1.5 percent. The slightly larger increase in importable labor requirements is due to the fact that investment in importables is more heavily subsidized than investment in exportables.

The elimination of the tax implicit in social security would have a major effect upon labor absorption. Taken alone, it would increase labor requirements by 13.3 percent in the importable industries and by 13.6 percent in the exportables. Taken together, the two policies would increase labor absorption per unit of output by 15.2 percent in importables and 14.9 percent in exportables. On the whole, the increase would be about the same in both industries, and the relative labor intensities would not be changed.

Table 2.23   **Total Labor Requirements in Industry under Assumed Changes in Policy, 1971 (Man-Years per One Million 1970 Cruzeiros Increase in Value of Production)**

Source of Increase in Demand	Changes in Policy Assuming Perfectly Elastic Supplies of Factors				Changes in Policy Given by (1) and (2) and Assuming Factor Supply Elasticities Equal to	
	No Change in Policy	Elimination of Tax on Labor (1)	Elimination of Subsidy to Capital (2)	Both (1) and (2) (3)	$\varepsilon_\ell = 1$, $\varepsilon_\kappa = 1$ (4)	$\varepsilon_\ell = 1$, $\varepsilon_\kappa = 2$ (5)
Import substitution	30.9	35.0	31.5	35.6	33.5	33.2
Exports	39.7	45.1	40.3	45.6	42.9	42.5

Source: See text.

Results for less than perfectly elastic factor supplies yield more modest changes in labor requirements. For the case of unitary supply elasticities, labor coefficients would increase by 8.4 percent in the importables and by 8.1 percent in exportables. For the case of a unitary labor supply elasticity and a capital supply elasticity of two, the increase in labor coefficients would be 7.4 percent for importables and 7.1 percent for exportables. Again, the relative labor intensities would not be affected.

Therefore we can conclude that the evidence on factor market distortions does not support the expectation that those effects have been highly significant. Of the two distortions examined here, social security legislation is more important. Nonetheless, the employment effect of eliminating both distortions would be considerable in absolute terms. For the case of unitary supply elasticities, their elimination would increase employment per unit of output by about 8 percent. Given the actual size of the labor force in manufacturing (about three million), that increase would imply the creation of 240,000 new jobs with no change in output.

2.6 Summary and Conclusions

Brazil has had both import substitution and export promotion phases in its trade regime. Although the import substitution policy was successful in increasing industrial output, employment did not grow accordingly. Employment growth in the export promotion period has been more substantial since Brazil's exports have been found to be labor-intensive.

Protection was decreased substantially and its cascaded structure reduced after 1965. Exports were subsidized through tax rebates and subsidies and through subsidized credit. The total subsidy to exports ranged from 15 to 30 percent, depending upon assumptions concerning individual components of the subsidy.

Brazil's production of exportables has higher labor requirements than its production of importables, and its exportable labor requirements have been increasing over time as the trade regime has expanded incentives to export. The pattern of exportable labor requirements by destination of exports was as anticipated from application of the HOS trade model; namely, exports to DCs embody more labor than exports to LDCs. Continued emphasis upon exports to developed nations, then, will generate greater employment than exports to LDCs.

The skill content of Brazil's exports is also lower than that of importables. Thus the export promotion policy currently followed will help generate employment for a growing unskilled labor force.

Two major distortions existed in the factor market—social security taxation and credit subsidization. Minimum wage legislation has not been effective. It is our judgment that the other distortions are not as important as incentives under the trade regime. However, eliminating social security taxation in particular could have significant employment effects. Its removal could potentially alter the wage-rental ratio in such a manner that labor absorption per unit of output would rise by about 8 to 15 percent, depending upon assumptions of supply elasticities. A reasonable assumption is that the supply of unskilled labor is perfectly elastic, so potentially the increase in manufacturing employment might be close to 450,000 workers. However, Brazil's trade strategy probably has had a more significant effect upon employment. Since the export promotion strategy began in 1965, manufacturing employment has increased by about 1.3 million workers, or 85 percent.

In general, then, Brazil's switch to an export promotion policy has been successful in increasing both manufacturing output and employment. Its experience is a valuable lesson for other developing nations.

Appendix A

Table 2.A.1   **Exports and Imports of Manufactures, 1959 (Values in Thousands)**

Manufacturing Sector	Exports		Imports	
	Cruzeiros	Dollars	Cruzeiros	Dollars
Nonmetallic minerals	41.013	279	2,022.328	11,565
Metal products	17.576	141	15,792.776	127,129
Machinery	140.774	946	22,962.948	223,031
Electrical equipment	11.861	75	7,754.279	64,005
Transportation equipment	85.659	980	18,896.798	211,626
Wood products	228.371	1,543	244.006	2,660
Furniture	.675	4	5.872	21
Paper products	.328	2	4,464.126	49,894
Rubber products	.856	5	152.235	974
Leather and hides	389.666	2,668	126.185	688
Chemicals	3,477.228	33,616	33,079.794	249,962
Pharmaceuticals	58.193	406	2,062.543	10,148
Perfumery	333.363	2,471	186.671	944
Plastics	—	—	4.857	31
Textiles	212.656	1,503	241.943	1,540
Clothing and footwear	13.552	91	4.085	23
Food	4,975.944	35,466	4,539.071	28,488
Beverages	2.151	15	719.765	2,275
Tobacco	12.126	80	21.075	197
Printing and publishing	3.097	52	718.579	7,432
Miscellaneous	34.885	276	2,848.458	17,842
Total manufactures	10,039.974	80,619	116,848.394	1,010,475
Grand total[a]	109,449.699	1,281,969	161,284.017	1,374,473

Source: Carvalho and Haddad (1978, tables A.4–A.7).
[a]All imports and exports.

Table 2.A.2   Exports and Imports of Manufactures, 1971 (Values in Thousands)

Manufacturing Sector	Exports		Imports	
	Cruzeiros	Dollars	Cruzeiros	Dollars
Nonmetallic minerals	93,161	17,639	184,009	35,360
Metal products	377,838	67,618	2,496,964	481,544
Machinery	407,632	77,054	3,808,103	757,441
Electrical equipment	152,156	28,529	1,463,777	281,111
Transportation equipment	145,996	27,249	1,755,988	337,989
Wood products	152,686	26,637	11,893	2,282
Furniture	14,767	2,793	1,586	303
Paper products	70,283	13,324	413,754	79,319
Rubber products	24,718	4,451	99,836	19,098
Leather and hides	101,781	14,139	15,606	3,001
Chemicals	288,912	129,206	3,258,198	621,726
Pharmaceuticals	21,573	4,073	237,114	45,867
Perfumery	63,591	12,110	49,955	9,639
Plastics	—	—	11,702	2,234
Textiles	186,554	33,433	224,577	44,650
Clothing and footwear	217,203	34,474	33,010	6,332
Food	808,300	150,553	491,364	94,822
Beverages	9,356	1,780	39,628	7,505
Tobacco	9,710	1,843	378	72
Printing and publishing	31,946	5,922	97,952	18,825
Miscellaneous	37,158	10,563	637,154	122,575
Total manufactures	3,215,321	663,390	15,332,548	2,971,695
Grand total[a]	15,373,766	2,903,856	19,218,408	3,701,449

Source: Carvalho and Haddad (1978, tables A.4–A.7).
[a]All imports and exports.

Table 2.A.3 **Imports and Exports According to the Manufacturing Sectors of the IBGE Matrix, 1970 (Thousands of Dollars)**

Sectors and Codes	Imports	Exports	Trade[a] Category
Mining	23,328	362,283	NRB
Fossil material and fuel exploration	304,420	—	NRB
Cement	7,857	17	MR
Glass	15,448	7,324	IM
Other nonmetallic minerals	7,528	2,436	MR
Iron and steel in primary forms	—	82,471	EX
Rolled steel	75,235	15,310	IM
Cast iron and steel	63,980	—	IM
Metallurgy of nonferrous metals	115,624	1,409	IM
Other metallurgical products	97,513	9,797	IM
Pumps and motors	30,454	2,592	IM
Parts for machinery	98,119	3,298	IM
Industrial machinery and equipment	290,548	23,905	IM
Agricultural machinery and equipment	18,553	1,459	IM
Machinery and equipment for office and domestic use	64,715	32,920	IM
Tractors and earth-moving machines	101,688	8,074	IM
Equipment for electrical energy	26,834	971	IM
Electrical cables and conduits	3,197	214	IM
Electrical material	46,809	7,999	IM
Electrical appliances	91,402	991	IM
Electronic material	17,821	2,151	IM
Communications equipment	79,872	4,856	IM
Automobiles Trucks and buses Parts for automotive vehicles	31,058	9,290	IM
Naval industry	38,592	4,493	IM
Railway stock and other vehicles	89,943	1,089	IM
Wood	1,240	38,358	EX
Furniture	183	1,511	MR
Cellulose and pasteboard	—	828	IM
Paper and cardboard	36,850	344	IM
Paper products	1,017	243	IM
Rubber	7,278	7,393	IM
Leather and hides	595	16,253	EX
Chemical elements and compositions	214,613	19,174	IM
Oil-refining and petrochemicals	47,791	15,027	IM
Coal derivatives	23,128	2	IM
Artificial threads and resins	51,751	575	IM
Raw vegetable oils	46,576	66,649	EX
Pigments (coloring matter), paints, solvents	—	6,531	MR

Table 2.A.3—*continued*

Sectors and Codes	Imports	Exports	Trade[a] Category
Other chemical products	148,732	7,368	IM
Pharmaceuticals	28,971	4,735	IM
Perfumery, soaps, and candles	3,638	8,762	MR
Plastics	2,629	159	IM
Processing of natural fibers	3	937	MR
Spinning and weaving of artificial fibers	20,379	773	IM
Spinning and weaving of natural fibers	5,771	43,552	EX
Other textile industries	8,749	6,264	MR
Clothing	5,888	3,014	MR
Footwear	33	7,914	EX
Agroindustry	71,007	89,436	MR
Sugar refining	2	134,493	EX
Oil-refining and preparation of vegetable fats for human consumption	1,008	844	MR
Other foodstuff products	5,661	81,468	EX
Beverages	6,949	16,542	MR
Tobacco	38	1,378	MR
Printing and publishing	15,668	2,388	IM
Miscellaneous	105,900	4,310	IM
Total	2,602,586	1,172,574	

Source: Carvalho and Haddad (1978, table A.8).
[a]Code: EX = exportable; IM = importable; MR = marginal protection.

Appendix B: The Relationship between Domestic and Export Prices

The following notation is used in the derivation below:

$P_d =$ internal demand price as viewed by the firm;
$P_f =$ internal supply price (does not include IPI but includes ICM on inputs);
$P_{fc} =$ internal factor cost per unit of output;
$P_x =$ international price f.o.b. in domestic currency;
$t_1 =$ ICM tax rate applied to P_f;
$t_2 =$ IPI tax rate applied to P_f;
$\bar{t}_1 =$ ICM credit premium equal to t_2 or equal to 0.13 if $t_2 > 0.13$;
$\bar{t}_2 =$ IPI credit premium equal to t_2 for $t_2 \leq 0.15$; and equal to 0.15 otherwise;
$t^* = \bar{t}_1 + \bar{t}_2$;
$t_3 =$ income tax rate;
$t_4 =$ tariff rate for imported inputs;
$t_5 =$ market interest rate (i) minus interest rate charged to loans given to export activities (r);
$q_1 =$ fraction of P_f corresponding to inputs subject to ICM tax;
$q_2 =$ fraction of P_f corresponding to inputs subject to IPI tax;
$q_3 =$ profits per unit of output as fraction of P_f;
$q_4 =$ value of imported inputs per unit of output as a fraction of P_f;
$q_5 =$ loans to export activities under special programs (interest rate $= r$) per unit of output as fraction of P_f.

Assume that the export firm receives (1) exemption from ICM, IPI, and from the import duty on inputs;[34] (2) transfers corresponding to the values of ICM and IPI that would have been paid;[35] (3) income tax exemption on export activities; and (4) subsidized interest rates on loans associated with exports. We can express the international price as the domestic price minus all these subsididy elements:

(A1)
$$P_x = P_d - t_1 P_f - t_2 P_f \frac{t_4}{1 + t_4} q_4 P_f$$

$$- t^* \left(P_x - \frac{q_4}{1 + t_4} P_f \right) - t_3 q_3 P_f - t_5 q_5 P_f.$$

After some transformation we obtain:[36]

(A2)
$$P_x = P_d \left[\frac{1 - (t_1 + t_3 q_3 + \dfrac{t_4 - t^*}{1 + t_4} q_4 + t_5 + q_5)}{(1 + t_2) \quad (1 + t^*)} \right].$$

We can write the export price as being the internal price at factor cost minus the implicit subsidy. First, note that

(A3) $$P_{fc} = P_d \left[\frac{1 - t_1 - \frac{t_4}{1 + t_4} q_4}{1 + t_2} \right],$$

since $P_x = P_{fc}$ if there is no subsidy.
Introducing P_{fc} in (A1), we obtain:

(A4) $$P_x = P_f - t^* \left(P_x - \frac{q_4}{1 + t_4} P_f \right) - t_3 q_3 P_f - t_5 q_5 P_f;$$

thus the subsidy is

(A5) $$S = t^* P_x + \left[-\frac{q_4 t^*}{1 + t_4} + t_3 q_3 + t_5 q_5 \right] P_f.$$

To see the effect of the export promotion policies based on these instruments, in terms of exporting price versus domestic price, let us assume the following values:

$t_1 = 0.13$, legal exporting ICM rate;

$t_2 = 0.10$, arbitrary value. Since the IPI rates vary widely, we are considering that on average it will range from 0.08 to 0.15;

$t_3 = 0.225$. The legal income tax rate is 0.3. Since a deduction of 25 percent is permitted if firms engage in special programs such as reforesting, SUDENE, SUDAM, or EMBRATUR, we assume that they will take advantage of these possibilities, and we consider the rate to be $0.75 \times 0.3 = 0.225$.

$t_4 = 0.25$, arbitrary value: The input import tariffs are very different according to the input. On average it might be between 0.15 to 0.25;

$t_5 = 0.08$. The annual interest difference can be approximated by $\frac{0.8 (i - r)}{3}$. Taking $i = 0.38$ for a given $r = 0.08$ for this difference;

$t^* = \bar{t}_1 + \bar{t}_2 = 0.2$. Given $t_1 = 0.13$ and $t_2 = 0.10$, we have $\bar{t}_1 = 0.1 = \bar{t}_2$ and therefore $t^* = 0.20$. Note that except for some special cases, the maximum value for t^* is 0.28;

$q_3 = 0.10$ arbitrary value;

$q_4 = 0.30$ arbitrary value;

$q_5 = 0.50$ arbitrary value.

If we consider all these tax cuts and credits we will obtain, using expression (A2), $P_x = 0.6026 \, P_d$, which implies that the export price can be 39.74 percent below the domestic price.

Since it is very difficult to obtain accurate information to formulate hypotheses about all ts and qs, it is convenient to consider only t_1, t_2, and t^*, which are more easily obtained. In this case the relationship between the export and the domestic prices is given by:

(A6)
$$P_x = \frac{1 - t_1}{(1 + t_2)\ (1 + t^*)} \, P_d.$$

Under the previous assumptions, $P_x = 0.6591 \, P_d$, that is, the export price is 34.1 percent lower than the domestic price. Note that under this more simple computation we obtain about 85 percent of the total difference between P_x and P_d calculated in the more complete formulation. Certainly, the assumptions about other ts and qs affect the accuracy of this approximation, but we think that using only t_1, t_2, and t^* we will cover about 80 percent of that difference in the relevant range of variation of those variables.

Appendix C: A Model Relating Factor Market Distortions to Factor Utilization

To investigate the effects of factor market distortions on factor use, consider the industrial sector consisting of n subsectors and assume that there are two factors of production, capital (K) and labor (L), used to produce industrial product, x_i, under a production function homogeneous of degree one, such that $x_i = \phi_i\ (K_i, L_i)$. Let us assume, also, that each factor is paid by value marginal product in all subsectors, and that the factor supply elasticities for the industrial sector are given by ϵ_K and ϵ_ℓ.

Under the above assumptions, the production equilibrium in the industrial subsectors can be expressed by the following system (eq. A7):
Factor substitution in production (for $i = 1, 2, \ldots, n$):

$$dlgK_i - dlgL_i = \sigma_i\ (dlgp_i + dlgt_{li} - dlgt_k - dlgt_{ki}).$$

Fixed output restrictions (for $i = 1, 2, \ldots, n$):

$$K_i dlgK_i = L_i\ dlgL_i.$$

Factor market equilibriums:

(A7)
$$\sum_{i=1}^{n} k_i dlgK_i = \epsilon_\kappa \, dlgp_k,$$

$$\sum_{i=1}^{n} l_i \, dlgL_i = \epsilon_\iota \, dlgp_l,$$

where

$K_i =$ capital used in subsector i;

$L_i =$ labor used in subsector i;

$\sigma_i =$ elasticity of substitution between capital and labor in the production of subsector i;

$$k_i = \frac{K_i}{\sum\limits_i K_i}; \quad l_i = \frac{L_i}{\sum\limits_i L_i};$$

$p_k =$ market rental value of capital in the industrial sector;

$p_l =$ market wage in the industrial sector;

$t_{ki} =$ distortions in the capital use as proportion of p_k in subsector i;

$t_{li} =$ distortions in the labor use as proportion of p_l in subsector i;

$\epsilon =$ factor supply elasticities for the industrial sector.

If we consider that σ_i (for $i = 1, 2, \ldots, n$), ϵ_κ, and ϵ_ι are known, we can solve (A7) given the actual use of factors (K_is and L_is) and the actual factor market distortions (t_{ki}s and t_{li}s), for the changes in K_is ($dlgK_i$), in L_is ($dlgL_i$) and in the factor market prices ($dlgp_l$ and $dlgp_k$). Thus, eq. A7 can be seen as a system of ($2n + 2$) independent equations in ($2n + 2$) unknowns, that is, $dlgK_i$ and $dlgL_i$ for $i = 1$, $2, \ldots, n$ and dp_k and dp_l. The system (A7) can be written in matrix form as:

(A8) $Bx = b$

To obtain the solution for (A8) we need to supply the matrix B and the vector b. In specifying B, we need to provide information on K_i and L_i and impose values for σ_i, ϵ_κ, and ϵ_ι. We consider the year 1970 and the twenty-one industrial subsectors, for the purpose of solving (A7), and taking the estimated values for σ_i from Macedo (1974); see column 5 in table 2.16. The values for K_i and L_i and consequently those for k_i and l_i are defined in terms of value, in such a way that they add up to the value added for sector i.

Since we have no information on the supply elasticities of capital and labor, we solve (A8) for different values of ϵ_κ and ϵ_ι: Three assumptions about ϵ_K and ϵ_ℓ are considered: (i) $\epsilon_K = \epsilon_\ell = \infty$; (ii) $\epsilon_K = \epsilon_\ell = 1$; and (iii) $\epsilon_K = 2.0$, $\epsilon_\ell = 1.0$. Section 2.3.3 of the text discusses the results in detail.

Notes

1. The interested reader is referred to Leff (1968) and Bergsman (1970) for more complete discussions of Brazilian economic development.

2. See also Villela and Suzigan (1973).

3. For more discussion of the trade regime, see Bergsman (1970), Baer (1965), and Fishlow (1975).

4. A recent study (Neuhaus and Lobato 1978) gives estimated ERPs for 1973 and 1975 for the more disaggregated (fifty-eight-activity) I-O classification used in section 2.4. These estimates could be grouped by trade category. They indicate a significant drop in effective protection in all categories since the earlier studies. Simple (unweighted) average ERPs for our trade categories in 1973 were 12 percent for exportables, 11 percent for importables, 18 percent for marginal trade items, and 12 percent for all manufactures. These low values make the estimates suspect, yet their magnitude suggests that protection has fallen considerably since the mid-1960s.

5. These benefits (not further discussed here) are associated with the simplification of exporting procedures; the marketing of Brazilian products abroad by the federal government; insurance against customer bankruptcies; special benefits to trading companies; sectoral programs; special incentives to foreign corporations to transfer operations to Brazil if they produce mainly for export; and tariff and tax exemptions on capital goods and raw materials imported by firms that have a pledge to export according to an approved plan.

6. In addition to IPI and ICM, other tax exemption measures include: (1) a drawback of import duties on all intermediate products entering into the production of an exported good (Decree-Law 53,967 [1964], extended by Decree-Law 37 [1968] and Decree-Law 68,904 [1971]); (2) rebates of other less important taxes on inputs, in the production and commercialization process of exports, like the tax on financial operation (IOF) and the tax on fuel and lubricants (IUCL); (3) exemption from import tariffs and other indirect taxes on machinery and equipment bought by firms that had a pledge with CACEX to export; and (4) exemption from income tax corresponding to export activities (Law 4,663 [1965], regulated by the Decree-Law 56,967 [1965]). For details, see Doellinger, Castro Faria, and Cavalcanti (1974); Fishlow (1975); Savasini (1975); Tyler (1976); and Castro Faria (1976).

7. Although the IPI and the ICM have been considered as value-added taxes, this is not always true, as we can see from the description of how they are applied and collected in chapter 4 of Carvalho and Haddad (1978). Since the main purpose of the tax reform that generated these two taxes was to avoid cascade taxing, a complete independent tax accounting system is necessary, and each firm has an accounting book for each tax.

8. The Resolução 71 was slightly modified recently by the Resolução 398 (December 1975), which unified all special credit programs granted to exports.

9. CACEX, or Carteria de Comércio Exterior, is the department of the Banco do Brasil that controls Brazil's foreign trade.

10. It is interesting to note that the computation with IPI tax rate equal to 0.08 produces results that almost coincide with independent estimates obtained by Fishlow (1975) and Savasini (1975).

11. The matrixes for 1959 and 1970 were constructed with data from the censuses of those years. The first one can be found in Rijckeghem (1969) and the second in IBGE (1976). The matrix for 1971 was constructed with data from the industrial tax (IPI) and is presented in Carneiro Leão et al. (1973). The matrixes are discussed in detail in Carvalho and Haddad (1978).

12. We call attention to the fact that the vectors of direct and total labor requirements on the two alternative definitions, value of production and value added, are highly correlated. The simple correlation coefficients between the vectors of direct and total requirements were equal to 0.92 and 0.95 for 1959, and 0.88 and 0.91 for 1971. Therefore the use of labor per value of production should not yield significantly different results, in relative terms, than labor per value added. Whenever the two calculations are made this is indeed the case, as we shall see below.

13. Estimates for 1970 using chapter 1's methodology are given in table 2.16. It should also be noted that labor requirements as estimated here encompass indirect labor only in the industrial sectors. The linkages with agriculture and services are not taken into account.

14. We have estimated that, *inclusive* of inputs from agriculture, the amount of employment attributable to exports of manufactures in 1970 was about twice that attributable to the production of import substitutes (i.e., 77.9 versus 34.7 per million cruzeiros of value of production). See Carvalho and Haddad (1978, chap. 6).

15. Lack of data for an alternative course imposes this procedure on us.

16. Labor coefficients for individual manufacturing sectors are thus implicitly weighted according to their share in the value of exports or imports. A logical alternative for inputs per unit of value added would be to weight according to the share of each sector in the value-added content of exports or imports.

17. West Germany, Belgium-Luxembourg, Denmark, France, Ireland, Italy, Netherlands, and United Kingdom.

18. Argentina, Bolivia, Chile, Colombia, Ecuador, Mexico, Paraguay, Peru, Uruguay, and Venezuela.

19. IBGE is working on a matrix for the agricultural sector, which will be completed in the near future.

20. This is not exactly true, since for some sectors at the two-digit level no subclassification is given. Therefore the matrix corresponds to a compromise between the two-digit and the three-digit classifications.

21. Twenty-one manufacturing sectors plus mining.

22. The categories for 1960 were (1) technicians and college graduates; (2) foremen (*mestres de contramestres*); (3) workers and apprentices; (4) other workers. For the 1970 census they were (1) technicians; (2) foremen and workers; (3) clerical workers. Rocca and Mendonca (1972) calculated an index in this fashion that is discussed in Carvalho and Haddad (1978, chap. 8).

23. The Two-thirds Law requires that two-thirds of a firm's labor force be Brazilian. Firms must report specific information giving nationality, skill categories, wages, education, and experience of their labor forces every April.

24. Obviously, schooling and job experience are not the only human capital content of the labor force, but other factors such as abilities and intelligence are not taken into account here.

25. The skill index for 1959 was obtained by first regressing the index of skill for 1970 on the sectoral wages paid and then applying those results to the wage structure of 1959.

26. Two observations in this context are in order. First, we are dealing here only with manufacturing. To the extent that exportables have more important linkages with the agricultural sector than importables, we should expect that the average skill content of exportables would fall relative to the one for importables once we take those linkages into account. Second, we are estimating skill content for importables produced with the Brazilian techniques, reflected in her input-output matrixes. It is perfectly possible, and probable, that import substitutes produced in Brazil are more labor-intensive and less skill-intensive than the same imports produced abroad.

27. Two studies analyze the existing regulations very carefully. One is Bacha, Mata, and Modenesi (1972), where the social security legislation is analyzed for its effects on labor absorption. The other is Kogut (1975), where the restrictions imposed on the use of labor at night and the effects on the possibility of industries adopting multiple shifts are analyzed.

28. This is the case of PIS (Program de Integração Social), the program that has as its main purpose a transfer of part of the profit to the labor force.

29. INPS is the Instituto Nacional do Previdencia Social, the agency responsible for administering the social security program in Brazil.

30. The rates on deposits at saving companies were fixed at 6 percent plus monetary correction, and the depositor also received a break in his income tax proportional to his average balance during the year, which increased the effective rate by at least two percentage points.

31. The rate of 10 percent plus monetary correction has been charged by the Financial Housing System to the general financing of home acquisition. For low-income housing the rate is smaller. Since the rate on bank lending has been kept under ceilings in the period 1965–75, we do not have evidence on the true market rates, which were higher than the ceilings owing to some widely used banking practices like the obligation of a minimum balance, a fee to open a credit line, and so on.

32. We are indebted to Arnold C. Harberger for suggesting this approach. Institutional barriers, high transaction costs, and the size of the industrial sector would justify the hypothesis of ϵ_κ and ϵ_ℓ not being infinity.

33. As in the case of perfectly elastic factor supplies, the percentage changes applied were adjusted for the initial position, which is taken to be already distorted.

34. Since the firm has the option of either executing the drawback on tariffs paid on inputs or receiving the IPI and ICM credit premium on those inputs, it would opt for the drawback only if $t_4 > t^*$.

35. Elements (1) and (2) do not represent double-counting. Element (2) is a subsidy equal to the exempted tax.

36. As mentioned in note 34, if $t^* > t_4$, the firm will not take the drawback on imported inputs and t^* will be applied to P_x and therefore q_4 should be considered equal to zero in equation (A4) below.

References

Bacha, Edmar L.; Mata, Milton da; and Modenesi, Rui Lyrio. 1972. *Encargos trabalhistas e absorção de mão de obra: Uma interpretação do problema e seu debate.* Rio de Janeiro: IPEA.

Baer, Werner. 1965. *Industrialization and economic development in Brazil.* Homewood, Ill.: Richard D. Irwin.

Bergsman, Joel. 1970. *Brazil: Industrialization and trade policies.* Oxford: Oxford University Press.

————. 1975. Politica de comercio exterior no Brasil. *Estudos Econômicos* 5(2):51–104.

Carvalho, José L. 1975. O setor industrial brasileiro. Ongoing research project at FGV/EPGE. Preliminary draft.

Carvalho, José L., and Haddad, Cláudio L. S. 1978. Foreign trade strategies and employment in Brazil. Rio de Janeiro: EPGE/FGV. Mimeographed.

Carneiro Leão, Antonio Sergio; Silva, Carlos Ribeiro da; Giestas, Elcio; and Nobrega, José. 1973. Matriz de insumo produto do Brasil. *Revista Brasileira de Econômia* 27(3): 3–10.

Castro Faria, Hugo Barros de. 1976. Incentivos fiscais as exportações brasileiras. Ongoing M.A. essay at FGV/EPGE. Second draft.

Doellinger, Carlos Von; Castro Faria, Hugo Barros de; and Cavalcanti, Leonardo Caserta. 1974. *A politica brasileira de comércio exterior e seus efeitos: 1967/73.* Rio de Janeiro: IPEA.

Fishlow, Albert. 1972. Origens e consequências da substituição de importações no Brasil. *Estudos Econômicos* 2, no. 6: 7–75.

————. 1975. Foreign trade regimes and economic development: Brazil. Mimeographed. Paper presented at a conference in Bogotá, Colombia.

Haddad, Cláudio L. S. 1974. Growth of Brazilian real output, 1900/1947. Ph.D. diss., University of Chicago.

Instituto Brasilero de Geografia e Estatistica (IBGE). 1976. *Matriz de relações interindustrialis: Brasil.* Rio de Janeiro: IBGE.

International Monetary Fund. Various years. International Financial Statistics. Washington, D.C.: IMF.

Kogut, Edy Luiz. 1975. *Estudo sobre o uso de turnos de trabalho na industria de transformação do Brasil.* Rio de Janeiro: EPGE.

Langoni, Carlos Geraldo. 1973. *Distribuição de renda e desenvolvimento econômico do Brasil.* Rio de Janeiro: Expressão e Cultura.

Leff, Nathaniel. 1968. *Economic policy-making in Brazil, 1947–1964.* New York: Wiley.

Macedo, Roberto B. M. 1974. Models of the demand for labor and the problem of labor absorption in the Brazilian manufacturing sector. Ph.D. diss., Harvard University.

Mincer, J. 1974. *Schooling, experience, and earnings*. New York: Columbia University Press.

Neuhaus, Paulo, and Lobato, Helena Maria. 1978. Proteção efetiva a industria no Brasil, 1973–1975. Rio de Janeiro: Fundação Centro de Estudos do Comércio Exterios. Mimeographed.

Rijckeghem, Willy van. 1967. Tabela de insumo produto: Brasil 1959. Rio de Janeiro: IPEA. Mimeographed.

————. 1969. An intersectoral consistency model for economic planning in Brazil. In *The economy of Brazil*, ed. H. S. Ellis. Berkeley: University of California Press.

Rocca, Carlos A., and Mendonca de Barros, José Roberto. 1972. Recursos humanos e a estrutura do comércio exterior. *Estudos Econômicos* 2(5): 89–109.

Savasini, José Augusto A. 1975. A study of export promotion: The Brazilian case. Ph.D. diss., Vanderbilt University.

Senna, José Julio. 1975. Schooling, job experience and earnings in Brazil. Ph.D. diss., Johns Hopkins University.

Tyler, William G. 1976. *Manufactured export expansion in Brazil*. Tubingen: J. C. B. Nohr.

Villela, Anival V., and Suzigan, Wilson. 1973. *Politica do governo e crescimento da econômia brasileira*. Rio de Janeiro: APEC.

3 Alternative Trade Strategies and Employment Implications: Chile

Vittorio Corbo and Patricio Meller

Introduction

Chile is an important case study for this volume because it provides a clear example of the antiemployment biases of import substitution strategies in developing countries. Since World War II, Chile has consistently used an overvalued currency, tariffs, and quantitative restrictions to promote manufactured import substitutes at the expense of agricultural and mining activities—whether for export or for domestic consumption. Under these policies, manufacturing output has increased at a modest pace, but manufacturing employment has shown little growth. For example, while manufacturing output was growing at an annual average rate close to 6 percent in the 1960s, manufacturing employment grew by slightly more than 3 percent annually. In fact, manufacturing employment in recent years is about the same as it was in the early 1950s.

A study of these policies is warranted to determine why they failed to generate employment in Chile. More important, the Chilean experience may provide a sobering lesson for policymakers in other developing

Vittorio Corbo is associated with Concordia University, Montreal, Canada; Patricio Meller is associated with CIEPLAN, Universidad de Chile, Santiago.

We are especially grateful to Anne O. Krueger and Hal Lary for detailed comments on earlier drafts of this study. We are also grateful to Narongchai Akrasanee, Hossein Askari, Ricardo Ffrench-Davis, James M. Henderson, Charles P. Kindleberger, Robert Lipsey, Constantine Michalopoulos, and Morton Stelcner for their comments. Seminars at CIEPLAN, Université de Montreal, University of Texas at Austin, United States Agency for International Development, and the Development Research Center of the World Bank provided many valuable insights. Skillful research assistance was provided by Veronica Corbo, Alireza Mohajer Va Pessaran, and José M. Vrljicak.

This study has been made possible by financial support provided by various institutions whose support is gratefully acknowledged: the USAID through funds provided to the NBER for this project, the Rockefeller Foundation, and the General Canada Council of Arts Research Funds of the Faculty of Arts and Sciences of Concordia University.

countries whose employment problems are even more severe than those of Chile.

The plan of this study follows that of other chapters in this volume. Section 3.1 below provides a brief overview of the Chilean economy and its trade regime;[1] section 3.2 presents the factor requirements estimates, and sections 3.3 and 3.4 analyze the effects of commodity and factor market distortions upon these factor requirements. Section 3.5 presents a dynamic analysis of factor proportions to determine the extent by which factor proportions responded to changes in trade policies during the 1960s.

Our study focuses upon the period 1960–70, and within this period the emphasis is upon the subperiod 1966–68. The major reason for this choice was data availability, namely a census of manufactures for 1967, which allowed us to make estimates of factor requirements. That year is a typical one, and its data should adequately describe the import substitution regime.

3.1   General Characteristics of the Chilean Economy: An Overview

3.1.1   Post–World War II Policy Developments

The two main events that shaped Chile's trade policies and industrialization patterns in the mid-twentieth century were the Great Depression and World War II. The fall in export earnings during the Depression (due mainly to price decreases) and the increase in the real foreign debt caused by the worldwide deflation created a strong drive for less dependence on the world economy. The interruption in international trade during and after World War II provided an additional incentive to developing countries to reduce their reliance on international trade through substituting domestic production for goods previously imported. A further impetus to this import substitution strategy (ISS) was given during the 1950s by the influence of the Economic Commission for Latin America (ECLA) under the leadership of R. Prebisch. Trade policies were influenced by the "Prebisch doctrine" concerning the long-term deterioration of the terms of trade of primary products (Askari and Corbo 1978). All of these events encouraged Chile and other Latin American countries to pursue the goal of industrialization through strong inducements for domestically oriented industrial programs.

In attempting to implement the import substitution strategy, a set of policies was designed to shift the domestic terms of trade in favor of industry as opposed to agriculture and mining. The trade policy pursued was a combination of overvalued currency, tariffs, and quotas. This resulted in a structure of effective protection rates that, in addition to discriminating against exports (especially agricultural and mineral products), was characterized by considerable dispersion in the rate of protection of industrial activities.

Table 3.1   Sectoral Composition of Gross Domestic Product, 1950–70

Economic Sector	Percentage Distribution							Average Annual Growth Rate	
	1950–54	1955–59	1960–62	1963–65	1966–68	1969–70		1950–59	1960–70
Agriculture, forestry, and fishing	15.5	12.7	11.1	10.4	10.3	9.3		−0.28	2.55
Mining	6.2	5.3	9.8	10.1	9.9	10.6		−0.11	4.87
Manufacturing	20.1	25.7	23.6	25.0	25.0	25.3		8.14	5.42
Construction	2.4	1.9	5.6	5.8	4.8	4.9		−0.08	2.38
Electricity, gas, water, and sanitary services	0.9	0.8	1.4	1.6	1.7	1.6		3.55	6.28
Transportation, storage, and communication	6.0	5.4	3.3	4.3	4.4	4.6		1.69	8.62
Wholesale and retail trade	19.4	19.5	21.7	20.9	21.1	21.3		3.42	4.13
Finance	3.0	2.4	2.5	2.4	2.7	4.1		−1.19	9.35
Ownership and dwellings	7.8	7.9	3.8	3.7	3.5	3.2		3.74	2.34
Public administration and defense	8.3	7.8	5.4	5.0	5.0	4.8		1.83	3.15
Services	10.4	10.6	11.8	10.8	10.8	10.3		3.21	3.09
Total	100.0	100.0	100.0	100.0	100.0	100.0		3.35	4.40

Source: Instituto de Economía (1963, tables 7 and 8); ODEPLAN (1971b).

Note: 1950–59 data were processed at 1960 market prices; 1960–70 data at 1965 market prices.

3.1.2   Growth and Structure of Production

The effects of the ISS can be observed from changes in the relative shares of the agricultural and manufacturing sectors since 1950 (see table 3.1). Together these sectors maintained an almost constant share of GDP from 1950 to 1970 (about 35 percent). However, the relative share of manufacturing increased from 20 percent to about 25 percent while that of agriculture fell continuously from 15 to about 9 percent. Most of the increase in manufacturing's relative share occurred in the late 1950s. Since then it has remained relatively constant. The real rate of growth of manufacturing output since World War II has been about 4 percent annually; that for agriculture has been about 2 percent.

Within the manufacturing sectors, those activities that, as of 1969–70, had the largest share in manufacturing value added were food-processing, textiles, clothing and footwear, transportation equipment, chemicals, and basic metals (see table 3.2). These six activities accounted for about 55 percent of total value added. The growth rate for value added in the entire manufacturing sector was 5.64 percent for the decade 1960–70.[2] However, there was a wide range in growth rates for individual activities. Five manufacturing activities had growth rates higher than 10 percent (paper and paper products, transportation equipment, electrical machinery and appliances, metal products, and chemicals). Five others had growth rates lower than 2 percent (clothing and footwear, printing and publishing, tobacco, leather and leather products, and furniture and fixtures). Two of these latter five industries have had negative growth rates.

The clothing and footwear industry was the largest employer in the manufacturing sector in the 1960s, although its relative importance decreased over time. Other relatively important sources of manufacturing employment were food processing, textiles, furniture and fixtures, metal products, and transportation equipment. Together, these six industries generated more than 63 percent of industrial employment.

The average annual growth rate of industrial employment was 3.14 percent during 1960–70. Six industries had employment growth rates over 5 percent (beverages, rubber products, petroleum and coal products, basic metals, electrical machinery and appliances, and chemicals). In contrast, four industries had employment growth rates lower than 2 percent (clothing and footwear, furniture and fixtures, nonelectrical machinery, and nonmetallic mineral products). The weight of the clothing and footwear industry in total employment, combined with its low employment growth rate (0.26%), has had a significant effect on the overall low manufacturing employment absorption.

The low growth rate of manufacturing employment in Chile appears to be due to the fact that industries that had high (value added) growth

Table 3.2 Sectoral Composition of Value Added and Employment in Manufacturing 1960–70

Chilean Code	Manufacturing Industry	Percentage Distribution (Annual Averages)								Average Annual Growth Rate		Total Employment-Value-Added Elasticity[a]
		1960–62		1963–65		1966–68		1969–70		1960–70		
		Value Added	Employment	Value Added	Employment	Value Added	Employment	Value Added	Employment	Value Added	Employment	
20	Food processing	11.87	11.71	11.09	12.37	12.09	12.82	12.30	12.49	6.28	4.12	0.66
21	Beverages	3.92	2.12	3.66	2.84	4.05	3.18	3.33	3.06	4.55	8.06	1.77
22	Tobacco	2.43	0.29	1.97	0.29	1.92	0.28	1.63	0.28	1.28	2.60	2.03
23	Textiles	10.75	9.17	10.84	9.48	10.53	9.66	9.93	9.50	4.65	3.70	0.80
24	Clothing and footwear	13.87	24.50	12.15	21.41	10.49	19.65	9.70	19.63	1.10	0.26	0.24
25	Wood and wood products	3.79	5.40	4.15	5.36	4.18	5.56	4.27	5.75	7.05	3.81	0.50
26	Furniture and fixtures	4.75	7.17	4.25	7.14	3.18	6.60	2.99	5.95	−0.53	1.07	** b
27	Paper and paper products	2.00	1.71	2.30	1.05	3.77	1.20	3.99	1.27	15.86	4.25	0.27
28	Printing and publishing	3.35	2.39	2.89	2.12	2.53	2.39	2.51	2.57	1.79	3.99	2.23
29	Leather and leather products	1.98	1.34	1.64	1.37	1.36	1.48	1.20	1.36	−0.51	3.91	** b
30	Rubber products	1.82	0.70	2.24	0.70	2.23	0.92	2.22	0.99	8.02	7.83	0.98
31	Chemicals	5.08	3.37	5.22	3.40	6.53	3.79	7.16	3.92	10.26	5.15	0.50
32	Petroleum and coal products	1.88	0.60	1.93	0.63	2.10	0.79	2.31	0.78	8.23	7.04	0.86
33	Nonmetallic mineral products	5.81	3.71	5.26	3.52	4.46	3.41	4.58	3.32	2.23	1.96	0.88
34	Basic metals	7.81	2.47	9.08	2.71	6.26	3.11	6.21	3.31	2.04	6.91	3.39

Table 3.2—continued

Chilean Code	Manufacturing Industry	Percentage Distribution (Annual Averages)								Average Annual Growth Rate		Total Employment-Value-Added Elasticity[a]
		1960–62		1963–65		1966–68		1969–70		1960–70		
		Value Added	Employment	Value Added	Employment	Value Added	Employment	Value Added	Employment	Value Added	Employment	
35	Metal products	4.32	6.42	5.30	7.18	6.02	6.67	6.05	7.26	10.31	4.22	0.41
36	Machinery except electrical	2.48	3.67	2.81	3.84	2.98	3.48	2.97	3.24	8.22	1.53	0.19
37	Electrical machinery and appliances	3.54	2.84	3.93	3.41	4.83	3.76	5.27	3.62	11.13	6.56	0.59
38	Transportation equipment	5.63	7.81	6.28	7.96	7.57	8.47	8.53	8.51	11.14	4.50	0.40
39	Other manufacturing	2.93	3.16	3.01	3.22	2.94	2.79	2.84	3.18	5.38	2.27	0.42
	Total percentage	100.00	100.00	100.00	100.00	100.00	100.00	100.00	100.00			
	Total value added (million 1965 escudos)	3,540.33		4,357.67		5,186.67		5,507.50		5.64		
	Total employment (thousands of persons)		434.23		483.03		535.53		556.80		3.14	0.56

Source to Table 3.2: CORFO (1972, pp. 10–11).
Note: Original data on value added were at 1965 market prices.
aPercentage increase in employment for each 1 percent increase in value added.
bNegative values (**) have been omitted.

rates had low employment–value-added elasticities. Basic metals, printing and publishing, tobacco, and beverages had high elasticities, but, with the exception of beverages, value added in these industries grew by 2 percent or less annually. Conversely, industries with low employment elasticities were nonelectrical machinery, paper and paper products, and clothing and footwear, of which nonelectrical machinery and paper products grew at annual rates over 10 percent.

3.1.3   Characteristics of Chile's Foreign Sector

Despite its import substitution bias, trade is very important to Chile. Both exports and imports increased from 10 percent of GDP in the 1950s to about 14 percent in the 1960s. The foreign trade sector plays a crucial role as a source of tax revenues for the government (supplying more than 25 percent of the total). Moreover, export earnings play a crucial role in providing a continuous flow of imported raw materials, certain basic consumption goods (sugar, coffee, meat, wheat, etc.), and above all the bulk of the capital goods required for the smooth functioning and growth of the economy.

The Composition of Trade

A dominant feature of the Chilean trade is the high concentration of export earnings in just one product, copper.[3] By the end of the 1960s, copper represented about 80 percent of exports and yielded about U.S. $900 million in foreign exchange per year. Most of the increase in the

Table 3.3   **Foreign Trade Indicators, 1950–70**

Time Periods	Exports/ GDP	Imports/ GDP	Merchandise Trade Surplus Yearly Average (Millions of U.S. Dollars)	Share of Copper in Commodity Exports[a]	Copper Price (U.S. Cents per Pound)	Terms of Trade[b] (1960 = 100)
1950–54	10.3%	8.9%	39.4	50.4%	23.6	92.8
1955–59	9.9	9.8	49.2	60.3	31.1	99.5
1960–62	13.5	14.7	−79.9	66.7	29.9	100.4
1963–65	13.7	13.3	− 2.1	63.6	32.8	104.4
1966–68	13.6	14.7	116.3	73.0	49.4	133.4
1969–70	13.7	16.2	157.9	78.0	63.3	153.3

Source: V. Corbo (1974, pp. 107–8); ODEPLAN (1971*b*).

Note: Underlying data for 1950–59 were expressed in 1960 prices, and those for 1960–70 in 1965 prices.

[a]1950–59 includes only large-scale copper mining; 1960–70 includes total copper mining exports. Manufactured copper goods are included in manufactured exports.
[b]Export price index divided by import price index.

export share from 10 to 14 percent of GDP was due to the increase in copper's share, in turn caused by abnormally high prices of copper in the period 1965–70. The second important group of exports consists of iron ore and nitrates. Their importance has declined over time from close to a 30 percent share at the beginning of the 1950s to about 10 percent by the end of the 1960s (table 3.4).

Manufactured exports were not quantitatively of major importance during 1950–70 either as a fraction of total Chilean exports (9.5 percent) or as a percentage of manufacturing output (less than 3 percent in 1967). This suggests that the external market did not play a major role in the Chilean industrialization of the 1950s and 1960s.

The relatively more important manufactured exports were processed foods, paper and paper products, and basic metals. Together these three industries provided more than 65 percent of manufactured exports (see table 3.5). Within processed foods, meat products and fish products (such as fish meal and frozen seafood) were the most important. Within the paper industry, the most important export products were cellulose and paper itself. Both of these export groups maintained a high level throughout the period. On the other hand, exports of basic metals were very unstable both in volume and in the type of goods exported. Iron and steel products alternated with manufactured copper products as the main goods exported by this industry.

Table 3.4   Composition and Growth of Commodity Exports, 1950–70

Time Period	Copper[a]	Rest of Mining	Agriculture and Fishing	Manufacturing	Total[b] (Millions of U.S. Dollars at Current Prices—Annual Averages)
1950–54	50.35%	28.60%	11.17%	9.55%	382.74[b]
1955–59	60.29	22.95	7.98	8.57	439.18[b]
1960–62	66.73	19.38	5.48	8.41	478.60
1963–65	63.58	19.51	4.28	12.63	593.34
1966–68	72.96	13.41	2.64	10.99	883.53
1969–70	77.99	10.02	2.55	9.44	1,149.70
Average annual growth rate (based on values in current U.S. Dollars)					
1950–59	4.51	−1.25	−3.11	4.40	2.02
1960–70	12.93	2.88	0.53	12.84	10.87

Source: Instituto de Economía (1963, p. 175); ODEPLAN (1971a, p. 421).
[a]See table 3.3, note a.
[b]Includes noncommercial exports which were 0.33 percent of total for years 1950–54 and 0.21 percent for years 1955–59.

The bias of the import substitution policies is clearly seen in the commodity composition of imports shown in table 3.6. Intermediate products and investment goods had the highest shares, fluctuating around 50 percent and 30 percent during the 1960s; the share of consumer goods imports was about 16 percent by the end of the 1960s. The average annual growth rate for 1960–70, at current values measured in United States dollars, was nonetheless substantial—6.73 percent. In other words, even at the end of the 1960s, annual spending on consumer goods imports exceeded U.S. $150 million. About 45–50 percent of these imports consisted of manufactured food and agricultural products, while motor vehicles accounted for 10–14 percent.

The Direction of Trade

During the 1960s, Chile succeeded in diversifying the destination of its exports, although most (90 percent) exports still are destined for developed nations. In the early 1960s, exports to the United States made up 40 percent of total exports; by the end of the decade, the United

Table 3.5   Composition of Industrial Exports, 1960–70

Chilean Code	Manufacturing Industry	Percentage Distribution			
		1960–62	1963–65	1966–68	1969–70
20	Food processing	25.69	25.83	31.53	26.97
21	Beverages	1.03	1.32	0.97	1.42
23 24	Textiles, clothing, and footwear	0.34	0.18	0.03	0.00
25 26	Wood and wood products, furniture and fixtures	5.86	3.59	3.81	7.42
27	Paper and paper products	17.84	10.03	21.97	26.59
28	Printing and publishing	0.26	0.77	1.70	1.89
29 30	Leather and leather products, rubber products	2.41	1.59	1.14	1.51
31	Chemicals	7.41	3.68	3.64	5.72
32	Petroleum and coal products	1.81	1.68	1.00	0.85
33	Nonmetallic mineral products	0.00	0.05	0.14	0.99
34	Basic metals	31.12	47.30	26.82	12.56
35 36	Metal products and machinery, except electrical	2.59	1.59	2.26	2.74
37	Electrical machinery and appliances	0.86	0.91	1.70	1.32
38	Transportation equipment	0.17	0.23	1.94	8.03
39	Other manufacturing	2.59	1.32	1.32	1.98
	Total	100.00	100.00	100.00	100.00
	Total (annual average in million U.S. dollars)	38.67	73.43	96.20	105.85

Source: CORFO (1972, pp. 14–15); ODEPLAN (1971a, p. 160).

Table 3.6   Composition and Growth of Imports, 1950–70

Time Period	Consumer Goods	Investment Goods	Intermediate Products	Total (Millions of U.S. Dollars at Current Prices—Annual Averages)
1950–54	31.67%	25.38%	42.95%	342.46
1955–59	29.73	34.26	36.01	417.24
1960–62	15.14	30.67	54.19	535.30
1963–65	13.11	27.18	59.71	588.20
1966–68	13.16	29.32	57.52	760.93
1969–70	16.11	31.36	52.53	955.75
Average annual growth rate (based on values in current U.S. Dollars)				
1950–59	3.61	9.62	0.93	4.26
1960–70	6.73	7.50	6.52	6.83

Source: 1950–59, Instituto de Economía (1963, p. 199); 1960–70, ODEPLAN (1971a, p. 425).

States share fell to 15 percent. The United Kingdom, France, and West Germany absorbed 33 percent of total exports in the early 1960s and 28 percent in the late 1960s. But the export share of other regions besides Latin America (mainly Japan and other European countries) rose from 20 to 45 percent. Exports to Latin American countries ranged around 10 percent of total exports over the decade.

Similarly, most (75 percent) Chilean imports originate in developed nations, although the origins have changed over time. The share of United States imports in total imports fell from 50 to 35 percent between 1950 and 1970. Likewise, the share of imports from the United Kingdom, France, and West Germany fell from 25 to 20 percent in the same period, while imports from countries outside Latin America rose from 1 to 20 percent. The share of Latin America imports fell from 23 to 17 percent in the 1950s, then increased over the 1960s to about 25 percent of total imports.

Balance of Payments

Chile has had chronic balance of payments problems ever since World War II. Although its merchandise trade balance has frequently been in surplus over this period (see table 3.3), its current account has continuously shown a deficit, largely because of repatriated profits on direct investment (mainly in large-scale copper mining). The current account deficits have been financed by capital inflows, principally associated with direct investment in large-scale mining (in the 1950s) and central government borrowing (in the 1960s). As we will see (section 3.1.4), these balance of payments problems contributed heavily to the development of the Chilean import substitution strategy.

3.1.4   The Trade Regime

The chronological history of Chile's trade regime can be divided roughly into periods before and after 1955.[4] Before 1955, policies were highly restrictive and enacted as ad hoc reactions to balance of payments problems. The policies after 1955 can best be described as "cycling," that is, switching back and forth from restrictive to more liberalized trade regimes. Even in the more liberalized phases, however, import substitution remained the central policy focus.

The Pre-1955 Period

The effect of the Great Depression on the Chilean economy led to the adoption of highly restrictive, ad hoc measures that reacted to balance of payments problems within a context of fixed exchange rates and high rates of inflation. Import and export procedures were often subject to arbitrary, endless regulations. Furthermore, institutional changes, frequent policy alterations, and the numerous exceptions to established regulations provided very uncertain and unstable rules for importers and exporters. In brief, the period before 1956 was characterized mainly by (1) quantitative restrictions (import and export quotas) applied with varying degrees of intensity; (2) a large number of exceptions to the general regime that affected an important proportion of total imports (such exceptions being related to special regimes, bilateral trade and compensation agreements, exemptions for government agencies, regional accords, and so forth, and (3) the establishment of an exchange control system with an overvalued domestic currency.

The Post-1955 Period

Policies after 1955 "cycled" back and forth from more to less restriction. There were three attempts to liberalize the trade regime: 1956–58, 1959–61, and 1965–70 (Behrman 1976, pp. 27–34). In all three cases, liberalization was not a goal per se but was one of the components of an overall stabilization program. Internal concerns (mainly related to inflation and income distribution) were paramount in causing these changes, although the influences of foreign payment obligations, speculation against the currency, capital flight, and donor and creditor country pressures were also felt. As Behrman (1976, p. 300) states, "Foreign-sector policy generally has been much more an appendage of domestic policy, albeit an important appendage, rather than vice versa."

In general, policies during 1956–70 gradually simplified and rationalized the trade regime and, toward the end of the period, decreased some of the bias in favor of import substitution as opposed to exports. Several measures were taken in this direction: (1) the bureaucratic and administrative procedures of export and import regulations were gradually reduced; (2) steps were taken to unify and stabilize the exchange rate in real terms and to keep the exchange rate close to its equilibrium level (especially during the subperiod 1965–1970 when a sliding-peg system was used); (3) import restrictions were reduced;[5] (4) some specific incentives for exports were introduced (e.g., a system of drawbacks up to 30 percent of the value of exports); and (5) improvements were made in the system of forecasting foreign exchange reserves and the balance of payments, thereby allowing more effective planning of external economic policies.

Owing to the important role of copper in export earnings, however, developments in the world copper market frequently played the crucial role in shaping the outcome of foreign trade policies. Furthermore, there is some suggestion that changes in the trade regime in this period were in response to fluctuations in real copper export revenues.

The Exchange Rate

During 1960–70, the Chilean escudo was always overvalued. Although the nominal exchange rate (escudos per unit of foreign currency) was frequently increased, internal inflation quickly resulted in overvaluation of the currency. Even with the sliding-peg policy of 1965–70, which provided a stable real exchange rate, the cost of foreign exchange was below the long-run equilibrium level (Behrman 1976, pp. 60, 129–30). Moreover, the wide dispersion in tariffs, quotas, and so on, dis-

Table 3.7		PPP-PLD-EERs for Imports and Exports, 1952–70 (1969 Escudos per U.S. Dollar)	
		Exports	
Time Periods	Imports	Copper Exports[a]	Other Exports
1952–54	9.12	3.39	— [b]
1955–59	10.60	7.58	8.91[c]
1960–62	10.29	8.37	8.72
1963–65	10.57	8.42	9.86
1966–68	10.59	8.63	9.82
1969–70	10.84[d]	8.95	10.65

Source: Ffrench-Davis (1973, pp. 266, 269).

Note: See chapter 1 for definition of terms. These rates do not include import premiums. See also note 7.

[a]Only large-scale copper mining.

[b]Not available.

[c]Excluding 1955.

[d]Data not available for 1970.

Table 3.8   **PLD-EERs for Major Production Sectors, 1950–70 (1965 Escudos per U.S. Dollar)**

Time Periods	Agriculture and Forestry	Mining	Manufacturing
1950–54	5.11	4.17	7.92
1955–59	5.14	3.99	8.19
1960–62	4.70	3.56	6.96
1963–65	4.46	3.35	6.45
1966–68	4.01	2.95	5.70
1969–70	3.91	2.20	5.14

Source: Behrman (1976, pp. 340–47).

Note: Data relate to imports. These rates are simple averages of exchange rates at a more disaggregate level (Behrman 1976, p. 347). See also note 7.

criminated against exports and shifted the domestic terms of trade in favor of the manufacturing sector. The effective exchange rates shown in tables 3.7 and 3.8 provide empirical support for these propositions.

Table 3.7 presents the effective exchange rates (EER) for imports and exports during 1952–70. Import EERs, which do not include premiums on import licenses, were higher than those for exports, although the difference decreased through time. Among exports there was discrimination in favor of noncopper exports that had an EER about 17 percent higher than the EER for large-scale copper mining. This rate applied only to the copper revenues used to buy domestic inputs and was mainly used as a tax for revenue purposes rather than to exploit any monopoly power in world copper markets.[6] The gap between the EER for imports and that for exports other than copper almost closed by the end of the 1960s, when the Chilean government became a partner in the copper corporations.

The EERs of table 3.8 show discrimination not only between exports and imports, but also between major Chilean production sectors. There was discrimination against mining and agriculture and discrimination in favor of manufacturing over the entire period.[7] Furthermore, mining was treated less favorably than agriculture, with EERs at least 20 percent lower than those of agriculture. These differences were undoubtedly further aggravated by quantitative restrictions.

Effective Rates of Protection

Effective rates of protection (ERP) and domestic resource cost (DRC) estimates given in Behrman (1976, pp. 137–40) are summarized in table 3.9. Our estimates by trade category (discussed below, section 3.2) are found in table 3.10.[8] Note first that ERPs were high and varied widely not only from industry to industry but also over time.

Table 3.9   **Nominal Protection Rates, Effective Protection Rates, and Domestic Resource Costs in Chile, Twenty-eight Sectors, 1961, 1967, and 1968 (Percent)**

Tradable Goods Sectors	Protection Rates Nominal (NPRs)			Effective Protection Rates (EPRs)			Domestic Resource Costs (DRCs)	
	1961 (1)	1967 (2)	1968[a] (3)	1961 (1)	1967 (2)	1968[a] (3)	1961 (1)	1968[a] (2)
1 Agriculture and forestry	43	1	19	50	− 7	15	250	111
2 Fishing	21			25				
3 Coal mining	37			31				
4 Iron mining	2		0	− 7	−12			180
5 Copper mining	0		0	−14	−10			60
6 Nitrate mining	1		0	− 6	−11			
7 Stone, clay, and sands	66			64				
8 Other mining	46		6	40		− 6		82
9 Food products	82	32	27	2,884	365	3	253	97
10 Beverages	122	7		609	−23		259	
11 Tobacco	106	0		141	−13		47	
12 Textiles	182	99		672	492			b
13 Footwear and clothing	255	23	29	386	16	5	1,916	52
14 Wood and cork	35	0	24	21	− 4	22	210	161
15 Furniture	129	0	30	209	− 5	18	241	73
16 Paper and paper products	55	44	27	41	95	14	683	164
17 Printing and publishing	72	0		82	−15		297	
18 Leather and leather products	161	25	15	714	18	−20	2,109	55
19 Rubber products	102	125		109	304		77	
20 Chemical products	94	38	24	89	64	14	356	75
21 Petroleum and coal products	50	55		45	1,140		47	
22 Nonmetallic mineral products	139	27		227	1			b
23 Basic metals	66	25	28	198	35	21	b	380
24 Metal products	59	80		43	92		217	
25 Nonelectrical machinery	84	56	12	85	76	− 9	150	59
26 Electrical machinery	105	162	26	111	449	10	131	50
27 Transportation equipment	84	150	21	101	271	1	118	56
28 Other manufacturing	125		18	164		4	175	41
Equally weighted arithmetic mean	83	48	18	254	168	3	419	106
Standard deviation	58	51	11	552	282	13	598	86
Range	255	162	30	2,898	1,127	42	2,109	339

Source: Behrman (1976, pp. 138–39).

[a]For subsectoral exports only.

[b]Value was negative, indicating that the total foreign exchange cost per unit exceeds the foreign exchange final product price.

Table 3.10   Average Nominal and Effective Rates of Protection by Trade Category, HOS Manufactures, 1967

Trade Category	ERP for Domestic Sales	Range		ERP for Export Sales	Range	
Exportables	37%	−25% to	100%	0%	−23% to 14%	
Importables	267	−15	to 1,830	2	−23	to 21
Noncompeting imports	155	−38	to 741	6	− 9	to 22
Total	233	−38	to 1,830	4	−23	to 22

Source: Based upon estimates in Corbo and Meller (1978*a*, appendix table IVA).
Note: Averages are unweighted averages of estimates for activities within a category; for a discussion of trade categories, see section 3.2.

Of the twenty manufacturing industries studied by Behrman (sectors 9 to 28 in table 3.9), half had ERPs greater than 100 percent in 1961. By 1967 the number of industries with such high ERP values had decreased to six. Manufacturing industries with consistently high ERPs were food processing, textiles, rubber products, electrical machinery, and transportation equipment. The relaxation of import restrictions during the 1960s is reflected in the decrease in the average ERPs from 254 percent to 168 percent in table 3.9.

The bias against exports is clearly seen in table 3.10. There was no effective protection on exports (for export sales), whereas importables received very high levels of protection (267 percent on domestic sales). In fact, exportable production for domestic sales had lower ERPs than importables, while export sales of importable production had positive ERPs.

The DRC estimates (table 3.9) coincide with the ERPs. They are systematically lower in 1968 than in 1961. This decrease probably indicates an improvement in the production efficiency of the Chilean manufacturing industries over time. Thus the years for which our estimates of the employment-trade relationship are made, 1966–68, were probably ones of greater efficiency and smaller variance in incentives than had prevailed earlier.

3.1.5   The Chilean Labor Market

Among the countries in the project, Chile's labor force bears the greatest resemblance to that of developed countries. Chile is a highly urbanized country. Even by 1960, 69 percent of the population (then 7.5 million) was urbanized. Population growth during the decade 1960–70 was just over 2 percent annually so that, despite continued urbanization, urban population grew at the fairly moderate rate of 3.7 percent annually. By 1970, 83 percent of the population was urban. That such a high fraction of the population is already urban suggests that out-migration from rural areas cannot continue at past rates; so, in that sense,

Chile's need to create new jobs is less pressing than the need of developing countries where the fraction of the population under labor force age is high, where the rate of population growth is more rapid, and where the fraction in rural areas is so great that important future out-migration to the cities can be expected.

During the 1960s, manufacturing output grew at an average rate of about 5 percent. Manufacturing employment in Chile, however, was virtually constant, as can be seen from table 3.11; it was at about the same level in 1970 as in 1963, and currently it is below that level. Chile's employment problem, therefore, is the failure of employment opportunities to grow. This has been reflected first in a substantial expansion in employment in the public sector, which has been an employer of last resort, and second in reported rates of open urban unemployment over 5 percent throughout most of the 1960s and even higher rates at

Table 3.11   Chilean Labor Market Data

Year	Population (Thousands) (1)	Labor Force (Thousands) (2)	Manufacturing Employment (1970 = 100)	Unemployment Rate (3)	Real Wage Rate (1970 = 100) (4)
1952	6,162	2,154	92[a]	4.9%	—
1960	7,583	2,427	96	7.1	55.7
1961	7,773	2,475	97	8.0	59.2
1962	7,961	2,523	98	7.9	62.0
1963	8.147	2,572	100	7.5	56.9
1964	8,330	2,622	103	7.0	59.2
1965	8,510	2,673	106	6.4	64.1
1966	8,686	2,725	104	6.1	75.6
1967	8,859	2,778	104	4.7	81.7
1968	9,030	2,833	104	4.9	86.9
1969	9,199	2,888	98	5.0	92.5
1970	9,369	2,950	100	6.1	100.0
1971	9,539	3,021	97	3.8	119.3
1972	9,711	3,094	108	3.1	108.2
1973	9,887	3,168	111	4.8	71.3
1974	10,068	3,244	107	9.2	67.6
1975	10,253	3,321	100	14.5	65.7
1976	10,443	3,405	91	13.7	70.3
1977	10,639	3,490	94	12.7	88.3
1978	10,840	3,578	93	10.9	99.4

Sources: Columns 1 to 3—from Ministerio de Hacienda, Exposición sobre el estado de la hacienda pública, January 1979; Column 4—from Departamento de Economía, Universidad de Chile, Comentarios sobre la situación Económica, second semester, 1978.

[a]Based on manufacturing employment in Santiago, Valparaiso, and Vine del Mar.

present. Only during the Allende years did the unemployment rate fall, and that decline was accompanied by a growth of manufacturing employment not associated with output increases.

There is ample reason on a priori grounds to believe that much of the failure of manufacturing and urban employment to grow in Chile may have been attributable to policies surrounding the determination of urban wages. As can be seen from table 3.11, urban wage rates in real terms almost doubled between 1960 and 1970, and that increase undoubtedly affected both the commodity composition of trade and the factor proportions with which outputs were produced. These subjects are discussed in more detail in section 3.4.

3.1.6 Inflation

Another chronic problem for Chile has been its very high rate of inflation. During 1950–70, the average annual increase in the GDP price deflator was in the neighborhood of 35 percent. The various relaxations of the trade regime after 1955 invariably were reactions to high rates of inflation in the preceding years (see Behrman 1976, chap. 1, for discussion), and usually the annual rate of inflation improved during the periods of relaxed restrictions. For example, during 1956–61 the annual rate of increase in the GDP deflator fell from about 50 to 10 percent. As restrictions were tightened in 1962, inflation rose to about 40 percent per year, and with the loosening of restrictions in the late 1960s, inflation fell back to about 20 percent annually. Thus, lower rates of inflation appear to be related to more liberal trade policies. However, inflation outpaced the rather substantial devaluations throughout the period, and the currency was continually overvalued (as mentioned earlier), thus decreasing incentives to export and increasing the need for restrictions on imports.

3.1.7 Summary

In the postwar era, Chile has consistently applied policies to encourage (with varying degrees of emphasis) the domestic production of manufactured goods previously imported. These policies have included, among other things, an overvalued currency, quantitative restrictions, and tariffs. Although they have been moderately successful in increasing domestic production of manufactures, they have not absorbed a significant amount of labor.

3.2 Trade Orientation, Factor Requirements, and Factor Proportions in Chilean Manufacturing

In this section we estimate the factor requirements (labor, capital, and skill) embodied in the production of Chilean HOS manufacturing activities. For this purpose we first classify manufacturing industries at the four-digit International Standard Industrial Classification (ISIC) level as being Heckscher-Ohlin-Samuelson (HOS) or natural resource based (NRB),[9] then we separate the HOS manufacturing industries into trade categories—that is, exportable, importable, or noncompeting import industries. Factor requirements and factor proportions are estimated for the first two types of industries.[10]

3.2.1   Classification of Industries by Trade Categories

The T_i statistic is used to separate activities into their respective trade categories (see chap. 1 for discussion). Exportable industries are those with a negative T_i; importable industries are those with a T_i falling between 0 and 0.75, and noncompeting imports have a T_i of more than 0.75.[11] To eliminate the effects of trade fluctuations, we used a three-year average for exports and imports over 1966–68 in our calculations.

With this procedure, seven four-digit industries were classified as exporting, sixty-six as import competing, and nine as noncompeting. That there are so few exporting HOS manufacturing industries is a reflection of the bias of the trade regime in favor of import-competing industries that prevailed in Chile for most of the 1950s and 1960s. The seven exporting industries are listed in table 3.12, which also gives a breakdown of exports by destination (DC and LDC) and estimates of factor intensities. Note the predominant role of canned fish in exports to DCs and pulp and paper in exports to LDCs. For both products, Chile had the opportunity to export the unprocessed counterpart (raw wood in the case of pulp and paper products, and fresh and simply preserved fish in the case of fish products), and thus we have initially classified both industries as HOS.[12] However, two factor-requirements estimates for exports are given below. One includes, and the other excludes, pulp and paper. The separate estimates are made because pulp and paper may be considered a borderline HOS good and because it receives special preferences in LAFTA. As we will see, the results are sensitive to whether it is included. The principal importable industries are listed in table 3.13. A full listing of industries in all categories is found in the Appendix (table 3.A.1), where their classification is indicated in each case by their T_i statistic.

Using three-year averages centered on 1967, 46 percent of Chile's total exports of manufactures, excluding copper products, went to DCs, and 54 percent went to LDCs. Within the LDCs, 99 percent went to Latin American Free Trade Association (LAFTA) members, and of this total 45 percent went to Argentina and 16 percent to Mexico.[13] However, for the HOS exportables in table 3.9, only 16 percent went to DCs (44 percent if pulp and paper are excluded).

Table 3.12   **Characteristics of Chile's HOS Export Industries**

ISIC Number	Industry	DVA per Unit of Output	Exports[a] (Thousands of U.S. Dollars) Developed Countries	Developing Countries	Total	Factor Intensities Labor[b]	Capital[c]	Skill[d]
3113	Canning and preserving of fruit and vegetables	.499	330	989	1,319	46.9	935.7	93.0
3114	Canning, preserving, and processing of fish, crustaceans, and similar foods	.582	1,868	31	1,899	69.5	1,575.9	93.6
3132	Wine industries	.301	518	416	934	55.1	2,218.7	143.9
3133	Malt liquors and malt	.623	—	1,363	1,363	21.5	487.4	87.1
3311	Sawmills, planing, and other wood mills	.411	413	1,334	1,747	121.2	934.9	223.1
3411	Manufacture of pulp, paper, and paperboard	.507	848	16,945	17,793	22.4	1,846.1	147.4
3901	Manufacture of jewelry and related articles	.543	67	—	67	112.7	208.5	480.9
	Total		4,044	21,078	25,122			

Source: Corbo and Meller (1978a, appendix tables III A, III B, and III C).

[a]Average for 1966–68. For the value in escudos of these flows, see Corbo and Meller (1978a).

[b]Number of persons employed per million escudos of direct DVA.

[c]Thousand escudos of fixed assets per million escudos of direct DVA.

[d]Number of skill units per million escudos of direct DVA.

Table 3.13   Characteristics of Chile's Main Import-Competing Industries

ISIC Number	Industry	DVA per Unit of Output	Imports[a] (Thousands of U.S. Dollars)			Factor Intensities		
			Developed Countries	Developing Countries	Total	Labor[b]	Capital[c]	Skill[d]
3513	Synthetic resins, plastic materials, and manmade fibers	.562	12,632	1,608	14,264	28.7	1,173.4	103.6
3514	Basic industrial organic chemicals, except fertilizer	.427	14,863	2,645	17,642	38.7	3,204.6	245.2
3710	Iron and steel basic industries	.465	25,357	1,780	27,166	34.4	1,914.4	243.8
3811	Cutlery, hand tools, and general hardware	.679	22,074	2,838	24,285	67.7	542.4	198.0
3813	Structural metal products	.488	28,718	766	29,672	71.5	773.2	235.1
3824	Special industrial machinery and equipment	.545	33,506	654	34,356	66.1	626.8	202.2
3829	Machinery and equipment except electrical n.e.c.	.615	33,208	2,846	36,271	42.5	642.4	160.3
3831	Electrical industrial machinery and apparatus	.597	23,307	420	23,772	54.0	379.7	190.3
3843	Motor vehicles	.587	28,715	1,757	30,559	20.3	237.0	90.1
3845	Repairs of aircrafts and aircraft parts	.851	14,753	0	14,753	83.0	127.4	348.7
	Total		237,113	15,314	252,427			

Source: Corbo and Meller (1978*a*, appendix tables III A, III B, and III C).

[a]Average for 1966–68. For the value in escudos of these flows, see Corbo and Meller (1978*a*).

[b]Number of persons employed per million escudos of direct DVA.

[c]Thousand escudos of fixed assets per million escudos of direct DVA.

[d]Number of skill units per million escudos of direct DVA.

Of Chile's imports of manufactures, 86 percent of the total (both in the importable group and in other manufactures) came from DCs and 14 percent came from LDCs. For imports from developing countries, 85 percent came from LAFTA countries, of which 58 percent came from Argentina and 11 percent from Mexico.

3.2.2 Procedures

In the estimates of factor requirements below, labor is measured by the number of persons employed. Capital is measured by the book value of fixed assets at 1967 prices less accumulated depreciation. Skill is approximated by dividing the wage bill by the unskilled wage in manufacturing to estimate the "blue collar" equivalent of the labor employed, then subtracting the number of persons actually employed (Corbo and Meller 1978a, appendix II, table XV).[14]

We encounter two problems related to weights in computing factor requirements for a basket of tradables. The first centers on the proper basket to use as weights. There are three alternatives: trade flows, domestic production, or total supply (production plus imports). The use of a trade-flow basket assumes that an import substitution (export promotion) strategy is implemented by increasing importable (exportable) production in proportion to actual imports (exports). The domestic production basket assumes that an import substitution (export promotion) strategy increases importable (exportable) production in proportion to current production. Finally, the use of a total supply basket for importables assumes that an import substitution policy increases domestic importable production in proportion to current consumption patterns.

The second problem is the choice of either value added or production weights. Leontief used value-of-production weights in his pioneering work on factors proportions of trade (Leontief 1953). But, since we focus upon HOS activities only, value-added weights are more appropriate for our purposes. Only value added in a given HOS manufacturing industry should be considered output of that industry, since the raw materials entering into the production are the output of other activities, principally NRB activities such agriculture and mining. Therefore using value-of-production weights may introduce an important NRB content into our HOS manufacturing activities. Value-added weights avoid this problem.

We initially tried all three baskets for weighting factor requirements. The results for importable production differed only marginally among the three baskets. In contrast, the results for exportables did differ according to the weights used. Calculations using domestic production weights generated labor requirements substantially higher and capital and skill requirements substantially lower than for the other two baskets. We thus opt for the trade weights, since neither domestic production nor total supply weights can be used to study the implications of trade upon factor requirements.

In computing direct factor requirements in trade, as given in table 3.13, we use as weights the shares of each industry in the direct value-added content of the basket of each tradable category considered. In computing direct plus indirect requirements, as in table 3.14, the weights are given by the shares of each industry in the direct plus home goods indirect value-added content of each category. Correspondingly, factor requirements cover only direct requirements in the first instance, whereas in the second they also include requirements in the home goods producing sectors that provide inputs directly and indirectly into the different tradable sectors.[15]

The results for labor requirements of importable products are very similar for DC and LDC weights. This is a consequence of the small variance in the sectoral labor to DVA coefficients and the large number of import-competing sectors considered.

3.2.3   Factor Requirements by Commodity Category

The factor requirements estimates given in tables 3.14 and 3.15 generally conform to expectations of a multicountry, multicommodity model (Jones 1977; Krueger 1977). Specifically, a basket of exportables to DCs uses more labor (per unit of DVA) than any other tradable category. However, there is some ambiguity caused by pulp and paper. As we will see below, the ranking of labor intensities is sensitive to whether it is included.

A major difference to be noted at the outset when comparing the results of table 3.14 with those of table 3.15 is the increase in labor requirements per unit of value added in all tradable categories when the computations include home goods indirect effects. This increase reflects the relatively high ratio of labor to value added in commercial services, which are an important supplier of inputs into the manufacturing sector. By contrast, capital requirements are moderately increased, and skill requirements are reduced, when measured on the broader basis.

A quick inspection of tables 3.14 and 3.15 suffices to show that the most striking result is the very high capital/labor ratio (col. 5) of Chile's HOS exports to other LDCs, much higher than for any other tradable category. It is more than twice as high as that for exports to DCs on a direct basis and still almost twice as high on a direct-plus-indirect basis. The difference stems from the much smaller labor inputs into HOS exports to LDCs rather than from differences in capital requirements. Like the capital/labor ratio, the skill/labor ratio is much higher in exports to LDCs than in exports to DCs, reflecting in this case both the lower labor content and the higher skill content of this trade flow. We also see that the results are heavily influenced by pulp and paper. In-

Table 3.14 Direct Factor Requirements and Factor Proportions in Exportables and Import Competing Products by Destination and Origin of Trade Flows, 1966–68

Tradable Category[a]	Weights[b] (1)	Labor[c] (2)	Capital[d] (3)	Skill[e] (4)	Capital/Labor Ratio (5) = (3) ÷ (2)	Skill/Labor Ratio (6) = (4) ÷ (2)
Exportables						
a. World		34.09 (63.80)	1,642.6 (1,125.1)	141.1 (125.0)	48.18 (17.62)	4.14 (1.96)
b. DCs		61.00 (71.40)	1,555.6 (1,477.3)	125.6 (119.8)	25.50 (20.69)	2.06 (1.68)
c. LDCs		28.92 (57.69)	1,659.3 (836.8)	144.1 (129.4)	57.37 (14.50)	4.98 (2.24)
Import competing products						
d. World		42.59	851.5	167.6	19.99	3.93
e. DCs		42.59	793.2	169.4	18.62	3.98
f. LDCs		42.45	1,151.2	157.3	27.12	3.71
Ratio of requirements	Exports and imports					
g. World (a ÷ d)	0.800	1.929 (1.321)		0.842 (.746)	2.410 (.881)	1.053 (.498)
h. DCs (b ÷ e)	1.432	1.961 (1.862)		0.741 (.707)	1.369 (1.111)	0.518 (.422)
i. LDCs (c ÷ f)	0.681	1.441 (.727)		0.916 (.823)	2.115 (.555)	1.342 (.604)

Note: Values in parentheses exclude pulp and paper from the HOS exportables and treat it as NRB.

[a]See tables 3.12 and 3.13 and appendix table 3.A.1 for composition of trade flows by major industries.

[b]Weights used are the value-added content of the trade flows specified.

[c]Number of persons employed per million escudos of direct DVA.

[d]Thousand escudos of fixed assets per million escudos of direct DVA.

[e]Number of skill units per million escudos of direct DVA.

Table 3.15   Direct Plus Home Goods Indirect Factor Requirements and Factor Proportions in Exportables and Import Competing Products by Destination and Origin of Trade Flows, 1966–68

Tradable Category[a]	Weights[a] (1)	Labor[b] (2)	Capital[c] (3)	Skill[d] (4)	Capital/Labor Ratio (5) = (3) ÷ (2)	Skill/Labor Ratio (6) = (4) ÷ (2)
Exportables						
a. World	58.46 (95.73)	1,733.7 (1,438.5)	122.4 (83.8)	29.65 (15.03)	2.10 (.88)
b. DCs	98.64 (111.03)	1,829.7 (1,815.7)	84.1 (71.9)	18.55 (16.35)	0.85 (.65)
c. LDCs	49.56 (84.61)	1,712.1 (1,164.2)	130.9 (92.4)	34.55 (13.76)	2.65 (1.09)
Import competing products						
d. World	60.10	983.4	145.6	16.36	2.42
e. DCs	59.97	910.2	147.7	15.18	2.46
f. LDCs	60.74	1,338.5	134.3	22.04	2.21
Ratio of requirements	Exports and imports					
g. World (a ÷ d)	0.973 (1.591)	1.763 (1.463)	0.841 (0.576)	1.812 (0.919)	0.868 (0.364)
h. DCs (b ÷ e)	1.645 (1.851)	2.010 (1.995)	0.569 (0.487)	1.222 (1.077)	0.345 (0.264)
i. LDCs (c ÷ f)	0.816 (1.393)	1.279 (0.870)	0.975 (0.688)	1.568 (0.624)	1.199 (0.493)

Note: Values in parentheses exclude pulp and paper from the HOS exportables and treat it as NRB.

[a]See table 3.11 for composition of trade flows and for weights used in computing factor coefficients.

[b]Number of persons employed per million escudos of direct plus home goods indirect DVA.

[c]Fixed assets per million escudos of direct plus home goods indirect DVA.

[d]Number of skill units per million escudos of direct plus home goods indirect DVA.

deed, when pulp and paper is excluded, the capital/labor ratio of Chile's HOS exports to other LDCs is the lowest among all tradable categories. However, the skill/labor pattern does not change when pulp is excluded.

It is also noteworthy that, when pulp and paper is included, the next highest capital/labor ratio is again found in Chile's trade with other LDCs, this time in its imports or, more specifically, its production of HOS goods competing with imports from LDCs. For such goods the capital/labor ratio is almost 50 percent greater than that for HOS products competing with imports from DCs. In this comparison, unlike that for exports, the difference in the ratios stems entirely from the capital side. The difference in labor inputs per unit of value added is negligible. Moreover, in contrast to exports, skill requirements are lower and therefore the skill/labor ratio is lower in goods competing with imports from LDCs than in those competing with imports from DCs. It is interesting that, at least in the aggregated factor requirements of tables 3.14 and 3.15, skill requirements do not seem to be closely related to capital inputs.

Observe next that Chile's total exports of HOS goods (strongly influenced by the LDC component) embody far more capital and slightly less labor and skill than do total imports, the latter being much more heavily weighted by trade with developed countries. These results seem anomalous for a less developed country like Chile. However, they are somewhat more expected if we consider only its DC trade. In DC trade, exports are far more labor-intensive than import-competing products, as one would anticipate, although they also use much more capital per unit of value added.[16] These results again are sensitive to the inclusion of pulp and paper. When this commodity category is excluded, Chile's total exports embody far more labor and capital and less skill than its imports—this result is entirely due to the change in factor requirements in Chile's trade with LDCs. Chile's exports to LDCs now embody more labor and less capital and skill than its imports from LDCs.

Sections 3.3 and 3.4 will consider some of the influences determining factor coefficients in Chile's trade. More immediately, however, some light is thrown on the question by examining the commodity composition of its trade. As we already noted with regard to table 3.12, exports to LDCs and to the world as a whole are dominated by the value-added content of the pulp and paper group, requiring heavy capital inputs and little labor per unit of value added. On the import-competing side, the results for LDCs, as table 3.13 indicates, are strongly affected by the value-added content of the first three product groups—synthetic resins and fibers, industrial chemicals, and iron and steel—all of which also have high capital requirements and low labor requirements. It is likely that the composition and factor requirements of Chile's manufacturing production and trade are strongly influenced by special trading arrangements within LAFTA, given the predominance of LAFTA trade in total LDC trade.

3.2.4 Net Factor Content of Trade

Using the average composition of a basket of tradables, we estimated factor requirements of a marginal change of one million escudos of international value added (IVA) in import-competing goods and in exportables.[17] In measuring the IVA content of exportables and import-competing goods, we converted DVA values to IVA ones using effective rates of protection for each four-digit ISIC industry. There are several problems in this approach. We may find, for example, that within a four-digit industry there are firms who export and firms who produce primarily for the domestic market. In a trade regime such as Chile's in the 1960s, with tariffs and quotas on imports and without fully compensating subsidies to exports, the ERP for the importable firm would be higher than that for the exportable firm. An industrywide value conceals this variation. Second, there is no careful and complete study of ERPs in the mid-sixties. The ERP estimates given earlier (section 3.1) are taken from a variety of sources. For importable production, the only study available for this period is De la Cuadra (1974), which covers only ninety-two commodities, of which eighty-three are of industrial origin. We use a procedure similar to Behrman's (1976) to allocate these commodities to a given four-digit ISIC sector.[18]

For exportable production, we use the rates given by Taylor and Bacha (1973), which pertain to the entire export production of a given three-digit ISIC manufacturing activity.

Bearing these data problems in mind, we present the factor requirements of exportables by destination and of import-competing goods by origin, distinguishing between developed and developing countries in table 3.16. The most important result that emerges is that the local production of HOS goods competing with imports from LDCs uses more of each factor than the production of goods destined to exports of LDCs. What this result shows is that Chile saves on all factors by trading with LDCs. In effect, local production of HOS goods competing with imports from LDCs would use more of each of the three factors per unit of IVA than any of the other baskets. (This result should be interpreted cautiously because of the weakness of the ERP rates used.)

Second, note that Chile's total exports are more capital-intensive and less labor- and skill-intensive than its total imports. In bilateral comparisons we now find that exports to DCs are more capital-intensive and less labor- and skill-intensive than importable production competing with imports from DCs. Another robust result is that, within exportables,

Table 3.16   Direct and Direct Plus Home Goods Indirect Factor Requirements in Exportables and Import Competing Products by Destination and Origin of Trade Flows: Tradables at International Prices, 1966–68

Tradable Category[a]	Weights[a]	Direct			Direct plus Home Goods Indirect		
		Labor[b]	Capital[c]	Skill[d]	Labor[e]	Capital[f]	Skills[g]
Exportables	Exports						
	a. World	36.95	1,780.4	152.9	52.75	1,564.2	110.4
	b. DCs	63.41	1,617.2	130.6	78.58	1,457.6	67.0
	c. LDCs	31.61	1,813.4	157.5	46.06	1,591.5	121.7
Import competing products	Imports						
	d. World	78.74	1,574.1	309.8	94.34	1,543.4	228.5
	e. DCs	75.21	1,400.6	299.1	90.77	1,377.8	223.6
	f. LDCs	104.34	2,829.7	386.6	116.70	2,571.5	258.1
Ratio of requirements	Exports and imports						
	g. World (a ÷ d)	0.469	1.131	0.494	0.559	1.013	0.483
	h. DCs (b ÷ e)	0.843	1.155	0.437	0.866	1.058	0.299
	i. LDCs (c ÷ f)	0.303	0.637	0.407	0.395	0.619	0.472

[a]See tables 3.12 and 3.13 for composition of trade flows. Weights used are the international value-added content of the trade flows specified.
[b]Number of persons employed per million escudos of direct IVA.
[c]Fixed assets per million escudos of direct IVA.
[d]Number of skill units per million escudos of direct IVA.
[e]Number of persons employed per million escudos of direct plus home goods indirect IVA.
[f]Fixed assets per million escudos of direct plus home goods indirect IVA.
[g]Skill units per million escudos of direct plus home goods indirect IVA.

the basket with DC weights is more labor-intensive and less skill-intensive than the one with LDC weights.

In terms of employment, we find that one million escudos of direct plus home goods indirect IVA in exports to DCs generates 78.58 jobs. Using an exchange rate of 5.132 escudos per dollar, the latter figure implies 40,327 jobs per 100 million dollars of IVA. This figure represents 10 percent of the manufacturing employment and about 1 percent of the total labor force in 1967.

3.3   Distortions in Commodity Markets: Protection and Factor Inputs

In this section we analyze the effects of distortions in commodity markets upon factor requirements and the factor proportions of exportables and importables. Our approach to this problem is twofold. First, we group industries in each of the two tradable categories according to their level of protection, then compare factor requirements for industries above and below the median protection rate. Second, we undertake an econometric analysis of the effect of the protection system on factor requirements and proportions. This analysis also provides a test of the implications of the Heckscher-Ohlin-Samuelson (HOS) theory for the pattern of trade.

We use the structure of effective protection as a measure of incentives accorded by the trade regime to different industrial activities. However, in the context of a general equilibrium model one can only show that the sector with the highest protection will attract resources. For the other sectors, nothing can be said a priori (see especially Bruno 1973). Nonetheless, empirical general equilibrium models built for some LDCs have shown that there is a high correlation between the partial equilibrium measure of ERP and the ex-post ERP derived from these models (Taylor and Black 1974; De Melo 1978). Thus the structure of effective protection can be used to capture the effects of Chile's trade regime.

Protection will generally affect factor requirements through two channels. First, it generates an overall import substitution or export promotion bias to the trade regime. Second, it may provide different incentives to individual activities within a commodity category. It thus may change the output mix of a given category, which in turn will change the overall factor requirements of that category. Both effects occurred during the period analyzed. The Chilean trade regime discriminated strongly in favor of import-competing activities. Furthermore, the wide range in ERPs within a category indicates that the regime affected the output mix of the category.

3.3.1   Factor Proportions in Above and Below Average Protected Industries

In table 3.17 we present our calculations of factor requirements for more and less protected exportable and importable activities. Less (more) protected importables are those with ERPs below (above) the median ERP of 76 percent. Less (more) protected exportables have ERPs below (above) the median of 3 percent.

The most important conclusion emanating from this table is that labor requirements in more protected activities are *always* below those of less protected activities. This is true for both importable and exportable categories and for both DC-LDC directions of trade. The trade regime thus appears to have encouraged industries with low labor requirements in both tradable categories.

Considering Chile's total trade, it is apparent that the more protected activities within each tradable category are more capital-intensive than less protected activities. Furthermore, the highest capital requirement per

Table 3.17   **Direct Plus Home Goods Indirect Factor Requirements and Factor Proportions in Exports and Import Competing Products by Destination and Origin of Trade Flows and Protection Levels, 1966–68**

Tradable Category	Weights (1)	Labor (2)	Capital (3)	Skill (4)	Capital/ Labor Ratio (5)	Skill/ Labor Ratio (6)
Exportables	Exports		*Above Median Protection Level*			
	World	44.39	1,852.6	151.8	41.73	3.42
	DCs	64.45	1,682.3	189.2	26.10	2.94
	LDCs	42.95	1,864.8	149.1	43.42	3.47
			Below Median Protection Level			
	World	91.98	1,450.3	52.4	15.77	0.57
	DCs	110.72	1,881.7	46.9	16.99	0.42
	LDCs	76.42	1,091.7	56.9	14.29	0.74
Import competing products	Imports		*Above Median Protection Level*			
	World	53.81	1,066.0	117.7	19.81	2.19
	DCs	53.32	931.4	116.7	17.47	2.19
	LDCs	55.99	1,514.9	121.6	27.06	2.17
			Below Median Protection Level			
	World	67.72	883.4	179.3	13.04	2.65
	DCs	66.93	888.0	180.2	13.27	2.69
	LDCs	73.78	854.8	169.2	11.59	2.29

Note: See tables 3.12 and 3.13 for composition of trade flows and for weights used in computing factor coefficients.

unit of DVA is for the most protected exports to developing countries. This bundle also has the lowest labor requirements per unit of DVA.[19] Another characteristic evident in table 3.17 is the high capital-intensity of goods competing with imports from developing countries produced by the industries with above-median protection level. These findings strongly suggest that most of the trade within LAFTA countries is done in capital-intensive and highly protected commodities.

Exports with above-median protection are more skill-intensive than exports with below-median protection. This result holds not only for total exports but also separately for exports to developed and to developing countries. On the other hand, the opposite result emerges in importable activities; those with above-median protection level have skill requirements on the average lower than sectors with below-median protection level.

These results pertain to direct plus home goods indirect effects. Computations for direct effects alone show the same pattern, but the differences in employment requirements in exportables between industries with above- and below-median protection levels are somewhat more pronounced when indirect effects are included.[20] This difference is due to the simultaneous operation of two forces: (a) very high shares of indirect value added in home goods; (b) higher labor intensity in home goods industries than in HOS industries and a differing importance of home goods in more and less protected tradable products. For the other primary factors, the pattern of results obtained for direct plus home good indirect effects is not affected.

To generalize, these results indicate that the structure of protection has created a bias in favor of the production of low labor-intensive and high capital-intensive commodities in both trade categories.

3.3.2 An Econometric Study

Next we proceed to a more disaggregated econometric analysis of the relation between net HOS imports (and also total imports), classified at a four-digit ISIC level, and factor inputs and protection of domestic production. The analysis is made separately for Chile's total trade and for its DC trade. In addition to searching for further evidence of the influence of protection upon the composition of production, we want to test the hypothesis that, in its trade with developed countries, Chile is a net importer of skills and capital and a net exporter of (raw) labor. We apply regression techniques in a manner similar to that of Hufbauer (1970), Baldwin (1971), and Branson and Monoyios (1977). Our initial model expresses factor inputs as stocks. Later the problem of chosing the appropriate scaling is treated as a problem of testing for heteroskedasticity.

The regression model is of the form:

Table 3.18   Commodity Composition of Trade: Regression Estimates for Chile's Trade with the World and with Developed Countries

Equation Number	Dependent Variable	Explanatory Variables					R^2	F Ratio
		Constant	LM	LS	K	AVERP		
1.1	NM (World)	12,124.1 (1.31)	−9.01 (−3.43)**	4.47 (4.71)**	−.046 (−.81)	708.3 (.53)	.337	8.6
1.2	M (World)	15,505.9 (1.71)	−9.80 (−3.81)**	4.75 (5.11)**	−.025 (−.45)	312.1 (.24)	.390	10.8
1.3	NM (Developed)	14,277.3 (1.72)	−10.33 (−4.39)**	4.66 (5.47)**	−.08 (−1.52)	35.0 (.03)	.351	9.2
1.4	M (Developed)	15,757.7 (1.87)	−10.17 (−4.26)**	4.63 (5.37)**	−.07 (−1.34)	−75.96 (−.06)	.351	9.2
		H*Constant	H*LM	H*LS	H*K	H*AVERP	R^2	
1.1'	H*NM (World)	11,632.6 (1.55)	−7.370 (−2.46)*	3.84 (3.77)**	−.03 (−.49)	535.1 (.48)	.192	
1.3'	H*M (Developed)	11,169.6 (1.72)	−8.113 (−3.02)**	4.00 (4.40)**	−.06 (−.99)	68.22 (.07)	.224	

Note: Terms in parentheses are t values. One asterisk and two asterisks indicate coefficients that, in a two-tailed test, are significantly different from zero at the .05 level and .01 level, respectively. The same convention applies for the testing of the whole model through F ratio test of R^2.

$$NM_i = \beta_1 + \beta_2 LM_i + \beta_3 LS_i + \beta_4 K_i + \beta_5\, AVERP_i + u_i,$$

where

> $NM_i =$ Net imports (imports minus exports) in 1966–68 of sector i (at the four-digit ISIC level) in thousands of escudos, where each trade flow has been converted from dollars to escudos using its own exchange rate.
>
> $LM_i =$ Labor (raw) employed in sector i, in thousands of persons.
>
> $LS_i =$ Skill in sector i, in skill units.
>
> $K_i =$ Capital stock in sector i, in thousands of escudos.
>
> $AVERP_i =$ Average effective rate of protection in sector i, as a percentage.[21]
>
> i is a four-digit import-competing or exporting industry.[22]

To verify the hypothesis mentioned above, the signs of β_2 and β_5 must be negative and those of β_3 and β_4 positive.[23] Table 3.18 summarizes our estimates. Equations 1.1 and 1.2 are estimated over seventy-three industries, of which sixty-six are importables and seven are exportables. The dependent variables are net imports and total imports. Equations 1.3 and 1.4 are estimated over seventy-three industries, but only DC trade is included. The dependent variables are the same as in 1.1 and 1.2.[24]

All estimates yield highly significant coefficients (with proper signs) for LM and LS. No pattern is observed on signs of the capital and ERP variables. These results lead to the conclusion that, in trade in manufactures, Chile implicitly imports skill and exports labor. The results for physical capital are ambiguous. The protection system, however, has no effect upon net imports, according to these estimates. The "bad showing" of the protection variable may be due in part to a problem of measurement errors for this variable. As we mentioned before, the ERP estimates are imperfect. They may be used for ranking incentives for individual sectors but not for accurately measuring the absolute levels of protection.

The next problem is to determine if the factor inputs and net imports should be scaled by some variable related to industry size. This question was raised by Stern (1975) and Harkness and Kyle (1975). Here, as in Branson and Monoyios (1977), we approach this question as an econometric problem of performing a constructive test for heteroskedasticity on the disturbances of equation 1. We test for heteroskedasticity and then reestimate the equations using generalized least squares. This procedure is equivalent to deflating or scaling the data before performing the regression. We proceed to test for heteroskedasticity in the disturbances in equations 1.1 and 1.3 following the procedure outlined by Park (1966).[25] The scaling performed is equivalent to dividing the dependent variable and the regressors by a function of production to express all variables in terms of intensities.

The results incorporating the corrections for heteroskedasticity appear at the bottom of table 3.18. Comparing the corresponding equations, we see that our main conclusion is not affected by the scaling of the variables.[26] The variables for raw labor and skill are significant with the proper signs; those for capital and protection are not significant.

3.4   Distortions in Factor Markets and Factor Requirements in Trade

Here we analyze the effects of factor market distortions (caused by the trade regime itself) upon factor requirements in Chilean manufacturing. We ignore factor market distortions resulting from other causes. That is, any distortion in the price of labor or capital or both brought about by public policies (including direct government intervention) not associated specifically with the trade regime will be excluded. However, the methodology developed here can be applied to evaluate factor market distortions not associated with the trade regime.

Our approach is to estimate production functions for each four-digit ISIC industry, then simulate the factor intensity under an undistorted factor price ratio. In the simulation, it is assumed that the only distortion is a subsidy to capital resulting from a preferential effective exchange rate for capital goods. For the period analyzed here, quantitative and other restrictions on capital goods imports were very minor (Ffrench-Davis 1973, pp. 96–107).

3.4.1   Technology in Chilean Manufacturing

Elsewhere[27] we have estimated production functions at the four-digit ISIC level. Here our procedures and results are briefly summarized. Translog functions with three factors (labor, skill, and capital) were estimated for forty-four four-digit ISIC industries[28] using cross-section data from the 1967 Chilean census of manufactures, disaggregated at the establishment level (11,468 establishments employing five or more persons.) We then tested the general translog model for constant returns to scale (CRTS). For forty-one out of forty-four sectors studied, the CRTS hypothesis could not be rejected at the 1 percent level. For these forty-one sectors, we tested further for a Cobb-Douglas technology. For thirty-five out of the forty-one sectors the Cobb-Douglas technology could not be rejected at the 1 percent level. For the six CRTS industries for which the Cobb-Douglas technology was rejected, we proceeded further to test for pairwise linear and nonlinear separability.[29] For the three sectors for which the CRTS hypothesis was rejected, we tested for complete global separability. In the three cases the null hypothesis was not rejected. For these three sectors we proceeded further to test for a Cobb-Douglas technology. In two cases the null hypothesis could not be rejected.

In our simulations under CRTS for the thirty-five sectors for which a Cobb-Douglas technology was not rejected, we use the estimated Cobb-Douglas function. For the six CRTS sectors for which the Cobb-Douglas technology was rejected (ISICs 3211, 3311, 3420, 3812, 3824, and 3829), we approximated our technology by the estimated Cobb-Douglas function. This was done to avoid the need for solving a nonlinear system of equations.

For the simulations of the three non-CRTS sectors, we used a non-CRTS Cobb-Douglas function. Again, only for two of these sectors was the Cobb-Douglas non-CRTS technology appropriate for use, based on the test results. For the third case (sector 3117), we used a non-CRTS Cobb-Douglas as a local approximation to avoid the nonlinearities involved.

Before we proceed to the simulation results, two complications should be noted. First, Cobb-Douglas functions could not be estimated for all seventy-three exporting and import-competing four-digit sectors because of insufficient observations in some sectors. The second problem is that the Cobb-Douglas function for sector 3559 was not well behaved; in particular, it is not monotonic in the capital input (i.e., there was a negative marginal product of capital). As a solution for these two problems, we approximated the technology for the sectors for which the function could not be estimated and for sector 3559. This was done by using for those sectors coefficients obtained as the simple average of the value-added elasticities of primary factors of the four-digit Cobb-Douglas functions belonging to the same three-digit industry. The value of the elasticities used in the simulations appears in Corbo and Meller (1978a, table 17).

3.4.2 Simulating the Effect of Factor Market Distortions

Having obtained estimates of production functions in Chilean manufacturing, we solved for an expression relating factor intensities to factor prices (see Appendix A), then used an estimate of the subsidy to capital to adjust factor prices and trace the effects of the factor price adjustment upon factor intensities.

All our estimates are for a cross section of 1967. Therefore, $q_{c,i} = q_{m,i} = 1.0$ (see Appendix A for notation). We assume further that $\delta^m{}_i = \delta^c{}_i$ and thus we obtain:

$$\frac{P^*{}_{k,i} - P_{k,i}}{P_{k,i}} = \left(\frac{e^*}{e} - 1\right)(1 - \lambda_i).$$

The value of λ_i for each of the seventy-three four-digit tradable sectors was obtained from the 1967 census of manufactures.[30] To estimate e^*/e, we need information on the equilibrium exchange rate and on the average tariff rate. The e^*/e ratio is equal to 1.30 $\times$ 1.0543 where 1.30 is the ratio between the equilibrium and the official exchange rate for 1967 as estimated by Taylor and Bacha (1973). The 1.0543 is the ratio between the average exchange rate and the exchange rate on investment goods. Thus, this last factor corrects for the lower tariffs on investment goods than on other imports. On the other hand, the 1.30 factor corrects for an absolute distortion between the price of tradables and the price of home goods.[31]

Now we adjust the market price of capital for the subsidy, then make new estimates of factor requirements and factor proportions under the new factor price ratio. We have run simulations for both the direct requirements only and for direct plus indirect requirements of home goods. Since the types of findings are very similar, we present in table 3.19 only those for direct plus indirect requirements of home goods. A comparison of these estimates with those actually observed (see table 3.16) shows that, when the subsidy to capital is eliminated, capital requirements for both exportables and import-competing products decrease about 19–23 percent, labor requirements increase about 6–8 percent, and skill requirements increase about 6–8 percent. The decrease in the capital/labor ratios is about 24–29 percent, and the skill/labor ratio remains practically constant.[32] The results imply that eliminating the preferential effective exchange rate on capital goods imports would have contributed significantly to creating employment in Chile's manufacturing sector.

3.5   Factor Requirements in Manufacturing: A Dynamic Analysis of the 1960s

The analysis of sections 3.2–4 centered upon the period 1966–68. In this section we extend our analysis to cover the entire decade of the 1960s. Two exercises are performed. First, we trace the evolution of the wage/rental ratio to determine how changes in relative factor prices might have affected factor requirements and altered the relative profitability of exportable and importable production. Second, we measure factor requirements in other periods of the 1960s to evaluate the robustness of our results for 1966–1968. In this regard our results indicate that the factor requirements for 1966–68 held, in general, throughout the decade.

The composition of tradables will be affected by changes in the wage/rental ratio, via changes in the overall profitability of individual industries. The evolution of the wage/rental ratio in 1960s is given in table

Table 3.19 Direct Plus Home Goods Indirect Factor Requirements and Factor Proportions in Exportables and Import Competing Products by Destination and Origin of Trade Flows: Simulation Experiment

Tradable Category	Weights (1)	Labor (2)	Capital (3)	Skill (4)	Capital/Labor Ratio (5) = (3) ÷ (2)	Skill/Labor Ratio (6) = (4) ÷ (2)
Exportables	Exports					
	a. World	62.94	1,348.1	132.5	21.42	2.10
	b. DCs	105.61	1,472.2	90.4	13.94	0.86
	c. LDCs	53.49	1,320.5	141.8	24.69	2.65
Import competing products	Imports					
	d. World	64.11	789.2	155.6	12.31	2.43
	e. DCs	63.95	730.6	157.9	11.42	2.47
	f. LDCs	64.87	1,072.7	143.8	16.54	2.22
Ratio of requirements	Ratio of exports to import requirements					
	g. World (a ÷ d)	0.982	1.708	0.852	1.740	0.864
	h. DCs (b ÷ e)	1.651	2.015	0.573	1.221	0.348
	i. LDCs (c ÷ f)	0.825	1.211	0.986	1.493	1.194

Note: See tables 3.12 and 3.13 for composition of trade flows and for weights used in computing factor coefficients. See table 3.14 for units used in factor coefficients.

3.20. Observe that it fell from 1960 to 1964, started to rise at the beginning of the Frei government (1965), declined slightly in 1967, then increased substantially in 1968 as the Frei government's stabilization program collapsed. After 1968 the wage/rental ratio decreased. From this evolution, we expect the production of labor-intensive goods to have been encouraged in the early 1960s, discouraged in the mid-1960s, and encouraged again in the late 1960s.

To evaluate the robustness of our results for 1966–68, we have calculated direct plus home goods requirements for trade flows in four of the five periods outlined in table 3.20 (the evolution on a direct basis is similar and is ignored here). These estimates are found by applying the estimated 1967 factor requirements to actual trade flows in each of these periods. The results of this exercise are given in table 3.21.

Observe that the main feature of these results is that our findings for the period 1966–68 hold in general for the other three periods; namely, exports have higher labor requirements than imports. Second, differences in the factor intensity of exports reflect shifts in their composition as trade policies were changed over the decade. Owing to space limitations, we focus only upon baskets with world trade weights. For exportables, when we compare the first two periods, there is a slight decrease in all three factor requirements. Then, between the second and third periods, there is a decrease in labor requirements and an increase in capital and

Table 3.20   **Evolution of Wage/Rental Ratio in Chilean Manufacturing**

Year	Wage Rate (Escudos per Worker)	Rental Price of Capital (Current E^{os} per E^{os} of Capital)	Wage/ Rental Ratio	Period Average
1960	803.2	.0396	20,282.8	19,857.4
1961	862.4	.0444	19,432.2	
1962	1,005.8	.0515	19,530.1	18,461.2
1963	1,454.0	.0836	17,392.3	
1964	2,131.8	.135	15,791.1	16,891.8
1965	2,878.8	.160	17,992.5	
1966	4,015.5	.213	18,852.1	19,067.5
1967	5,247.2	.292	17,962.9	
1968	7,785.3	.382	20,380.4	
1969	11,226.9	.585	19,191.3	18,649.0
1970	15,752.8	.870	18,106.7	

Sources: The wage rate in the industrial sector is taken from ODEPLAN (1971a, p. 182), and the rental price of capital is computed as described in M. Corbo (1974, pp. 154–55, p. 224).

skill requirements. In terms of factor proportions, the capital/labor ratio and the skill/labor ratio increased by 34.9 percent and 49.6 percent, respectively, from the second to the third period (this period coincides with the increase in the wage/rental ratio of the Frei government). After 1968 there is an increase in the requirements of labor and skill and a slight decrease in capital requirements.

Table 3.21   **Direct Plus Home Goods Indirect Factor Requirements in Exports and Import Competing Products by Destination and Origin of Trade Flows: Dynamic Evolution**

Periods	Weights	Labor	Capital	Skill
1962–63	Exports			
	World	77.56	1,738.3	113.2
	DCs	113.06	1,912.6	55.4
	LDCs	74.13	1,740.0	121.2
	Imports			
	World	60.91	1,030.6	155.8
	DCs	61.55	892.9	158.2
	LDCs	56.55	1,804.5	138.2
1964–65	Exports			
	World	75.15	1,651.6	105.2
	DCs	111.45	1,802.1	74.8
	LDCs	81.54	1,613.0	99.4
	Imports			
	World	59.08	1,153.8	145.2
	DCs	60.16	941.6	146.2
	LDCs	54.25	2,008.3	139.6
1966–68	Exports			
	World	58.46	1,733.7	122.4
	DCs	98.64	1,829.1	84.1
	LDCs	49.56	1,712.1	130.9
	Imports			
	World	60.10	983.4	145.6
	DCs	59.97	910.2	147.7
	LDCs	60.74	1,338.5	134.3
1969–70	Exports			
	World	62.32	1,781.4	139.6
	DCs	105.04	1,842.4	97.8
	LDCs	59.62	1,772.6	141.6
	Imports			
	World	60.71	987.7	150.9
	DCs	60.71	927.6	150.4
	LDCs	59.78	1,338.7	138.2

Note: See tables 3.12 and 3.13 for composition of trade flows and for weights used in computing factor coefficients. See table 3.14 for units used in factor coefficients.

For importable goods, labor and skill requirements are more stable throughout the four periods. Capital requirements for these goods increase from the first to the second period, then they decrease from the second to the third period. After 1968 they become fairly constant. This evolution is due to the changes in the composition of goods competing with imports from the developing world and, hence, changes in their capital requirements. Capital requirements of a basket of goods competing with imports from developing countries decreased substantially after the mid-1960s.

These patterns are expected, given the "cycling" of the trade regime in the period. As we mentioned earlier, Chile's trade regime was relatively liberal in the early 1960s, became more restrictive in the mid-1960s, and became liberal again in the late 1960s. Presumably, then, factor requirements at the beginning and end of the decade ought to have better reflected its comparative advantage than factor requirements in the mid-1960s. That is, its labor requirements ought to have been higher and skill and capital requirements lower in periods of trade liberalization than in periods of trade restrictiveness. The estimates shown in table 3.21 generally coincide with these expectations.

3.6 Concluding Remarks

The main conclusions of this study may be summarized as follows:

1. With regard to the composition and direction of Chile's trade, one important feature is its failure to develop a significant volume of HOS exports, especially in trade with developed countries. This failure reflects in considerable part the strong emphasis over the last several decades on import substitution and hence on the production of import-competing HOS goods. The small size of the HOS component in Chile's exports also reflects the country's considerable endowment in natural resources and their major contribution to its exports, as exemplified by refined copper. Indeed, the natural resource factor plays also some role in the production of goods here treated as HOS exports, notably pulp and paper, which dominate exports to other LDCs—chiefly neighboring countries in LAFTA—and various fish, meat, and vegetable products figuring prominently in exports to developed countries.

2. The factor content of Chile's trade in HOS goods is most strikingly marked by the high capital and low labor requirements of its exports to other LDCs and, therewith, the relatively small contribution made by those exports to employment in Chile. In particular, comparing the factor requirements and factor proportions of baskets of tradables with equal DVA content we have found:

HOS exports to DCs are more labor- and capital-intensive and less skill-intensive than Chile's production of HOS goods competing with imports from DCs. Thus, in its trade with DCs, Chile implicitly exports labor and capital and imports skill.

HOS exports to LDCs are more capital-intensive and less labor- and skill-intensive than Chile's production of HOS goods competing with imports from LDCs. The labor and capital requirements of Chile's trade with LDCs are strongly dominated by pulp and paper, a commodity group that has had preferential treatment within LAFTA. Indeed, when exports of pulp and paper are excluded, we found that Chile's HOS exports to LDCs are more labor-intensive and less capital- and skill-intensive than its imports from LDCs. These results suggest that trading arrangements within LAFTA may have been such as to place demands on members' scarce capital resources while giving less inducement to creation of employment.

In exportables (including indirect effects), Chile's exports to DCs are more capital-intensive and less skill-intensive than export to LDCs. These patterns are not affected by the treatment of the pulp and paper sector.

In import-competing products, Chile's imports from DCs are more skill-intensive and less capital-intensive than imports from LDCs. Labor requirements are almost the same for both baskets.

3. The measurement of factor coefficients in terms of international value added is handicapped by lack of good data on effective protection needed for this calculation. Subject to these qualifications, it appears that Chile's production of HOS goods competing with imports from other LDCs would use more labor, capital, and skill per unit of IVA than any of the other trade flows examined. Thus it appears that Chile saves on all factors through its trade with LDCs.

4. Analysis of the effects of trade regime on factor requirements and factor proportions, by major trade categories, indicates that in general the structure of protection has created a bias in favor of the production of low labor-intensive and high capital-intensive commodities. This applies to both exporting and import-competing industries.

5. Concerning the effects of distortions in factor prices brought about by the trade regime and related commercial policies, we estimated an equilibrium price of capital services above the observed price. In studying the effect of this distortion on factor requirements, we find that, when the distortion is present, labor and skill requirements are about 6–8 percent lower and capital requirements are about 19–23 percent higher than without the distortion. The capital/labor ratio would thus be about 25 percent lower without distortions.

6. When we extend the study to other periods in the 1960s, we find that our results and conclusions are still valid for the decade as a whole.

7. As a concluding observation, we judge that a significant, though not spectacular, amount of employment could be created through export

expansion. Chilean exportables to the developed world generated about 40,000 employment opportunities per $100 million of IVA, which is probably a feasible annual increase in export levels; this would represent an annual increase in manufacturing employment of about 11 percent (equal to about 1 percent of the total labor force). The Chilean basket of exportables to developed countries would generate about 20 percent more employment opportunities per unit of IVA than the basket of exportables to LDCs.

Appendix A: Relationship of Factor Intensities to Factor Prices

Start with an aggregate production function at the industry level given by:

$$(A1) \qquad Y_i = A_i \, LM_i^{\alpha_1} LS_i^{\alpha_2} K_i^{\alpha_3}.$$

Then introduce the following first-order conditions for cost minimization:

$$(A2) \qquad \frac{\partial Y_i / \partial LM_i}{\partial Y_i / \partial LS_i} = \frac{w}{P_{s,i}},$$

$$(A3) \qquad \frac{\partial Y_i / \partial LM_i}{\partial Y_i / \partial K_i} = \frac{w}{P_{k,i}},$$

where w is the wage rate of unskilled labor, $P_{s,i}$ is the price of a unit of skill,[33] and $P_{k,i}$ is the price of capital services. Using equations (A1), (A2), and (A3), solve for K_i/Y_i, LM_i/Y_i, and LS_i/Y_i as a function of relative factor prices and the level of value added. These solutions are:

$$(A4) \qquad \frac{LM_i}{Y_i} = C \left(\frac{\alpha_1}{\alpha_3} \frac{P_{k,i}}{w} \right)^{\frac{\alpha_3}{\alpha_1 + \alpha_2 + \alpha_3}}$$

$$\times \left(\frac{\alpha_1}{\alpha_2} \frac{P_{s,i}}{w} \right)^{\frac{\alpha_2}{\alpha_1 + \alpha_2 + \alpha_3}}$$

$$(A5) \qquad \frac{LS_i}{Y_i} = C \left(\frac{\alpha_1}{\alpha_3} \frac{P_{k,i}}{w} \right)^{\frac{\alpha_3}{\alpha_1 + \alpha_2 + \alpha_3}}$$

$$\times \left(\frac{\alpha_1}{\alpha_2} \frac{P_{s,i}}{w} \right)^{- \frac{\alpha_1 + \alpha_3}{\alpha_1 + \alpha_2 + \alpha_3}}$$

(A6)
$$\frac{K_i}{Y_i} = C \left(\frac{\alpha_1}{\alpha_3} \frac{P_{k,i}}{w} \right)^{- \frac{\alpha_1 + \alpha_2}{\alpha_1 + \alpha_2 + \alpha_3}}$$

$$\times \left(\frac{\alpha_1}{\alpha_2} \frac{P_{s,i}}{w} \right)^{\frac{\alpha_2}{\alpha_1 + \alpha_2 + \alpha_3}},$$

where
$$C = A_i^{\left(- \frac{1 - \alpha_1 - \alpha_2 - \alpha_3}{\alpha_1 + \alpha_2 + \alpha_3} \right)}$$

$$\times Y_i^{\left(\frac{1 - \alpha_1 - \alpha_2 - \alpha_3}{\alpha_1 + \alpha_2 + \alpha_3} \right)}.$$

Then, differentiating these expressions, we obtain the change in factor intensity as a function of the change in factor prices:

(A7)
$$d \frac{LM_i}{Y_i} = \frac{LM_i}{Y_i} \left(- \frac{\alpha_2 + \alpha_3}{\alpha_1 + \alpha_2 + \alpha_3} \, dln \, w_i \right.$$

$$+ \frac{\alpha_2}{\alpha_1 + \alpha_2 + \alpha_3} \, dln \, P_{s,i}$$

$$\left. + \frac{\alpha_3}{\alpha_1 + \alpha_2 + \alpha_3} \, dln \, P_{k,i} \right);$$

(A8)
$$d \frac{LS_i}{Y_i} = \frac{LS_i}{Y_i} \left(\frac{\alpha_1}{\alpha_1 + \alpha_2 + \alpha_3} \, dln \, w_i \right.$$

$$- \frac{\alpha_1 + \alpha_3}{\alpha_1 + \alpha_2 + \alpha_3} \, dln \, P_{s,i}$$

$$\left. + \frac{\alpha_3}{\alpha_1 + \alpha_2 + \alpha_3} \, dln \, P_{k,i} \right);$$

(A9)
$$d \frac{K_i}{Y_i} = \frac{K_i}{Y_i} \left(\frac{\alpha_1}{\alpha_1 + \alpha_2 + \alpha_3} \, dln \, w_i \right.$$

$$+ \frac{\alpha_2}{\alpha_1 + \alpha_2 + \alpha_3} \, dln \, P_{s,i}$$

$$\left. - \frac{\alpha_1 + \alpha_2}{\alpha_1 + \alpha_2 + \alpha_3} \, dln \, P_{k,i} \right).$$

These expressions are local approximations (i.e., valid only for a given level of output) around Y_i for the non-CRTS case and global (independent of the level of output) with $\alpha_1 + \alpha_2 + \alpha_3 = 1.0$ for the CRTS case.

Distortions in Price of Capital Services

Next we must adjust the price of capital services upward to correct for the subsidy resulting from the existence of a preferential effective exchange rate for capital goods imports.

The market price of capital services is given by:

(A10) $\qquad P_{k,i} = q_{c,i}\,\lambda_i(r_i + \delta_i^c) + q_{m,i}\,(1 - \lambda_i)\,(r_i + \delta_i^m),$

where λ_i is the share of construction in the total capital stock, $1 - \lambda_i$ is the share of machinery and equipment in the total capital stock, $q_{c,i}$ ($q_{m,i}$) is the price of one unit of construction (machinery and equipment), δ_i^c (δ_i^m) is the depreciation rate for construction (machinery and equipment) capital, and r_i is the cost of capital.

On the other hand, the distortion-free price of capital services is given by:

(A11) $\qquad P_{k,i}^* = q_{c,i}\,\lambda_i\,(r_i + \delta_i^c) + q_{m,i}\,(1 - \lambda_i)\,(r_i + \delta_i^m)\,\dfrac{e^*}{e},$

where e^* is the equilibrium effective exchange rate and e the effective exchange rate for imported capital goods.

Finally, the percentage change in the rental price of capital services resulting from eliminating the distortions is given by:

(A12) $\qquad \dfrac{P_{k,i}^* - P_{k,i}}{P_{k,i}}$

$$= \dfrac{q_{m,i}\,(1 - \lambda_i)\,(r_i + \delta_i^m)\,(e^*/e - 1)}{q_{c,i}\,\lambda_i\,(r_i + \delta_i^c) + q_{m,i}\,(1 - \lambda_i)\,(r_i + \delta_i^m)}$$

Table 3.A.1 Foreign Trade Participation of Chilean Manufacturing Industries—Computation of T Statistic

Industry (ISIC)	Exports[a] (Average, 1966–68) (1)	Imports (Average, 1966–68) (2)	Net Production (1967) (3)	Consumption (4)	Trade Classification Coefficients $\frac{(4)-(3)}{(4)}$ (5)
3111 Slaughtering, preparing and preserving meats	142,982	100,103	1,478,860	1,435,980	−.02986
3112 Dairy products	0	73,759	382,102	455,862	.16180
3113 Canning and preserving of fruits and vegetables	9,129	5,477	140,001	136,350	−.02678
3114 Canning, preserving, and processing of fish, crustaceans, and similar foods	8,826	42	142,856	134,072	−.06551
3115 Vegetable and animal oils and fats	4,925	64,935	304,685	364,695	.16454
3116 Grain mill products	3,627	46,452	628,336	671,161	.06390
3117 Manufacture of bakery products	9	676	585,836	586,503	.00113
3118 Sugar factories and refineries	0	93,011	350,154	443,165	.20987
3119 Cocoa, chocolate, and sugar confectionery	489	7,032	127,428	133,972	.04884
3121 Manufacture of food products n.e.c.	2,543	77,835	330,126	405,418	.18571
3122 Prepared animal feeds	0	907	87,247	88,153	.01028
3131 Distilling, rectifying, and blending of spirits	26	2,662	153,225	155,861	.01691
3132 Wine industries	8,205	114	432,174	424,083	−.01907
3133 Malt liquors and malt	11,935	26	161,916	150,007	−.07938
3134 Soft drinks and carbonated waters industries	0	9	171,246	171,255	.00005
3140 Tobacco manufactures	0	263	172,548	172,811	.00152
3211 Spinning, weaving, and finishing of textiles	48,909	171,440	1,278,940	1,401,470	.08743
3212 Made-up textile goods except wearing apparel	132	69,419	26,524	95,811	.72316
3213 Knitting mills	13	1,877	413,309	415,172	.00448
3214 Manufacture of carpets and rugs	0	1,493	22,281	23,775	.06281
3215 Cordage, rope, and twine	0	20,391	22,723	43,114	.47295

Table 3.A.1—*continued*

Industry (ISIC)	Exports[a] (Average, 1966–68) (1)	Imports (Average, 1966–68) (2)	Net Production (1967) (3)	Con-sumption (4)	Trade Classification Coefficients $\frac{(4)-(3)}{(4)}$ (5)
3219 Textiles n.e.c.	13	2,484	1,584	4,055	.60946
3220 Wearing apparel, except footwear	40	28,783	587,654	616,397	.04663
3231 Tanneries and leather finishing	0	13	202,442	202,455	.00006
3233 Products of leather and leather substitutes except footwear	30	4,500	31,894	36,364	.12291
3240 Footwear, except vulcanized or molded rubber or plastic footwear	493	10,076	374,045	383,627	.02497
3311 Sawmills, planing, and other wood mills	12,167	1,741	506,528	496,102	−.02101
3312 Wooden and cane containers and small caneware	14	3,434	19,565	22,985	.14877
3319 Wood and cork products n.e.c.	801	75,481	19,971	94,652	.78900
3320 Furniture and fixtures, except primarily of metal	369	58,265	163,909	221,805	.26102
3411 Pulp, paper, and paperboard	141,180	37,862	316,845	213,527	−.48386
3412 Containers, and boxes of paper and paperboard	0	3,896	42,645	46,540	.08370
3419 Pulp, paper, and paperboard articles n.e.c.	2,110	5,332	9,838	13,059	.24666
3420 Printing, publishing, and allied industries	13,266	92,671	421,550	500,954	.15850
3511 Basic industrial inorganic chemicals, except fertilizers	40,196	82,383	112,191	154,377	.27326
3512 Fertilizers and pesticides	750	21,204	34,719	55,173	.37072
3513 Synthetic resins, plastic materials and man-made fibers except glass	24,120	109,190	182,965	268,035	.31738
3514 Basic industrial organic chemicals, except fertilizers	3,705	134,742	16,459	147,496	.88841
3521 Paints, varnishes, and lacquers	0	7,938	128,250	136,188	.05828
3522 Drugs and medicines	130	83,140	248,174	331,184	.25064
3523 Soap and cleaning products, perfumes, cosmetics, and other toilet preparations	15	8,528	270,317	278,829	.03052
3529 Chemical products n.e.c.	3,942	51,020	137,645	184,723	.25485

Table 3.A.1—continued

Industry (ISIC)	Exports[a] (Average, 1966–68) (1)	Imports (Average, 1966–68) (2)	Net Production (1967) (3)	Con-sumption (4)	Trade Classification Coefficients $\frac{(4) - (3)}{(4)}$ (5)
3530 Petroleum refineries	34	50,444	651,882	702,292	.07177
3540 Miscellaneous products of petroleum and coal	0	1,683	84,128	85,811	.01961
3551 Tire and tube industries	68	27,551	169,117	196,601	.13979
3559 Rubber products n.e.c.	2,935	72,037	84,124	153,226	.45098
3560 Plastic products n.e.c.	12,960	96,980	214,140	298,161	.28179
3610 Pottery, china, and earthenware	86	3,660	61,393	64,968	.05502
3620 Glass and glass products	503	26,692	135,225	161,414	.16224
3691 Structural clay products	96	38,444	26,044	64,391	.59553
3692 Cement, lime, and plaster	578	4,324	171,375	175,121	.02139
3695 Fiber-cement products	0	867	49,685	50,552	.01714
3699 Nonmetallic mineral products n.e.c.	268	26,607	90,141	116,480	.22612
3710 Iron and steel basic industries	52,046	290,745	697,687	936,386	.25491
3729 Nonferrous metal basic industries, except copper	87,772	98,924	17,466	28,618	.38969
3811 Cutlery, hand tools, and general hardware	822	165,033	40,464	204,675	.80229
3812 Furniture and fixtures primarily of metal	0	2,929	102,244	105,173	.02784
3813 Structural metal products	1,529	201,641	160,244	360,356	.55531
3814 Metal containers and metal housewares	20	11,553	272,287	283,819	.04063
3815 Cable, wire, and their products	0	3,208	97,424	100,632	.03187
3819 Fabricated metal products except machinery and equipment n.e.c.	170	8,447	116,803	125,080	.06617
3822 Agricultural machinery and equipment	27	25,871	44,147	69,990	.36924
3823 Metal and woodworking machinery	14	65,823	31,014	96,823	.67968

Table 3.A.1—*continued*

Industry (ISIC)	Exports[a] (Average, 1966–68) (1)	Imports (Average, 1966–68) (2)	Net Production (1967) (3)	Con-sumption (4)	Trade Classification Coefficients $\frac{(4) - (3)}{(4)}$ (5)
3824 Special industrial machinery and equipment except metal and woodworking machinery	428	233,472	19,829	252,873	.92158
3825 Office, computing, and accounting machinery	673	56,608	38,290	94,225	.59363
3829 Machinery and equipment except electrical n.e.c.	4,859	246,485	420,363	661,989	.36500
3831 Electrical industrial machinery and apparatus	653	246,552	41,605	287,503	.85528
3832 Radio, television, and communication equipment and apparatus	3,920	127,020	285,359	408,458	.30137
3833 Electrical appliances and housewares	0	2,987	27,612	30,599	.09761
3839 Electrical apparatus and supplies n.e.c.	11,326	75,277	141,881	205,832	.31069
3841 Shipbuilding and repairing	0	677	89,428	90,105	.00750
3842 Railroad equipment	11	84,098	178,597	262,685	.32010
3843 Motor vehicles	366	338,911	594,367	932,912	.36289
3844 Motorcycles and bicycles	0	3,671	15,702	19,373	.18948
3845 Repairing of aircraft and manufacture of aircraft parts	1,076	163,616	10,923	173,464	.93703
3849 Transport equipment n.e.c.	0	233	2,724	2,957	.07875
3851 Professional and scientific equipment n.e.c.	288	105,647	16,976	122,334	.86123
3852 Photographic and optical goods	78	18,665	15,920	34,508	.53865
3901 Jewelry and related articles	743	111	19,119	18,487	−.03419
3902 Musical instruments	11	4,869	1,024	5,882	.82586
3903 Sporting and athletic goods	55	6,455	1,483	7,882	.81186
3909 Manufacturing industries n.e.c.	0	11,867	64,650	76,517	.15508

[a]Columns 1–4 are in thousands of escudos.

Notes

1. We recommend Behrman (1976) and Corbo (1974) to the reader interested in greater detail on Chilean economic development. A more detailed analysis of alternative trade strategies and employment in Chile and the complete set of data used in this study are found in Corbo and Meller (1978a), available for the cost of reproduction from the National Bureau of Economic Research.

2. Note that this value is slightly different from that given in table 3.1, owing to different data sources.

3. Most studies indicate conclusively that Chile has a comparative advantage in the production of this resource-based commodity. Hence there is need to design a policy to stabilize copper earnings. This is readily seen by the fact that changes in the price of copper have an important effect upon trade surpluses (see table 3.3). The high copper prices in the late 1960s allowed the banking system to accumulate, by 1970, the highest level of net international reserves in twenty years (U.S. $343.5 million). Also, one should note the impressive improvement in Chile's terms of trade at the end of the 1960s (table 3.3). This behavior depends in a very important way upon the trend in the price of copper.

4. For a more detailed analysis see Ffrench-Davis (1973) and Behrman (1976).

5. The main tools to control imports were: (1) import restrictions with a list of "allowed goods"; (2) prior deposits on imports; and (3) tariffs, generally high but with a wide range of rates.

6. The major reason for this type of discrimination was the foreign ownership of large-scale copper mining. Thus the exchange rate was used as a device to tax large-scale copper mining.

7. It will be noted that EERs in tables 3.7 and 3.8 show different levels and different time trends. The difference in levels arises because table 3.7 is in terms of 1969 escudos per dollar, whereas table 3.8 is in 1965 escudos. The difference in trends arises because the EERs in table 3.7 are "purchasing-power-parity-adjusted" (i.e., multiplied by the ratio of the foreign price level to the domestic price level), whereas the EERs in table 3.8 are "price-level-deflated" (i.e., deflated by the Chilean GDP deflator). Furthermore, the sources cited for the tables report quite different methodologies for computing the EERs. Behrman's EERs are based on direct price comparisons for 220 commodities between Chile and the United States. Ffrench-Davis's EERs are based on comparisons of the total cost of imported commodities with their c.i.f. prices. Thus, he transforms each explicit import cost into an ad valorem tariff equivalent that is added to the c.i.f. price.

8. All estimates use price comparisons to estimate nominal protection and the Corden method to calculate ERPs.

9. See chapter 1 for a discussion of this distinction. Particularly important among the products here classified in the NRB category are refined copper (ISIC 3721) and meat meal and fish meal (SITC 081.4, which, for Chile, consists mainly of fish meal).

10. In Corbo and Meller (1978a) we also study the factor proportions and requirements of noncompeting import industries.

11. We also experimented with 0.90 as a cutoff point for the classification of industries in the import-competing and noncompeting import categories. The factor requirements in import-competing industries were only marginally affected when this alternative was used.

12. Indeed, over the period studied Chile did export significant amounts of both raw wood and fresh or simply preserved fish (such exports being here classified as NRB).

13. For details of these trade flows by four-digit ISIC sectors and by countries, see Appendix I, section III, of Corbo and Meller (1978a).

14. This way of defining "skill" assumes that all differences in wage rates within the manufacturing sector can be attributed to skill differences and that there is perfect substitution among different types of labor. The only evidence we have for Chile on earnings within the manufacturing sector (M. Corbo 1974), shows that a substantial proportion of the variance in labor earnings can be accounted for by human capital characteristics of the labor force. This way of measuring skill has been popularized by Griliches and used extensively in the testing of trade theories (see especially Stern 1975).

15. The treatment of home goods in computing factor requirements has been discussed in the introductory chapter of this volume. For Chile a problem arises because of the lack of a cost structure for each of the eighty-two four-digit ISIC industries used in computing direct factor requirements. There is available, however, a fifty-four-sector input-output table for 1962. Of the fifty-four sectors, twenty-four are manufacturing sectors that correspond closely to the ISIC classification at the three-digit level. We use this source to compute value added and factor requirement multipliers at the level of disaggregation provided by the I-0 table. For details on the derivation of these multipliers see Corbo and Meller (1978a, chap. 3). Then we use the same multiplier for all four-digit industries belonging to a given three-digit industry of the I-0 table. This procedure assumes that each four-digit industry belonging to a three-digit group has the same intermediate structure with respect to home goods.

16. Initially (Corbo and Meller 1978a, chap. 3) we treated Argentina and Mexico separately, but the factor requirement of Chile's trade with these two countries was not too different from the ones for Chile's trade with other LDCs. Thus we decided to include these two countries in the LDC group.

17. This procedure assumes that the marginal basket uses the same technology as the average one (see Lydall 1975, pp. 26–27, for a discussion of the validity of this assumption) and that the output mix is the same. For effective rates of protection see Corbo and Meller (1978a, Appendix I, table IV-A).

18. For effective rates of protection see Corbo and Meller (1978a, Appendix I, table IV-A).

19. These results are again dominated by the ERP of, and factor requirements in, the pulp, paper, and paperboard industry.

20. We also computed direct plus total indirect effects, and the pattern of results is similar to the one for direct plus home goods indirect effects. The difference in labor requirements by protection level within a given tradable category was even higher than for direct plus home goods indirect effects owing to the greater labor intensity of agricultural products that have a heavier weight as inputs in the industries with lower protection level.

21. This variable is defined as the weighted average of the effective rate of protection of import-competing industries (ERPM) and the effective rate of protection of exporting industries (ERPX), where the weights are import-competing production and exports, respectively.

22. We also used, as did Baldwin (1971), a concentration index as an explanatory variable, but it was never significant.

23. The simple correlation in the sample between LM and LS is 0.90, and between LS and K it is 0.63, both of which are significantly different from zero at the .01 level. Furthermore, NM is positively correlated with LM, LS, and K: the simple correlation coefficients are 0.26, 0.46, and 0.32, respectively, all of them significant at a .01 level.

24. On the other hand, when we ran equations using total exports as dependent variables the results were very poor, and they are not reproduced in the table. No coefficient was significantly different from zero at the .05 significance level. These results are due in part to the behavior of the dependent variable. In nineteen out of the seventy-three exporting and import-competing tradable sectors, total exports are zero, and in many other sectors they are very small. Furthermore, it is meaningless to estimate this equation for exporting sectors only, because of the small number of degrees of freedom available.

25. In the Park test, the squared residuals of the original regression are regressed on a function of some size variable. In our computations, we used as a size variable the output of the sector and the consumption of the sector. The results were better for the first variable, and they are the ones we present here.

We proceed now with one equation at a time. When the residuals of equation 1.1 were regressed as a function of PRO, the best fit was for the following equation:

$$e^2{}_i = 1.396 \times 10^9 + 6221.7\,PRO \qquad\qquad R^2 = .039,$$
$$\quad (1.05) \qquad\qquad (1.69)$$

where e_i is the residual of the regression and PRO is production. In the case of the residuals of equation 1.3, the best fit was for the following equation:

$$e^2{}_i = 1.018 \times 10^9 + 5436.58\,PRO \qquad\qquad R^2 = .040.$$
$$\quad (.90) \qquad\qquad (1.73)$$

The correction for heteroskedasticity is performed by creating a diagonal matrix H whose ith diagonal element (d_{ii}) is given by the reciprocal of the square root of the right-hand side terms in the equations for $e^2{}_i$ above. Then all the original variables are premultiplied by the diagonal matrix H. This procedure is equivalent to a deflation of the original variables.

26. We also used $ERPM$ in the equation for imports, but the results were of the same form; that is, the protection variable was never significant even at a .10 level.

27. Corbo and Meller (1978a, b). For a fuller discussion of the implications of technology for the pattern of trade see Corbo and Meller (1978b).

28. We could not estimate a production function for all the seventy-three exporting and import-competing sectors owing to a lack of degrees of freedom for some sectors.

29. For details of the results see Corbo and Meller (1978a).

30. Instituto Nacional de Estadísticas (1970, pp. 40–45).

31. In Corbo and Meller (1978a), we also simulate the joint effect of this increase in the price of capital services together with a 10 percent decrease in the minimum wage rate.

32. We have also studied the effect of distortions on factor requirements and factor proportions measuring value added at international prices. When compared with the results of table 3.16, the same pattern emerges: the removal of distortions yields a 6–8 percent increase in labor and skill requirements and a substantial decrease in capital requirements. This pattern of results is found for both the direct effect and the direct plus home goods indirect effect. As in section 3.3, we also grouped the tradables by protection level and studied the factor requirements and factor proportions of trade for two sets, one with tradables with rate of protection above the median and the other with rate of protection below the median. When we compare the results with those in section 3.3, the pattern is again similar for corresponding baskets; we observe an increase in labor and skill requirements and a substantial decrease in capital requirements and in the capital/labor ratios. For details of these results see Corbo and Meller (1978a).

It should be mentioned that these simulation results correspond to the substitution effect, that is, movements along an isoquant. The full effect on factor requirements, measured above, would therefore take time to materialize. Moreover, output adjustments are neglected.
33. Skill is expressed in units of unskilled labor. Therefore its price is also equal to the minimum wage.

References

Askari, H., and Corbo, V. 1978. Export promotion: Its rationale and feasibility. *Pakistan Economic and Social Review.*

Baldwin, R. 1971. Determinants of the commodity structure of U.S. Trade. *American Economic Review* 60 (March): 126–46.

Behrman, J. R. 1976. *Foreign trade regimes and economic development: Chile.* New York: Columbia University Press for NBER.

Branson, W. M., and Monoyios, N. 1977. Factor inputs in U.S. trade. *Journal of International Economics* 7 (May): 111–31.

Bruno, M. 1973. Protection and tariff change under general equilibrium. *Journal of International Economics* 3 (August): 205–25.

Corbo, M. 1974. Schooling, experience and wages in Santiago, Chile. Ph.D. diss., University of Chicago.

Corbo, V. 1974. *Inflation in developing countries.* Amsterdam: North-Holland.

Corbo, V., and Meller, P. 1977. The substitution of labor, skill and capital in Chilean manufacturing. In manuscript. Available on request from the authors.

———. 1978a. Alternative trade strategies and employment implications: Chile. In manuscript. Available from NBER.

———. 1978b. The substitution of labor, skill, and capital: Its implication for trade and employment. In *Trade and employment in developing countries.* Vol. 2. *Factor supply and substitution,* ed. Anne O. Krueger. Chicago: University of Chicago Press. Forthcoming.

———. 1979. The translog production function: Some evidence from establishment data. *Journal of Econometrics* 10 (June): 193–99.

CORFO. 1972. *Datos básicos sector industrial manufacturero período 1960–70.* Santiago: División de Planificación Industrial.

de la Cuadra, S. 1974. La protección efectiva en Chile. Documento de Trabajo no. 22. Duplicated. Santiago. Instituto de Economía Universidad Católica.

De Melo, J. A. P. 1978. Protection and resource allocation in a Walrasian trade model. *International Economic Review* 19 (February): 25–43.

Departamento de Economía, Universidad de Chile. 1978. Comentarios sobre la situación económica. Second semester.

Ffrench-Davis, R. 1973. *Políticas económicas en Chile 1952–1970*. Santiago: Universidad Católica de Chile.

Harkness, J., and Kyle, J. F. 1975. Factors influencing United States comparative advantage. *Journal of International Economics* 5 (May): 153–65.

Hufbauer, G. C. 1970. The impact of national characteristics and technology on the commodity composition of trade in manufactured goods. In *The technology factor in world trade*, ed. R. Vernon. New York: Columbia University Press for NBER.

Instituto de Economía. 1963. *La economía de Chile en el período 1950–63*. Vol. 2. Santiago: Universidad de Chile.

Instituto Nacional de Estadísticas. 1970. *IV censo nacional de Manufacturas*. 2 vols. Santiago.

Jones, R. 1977. *Two-ness in trade theory: Cost and benefits*. Princeton Special Studies Series. Princeton: Princeton University Press.

Krueger, A. 1977. *Growth distortions and patterns of trade among many countries*. Princeton Studies in International Finance. Princeton: Princeton University Press.

Leontief, W. W. 1953. Domestic production and foreign trade: The American capital position re-examined. *Proceedings of the American Philosophical Society* 97: 331–49.

Lydall, H. F. 1975. *Trade and employment*. Geneva: International Labor Organization.

Ministerio de Hacienda. 1979. Exposición sobre el estado de la hacienda pública, January.

ODEPLAN. n.d. Cuadro de transacciónes intersectoriales para la economía Chilena–1962.

————. 1971*a*. *Plan de la economía nacional: Antecedentes sobre el desarrollo Chileno, 1960–70*. Santiago.

————. 1971*b*. *Cuentas nacionales de Chile*. Santiago.

Park, R. E. 1966. Estimation with heteroskedastic error terms. *Econometrica* 34 (October): 888.

Stern, R. M. 1975. Testing trade theories. In *International trade and finance: Frontiers for research*, ed. P. Kenen. Cambridge: Cambridge University Press.

Taylor, L., and Bacha, E. 1973. Growth and trade distortions in Chile and their implications in calculating the shadow price of foreign exchange. In *Analysis of development problems: Studies of the Chilean economy*, ed. R. S. Eckaus and P. M. Rosenstein-Rodan. Amsterdam: North-Holland.

Taylor, L., and Black, S. 1974. Practical general equilibrium estimation of resource pulls under trade liberalization. *Journal of International Economics* 4 (February): 37–57.

4 International Trade Strategies, Employment, and Income Distribution in Colombia

Francisco E. Thoumi

4.1 Introduction

Colombia is an interesting country to study for this project because it has experienced both import substitution and export promotion trade strategies and because it faces severe employment problems. From World War II until 1967, Colombia followed well-defined import substitution policies. During this period the Colombian manufacturing sector evolved from producing mostly consumer goods to producing intermediate and capital goods as many import substitution industries developed. In this environment, natural resource based (NRB) commodities accounted for the bulk of exports. In 1960 coffee accounted for 72 percent of total exports, while manufactures made up only 2 percent of the total.

In 1967, after a balance of payments crisis, Colombia changed the focus of its trade policies. The change was not abrupt. Its purpose was to make the development of export industries more attractive than the further development of import substitution industries. However, at the same time, Colombia hoped that industries that had developed efficiently under the import substitution strategy would find it profitable to begin exporting. Thus the new policy was intended to improve the profitability of export sales relative to domestic sales for new and existing producers. The resulting opening of the economy was dramatic, and the composi-

Francisco E. Thoumi is associated with the Inter-American Development Bank.

The opinions expressed here are the author's and do not represent those of the Inter-American Development Bank. The basic research was undertaken concurrently with teaching at George Washington University. The author wishes to extend thanks to Anne O. Krueger, Hal B. Lary, John E. Elac, Hugh Schwartz, and Peter Wogart for their helpful comments on a previous version of this paper, to José Sidaoui for his computer assistance, and to Elba Planells for her patient typing.

tion of exports changed drastically. By 1976, manufacturing exports accounted for 21 percent of total exports, and coffee's share had fallen to less than 50 percent.

Colombia's employment problems are similar to those afflicting many other LDCs. Population growth has been rapid, with the urban population rising at an even more rapid rate. During its import substitution phase, growth of manufacturing employment was dismal. In the last ten years of import substitution, manufacturing employment growth averaged 1 percent per year. In its last five years, manufacturing output rose at an annual rate of 5.5 percent, but manufacturing employment did not increase at all. One of the purposes of the export promotion policy was to increase employment opportunities in the manufacturing sector. To a certain degree this increase has occurred, although it has not been as strong as that experienced in some other countries. Since 1967, manufacturing employment has been growing at annual rates of 3 to 4 percent. This growth is not as large as, say, that of Brazil, which experienced increases in manufacturing employment on the order of 6 to 7 percent annually after adopting export promotion policies.

Although there have been extensive studies of the progress of the Colombian economy, its dependence upon coffee exports, and its import substitution policies (e.g., Berry and Thoumi 1977; Díaz-Alejandro 1976b; Thoumi 1978), there has been no study of the employment effects of the export promotion strategy. Thus, Colombia should make an interesting comparison to other export-oriented countries largely because its policies have been relatively less successful (though certainly not unsuccessful) in generating employment opportunities.

My analysis focuses upon the years 1970 and 1973.[1] Data availability was the primary reason for this choice. However, comparing labor requirements between the two years will permit inferences about the progress of the export promotion policies started in 1967. The 1970 estimates then will refer to the early phase of export promotion; the 1973 estimate will refer to the later phase.

4.2   An Overview of the Colombian Economy

4.2.1   Patterns of Growth

Colombia has many characteristics in common with other LDCs.[2] Its per capita income was approximately $630 in 1976, somewhat below the average for the "middle-income developing countries" (MDC) estimated by the World Bank. Growth in real GNP during the past thirty years has averaged approximately 5 percent per year, although growth has not been smooth by any means. From 1950 to 1956, growth in GNP averaged 5.23 percent; from 1956 to 1967, the annual average growth rate fell to 4.57 percent; from 1967 to 1972, it averaged 6.08 percent. This rate has increased in more recent years to about 6.5 percent (see *Coyuntura Económica*, various issues), with the exception of 1975, when GNP grew only 1.8 percent as a result of the world recession and restrictive internal macroeconomic policies. The composition of GNP has changed substantially since, as formal manufacturing and services have grown at a faster rate than GNP, while agriculture has grown at a lower rate. The national accounts (*Cuentas nacionales* 1973, 1977) indicate that agriculture's share of GNP declined from 35.9 percent in 1950 to 26.7 percent in 1972. Total manufacturing's share, including the informal sector, grew from 17.8 percent to 20.2 percent. Underlying this, the rate of growth of the formal manufacturing sector has consistently outpaced GNP by approximately 1 percent per year during the past fifteen years. The shares of mining, personal services, government services, and transport have remained stable, while the shares of commerce, communications, electricity, gas and water, construction, and banking, insurance, financial, and real estate services have all increased significantly. Particularly large percentage changes took place in communications and electricity and other utilities, reflecting both the large infrastructure expenditures by the government in the fifties and sixties and also the increased degree of urbanization and internal economic integration of the country.

4.2.2 International Trade

Pattern and Composition of Trade

Colombia's exports consist principally of NRB products (of which coffee is the most important), destined mainly for the developed capitalist world. Its imports are mostly manufactured goods, again mainly originating from developed nations. However, it is perhaps not quite as dependent upon trade as some LDCs for its economic well-being and, to a degree, has succeeded in diversifying both the composition and the destination of its exports.

Colombia's international trade has grown at an accelerating rate since 1960. Table 4.1 shows that commodity exports (in current prices) rose by 16 percent between 1960 and 1965, by 35 percent between 1965 and 1970, and by 102 percent during the following five years. Commodity imports behaved somewhat erratically; they declined 16 percent between 1960 and 1965 and then increased sharply as dollars became available because of increased exports. During the 1960s the share of exports in GNP fluctuated between 12.8 and 14.3 percent, and that of imports ranged from 12.4 to 16.2 percent. More recently (1976), official figures show a decline in the share of exports in GNP to 11.8 percent and a decline in the share of imports to 12.0 percent. These figures, which

Table 4.1   Growth of Colombia's Foreign Trade, 1960 to 1975 (Values in Millions of U.S. Dollars)

Year	Exports	Coffee	DCs	LDCs	Imports	DCs	LDCs
1960	463.9	72%	94%	6%	541.1	89%	11%
1965	539.5	64	87	13	452.7	88	12
1970	727.6	64	86	14	843.7	90	10
1973	1,191.4	50	84	16	1,061.5	87	13
1975	1,468.2	46	79	21	1,494.8	87	13
			Percentage Change				
1960–65	16%	3%	7%	150%	−16%	−18%	−10%
1965–70	35	36	40	12	86	91	66
1970–75	102	44	72	324	77	72	122

Source: International Monetary Fund, *Direction of Trade*, computer tapes, 21 July 1977.

would mean a decline in the trade share in spite of the export drive and simultaneous lowering of tariffs, may be biased downward because contraband has probably increased.

Colombia has become less dependent upon NRB and coffee exports. In 1960, NRB commodities formed 98 percent of exports, of which coffee was 72 percent. In 1970 the share of NRB commodities in total exports had fallen to about 85 percent; that for coffee was 64 percent. By 1973 NRB products formed 65 percent of exports; coffee's share had fallen yet further to 50 percent.

The relative importance of exports to developed nations has fallen at the same time that the relative shares of NRB and coffee exports have fallen. In 1960, 94 percent of Colombia's exports were destined for DCs, of which the United States and Germany were most important. By 1975 the DC share in total exports had decreased to 79 percent. Its major LDC destinations were other Latin American countries, especially Ecuador, Peru, Panama, and Venezuela.

Colombian imports are mostly manufactured products and originate mostly in the developed countries (see tables 4.1 and 4.2). The course of imports has not changed much in the past twenty years, about 87 percent of imports originating in DCs. However, the relative share of the United States fell from 50 percent in the early 1960s to 46 percent in 1970 and 41 percent in 1973, while that of other DCs rose from 35 percent to 40 and 44 percent in the same time periods. The content of imports has also remained relatively stable. Manufactured imports were 95 percent of all imports in the early 1960s, 94 percent in 1970, and 89 percent in 1973.

It has been argued (Díaz-Alejandro 1976b) that the export promotion policies followed by the Colombian government have benefited NRB products, which probably would have been exported independently of the export promotion policies—for example, cotton, sugar, coffee, tobacco, and bananas. However, the substantial increase in the importance of HOS exports in the 1970s indicates that the export promotion policies have affected HOS exports more than NRB exports. In general, growth rates (of the value of exports) for NRB exports have been lower than those for HOS exports despite booming world markets for NRB commodities (e.g., the export price of Colombian coffee increased by close to 200 percent between 1970 and 1975). It seems clear then that HOS exports have been more responsive to domestic price incentives than NRB commodities, whose exports depend upon weather and international price fluctuations.

Although HOS exports grew across the board, their most substantial growth was in exports to developed countries other than the United States. Exports to these countries increased ninefold to exceed the exports to the United States by 26 percent when HOS is defined to include all the manufacturing sector, and by 90 percent when the HOS definition excludes petrochemicals, jewelry, and sugar. The share of HOS exports going to the United States declined by over 15 percentage points between 1970 and 1973 under the different HOS definitions used (see table 4.2). The share going to other developed countries increased by about 20 percentage points. The share of LDCs in HOS exports decreased by about 8 percentage points when sugar, petrochemicals, and jewelry are included in the HOS sector and by about 5.5 percentage points when these products are excluded.

Table 4.2 also shows the share of HOS goods in total exports in 1970 and 1973. The striking feature is the dramatic increase of HOS exports as a percentage of total exports to nearly all destinations, with the most significant increases being in the HOS share of exports to other developed countries, the Andean Group, and other Latin American countries. Their share of HOS exports in total exports increased from 14.9 percent to 35.5 percent when all manufacturing except sugar is defined as the HOS sector and from 12.7 percent to 29.9 percent when all food manufacturing is excluded from the HOS category. They increased their shares in other DC exports from 3.5 to 30.2 percent, in Andean Group exports from 36.3 to 78.5 percent, and in other Latin American exports from 36.4 to 54.6 percent.

The evidence thus suggests that the switch in trade policies that improved the relative attractiveness of exports after 1967 had a cumulative effect. In the early post-1967 years many NRB exports benefited from the export incentives system, while the effect of these policies on HOS exports was not being fully felt. However, as time passed without drastic changes in export oriented policies, entrepreneurs gained confidence in

Table 4.2   Colombian Exports and Imports by Country Groupings and Share of HOS Goods in Exports, 1970 and 1973

		United States	Other Developed Countries	Venezuela	Andean Group	Central America and Caribbean	Other Latin American Countries	Other Less Developed Countries	Socialist Countries	Total
				Country Distribution of Trade (%)						
Total exports	1970	39.0	39.0	.9	7.3	3.6	2.1	.2	.7	100
	1973	36.5	43.6	1.8	5.6	6.6	1.8	.4	3.7	100
HOS exports— all manufactures	1970	43.3	14.5	4.5	15.7	17.0	4.6	.2	.1	100
	1973	27.8	35.3	4.2	11.5	14.8	2.7	.7	3.0	100
HOS exports excluding sugar, petrochemicals, and jewelry	1970	32.1	12.5	6.0	19.6	22.1	6.1	1.1	.5	100
	1973	17.2	33.0	6.3	17.2	21.0	4.0	.9	.4	100
Total imports	1970	46.4	39.5	1.1	4.3	.9	4.4	.8	2.6	100
	1973	41.0	43.5	.7	4.0	.9	7.0	1.2	1.7	100
Manufactured imports	1970	47.1	41.1	1.1	3.3	1.0	3.4	.3	2.7	100
	1973	37.7	47.7	.8	4.0	.8	6.6	.5	1.9	100
				Share of HOS Exports in Total Exports (%)						
HOS exports excluding sugar	1970	15.4	3.5	81.5	36.3	80.9	36.4	51.8	9.6	14.9
	1973	25.6	30.2	88.5	78.5	85.0	54.6	50.2	2.8	35.5
HOS exports excluding all processed foods	1970	13.3	3.2	69.2	30.2	66.0	34.7	51.5	7.1	12.7
	1973	23.2	23.5	71.9	67.0	73.3	53.9	49.2	2.0	29.9

Source: Computations derived from DANE (1970–73, 1970; see Appendix A). These computations are hereafter referred to as "author's computations."

the stability of these policies and began to invest in manufacturing plants to supply world markets. The full effect of this process had not been felt by 1970; thus the large increase in manufactured exports between 1970 and 1973.

Balance of Payments

Balance of payments problems have frequently shaped Colombia's trade policies. During its import substitution phase, Colombia typically encountered balance of payments difficulties (see table 4.3). Policy-makers responded to these problems by increasing import licensing, introducing multiple exchange rates, and generally tightening the stringency of exchange controls. The change in policy directions of 1967 was itself partially due to a balance of payments crisis. In mid-1965, foreign exchange reserves were down to $56 million, their lowest level since 1957 and half that of a year earlier. From 1965 to 1966, merchandise imports rose (in current terms) by nearly 50 percent while exports fell by 6 percent. Reserves fell still further. A crisis ensued, and after consultation with domestic and international officials the exchange system was changed to a crawling peg (as characterized by Díaz-Alejandro 1976*b*, p. 206), and the nature of the trade regime was altered substantially.

The Exchange Rate

Colombia has used a multiple exchange rate system[3] since World War II with periodic changes in rates and classifications of different exports and imports. In some periods, various rates have been allowed to float. In general, it can be said that the peso was consistently overvalued and that exports were discriminated against during the import substitution phase, although the degree of overvaluation varied as exchange rates

Table 4.3   **Colombian Balance of Payments, 1957–74 (Annual Averages in Millions of Current U.S. Dollars)**

	1957–62	1963–66	1967–70	1971–74
1. Coffee exports	337	366	380	513
2. Merchandise exports	519	562	657	1,123
3. Merchandise imports	467	537	632	1,061
4. Trade balance	52	25	25	62
5. Net services and transfers	−86	−171	−227	−201
6. Current account balance	−34	−146	−202	−263
7. Net long-term capital	32	151	211	244
8. Net short-term capital	−31	31	38	13
9. Errors	1	− 42	0	61
10. Sum (6) + (7) + (8) + (9)	−32	− 6	47	55

Source: International Monetary Fund, *International Financial Statistics* (various years).

adjusted infrequently in the face of chronic inflation. Since 1967 the degree of overvaluation has fallen. Hutcheson and Schydlowsky (1976) indicate that it was about 25 percent. The average annual rate of inflation for 1961–72 was 11.25 percent (Gomez-Otalora and Pardo-Vargas 1973). Inflation accelerated to 24 percent in 1973, then 26 percent in 1974, and declined to 18 percent in 1975 (see *Coyuntura Económica* 1 [April 1976]: 36). Growth of the money supply resulting from continued large budget deficits is probably the main cause of inflation (see Barro 1973). For example, the money supply in 1972 was twenty-five times greater than it was in 1960, while the government ran annual budget deficits exceeding 800 million pesos over the period.

The Trade Regime

After World War II, Colombia's international reserves diminished as the demands for many commodities not available during the war were satisfied. Simultaneously, coffee prices declined and the government reacted to the ensuing balance of payments problems with a combination of devaluations and protectionist policies favoring industrial development and penalizing agriculture. A boom in coffee prices from 1953 to 1956 allowed consumer goods imports to increase. Thus, competition for some domestic industries increased, but the fundamentally protectionist policies continued to encourage many new industries under the umbrella of cheap foreign exchange obtained from coffee, which was used to import machinery, technology, and intermediate goods. A precipitous fall in coffee prices from one dollar a pound in September 1956 to approximately thirty-five cents per pound in 1961 caused still more restrictions to be placed on imports.

In 1960 tariff laws were thoroughly revised. In effect the tariff was "modernized"; that is, a tariff structure was developed following some rules that rationalized the tariff already in existence, which had resulted from changes induced by balance of payments problems, specific lobbyists' pressures, and government priorities. Specific tariffs were abolished almost completely and a system of ad valorem tariffs was established, which increased "rationally" as the "degree of elaboration of a commodity and its technological complexity" increased. The tariff structure was complemented by the creation of three lists in which all tariff items were classified: prohibited, license-required, and free (no license required) imports. The composition of these lists varied, depending on short-term balance of payment conditions. In times of difficulty, the prohibited import list grew as the free list declined,[4] and vice versa.

Protection was also provided by indirect protective measures, such as prior import deposits, which were introduced as an anti-inflationary policy aimed at controlling the money supply. Another important protectionist measure was the "law of basic industries," which gave an income tax exemption to firms using intermediate goods produced by Paz-del-Rio, the government-supported steel mill that had been in operation for a few years with a dismal record.

Trade policies had some interesting loopholes; for example, the tariff did not apply to imports by the government and by the Catholic church. Furthermore, any importer attempting to bring in a "complete production process" could apply for a "global license" that would establish a single tariff for all the machinery and equipment imported. Since the tariff would be determined by that of "the machine that characterized the process," importers had a good idea of which tariff they could obtain and thus would apply for global licenses only if they expected a lower rate.

The general incentive system also included price controls, mostly on agricultural commodities, and capital subsidies. The latter were applied through portfolio requirements and interest-rate ceilings imposed on the banking system.

By the early 1960s the "easy import substitution" period was nearly over. To continue the import substitution process, it was necessary to develop intermediate and capital goods industries, many of them capital-intensive (e.g., the chemicals and petrochemical industries absorbed 25 percent of total investment in manufacturing from 1962 to 1967; Thoumi 1971). The government participated heavily in the industrial development at this stage, mainly through the Instituto de Fomento Industrial (IFI), whose assets skyrocketed in constant 1958 pesos from 35 million in 1958 to 1,962 million in 1972 (Thoumi 1978). The IFI's investments were coordinated with private sector projects; it undertook projects complementary to private sector investments that were not developed by private firms because of their high risk or the large amount of capital needed.

In summary, by 1967 Colombia had an incentive structure that provided heavy protection to the manufacturing sector, penalized the agricultural sector, provided higher protection to finished products and consumer goods than to unfinished products and capital goods, but which did not exclude the possibility of heavily protecting specific intermediate and capital goods industries through protection of individual plants and which penalized employment creation in manufacturing.[5]

After the balance of payments crisis of 1966, trade policies were thoroughly altered. The main features of the new policies were a commitment to generating exports of manufactures and an abandonment of the fixed exchange rate policy. Decree 444 was the major policy tool. It allowed the president to change the exchange rate periodically, creating, in practice, a crawling-peg system. A set of export incentives was also created. These included a flat 15 percent subsidy granted on the value of "nontraditional" exports,[6] the extension of credit for exporters, and the establishment of a legal framework that regulated the establishment of free zones. Simultaneously, the government made a commitment to simplify the bureaucratic requirements of the temporary import and tariff drawback systems that had been in existence for some time but were not operating efficiently.

As I mentioned earlier, the policy change was not a clear shift from import substitution industrialization to export oriented industrialization. Import substitution manufactures had large investments and had been supplying most of the manufactured consumer goods available in Colombia. The new policies were not aimed at forcing those industries to compete with imports in the domestic markets. Nominal protection and import restrictions remained at a high level. However, the profitability of export oriented activities became more attractive relative to that aimed at supplying the domestic market. New export industries were developed, and industries that had developed efficiently under import substitution policies were encouraged to expand output for exports.

4.2.3   Labor Market

Employment creation has been perceived as a major problem in Colombia.[7] Its population growth rate was high, with intercensal data showing a 3.12 percent annual population growth rate for 1951–64, followed by a 2.82 percent growth rate for 1964–73.

Population growth has been accompanied by substantial rural-urban migration and one of the highest rates of urbanization in the world.[8] The Colombian population was 69.1 percent rural in 1938 and became 60.9 percent urban in 1973. The urban population grew at a rate of 5.36 percent per year between 1951 and 1964 and at the lower rate of 3.74 percent between 1964 and 1973. Urbanization has encompassed at least thirty cities. Bogotá has increased its share of the total population from 5.8 percent in 1951 to 12.2 percent in 1973. However, this increase has not made Bogotá significantly bigger relative to other cities, for they have increased their population shares in similar proportions.

Contrasted with these high rates of urban population growth, manufacturing employment has grown rather slowly. From 1956 to 1966 it grew at an annual average rate of 1 percent. Thereafter it has averaged about 3 percent annually. However, that higher rate has been insufficient to absorb even the natural rate of population increase, much less immigrants to urban areas.

Urban open unemployment in Colombia thus was high by MDC standards, although not abnormally high by LDC levels. As in most LDCs, unemployment data are difficult to evaluate, since time-series data are hard to come by and, when found, are not rigorously comparable through time. A recently published series (Asociación Nacional de

Instituciónes Financieras 1976) that puts together data for Bogotá, Medellín, Cali, and Barranquilla from 1963 to 1976 shows rising open unemployment in Bogotá between 1963 (7.9 percent) and 1967 (12.2 percent), followed by a period of declining unemployment to 6.8 percent in 1972. Then there was a sharp rise to 11.9 percent in June 1974, followed by a milder drop to 8.5 percent in October 1975 and an increase to 10.1 percent in February 1976. During this same period, open unemployment in Medellín was more stable, ranging from a low of 10.8 percent in 1965 to a high of 14.2 percent in 1972. Open unemployment rates in Cali and Barranquilla are chronically substantially higher than the ones of Bogotá, averaging 40 percent to 60 percent more. Recent work by Berry (1975) shows that a substantial number of the openly unemployed in the cities are city-born, have higher than average education, and are under thirty years of age. Apparently, members of this group have some means of subsistence (family) and are unemployed because they are not able to find jobs that satisfy their expectations.

Disguised unemployment in the cities has also apparently been high. The International Labor Organization (ILO) report on Colombia (1970) points out that the participation rates in the labor force tend to be lower in Colombia than in other Latin American countries, findings that suggest a substantial level of disguised unemployment. The ILO rough estimates put the urban disguised unemployment level somewhere around 13 percent. Rural open and disguised unemployment are also believed to be high, but no data exist on the subject.

Poverty is a bigger issue in Colombia than unemployment, not only because of the low income per capita, but also because of the concentration of income. Berry and Urrutia (1975) estimated that in 1964 the wealthiest 10 percent of urban population (excluding absentee landlords who reside in urban centers) received approximately 43 percent of urban income, and the richest 1 percent received 12 percent.

Income distribution in rural areas is still more concentrated; the richest 10 percent received 51 percent of the income, and the top 1 percent got 23 percent. In the urban areas the poorest 40 percent got only 9.5 percent of the income, while in the rural areas the comparable group took approximately 12 percent of the income.

Real wages in the manufacturing sector rose during the import substitution and early export promotion periods. They were 3.55 pesos per hour (1970 prices) in 1958, 5.73 pesos per hour in 1967, and 6.66 pesos per hour in 1971. Thereafter, they have fallen to 5.49 pesos per hour in 1975, the latest year for which data are available.

Real wages are affected in the formal sector by an array of legislative measures, which include minimum wage regulation, paid holidays, layoff costs, transport subsidies, paid vacations, paid holidays, contribution to the social security institute, which provides mainly health services, and a Christmas bonus equal to one month's salary if the employee has worked the full year (or a fraction of a month's salary equal to the proportion of the year worked). All these legal fringe benefits amount to approximately 40 percent of the salary base.

All large manufacturing firms pay the legal fringes, and in many instances they provide extra ones such as education and food subsidies. It is widely believed that small firms escape payment of some of the legal fringe benefits.

The effect of the minimum wage legislation is extremely difficult to determine, since changes in the legislated minima have frequently lagged inflation increases, and thus minimum levels set by the government have been below prevailing wages at times.

4.2.4   The Structure of Production

The Colombian manufacturing sector, the focus of this study, forms a sizable share of GDP (about 20 percent). Industries classified as export-ables (see section 4.4 below) generated about 52 percent of domestic value added in manufacturing (in 1970) and employed about 53 percent of the manufacturing labor force. Industries classified as importables generated 38 percent of manufacturing value added and employed 36 percent of its labor force. Production not competing with imports generated 10 percent of manufacturing value added and employed 10 percent of the labor force.

4.3   Effective Protection in Colombia

The most rigorous studies of effective protection in Colombia are Hutcheson (1973) and the revised study by Hutcheson and Schydlowsky (1976).[9] Their estimates include effects of quotas, subsidies, currency overvaluation, and other government interferences in trade. The Corden method was used and price comparisons were made when appropriate. Their estimates, protection on domestic sales, are given in table 4.4. Note that in general the ERPs, contrary to what is normally expected, tend to be lower than the nominal protection figures. This is because the ERPs adjust for currency overvaluation. These estimates indicate that ERPs were negative for coffee and mining and low for processed foods, construction materials, and "simple" intermediate goods; they were somewhat higher for beverages and tobacco, "complex" intermediate goods, and machinery, and higher still for nondurable consumer goods, durable consumer goods, and transportation equipment. Thus, protection for domestic sales retained the cascaded effect found in the import substitution period. Separate calculations of simple average ERPs for our trade categories (discussed in section 4.4 below) correspond to these estimates. The average (unweighted) ERP for activities classified

Table 4.4   **Nominal and Effective Protection in the Manufacturing Sector, 1969**

Aggregated Groupings	Nominal Protection	Effective Protection[a]
Agriculture, forestry, and fishing	−12.3%	−13.3%
Noncoffee agriculture, forestry, and fishing	2.3	2.2
Mining	− 9.0	− 8.9
All primary products	−12.0	−13.0
Processed foods	2.6	8.4
Processed foods excluding sugar	4.4	12.1
Beverages and tobacco	23.0	20.3
Construction materials	4.5	3.4
Intermediate products I ("simple")	11.4	12.2
Intermediate products II ("complex")	26.4	18.3
Nondurable consumer goods	36.8	30.5
Durable consumer goods	49.1	36.5
Machinery	33.0	25.0
Transportation equipment	138.6	135.2
All manufactures	19.5	18.6
All manufactures excluding beverages and tobacco	19.3	18.5
All manufactures excluding sugar	20.7	20.0
All sectors	2.7	− 1.9
All sectors excluding coffee, mining, and sugar	12.5	10.0
All exports	−15.1	−16.5
All exports excluding coffee, mining, and sugar	13.0	26.0
All manufactured exports excluding sugar	13.0	34.1

Source: Hutcheson and Schydlowsky (1976) and Hutcheson's unpublished data. Appendix table 4.A.1 shows nominal and effective protection rates for the disaggregated manufacturing sector (four digits). See also the note to table 4.A.1 for the effect of currency overvaluation on the relative levels of nominal and effective protection rates. All weights are international value added.

[a]Corden method of computation employed.

as exportables for purposes of estimating labor requirements in 1970 was 10 percent; that for importables was 22 percent; and that for noncompeting importable production was 52 percent. All estimates refer to protection on domestic sales. Exportables tended to fall into the processed food, construction materials, and "simple" intermediate products groups, while noncompeting importable production was likely to fall in the machinery and transportation equipment groups. There were differences between the effective protection rates in the domestic and foreign markets (not shown in table 4.4) owing to the effect of price controls, especially in the food sector, and the subsidies of the export incentive system. Exports of processed foods were highly protected while exports of construction materials and simple intermediate products were mildly subsidized, as were the average manufactured products. A comparison of these rates with those for domestic sales shows that the domestic market in 1969 was more attractive than the export markets for industries producing capital goods, intermediate products, nondurable and durable consumer goods, and transportation equipment. The opposite was true of construction materials and processed foods, except beverages and tobacco. Thus, activities classified as exportables below (section 4.4) tended to have higher ERPs on export sales relative to domestic sales. However, activities classified as importables had higher ERPs in domestic markets than those for exportables and importables in foreign markets. Thus, while importables received incentives to export, the restrictions on imports in the domestic market continued to make it a more attractive place to sell.

Since this study focuses upon 1970 and 1973, it is important to note how policy changes in 1970–73 might have altered these 1969 estimates. First, the crawling-peg exchange system was maintained, thus keeping the real exchange rate at a fairly constant level (see *Coyuntura Económica*, various issues). Therefore the degree of currency overvaluation probably was unchanged. Likewise, the export incentive system was maintained, but the export subsidy was raised to 20 percent in 1972. Export ERPs would have increased thereafter.

The general trend toward a more open economy continued; many commodities were transferred from the prohibited list to the license-required list, and many others moved from the license-required to the free list. The number of import license applications approved increased; by the end of 1973 more than 90 percent were approved. Complementary to the relaxation of licensing policies, the average level of tariffs was lowered. These trends suggest that protection on domestic sales would have fallen.

In 1969 Colombia joined the Andean Common Market. The Andean Group's policies have emphasized the coordinated development of new industries and have deemphasized trade in products already manufactured in the region before the Common Market's creation. Protection within the Common Market thus would have increased export ERPs for exports whose major destination is the Andean Group. Between 1970 and 1973 (see table 4.2), exports to the Andean Group did not increase as rapidly as exports in general. This was true for both NRB and HOS exports. However, the share of HOS exports in total Andean Group exports rose dramatically, so it is likely that export ERPs for HOS goods in Andean trade increased. Nonetheless, the overall extent of this increase probably was small since the Andean Group absorbed so little (15 percent) of Colombia's HOS exports.

Finally, the Pastrana government, which took office in the middle of 1970, changed the overall thrust of Colombia's development strategy. It assigned first priority to the expansion of the construction sector. Export incentive policies continued, however, while import substitution industries lost their privileged position as resources were diverted from the import substitution sector to construction. These changes would imply a reduction in ERPs for import substitutes and for domestic sales in general.

To summarize, in 1969 the structure of protection (for domestic sales) retained its cascaded effect from the import substitution phase, although the degree of cascading was probably lower. Protection in export markets was provided all HOS manufactures. Those later classified as exportables for purposes of calculating labor requirements naturally had higher ERPs on foreign sales than domestic sales. While importables received some incentives to export, they were more protected in domestic than foreign markets.

Changes in the trade regime since 1969 probably had the net effect of increasing protection somewhat on exports and decreasing protection on import sales. Major causes of these changes were an increase in the export subsidy, a continued relaxation of import controls, and a general decrease in tariff rates.

4.4 Factor Proportions in Colombian Trade

4.4.1 Sectoral Classification

For Colombia it was possible to undertake the analysis of factor proportions in trade on the basis of a four-digit ISIC-II classification. For the industries where foreign trade was not negligible, trade is classified according to the T statistic, defined in the introductory chapter as follows: if $T < 0$, the industry was classified as a producer of exportable goods; if $0 < T < 0.4$, the industry was defined as a producer of import-competing goods; if $0.4 < T < 1.0$, the industry was defined as a producer of non-import-competing goods. The value of 0.4 was chosen to separate the import-competing from the non-competing import industries because there were few industries for which the T statistic was close to 0.4.[10] When foreign trade was negligible, the industry was defined as a producer of nontraded commodities.

The agriculture and mining sectors were unambiguously classified as NRB. Various alternative classifications were employed for the manufacturing sector to account for the fact that some HOS activities are NRB-related. The first classification categorized all manufacturing activities as HOS. The second eliminated sugar refining. The third eliminated all food manufacturing (classifying those activities as NRB). The fourth eliminated sugar, petrochemicals, and jewelry (all defined as NRB). Finally, a fifth eliminated all food manufacturing, petrochemicals, and jewelry. Use of these alternative classifications was motivated by particular difficulties surrounding the commodities indicated. For the food-processing branches, there is a question whether they need to be located near the raw material source. Petrochemicals raise a similar question. The jewelry branch is unique because of losses (stealing) of government output and repeated exporting of the same gems to collect the export subsidy (see below). These phenomena cast considerable doubt on the reliability of the jewelry statistics.

The T statistic was computed for both 1970 and 1973 with the classifications of exportable, import-competing, and non-competing goods varying substantially between the two years. Of the seventy-eight tradable manufacturing industries, sixteen switched classification. These industries accounted for 19 percent of total manufacturing value added in 1970. Nine import-competing industries in 1970 became exporters, while four industries went the opposite way. Two non-competing industries turned into import-competing, and one import-competing turned into non-competing. These changes are shown in table 4.5 below. That the largest change in classification was from import-competing to exporting reflects policy changes between 1970 and 1973 which made exporting more attractive relative to import substitution.

For this study, I decided to use the classification resulting from the 1973 data, despite the fact that international markets were exceptional

Table 4.5   Changes from 1970 to 1973 in Classification of Industries by Major Trade Categories

1970 import-competing industries turned exporters by 1973
    3111 Meat products
    3122 Animal feeds
    3140 Tobacco
    3212 Made-up textiles
    3215 Cordage and rope
    3319 Other wood and cork products
    3412 Containers and boxes of paper and paperboard
    3691 Structural clay products
    3812 Metal furniture and fixtures

1970 export industries turned import-competing by 1973
    3113 Canning of fruits and vegetables
    3116 Grain mill products
    3119 Cocoa and chocolate products
    3219 Other textiles

1970 noncompeting industries turned import-competing by 1973
    3710 Iron and steel basic industries
    3841 Shipbuilding and repairing

1970 import-competing industry turned noncompeting by 1973
    3512 Fertilizers and pesticides

in that year. This year is likely to be a better reflection of the present economy, since the trend toward a more open economy has continued. The classification of two industries, however, was modified. According to the trade statistics, refined petroleum and petroleum and coal products were net exports in 1973, owing to a Colombian government policy that until very recently kept oil prices at the lowest level in the world. Colombia's oil production has dwindled, however, and today Colombia has become a net importer of oil products. Furthermore, in the early 1970s the petrochemical industries were net exporters, since they were exporting at marginal costs products from domestic plants that were larger than needed by the domestic market. These "excess capacity" exports have disappeared. For these reasons, the refining and petrochemical industries are here classified as import-competing rather than as exporting.

It should be noted that this study deals only indirectly with the agricultural, mining, and services sectors of the economy. The lack of meaningful data (see Appendix A) constrains any comprehensive empirical study of those sectors.[11] This omission means that conclusions reached herein are valid primarily for the manufacturing sector.[12] It should also be noted that changes over time in average labor or skill ratios reflect changes in the relative size, and weight, of the components of the trade flows distinguished and not changes in factor inputs into individual industries. This follows from the fact that (as reported in Appendix A) the basic input and output data used are all for the year 1970.

The following activities were classified as major HOS exportables (see appendix table 4.A.1 for their respective ISIC codes and table 4.6 for factor intensities: meat, dairy products, fish packing, bakery, sugar, and prepared animal feeds among the food processing industries; tobacco; all textile branches with the exception of the small "other textiles"; apparel, shoes, and fur and leather and their products; wood and cork products; cardboard containers; tires and tubes; pottery, glass, structural clay products, and cement; metal furniture; and jewelry. Most of these classifications are expected, but a few comments are in order. Cardboard containers are exported mostly as packing for other exports, but they are classified separately so that the cardboard box producer can collect the export subsidy. Tires have been exported to South and Central America since the early 1960s. These exports have not been continuous, since they tend to occur when the domestic producers have excess capacity owing to large indivisibilities in production. Structural clay products and cement are exported from the northwest coast of Colombia to the Caribbean countries, since their transportation costs are lower than those in the interior of Colombia.[13] The list of exportables coincides

Table 4.6   Factor Intensities in Major HOS Exportable and Importable
                   Production, 1970

Industry	ISIC Code	Total Labor Remuner- ation/ Value Added	Direct Labor/ Domestic Value Added (Man-Years/ Million Pesos)	Ratio Male to Female Blue- Collar Employ- ment	Per- centage of Labor Force Blue- Collar
Exportables					
Bakery products	3117	.51	37.7	1.608	76%
Sugar	3118	.87	17.0	60.832	81
Food products n.e.c.	3121	.34	11.3	2.202	70
Tobacco	3140	.14	3.1	1.850	80
Spinning, weaving	3211	.36	14.1	1.378	82
Knitting mills	3213	.71	32.9	.599	82
Cotton fabrics	3216	.56	16.0	5.343	87
Wearing apparel	3220	.52	40.6	3.021	85
Nonmetallic mineral products n.e.c.	3699	.46	20.4	28.200	79
Importables					
Grain mill products	3116	.15	8.8	1.462	78%
Pulp and paper	3411	.48	9.4	8.058	71
Printing and publishing	3420	.62	23.7	2.786	73
Drugs	3522	.52	12.9	.559	51
Soap and cosmetics	3523	.43	14.4	1.635	52
Iron and steel	3710	.69	20.6	102.368	75
Fabricated metal products	3819	.47	21.8	5.056	80

Source: Calculated from data outlined in Appendix A.
Note: "Major" means more than 300 million pesos of domestic value added.

in general with what one can a priori define as labor-intensive branches,
with the exception of sugar, glass, cement, and rubber tires.

The import-competing industries are: canning, oils and fats, grain mill
products, and candy and other foods among the food processors; wine
and hard alcohol; "other textiles"; pulp and paper and their products;
printing; paints, medicines, and soaps and cosmetics; petroleum refining
and its derivatives; rubber products except tires and tubes; plastic products; other nonmetallic minerals; iron and steel; cutlery, hand tools,
and general hardware; structural metal products; fabricated metal
products; other electrical apparatus; shipbuilding, bicycles, and other
transportation equipment; and manufacturing industries not elsewhere
classified. This list also is predictable, since it includes some of the old
import substitution industries, such as pulp and paper, iron and steel,
paints, medicines, soaps and cosmetics, petroleum and its derivatives,
rubber products, and metal products, which have developed for more
than fifteen years, capturing a very large share of the domestic market.

The noncompeting industries include: industrial chemicals; fertilizers; synthetic resins and manmade fibers; other chemical products; industrial nonferrous basic metals; engines; all types of machinery and equipment; radio, television, and electrical appliances; railroad equipment; motor vehicles; aircraft; professional and scientific equipment; photographic equipment; watches; and musical instruments and sporting goods. Some of these industries require, or include subgroups that require, very advanced technology, such as many industrial chemicals, fertilizers, and aircraft. Others need a very well-developed industry for their inputs, such as synthetic resins and fibers, which require a very substantial petrochemical industry, and engines and most machinery, which require good iron, steel, and other basic mineral industries. Still other groups depend upon very accurate equipment and skills not well developed in Colombia: for example, photographic equipment, watches, and musical instruments. The radio, television, and household appliances industries, in spite of having a fairly long history in Colombia, are also noncompeting owing to some peculiar obstacles to their development. The small appliance industries have not been able to grow rapidly despite high protection because of significant amounts of smuggling. The large appliance industry has had particular difficulties with the low-quality sheet metal produced domestically. Policies protecting the domestic steel industries require it to use this low-quality input. Many of the other noncompeting branches fall into the machinery category. Colombia produces some simple machines and parts, but it does not produce machines that require the use of alloys or any sophisticated metal process. Thus, in most of these branches, imports do not compete with domestic production, since there is little or none of the latter.

The only manufacturing branches here identified as nontraded or home goods are beer and soft drinks. Note also that construction, transportation, utilities, insurance and banking, and personal services are treated as home goods when calculating indirect requirements from the input-output table.

4.4.2 Employment and Skill Requirements by Trade Category

Direct Requirements

Direct requirements by skill category (see Appendix B for discussion of categories) per unit of DVA and IVA for trade categories are given in table 4.7. The weights used in aggregation are value added in domestic production.

Observe that the results are as expected from the HOS model, given that Colombia's comparative advantage lies in labor-intensive production. Industries classified as exportables had ratios of blue-collar and total employment to domestic value added twice as large as those of the importable group, and 50 percent higher than in the noncompeting industries. The same result holds, although the magnitude differs as one moves from DVA to IVA measures. The small change in the labor requirements for exportables and the larger changes for importables and noncompeting production are due to the higher effective protection in these latter industries.

Several comments are in order concerning the interpretation of the results for noncompeting production. A priori, one would have expected these industries to have the lowest labor requirements. That they do not is due to several factors. First, the values are based upon domestic coefficients. Had these been adjusted as suggested in chapter 1, they undoubtedly would have been lower. Second, there is a problem of aggregation in these activities. Domestic production is not always comparable to imports, especially in machinery industries where Colombia imports machinery and electrical equipment not produced domestically and produces spare parts and simple machines whose production is labor-intensive. Finally, the importable group contains some of the large capital-intensive import substitution projects developed during the sixties that supply most of what the country consumes. Industries in which these projects are located then will have low labor coefficients and reduce the overall importable estimates accordingly.

In general, my results indicate that exportables have a much larger direct employment generation effect than the import substitution industries. Berry and Díaz-Alejandro (1977) and Díaz-Alejandro (1976a) have suggested that manufactured exports are more capital-intensive than

Table 4.7   Labor Intensity of Manufacturing Production by Major Trade Categories, 1973 (Number of Workers per Million 1970 Pesos of Direct Value Added)

Trade Category	Total Employ-ment	Blue-Collar Workers	White-Collar Workers	Manage-ment
Per unit of domestic value added				
Export industries	29.1	23.9	3.6	1.6
Import-competing industries	15.5	11.0	3.2	1.3
Noncompeting industries[a]	21.7	16.3	3.8	1.6
Per unit of international value added				
Export industries	29.3	24.0	3.6	1.7
Import-competing industries	18.0	13.1	3.7	1.7
Noncompeting industries[a]	27.8	20.8	4.8	2.2

Source: Author's computation (see Appendix A).
Note: Weights are DVA of domestic production.
[a]Values refer to domestic coefficients and are not adjusted in the manner suggested in chapter 1.

the products sold in the domestic market. This hypothesis is based on two facts: the firms that export are larger than the average, and larger firms are more capital-intensive. However, I (Thoumi 1979) have suggested that the shift in international trade strategies toward a more open economy increased the labor intensity of Colombian manufacturing as investment moved toward the most labor-using industries. My evidence corroborates this latter suggestion: export industries were substantially more labor-using than the import substitution ones. Unfortunately, I could not investigate Berry's and Díaz-Alejandro's hypothesis more fully, since it was impossible to obtain data on labor coefficients by firm size within an industry.[14] It is important to note, however, that the high degree of disaggregation used here minimizes interindustry variations in ratios of employment to value added. Furthermore, the average labor coefficients for each industry are closer to the ratios of the larger than of the smaller plants, since the larger plants have more weight than the smaller ones. Thus, while more research should be encouraged in this field, it can be concluded with some confidence that export oriented products are more labor-intensive per unit of value added than the import substitution ones.

The data available also gave a breakdown of employment by sex. Out of curiosity, I calculated the ratio of male to female blue-collar workers (hereafter M/F ratio) for each trade category (again weighting by value added of production). This ratio was smaller for exports (18.7) than for importables (22.3) and noncompeting production (24.5). When all foods and petrochemicals were excluded from the export branches, the M/F ratio dropped to 12.9. A comparison of the actual exports of 1970 and 1973 indicates that Colombian exports were becoming even less male-intensive; exports that were growing most rapidly tended to be significantly more female-intensive than exports on the average.[15]

One characteristic of Colombia is its lack of centralization. It not only has many urban centers, but also has various geographic regions clearly separated from each other. Three mountain ranges, thick tropical jungles, swamps, and tropical diseases have made internal communications and trade difficult.[16] Most of the rivers are not easily navigated, and transportation routes were very primitive until recently. Even today there is no overland communication with Panama or between the populated areas of Colombia and the one-fifth of the Colombian surface covered by the Amazon jungle. The natural regionalization of the country has allowed the development of ethnic subgroups with specific characteristics, including varying attitudes toward economic policies and entrepreneurship.[17]

To test whether these regional differences were important, I divided exports by origin into five categories, then calculated blue-collar labor requirements for these exports. The categories are: the Caribbean coast;

the "Llanos," or eastern prairies; Nariño, or the southern border; the northeast border (north of Santander); and the center of the country. The first four regions' exports to other countries can be considered as "border" trade induced by low international transportation costs. It is expected that the center's exports would be more labor-intensive than border exports, since the center needs a greater comparative advantage to export in the presence of high transportation costs. The data in table 4.8 support this hypothesis: blue-collar employment per unit of domestic value added was higher for the center's exports than for the exports of any of the other regions. Exports from the Caribbean region were particularly capital-intensive for 1970. However, when petrochemicals were eliminated, the coefficient for that region's manufactured exports increased notably—to 20.0 in 1970 and 26.2 in 1973 for "all manufactures." It is also apparent that the difference between the center's coefficient and the other regional coefficients declined between 1970 and 1973; this decline was probably caused by the development of some very labor-intensive exports in the border areas, especially in the Caribbean, where offshore assembly industries were established and increased exports rapidly.

Labor Skills and Salaries

Skill requirements are likely to affect Colombian comparative advantage. Specifically, we expect export industries to be less skill-intensive than import-competing industries, and exports to low-income countries to be more skill intensive than exports to high-income countries. It is very difficult to define skills theoretically and to measure them empirically (see Appendix B). Nevertheless, I decided to use two proxies to measure skills; the average remuneration per unit of labor and the ratio of the number of white- to blue-collar workers (hereafter the W/B ratio).

Table 4.8   Labor Intensity of Manufacturing Production by Export Industries According to Region of Origins within Colombia, 1970 and 1973 (Blue-Collar Employment per Million 1970 Pesos of Domestic Direct Value Added)

Region	All Manufactures		All Manufactures Except Processed Foods	
	1970	1973	1970	1973
Caribbean	11.5	20.0	6.1	14.6
"Llanos"	19.6	24.5	19.3	24.5
Nariño	19.5	26.5	14.5	26.2
Northeast border	19.8	17.4	19.8	17.4
Center	22.1	26.8	24.8	28.3

Source: Author's computations (see Appendix A).

Table 4.9 shows average remuneration for various types of labor in the trade categories for manufactures. Several interesting observations arise for these data. First, the average blue-collar total remuneration, which includes fringe benefits, is remarkably close in all categories, indicating that the average skill of blue-collar workers tends to be similar in every category. This finding is consistent with the beliefs of various entrepreneurs and officials of SENA,[18] who consider that the cost and time of training good blue-collar workers for the various manufacturing industries is fairly constant. If this is so, the value of the human capital of the blue-collar workers in the various categories, and thus their skill levels, would tend to be constant.

The same statement is true when comparing average white-collar remuneration in the export, import-competing, and noncompeting categories. The variations in managerial remuneration are to be expected; these data are much less reliable than the other wage data, since in many plants it is impossible to separate the remuneration of the manager from that of the owners. However, high managerial salaries appear to be concentrated in the import-competing and noncompeting industries. These are the ones that benefit from the highest effective protection levels (see table 4.11). Since the rent created by protection is expected to rise as protection increases, managers are probably in a better position to capture a share of this rent than blue- and white-collar workers, who face more competitive labor markets.

The last column of table 4.9 indicates that the W/B ratio increases as one goes from export to import-competing to noncompeting industries. This ratio reflects the average "skill content" of the product as well as the degree of competition of the markets in which the products are sold (see Appendix B). These results are expected. Either Colombia exports

Table 4.9   **Indicators of Skill Content by Trade Category, 1973**

	Export Industries	Import-competing Industries	Non-competing Industries
Average annual remuneration[a]			
All employees	26,200	28,580	28,220
Blue-collar workers	22,590	21,750	21,250
White-collar workers	38,050	38,470	40,510
Management	40,320	53,340	52,530
Ratio of white-collar to blue-collar workers	.151	.291	.233

Source: Author's computations (see Appendix A).
[a]Average in 1970 pesos, weighted by domestic value added of production in each four-digit industry in 1973.

products with lower skill contents than those produced for the domestic market, or domestic marketing requires a larger number of salesmen than the international market, or both.

4.4.3 Indirect Effects

The only way to derive the indirect effects generated by export, import-competing, and noncompeting manufacturing industries was to use the Colombian 1970 input-output matrix. This matrix has only thirty-one producing sectors; thus the level of aggregation is much higher than that used in other parts of this chapter. The nonfood manufacturing sector was disaggregated into ten branches. Agricultural-based manufacturing was disaggregated into seven branches. Six industries were treated as home goods: utilities, construction, transportation, communications, insurance and banking, and personal services. The indirect effects on output, value added, and total wages and salaries in these sectors were estimated. It was not possible to determine the effects on employment directly, because there were no employment data compatible with the matrix.

Table 4.10 shows the indirect effects in pesos generated by a one-peso increase in direct value added. The import-competing HOS industries have a much larger indirect effect on the economy than the export-oriented HOS industries. Noncompeting industries fall in between, although they are closer to the export sector. These results can be understood when the nature of the component industries is considered. The import-competing branches of Colombian manufacturing include the heaviest (more capital-intensive) industries in the country. These industries are also the most energy- and water-intensive, and the ones in which transportation costs for their inputs are the highest. The high capital intensity also results in higher banking and insurance inputs.

Table 4.10   Indirect Effects on Home Goods of HOS Manufacturing Production by Trade Categories, 1973 (Increase, in 1970 Pesos, Generated by One Peso of Direct Value Added)

Trade Category	Output (1)	Value Added (2)	Wages and Salaries (3)
Exports	.202	.145	.076
Import-competing	.307	.221	.115
Noncompeting	.226	.163	.087

Source: See text.

4.4.4   Changes in Manufacturing Industry Classification

Changes in the T Statistic and in the Composition of Trade Categories

As I noted earlier, and as is set out in table 4.5, sixteen manufacturing industries changed classification between 1970 and 1973 according to the T statistic. Five of them were food processors. These changes were probably caused by changes in world prices and domestic subsidies. Meat and prepared animal feeds turned from importable to exportable as their world prices increased. Canning, grain mill products, and cocoa turned from exportable into importable production. The only nonfood or tobacco branch that shifted from exportable to importable was "other textiles," a relatively unimportant catchall branch.

Apart from the latter and from food and tobacco, the only industry that become noncompeting was fertilizers and pesticides, which changed because of the skyrocketing fertilizer prices in the world market in 1973.

Some of the classification changes seem to be the result not of general policies but rather of specific developments and particular policies. Tobacco is a very special case because fluctuating excise taxes in Colombia have generated great swings between legal and illegal imports. The switch in T statistic between 1970 and 1973 happened because in the latter year large amounts of cigarettes were smuggled into the country. The high world price of steel in 1973 lowered steel imports and even allowed the normally inefficient Paz del Rio steel mill to export some of its products so that the sector moved from the noncompeting to the importable category. Between 1970 and 1973, Conastil, an IFI-financed plant that produces small fishing boats, began to operate. Because the production of these small boats is very labor-intensive, Colombia developed a sizable amount of exports, and this industry became import-competing rather than noncompeting.

Effective Protection and Classification Changes

Effective protection levels could also have affected classification changes. Thus, importable activities with low levels of protection were more likely to become exporters than more protected ones. Likewise, highly protected export sectors were more likely to become import-competing than less protected ones. Similar expectations hold for the switches between the import-competing and noncompeting categories.

Unfortunately, the available data on effective rates of protection did not cover all eighty four-digit manufacturing branches, and thus no formal test of these hypotheses could be made. However, the data available could be used to "suggest" a relationship between effective protection and the nature of the classification changes. Table 4.11 shows unweighted effective protection averages derived from estimates for forty-eight industries assigned to various categories. For those forty-eight industries, this table shows that (1) exports had the lowest ERPs; (2) noncompeting industries had the highest ERPs; (3) industries that were exporters in 1970 and became import-competing in 1973 had higher ERPs than the 1973 export industries; and (4) the 1970 import-competing industries that became exporters had significantly lower protection than those classified as import-competing in 1973.

The results strongly suggest that lower protection is associated with industries that became exporters, while changes in the opposite direction are associated with higher protection.

Employment and Classification Changes

We next made estimates of labor coefficients and average remuneration of industries that switched trade categories from 1970 to 1973. These are shown in table 4.12. Note that the labor coefficients of import-competing industries in 1970 that became exporters by 1973 were 46 percent of the average of 1973 export branches (see table 4.12). Also, the average remuneration paid in these industries was 32 percent higher than the average paid by export industries, as is shown by comparing tables 4.12 and 4.9. These results are due to changes among the food industry group.

When nonfood industries were considered separately (column 2 of table 4.12), their labor requirements were 13 percent greater and their average remuneration 34 percent lower than similar averages for exportables. Those export industries that became import-competing had lower labor coefficients and slightly lower than average remuneration, while the noncompeting industries that turned import-competing had both

Table 4.11   Effective Protection and Branches That Switched _T_ Classification between 1970 and 1973

	Number of Industries for Which Effective Protection Estimates Are Available	Effective Protection, 1970[a]
All manufacturing	48	19.0%
Export industries (1973)	16	9.2
Export industries turned import-competing	4	16.0
Import-competing industries turned exporters	4	11.0
Import-competing industries (1973)	16	18.2
Noncompeting industries turned import-competing	1	15.1
Noncompeting industries (1973)	15	30.2

Source: Hutcheson and Schydlowsky (1976) and author's computations.
[a]Unweighted averages. Corden method of computation employed.

Table 4.12   Labor Intensity and Average Remuneration in Industries That Changed *T*-Statistic Classification between 1970 and 1973

	Import-Competing Turned Exporter		Export Industries Turned Import-Competing		Noncompeting Turned Import-Competing—Two Industries (5)	Import-Competing Turned Noncompeting—One Industry (6)
	Nine Industries (1)	Excluding Food and Tobacco—Six Industries (2)	Four Industries (3)	Excluding Food—One Industry (4)		
Number of workers per unit of DVA						
Total employment	13.5	32.9	11.3	40.1	21.1	11.9
Blue-collar workers	10.8	27.3	8.5	33.1	15.9	7.1
White-collar workers	1.8	3.5	2.1	4.9	4.5	3.4
Management	.9	2.1	.7	2.8	.7	1.4
Average remuneration[a]						
All employees	34,580	17,240	19,220	19,320	33,400	39,150
Blue-collar workers	27,950	14,940	14,810	13,410	39,720	27,330
White-collar workers	48,840	29,630	31,670	28,770	38,220	50,180
Management	47,250	23,210	38,070	28,790	56,660	72,230

Source: See text.
[a]In 1970 pesos.

higher employment coefficients and higher remuneration; the importables that turned noncompeting had very low employment coefficients and very high remunerations.

On the whole, then, if we exclude the food sector (whose exports and imports are subject to fluctuations caused by domestic crop fluctuations and international price changes), labor-intensive manufacturing industries were more likely to move in the "correct" direction (i.e., toward lower T values). Movement in the opposite direction, however, could not be statistically verified from the data analyzed here because, as I noted above, only two nonfood industries moved to a higher T classification.

4.4.5   Employment and Skill Requirements Associated with Exports

Direct Employment

Table 4.13 gives labor coefficients per million pesos of domestic and international value added in the production of HOS goods exported to various country groupings. The overall results indicate that exports to developed countries other than the United States generated significantly more employment per unit of DVA than exports to LDCs. Surprisingly, the DVA labor coefficients for exports to the United States were remarkably close to the corresponding coefficients for exports to LDCs. However, when petrochemicals, sugar, and jewelry were excluded, exports to the United States were more labor-using than those of LDCs. These re-

Table 4.13   Labor Intensity of HOS Exports by Destination, 1970 and 1973 (Number of Workers per Million 1970 Pesos of Direct Value Added)

Destination	All Manufactures		All Manufactures Except Sugar, Petrochemicals, and Jewelry	
	1970	1973	1970	1973
Per unit of domestic value added				
United States	22.1	24.4	29.1	37.0
Other developed countries	34.7	38.8	44.4	46.7
Less developed countries	21.6	24.0	21.6	25.1
Total exports	23.8	29.1	28.6	35.5
Per unit of international value added				
United States	25.0	25.8	43.2	52.2
Other developed countries	40.8	44.0	62.8	72.2
Less developed countries	25.4	31.6	30.4	40.1
Total exports	27.6	33.9	38.8	47.2

Source: Author's computations.

sults tend to corroborate the notion that, in general, manufactured exports to developed countries were produced by manufacturing branches that were more labor-intensive than those producing goods exported to LDCs.

A further breakdown of exports to LDCs indicated that exports to Central America and the Caribbean were more labor-intensive than those to other LDCs or to the United States, using both IVA and DVA estimates. The high labor coefficients of these exports can probably be explained by the fact that the Central American and Caribbean countries have a less diversified manufacturing sector than do the other Latin American and less developed countries with which Colombia trades. Also, the Central American and Caribbean countries have far fewer nontariff barriers than do the other Latin American countries. To export to one of the latter, it is necessary to find a commodity not produced in large quantities in that country. Since the manufacturing structures of those countries are similar to Colombia's, such a commodity necessarily must be either skill-intensive or capital-intensive. By contrast, there were at least some labor-intensive goods produced in Colombia, as well as in other Latin American countries, that could be exported to Central America.

A comparison of the 1970 and 1973 data in table 4.13 shows a substantial increase in the employment coefficients of exports over that brief period. Similar estimates by labor category (not shown in the table) indicate further that managerial labor requirements increased faster than those for any other job category, followed by blue-collar employment and white-collar employment. (Average total labor requirements per unit of DVA for all exports increased by 22.3 percent; the average for blue-collar employment increased by 24.2 percent; the average for white-collar employment increased by 8.5 percent; and the average for managerial employment increased by 33.7 percent.) These changes were principally due to the changing composition of exports.

We pointed out earlier that exports were less male-intensive than other trade categories in 1970. We calculated these ratios for 1970 and 1973 exports by destination. These are given in table 4.14. Observe that exports to DCs other than the United States have much lower male intensities than exports to other destinations. When processed foods and petrochemicals were excluded from the estimates, the ratio for exports to the United States fell by more than half and was only 60 percent of that for exports to LDCs. These results suggest first that the male intensity of exports to DCs was substantially less than that of exports to LDCs and that the difference widened from 1970 to 1973. That exports became less male-intensive overall from 1970 to 1973 is expected, since many labor-intensive exports were also female-intensive, as in garment production and assembly plants.

Table 4.14   Ratio of Male to Female Blue-Collar Workers in Colombian
               HOS Export Sectors, 1970 and 1973

Sector		Total Exports	United States	Other Developed Countries	Less Developed Countries
All manufactures	1970	26.3	30.9	27.8	21.0
	1973	18.7	25.2	9.3	19.8
All manufactures	1970	22.5	27.3	8.2	22.1
except processed foods	1973	16.5	22.2	7.1	21.9
All manufactures	1970	16.8	13.9	8.2	21.8
except processed foods	1973	12.9	10.5	6.3	17.5
and petrochemicals					

Source: Author's estimates.

Skills and Salaries

Table 4.15 presents results of calculations of white- to blue-collar worker ratios by destination of exports. Note that the ratio of white- to blue-collar workers used in the production of HOS exports was significantly lower for exports to the United States and other DCs than for exports to most other destinations. The highest ratio was registered for exports to Colombia's neighbors, Venezuela and the Andean Group, with which Colombia had active border trade and integration agreements. From these ratios one can conclude that exports to the developed countries tended to create a greater number of blue-collar jobs per white-collar job than exports to the rest of the world. Inasmuch as the W/B ratio is a measure of the skill content of a product, one can also conclude that exports to the developed world were significantly less skill-intensive than exports to LDCs.

The W/B ratio for total exports declined by approximately 15 percent between 1970 and 1973. The ratios for exports to all country groupings except "other Latin America" also declined. The sharpest drop (23 percent) took place in the Venezuelan ratio. The increase in the ratio of the rather limited exports to "other Latin America" was a moderate 9 percent. Between 1970 and 1973 there was a very strong trend for low-skill exports to increase more rapidly than skill-intensive exports. The effect of the export-oriented policies was therefore larger on low-skill than on high-skill industrial branches.

The data on remunerations in exports by trade category (table 4.16) tend to confirm the preceding conclusion, since the average (in 1970 pesos) for every export destination except other DCs declined substantially between 1970 and 1973. The table also shows that total manufactured exports to the United States produced the highest average remuneration. However, when sugar, petrochemicals, and jewelry were

Table 4.15　　Ratio of White-Collar to Blue-Collar Workers in Production of HOS Exports, 1970 and 1973

Year	Total Exports	United States	Other Developed Countries	Venezuela	Andean Group	Central America and Caribbean	Other Latin American Countries	Other Less Developed Countries	Socialist Countries
1970	.172	.157	.138	.245	.242	.169	.183	.198	.136
1973	.150	.137	.129	.194	.211	.155	.201	.191	.131

Source: Author's estimates.
Note: Unweighted average of the ratios for the five alternative classifications of HOS exports as defined in text (section 4.4.1).

excluded, the average generated by exports to the United States dropped to the second lowest position, higher only than that for exports to other DCs. Excluding the three industries mentioned, we can conclude that exports to DCs were less skill-intensive than exports to LDCs. Also, as the ratio of white- to blue-collar workers could be an indication of the degree of competition in Colombia's markets, the data suggest that industries that exported to the DCs tended to have more competitive markets than those that exported to LDCs.

4.4.6   Factor Proportions in Colombian Imports

Table 4.17 shows the total, blue-collar and white-collar employment per million dollars of international value added of imports of manufactures. The labor coefficients used here are derived from the United States census. They are assumed to reflect international coefficients. One interesting result is the similarity of most of the employment coefficients for the various country groupings. This may be due to the level of aggregation used, since the higher the level of aggregation, the more similar will be labor requirements for imports from various sources. On the average, the labor intensity of total imports declined slightly between 1970 and 1973, although this decline was not statistically significant. However, the labor intensity of imports from some particular countries did change markedly. Imports from the Andean Group were 33 percent less labor-intensive than the overall average in 1970 but exceeded the average by 11 percent in 1973. This change can be readily explained as the result of the Andean Group import liberalization program begun in 1971, according to which Colombia eliminated nontariff restrictions on imports from Common Market members and also eliminated tariffs for a special subset of imports from Bolivia and Ecuador, the least developed Andean Group countries. This special subset included some very

Table 4.16   **Average Total Employment Remuneration in HOS Exports by Destination, 1970 and 1973 (in 1970 Pesos)**

Sector		Total	United States	Other Developed Countries	Less Developed Countries
All manufactures	1970	34,830	42,650	27,990	28,930
	1973	27,000	37,340	18,070	26,820
All manufactures except sugar	1970	32,410	40,760	25,960	28,930
	1973	25,130	35,520	17,180	26,820
All manufactures except sugar, petrochemicals, and jewelry	1970	21,180	20,850	15,580	28,930
	1973	19,520	18,680	15,710	26,820

Source: Author's computations.
Note: The computations in this table relate to total exports of HOS goods, including those originating in import-competing and noncompeting industries.

Table 4.17 Labor Intensity of Imports of Manufactures, 1970 and 1973 (Number of Workers per Million Dollars of International Value Added of Imported Goods)

		Total Imports	United States	Other Developed Countries	Venezuela	Andean Group	Central America and Caribbean	Other Latin American Countries	Other Less Developed Countries	Socialist Countries
Total employment[a]	1970	43.9	42.8	46.2	46.3	32.0	43.2	43.4	45.3	45.4
	1973	42.7	42.5	42.5	42.5	47.2	35.0	44.1	55.4	38.5
Blue-collar employment	1970	32.3	30.8	34.3	37.1	25.2	32.7	30.4	36.0	36.1
	1973	30.6	30.4	30.0	32.6	37.8	24.6	31.8	45.2	28.4
White-collar employment	1970	11.6	11.9	11.9	9.2	6.8	10.5	13.0	9.3	9.3
	1973	12.1	12.1	12.5	9.9	9.4	10.4	12.3	10.2	10.1

Source: Author's computations.

[a]Total employment is exclusive of management.

labor-intensive items such as cotton jackets. Other large changes in labor coefficients were found in imports from Central America and the Caribbean and from socialist countries, which became less labor-intensive, and in imports from other LDCs, which became more labor-intensive.

Colombia's manufacturing sector is well diversified. More than 90 percent of manufactured consumer goods sold in the country are either produced or assembled domestically behind tariff walls. The greater part of imports is made up of intermediate and capital goods. Thus, most manufactures typically produced by LDCs are not imported. This is probably why the average labor coefficients for most of the country groupings were close to the overall average. And when tariff rates on some consumer goods items are reduced for certain countries, imports of such goods from those countries increased. This explains why special tariff concessions to Ecuador and Bolivia had an effect on their exports to Colombia and thus on the labor coefficients.

4.4.7 Employment and Income Distribution Effects of International Trade Strategies

Given the data available, it was impossible to estimate the effects of various trade strategies on the size distribution of income of Colombia. However, the evidence collected provided indications on which social groups tended to benefit the most from the development of exportable, import-competing and noncompeting manufacturing activities. Table 4.18 provides a summary of data relevant to the income distribution effects of the manufacturing groups considered.

The results suggest that the average compensation in the import-competing sector was slightly higher than in the noncompeting sector and 9 percent higher than in the export sector. The higher remuneration in the import-competing sector was due to higher management compensation and not to higher wages and salaries for blue- and white-collar workers (see table 4.9).

Direct employment per unit of value added generated by the export sector was almost twice that created by the import-competing sector. The employment difference was almost totally accounted for by blue-collar workers.

Total remuneration as a percentage of value added was highest by far in the export sector, followed by the noncompeting and import-competing sectors. This ranking was unchanged if indirect salary effects were taken into account. On this basis, the wage and salary share in value added was approximately 60 percent higher in exports than in importables.

In sum, it seems clear that, in terms of direct effects, export-oriented manufacturing created substantially more blue-collar jobs than import-competing manufacturing; wages in both sectors were almost equal; and

Table 4.18 Employment and Labor Remuneration in Four Trade Categories, 1973

Trade Category	Total Workers per Million Pesos of DVA[a] (1)	Blue-Collar Workers per Million Pesos of DVA (2)	White-Collar Workers per Million Pesos of DVA (3)	Ratio of White-to Blue-Collar Employment (4)	Average Remuneration (1970 Pesos) (5)	Total Remuneration as Percentage of DVA	
						Direct Only (6)	Direct and Indirect[b] (7)
Exports	29.1	23.9	3.6	.151	26,200	76.2%	73.2%
Import-competing	15.5	11.0	3.2	.291	28,580	44.3	45.7
Noncompeting	21.7	16.3	3.8	.233	28,220	61.2	60.1

Source: Author's computations.

Note: Columns 1 through 6 relate to direct employment only, whereas column 7 includes also indirect employment.

[a]Including management; see tables 4.7 and 4.9.

[b]Direct plus indirect remuneration divided by direct plus indirect value added; i.e. (column 6 + column 3 of table 4.10) ÷ (1 + column 2 of table 4.10).

total labor remuneration was higher in exports. This last point was still valid after measurable indirect effects were taken into account. Thus, given the evidence available, it can be concluded that emphasis upon export promotion produced more egalitarian effects on income distribution than emphasis upon import substitution in the period before 1967.

4.5 Conclusions

My analysis has shown that export-oriented manufacturing branches were significantly more labor-intensive than the import-competing and noncompeting branches. This does not mean that some of Colombia's exports have not been and are not now capital-intensive, since examples of such exports can be found. On the average, however, the results clearly showed that exports were more labor-intensive. Furthermore, the results showed that, as the economy became more open, the labor intensity of exports increased. As one would expect, exports to LDCs were less labor-intensive and less female-intensive than exports to DCs. On the import side, a strong similarity was found in the labor intensity of imports from DCs to LDCs.

The opening of the economy that began in 1967 also had an effect on the shares of NRB and HOS goods in exports. With the economy opening, the comparative advantage of the country in labor-intensive production was observable in the substantially higher increase in HOS export production relative to NRB exports; the strength of this trend was found even in the presence of increasing commodity prices.

Estimated indirect effects on home goods production also gave expected results. Home goods indirect labor affected import-competing industry more than other sectors, since they are more intensive in the use of energy, transportation, and banking services, all of which are relatively labor-using. Even including indirect effects, however, production for export still provided appreciably greater employment opportunities than import-competing production insofar as can be judged by the relative share of labor remuneration in total value added.

Export production had more egalitarian effects on income distribution than import-competing production. This was true even when the indirect effects on home goods were taken into account.

In general, all these results are expected in an economy that responds well to price incentives. They suggest that any incentive-oriented economic policy (import substitution or export promotion) will be effective, since Colombian entrepreneurs appear to respond well to traditional policy instruments. However, given Colombia's employment problems and experience with import substitution, my results provide a strong argument for continuation of Colombia's export promotion regime.

Appendix A: Data Sources

Employment, Skills, and Value-Added Data

The 1970 census of manufactures was used to obtain employment, skills, and value-added data at the four-digit level of the ISIC-II classification. The census provides information on the number of various types of workers employed in manufacturing: white-collar, blue-collar, and managers. Unfortunately, no information is available on the number of hours worked; thus all labor measures used in this study are based on the number of workers and not on the flow of services of labor.

The census data were used to derive value-added figures for each four-digit sector. The value-added figures were obtained by subtracting from the output data all intermediate goods purchases plus payments for services and raw materials. No deduction for depreciation was made, since no data on fixed capital are available. The value-added data are used as a proxy for capital stock because it was impossible to find data on capital.

No direct information on labor skills was available. Data on salaries and wages and on ratios of white- to blue-collar workers are used as proxy variables for skills (see Appendix B), as is the female-intensity of different sectors (with the strong presumption that under prevailing conditions women are, on the average, significantly less skilled than men).

Trade Data

International trade data were obtained from the trade yearbooks for 1970 and 1973 (DANE 1970–73). All exports and imports of Colombia were reclassified at the four-digit ISIC-II level to make them comparable to the manufacturing census data.

Following our beliefs about the relevance of the various trade partners of Colombia, the trade data were also assembled according to the following country groupings: (1) the United States, the largest single trade partner of Colombia; (2) all the other developed capitalist countries; (3) Venezuela, a country with which there is a large amount of trade, both legal and illegal; (4) the Andean Group countries (notice that in 1973 Venezuela had not joined and Chile was still a Common Market member and thus was included in this category); (5) the Central American and Caribbean countries, which have generally followed less protective policies than other LDCs and with which Colombia has low natural barriers, since the Caribbean supplies a cheap transport route; (6) the rest of Latin America (all these countries are members of the Latin American Free Trade Association—LAFTA, an integration scheme that has developed a few bilateral and multilateral trade agreements in which Colombia participates); (7) the other LDCs; (8) the socialist European and Asiatic countries with which all trade takes place through bilateral agreements and where natural resource endowments play a lesser role in determining the composition of trade.

Other Data

Two other main sources of data were used in this study: the Colombian input-output table for 1970, and an effective protection study done by Thomas Hutcheson and Daniel Schydlowsky (1976) with 1970 data. The 1970 input-output table is unfortunately very aggregated, with only thirty-one sectors. Therefore, indirect effects could be determined only in a very approximate way, and estimates are given here only for output, value added, and wages and salaries. No estimates are offered for employment, since, for example, the indirect employment effects of the manufacturing branches of the 3111 to 3119 ISIC codes are estimated only globally and cannot be broken down by manufacturing branch.

The effective protection study is of very high quality. It is based on a survey of product prices and thus reflects actual domestic prices, not estimated prices. The study not only takes into account tariffs, licenses, and other foreign trade barriers, but also includes capital and other subsidies that affect the level of protection provided by the government's intervention in the market mechanism. Unfortunately, the survey provides effective protection data for only fifty-six branches of the eighty four-digit ISIC-II branches (table 4.A.1).

Table 4.A.1   **Nominal and Effective Protection of Manufactures in Colombia, 1969**

ISIC No. Manufacturing Branch	Nominal Pro-tection	Effective Pro-tection	Trade Cate-gory[a]
3111 Slaughtering, preparing, and preserving of meat	6.3%	7.3%	X
3112 Manufacture of dairy products	15.0	11.8	X
3113 Canning of fruits and vegetables	41.6	30.2	M
3114 Canning, preserving, and processing of fish and crustaceans	30.8	11.1	X
3115 Manufacture of vegetable and animal oils	13.7	9.2	M
3116 Grain mill products	−4.8	17.8	M
3117 Manufacture of bakery products	0.0	−3.2	X
3118 Sugar factories and refineries	−9.8	−8.6	X
3119 Manufacture of cocoa, chocolate, etc.	20.8	16.3	M
3121 Manufacture of food products n.e.c.	9.6	2.3	X
3131 Distilling, rectifying, and blending spirits	51.0	42.5	M
3132 Wine industries	51.0	29.9	M
3140 Tobacco manufactures	0.0	0.0	X
3211 Spinning, weaving, and finishing of textiles	23.4	11.8	X
3212 Manufacture of made-up textile goods except wearing apparel	0.0	−0.3	X
3213 Knitting mills	46.1	30.4	X
3215 Cordage, rope, and twine industries	9.3	7.8	X
3219 Textiles n.e.c.	15.7	3.3	M
3220 Wearing apparel except footwear	22.0	13.6	X
3231 Tanneries and leather finishing	18.8	11.2	X
3233 Production of leather and leather substitutes, except footwear and wearing apparel	29.8	21.3	X
3240 Footwear, except vulcanized or plastic footwear	0.7	0.4	X
3311 Sawmills, planing, and other wood mills	9.4	7.2	X
3319 Wood and cork products n.e.c.	8.2	5.1	X
3320 Furniture and fixtures	8.0	4.9	M
3411 Pulp, paper, and paperboard	24.2	14.1	M
3412 Containers and boxes of paper and paperboard	22.4	14.6	X
3511 Basic industrial chemicals except fertilizers	41.9	32.7	NC
3513 Snythetic resins, plastic materials and manmade fibers, except glass	61.7	35.4	NC
3521 Paints, varnishes, and lacquers	49.5	49.8	M
3522 Drugs and medicines	85.7	64.3	M
3523 Soap and cleaning preparation, perfumes, cosmetics, etc.	16.3	6.8	M
3529 Chemical products n.e.c.	54.8	56.0	NC
3530 Petroleum refineries	−9.8	5.2	M
3540 Products of petroleum and coal	15.0	11.4	M
3551 Tire and tube industries	10.0	4.4	X
3559 Rubber products n.e.c.	29.5	24.3	M

Table 4.A.1—*continued*

ISIC No. Manufacturing Branch	Nominal Pro-tection	Effective Pro-tection	Trade Cate-gory[a]
3620 Glass and glass products	36.0	5.1	X
3692 Cement, lime, and plaster	1.1	1.3	X
3699 Nonmetallic mineral products n.e.c.	85.6	61.2	X
3710 Iron and steel, basic industries	30.2	17.6	M
3720 Nonferrous metal, basic industries	43.4	25.6	NC
3811 Cutlery, hand tools, and general hardware	23.1	21.7	M
3812 Manufactures of furniture and fixtures, primarily of metal	33.2	4.6	X
3813 Structural metal products	33.2	4.6	M
3819 Fabricated metal products, except machinery and equipment n.e.c.	14.2	4.9	M
3822 Agricultural machinery and equipment	18.8	12.3	M
3824 Special industrial machinery and equipment, except metal and woodworking machinery	29.7	21.1	NC
3830 Electrical industrial machinery and apparatus	42.3	33.2	NC
3832 Radio, television, and communication equipment and apparatus	85.8	72.5	NC
3833 Electrical appliances and housewares	91.0	65.0	NC
3839 Electrical apparatus and supplies n.e.c.	192.9	123.5	M
3843 Motor vehicles	142.8	139.6	NC
3844 Motorcycles and bicycles	68.7	41.7	M
3901 Jewelry and related articles	0.1	−0.5	X
3909 Manufacturing industries n.e.c.	67.9	69.0	NC

Source: Hutcheson and Schydlowsky (1976), and Hutcheson's unpublished data.
[a]Code: X = exportable, M = importable, NC = noncompeting production.

Appendix B: A Note on Labor Skills and Their Measurement in Colombia

The decision to introduce skills in a study of this nature is based on the belief that there exist various types of labor that are important in determining total output, length of time of the production process, and so forth. A priori, these various skills or qualities of labor are not defined in the same dimension, and thus they are not directly comparable; for example, the skills of a wood-carver and those of a truck driver are not directly comparable. To compare these various skills it is necessary to use a function that weights all the skills being considered. The theory of human capital provides such a weighting function, since it offers a method of valuing each type of labor. If we rely basically on the assumption that the supply of different types of skills is highly elastic, under competitive conditions, the wage paid each type of labor can be interpreted as representing the value of the raw labor used (unskilled time) plus the value of the skills embedded in marginal individuals providing the labor services. Total labor remuneration can thus be used as a proxy measure for the quantity of skills used in a production process.

Wages and salaries have to be used carefully in Colombia, because they are somewhat distorted by the following factors: minimum wage laws, extensive labor unionization in the manufacturing sector, and possible observation of disequilibrium conditions. Minimum wage laws establish a floor for wages in all areas of the country and assign differentiated wages by region and economic sector (agriculture vs. manufacture). The degree of compliance with these laws varies a great deal, and there is no way to measure the degree of evasion. However, minimum wage laws are generally enforced in the large cities and in manufacturing establishments with more than ten employees. Owing to the persistent inflation experienced in Colombia and to the lag in the adjustment in minimum wage floors, minimum wages have not always been binding. It is frequently stated that labor unions used the minimum wage levels as benchmarks in their salary demands. To conclude, while it is widely believed that minimum wage laws and unions have an effect on wage levels, there is no quantification of the magnitude of this effect.

Certain wages and salaries in Colombia are likely to be at levels different from what they would be in long-run equilibrium. In an economy where many new products and plants are developed every year, some types of labor will likely be in short supply. Individuals with the necessary skills are in a position to command salaries well above their social replacement costs, which in the long run are determined by the costs of training. While these conditions point out the difficulties in using wages and salaries as a proxy for skill levels in Colombia, they were nonetheless used in the absence of a better measure.

Census data were used to obtain labor remuneration for three types of workers: blue-collar, white-collar, and managerial. The blue-collar and white-collar data are believed to be of good quality. However, the managerial data are of lower quality, since in many small plants there is no separation between ownership and management. Thus the managerial remuneration is only an accounting cost and does not necessarily represent what the manager actually gets. Furthermore, in the corporate sector many managers get part of their salary in kind so that they can avoid paying income taxes. These payments in kind are not included in the data.

The ratio of white- to blue-collar workers is also taken as a proxy for skills used in production, because it is believed that white-collar workers are employed in jobs that are not directly related to the production process but arise from market imperfections. Such jobs include those held by employees who are used to get import and export licenses, to influence price controls, and so forth. Also, many sales jobs have been created by oligopolistic market structures and product-differentiation advertising, and other sales efforts have to be made to maintain a plant's market share. To summarize, the white-collar workers employed by a plant include not only engineers and production workers but also non-production-related employees. Therefore the ratio of white- to blue-collar workers reflects the quality and skills of the production supervisory staff as well as market imperfections and government intervention. Unfortunately, there is no way to separate these three elements.

In this study, therefore, two skill measures have been used: the level of labor remuneration and the ratio of white- to blue-collar workers. As I pointed out above, both have to be employed with reservations. Both are used as they reflect different skill requirements of the various production processes. Salaries can be used to compare various skills within a labor classification, that is, skill differences among blue-collar workers of various industries. The W/B ratio can be used to reflect different supervisory, research, and engineering requirements of the various manufacturing branches.

Notes

1. In some respects 1973 was not a typical year: international inflation was running high, and it was a boom year for the world economy during which "shortages" of many commodities developed. These factors probably affected Colombian trade in 1973, since imports of NRB commodities were discouraged while exports of such commodities were encouraged by high prices. Furthermore, shortages of intermediate goods hampered domestic production of some manufactured goods and, thus, exports of manufactures.

2. A more detailed overview of Colombian development can be found in Díaz-Alejandro (1976b).

3. For a complete discussion of the exchange regime, see Díaz-Alejandro (1976b).

4. An excellent analysis of the Colombian trade system and history in recent years is found in Díaz-Alejandro (1976b).

5. These biases were still present in 1969, the date for which good effective protection estimates exist.

6. The subsidy was also income tax free.

7. Recently there have been some drastic changes in Colombia that have improved the employment picture. The description in this section pertains to the situation prevailing during the period to which the study applies—the 1960s and early 1970s. Several factors have altered the outlook: (1) Colombia has had one of the most dramatic declines in rate of population growth of any country, with the rate falling from about 3.3 percent in the 1950s and early 1960s to less than 2 per-

cent in the late 1970s; and (2) the boom produced by the high coffee prices, and the development of marijuana and cocaine industries, has produced a very large source of income, which in turn has had a large effect on employment.

8. See Conroy (1976) for a detailed analysis of this phenomenon; data mentioned here are taken from his study.

9. Protectionist policies have changed since these studies were made, as the 1970s have witnessed a continuation of the trade liberalization policies begun in 1967. However, the effective protection estimates for 1969 are suitable here because they are only one year away from the manufacturing census used in the latter part of this chapter.

10. This figure (0.4) is lower than the one used to divide import-competing and noncompeting industries in many other country studies presented in this volume. The T statistic for Colombia was clearly bimodal for values between zero and one, with modes at about 0.25 and 0.65. Furthermore, most of the noncompeting industries are either metal-manufacturing branches that contain a great number of products with different patterns of behavior or industries in which imports tend to be quite different from domestic products and thus are noncompeting.

11. The Colombian agricultural sector has not been studied extensively; however, the interested reader could look at Junguito (1974).

12. For example, the finding that manufactured exports are on the average more labor-intensive than import-competing manufactured products cannot be extended to the agricultural sector, where the opposite may take place (further discussed below).

13. For an explanation of the rationale for the geographic divisions used, see Appendix A.

14. The size breakdown is not available at the four-digit level of disaggregation used in this essay. Such detail would violate the confidentiality of the census data, since it would allow the identification of many firms.

15. This issue is discussed further below. See table 4.14.

16. These obstacles, in the view of many historians, played a major role in the dissolution of the Gran Colombia, which in the nineteenth century included what today are Colombia, Ecuador, Panama, and Venezuela.

17. See the works of Hagen (1962) and Lopez-Toro (1970), in which the regional development of entrepreneurial abilities in Antioquia are studied.

18. Servicio Nacional de Aprendizaje, a government organization in charge of a large vocational training program in Colombia.

References

Ahluwalia, M. S. 1974. Income inequality: Some dimensions of the problem. *Redistribution with growth*, ed. Chenery et al., chap. 1. London: Oxford University Press.

Asociación Nacional de Instituciónes Financieras. 1976. *Empleo y desempleo*. Bogotá.

Banco de la República. 1973. *Cuentas nacionales, 1968–1972*. Bogotá: Banco de Republica.

————. 1977. *Cuentas nacionales, 1950–1976*. Bogotá: Banco de Republica.

Barro, R. J. 1973. El dinero y la base monetaria en Colombia, 1967–1972. *Revista de Planeación y Desarrollo* 5, no. 2:68–87.

Berry, R. A. 1975. Open unemployment as a social problem in urban Colombia: Myth and reality. *Economic Development and Cultural Change* 23 (January):276–91.

Berry, R. A., and Díaz-Alejandro, C. F. 1977. Trade policies and income distribution in developing countries: Some necessary complications and some preliminary soundings in Colombia. Mimeographed.

Berry, R. A., and Thoumi, F. E. 1977. Import substitution and beyond: Colombia. *World Development* 5:89–109.

Berrry, R. A., and Urrutia, M. 1975. *La distribución del ingreso en Colombia*. Medellín: La Carretta.

Conroy, M. E. 1976. Urbanization, internal migration, and spatial policy in Colombia. Mimeographed. Washington, D.C.: International Bank for Reconstruction and Development.

Departmento Administrativo Nacional de Estadística (DANE). 1970. *Censo manufacturero nacional 1970*, Bogotá: DANE.

———. 1970–73. *Anuario de comercio exterior*. Bogotá: DANE.

Díaz-Alejandro, C. F. 1976a. Efectos de las exportaciónes no tradicionales sobre la distribución del ingreso: El caso Colombiano. *Revista de Planeación y Desarrollo* 8(3):5–20.

———. 1976b. *Foreign trade regimes and economic development in Colombia*. New York: National Bureau of Economic Research.

Fedesarrollo. *Coyuntura Económica*. Various issues.

Gomez-Otalora, H., and Pardo-Vargas, F. 1973. Las tasas de interés en Colombia: Perspectiva general. Bogotá: Fedesarrollo.

Hagen, E. E. 1962. *The Theory of social change*. Homewood, Ill.: Dorsey Press.

Hutcheson, T. 1973. Incentives for industrialization in Colombia. Ph.D. diss., University of Michigan.

Hutcheson, T.; and Schydlowsky, D. 1976. Incentives for industrialization in Colombia. Mimeographed. Washington, D.C.

International Labor Organization. 1970. *Hacia el pleno empleo*. Bogotá: Banco Popular.

Junguito, R. 1974. El sector agropecuario y el desarrollo económico Colombiano. In *Lecturas sobre desarrollo económico Colombiano*, ed. H. Gomez-Otalora and E. Wiesner. Bogotá: Fedesarrollo.

Lopez-Toro, A. 1970. *Migración y cambio social en antioquia durante el siglo diez y nueve*, Bogotá: Universidad de Los Andes.

Thoumi, F. E. 1971. Evolución de la industria manufacturera fabril, 1958–1967. *Boletín Mensual de Estadística*, no. 236.

———. 1976. El Pacto Andino: Acierto o desatino para Colombia? *Revista de Planeación y Desarrollo* 8:263–74.

————. 1979. Industrial development and policies during the national front years. In *Politics of Compromise: Coalition government in Colombia*, ed. R. A. Berry, R. Hellman, and M. Solaun. New York: Transaction Books.

5   Alternative Trade Strategies and Employment in Indonesia

Mark M. Pitt

Introduction

The trade-employment relationship in Indonesia is of particular interest for a number of reasons. First, Indonesia is a large country. With a population of approximately 140 million (1978), it is the third largest developing country in the world after China and India. The sheer size of its domestic market would allow it to produce a wide range of commodities if the state intervened sufficiently in trade. Second, Indonesia has a rapidly expanding labor force. It is projected to increase by nearly 12 million (or 29 percent) over the decade 1971–81 (*BPS, Statistical Pocketbook, 1974–75*, p. 68). By the year 2000 the total labor force will more than double, and the urban labor force may quadruple relative to 1970 levels (Speare 1978, p. 99). Providing productive employment for this burgeoning labor force presents Indonesia with difficult challenges over the coming decades, and employment creation is given highest priority in planning documents. Third, real gross domestic product increased at a relatively rapid pace (7.2 percent per annum) from 1968 to 1976. Much of this growth was due to recovery from a lengthy period of economic mismanagement and stagnation and to the rapid growth of the petroleum sector and other extractive sectors. Over the same period, manufacturing value added grew at an average rate of 11.1 percent and increased its share of GDP to 11.1 percent in 1976. Fourth, the dearth of prior research evaluating the Indonesian trade regime and its

Mark M. Pitt is associated with the University of Minnesota.

The comments of Anne O. Krueger, Narongchai Akrasanee, and Hal Lary on drafts of this paper are greatly appreciated. This research would not have been possible without the assistance of the Biro Pusat Statistik in Jakarta. Competent research assistance was provided by Paitoon Wiboonchutikula, Jacob Shemer, Makio Suura, and Abdessatar Ouanes. Any errors are my responsibility.

effect on resource allocation has heretofore precluded comparison of the Indonesian experience with that of other developing countries.

Finally, the nature of the trade-employment relationship is of particular policy relevance in the Indonesian case. Indonesia appears to be approaching a key juncture in its trade regime. Since the dramatic trade liberalization of the late 1960s, Indonesia has had a relatively open foreign sector with full exchange convertibility and the complete absence of foreign exchange licensing. Attracted in part by the wide array of fiscal and tariff incentives offered to domestic and foreign investment, new investment has played an important role in postliberalization growth. In manufacturing, foreign investment contributed nearly half of all new investment between 1967 and 1973. Much of this investment took place in activities where protection was greatest or where entry of new firms was controlled. Recent events indicate that the growth of manufacturing investment and output may be expected to slow in coming years. Excess capacity has already become a significant problem in many industries and has led to calls for increased protection. The government's response has been to increase quantitative restrictions on imports and to state publicly that it believes imports should not be permitted unless domestic production is fully utilized (Grenville 1977, p. 25). Another sign of a future slowdown in the growth of manufacturing is the decline in the rates of both new foreign and private domestic investment. The recent economic climate has prompted some observers to deem Indonesia "one of the least attractive foreign investment sites of Asia, particularly outside of the extractive sector" (Arndt 1977, p. 13). Nevertheless, public-sector enterprises seem to be enjoying vigorous growth. Hopes of increased exports of manufactures, however, have not materialized. In spite of a higher rate of inflation relative to its trading partners (including the United States), large oil earnings have permitted the rupiah exchange rate vis-à-vis the dollar to remain unchanged since 1971, thereby raising the relative costs of actual and potential manufactured exports. Thus, the seeds for a more inward-oriented manufacturing development strategy exist. The trade-employment relationship examined here for the year 1971 is for an economy whose trade regime may be entering a new phase.

5.1   The Indonesian Economy since 1950

5.1.1   Phases in Indonesian Economic Growth

From 1950,[1] when Indonesians took complete control of their government from the Dutch, until the present time the Indonesian economy has gone through four phases, roughly delineated by the years 1950–57, 1958–65, 1966–71, and 1972 to the present.

1950–57

1950 marked the end of a decade during which Indonesia was first subject to Japanese occupation and then engaged in a struggle for independence. The next seven years were a period of reconstruction. Rates of real per capita income growth were low but positive. The end of the commodity price boom after the Korean War necessitated a dramatic reduction of imports from their heady levels of 1951–52. This was accomplished by imposing quantitative restrictions and by introducing a number of trade devices that were to be employed again and again over the next dozen years: import entitlement schemes, prepayment requirements, and import surcharges. The government relied heavily on taxes on trade, which contributed an average of more than 40 percent of net government revenue over the period. At the same time, rising government budget deficits led to inflation, which reached double-digit levels by 1955.

Although good data are unavailable, manufacturing value added probably grew somewhat faster than GDP over this period. High levels of protection were provided by quotas and high tariff rates on finished consumer goods and by low duty rates on raw materials and capital goods. Industries regarded as essential received priority in the allocation of foreign exchange. Government agencies were established to distribute some raw materials, such as weaving yarns, at subsidized prices. One result was an expansion of capacity in the presence of its underutilization because raw material allocation among firms was based on their productive capacity (Suhadi 1967, p. 225). The "essential" industries that received priority in the allocation of foreign exchange utilized only 60 percent of capacity in 1958, less essential industries operated at only 20 percent of capacity, and manufacturing as a whole operated at about 40 percent (Suhadi 1967, p. 225).

1958–65

The period 1950–57 came to an end after the last and broadest of several short liberalization attempts that characterized the period. Temporary liberalization of the highly restrictive import-licensing system was achieved through the Bukti Ekspor (literally, "proof of export") system (BE), an import entitlement scheme, introduced in June 1957. The BE system was ended when President Sukarno set out to implement his concept of "guided economy" based on an aversion to foreign capital and the market process. Because of economic mismanagement, 1958–65 was economically dismal by any measure. Per capita national product was below its 1958 level in all the succeeding years of this phase. Inflation intensified to three-digit magnitudes by 1962.[2] Import restrictions continued, and exports suffered since the effective exchange rate (EER) was not adjusted as rapidly as domestic prices were rising. With export receipts falling, cuts in imports were necessary. Food shortages mandated the use of much of the available foreign exchange for food imports. As a result, imports of raw materials were cut back drastically.

At the end of this period of trade restriction and economic mismanagement, Indonesia found herself in desperate economic straits. The average price level in 1966 was more than 1,000 percent of that in 1965. Total foreign debt at the end of 1965 was almost $2.4 billion, much of it owed to the Soviet Union for military equipment. Debt repayment due in 1966 was $530 million—78 percent of the value of exports in that year. Recorded values of imports and exports were below the average levels of the ten previous years. Domestic manufacturing was operating at only 20–30 percent of capacity, and government rice godowns (storage) were empty following the prohibition of further rice imports decreed by President Sukarno in 1964.

1966–71

After an abortive coup on 30 September 1965, a new government emerged, headed by General (later President) Suharto, which relied heavily on a group of Western-trained economists. Beginning in 1966, they embarked on a successful program of stabilization and trade liberalization and achieved remarkable economic growth in spite of the obstacles present when the program began.

Indonesian national product data for the decade of the 1950s and early 1960s are notoriously poor. The available data indicate that per capita rates of growth turned negative in the late 1950s. It is estimated that per capita product in 1963 was 7 percent less than it was five years earlier (Nugroho 1967, p. 450). It was not until at least 1968 that per capita product reached the levels achieved in the 1950s. Thereafter, as noted above, real GDP grew relatively rapidly, with growth most pronounced in exports and manufacturing. During the early 1960s manufacturing's share of GDP had actually fallen marginally (see table 5.1), and real manufacturing value added in 1966 was less than it was in 1961. After 1968 manufacturing value added grew two-thirds faster than GDP.

During the late 1950s and early 1960s, restrictions on imports of raw materials resulted in excess capacity and a declining share of total manufacturing value added for those sectors dependent on imported inputs and spare parts. As table 5.2 illustrates, the share of manufacturing value added originating in importable activities (defined simply as all sectors except the manufacture of food, beverages, tobacco, wood, and rubber) declined dramatically throughout the period of import stringency but increased after liberalization began.

Table 5.1   Gross Domestic Product by Industrial Origin and by Expenditure Category, 1960–76

GDP by Industrial Origin	1960[a]	1965[a]	1971[a]	1971[b]	1976[b,c]
Agriculture	53.9%	52.4%	45.9%	43.6%	36.1%
Farm crops	(34.3)	(33.1)	(29.7)	(25.6)	(21.5)
Others	(19.6)	(19.3)	(16.2)	(18.0)	(14.6)
Mining	3.7	3.7	5.6	9.8	11.6
Manufacturing	8.4	8.3	9.4	8.8	11.1
Electricity, gas, water	0.3	0.4	0.5	0.4	0.6
Construction	2.0	1.7	3.0	3.0	4.7
Transportation	3.7	3.5	3.6	3.8	4.2
Services	28.2	30.0	32.0	30.6	31.7

GDP by Expenditure Category (Current Market Prices)	1960–64	1965–69	1970–74	1975–76
Private consumption expenditure	83.4%	90.4%	73.6%	68.4%
General government consumption expenditure	8.7	7.3	9.6	10.1
Gross domestic capital formation	8.8	8.0	16.5	20.5
Exports	9.9	9.3	18.2	22.3
Imports	−10.8	−15.0	−17.9	−21.3
Gross domestic product	100.0	100.0	100.0	100.0

Source: Biro Pusat Statistik (1969, 2:519); Biro Pusat Statistik, *Statistical Pocketbook of Indonesia*, 1974–75, p. 512; Arndt (1977, p. 31).

Note: There are no comparable figures before 1958.

[a]At 1960 prices.

[b]At 1973 prices.

[c]Preliminary.

The low rate of growth during the 1960s can be attributed in part to the low rate of gross domestic capital formation. Data on GDP by type of expenditure, given in table 5.1, show that gross domestic capital formation was only 8.8 percent of GDP in 1960–64 and 8.0 percent in 1965–69. Spurred by the economy's new health and the growth of the extractive sectors, the rate of capital formation more than doubled in 1970–74 over the preceding period and rose even further in 1975–76.

1972 to the Present

Indonesia's high rate of growth has continued since 1972, thanks in large part to a continuation of its relatively liberal policies. As I mentioned above, real GDP grew at a relatively rapid rate of 7.2 percent annually from 1968 to 1976 while manufacturing grew at an even faster annual rate of about 11 percent. Consequently its share in GDP rose from 9 to 11 percent from 1971 to 1976.

Nonetheless, policies in recent years have regressed from their relative liberalness in the prior period. For example, recent studies (e.g.,

Table 5.2   **Share of Import-Competing Sectors in Total Manufacturing Value Added and Employment**

	1958	1961	1963	1966	1971	1972
Value Added						
Large establishments[a]	48.7%	47.5%	28.4%	12.6%	26.5%	—
Large and medium establishments	—	—	31.9	18.8	35.9	37.1
Employment						
Large establishments	54.5%	68.9%	36.5%	36.8%	26.0%	—
Large and medium establishments	—	—	41.8	40.2	32.2	34.7

Source: Biro Pusat Statistik, *Pendapatan nasional Indonesia 1958–62*; Biro Pusat Statistik, *Pendapatan nasional Indonesia 1960–68*; Biro Pusat Statistik, *Statistik industri* (1971 and 1972).
Note: "Import-competing sectors" here includes all manufacturing except food products, beverages, tobacco, wood products, and rubber products. These products account for the remainder of manufacturing value added and employment.
[a]Large establishments are defined as enterprises without mechanical power employing 100 or more persons or with mechanical power employing 50 or more persons. Medium establishments are defined as enterprises without mechanical power employing 10–99 persons or with mechanical power employing 5–49 persons.

Grenville 1977, p. 25) report that there have been substantial increases in import duty collections. Quantitative restrictions, duty prepayment, and restricted credit access now apply to imports of textiles and some other commodities. Thus, as I suggested in the introduction, Indonesia is at a crucial juncture in its development.

5.1.2   International Trade

Trade Patterns

Table 5.3 shows the changing composition of Indonesia's exports and highlights the importance of two commodities, rubber and petroleum, in total exports. Rubber was dominant in the 1950s, when it constituted more than 50 percent of export returns. With dramatically higher production and prices, petroleum has recently dominated exports, accounting for almost three-quarters of export proceeds in 1975. By 1972 rubber had fallen to third among export commodities, overtaken by rapidly growing exports of forest products. Table 5.4 presents greater detail on the commodity composition of Indonesian exports in 1960–62 and 1970–72. The table also shows the contributions of different manufacturing sectors broadly defined to include all HOS exportables (as classified below in section 5.3).[3] (This breakdown is confined to 1971, being derived from the input-output table for that year.) So defined, exports of manufactures consisted mainly of processed agricultural and forestry products, among which smoked and remilled rubber was the dominant item.

Table 5.3   Composition of Exports and Imports, 1950–76 (in Millions of Dollars and in Percent)

Year	Exports				Imports			
	Rubber	Petroleum	Other	Total	Consumer Goods	Raw Materials	Capital Goods	Total
1950–53	421.3 (45)	174.1 (18)	351.7 (37)	947.1	358.6 (48)	266.5 (35)	131.2 (17)	756.4
1954–57	348.9 (38)	247.3 (27)	316.9 (35)	913.1	259.0 (35)	328.4 (45)	142.7 (20)	731.1
1958–61	341.2 (41)	262.4 (32)	225.2 (27)	828.8	198.1 (33)	266.8 (44)	135.2 (23)	600.1
1962–65	250.3 (36)	255.9 (36)	196.7 (28)	702.9	215.6 (34)	219.8 (35)	200.4 (31)	635.8
1966–69	198.5 (27)	280.8 (38)	252.8 (35)	732.1	236.1 (35)	249.6 (38)	182.3 (27)	668.0
1970–73	263.9 (14)	861.5 (47)	707.1 (39)	1,832.5	340.5 (21)	593.9 (37)	664.5 (42)	1,598.8
1974–76	457.4 (6)	5,534.0 (72)	1,671.3 (22)	7,662.7	766.8 (16)	1,855.8 (39)	2,140.6 (45)	4,763.2

Source: Biro Pusat Statistik, *Ekspor* (various issues).

Note: Figures are annual averages for the years indicated.

Table 5.4 **Composition of Exports**

Composition of Total Exports by Main Commodities

Commodity	1960–62 Millions of $	%	1970–72 Millions of $	%
Rubber	327.0	43	221.5	16
Petroleum and derivatives	232.2	30	612.5	44
Tin ore concentrate	42.2	6	74.3	5
Copra and copra cakes	30.8	4	25.8	2
Tea	24.7	3	25.9	2
Palm oil and kernels	23.3	3	45.1	3
Tobacco	23.2	3	16.4	1
Coffee	13.3	2	67.2	5
Pepper	18.1	2	16.0	1
Wood	1.5	*	161.6	12
Hard cordage fibers	2.5	*	0.1	*
Edible crustaceans	—		16.4	1
Others	29.9	4	107.7	8
Total	768.7		1,390.6	

Composition of Manufacturing Sector Exports by Industry of Origin[a]

Sector	1971 Millions of $	%
Smoking and remilling of rubber (94)	262.1	57
Coffee grinding (58)	55.3	1
Vegetable and animal oils and fats (50)	51.4	1
Tea processing (59)	28.9	6
Processed tobacco (64)	15.2	4
Dried cassava and tapioca flour (53)	15.0	3
Coconut oil and cooking oil (49)	12.1	3
Tanneries and leather finishing (74)	5.7	1
Sawmills, planing, and other wood processing (77)	1.9	*
Canning and preserving of fish and other seafoods (48)	1.7	*
Batik industries (69)	1.1	*
Other manufacturing industries	7.1	2
Total	457.4	

Sources: Commodity exports: Biro Pusat Statistik, *Ekspor* (various issues); sector exports: unpublished 1971 input-output table for Indonesia constructed by Biro Pusat Statistik. (See also note 14.)

*Less than 0.5 percent.

[a]Includes only exports of sectors classified as HOS exportables (see Section 5.3). Numbers in parentheses refer to input-output code, as in table 5.A.1. Trade data from the input-output table are not always consistent with official trade figures. For example, the table indicates that exports from the rubber milling sector exceed official commodity exports of all rubber. No explanation for this discrepancy is available.

Indonesia's import composition (see table 5.3) has reflected the orientation of the trade regime. During the 1950s raw materials were more than 45 percent of total imports, reflecting the priority in foreign exchange allocation given the sheltered manufacturing sector. However, raw material imports suffered most when imports had to be reduced because of decreased export earnings in the early 1960s. They fell from an average annual level of $328 million in 1954–57 to $220 million in 1962–65. With increased availability of foreign exchange in the 1970s, all imports grew, but capital goods imports grew the fastest, reflecting in part the high level of capital formation. Capital goods imports in 1974–76 made up 45 percent of total imports and were nearly twelve times their dollar volume in 1966–69.

The pattern of commodity trade by country has also altered substantially in recent years. Of particular note is the increased importance of Japan as a trading partner. Japan's share of Indonesia's exports rose from 6 to 46 percent from 1960–62 to 1970–72. Much of this increase is due to Japan's position as the major importer of Indonesia's crude petroleum; nevertheless, Japan's share of nonoil exports in 1970–72 was more than 22 percent. Japan also became Indonesia's largest source of imports, accounting for almost one-third of the total in 1970–72. The share of imports from LDCs (including Singapore and Malaysia) doubled between 1960–62 and 1970–72 to account for a quarter of the import total.

Balance of Payments

Table 5.5 gives data on Indonesia's balance of payments for selected years over the period 1960–76. In these years the trade balance was always in surplus, while the goods and services balance was always in deficit. Much of the recent growth in the services deficit is due to increased profit remittances of foreign-owned firms. Private capital inflows became substantial in the early 1970s and were almost $500 million in 1973. The 1975–76 net private capital outflow principally represents short-term debt repayment by PERTAMINA (the state-owned oil company), balanced to some extent by loans that appear on the official transfers and capital account.

The Trade Regime

Here I attempt to summarize salient features of Indonesia's highly complex trade policies. A longer discussion is found in section 5.2.

In the 1960s Indonesia's trade regime was characterized by (1) a system equivalent to legal underinvoicing designed to subsidize exports; (2) foreign exchange allocation based upon the degree of their "necessity" of imports, either as consumption goods (e.g., rice, pharmaceuti-

Table 5.5   Indonesia's Balance of Payments, Selected Years 1960 to 1975–76 (Millions of U.S. Dollars)

	1960	1965	1971	1975–76[a]
Exports, f.o.b.	881	634	1,307	5,011[b]
Imports, f.o.b.	749	610	1,226	4,479[c]
Trade balance	132	24	81	532
Services	−216	−272	−511	−1,386
Goods and services balance	− 84	−248	−430	− 854
Special drawing rights	0	0	28	0
Private capital	20	18	156	− 131
Official transfers and capital	163	253	285	571
Errors and omissions	− 3	− 35	− 96	− 353
Monetary movements	− 96	12	57	364

Sources: Bank Indonesia, *Indonesian Financial Statistics* (various issues).
[a]Fiscal year 1 April to 31 March.
[b]Net of oil imports.
[c]Non-oil imports.

cals) or as intermediate inputs; (3) chronic overvaluation of the exchange rate because of the high rate of inflation; and (4) the existence of widespread smuggling. In the late 1960s the system was simplified, foreign exchange controls were lifted, the exchange rate structure was unified, and legal underinvoicing was eliminated. Thus, by the early 1970s (the focus of the study) the trade regime had become relatively liberal. Foreign exchange controls no longer existed and, in general, protection was moderate. The structure of protection had a definite import substitution bias. ERPs were highest for importables and low, if not negative, for exportables. Since the early 1970s, policies have become more restrictive (as mentioned earlier) although not enough to eliminate their general open and liberal character.

Exchange Rates

The existence of chronic inflation has meant that exchange rates have been chronically overvalued and that a substantial share of international trade occurred through illegal channels (see section 5.2 for details). From 1950 to 1972, prices rose by a factor of 42,000; that is, in 1972 prices were 42,000 times greater than they were in 1950! The black market exchange rate has been consistently above the effective rate, with differentials ranging from 10 to over 1,100 percent. Currency devaluations have occurred only infrequently (except for a period of floating rates from 1967 to 1970), causing wide variation in price level deflated effective exchange rates. However, since liberalization in the late 1960s, the degree of overvaluation has been small relative to that of the 1950s and early 1960s.

5.1.3   The Structure of Production

Like most developing countries, Indonesia is heavily dependent upon NRB production. Close to 50 percent of GDP originates in NRB production, and about 80 percent of the population is found in rural areas. However, the relative importance of NRB production has decreased while that of manufacturing has increased, especially since the late 1960s. In 1971 manufacturing produced about 9 percent of GDP and employed 6 percent of the labor force.

Most manufacturing activities are located in import substitution activities. Activities categorized as importables (see section 5.3 for details) generated nearly 60 percent of domestic value added (DVA) in manufacturing (excluding petroleum refining). Exportables generated 40 percent of DVA, and production that did not compete with imports generated about 1 percent of DVA. Most importable activities could be classified as processed food and consumer goods industries. Major exportables consist of processed NRB goods, for example, canned fish, sawmill products, and milled rubber.

5.1.4   The Indonesian Labor Market

Growth and Structure

Indonesia's population growth rate is not high in comparison with that of other large developing countries. It averaged 2.1 percent per annum over the period 1961–71, substantially less than Brazil's and Pakistan's 2.9 percent and Thailand's 3.0 percent but only slightly less than India's 2.3 percent. The labor force growth rate of 1.8 percent has been less than that of population. The share of population under fifteen years of age stood at 44 percent in 1971, and 61 percent of those ten years of age or older were literate.

As I mentioned above, the Indonesian labor force is still primarily rural and agricultural. According to the 1971 population census (*Penduduk Indonesia*), only 14.7 percent of the 1971 labor force was urban, and 6.2 percent of the total labor force was engaged in manufacturing compared with 60 percent in agriculture. The manufacturing labor force in urban areas was only 23 percent of the total manufacturing labor force in 1971. Indeed, according to official figures, the urban manufacturing labor force declined in absolute terms from 1961 to 1971 while the rural manufacturing labor force nearly doubled. Sundrum (1975, pp. 60–62) has adjusted this population census data to reflect differences in the definition of an "urban area" between 1961 and 1971. His adjusted figures reveal an absolute increase in the urban manufacturing labor force (of 46 percent compared with rural's 59 percent); however, the share of the manufacturing labor force in urban areas still declined (from 36.9 to 33.9 percent). This may be a reflection of the decline of import-competing sectors during the 1960s (see table 5.2), since these sectors were composed of firms that were more urban than the agricultural processing sectors that composed the remainder of manufacturing. Most evidence indicates that this trend has been halted and probably reversed during the 1970s.

Over the period 1961–71, manufacturing employment grew at a 3.3 percent annual rate and increased its share in total employment from 5.7 to 6.8 percent.[4] Table 5.6 provides the data. This rate of growth was not constant over time. During the period of greatest economic decline

Table 5.6   **Labor Market Conditions in Indonesia**

				Rates of Growth		
	1961	1965	1971	1961–65	1965–71	1961–71
1. Population (millions)	97.4	105.4	120.1	1.97	2.18	2.09
2. Labor force (thousands)	34,578	36,543	41,261	1.38	2.02	1.77
3. Employment (thousands)	32,709	35,698	37,628	2.19	0.88	1.40
4. Manufacturing employment (thousands)	1,856	2,059	2,573	2.59	3.71	3.27
5. Manufacturing value-added (Rp billion, constant 1960 prices)						
Large and medium enterprises	24.5	22.7	41.8	−1.91	10.18	5.34
Small enterprises	12.1	12.7	15.8	1.21	3.64	2.67
Total	36.6	35.6	57.6	−0.69	8.02	4.53
6. Real annual wage in manufacturing (thousands of 1973 rupiahs):						
Large enterprises	69.5	51.4	74.1	−7.54	6.10	0.64
Medium enterprises	35.0	23.5	37.6	−9.96	7.83	0.72
7. Rate of unemployment (%)	5.4	2.3	8.8			
8. Elasticity of manufacturing employment (with respect to value added)				−4.00	0.40	0.67

Sources: Row 1: Biro Pusat Statistik, *Statistical Pocketbook of Indonesia*, 1974–75, p. 23.

Row 2: 1961: Biro Pusat Statistik (1963), p. 12; 1965: Biro Pusat Statistik (1967), p. 1; 1971: Biro Pusat Statistik (1975), p. 218.

Row 3: 1961: Biro Pusat Statistik (1963), p. 12; 1965: Biro Pusat Statistik (1967), p. 1; 1971: Biro Pusat Statistik (1975), p. 166.

Row 4: 1961: Biro Pusat Statistik (1963), p. 32; 1965: Biro Pusat Statistik (1967), p. 37; 1971: Biro Pusat Statistik (1975), pp. 218–19.

Row 5: Biro Pusat Statistik, *Statistical Pocketbook of Indonesia*, various issues.

Row 6: Table 5.7.

Row 7: (Row 2 − row 3) ÷ (row 2). Figures are not comparable over time.

Row 8: Calculated as the change in manufacturing employment (row 4) divided by the change in manufacturing value added (row 5) over the same time period.

(1961–65), the growth rate of manufacturing employment was somewhat slower than in the succeeding period of economic advance (1965–71). However, the increase in manufacturing employment during 1961–65 coincided with an absolute decline in manufacturing employment. This phenomenon may be explained by a number of factors. First, labor productivity tends to fall as excess capacity rises because firms find it more difficult to lay off labor relative to capital. Second, the 26 percent fall in real manufacturing wages paid by large-scale firms over this period may have led to factor substitution. Third, employment may have risen because the composition of output shifted dramatically toward more labor-intensive sectors. Table 5.2 indicates that the share of import-competing sectors in total large firm value added and employment declined from 47.5 to 28.4 percent and from 68.9 to 36.8 percent respectively between 1961 and 1966. It would be expected that import-competing sectors would have a smaller labor requirement per unit of domestic value added than other sectors. The evidence presented in section 5.4 bears out the validity of this assertion for 1971. Also note that the fall in manufacturing value added is entirely attributable to large and medium-size firms and that small firm output actually increased. Small firms in Indonesia are substantially more labor-intensive than larger firms.[5]

Wage Behavior

The Indonesian labor market has operated in the absence of significant government intervention. It was not until 1975 that minimum wage regulations were enacted, and even these regulations covered a limited set of industries in certain regions. A law enacted in 1964 required private firms to obtain government approval before dismissing more than ten workers and to pay indemnity. The number of employees covered by this act was relatively small, and according to Arndt and Sundrum (1975, p. 377) enforcement was of doubtful effectiveness. However, the government encouraged the use of capital by subsidizing credit, providing customs duty exemptions, and tax holidays, and offering other incentives to new investment.

The behavior of real wages over the past twenty-five years suggests that wage determination occurs in an undistorted labor market. Every indication is that real wages fell by at least half from the early 1950s to the mid-1960s, then rebounded just as dramatically by 1971.[6] Table 5.7 provides time-series data on wage rates in different types of employment. In column 1, note that the real annual wage in 1973 rupiahs in all large-scale manufacturing fell from the initial level of Rp 110,300 in 1954 to Rp 46,000 in 1962. This represents nearly a 60 percent fall in real wages over eight years. Real wages remained near this level until 1967, and by 1973 had returned to 77 percent of their 1954 levels.[7]

Table 5.7   Real Wages in Indonesia, 1951–73

Year	Average Yearly Wage in Large-Scale Manufacturing (1973 Rupiahs) (1)	Average Yearly Wage in Medium-Scale Manufacturing (1973 Rupiahs) (2)	Average Monthly Wage on Estates (1966 Rupiahs) (3)
1951	—	—	413
1952	—	—	524
1953	—	—	545
1954	110,300	—	431
1955	102,600	—	367
1956	100,400	—	384
1957	97,600	—	394
1958	80,500	27,500	344
1959	78,400	35,000	309
1960	71,600	33,300	314
1961	69,500	35,000	278
1962	46,000	20,700	—
1963	50,400	20,800	202
1964	46,800	—	—
1965	51,400	23,500	—
1966	55,200	18,700	268
1967	67,800	—	275
1968	—	—	238
1969	—	—	291
1970	—	—	348
1971	74,100	37,600	348
1972	83,700	43,200	353

Source: Cols. 1 and 2: Biro Pusat Statistik, *Statistical Pocketbook of Indonesia* (various issues, 1956–63); *Pendapatan nasional Indonesia* (various issues); *Statistik industri* (issues of 1971–73); and unpublished data from Biro Pusat Statistik. Col. 3: Papanek (1974), pp. 16–17.

Real wage data for some nonmanufacturing sectors demonstrate a pattern similar to that of manufacturing. Data on the average monthly wage (including payments in kind) paid on estates in constant 1966 rupiahs indicate a trend similar to that of the other time series.[8] Real wages in large-scale manufacturing and on estates fell by almost equal percentages (54 percent) between 1954 and 1963, then by 1973 they both regained a real wage of about 75 percent of that of 1954.

Two other characteristics of the movement of real wages are worth noting. First, real wages in medium-scale manufacturing seem to have increased faster from the mid-1960s until 1973 than large-scale manufacturing wages, closing some of the wide gap between them. Second, during the period when real wages were falling, skilled workers (defined here as employees paid by the month) suffered a greater loss in real wages than unskilled workers (employees paid by the day or week). The 1961 annual real wage of unskilled workers in 1973 rupiahs was 41 percent lower than its 1954 level of Rp 79,500, while the skilled wage fell 51 percent from its 1954 level of Rp 295,700.

That real wages fell during a period of two- and three-digit inflation and falling per capita income is not unexpected. That they fell by the magnitude indicated by the data of table 5.7 is surprising. Apparently the fall and subsequent rebound of the real manufacturing wage was due to the absence of government policies that might distort wages.

5.1.5 Summary

Indonesia's economic performance has been relatively impressive in the last decade. After a disastrous period in which GDP and manufacturing output fell, both have increased substantially since 1968. One factor affecting this performance has been a gradual easing of foreign exchange and trade restrictions. However, Indonesia's trade regime still must be characterized as having an overall import substitution bias.

5.2 The Foreign Trade Regime and Effective Exchange Rates

5.2.1 Trade Liberalization: 1966–71

The six-year process of trade liberalization began in February 1966 with the introduction of yet another import entitlement certificate known as Bonus Ekspor (export bonus), which had the same acronym, BE, as the Bukti Ekspor of 1957–58, mentioned in section 5.1. Exporters were granted certain percentages of their surrendered export receipts in the form of BE certificates. The remainder of their surrendered export receipts were exchanged at the official rate of Rp 10 = $1. Initially, the BE certificate represented a nonsalable right to foreign exchange for the import of certain goods on the "BE list." The share of export receipts that were exchanged for BE certificates was increased twice in 1966 alone, and with the last increase BEs were made freely salable. After July 1967, all surrendered export receipts were exchanged for BE certificates.

Other elements of the foreign trade regime during this period included legal underinvoicing (the check-price overprice system), exchange controls, and a unification of the exchange system. Each is discussed below.

The Check-Price Overprice System:

A system called check-price overprice (identical to legal underinvoicing) played an important role by subsidizing exports in the 1960s. *Overprice* is the foreign exchange retained when actual export receipts exceed a stated surrender price or *check-price*. Although this foreign exchange retention had been tacitly recognized earlier, it was given legitimate status by the Foreign Exchange Law of 1964 and became known as Devisa Pelangkap (Complementary Foreign Exchange), or DP exchange.

Regulations enacted in 1965 permitted DP exchange earned as overprice to be used for importing or to be sold once. Sale of DP exchange could be legally accomplished only through foreign exchange banks at agreed prices. Imports using DP exchange did not require a license, but they bore additional import duties. Because of these restrictions on its sale and use, only a small part of the overprice (DP) was surrendered by most exporters. Unreported overprice was kept as cash abroad or used as free foreign exchange (Siahaan 1969, p. 26). In 1967 restrictions on the use and sale of DP exchange were greatly loosened, and a market for DP exchange was established in Jakarta.

In table 5.8, the overprice for natural rubber sheets (RSS I) has been calculated quarterly for the period 1965 I through 1970 I. The overprice margin (or the degree of legal underinvoicing), defined as the share of overprice in total realized price, varied widely over the period. After a severe reduction in mid-1967, the overprice was restored in 1968 and remained at a comparatively high level until the check-price overprice system was terminated in April 1970. After April 1970, illegal underinvoicing of exports may still have continued, although there was only a small incentive to do so.

The importance of overprice in exporter receipts is demonstrated by the large share of overprice earnings in the effective exchange rate (EER). At the time the check-price overprice system was terminated, overprice accounted for nearly half of the rupiah earnings per dollar of rubber export. For example, the Bank Indonesia officially estimated that, in the 1969–70 fiscal year, the overprice margin of nonoil exports was 26.4 percent. Thus, these overprice margins varied over time and over commodities that depended to a large degree upon the administrative ability of the Ministry of Trade to reset check-prices in line with world price movements. The use of this overprice system also meant that export data at the commodity level were undervalued for the years when the system operated (1965–70), since exports were recorded at their check-prices rather than their realized prices.

Regulation of Imports

In 1966, imports were classified into five categories, officially described as follows:

Category I: Essential commodities; for example, rice, fertilizers, textbooks, pharmaceuticals.

Category II: Raw materials and auxiliary goods, semifinished products and capital goods that are foreign exchange earning or saving.

Category III: Raw materials, auxiliary goods, and semifinished products intended for domestic consumption.
Category IV: Other goods (mostly finished consumer goods).
Category V: Prohibited goods.

Table 5.8   **Check-Price Overprice System for Rubber, 1965–70**

	Average Check-Price of Rubber (Cents/Lb.) (1)	Average New York Spot Price of Rubber (Cents/Lb.) (2)	Overprice[a] (Legal Under-invoicing) (Cents/Lb.) (3)	Overprice Margin[b] (Percent) (4)	Overprice Earnings as Percentage of EER for Rubber (5)
1965					
I	18.02	26.05	5.83	24.4	50.4
II	20.45	27.57	4.92	19.4	42.5
III	21.83	24.97	0.94	4.1	11.2
IV	19.37	24.17	2.60	11.8	36.3
1966					
I	20.00	25.37	3.17	13.7	36.2
II	18.92	23.93	2.81	12.9	38.0
III	18.21	22.90	2.49	12.0	28.3
IV	17.25	22.07	2.62	13.2	23.3
1967					
I	15.45	21.10	3.45	18.3	31.9
II	13.97	21.20	5.03	26.5	42.1
III	14.86	19.27	2.21	12.9	19.9
IV	14.42	18.07	1.45	9.1	12.9
1968					
I	13.53	17.10	1.37	9.2	12.9
II	13.88	19.27	3.19	18.7	26.0
III	13.12	20.63	5.31	28.8	37.8
IV	13.17	22.37	7.00	34.7	45.5
1969					
I	13.58	23.70	7.92	36.8	45.4
II	14.33	26.60	10.07	41.3	49.1
III	15.00	24.27	12.07	44.4	52.2
IV	15.38	25.10	7.52	32.8	40.0
1970					
I	13.88	24.30	8.22	37.2	44.7

Sources: Check prices: *Warta Perdagangan* and *Business News* (Jakarta); New York spot prices: *Commodity Yearbook*; effective exchange rates: Pitt (1977), p. 53.
Note: Calculations are for rubber smoked sheet I (RSS I).
[a]Calculated as (col. 2 − 2.2) − col. 1; deduction of 2.2 cents/lb. corrects New York spot price to f.o.b. net.
[b]Calculated as col. 3/(col. 2 − 2.2).

The differing types of exchange were restricted to the import of commodities from certain import categories as outlined below:

Types of Exchange	Eligible Import Categories
BE certificates	Commodities from the "BE list" (composed of a restricted set of commodities)
Provincial foreign exchange allocations	I, II, and III
DP (Complementary Exchange)	I, II, III, and IV
Foreign exchange from the Foreign Exchange Fund	Subject to license
Aid-BEs	Aid-BE lists, usually more restrictive than the ordinary BE list

Aid-BEs were foreign credits and grants sold by the government to importers in the form of BE certificates. The Aid-BEs were sold at a substantial discount from export BEs because their use was restricted to imports from the donor country, lists of commodities eligible for import were usually more restrictive, and delivery lags were longer.

In 1967 the BE list was revised, and imports paid with provincial foreign exchange were restricted to the commodities on the BE list. In addition, a DP list was formulated that included all items importable with DP exchange that were not on the BE list. Special Aid-BE lists remained for each donor country. The relative importance of these types of import financing is evident in table 5.9. Note the large share of imports financed by foreign aid, almost 30 percent in 1967 and 1968.

Imports were also subject to special licensing, varying degrees of prepayment, import duties, surtaxes, luxury taxes, and "excess profits" tax.

Exchange Rate Unification

In May 1968 the special Aid-BE rate was abolished. However, since Aid-BE credits were tied to donor countries, and since lists of goods that could be imported with Aid-BE exchange were more restrictive than ordinary BE exchange, special credit inducements were provided to encourage their use.

In April 1970 the dual exchange rate system was ended and the check-price overprice system was abolished.[9] The markets for BEs and DP exchange were merged, and the exchange rate was set at Rp 378 = $1. This was the DP exchange rate before exchange rate unification.

Table 5.9   **Total Import Financing, 1966–71/72 (in Millions of U.S. Dollars)**

Financed by	1966	1967	1968	1969	1970/71[a]	1971/72[a]
Export BEs/general						
foreign exchange	340	384	416	475	419	361
Aid-BEs	128	238	240	285	346	393
Program aid	(96)	(145)	(103)	(101)	(125)	(139)
Food aid	(—)	(6)	(30)	(32)	(39)	(40)
PL 480	(32)	(25)	(89)	(90)	(105)	(111)
Project aid	(—)	(62)	(18)	(62)	(77)	(103)
DP and free foreign						
exchange	68	114	94	125	32	42
Direct investment	—	1	1	21	65	121
Merchants L/C	0	0	0	0	146	238
Subtotal	536	737	751	906	1,008	1,155
Imports of oil companies	68	68	80	87	94	132
Total	604	805	831	993	1,102	1,287

Source: Bank Indonesia Report, various years.
[a]Fiscal year.

While this rate was nominally floating, the Bank Indonesia intervened in the market to support it.

The exchange rate unification meant that the more essential commodities on the BE list no longer enjoyed a more favorable exchange rate than other imports that could previously be financed only with DP exchange. When credit costs are taken into account, imports with BE exchange may have actually been more expensive than imports with DP exchange. Importing with BE exchange was relatively more expensive because cheap foreign credit was available only to DP exchange financed imports. At one time, commodities on the BE list made up more than half of the value of imports financed with DP exchange (Simpkin 1970, p. 6).

The devaluation of 23 August 1971 to Rp 415 per dollar was Indonesia's last official devaluation. It marked the end of a liberalization phase that had transformed Indonesia's trade regime from one of the more restrictive among LDCs to one in which there was full exchange convertibility and a complete absence of foreign exchange licensing.

5.2.2   Effective Exchange Rates

To determine the effects of this complicated succession of foreign exchange policies on returns from exporting, the effective exchange rate (EER_x) for rubber exports has been calculated. Although there were periods when literally dozens of EERs for various exports existed, for the purpose of this research the rubber exchange rate is an adequate proxy for an average EER_x weighted by the value of exports. One reason this is true is that rubber would carry an enormous weight in such an average calculation. From 1950 to 1969, rubber exports contributed on the average about 57 percent of all nonmineral exports. In addition, rubber's EER over that period usually lay somewhere near the middle of a ranking of the EERs of major agricultural exports. Pepper, tea, and kapok had somewhat higher EER_xs, while copra and coffee often had lower EER_xs. Other less important exports often had the highest EER_xs, but they would carry very little weight in a weighted average.

The EER_xs presented in table 5.10 were calculated by summing the values of all trade policy instruments, including such things as the value of import entitlement certificates, foreign exchange retention, and export taxes and premiums. The EER_x thus calculated may differ, however, from the rate actually realized, because of illegal transactions.

The importance of the export incentive schemes meant that changes in the official registered exchange rates did not significantly alter the EER_x. For example, the gross devaluation of 200 percent in 1952 (from Rp 3.8 to Rp 11.40) resulted in a net devaluation of 12.5 percent. Likewise, gross devaluations of 294 percent, 22,000 percent, 16 percent, and 10 percent in 1959, 1965, 1970, and 1971 resulted in net devaluations of 19 percent, 300 percent, 8 percent, and 10 percent respectively.

Table 5.10 also presents an index of the estimated annual average price level deflated effective exchange rate (PLD-EER_x) for natural rubber.[10] The tremendous variance in the PLD-EER_x index shows the effects of a consistently rapid rise in domestic prices countered from time to time by devaluation.

Notes to Table 5.10

Source: Pitt 1977, pp. 56, 66.

Note: Col. 1: Effective exchange rate for (rubber) exports expressed in old rupiahs through 1965 and thereafter in new rupiahs resulting from the thousand-to-one currency conversion of December 1965.

Col. 2: Cost-of-living index for a government worker in Jakarta linked with the sixty-two-item Jakarta cost-of-living index (expressed in old rupiah equivalent after 1965).

Col. 3: Col. 1 deflated by col. 2 (and, from 1966 on, multiplied by 1,000 to adjust for currency conversion in December 1965) and converted to index series with 1971 as base year.

Col. 4: See text (and, for currency conversion, see note on col. 1).

Col. 5: Percentage excess of domestic price over world price (less transportation costs), latter being converted at rates given in col. 1. As explained in text, the term "disparity" is no longer appropriate for differentials after 1965.

Col. 6: Realized effective exchange rate for exports; i.e., col. 1 increased by percentage in col. 5.

Col. 7: Col. 6 adjusted in same way as col. 1 in col. 3.

Col. 8: Effective exchange rate for imports adjusted like col. 1 in col. 3. For further explanation of concepts, see text and chapter 1.

Table 5.10   Exchange Rates, Variously Defined and Adjusted, Annual Averages, 1950–72

Year	EER_x (Rp per \$) (1)	Cost of Living Index (1953 = 100) (2)	Index of $PLD\text{-}EER_x$ (1971 = 100) (3)	Free Exchange Rate (Rp per \$) (4)	Price Disparity for Rubber (%) (5)	$REER_x$ (Rp per \$) (6)	Index of $PLD\text{-}REER_x$ (1971 = 100) (7)	Index of $PLD\text{-}EER_m$ (1971 = 100) (8)
1950	7.08	60	77.4	24.65	20.34	8.52	96.24	244.6
1951	7.60	85	58.7	16.17	11.31	8.46	67.46	119.5
1952	9.41	92	67.1	19.63	13.71	10.70	79.06	102.2
1953	11.60	100	76.1	27.32	2.33	11.87	80.48	123.3
1954	12.52	103	79.7	31.98	13.10	14.16	93.21	158.5
1955	11.07	127	57.2	39.13	42.01	15.72	83.94	203.7
1956	11.84	142	54.7	33.33	21.71	14.41	68.82	140.8
1957	17.33	159	71.5	43.65	16.96	20.27	86.47	142.4
1958	29.55	225	86.1	71.74	27.24	37.60	113.33	170.6
1959	32.21	280	75.5	130.82	49.92	48.29	116.95	250.6
1960	37.52	367	67.1	285.17	100.21	75.12	107.40	270.4
1961	40.50	487	54.6	186.67	58.59	64.23	89.44	199.2
1962	136.50	1,324	67.6	760.42	32.75	181.21	92.81	217.6
1963	320.55	2,927	71.8	1,456.00	30.42	418.05	96.85	201.2
1964	788.35	6,106	84.7	3,004.00	18.29	932.52	103.57	205.4
1965	2,683.00	24,715	71.3	14,083.00	33.85	3,591.18	98.54	256.9
1966	36.00	283,166	82.8	105.67	− 4.66	34.32	82.20	182.7
1967	103.38	763,222	88.9	172.25	−12.17	90.80	80.68	132.6
1968	269.03	1,719,762	102.6	386.67	.04	270.12	106.51	133.8
1969	318.23	2,020,089	92.3	408.42	2.80	327.13	109.81	131.9
1970	333.65	2,262,000	98.6	388.59	.54	335.44	100.56	113.6
1971	353.88	2,321,500	100.0	397.33	− 3.26	342.34	100.00	100.0
1972	373.50	2,562,600	95.6	418.00	− .02	372.89	98.68	86.6

In addition to the *PLD-EER$_x$*, the ratio of the *EER* to the black-market or free-market rate of exchange gives some indication, albeit uncertain, of the rupiah's overvaluation.[11] Illegal transactions in international trade characterized the 1950s and 1960s, with substantial quantities of foreign exchange being traded through black markets. In many years the black-market rate of exchange was many times greater than the effective rate. At its peak in early 1960, the black-market rate was almost eleven times the *EER$_x$*, and over the five years 1960–64 it averaged more than five times as great. Since the black-market rate represents the exchange rate for foreign exchange earned in smuggling, these disparities indicate that there were enormous incentives to smuggle.

It is well known that the smuggling of agricultural exports—rubber and copra in particular—was widespread. Because smuggling was a significant share of export trade, the *EER$_x$* calculations for rubber that have been presented may not be good measures of the returns from export trade; logically it might be expected that smuggled rubber earned a greater rupiah return per dollar of export than legally exported rubber. And, indeed, one phenomenon that characterized Indonesian trade in the presence of smuggling was the existence of price disparity that is defined as the positive difference between the domestic price and the world price of an exported commodity converted at the legal effective exchange rate. The existence of price disparity indicates that some of the higher returns from smuggling vis-à-vis legal trade are passed back to producers in the form of higher domestic prices.[12]

In table 5.10 annual estimates of price disparity caused by smuggling of rubber are presented, with price disparity being measured as a percentage:

$$\frac{P^d - (EER_x \cdot P^w)}{EER_x \cdot P^w} \times 100,$$

where P^d = domestic price of rubber in rupiahs at Jakarta
     EER_x = legal effective exchange rate for rubber
     P^w = international trade price of rubber; here it is based on the f.o.b. price of rubber at Singapore less transportation costs.

The effect of smuggling on the domestic price of rubber over much of the 1950s and 1960s is demonstrated by these calculations. Over 1959–65, smuggling increased the domestic price of rubber by more than 46 percent on the average beyond the price that would have existed in its absence. In the year 1960 the domestic price was about double the legal trade price. Kenneth Thomas (1966, p. 102) claims that price disparity exceeded 160 percent in September 1965. After the reforms of 1966, price disparity fell markedly, as can be seen from column 5 of table 5.10. Indeed, in some years the domestic price was slightly below the world price.

It is clear that over a number of years smuggling, working through the mechanism of price disparity, counterbalanced a significant amount of the price distorting effects of government trade policy. The effective exchange rate for all exports that was actually realized, $REER_x$, was $(EER_x) \times (1 + \text{price disparity})$. The $REER_x$ for rubber is presented in table 5.10. The $REER_x$s imply a level of price distortion considerably less than is implied by the EER_xs. In addition, in table 5.10 there is also an index of $PLD\text{-}REER_x$. These calculations suggest that, during 1958–65, generally regarded as the period of greatest government intervention in the trade sector, the realized rupiah return to a dollar's worth of rubber export was, surprisingly, on the average slightly greater, in real terms, than it was at the end of the liberalization period in 1971.

The $PLD\text{-}EER$ for imports presented as an index in table 5.10 is calculated by comparing domestic and international import price indexes and deflating by the increase in domestic prices. Keeping in mind the potential error in such a calculation owing to aggregation and smuggling, note that the calculated $PLD\text{-}EER_m$ was at its highest level in 1959–65, when the value of total imports was lowest and subject to the greater restrictions. It was low in 1951–53, reflecting the freeing of imports as a result of the Korean War commodity price boom, but it leaped in 1955 when foreign exchange allotments for consumer goods were sharply curtailed. As the trade regime was liberalized, the $PLD\text{-}EER_m$ fell sharply, dropping nearly two-thirds from 1965 to 1972. Thus the estimated $PLD\text{-}EER_m$ seems to have moved in accordance with the nature of the trade regime.

5.2.3 The Current Phase: 1972 to the Present

As I mentioned earlier, there has been a definite movement toward increased protection of import-competing industries since 1972. However Indonesia's trade policies remain generally more liberal than those in other large LDCs. Examination of tariff schedules imposed since 1971 cannot provide information on whether protection from tariffs has increased without information on tariff collection rates, which tend to differ markedly from scheduled rates. Although a sectoral breakdown of tariff collections is unavailable for the years since 1971, it has recently been reported that there have been substantial increases in import duty collections (Grenville 1977, p. 25). In addition, the use of check-prices on imported commodities on which customs duties and import sales taxes are calculated has recently emerged as a protective device. For example, the check-prices on some textiles were raised by as much as 75 percent in 1975 alone. Imports of textiles and other commodities have also faced increased quantitative restrictions, import duty prepayment, and restricted access to credit. On the other hand, exports have benefited from the reduction of the 10 percent export tax.

The government has also had a growing influence on factor markets. Minimum wage regulations have been enacted for a limited set of industries in certain regions, and more are promised. The government has further encouraged the use of capital-intensive technologies by subsidizing credit and providing customs duty exemptions, tax holidays, and other incentives to new investment. On the other hand, it has acted to protect small-scale firms by exempting from sales and excise taxes weaving, knitting, and cigarette products originating from factories using nonmechanized technologies. Nevertheless, most observers agree that the recent new investment in manufacturing is very capital-intensive relative to existing plants.[13] This is particularly true for the increasingly large public sector (including PERTAMINA) investments. After examining public sector investments, McCawley and Manning (1976, p. 27) conclude that "it would be difficult to prepare a more capital intensive set of projects. Thus, despite the official emphasis that is given to the need to create jobs, in practice the goal of employment creation has received low priority." In brief, current trade strategy seems to be moving away from a liberalized foreign sector and the express goal of employment creation.

5.3   Effective Protection in Indonesian Manufacturing

5.3.1   Procedures

The 1971 input-output table for Indonesia provides much of the basic data necessary for the ERP estimates.[14] The table includes 32 agriculture, livestock, forestry, and fishing activities, and 12 mining, 82 manufacturing, and 45 service or other activities. Four of the 171 activities had no domestic production in 1971, so there were 167 producing industries. For this study 2 activities were disaggregated to bring the total number of producing activities to 169, of which 83 were in manufacturing. The bulk of cottage and small-scale agricultural processing such as hand pounding of rice and peasant sugar refining were treated as manufacturing value-added activities and included with similar processes occurring in larger-scale production units.

To estimate nominal protection, I relied heavily upon vectors of customs duty and import sales tax collections and the c.i.f. value of imports included in the input-output table. These provide appropriate measures as long as tariffs are the only trade restriction and domestic taxes are not a factor. However, price comparisons were used to measure nominal protection in activities where imports were prohibited.[15] In addition, goods whose import is performed solely by or for government agencies have also had their nominal protection estimated in this manner. In 1971 these government-imported commodities were rice, cloves,[16] wheat flour, fertilizer, pesticides and inputs into pesticide production, and sugar.

Besides tariffs, I had to consider a variety of other protective devices in making my ERP calculations. These included an import sales tax, a withholding tax on corporate income, special exchange rates, export taxes, and, finally, the existence of illegal transactions. Each is discussed below.

Imported commodities are exempt from the domestic sales tax, and thus the import sales tax is not entirely protective. Collected at the same time as the customs duty and using the same tariff nomenclature, the import sales tax differs from the customs duty by both its rate of levy (and collection) and its base, which is the c.i.f. price of the import plus the customs duty and a 5 percent markup to cover presumptive storage, transport, and other costs. The domestic sales tax is not harmonized with the import sales tax. Only rarely does the domestic sales tax completely offset its import counterpart. The computation of the extent of the offset is complicated by a change in the tax schedule that went into effect in July and August of 1971.

Another complication in computing ERPs arises because of the MPO tax, a withholding tax on corporation income.[17] It is paid to the government, at an ad valorem rate by the MPO collector on behalf of the purchaser, who can credit this amount against his corporation income tax liability. On domestic sales, the MPO rate was 2 percent in 1971, with the seller usually acting as MPO collector. For imported goods, the MPO rate was 3 percent except for commodities imported with a merchant's letter of credit (L/C), for which the rate was 6 percent. The tax was not collected on exports. In the 1971–72 fiscal year, imports with a merchant's L/C were 20 percent of all imports and 37 percent of all imports excluding those financed by foreign aid and direct investment. For imports, banks usually act as collector, probably making evasion more difficult than for domestic sales. About one-half of all MPO revenue is collected from imports.

While the MPO increases the price of a commodity to a firm by its rate of collection, it may not affect a firm's decision-making if the levy is merely treated as an advance payment on its profits tax. In that case the only protective effect of the discriminatory MPO rate on imports would be the relatively minor cost of additional tax prepayment.

However, because of the presumptive nature of the base of the corporation income tax, the firm may choose not to claim an MPO tax credit.[18] For tax collection purposes, profits are presumptively determined as a margin on sales, which in turn are a presumptive markup on cost. The total MPO credit claimed by the firm presumably indicates the firm's cost and thus, up the chain of margins, the firm's presumed profit. It may be to a firm's advantage to underreport MPO tax credits and thus reduce presumptive profit. Therefore the MPO tax is considered a sales tax and, for sectors subject to MPO tax, nominal protection in the estimates presented here includes a 1 percent MPO protective effect. This is a low estimate because the 4 percent protective effect of MPO on imports with merchants' L/C has been ignored. This is somewhat offset by exemptions on MPO payment given firms under tax holiday and other special cases.

Special exchange rates took two forms in 1971: fixed subsidized rates of exchange to import weaving yarns under the PL-480 program and raw cotton; and special rates of exchange for the import of restricted lists of commodities from certain origins with aid foreign exchange (*Devisa Kredit*). On average during 1971, these special exchange rates represented a subsidy of 46.7 percent for raw cotton and 68.0 percent for PL-480 weaving yarns.[19] These are taken into account in the ERP estimates below.

Incentives for the use of aid foreign exchange beginning January 1971 included a reduced prefinancing requirement for aid exchange imports from most origins and an interest rate discount for credit. Concurrent with the official devaluation of 23 August 1971, a system of rebates to the official exchange rate of Rp 415 varying by country of origin was instituted for the import of goods with aid foreign exchange.[20] Although nearly 24 percent of all imports in 1971 were paid for with aid foreign exchange (excluding imports under food and project aid), it was ignored in calculating ERPs for two reasons. First, it was not possible to determine the rate of subsidization by sector, and, second, the aid exchange rebates probably only offset the additional cost of their use.

In 1971 exporters were required to surrender 10 percent of their export proceeds as an export tax. Exempted were the export of "finished goods and handicrafts" as defined by commodity lists. The lists do not seem entirely consistent; for example, tea was considered a finished good, while coffee, rubber, vegetable oils, and almost all other NRB and processed NRB goods were not. In addition, rubber, coffee, copra, and pepper exports were subject to a cess and rehabilitation levy on a per kilogram basis. These levies were substantially reduced in mid-1971. In addition, copra was also subject to regional levies, and coffee needed International Coffee Agreement stamps in order to be exported to International Coffee Organization (ICO) member nations. Finally, certain exports were prohibited with protective intent, namely, lower grades of rubber and chinchona bark, the raw material of quinine. All the above have been incorporated into the protection estimates.

Under Indonesia's Sales Tax Act, export shipments are exempt from paying the domestic sales tax. In addition, the minister of finance can exempt from sales tax commodities that by nature are destined for export, although they may be utilized locally in intermediate stages. Nevertheless, according to Cnossen (1973, p. 31) these provisions are not observed in practice. Therefore, in the ERP computations it is assumed that domestic sales taxes are levied on exports.

Illegal transactions, traditionally an important facet of Indonesian foreign trade, are potentially the most troublesome source of error in calculating protection rates. Two aspects of illegal import transactions may be important: importers may pay less than the listed tariff rate on the true value of the import, or they may pay the listed tariff on an underinvoiced import value.

Richard Cooper (1974) has verified the quantitative importance of the first aspect (paying less than the stated tariff rate) through a comparison of actual tariff collections and the listed legal tariffs. Not all of the difference between theoretical and actual tariff collections can be attributed to illegal transactions. There are a number of legal tariff exemptions, including imports for direct investment by both foreign and domestic firms, imports for aid projects, and numerous special exemptions by the Ministries of Finance and Trade.[21] Nevertheless, exempt imports explain only a small part of the difference between theoretical and actual tariff collections.

Even if importers pay the listed tariff, there may still be evasion of tariffs if the commodity is underinvoiced. Recall that actual tariff collections are the starting point for most of the nominal protection calculations. Thus underinvoicing can create a real problem because tariff collections are divided by the listed (underinvoiced) c.i.f. values of imports to obtain tariff rates and therefore protection is overestimated. However, the computed estimates will be reliable if all imports are correctly valued at customs and if illegal transactions occur only via the underpayment of trade taxes. That is, the actual tariff collections, although underpaid (less than implied by the listed tariff) would measure protection on the actual c.i.f. price.

Using data on foreign and domestic prices for a number of imported commodities for the years 1969 and 1971, Cooper econometrically estimated the relationship between observed domestic prices and scheduled tariff rates. Employing his results and the observed relationship between actual tariff collections and scheduled tariff rates, I performed an analysis to determine if the use of tariff collection data and declared import values results in a systematic underestimate (or overestimate) of actual domestic prices. There was no evidence that nominal rates of protection calculated with tariff collections data would be systematically biased, only that the error of the estimates may be large.[22]

Finally, adjustments had to be made in activities where intermediate inputs were commodities in the same sector as the final output but with differing nominal rates of protection. This was particularly important in assembly industries, where commodities in a completely knocked down (CKD) condition enter with a tariff discount.

5.3.2 The Structure of Protection

Estimates of nominal and effective protection for Indonesian manufacturing activities for the year 1971 are given in the Appendix (along with their input-output code numbers and names). Aggregates for tradable categories are presented in table 5.11, and values for major exportables and importables are given in table 5.12.

Classification of Activities

Forty-six activities were classified as home goods. Most of these were service activities, but also included are sugarcane (I-0 code no. 11), coffee (16), tea (17), dairy products (23), poultry products (26), stone quarrying (40), and repairing of motor vehicles (118). A few service activities in which trade was substantial were not considered home goods. Paddy (1) and cassava (3), which enter trade in small amounts, might marginally be considered home goods but were classified as natural resource based (NRB) tradables in the following analysis.[23]

All agriculture, forestry, livestock, fishing, mining, and quarrying activities not considered home goods were classified as NRB tradables, as was nonferrous metal refining (103).

Table 5.11   Distribution of Effective Protection in Indonesian Manufacturing, 1971

HOS Manufacturing Tradable Group	Effective Rates of Protection
1. Exportables	−11%
2. Importables (excluding negative IVA activities)	46
Activities with lowest protection	−13
Excluding processed NRBs	26
Activities with medium protection	55
Excluding processed NRBs	132
Activities with highest protection	279
Excluding processed NRBs	473
3. All importables (including negative IVA activities)	66
4. Noncompeting importables	15
5. All importable sectors (3 and 4)	65
All HOS tradable sectors (1, 3, and 4)	33

Source: Appendix table 5.A.1.

Note: Calculated as $\left(\dfrac{\Sigma\, DVA_i}{\Sigma\, IVA_i} - 1 \right) \times 100$, where i indexes the activities in a tradable group.

Table 5.12   **Characteristics of Major HOS Exportables and Importables, 1971**

Industry	Nominal Protection	Effective Protection	T_i	with DCs Trade[a]
Exportables				
Canned and preserved fish and seafoods	0%	1%	— .00	98%
Coconut oil and cooking oil	−10	68	— .06	100
Vegetable oils, animal oils, and fats	−10	−12	— .83	98
Dried cassava and tapioca flour	−10	−19	— .22	100
Coffee grinding	−15	−19	— .60	95
Tea processing	0	0	— .66	99
Processed tobacco	−10	−27	— .13	98
Tanneries and leather finishing	0	− 4	— 1.08	93
Sawmills	0	1	— .00	95
Smoking and remilling of rubber	−11	−11	−104.8[b]	96
Importables				
Canned and preserved meat	5	50	.00	80
Rice milling and polishing	−13	−15	.05	69
Sugar refining	30	154	.08	15
Soybean products	0	25	.03	62
Cigarettes	82	556	.00	96
Spinning industries	− 8	134	.40	49
Weaving industries	44	Neg. IVA	.19	75
Wearing apparel	55	199	.02	79
Printing, publishing	25	42	.30	97
Soap	41	701	.03	78
Motor vehicles	110	526	.52	99

Source: Appendix table 5.A.1, 5.A.2.

Note: Activities with production in excess of 25,000 million rupiahs.

[a]Trade refers to exports for exportables and imports for importables.

[b]Owing to a fall in inventories, export exceeded production, and therefore the calculated value for T is positive. A sector is exportable if $T_i < 0$ or $T > 1$; the latter values can occur only if inventories are reduced.

All activities classified as HOS tradables were manufacturing activities. These industries were further classified as either exportable, importable, or noncompeting, following the T statistic methodology described in chapter 1. Exportables had a negative T_i, importables had T_is between 0 and 0.8, and noncompeting had T_is greater than 0.8.

These values are calculated only for the year 1971. For those activities whose value of T was close to 0 or 0.8 or where there was a priori knowledge of significant trade fluctuations, reference was made to the trade data of succeeding and preceding years in making the ultimate classification. Thus the fertilizer (84), railroad equipment (115), and aircraft (119) industries were classified differently than the 1971 T statistic would indicate.[24]

HOS tradables were further subdivided into those considered to process NRB goods and those that do not. The processed NRB subgroup as used here covers certain manufacturing activities that, with the input-output information available at the time of preparing this analysis, could not be clearly separated between the NRB stages necessary to turn a raw material into a tradable product and further HOS stages of processing. Coffee provides a good illustration on the side of Indonesia's exports. Although the coffee growing activity (I-0 code number 16) is properly categorized as NRB, the value added in the coffee roasting and grinding activity (58) embraces certain additional NRB states such as the sorting and drying needed to make the product tradable and further HOS processing beyond that point. A similar mixture of NRB and HOS stages is found in tapioca (53) and tea processing (59) among export industries and in rice milling (51) and sugar refining (56) among importable industries. These industries are accordingly classified as processed NRBs in the following analysis. Given the importance of the smoking and remilling of rubber (I-0 code 94) as an export industry, it should be noted that this industry is not here classified as a processed NRB but rather as "other HOS." The reason is that natural rubber can be exported in cruder form, processed just sufficiently to allow it to be traded, and as such would be considered an export from the rubber-tapping activity (10).[25]

In analyzing the structure of protection and factor proportions in various classes of HOS tradables, two activities were excluded ("petroleum refining" [91] and "other petroleum and coal products" [92]) because of a lack of data on factor requirements (except for the wages and salaries data of the input-output table). With their huge value added (almost 15 percent of total value added in HOS industries), any error in estimating their factor requirements would lead to a correspondingly large error in the aggregate results.[26]

The Distribution of ERPs over Commodity Categories

The distribution of average ERPs by commodity category is presented in table 5.11. Importable activities excluding those with negative international value added were ranked by ERPs. This ranking was then divided into three groups of equal domestic value added, and the groups were labeled as "lowest protection," "medium protection," and "highest protection" sectors.

Eight activities had negative value added at international prices, all of them HOS importables. Four of them were textile industries, including the large weaving sector. This is somewhat surprising, since other Asian

LDCs have efficient textile industries, often with large export volume. For the Indonesian weaving industry, nominal protection was not extraordinarily high (44.3 percent); it was largely the subsidy given cotton yarn imports that resulted in the finding of negative IVA. Of course there may be some components of this sector with positive IVA.

Negative ERPs were found to occur in fifteen of the manufacturing activities reported in table 5.A.1. Of these fifteen activities, eleven were HOS exportables, three were noncompeting importables, and one was a processed NRB HOS importable (rice milling). The large number of HOS exportables with negative protection indicates the lack of attention to exports, and the consequent disincentives for them, that characterized the Indonesian trade strategy in 1971.

Since eleven out of fifteen exportable industries had negative rates of protection, it is not surprising that, as a group, exportables had negative effective protection of −11 percent. The trade regime quite definitely favored importables, with their overall rate of protection of 66 percent. Indonesia, like many other countries in this study, did not provide high levels of protection to noncompeting importables, particularly if they produced capital goods. These industries had a relatively low 15 percent ERP.

The least-protected activities in the importable group had negative effective protection. This is due mainly to the negative protection afforded the large rice milling sector. When rice milling and the other processed NRB importables (sugar refining) were excluded, protection was positive. The protection afforded the most-protected industries in the importable group was six times that afforded all nonnegative IVA importable industries. These results indicate the wide range of incentives given to the various manufacturing sectors.

5.4   Factor Proportions in Indonesian Trade in Manufactures

5.4.1   The Measurement of Factor Inputs

For HOS importable and exportable activities, nine measures of factor use were employed: four types of labor, one measure of skills, and four measures of capital.

Four surveys were drawn upon to estimate labor coefficients. The total labor requirements per million rupiahs of DVA in importable and export industries were calculated from a 1973 industrial survey carried out by the Biro Pusat Statistik of Indonesia covering large and medium-size firms.[27] These data were augmented by a 1973 sample survey of small firms (Biro Pusat Statistik 1974) in a limited number of industries and a new 1974–75 industrial census of household and cottage industries (Biro Pusat Statistik 1976–77). The data permitted measurement of labor requirements in terms of man-days and are believed superior to data derived from the input-output table.

Labor requirements were disaggregated into manager, other white-collar, male operative, and female operative man-days on the basis of a 1971 industrial survey (BPS, *Statistik Industri* 1971). The 1971 survey contained information on the number of employees of each of these four types by sector. The proportion of each type of employee in the total employees of each sector was then multiplied by the total labor requirements in man-days obtained from the 1973 data to yield the final man-days disaggregations. For this purpose it is assumed that man-days per employee did not differ across the various employee types and that the employee composition did not change from 1971 to 1973.[28]

The measure of skills used is based on estimates of the average wage per man-day calculated from the 1973 industrial survey of large- and medium-size firms. The wage for unskilled labor was taken to be the average wage of the five HOS tradable sectors reporting the lowest average wage—Rp 125 per man-day. Pure skill-days per million rupiahs of value added for sector i was then computed as the ratio of the wage in the ith industry to the unskilled labor wage times total man-days per million rupiahs of domestic value added. Other measures of skill intensity can be derived from the labor requirement disaggregation, for example, the ratio of white-collar to blue-collar man-days.

There are four capital requirement measures, two based on the horsepower of installed machinery and two on energy utilization. The horsepower measures are for prime movers and electric motors. Horsepower of prime movers—that is, machines that use nonelectrical sources of energy—may represent a less sophisticated type of capital. Such machinery is prevalent in food processing and other activities located in rural areas where electricity is unavailable. For example, prime-mover horsepower predominates in the large rice milling and tapioca sectors. The two energy-related measures of capital are electricity consumption in kilowatt-hours and the value of all energy consumed.

For noncompeting importables, factor requirements were taken from the 1973 United States *Annual Survey of Manufactures* (United States 1976). Labor requirements in man-days are the only measure of factor requirements available from United States data that are comparable to the Indonesian data. Because domestic factor proportions differ between the United States and Indonesia, using the United States data directly would underestimate labor requirements. Therefore the data are adjusted by the ratio of the labor input in a set of industries in Indonesia to the labor input in the same set of industries in the United States. Most of the industries chosen in calculating this correction factor are industries classified as noncompeting in which some domestic production nonetheless exists.

5.4.2   Factor Proportions: Direct Requirements

Table 5.13 presents data on direct factor requirements per unit of value added in HOS exportable and importable activities. Table 5.14 gives estimates for major exportables and importables (a complete listing is found in appendix table 5.A.2.) For aggregating the exportable industries, the value-added content of production is used as a weight; for the import-competing sectors, each sector is weighted by domestic value added of domestic production plus the domestic value-added content of imports.[29] The table also presents data with HOS processed NRB activities excluded.

The data in table 5.13 indicate that exportable industries use twice as much labor per unit of DVA as importables. Exportables use more of each type of labor, but ratios vary markedly over labor types. White-collar labor is a greater share of total labor requirements in importable industries than in exportable industries. Since white-collar labor typically embodies more human capital than operative labor, the indication is that importables are more skill-intensive. This is borne out by the skill-day requirement data.

All four measures of capital use indicate a greater capital requirement by importables than by exportables. Importables use nearly two and one-half times the horsepower, twice the energy expenditure, and one and one-half times the electricity consumption per unit of domestic value added as exportables.

These results are basically unchanged if processed NRB industries are excluded from the analysis. As might be expected with her relative abundance of unskilled labor, Indonesia's exportables are clearly more labor-intensive and less skill-intensive than her importable industries.

5.4.3   Factor Requirements by Trade Origin and Destination

Trade flows were disaggregated among seven origin/destinations: Japan; Singapore and Hong Kong; other developed countries; member countries of the Association of South-East Asian Nations (ASEAN) except Singapore; South Korea and Taiwan; socialist countries; and other less developed countries. A serious problem centers on the role of Singapore and Hong Kong as an entrepôt for Indonesian exports. Although some of the Indonesian exports they receive are reprocessed, most are merely reexported, primarily to developed countries. By far the most important commodity to enter this trade is milled natural rubber. Thus, for purposes of aggregating the seven origin/destinations into two—developed countries and less developed countries—trade with

Table 5.13   **Summary Table: Direct Factor Requirements, Exportable and Import-Competing HOS Manufacturing Sectors (Requirements per Million Rupiahs of Value Added)**

Factor	Exportable Sectors per Unit of DVA		Import-Competing Sectors per Unit of DVA		Exportable Sectors per Unit of IVA		Import-Competing Sectors per Unit of IVA	
	(a)	(b)	(a)	(b)	(a)	(b)	(a)	(b)
Total man-days	2,175	1,644	1,038	950	2,230	1,754	1,159	1,116
Manager man-days	55	33	50	35	57	29	54	50
Other white-collar man-days	214	152	150	144	273	228	201	207
Male operative man-days	1,118	843	636	536	1,292	1,016	750	698
Female operative man-days	787	617	203	235	608	481	154	161
Skill-days	1,175	1,263	1,451	1,576	1,809	1,929	2,983	3,314
Prime mover (horsepower)	4.77	6.30	9.67	6.07	4.46	3.14	13.91	13.43
Electric motor (horsepower)	2.46	2.33	7.99	10.50	2.53	1.52	23.39	27.22
Total horsepower	7.23	8.63	17.66	16.58	6.99	4.67	37.30	40.65
Electricity used (kwh)	2,386	2,448	3,886	5,130	4,367	6,133	12,639	14,724
Energy consumed (Rp 000)	44.59	45.45	91.42	96.90	29.97	20.96	214.45	237.00

Source: Author's computations as described in text.

Note: Col. a: All sectors in tradable classification; col. b: Processed NRB sectors excluded.

Table 5.14 **Direct Factor Requirements in Major HOS Importables and Exportables Labor (Man-Days/Million Rupiahs of DVA)**

Industry	Total	Man-agers	Skill-Days	Total Horsepower
Importables				
Canned and preserved meat	514	21	1,069	5.93
Rice milling and polishing	1,150	105	2,383	24.83
Sugar refining	1,571	37	2,438	8.08
Soybean products	3,253	88	3,695	8.59
Cigarettes	52	0	490	.35
Spinning industries	304	5	1,398	15.01
Weaving industries	870	14	1,802	10.13
Wearing apparel	1,990	63	5,508	1.75
Printing and publishing	102	3	266	95.58
Soap	468	16	2,134	1.85
Motor vehicles	440	25	2,893	7.26
Exportables				
Canned and preserved fish and seafood	1,335	41	1,324	4.78
Coconut oil and cooking oil	792	23	2,281	6.50
Vegetable oil, animal fats and oils	600	17	2,400	6.50
Dried cassava and tapioca flour	2,462	128	2,796	37.25
Coffee grinding	3,876	196	6,822	15.61
Tea processing	3,715	40	4,012	7.59
Processed tobacco	4,057	46	2,953	.77
Tanneries and leather finishing	940	38	2,218	22.32
Sawmills	1,023	38	3,396	28.13
Smoking and remilling of rubber	2,300	35	4,968	3.72

Source: See text.

Singapore and Hong Kong is considered trade with developed countries. The quantitative importance of considering export trade via Singapore and Hong Kong trade with developed countries is highlighted by the fact that, if they were considered an LDC destination, then only 3.7 percent of HOS exports (and 36.6 percent of HOS exports excluding rubber) to LDCs would be to destinations besides Singapore and Hong Kong. The value of all HOS exports to LDCs excluding Singapore and Hong Kong in 1971 was $16.75 million.[30]

Table 5.15 shows that labor requirements for exports to developed countries are virtually the same as labor requirements for exports to less developed countries. Exports to less developed countries also require 22 percent more skill-days and more capital (by two out of three measures) than exports to developed countries. If processed NRB industries are excluded, as also shown in table 5.15, exports to developed countries require less labor, skills, and capital (by every measure) than exports to less developed countries.

Table 5.15 **Direct Factor Requirements per Unit of DVA by Trade Destination or Origin (per Million Rupiahs of Domestic Value Added)**

Trade Origin or Destination	Total Man-Days (a)	(b)	Skill-Days (a)	(b)	Horsepower (a)	(b)	Electricity (Kwh) (a)	(b)	Energy (Rp 000) (a)	(b)
Exportable HOS Manufacturing Industries										
Developed countries	2,176	1,630	1,166	1,256	7.14	8.52	2,384	2,434	45.11	45.22
Japan	1,398	1,359	434	400	4.05	3.85	2,432	2,434	44.72	44.93
Singapore and Hong Kong	2,259	2,085	1,460	1,723	5.35	9.33	5,822	4,261	49.63	42.41
Other DCs	2,327	1,541	1,250	1,316	8.31	9.45	1,448	1,796	43.97	46.28
Less developed countries	2,149	2,105	1,421	1,472	9.72	12.42	2,427	2,892	30.73	52.90
ASEAN except Singapore	3,233	2,501	726	913	5.65	10.59	1,475	1,705	48.90	60.75
South Korea and Taiwan	3,197	1,368	484	2,073	5.45	24.53	681	1,402	26.18	73.99
Socialist countries	2,492	2,139	2,558	2,478	7.88	5.96	7,310	9,168	15.08	15.84
Other LDCs	1,392	2,305	1,449	629	12.77	3.88	1,338	758	26.86	40.98
Import-Competing HOS Manufacturing Industries										
Developed countries	994	946	1,523	1,603	18.76	17.54	4,264	5,211	89.61	94.10
Japan	793	716	1,454	1,502	16.36	14.54	4,176	4,983	98.89	105.17
Singapore and Hong Kong	1,164	1,162	1,538	1,541	11.69	11.71	7,650	7,680	68.81	68.66
Other DCs	1,066	1,017	1,562	1,706	22.64	22.41	3,200	4,246	90.55	97.66
Less developed countries	1,177	921	1,202	1,413	14.24	11.18	2,617	4,842	89.30	95.82
ASEAN except Singapore	1,124	1,028	1,294	1,505	21.95	13.01	1,359	4,364	85.61	136.84
South Korea and Taiwan	889	741	1,225	1,303	10.34	10.83	5,951	6,899	122.82	127.90
Socialist countries	1,281	945	1,117	1,406	8.95	9.96	2,278	3,061	87.23	72.98
Other LDCs	1,201	1,038	1,253	1,535	18.05	14.21	3,142	8,283	76.48	71.88

Source: Author's computations as described in text.

Note: (a) All sectors in tradable classification; (b) processed NRB industries excluded.

For importable industries, imports from less developed countries are estimated to require over 18 percent more labor than imports from developed countries and less capital by every measure; both the skill-day data and the share of white-collar in total labor supplied indicate a greater abundance of skills required in imports from developed countries than in imports from less developed countries. The estimated capital/labor ratios for products competing with imports from developed countries are 1.56, 1.93, and 1.19 times those for products competing with imports from less developed countries, according to the horsepower, electricity, and energy proxies, respectively.

When processed NRB industries are excluded, the factor requirement estimates are mixed for importables competing against various sources. Imports from developed countries now require more labor as well as more skill and capital (by two of three measures) than imports from less developed countries. If Singapore and Hong Kong are considered LDCs, however, labor requirements of imports from that group will again exceed those of imports from DCs (1,062 versus 889).

The HOS model of trade with many commodities and countries predicts that noncompeting imports would utilize more of a country's scarce resource and less of its abundant resource than competing imports or other tradables. Table 5.16 clearly supports this contention. Noncompeting imports would require only about one-fifth the labor per unit of DVA that is required in importable sectors. Furthermore, noncompeting imports from DCs embody slightly less labor per unit of DVA than imports from LDCs.[31]

Table 5.16   Direct Labor Requirements in Noncompeting HOS Activities by Import Origin

Origin	Man-Days per Unit of DVA	Man-Days per Unit of IVA
Total	208	229
Developed countries	207	229
Japan	211	233
Singapore and Hong Kong	209	223
Other DCs	200	226
Less developed countries[a]	214	230
ASEAN except Singapore	207	221
South Korea and Taiwan	220	239
Socialist countries	209	222
Other LDCs	203	221

Source: Author's computations as described in text.
[a]Including socialist countries.

5.4.4   Direct Plus Indirect Home Goods Requirements

For computing direct and home goods indirect factor requirements for Indonesian HOS tradable classifications, total man-day labor requirements are the only measure of factor use available. Even if data on horsepower or energy consumption were available for home goods activities, they would be poor measures of the capital services provided in these predominantly service and agricultural sectors. Direct and home goods indirect labor requirements per million rupiahs of direct and home goods indirect value added for various classifications of Indonesian HOS tradables are presented in table 5.17. There is only a minor difference between the direct and the direct plus indirect results. Exportable labor requirements fall slightly, while those of importable activities remain practically constant. This implies that home goods labor requirements are close to those of importables. In summary, these estimates provide results that mirror those from the analysis of direct requirements only.

5.4.5   Net Factor Content of Trade

The HOS factor proportions explanation of trade predicts, among other things, that a labor-abundant country like Indonesia will import commodities with a higher capital/labor ratio than those it exports. In particular, with balanced trade, it predicts that Indonesia will be a net exporter of labor and a net importer of capital. The net factor content of trade, the statistic necessary to test this proposition, measures the net factor content of a representative basket of exports and competing imports leaving the trade balance unchanged. To correctly test the HOS proposition, trade flows should be partitioned between less labor-abundant and more labor-abundant areas. Since Indonesia probably lies near the bottom of a ranking of all countries by capital/labor ratios, it might be expected that the Indonesian net factor content of trade to every broad grouping of countries will reflect a net export of labor.

The conversion of factor requirements per unit of DVA into international value-added terms for reasons explained in chapter 1 was accomplished by applying the calculated *ERP*s. In aggregating exportable and importable industries for the net factor content of trade calculation, the weighting system used is the actual international value-added content of the 1971 basket of competing imports and exports. The resulting statistic thus differs from the calculated factor requirements at domestic prices by both the prices used and the system of weights.

An examination of the IVA columns of table 5.13 reveals that, with balanced trade, Indonesia is clearly a net exporter of labor and a net importer of capital and skills. The capital/labor ratio of her imports is from six to fourteen times that of her exports, depending on the capital

Table 5.17 Direct and Home Goods Indirect Labor Requirements by Trade Destination or Origin (Total Man-Days per Million Rupiahs of Direct and Home Goods Indirect Domestic Value Added)

HOS Manufacturing Sectors	Total, All Countries	Developed Countries				Less Developed Countries[a]				
		Total	Japan	Singapore and Hong Kong	Other DCs	Total	ASEAN Except Singapore	South Korea and Taiwan	Socialist Countries	Other LDCs
All Sectors in Tradable Classification										
Exportable sectors										
Per DVA	1,990	1,989	1,270	2,092	2,129	1,975	2,865	2,864	2,234	1,221
Per IVA	2,060	2,056	1,175	1,937	2,188	2,093	2,240	1,676	1,894	2,154
Import-competing sectors										
Per DVA	1,038	998	816	1,142	1,057	1,171	1,122	964	1,276	1,184
Per IVA	1,245	1,208	1,103	1,699	1,183	1,447	1,213	1,318	1,744	1,264
Processed NRB Sectors Excluded										
Exportable sectors										
Per DVA	1,514	1,503	1,241	1,916	1,425	1,932	2,242	1,295	1,978	2,081
Per IVA	1,623	1,625	1,057	1,847	1,533	1,711	1,588	1,528	1,811	1,378
Import-competing sectors										
Per DVA	960	961	749	1,140	1,016	924	1,108	835	951	1,036
Per IVA	1,222	1,224	1,115	1,696	1,194	1,143	1,731	1,188	1,231	1,099

Source: Same as table 5.11.

[a]Including socialist countries.

measure used. With processed NRB industries excluded, the estimated capital/labor ratios of imports range from four to eighteen times that of exports. Imports also embody 65 percent more skill-days than exports and more than three times as many skill-days per man-day of direct labor, a result not significantly altered by the exclusion of processed NRB sectors.

Table 5.18 provides the data needed for bilateral tests of the HOS propositions with respect to the net factor content of trade. There it is seen that for all nine trade destinations and origins specified Indonesia is a net exporter of labor. For all three measures of capital Indonesia is a net importer of capital in trade with all nine destinations, with the sole exception of the electricity consumption measure in trade with socialist countries. In addition, Indonesia is a net importer of skill-days from eight of nine trading areas, socialist countries again being the exception. When processed NRB industries are excluded from the calculations, the results are nearly the same as those based on the full set of HOS tradable sectors; however, the two exceptions noted above disappear.

The results including both direct and indirect labor requirements and value added at international prices are found in table 5.17. There it may be seen that exports embody more labor than competing imports regardless of the inclusion or exclusion of processed NRB sectors. Bilateral tests using all HOS manufacturing sectors yield similar results for trade with both developed and less developed countries but, if raw-material-based sectors are excluded, not for trade with Japan and ASEAN countries except Singapore.

5.5   Factor Proportions and the Height of Protection

In this section the influence of the trade regime on the commodity composition of trade is examined. If the levels of protection provided vary among industries, the commodity composition of trade, and hence its factor composition, are likely to be affected.

To test this proposition, we again aggregate importable industries by three levels of protection. It would be expected that, the closer an industry lies to Indonesia's comparative advantage, the less protection is needed to enable it to produce domestically. Thus it is expected that least-protected industries would be the least capital- and skill-intensive.

Factor requirements data for each of the three groups are presented in table 5.19, weighted in the same manner as direct factor requirements. Note that the only direct absolute factor requirement that changes monotonically over the three groups is skill-days. But two capital-labor ratios, electricity per man-day and energy per man-day, rise monotonically. It is interesting that industries with medium protection have the greatest absolute labor and capital requirements (by every measure).

Table 5.18   Direct Factor Requirements per Unit of IVA by Trade Destination or Origin (per Million Rupiahs of International Value Added)

Trade Origin or Destination	Total Man-Days (a)	(b)	Skill-Days (a)	(b)	Horsepower (a)	(b)	Electricity (Kwh) (a)	(b)	Energy (Rp 000) (a)	(a)
Exportable HOS Manufacturing Sectors										
Developed countries	2,229	1,750	1,800	1,928	6.99	4.65	4,352	6,113	30.47	21.06
Japan	1,273	1,119	1,693	1,639	6.33	5.77	3,038	3,274	25.43	26.56
Singapore and Hong Kong	2,077	2,003	2,174	2,255	3.72	3.65	8,351	8,517	17.95	13.90
Other DCs	2,372	1,653	1,653	1,730	8.41	5.23	2,832	4,759	36.13	25.50
Less developed countries	2,257	1,856	2,043	1,961	6.98	5.03	4,762	6,648	16.81	18.50
ASEAN except Singapore	2,494	1,737	1,627	1,366	7.88	5.28	1,612	2,848	30.08	30.28
South Korea and Taiwan	1,792	1,624	746	1,108	6.33	11.17	721	903	13.58	28.99
Socialist countries	2,082	1,962	2,286	2,280	5.20	4.39	7,771	8,628	13.16	13.51
Other LDCs	2,528	1,486	1,899	1,106	10.30	6.25	615	1,589	16.57	30.54
Import-Competing HOS Manufacturing Sectors										
Developed countries	1,124	1,127	3,172	3,395	39.71	41.75	13,069	14,398	215.41	231.14
Japan	983	982	3,231	3,411	33.02	34.00	15,409	16,650	256.64	272.90
Singapore and Hong Kong	1,624	1,620	3,851	3,863	43.31	43.46	15,725	15,788	233.45	233.83
Other DCs	1,130	1,129	3,018	3,292	43.40	46.69	11,105	12,596	185.72	202.20
Less developed countries	1,345	1,015	1,960	2,594	24.25	30.75	10,309	17,652	209.28	292.61
ASEAN except Singapore	1,081	1,268	1,814	3,446	25.12	33.76	5,455	16,336	187.36	460.11
South Korea and Taiwan	998	825	2,164	2,268	26.91	28.70	20,141	22,319	343.13	366.65
Socialist countries	1,669	1,074	1,950	2,459	21.35	28.66	7,710	11,988	192.07	224.68
Other LDCs	1,211	968	1,976	2,823	27.84	37.57	13,661	26,463	152.55	216.04

Source: Author's computations as described in text.

Note: Col. a: All sectors in tradable classification.

col. b: Processed NRB sectors excluded.

Table 5.19 **Direct Factor Requirements per Unit of DVA and Height of Protection**

Factor Requirements	Exportables	Importables		
		All HOS Imports	With Lowest Protection	With Medium Protection	With Highest Protection
	Per Million Rupiahs of Domestic Value Added			
Total man-days	2,175	1,038	1,130	1,326	752
Skill-days	1,175	1,451	1,225	1,200	1,958
Total horsepower	7.23	17.66	27.20	24.74	6.26
Electric motor horsepower	2.46	7.99	7.35	17.43	2.05
Electricity (kwh)	2,386	3,886	3,105	5,524	3,791
Energy (Rp 000)	44.59	91.42	81.85	103.19	90.84
Electricity per man-day	1.10	3.74	2.75	4.17	5.04
Skill-days per man-day	0.54	1.40	1.08	1.02	2.60
Energy (Rp) per man-day	20.50	88.07	72.43	77.82	120.80
	Ratios of LDC to DC Factor Requirements[a]			
Total man-days		1.184	1.024	1.104	1.115
Skill-days		0.789	0.999	0.711	0.863
Total horsepower		0.759	0.928	0.343	1.137
Electric motor horsepower		0.366	0.288	0.198	1.237
Electricity (kwh)		0.614	0.182	0.343	1.819
Energy (Rp 000)		0.996	0.859	0.985	1.157

Source: Author's computations as described in text.

[a]More precisely, ratios of factor requirements of products competing with imports from LDCs to factor requirements of products competing with imports from DCs.

Most-protected industries, which might be expected to be inefficient, nevertheless seem to use both less labor and less capital to produce one million rupiahs of DVA than do the other groups.[32] However, the correct measure of efficiency would be in terms of factor requirements per unit of IVA, because otherwise the inefficiency of highly protected industries is disguised by their inflated domestic value added. Using this measure (see table 5.20), note that the most-protected industries use more labor, skills, and capital (by two out of the three measures) than do other import-competing sectors. Exportables use by far the most labor, but they use much smaller inputs of capital than any importable group.

An explanation is possible for the odd behavior of some of the factor proportions data of table 5.19. The least-protected group is composed of only six industries, which include two capital goods industries, electrical machinery and apparatus (109) and shipbuilding, boatbuilding, and repairing (114), as well as one activity on the margin of being noncompeting, fertilizer (84). These industries are very capital-intensive according to our capital proxy measures and, because their volume of trade is large, they carry a heavy weight in the factor requirement computation. It also seems likely that in the case of electrical machinery and shipbuilding imported commodities may differ substantially from domestically produced commodities. Therefore the data for the least-protected group should be viewed with caution. For the most-protected group, it appears likely that the capital measures, particularly horse-power, are poor measures of real capital services provided to the activities involved. For example, the horsepower (and other capital) requirements in the drug, motor vehicle assembly, cosmetics, cigarettes, and storage and dry battery industries are very low compared with their relative capital intensity in other countries. Probably the capital requirements data available do not adequately measure the more complex types of capital used in these industries. The same may be true for all activities; thus my capital requirements estimates generally should be viewed with some caution.

As would be expected, table 5.19 shows that capital requirements of products competing with LDCs are lower than capital requirements of products competing with DCs for both medium- and least-protected sectors. The difference is particularly striking for the electric motor horsepower and electricity consumption measures, which represent more sophisticated capital than the other measures. The contrary results for the most-protected industries are perhaps also due to the inadequacy of the capital proxies used in measuring the flow of real capital services to these sectors.

It is also of interest to check whether new investment by activity is related to the height of protection. Table 5.21 presents data on fixed capital formation obtained from manufacturing surveys, which, though limited to two years, permit some tentative observations to be made. The data indicate that in 1972–73 fixed capital formation per unit of DVA in import-competing sectors was 24 percent higher than in exportable sectors. The difference in capital formation between least-

Table 5.20   Direct Factor Requirements per Unit of IVA and Height of Protection (per Million Rupiahs of International Value Added)

Factor Requirements	Exportable Sectors	All HOS Import-Competing Sectors	Import-Competing Sectors With Lowest Protection	With Medium Protection	With Highest Protection
Total man-days	2,230	1,159	373	1,565	1,794
Skill-days	1,809	2,983	721	2,250	7,780
Total horsepower	6.99	37.30	28.59	49.22	32.77
Electric motor horsepower	2.53	23.39	17.83	37.63	10.15
Electricity (kwh)	4,367	12,639	10,139	10,673	19,746
Energy (Rp 000)	29.97	214.45	85.46	185.14	468.54

Source: Author's computations as described in text.

Table 5.21   Fixed Capital Formation, 1972–73, and Height of Protection

Tradable Group	New Fixed Capital Formation per Unit of Domestic Value Added
Exportables	.250
Excluding rubber milling (94)[a]	.216
Import-competing	.310
Sectors with lowest protection	.300
Excluding fertilizer (84) and electrical machinery (109)	.194
Sectors with medium protection	.303
Sectors with highest protection	.228
Excluding cigarettes (65)	.284
Negative IVA sectors	.498

Source: Biro Pusat Statistik, Statistik industri (1972, 1973).
[a]Numbers refer to input-output code.

protected and medium-protected sectors is not very striking. If the fertilizer (84) and electrical machinery (109) industries are excluded from least-protected groups, the rate of capital formation falls markedly. Rice milling predominates in the remaining figure. Most-protected industries have a lower rate of capital formation than both least- and medium-protected industries. Since they are unable to export, growth in these industries is constrained by the size of the domestic market. Some of the largest industries in the group—cigarettes and motor vehicles, for example—also have new capital formation strictly controlled or prohibited by the government investment board.

Industries with negative IVA are found to have the highest rate of fixed capital formation among all groups investigated. Since negative IVA implies that domestic production is absolutely inefficient, the indication is that the trade regime is providing above-average incentives to the least desirable activities.

5.6 Summary and Conclusions

In examining the factor requirements of bundles of manufactured tradables containing one million rupiahs of DVA, it was found that HOS exportable manufacturing industries required twice as much labor as importable industries but substantially less capital and skills. When trade was partitioned between developed and less developed countries for origins and destinations, it was not possible to conclude definitively that Indonesian exportable production destined for DCs had a lower capital-labor ratio than that bound for LDCs, although the evidence pointed in that direction. The reason for the ambiguity hinged on inadequate proxies for capital and the question of how trade with Hong Kong and Singapore should be treated. However, in every case skill-labor ratios were lower for exports to DCs than to LDCs. Second, my results did indicate that the capital-labor ratio of imports from developed countries exceeded that of imports from less developed countries.

In comparing the factor requirements of baskets of tradables containing equal quantities of value added at international prices, it was found that Indonesia was clearly a net exporter of labor and net importer of capital and skills in her trade in HOS manufactures; when trade was partitioned between developed and less developed countries, the above result still held in every case.

The results above hold irrespective of whether factor requirements are measured by direct or direct plus home goods indirect coefficients.

An examination of the height of protection and factor proportions found that when importable activities were partitioned into three groups based on their effective protection, capital/labor ratios were higher (by two of three measures) the greater the effective protection afforded the group. The most-protected industries used only 61 percent of the labor of all least-protected industries, though industries with medium protection used more labor than least-protected industries.

Eleven out of fifteen HOS manufacturing sectors that had negative rates of protection were exportable sectors, and on average HOS exportables received negative effective protection. On the other hand, substantial protection was afforded importable industries. Indeed, eight HOS importable industries were found to have negative international value added. Noncompeting importables had low ERPs. Thus the incentive system was definitely biased against exports and favored importable industries.

An important result of this research is an estimate of the employment trade-off implicit in Indonesia's choice of trade strategy. It has been noted that, since the conclusion of a period of dramatic trade liberalization in 1971, the Indonesian trade regime has tended to become more restrictive. In particular, levels of protection seem to have increased recently in response to emerging excess capacity in certain industries. The employment cost of following an import substitution strategy in Indonesia is severe. One million dollars of increased value added from manufactured exports generates 57 percent more employment than an equivalent reduction in competing imports. If manufactured exports were to increase by 15 percent per year, a rate of growth that should be readily attainable,[33] the employment necessary to produce these exports would rise from its 1971 level of 374,000 full-time equivalents to almost 1.7 million by 1981. This increase would be enough to employ about 11 percent of the projected growth in the labor force over that period.

Appendix

Table 5.A.1   Protection in Indonesian Manufacturing, 1971

Input-Output Code	Sector	Nominal Protection $(pd/pw - 1) \times 100$	Effective Protection $(DVA/IVA - 1) \times 100$	Trade Classification
45	Canning and preserving of meat	5.0%	50.0%	HOS-MC
46	Dairy products	74.0	Neg. IVA	HOS-MC
47	Canning and preserving of fruits and vegetables	80.0	5,400.0	HOS-MC
48	Canning and preserving of fish and other seafoods	0	1.0	HOS-X
49	Coconut oil and cooking oil	−10.0	67.8	HOS-X
50	Vegetable and animal oils and fats	−10.0	−12.3	HOS-X
51	Rice milling, cleaning, and polishing	−13.0	−14.7	HOS-MC
52	Wheat flour and other grain mill products	−18.0	471.8	HOS-MC
53	Dried cassava and tapioca flour	−10.0	−19.0	HOS-X
54	Bread and bakery products	89.1	Neg. IVA	HOS-MC
55	Noodles, macaroni, and similar products	0	35.4	HOS-MC
56	Sugar refining	26.0	52.7	HOS-MC
57	Cocoa, chocolate, and sugar confectionery	29.8	154.3	HOS-MC
58	Coffee grinding	−15.0	−18.7	HOS-X
59	Tea processing	0	0.4	HOS-X
60	Soybean products	0	24.9	HOS-MC
61	Other food products n.e.c.	10.9	35.8	HOS-MC
62	Alcoholic beverages	38.1	92.6	HOS-MC
63	Soft drinks and carbonated water	67.0	1,172.7	HOS-MC
64	Processed tobacco	−10.0	−27.0	HOS-X

Table 5.A.1—continued

Input-Output Code	Sector	Nominal Protection $(pd/pw - 1) \times 100$	Effective Protection $(DVA/IVA - 1) \times 100$	Trade Classification
65	Cigarettes	81.7	555.8	HOS-MC
66	Spinning industries	− 7.6	134.3	HOS-MC
67	Weaving industries	44.3	Neg. IVA	HOS-MC
68	Textile bleaching, printing, dyeing, and finishing, excluding batik	10.0	22.2	HOS-MC
69	Batik industries	0	−37.9	HOS-X
70	Knitting industries	75.0	Neg. IVA	HOS-MC
71	Made-up textile goods, excluding wearing apparel	78.3	Neg. IVA	HOS-MC
72	Wearing apparel, excluding footwear	55.3	198.6	HOS-MC
73	Carpets, rugs, ropes, and other	34.9	Neg. IVA	HOS-MC
74	Tanneries and leather finishing	0	− 4.4	HOS-X
75	Leather products, excluding footwear industries	0	− 9.6	HOS-X
76	Footwear of leather	63.4	180.8	HOS-MC
77	Sawmills, planing, and other wood processing	0	.5	HOS-X
78	Wood and cork products	0	− 1.9	HOS-X
79	Furniture and fixtures, excluding those primarily of metal	32.2	353.3	HOS-MC
80	Pulp, paper, and cardboard	30.4	67.0	HOS-MC
81	Paper products	44.1	72.2	HOS-MC
82	Printing, publishing, and allied industries	25.0	42.1	HOS-MC
83	Basic industrial chemicals, excluding fertilizers	8.1	18.6	HOS-NC
84	Fertilizers and pesticides	0	− 8.9	HOS-MC
85	Paints, varnishes, and lacquers	65.0	297.4	HOS-MC
86	Drugs and medicines	37.4	107.2	HOS-MC
87	Soap and cleaning preparations	41.3	701.0	HOS-MC

Table 5.A.1—*continued*

Input-Output Code	Sector	Nominal Protection $(pd/pw - 1) \times 100$	Effective Protection $(DVA/IVA - 1) \times 100$	Trade Classification
88	Cosmetics	38.8	143.8	HOS-MC
89	Matches	76.6	317.6	HOS-MC
90	Other chemical industries	27.9	Neg. IVA	HOS-MC
91	Petroleum refining	−12.0	Unclassified	Unclassified
92	Other petroleum and coal industries	− 6.0	Unclassified	Unclassified
93	Tires and tubes	57.0	Neg. IVA	HOS-MC
94	Smoking and remilling of rubber	−11.0	−11.7	HOS-X
95	Other rubber products	31.2	194.9	HOS-MC
96	Plasticware	34.0	129.0	HOS-MC
97	Ceramics and earthenwares	64.0	189.2	HOS-MC
98	Glass and glass products	40.8	92.5	HOS-MC
99	Structural clay products	46.4	90.2	HOS-MC
100	Cement	21.5	159.0	HOS-MC
101	Other nonmetallic mineral products	36.3	104.7	HOS-MC
102	Iron and steel	4.3	7.2	HOS-NC
103	Nonferrous basic metals	0	0	NRB-X
104	Cutlery, hand tools, and general hardware	27.9	77.0	HOS-MC
105	Furniture and fixtures, primarily of metal	21.0	69.9	HOS-MC
106	Structural metal products	13.0	29.8	HOS-MC
107	Other fabricated metal products	18.6	50.1	HOS-MC
108	Nonelectrical machinery	4.7	5.3	HOS-NC
109	Electrical machinery and apparatus	12.8	16.3	HOS-MC
110	Radio, television, and communication equipment and apparatus	46.8	217.0	HOS-NC

Table 5.A.1—*continued*

Input-Output Code	Sector	Nominal Protection $(pd/pw - 1) \times 100$	Effective Protection $(DVA/IVA - 1) \times 100$	Trade Classification
111	Electrical appliances and housewares	44.8	96.4	HOS-NC
112	Accumulator and dry battery industries	47.0	193.1	HOS-MC
113	Other electrical apparatus and supplies and repairing	12.7	10.3	HOS-NC
114	Ship and boat building and repairing	4.7	1.5	HOS-MC
115	Railroad equipment	.2	− 3.5	HOS-NC
116	Motor vehicles	110.0	525.7	HOS-MC
117	Motorcycles, bicycles, and other vehicles	55.8	204.3	HOS-MC
118	Repairing of motorized and nonmotorized vehicles	Home good	Home good	Home good
119	Aircraft	9.6	− 1.9	HOS-NC
120	Professional and scientific equipment	8.3	18.4	HOS-NC
121	Photographic and optical goods	13.8	16.1	HOS-NC
122	Watches and clocks	59.1	Nonproduced	HOS-NC
123	Jewelry and related articles	21.5	101.2	HOS-MC
124	Musical instruments	41.0	151.1	HOS-NC
125	Sporting and athletic goods	48.4	419.9	HOS-MC
126	Other manufacturing industries	0	−13.3	HOS-X
172	Kretek (clove cigarettes)	0	−23.1	HOS-X
173	Other nonproduced manufacturing	38.0	Nonproduced	HOS-NC

Note: HOS-MC = Heckscher-Ohlin-Samuelson import-competing tradable.
HOS-NC = Heckscher-Ohlin-Samuelson noncompeting importable.
HOS-X = Heckscher-Ohlin-Samuelson exportable.
NRB-X = Natural resource based exportable.

Table 5.A.2   **Labor Requirements, Trade Patterns, and Wages in Indonesian Manufacturing, 1971**

Industry Code[a]	Labor Requirements (Man-Days per Million Rupiahs of DVA) Direct	Direct plus Indirect	Wages per Man-Day (Rupiahs)	Trade[b] with DCs (Millions of Rupiahs)	Trade[b] with DCs (%)
Exportables					
48	1,335	1,256	124	667	98
49	792	788	360	4,713	100
50	600	602	500	19,633	98
53	2,462	2,149	142	5,861	100
58	3,876	3,212	220	20,496	95
59	3,715	4,008	135	11,227	99
64	4,057	3,624	91	5,810	98
69	3,261	2,920	160	392	91
74	940	919	295	2,086	93
75	2,161	2,028	195	24	100
77	1,023	999	415	691	95
78	5,000	4,331	125	357	83
94	2,300	2,119	270	98,263	96
126	2,235	2,109	160	2,179	94
172	715	708	184	4	100
Importables					
45	514	516	260	180	80
46	128	178	731	8,147	99
47	1,615	1,510	296	214	38
51	1,150	1,123	259	20,083	69
52	104	243	768	4,782	100
54	2,066	2,150	235	295	83
55	2,688	2,606	210	0	0
56	1,571	1,556	194	1,317	15
57	626	627	294	171	62
60	3,253	3,085	142	948	95
61	1,747	1,631	196	1,490	97
62	156	235	1,086	1,004	91
63	245	294	609	268	89
65	52	104	1,179	48	96
66	304	375	575	8,712	49
67	870	847	259	14,915	75
68	825	792	291	0	0
70	2,105	1,910	162	324	81
71	1,358	1,334	213	1,070	82
72	1,990	1,951	346	960	79
73	1,546	1,440	253	2,670	56
76	845	840	295	134	89

Table 5.A.2—*continued*

Industry Code[a]	Labor Requirements (Man-Days per Million Rupiahs of DVA)		Wages per Man-Day (Rupiahs)	Trade[b] with DCs (Millions of Rupiahs)	Trade[b] with DCs (%)
	Direct	Direct plus Indirect			
79	3,894	3,669	225	227	76
80	290	313	698	11,549	79
81	178	196	994	741	87
82	1,406	1,362	326	12,984	97
84	116	209	943	13,824	99
85	517	319	537	*	100
86	243	315	390	6,556	92
87	468	475	570	731	78
88	504	522	691	1,599	82
89	2,566	2,433	157	4	83
90	806	778	281	6,122	96
93	241	297	713	3,485	97
95	1,067	1,045	180	1,802	96
96	1,902	1,752	200	3,045	89
97	452	799	561	1,379	61
98	650	1,064	340	2,860	72
99	3,240	3,139	160	857	92
100	133	833	920	5,355	66
101	2,840	2,817	195	1,298	98
104	1,149	1,108	244	2,252	87
105	1,200	1,145	319	1,657	94
106	170	201	561	8,866	99
107	1,115	1,092	329	11,835	89
109	132	208	910	23,014	95
112	526	537	445	1,892	64
114	488	491	1,016	606	98
116	440	457	822	65,016	99
117	134	157	492	7,916	76
123	3,000	2,796	160	459	100
125	1,546	1,429	210	257	97

Source: Pitt 1977.
*Less than 0.5 million rupiahs.
[a]See table 5.A.1 for name of each industry.
[b]Trade refers to exports for exportables and imports for importables.

Notes

1. For a complete review of Indonesian economic development, see Booth and McCawley (1980) and the "Survey of Recent Developments" found in each issue of the *Bulletin of Indonesian Economic Studies*.

2. The Jakarta cost-of-living index is presented in table 5.10.

3. Determining the value of Indonesia's manufactured exports is complicated by the problem of defining a "manufactured" export and by the problem of reexport. A recent analysis by Arndt (1977) of the Indonesian trade minister's claim that 1976 industrial exports totaled $220 million is an enlightening example. After eliminating processed goods such as sawn timber, vegetable oils, and crumb rubber, Arndt noted that much of the SITC classification "manufactured goods" was accounted for by tin, unwrought and in bars, and most of the $53.2 million of "machinery and transportation equipment" consisted of reexport. The items that he claims can plausibly be considered manufactured exports totaled only $9.6 million out of $2.4 billion in nonoil exports in 1976.

4. The data also indicate that females accounted for most of the increase in manufacturing employment over this period.

5. There are some serious pitfalls in comparing Indonesian census data over time. Gavin Jones (1978) provides a number of alternative measures of employment growth by making various corrections to the census data.

6. This phenomenon was first examined by Papanek (1974).

7. The data suffer from a number of weaknesses. First, average manufacturing wages may have changed because the commodity composition of manufacturing changed somewhat over this period. Second, because of the highly variable rates of capacity utilization over the period, the data may not represent "payment per year of labor services," since employees may have worked part time. The problem of payment in kind does not appear important because the data supposedly include such payment valued at market prices. The problem of manufacturing's changing commodity mix was partially resolved by calculating real wages for one manufacturing subsector (textiles). As a whole, the textile real wage demonstrates the same downward slide as manufacturing except for a larger decline in textile wages in 1965–67. This drop may represent the extremely low levels of capacity utilization of those years.

8. This is also true for a time series on household servant wages in Jakarta. Papanek (1974, p. 12) notes that real wages on estates in 1938 were probably 15 percent higher than in any subsequent year.

9. However, aid foreign exchange (Devisa Kredit) continued to receive a special rate of Rp 326 until December 1970.

10. The price-level deflator is the cost-of-living index for a government worker in Jakarta linked with the sixty-two-item Jakarta cost-of-living index.

11. The ratio of the black-market rate to the EER_x may not be a good indicator of the EER_x's overvaluation for at least two reasons. For one thing, pressure on the black-market rate may come from a desire to export capital abroad when it is legally prohibited. In the case of Indonesia, the leaps in the black-market rate in late 1959 and early 1960 were in part due to severe government actions against Chinese entrepreneurs, which resulted in a surge of Indo-Chinese capital out of the country. Second, the black-market rate reflects exchange restrictions not only on exports but also on imports. Given an EER for exports, the black-market rate would be higher the greater the restrictions on imports.

12. A theory of smuggling that explains the simultaneous existence of legal trade, smuggling, and price disparity is found in Pitt (1978). The theory presented there considers legal trade and smuggling as activities carried out by the same firms. A large share of smuggling takes the form of misinvoiced, misgraded, and misweighed legal trade. The greater the legal export, the easier it is to hide smuggling from enforcement agencies and therefore the less costly smuggling will be. Thus legal trade can be viewed as an input into the smuggling activity. Price

disparity exists because firms will bid the price of the smuggled commodity above its legal trade return as long as profit can be made in combined smuggling and legal trade.

13. Lee and Pitt (1978) found that new weaving firms in Indonesia are much more capital-intensive than older firms. The newest quintile of firms in their sample had a capital/labor ratio two and one-half times as great as the oldest quintile of firms and 31 percent greater than average.

14. The table also serves as the basis for the sectoral disaggregation of the employment calculations that follow. It should be noted that the 171-sector input-output table for Indonesia used in this research is not identical to that published by the Biro Pusat Statistik (1976). In the published 175-sector table, small-scale agriculture processing activities are considered separate sectors or are aggregated into the NRB agricultural activity.

15. Had the data been available, price comparisons would have been used to check nominal protection estimates in all sectors.

16. Large quantities of cloves ($30.4 million in 1971) are imported for use in the kretek (clove cigarette) industry.

17. MPO is the acronym for *menghitung pajak orang-lain*, literally, "to count the tax of another person." The name is derived from the fact that the seller of a taxed commodity usually withholds the tax on behalf of the purchaser.

18. Richard and Peggy Musgrave, in an unpublished memorandum, provide the following analysis:
"Assume that for a firm the only cost is the price of merchandise purchased. The profits tax T equals:

$$T = tP - Z$$

where P is profits, t the profit tax rate, and Z the MPO credit claimed. Furthermore, assume that profits are estimated by a margin m on sales S, so

$$P = mS,$$

and that sales are determined as a markup u on cost C, so

$$S = (1 + u)C.$$

Cost can be presumptively determined on the basis of Z, so that

$$C = Z/g$$

where g is the MPO tax rate. Thus, substituting and solving for T, one obtains

$$T = t\left(\frac{m(1 + u)}{g} - 1\right)Z$$

and since

$$u = \frac{m}{1 - m} \text{ then } T = t\left[\frac{m(1 + m/1 - m)}{g} - 1\right]Z$$

When $g = .02$, the term in the brackets is positive when m exceeds 1.96 percent. Since m would typically be above that, the tax increases with Z and the firm would decrease its tax liability by underreporting Z its MPO credit."

19. The special exchange rates for cotton and weaving yarn have been adjusted since 1970 as follows:

Beginning Date	Raw Cotton Exchange Rate per U.S. $1	Exchange Rate of General Foreign Exchange per U.S. $1
3 July 1969	Rp 170	Rp 326
23 Feb. 1971	Rp 215	Rp 378
18 Jan. 1972	Rp 271	Rp 415

Weaving Yarn Ex-PL 480

Beginning Date	*Exchange Rate per U.S. $1*	*Exchange Rate of General Foreign Exchange per U.S. $1*
5 July 1969	Rp 125	Rp 326
3 May 1972	Rp 150	Rp 415

20. The rebate schedule was as follows:

Country of Origin	*Rebate per U.S. $1*
United States and Canada	Rp 60
Netherlands, West Germany, France, Belgium, and the United Kingdom	Rp 40
Australia and New Zealand	Rp 30
Untied aid foreign exchange from United States	Rp 30
Japan	Rp 20

21. These categories accounted for nearly 20 percent of imports (excluding imports of oil companies) in fiscal year 1971/72.

22. This does not imply that underinvoicing does not occur, only that it does not seem to bias the estimates. Special costs associated with illegal transactions, such as side payments to customs officials, may be offsetting the benefits of undervaluation.

23. Textile bleaching, printing, dyeing, and finishing except batik (68), a sector for which there is no trade attributed by the 1971 input-output table, is nonetheless considered a tradable. The absence of any reported trade in the sector is attributable to the inflexibility of the trade statistics. All textiles, printed and dyed or not, enter as weaving sector imports with no attribution of the printing and dyeing activity to that sector. The sector is considered import-competing because it is protected both by higher tariffs on the import of dyed and printed textiles relative to undyed and unprinted textiles and because there are prohibitions on the import of certain varieties of textiles only if they are printed.

24. Examination of trade data for years adjacent to 1971 indicates that railroad and aircraft equipment imports in 1971 were less than average and that those sectors should be classified as noncompeting imports rather than import-competing. Fertilizer had a 1971 value of T that was borderline, 0.81, and in light of rapidly growing productive capacity in this sector, fertilizer was classified as import-competing.

25. Traditionally, a substantial share of of crudely milled Indonesian rubber has been exported to Singapore for remilling and reexport. However, prohibitions on the export of lower grades of rubber, in effect in 1971, diverted most rubber exports through the smoking and remilling sector.

26. It is not clear to which trade classification petroleum refining would belong. Most exports are refined by-products for which sufficient market does not exist in Indonesia, while imports consist of more basic products such as kerosene. According to Johnson (1977, p. 43), most of the refined exports consist of low-sulfur waxy residue. With trade in petroleum products under the control of the state petroleum monopoly, PERTAMINA, it may be that, under an efficient pattern of resource allocation, the value of T might be positive rather than marginally negative.

27. The survey is the *Survey Perusahaan Industri 1973.* Man-days were calculated in the following manner: firms reported the number of days they were in operation during each quarter and the number of employees at the middle of each

quarter, and the two figures were multiplied and summed over the four quarters. The detailed employment data were coded from firm questionnaires for this research. Aggregated data from the survey were published as Biro Pusat Statistik *Statistik Industri 1973* (2 vols.), Jakarta 1975.

28. Because part-time operatives may be more prevalent than part-time white-collar employees, the first assumption may not be strictly true and operative man-days may be overestimated, but not consequentially.

29. These weights are chosen because it is felt that increments in manufacturing value added would be more in proportion to the sectoral composition of consumption than production. The factor requirements calculations therefore represent requirements for incremental units of domestic value added.

30. Even if trade via Singapore and Hong Kong were not of an entrepôt nature, it would not be a misspecification to label them developed countries, since only the correct ranking of countries by factor endowments is of concern. Classified as LDCs, Singapore and Hong Kong would likely be the best capital-endowed among them; if classified as DCs they would be among the least well-endowed. Since Indonesia is near the bottom of a capital-intensity ranking, its position is of no importance here. Therefore Singapore and Hong Kong can be considered developed countries for both import and export trade. Any significant change in the results for imports that would come about by considering them as LDCs will be noted.

31. Although this difference is small, the variance of these sectoral labor coefficients is also small.

32. This might possibly be explained by the presence of large economic profits earned by firms in these oligopolistic sectors.

33. A 15 percent rate of growth of manufactured exports is small relative to the rate of growth projected by "The Study of Long-Term Growth Perspectives" supervised by the Indonesian minister of state for research and reported in Sumitro Djojohadikusumo (1977, p. 26). They estimated a growth rate of manufactured exports of 39.2 percent per annum over the period 1974–80 and 25.2 percent over 1980–85. Since they define manufactured exports much more narrowly than here, their projections are not applicable.

References

Arndt, H. W. 1977. Survey of recent developments. *Bulletin of Indonesian Economic Studies* 13 (3):1–33.

Arndt, H. W., and Sundrum, R. M. 1975. Wage problems and policies in Indonesia. *International Labour Review* 112 (5):369–87.

Bank Indonesia. *Bank Indonesia report.* Annual. Jakarta.

————. *Indonesian financial statistics.* Monthly. Jakarta.

————. *Report for the financial year.* Annual. Jakarta.

Biro Pusat Statistik (BPS). 1963. *Sensus penduduk 1961* (Series S, P. II). Jakarta.

————. 1967. *Angkatan kerdja penduduk Indonesia (Ringkasan)* (Survey Social Ekonomi Nasional Tahap Kedua Laporan no. 2A). Jakarta.

————. 1969. *Almanak Indonesia 1968*. 2 vols. Jakarta: BPS.

————. 1974. *Survey industri kecil dan kerajinan rumah tangga, Januari–April 1973*. Jakarta: BPS.

————. 1975. *Penduduk Indonesia* (series D). Jakarta.

————. 1976. *Tabel input-output Indonesia*. 2 vols. Jakarta: BPS.

————. 1976–77. *Industri/kerajinan rumah tangga* (Sensus industri 1974–75). 4 vols. Jakarta: BPS.

————. N.d. *Impor: Menurut jenis barang dan negeri asal*. Annual; title varies. Jakarta: BPS.

————. N.d. *Ekspor: Menurut jenis barang, negeri asal dan pelabuhan ekspor*. Annual; title varies. Jakarta: BPS.

————. N.d. *Pendapatan nasional Indonesia*. Serial; irregular. Jakarta: BPS.

————. N.d. *Statistik industri*. Annual since 1970. Jakarta: BPS.

————. N.d. *Statistical pocketbook of Indonesia*. Annual. Jakarta: BPS.

Booth, Anne, and McCawley, Peter. 1980. *The Indonesian economy during the Soeharto era*. Kuala Lumpur: Oxford University Press.

Business News (also known as *Business News Analisa*). Newspaper. Jakarta.

Cnossen, Sijbren. 1973. *The Indonesian sales tax*. Deventer, Netherlands: Kluwer.

Commodity yearbook. Annual New York: Commodity Research Bureau, Inc.

Cooper, Richard N. 1974. Tariffs and smuggling in Indonesia. In *Illegal transactions in international trade*, ed. Jagdish Bhagwati. Amsterdam: North-Holland.

Grenville, S. A. 1977. Survey of recent developments. *Bulletin of Indonesian Economic Studies* 13(1):1–32.

Johnson, Mark. 1977. Oil I: Recent developments. *Bulletin of Indonesian Economic Studies* 13(3):34–48.

Jones, Gavin. 1978. Sectoral employment–output coefficients in Indonesia since 1961. *Bulletin of Indonesian Economic Studies* 14(1):80–92.

Lee, Lung-Fei, and Pitt, Mark M. 1978. *Pooling cross section and time series data in the estimation of stochastic frontier production function models*. Discussion paper no. 78-98, Center for Economic Research, Department of Economics, University of Minnesota.

McCawley, Peter, and Manning, Chris. 1976. Survey of recent developments. *Bulletin of Indonesian Economic Studies* 13(3):1.

Nugroho. 1967. *Indonesia facts and figures*. Jakarta.

Papanek, Gustav. 1974. *Real wages: The effect of growth and inflation on workers income, income distribution and labor costs*. Typescript dated 10 December, n.p.

Pitt, Mark M. 1977. Foreign trade regime. In manuscript.

————. 1978. A theory of smuggling with application to Indonesia. Mimeographed.

Siahaan, Luckman. 1969. *Export problems of Indonesia: An evaluation of the October 3, 1966 regulations.* Jakarta: National Institute of Social and Economic Research (LEKNAS), Indonesian Institute of Science (LIPI).

Simkin, C. G. F. 1970. Survey of recent developments. *Bulletin of Indonesian Economic Studies* 6(1):1–16.

Speare, Alden, Jr. 1978. Alternative population distribution policies. *Bulletin of Indonesian Economic Studies* 14(1):93–106.

Suhadi Mangkusuwondo. 1967. *Industrialization efforts in Indonesia. The role of agriculture and foreign trade in the development of the industrial sector.* Ph.D. diss., University of California, Berkeley.

Sumitro Djojohadikusumo. 1977. Strategic variables in Indonesia's long-term growth. *Ekonomi dan Keuangan Indonesia* 25(1):17–33.

Sundrum, R. M. 1975. Manufacturing employment 1969–71. *Bulletin of Indonesian Economic Studies* 12 (1):58–65.

Thomas, Kenneth. 1966. "Price disparity" in export trade. *Bulletin of Indonesian Economic Studies* 2(4):101–2.

United States Department of Commerce, Bureau of Census. 1976. *Annual survey of manufactures 1973.* Washington, D.C.: U.S. Government Printing Office.

Warta Perdagangan. Monthly magazine. Jakarta.

6   Trade Strategies and Employment in the Ivory Coast

Terry Monson

6.1 Introduction

The Ivory Coast is a small, prosperous West African coastal nation that shares borders with Ghana, Guinea, Liberia, Mali, and Upper Volta. Its prosperity is due in large part to the trade, development, and employment policies it has followed since it gained independence from France in 1960. These policies can be characterized as "open" or "liberal" in the sense that traditional natural resource based (NRB) exports have been emphasized, markets are relatively free from government intervention, protection is moderate, and foreign capital and labor inflows are encouraged. These policies have resulted in sustained economic growth, a heavy dependence upon international trade, relatively few factor market distortions, production patterns similar to those expected under free trade, and an unusual modern sector labor force in which half of the workers are either European expatriates or migrant Africans from neighboring countries.

Terry Monson is associated with Michigan Technological University.

Many individuals and organizations helped make this study possible. H. Jacques Pegatienan, director of the Centre Ivoirien de Récherche Economique et Sociale, aided in data collection and provided valuable commentary during the course of this study. The Development Research Center of the World Bank allowed the author to use its protection estimates in constructing his description of the trade regime. Steven Rinkeviczie and Gordon Hein helped compile and analyze the data. Major parts of the funding for the project are from the United States Agency for International Development, through the National Bureau of Economic Research. The Graduate School of Illinois State University (where the author was employed while most of the research was being undertaken) contributed supplementary funding. Michigan Technological University provided computer time. However, the usual disclaimer applies: the author is solely responsible for opinions and errors of omission or commission.

239

In some respects these policies are similar to those currently practiced by some of the other countries studied in this volume. They differ, however, in having been consistently applied and in their emphasis upon encouraging inflows of both capital and labor. The latter point is especially important. The Ivory Coast is not as labor-abundant as some LDCs. Historically it has been an importer of labor, both skilled expatriates and unskilled African migrants. The reasons for this migration have been a relatively low population density and an inadequate educational structure.[1]

Ivorian policies and their ensuing trade and development patterns are instructive in their own right. More important, the employment implications of these policies have never been fully analyzed. Thus I propose to examine the Ivorian pattern of trade and its effects upon employment. The focal years for the analysis are 1972–73. These years were chosen because of the availability of data and of complementary research on the trade regime.[2]

Fact Sheet: Ivory Coast
Population (1975 Census): 6,670,912
Area: 127,500 square miles
Population density: 52 persons per square mile
Capital: Abidjan
President: Felix Houphouet-Boigny
Date of independence (from France): 7 August 1960
Gross Domestic Product per capita (1976): FCFA 159,980, U.S. $680
(converted at the exchange rate current in early 1978)
Currency: Franc de la communauté financière africaine (FCFA)
Par value: FCFA 50 = French franc 1
Exchange rate on the U.S. dollar, early 1978: FCFA 235 = U.S. $1

Abbreviations Used in This Study
ACP: African, Caribbean, and Pacific (EEC associates signatory to the Lomé Treaty)
BCEAO: Banque Centrale des Etats de l'Afrique de l'Ouest
CEAO: Communauté Economique de l'Afrique de l'Ouest
EEC: European Economic Community
OCAM: Organisation Commune Africaine et Malagache
UDEAO: Union Douanière des Etats de l'Afrique de l'Ouest
UMOA: Union Monétaire Ouest Africaine

6.2 An Overview of the Ivory Coast Economy

6.2.1 Salient Features of Ivorian Growth

When the Ivory Coast became independent from France in 1960, the economy was primarily rural.[3] About 80 percent of the population resided in rural areas; natural resource based (NRB) products accounted for 43 percent of GDP, and the three major NRB exports (coffee, cocoa, and logs) generated 87 percent of export revenue. By contrast, the manufacturing sector was small and accounted for only 8 percent of GDP (see table 6.1).

Since then Ivorian growth has been phenomenal. During 1960 to 1976, real GDP quadrupled and real GDP per capita almost doubled.[4] This represented a 7.5 percent annual growth rate in real GDP and 3.5 percent in GDP per capita.[5]

Ivorian growth has been based largely upon export promotion. There was heavy emphasis upon the expansion of the three traditional NRB exports, coupled with diversification into new NRB activities (e.g.,

Table 6.1   **Selected Aggregate Data on the Ivory Coast Economy**

	1960	1972	1976
GDP (billion FCFA)			
Current prices	143	473	1,117
1970 prices[a]	203	470	687
GDP per capita (thousand FCFA)			
Current prices	38	79	160
1970 prices[a]	54	78	98
Breakdown of GDP (percentage at producers' prices)			
NRB production	43	32	32
HOS production	8	17	15
Services and others[b]	49	50	53
Exports f.o.b. (billion FCFA)	45	140	393
Percentage of GDP	32	32	35
Percentage of tradable production	70	77	80
Per capita (thousand FCFA)	12	26	56
Manufacturing output per capita (FCFA)			
Current prices	2,950	12,060	19,300
1970 prices[a]	4,195	12,000	11,910
Consumer price index (1970 = 100)			
European families	70	101	163
African families	74	109	175
Exchange rate (FCFA/U.S. $1)[c]	247	252	239
Export prices and terms of trade			
Index of prices of three major exports (1970 = 100)	90	81	215
Index of average export-import price ratio (1970 = 100)[d]	46	96	115

Source: Most data based upon information in BCEAO, "Indicateurs economiques," (various years).

[a]For lack of more appropriate price indexes, the consumer price index for African families was used to deflate GDP and manufacturing output to 1970 prices.

[b]"Others" includes construction, water, energy, mining, and transportation.

[c]The exchange rate is the trade conversion factor given in IMF, *International Financial Statistics* (various years).

[d]Index of the ratio of average export prices f.o.b. to average import prices c.i.f. with no adjustment made for changes in the composition of trade.

cotton, fruit, palm products). From 1960 to 1976, real production of NRB commodities rose by 150 percent, and the export volumes of cocoa, coffee, and logs rose by 120 percent, 110 percent, and 215 percent, respectively. Industrialization came later in the 1960s with an initial emphasis upon transforming NRB products for export (e.g., processed cocoa products, lumber, and instant coffee). Finally, in the late 1960s and early 1970s, new export and import substitution industrial activities were established. Beginning from a small base ($45 million in 1960), the real value of manufacturing output quintupled from 1960 to 1976 while its share of GDP rose from 8 to 15 percent (an average annual real growth rate of manufacturing output of 11 percent). Manufacturing sector employment quadrupled in the same period, implying an employment-output elasticity with respect to labor of 0.8.

As a consequence of these policies, the Ivorian economy has retained its rural character, as well as its dependence upon NRB exports as a basis for growth. Sixty percent of the population still resides in rural areas. Coffee, cocoa, and logs remain the major exports, together generating two-thirds of export revenues, and NRB production accounts for one-third of GDP. However, the manufacturing sector has grown and now generates more than one-fourth of exports.

6.2.2   The Structure of Ivorian Production

Production in the Ivory Coast is concentrated in informal or artisanal activities.[6] In our year of reference (1972), artisanal activity employed 88 percent of the labor force and generated one-third of GDP. It is found in nearly all lines of production but is most predominant in natural-resource-based activities. For example, all coffee and cocoa exports are grown on small peasant farms classed as artisanal activity. Artisanal activity is also found in some HOS and home goods production, although in most cases it is relatively unimportant.

Modern-sector manufacturing is relatively small, despite impressive gains in its relative size in the postindependence period. In 1972 it generated 17 percent of GDP (versus about 8 percent in 1960) and employed about 6 percent of the labor. For reasons to be enumerated later (see section 6.3), it will be the focus of most of the analysis in this study.

6.2.3   International Trade and the Ivorian Economy

Introduction

The Ivory Coast is heavily dependent upon international trade for its well-being. Since independence, exports have accounted for slightly more than one-third of GDP. The geographic pattern of trade has not changed substantially. Approximately 85 percent of its trade is with industrialized nations, the strongest ties being with France and the EEC. However, policies encouraging manufactured exports have had some effect. HOS exports rose from 5 percent of total exports at independence to 28 percent in 1976.

Ivorian trade policy has a two-pronged strategy. To encourage manufactured exports (mainly processed NRB products), there are high exit taxes on NRB exports[7] and lower exit taxes (or none at all) on manufactured exports. To encourage import substitution activities (especially in consumer goods industries), there is tariff cascading and a moderate but growing use of quotas and other nontariff barriers (see discussion in section 6.3).[8] Relative to most LDCs, however, the Ivorian trade strategy is outer-oriented, and the level of protection for import substitution industries has been fairly moderate.

Institutional Characteristics

The Ivory Coast, like most other former members of the French West African colonial federation (*Afrique Occidentale Française*), has maintained close monetary and trade relationships with France and other French West African countries. It is a member of the West African Monetary Union (UMOA).[9] France guarantees the convertibility of the UMOA currency (FCFA or *Franc de la Communauté Financière Africaine*) into French francs at a rate of FCFA 50 to the franc, while the UMOA keeps external reserves in an operations account at the French Treasury. The Ivory Coast belongs to several West African organizations aimed at promoting trade and development[10] and maintains special bilateral agreements with its major Francophone trading partners. However, these agreements have had only a marginal effect upon the direction and content of Ivorian trade.

The Composition of Trade

Table 6.2 breaks down Ivorian foreign trade by major export products and by major categories of imports in 1960, 1972, and 1976 and gives their growth rates (in nominal terms) for the postindependence period. Since the exchange rate hardly altered over the period, while the Ivorian price level was fairly stable, the real volume of trade is fairly well represented by these figures.

As mentioned above, NRB products still generate most export revenue, although their relative importance has fallen over time. Cocoa, coffee, and logs accounted for two-thirds of exports in 1976 (U.S. $1.1 billion) versus 87 percent in 1960. Tropical fruit (pineapples and bananas), cola nuts, rubber, palm kernels, and a variety of other agricultural products accounted for the remaining NRB exports.

Manufactured goods generated 28 percent of export receipts in 1976 compared with 5 percent in 1960. Their growth rate has been twice as high as that for NRB exports and reflects the emphasis upon encouraging processed NRB exports. In 1976 they were valued at about $450 million, versus about $9 million in 1960. Processed NRB exports grew from 2 to 14 percent of total exports, while the share of exports produced by activities in our importable categories (see section 6.3) rose from 3 to 14 percent in the postindependence period. In recent years,

Table 6.2   The Composition and Growth of Ivory Coast Exports and Imports

	Values, 1976 (Billion FCFA)	Compounded Annual Nominal Growth Rate, 1960–76[a]	Breakdown by Percentage of Total Trade		
			1960	1972	1976
Exports					
NRB	283.4	12.8	95.0	73.5	72.1
Cocoa	71.4	13.2	22.5	16.2	18.2
Coffee	132.8	12.4	46.6	26.4	33.8
Logs	62.4	14.0	17.6	23.3	15.9
Other NRB	16.8	9.9	8.3	7.6	4.2
HOS	109.6	27.7	5.0	26.5	27.9
Processed cocoa	19.9	*	—	3.4	5.1
Canned coffee	2.4	*	—	0.9	0.6
Canned fruit	8.1	18.6	1.2	2.5	2.1
Palm oil	7.8	*	—	1.6	2.0
Lumber, plywood	12.1	21.1	1.3	3.4	3.1
Canned fish	3.1	*	—	0.5	0.8
Refined petroleum	15.2	*	—	2.1	3.9
Other HOS	40.5	25.3	2.5	12.1	10.3
Total exports	392.5	14.7	100.0	100.0	100.0
Imports[b]					
Foodstuffs	37.4	11.1	17.7	16.2	12.0
Chemicals, plastics, rubber	29.6	14.4	9.1	8.8	9.5
Textiles	19.0	6.0	19.8	10.0	6.1
Machinery	66.1	18.8	11.1	19.6	21.2
Vehicles	45.5	10.6	18.2	12.6	14.6
Metals, metalwork	34.6	14.2	11.1	8.7	11.1
Construction material	7.5	19.0	2.1	2.6	2.4
Other[c]	72.3	60.0	10.9	21.6	23.2
Total imports	311.6	14.1	100.0	100.0	100.0

Source: Calculated from data in RCI, Ministère de l'Economie, *Statistiques du commerce exterieur* (1960, 1972), and BCEAO (1976).

[a]Asterisks (*) in the growth rate column indicate that there was no product in 1960.

[b]Imports exclude crude oil, which represented 5.3 percent of 1960 imports, 5.6 percent of 1972 imports, and 11.1 percent of 1976 imports.

[c]See note 11 for reservations regarding the size and growth rate of "other" imports.

revenue from processed NRB exports has increased more rapidly than that from other HOS and unprocessed NRB exports.

Although import growth rates have paralleled those for exports, there have been changes in their composition. For the entire postindependence period (1960–76), the most noticeable changes were decreases in the shares of foodstuffs, vehicles, and textiles, all of which are important import substitution activities, and an increase in the share of machinery imports.[11]

Direction of Trade

Approximately 85 percent of the Ivory Coast–international trade is with developed countries, mainly the EEC. However, the LDC share has increased in recent years. On the import side, the increase represents higher prices for crude oil;[12] on the export side, the increase represents larger sales of manufactures, particularly canned coffee, textiles, lumber, and petroleum.

Typically, the Ivory Coast runs a large trade deficit with France and (because of crude oil imports) with LDCs other than those in West Africa. This deficit is compensated for by surpluses with other DCs and West African LDCs. In 1976 the deficit with France was 20 billion FCFA (about U.S. $90 million), while surpluses with other DCs and West Africa were 42 billion FCFA and 15 billion FCFA (U.S. $185 million and U.S. $68 million), respectively. It is likely that this pattern of trade will continue in the near future.

Balance of Payments

Table 6.3 gives balance of payments accounts for 1963, 1972, and 1975. The principal features seen from these data are large surpluses in the Ivory Coast's merchandise trade, still larger deficits in services and unrequited transfers, and substantial capital inflows. In the postindependence period, the merchandise balance has never been negative, and other current account elements have never been positive. One of the largest elements of the service account is the transfer abroad of earnings on foreign direct investment in the Ivory Coast. Such transfers averaged FCFA 17.1 billion (U.S. $70 million) annually from 1970 to 1975. Private unrequited transfer deficits are large because they represent repatriated earnings of the foreign workers in the Ivory Coast. The deficits in the service and unrequited transfer accounts usually outweigh the trade account surplus, thus putting the current account in deficit.

The current account deficit has been offset in most years by capital inflows. In the 1960s private direct investment inflows were most significant. However, long-term borrowing, both private and governmental, has increased dramatically in recent years (IBRD 1977).

Table 6.3   Ivory Coast's Balance of Payments, 1963, 1972, and 1975 (Values in Billion FCFA)

	1963	1972	1975
Current account	−0.5	−29.7	− 82.3
Goods and services	0.5	−17.2	− 51.9
Merchandise	9.0	34.3	48.7
Services	−8.5	−51.5	−100.6
Direct investment revenue	−5.1	−14.4	− 29.3
Other services	−3.4	−37.1	− 71.3
Unrequited transfers	−1.0	−12.5	− 30.4
Private	−5.4	−20.8	− 38.1
Government	4.4	8.3	7.7
Nonmonetary capital	5.9	9.2	44.1
Direct investment	2.6	4.7	17.4
Other private long-term capital	2.1	7.2	20.2
Central government	1.2	1.2	11.3
Other	—	− 3.9	− 4.8
Errors and omissions	−1.0	0.1	2.8
Total (current account, non-monetary capital, errors and omissions)	4.4	−20.6	− 35.4

Source: IMF (1970), BCEAO (1977). Data for years before 1963 and after 1975 are not available.

Exchange System

The Ivory Coast shares a common currency with other UMOA members. Its parity of FCFA 50 to the French franc has been unchanged since independence. The FCFA-dollar rate has ranged from about FCFA 200 to FCFA 280 per dollar and is currently about FCFA 235. Effective exchange rates (EER) vary from product to product, since most NRB exports are subject to sizable exit duties, and imports are subject to varying degrees of protection (see discussion below in section 6.3). In 1972 EERs ranged from FCFA 159 per dollar (exports of cocoa) to FCFA 386 per dollar (imports of shoes).

Price level deflated effective exchange rates (PLD-EER) were relatively constant in the 1960s, since domestic inflation was moderate (about 3 percent per year) and neither nominal nor effective exchange rates fluctuated widely. PLD-EERs have decreased in recent years because of an acceleration of inflation (about 10 percent per year since 1970) and a mild appreciation of the French franc vis-à-vis the dollar.

Trade Regime

There have been three phases in Ivorian commercial policy: (*a*) the period from 1960 to 1972, during which incentives for processing of

NRB products were not extreme and most import substitution activities were accorded relatively equal and moderate protection; (*b*) the period from 1973 to mid-1975, which followed a tariff reform designed to encourage greater processing to NRB exports and production of import-competing finished consumer goods; and (*c*) 1975 to the present, in which protection has been generally increased.

Before the 1973 tariff reform, export duties averaged about 15 percent of the f.o.b. value of exports, and import duties were about 34 percent of the c.i.f. value of imports.[13] Export duties were relatively uncascaded. For example, exit duties on logs and lumber ranged from 1 to 11 percent before the reform; after the reform, logs became subject to duties ranging from 27 to 50 percent, while plywood and lumber were subject to duties of 2 and 2–15 percent, respectively. For most other exports, the exit duty on the unprocessed products remained constant, and duties on processed NRB products fell precipitously. Consequently, export duties as a percentage of f.o.b. export values fell slightly in the postreform period (from 1973 to 1976, this ratio averaged 11 percent).

In the postreform period import duties were more cascaded; this reflected an effort to promote domestic import-competing production of finished goods. For example, textiles and clothing both were subject to tariffs of approximately 20 percent until 1972; after 1972, textiles were subject to rates ranging from 20 to 30 percent and clothing to rates ranging from 30 to 45 percent.

Import restrictions increased after mid-1975. Before that time, imports from the EEC enjoyed preferential treatment by being subject to only one of the two entry duties.[14] In 1975 the Lomé Treaty renegotiated trade arrangements between the expanded EEC and its African, Caribbean, and Pacific (ACP) associates. Essentially, this treaty offered duty-free entrance of most ACP exports to the EEC and eliminated requirements for reciprocal treatment of EEC exports to ACP associates. In mid-1975 the Ivory Coast began applying both entry duties to EEC imports, thus effectively raising duties on most imports. In 1976 import duties were 38 percent of the c.i.f. import value compared with 30 percent in 1973–74. This change is one manifestation of a policy shift favoring greater protection of domestic industry. There is also a new requirement that import orders above FCFA 500,000 (about U.S. $2,000) are now subject to inspection and price comparison with similar products on the world market.[15] Another reflection is an apparent increase in the use of quantitative restrictions, particularly for textile imports.

6.2.4   The Ivory Coast Labor Market

Unlike many other LDCs, the Ivory Coast has suffered from a deficiency of labor. To meet this deficiency, it has had to rely upon migrant labor—unskilled labor from neighboring African countries (mainly Mali and Upper Volta) and skilled expatriate labor. However, labor market conditions are changing owing to a high population growth rate (4 percent per annum) and a high rural-urban migration rate.

As table 6.4 shows, population increased by 80 percent between 1960 and 1975. In the same period, urban population nearly quintupled while that of Abidjan (the capital) quintupled. The high urban population growth rate has generated a high urban unemployment rate. An approximate estimate would place such unemployment at about 25 percent today.[16]

The high population growth rate is due to a combination of high reproduction rates and migration from neighboring countries. Historically, the Ivory Coast has imported labor for employment in rural areas. The migration was due in part to a relatively low population density (about 52 per square mile versus more than 100 in neighboring Ghana, with which it has been frequently compared—e.g., Berg 1971). The current African migrant population is estimated at two million (den Tuinder 1978, pp. 6–7). Most migrants work in the agricultural sector or as unskilled labor in modern sector activities.

In addition to migrant Africans, there is a sizable expatriate population in the Ivory Coast (estimated at 50,000 by den Tuinder 1978).[17] Expatriates are usually employed in the most skilled occupations. Originally they were imported to fill manpower gaps at independence. Since

Table 6.4   Labor Market Conditions in the Ivory Coast

	1960	1965	1970	1975
Population (thousands)[a]	3,500	4,303	5,125	6,700
Number urban	502	946	1,435	2,300
Percentage urban	14	22	28	34
Located in Abidjan	200	340	590	1,000
Manufacturing employment[b]	10,000	20,770[d]	33,352	43,243[e]
Real wage index (1970 = 100)[c]				
Minimum industrial wage	83.7	93.0	100.0	108.7
Average manufacturing wage	n.a.	93.1[d]	100.0	106.3[e]

[a]Population data from den Tuinder (1978, p. 125) and Ministère du Plan (1967).
[b]Employment data for 1965, 1970 and 1975 are taken from Chambre d'Industrie (1975). The 1960 employment value is the author's estimate based upon IMF data (1970, p. 260). Urban employment refers to settlements over 4,000.
[c]The minimum real wage is the nominal minimum wage in manufacturing, deflated by the African consumer price index in BCEAO. It does not include other charges for family allowances, social security, etc. (*charges sociales*). The index of average manufacturing wages is based upon actual wages paid by Chamber of Industry members deflated by the African consumer price index.
[d]1966.
[e]1974.

then, their presence has been required to meet continued manpower needs created by the country's pace of development.

Tables 6.5 and 6.6 give my estimates of the structure of employment in the Ivory Coast in 1972. Only 12 percent of the labor force was involved in modern sector activity. The remaining 88 percent was concentrated in "artisanal" or "informal" sector activity, particularly in NRB activities. Of the modern sector labor force, only one-half was Ivorian. Migrant Africans (MA) formed 45 percent of the modern sector labor force, and non-African (NA) expatriates composed the remaining 5 percent.

Each nationality group predominated a particular occupational or skill category (table 6.6). Non-Africans occupied about three-quarters of the management positions; migrant Africans filled slightly more than half the unskilled positions; and Ivorians constituted two-thirds of the skilled occupations.[18]

There are legislated minimum wages for nearly all levels of employment in the Ivory Coast. The two most important are the minimum wages in industry and plantation agriculture. The real minimum industrial wage was relatively constant in the 1960s, hovering around 85 percent of its 1970 value as adjustments to the nominal minimum wage were made periodically to account for inflation. However, the nominal minimum agricultural wage was adjusted less frequently and by relatively smaller amounts. Thus, the ratio of real minimum wages in industry and agriculture widened gradually over the 1960s and probably contributed to the increasing flow of population to urban areas. More recently, the real minimum wage in industry has increased dramatically. From 1969 to 1976, it rose by about 40 percent. It is now about three times the minimum agricultural wage and more than double the minimum industrial wage in the neighboring countries that supply unskilled labor.[19] As a consequence, rural-urban migration has intensified and urban unemployment has become a more significant problem.

Other wages are primarily market-determined in the Ivory Coast. In my discussion of factor market distortions below (section 6.6), I will observe that modern sector wages are usually above the minimum in skill categories other than unskilled labor. In the urban informal sector, wages have historically been approximately 20 percent below the minimum industrial wage (as best one can determine). Thus the only significant distortion in the labor market appears to be the artificially high minimum wage for unskilled industrial labor.[20]

6.2.5   Capital Market Policies

Since independence, the Ivory Coast has applied an investment code to attract foreign direct investment. This code allows capital goods to be underpriced, since it contains provisions for tax holidays, duty-free

Table 6.5   Estimated Employment by Nationality and by Production Category, 1972

Production Category	Modern Sector Activities[a]				Artisanal Activities	Grand Total and Percentage of Total Employment
	IVOR	MA	NA	Total		
NRB						
Number	18,339	445	1,350	55,134	1,347,333	1,401,416
Percentage of total in category	1.3	2.5	0.1	3.9	96.1	81.8
HOS						
Number	23,026	14,228	1,486	38,740	63,427	102,167
Percentage of total in category	22.5	13.9	1.5	37.9	62.1	6.0
Home goods						
Number	59,471	41,614	7,489	108,574	100,427	209,001
Percentage of total in category	28.5	19.9	3.6	51.9	48.1	12.2
Total						
Number	100,896	91,247	10,325	202,468	1,511,187	1,713,655
Percentage of total	5.9	5.3	0.6	11.8	88.2	100.0

Source: Monson 1978.

[a]IVOR = Ivorian; MA = migrant African; NA = non-African.

Table 6.6   **Estimated Employment in Modern Sector by Skill Level, 1972**

	Modern Sector Activities[b]			
Skill Level[a]	IVOR	MA	NA	Total
Management				
Number	1,666	525	6,178	8,369
Percentage distribution	20.0	6.3	73.8	4.2[c]
Skilled				
Number	28,786	10,093	4,081	42,960
Percentage distribution	67.0	23.5	9.5	21.2[c]
Unskilled				
Number	70,444	80,629	66	151,139
Percentage distribution	46.7	53.3	—	74.6[c]
Total				
Number	100,896	91,247	10,325	202,468
Percentage distribution	49.8	45.1	5.1	100.0

Source: Monson 1978.

[a]Management refers to management and technicians; skilled refers to supervisors and skilled blue- and white-collar labor; and unskilled includes semi-skilled white- and blue-collar labor, unskilled workers, and apprentices.

[b]IVOR = Ivorian; MA = migrant African; NA = non-African.

[c]Percentage of total employment in modern sector.

import of equipment and inputs, and tax rate guarantees (for details see section 6.3). The code has been used by most investors in modern sector manufacturing. In 1972 production of firms most favored under the investment code was 65 percent of total modern HOS production. About 80 percent (in 1972) of modern HOS activity was owned by foreign interests. The net effect of the investment code is an indirect subsidy to capital and therefore the encouragement of higher capital intensities.

Fragmentary evidence from member firms of the Ivory Coast Chamber of Industry (Chambre d'Industrie 1975) appears to justify the claim that factor market distortions have favored capital utilization. Using employment, capital stock, and production data for these firms, and making crude adjustments for inflation,[21] I calculated incremental capital/labor ratios and employment elasticities for 1968–74. Table 6.7 gives my estimates. Note that in 1968–71 the employment elasticities roughly correspond to those mentioned earlier (0.8). After 1971 the estimates fall dramatically. My calculations further indicate that the ratio of the real undepreciated capital stock to employment rose some 60 to 70 percent over the period to about FCFA 4 million per worker by the end of 1974 ($16,000, converted at the exchange rate of FCFA 250 per U.S. dollar). It seems probable that these changes can be attributed, in large part, to more capital-intensive technologies, influenced by provisions of the investment code as well as to an increasing real minimum industrial wage.

Table 6.7   Incremental Capital/Labor Ratios,
Employment Elasticities, 1968–74

Year	Incremental Capital/Labor Ratio (Billions FCFA/Man-Year)	Employment Elasticity with Respect to Output
1968	2.220	.77
1969	2.513	.68
1970	4.183	1.08
1971	4.337	.74
1972	3.723	.42
1973	4.562	.42
1974	12.525	.16

Source: Calculated from data in Chambre d'Industrie (1975). Annual investment deflated by the building materials index to obtain real investment; output deflated by the value of the consumer price index. Data cover all firms registered with the Chamber of Industry except public utilities.

6.2.6   Other Considerations

Inflation

Inflation has not been an important consideration in the Ivory Coast. During the 1960s and early 1970s, prices rose, on average, at about 3 percent per year. More recently, price increases have been about 10 percent per annum.

Income Distribution

Income distribution also has not been a problem in the Ivory Coast. In general, incomes are relatively evenly distributed in comparison with other African countries. World Bank estimates (den Tuinder 1978, p. 135) place the percentage of income received by the lowest 40 percent of income earners at 20 percent and that earned by the top 20 percent of income earners at 51 percent. The comparative evenness occurs because, through NRB exports are subject to exit taxes, the taxes are less than those of many other countries. Thus, peasant farmers of cocoa and coffee, who form the bulk of the labor force, are better treated than farmers elsewhere. Additionally, the Ivory Coast has had an effective extension service aimed at improving agricultural productivity so that output has increased remarkably since independence.

6.2.7   Summary

The Ivory Coast has enjoyed an enviable record of economic growth since independence. This growth is due to its emphasis upon traditional exports to developed countries, coupled with a dependence upon foreign labor and capital. Employment generation, though not a problem in the past, has become one today as a result of a high population growth rate, a continued migration of labor from neighboring countries, and a high rural-urban migration.

6.3   The Structure of Production

In this section I classify Ivorian production following the methodology described in chapter 1. Activities are first separated into NRB, HOS, or home goods according to the nature of their production, then the statistic T_i is used to classify NRB and HOS production as exportables, importables, or noncompeting production.[22] In general, exportables are those activities with a negative T_i; importables have T_i statistics between zero and 0.75; and noncompeting production has T_i statistics greater than 0.75 (with certain exceptions described below). I further separated HOS importables into those that would exist "naturally," those whose primary competition is from developed countries (DCs), and those whose primary competition is from less developed countries (LCDs). The DC-LDC separation was not made for HOS exportables or NRBs because of the limited number of activities in each category (five HOS exportables and seven NRB activities). Tables 6.8 and 6.9 summarize my categorizations.

Table 6.8   Characteristics of Ivorian Exportable Production, 1972

Activity	Major Ivorian Products	Modern Sector Value Added as a Percentage of the Activity's Total Value Added	T_i	Exports (Millions FCFA)	
				DCs	LDCs
NRB production					
Coffee	Green coffee beans	0.0%	− 5.212	41,710	2,149
Cocoa	Green cocoa beans	0.0	−14.913	23,739	192
Other exports	Agriculture, rubber, fruit	5.8	− 5.578	8,270	1,867
Logs		87.0	− .517	30,831	1,725
HOS production					
Canned fruit	Pineapple	100.0	− 7.244	4,450	72
Canned coffee	Instant coffee	100.0	− 2.285	514	774
Processed cocoa	Cocoa butter, powder	100.0	− 8.503	5,591	17
Edible oils	Palm oil	94.0	− .355	2,842	355
Lumber	Sawn lumber, plywood	100.0	− 1.313	4,086	732

Source: Monson 1978, tables I–1, I–5, III A–B.

Table 6.9   **Characteristics of Ivorian Importable Production**

Activity	Major Products	Modern Sector Value Added as a Percentage of the Activity's Total Value Added	T_i	Imports (Millions FCFA) DCs	Imports (Millions FCFA) LDCs
NRB production					
Traditional	Agriculture, livestock, grains	1.0%	.149	2,552	6,509
Fishing	Fish	65.0	.227	1,037	238
HOS production					
Competitive importables					
Bakeries	Bread, biscuits	79.0	.023	195	3
Other milled products	Milled rice	6.0	.343	1,268	1,274
Beverages	Beer, soda	100.0	.354	1,441	1,324
Other processed food	Processed meat, candy	27.0	.045	1,773	523
Wood products	Furniture	43.0	.134	828	13
Paper	Boxes, toilet paper	100.0	.621	3,283	187
DC competing importables					
Paint	Paint	100.0	.135	289	30
Soap	Soap	100.0	.257	1,158	5
Plastic products	Dishes, packaging	100.0	.180	638	13
Other chemicals	Matches, glue	100.0	.810	4,579	52
Rubber	Tires, mattresses, latex	100.0	.526	2,760	33
Cement	Cement	100.0	.472	4,959	65
Autos (assembly)	Autos, trucks	100.0	.735	14,533	15
Other vehicles	Boats, bicycles, motorcycles	100.0	.531	2,382	0
Metalwork	Fabricated metal products	67.0	.469	7,575	117
Printing, diverse	Printing, miscellaneous	37.0	.413	2,488	279
LDC competing importables					
Flour	Flour	100.0	−.073	33	23
Tobacco	Cigarettes, cigars	100.0	.571	6,417	1,525
Textiles	Textiles	100.0	.122	5,607	2,202
Clothing	Clothing	32.0	.535	3,921	596
Shoes	Plastic shoes	70.0	.329	1,164	380
Petroleum refining	Petroleum products	100.0	−.058	911	817
Fertilizer	Fertilizer	100.0	.105	611	237
Noncompetitive importables					
Minerals	Diamonds	100.0	.703	464	6,788
Machinery	Machinery	100.0	.893	21,468	197
Basic chemicals	Essential oils	100.0	.881	3,636	63

Source: See table 6.8.

6.3.1 NRB Activities

The seven NRB activities given in tables 6.8 and 6.9 generated about one-third of GDP and employed about 80 percent of the Ivorian labor force. Artisanal activity (defined above in section 6.2) dominates NRB production, employing 96 percent of the NRB labor force and producing 75 percent of NRB output. As implied by the column "Modern Sector Value Added as a Percentage of the Activity's Total Value Added," artisanal activity is confined mainly to cocoa and coffee production for export and production of traditional foodstuffs (yams, manioc, rice, etc.) for domestic consumption. Modern sector activities are found in logging, other export (larger plantation) agriculture, fishing, and minerals.

NRB export activities include traditional coffee, cocoa, and log exports and newly developed agricultural exports (palm products, fruit). NRB importable activities include traditional agriculture and fishing. The sole NRB noncompeting importable is minerals. In 1972 there was some diamond mining in the Ivory Coast that has since ceased. Imports in the minerals category include mainly crude oil for local refining.

6.3.2 HOS Activities

The thirty-two HOS industries in tables 6.8 and 6.9 generated 17 percent of GDP and employed 6 percent of the labor force in 1972. Five HOS industries had T_i statistics considerably less than zero and were characterized as exportables,[23] twenty-three were categorized as importables, and two were classed as noncompeting importables.

All five HOS exportables used domestically produced NRB inputs, thus raising the question whether they should be categorized as NRB or HOS activities. However, in all cases the unprocessed input could be exported for processing elsewhere, thus necessitating the HOS classification.[24] In 1972 these activities accounted for 17 percent of HOS production and 14 percent of exports. They employed 35 percent of the modern HOS labor force, and 65 percent of their production was exported (primarily to developed countries with the exception of canned coffee, for which West African LDCs constituted 60 percent of the export market).

In the HOS importable category, six activities receive "natural" protection and are called "competitive" importables; seven compete against LDC source imports; and the remaining ten compete against DC source imports.[25] The "naturally" protected industries require little, if any, protection, since they process raw materials found in the Ivory Coast (rice milling, processed food, furniture) or are borderline nontradables (bakeries and biscuits, beverages, paper). In 1972 they accounted for 21 percent of HOS production. The LDC-competing importables made up 39 percent of HOS production and employed 27 percent of the modern HOS labor force while the DC-competing importables made up 21 percent of HOS production and employed 18 percent of the modern HOS labor force in the same year.

Only two HOS activities were categorized as noncompeting importables (machinery and basic chemicals). Their production accounted for less than 2 percent of HOS production. Note that the activity "other chemicals" was categorized as a competing importable despite a fairly high T_i (0.81). This was due to the level of aggregation and the fact that there was significant Ivorian production in the category.

Artisanal activity was also significant in the HOS sector. The artisanal sector employed 62 percent of the total HOS labor force but accounted for only 15 percent of the value of total HOS production. Actually, most artisanal production classified in an HOS activity in the Ivorian national income accounting nomenclature was nontradable (e.g., shoe repair in the shoe manufacturing industry, cabinetmaking in the wood products industry, etc.). Whenever artisanal activity is nontradable in nature, I will treat it as a home good in my factor requirements estimates (section 6.5).

6.3.3   Home Goods

The remaining share (50 percent) of GDP originated in the tertiary sector. Services and commercial activities accounted for 58 percent of tertiary production, while construction, transportation, electricity and water composed the rest.

6.4   The Trade Regime

As discussed above (section 6.2), the Ivory Coast's trade regime is relatively uncomplicated and probably somewhat less restrictive than that of most LDCs. The trade regime in the period under study (1972–73) was characterized by tariff cascading, exit taxes on NRB exports, and concessions under the investment code.[26] Each is discussed in turn below.

6.4.1   Policies Affecting Importable Activities

The two major forms of incentives offered for domestic production of importables were tariffs and quantitative restrictions. Additionally, two firms (one in fertilizers, the other in chemicals) received direct subsidies, and some firms obtained preferential credit terms. However, these latter preferences were relatively minor.

The Ivory Coast's tariff code is fairly simple. Most duties are ad valorem and escalate according to the degree of processing.[27] In 1973 there were two entry duties. EEC source imports were subject to one of these duties, and imports from most other sources were subject to both duties. The major exception to this pattern was imports from member countries of the former West African customs union (UDEAO), which were subject to one-half the duty of those levied on EEC goods.[28]

Prior authorization of imports, quotas, and import prohibitions were used in 1973. However, they were not very significant. Imports were categorized into three groups: prohibited, restricted, and liberated.[29] All restricted imports were subject to country quotas. Imports from the EEC and other countries with which the Ivory Coast had commercial agreements were granted priority. Licenses for liberated imports were readily obtained.

6.4.2   Policies Affecting Exports

Exit taxes were the most significant policy instrument influencing exports. NRB export activities were also affected by specialized government organizations that provided extension services, offered subsidized inputs, and acted as marketing agents for the products concerned (Elliott 1974). HOS export activities tended to be concentrated in firms that have received concessions under the investment code.

Exit taxes applied to all NRB exports and some processed NRB exports. Rates on NRB exports were higher on traditional products (such as coffee, cocoa, and logs) than on newly developed products (such as palm oil and latex). The rates were ad valorem and were applied to officially fixed prices (*valeurs mercuriales*). Since neither the tax rate nor the official price changed frequently, the tax became specific in nature. In 1973 the taxes ranged from approximately 2 percent (palm oil), to 16 percent (coffee), and 30 percent (cocoa) of the average 1973 f.o.b. price of the export.[30]

Aside from the export tax, there was a marketing board (*Caisse de Stabilisation et de Soutien des Prix des Production Agricoles*) for coffee, cocoa, and cotton, whose stated purpose was to stabilize prices paid to producers. In practice it had accumulated fairly large surpluses (e.g., $60.4 million in 1973/74)[31] that were reallocated to agricultural activities into which the Ivory Coast wished to diversify. Since the Caisse had control over these exports, its surpluses acted as an additional tax on producers. In 1973 the producer price for coffee and cocoa was about 60 percent of the f.o.b. price less fees paid the exporting agent; in 1975 these ratios were about 65 percent for cocoa and 55 percent for coffee.

The only significant taxes on major HOS exports were applied to processed cocoa (about 15 percent), lumber (5–15 percent), and plywood (2 percent). Since they were considerably less than those on the unprocessed product, they amounted to an indirect incentive to process cocoa and logs domestically.

Firms exporting manufactures could, in principle, import inputs duty-free. In practice, regulations on separate storage plus the administrative lag in obtaining permission for importing restricted this benefit to a few large exporting firms.

With the exception of lumber, HOS production was concentrated in the hands of firms receiving concessions under the investment code (discussed below). These concessions, combined with indirectly subsidized local inputs, tended to provide fairly high levels of protection.

6.4.3 The Investment Code

The Ivorian investment code offered a generous set of tax incentives to attract direct foreign investment. There were two categories of private firms established under the code: priority firms (*entreprises prioritaires*) and common-law firms (*entreprises de droit commun*). Common-law firms were exempted from profit taxes (currently 40 percent) for five years and received several other minor tax concessions. Priority firms received a ten-year profit tax exemption, duty-free import of equipment (to establish the plant) and of inputs (for ten years), and a guarantee that tax rates applicable at the time the priority agreement was made would apply for up to twenty-five years. (This was especially important because the profit tax rate increased from 33 to 40 percent between 1971 and 1976.) In return, their activities were subject to yearly analysis by the Planning Ministry, and price increases had to be approved by the Ministry of Finance.

As of January 1975, eighty-two firms had been granted priority status. While most major exporting firms had this status, the bulk of priority firms (80 percent) were engaged in importable activities. Industries in which priority firm production was important included textiles, petroleum refining, fertilizers, metalworking, and automobile assembly.

6.4.4 Levels of Protection

Table 6.10 gives estimates of protection for the various commodity categories described above. The estimates are based upon direct price comparisons and include effects of QRs whenever appropriate.[32]

In general, protection was moderate, although neither low[33] nor uniform across commodity categories. NRB activities were less protected than HOS activities, and exportables were less protected than importable activities, regardless of whether they were NRB or HOS importables.

All NRB activities had ERPs equal to or less than zero with the exception of fishing (46 percent). Exit taxes on NRB exports, especially traditional exports, caused the low ERP estimate for NRB exports. The ERPs for coffee, cocoa, and logs were −45, −44, and −36 percent, while the ERP for other export agriculture was −16 percent.

On average, HOS exportables received slightly greater protection than HOS importable activities. However, when competitive HOS importable activities are excluded, exportables receive significantly less protection

Table 6.10   **Weighted Average Protection by Commodity Category, 1973**

| | Nominal Protection | | |
	Output	Tradable Inputs	Effective Protection
Exports	−26%	8%	−36%
NRB	−28	9	−40
HOS	2	−7	35
Importables	4	7	13
NRB	3	5	3
HOS	6	10	29
Competitive	− 6	15	−21
Requiring protection	20	6	84
From DC imports	18	5	45
From LDC imports	24	7	139
Noncompeting imports	24	7	101
Total	2	8	−28

Source: The averages are computed from data found in the statistical appendix to this study (Monson 1978). The weights are the IVA of domestic production of each activity within a commodity category. The ERP estimates include premiums on import licenses. See also note 32.

than HOS importables requiring protection (ERPs of 35 and 84 percent, respectively). Within the latter category, those activities requiring protection from DCs were less protected than those requiring protection from LDCs (ERPs of 45 and 139 percent, respectively).

The ERPs on HOS exports were positive because, though exports received little protection on output, their major domestically produced inputs were available at less than world market prices. For example, sawmills obtained logs at the world market price minus the exit tax normally paid on log exports. The one activity (canned coffee) that had an extreme ERP (6,111 percent) had a very low international value added owing to this subsidy.[34]

All "competitive" importables had negative ERPs except the wood products industry (ERP of 115 percent), which enjoyed fairly high nominal protection on output (28 percent) and whose inputs were only moderately taxed (3 percent). All other activities in this category paid substantial taxes on tradable inputs and received little, if any, protection on their output, a result caused, in part, by the small representation of priority firms (13 percent) in the category's production.[35]

The averages given in the table conceal wide variations and several extreme estimates. The extremes were canned coffee (noted above) and flour (an ERP of 1,124 percent). In the category of DC importables, paint, other chemicals, and metalwork had ERPs greater than or close to 100 percent, while rubber, cement, autos, and other vehicles had low or, in the case of cement, even negative ERPs. Those with ERPs near the average for this category were soap, plastics, and printing and diverse industries. In the LDC-importable category, tobacco had a negative ERP (−3 percent), petroleum refining received below-average protection (91 percent) and clothing about average (137 percent), while textiles (194 percent), shoes (239 percent), fertilizer (278 percent), and flour received above-average protection.

To summarize, in 1973 the Ivorian trade regime was probably somewhat less restrictive than that of most LDCs. It had a cascaded tariff structure that protected LDC importables more than DC importables. NRB exports were taxed mainly to raise fiscal revenues, and HOS exports received moderate effective protection because of implicit subsidies on inputs.

6.5   Factor Requirements and the Ivory Coast's Net Factor Content of Trade

The foregoing discussion suggests features of the Ivorian economy that may be useful in theorizing about Ivorian patterns of trade and specialization and their employment implications.

Relatively speaking, the Ivory Coast is a "Third," not a "Fourth," World country. Its per capita income (U.S. $700 in 1976) is high in relation to many (especially African) LDCs. Its population density is relatively low, and agricultural expansion has occurred more through increases in land under cultivation than through the use of intensive production techniques. Finally, foreign capital and labor have played integral parts in its development efforts.

These considerations imply that the Ivory Coast fits the category "underdeveloped" better than "poor" in the context of Krueger's three-factor model (1977). Its development pattern has followed that outlined in her analysis. Since independence, its high land-labor ratio has caused agricultural wages to be high in comparison with those in many LDCs. Development began with expansion of agricultural activities then later moved toward manufacturing as the liberal investment code encouraged foreign capital inflows. However, manufacturing wages also had to be high in order to induce rural-urban migration, although not so high as set by the minimum wage for unskilled labor. Manufacturing activities, then, ought to be somewhat more heavily weighted toward more capital-intensive production than in many LDCs. A reasonable assumption is that the Ivory Coast manufacturing capital-labor ratio falls between those of more developed countries and "poorer" LDCs (i.e., those with low land-labor ratios).

If this contention is true, then theory predicts that the capital intensity of manufactured (HOS) exports to more capital-abundant (DCs) nations will be lower than the capital intensity of manufactured exports to LDCs. Similarly, the capital intensity of production of commodities competing with imports from DCs will be higher than that of commodities competing with imports from LDCs. Extending this analysis to employment levels, theory then predicts that export trade with DCs will utilize relatively more labor than trade with LDCs. Since most trade is with developed nations, Ivorian exports should be generally more labor-intensive than the country's imports.

In this section, I will examine the factor content of trade to determine if these expectations are generally confirmed.

6.5.1 Procedures

At the time this study was undertaken data for 1973, the year of my protection estimates, were not available to estimate labor coefficients and the net factor content of trade. However, 1972 data were available, which allowed me to disaggregate the twenty-seven-activity input-output table into forty-nine activities. Likewise, good employment data could be found for most activities for 1972. In cases where 1972 employment data were inadequate, data from other years in the period 1971 to 1974 were adjusted to 1972 levels.[36] I believe this 1972 data set provides a good description of the Ivorian economy in the early 1970s and that it can be used to generalize about economic conditions in 1973, the year of my protection estimates.

I proceeded to use this data to estimate labor coefficients for each occupational category mentioned earlier (management, skilled and unskilled labor) for modern sector activities. No corresponding breakdown was possible for artisanal activities. The units used in the estimates were man-hours per million FCFA of domestic value added (in 1972, one million FCFA was approximately equal to U.S. $4,000). Detailed estimates by activity are given in table 6.A.1. I then aggregated these estimates by major trade categories in table 6.11 (using value added in domestic production as weights) and used these, in turn, to compute the net factor content of trade in table 6.12. Two separate estimates were made—one for all tradables and a second that focused more narrowly upon modern HOS tradables only.

The reason for the two estimates was the large artisanal component of Ivorian production. Recall that artisanal activity produced three-fourths of NRB output and one-third of GDP and employed close to 90 percent of the labor force in 1972. Artisanal production posed three problems for the analysis—its inadequate data base, its probable dependence upon resources specific to the country, and an uncertainty about the extent to which it can continue to foster economic growth.

Operationally, the first problem was most severe, since artisanal employment data were sketchy at best and fraught with problems of seasonality, the treatment of family labor, multiple products, and so on.[37] The second problem raised some theoretical issues, since artisanal production consists mainly of NRB goods, all of which can be produced economically only in tropical areas. To a certain degree, their production probably was dependent upon resources specific to the country. The third problem was potentially most important. While artisanal activity has accounted for past growth, it is likely that future growth will depend much more upon expansion of modern plantation agriculture and manufacturing activities as good arable land becomes scarcer. Stryker (1974, p. 65) suggests that "today, much of that land has a relatively high opportunity cost in terms of cocoa or coffee which may be grown." Expansion of NRB production will have to come increasingly from higher yields and diversification into new crops.[38]

For these reasons, I present the two estimates. The "all tradables" estimate (including artisanal and modern HOS and NRB tradables) should be interpreted (cautiously, given the data problems) as explaining what did happen to employment in the first fifteen years after independence; the modern HOS estimate should be interpreted as explaining what might happen if growth centers upon manufacturing activities. Given the qualifications concerning inadequate data and specific resources, I feel more comfortable emphasizing the HOS estimates.

6.5.2   Factor Requirement Estimates by Trade Category

Table 6.11 gives, by major trade categories, estimates of total labor requirements (direct plus indirect in home goods) per unit of DVA and IVA using value added in production as weights. The first four columns break down the DVA estimates for the modern sector by skill level, and the next two columns add artisanal employment. Values in the column entitled "grand total" are the relevant ones to compare labor requirements per unit of DVA in the various commodity categories. The column to the far right converts the estimates to show total requirements per unit of IVA.

Labor requirements per unit of value added for the "all tradables" categories, both exports and imports, are dominated by the artisanal labor component and are very large in comparison with those for the modern HOS categories, attesting to the high labor intensity of artisanal production. For example, the unit labor requirements for tradable NRBs (largely artisanally produced) are far larger than those for HOS tradables. These differences were symptomatic that Ivorian comparative advantage in 1972 lay in labor-intensive NRB production. In comparing the DVA and IVA estimates for all export tradables, one sees that labor requirements are much lower for the IVA than for the DVA calculations.

Table 6.11   Total Labor Requirements by Major Trade Category, 1972

	Man-Hours per Million FCFA of DVA[a]					Total Man-Hours per Million FCFA of IVA
	Modern Sector[b]					
Trade Category	Man	Sk	Unsk	Total[c]	Arti-sans	Grand Total	
Exportable production							
All tradables	28	167	1,151	1,346	16,496	18,993	11,533
NRB exports	25	143	1,158	1,326	18,607	19,933	12,219
Modern sector HOS exports	53	383	2,026	2,463	25	2,488	3,647
Importable production							
All tradables	22	124	467	612	9,693	10,305	10,272
NRB importables	7	25	186	219	12,468	12,687	13,107
Modern sector HOS importables	64	406	1,352	1,823	16	1,839	2,577
Competitive	75	449	1,953	2,477	24	2,501	1,707
All requiring protection	61	394	1,183	1,638	14	1,652	3,290
From DC imports	60	387	1,053	1,500	20	1,520	2,334
From LDC imports	61	399	1,273	1,733	10	1,743	4,372

Source: Derived from appendix table 6.A.1.
[a]Direct plus indirect labor in home goods. Weights are value added of domestic production.
[b]Man = management; Sk = skilled; Unsk = unskilled.
[c]Components may not sum to total because of rounding errors.

The negative ERPs of exports were the primary cause here. For importable activities the difference was negligible, since NRB importables dominated production (generating about 70 percent of the DVA of tradable ICAs), and international and domestic value added were similar because of low protection (see table 6.11). It would be consistent with my hypothesis that the Ivory Coast's manufacturing capital/labor ratio fell between those of DCs and other LDCs if labor requirements for exports were greater than those for importables and if, within the importable category, goods competing with imports from DCs had lower labor requirements than goods competing with imports from LDCs. The results presented in table 6.11 generally follow this pattern. Reading down the "grand total" column, we observe that the labor requirement per million FCFA of DVA in export production (2,488 man-hours) was 50 percent greater than for all importables requiring protection (1,652), and LDC-competing importables used 15 percent more labor than DC-competing importables (1,743 and 1,520 man-hours, respectively).[39]

I separated competitive HOS importables from HOS importables requiring protection because I had no a priori notion of where they would fall in a ranking of commodity categories by labor coefficients. They might be competitive because of the availability of NRB inputs at low (export) prices in the Ivory Coast or because of high transport costs for the commodity. Either way, there was no presumption about labor requirements. Alternatively, they might require little protection since they were labor-intensive goods and embodied Ivorian comparative advantage.

The labor coefficients for competitive HOS importables in table 6.11 suggest that there might be some validity in the latter speculation, since they used about the same labor per unit of DVA as HOS exports (2,501 versus 2,488 man-hours). Moreover, a trade-weighted estimate was 23 percent below that using production weights (1,930 versus 2,501 man-hours), suggesting that imports in this group were more heavily weighted with capital-intensive goods than domestic production within the same category.

Turning now to the labor coefficients by skill categories, in table 6.11 we first observe that the absolute values of the management and skilled labor requirements, per unit of DVA, did not vary much between exports and importables requiring protection. Differences in total labor requirements were found mainly in the unskilled labor coefficients. All differences in the unskilled category were expected. Those for exports were larger than importables requiring protection and, among the latter, those for LDC-competing importables were larger than DC-competing importables but smaller than exportables.

The proportion of skilled workers and managers was higher in all categories of importable activities than in exportable production. Management constituted 2.1 percent and skilled labor 15.4 percent of workers per unit of DVA in exportables. For importable production, the figures were 3.0 and 17.9 percent for competitive protection and 3.7 and 23.8 percent for all requiring protection.

For HOS trade categories other than competitive importables, labor coefficients increased as I changed from DVA to IVA measures. This change was most noticeable in protected importables competing with LDCs. Even with these changes, it was still true that exportables used more labor (per unit of IVA) than all importable categories (except LDC importables), indicating that the moderate levels of protection in the Ivory Coast limited, at least to some extent, the degree of inefficiency of these industries. Comparison of the increases in each case indicates the degree of relative inefficiency. For HOS exportables, labor coefficients rose by 47 percent; for all importables requiring protection, they rose by 99 percent; for DC importables, by 53 percent, and for LDC importables, by 151 percent.[40]

6.5.3   Net Factor Content of Trade

For the net factor content of trade estimates, I computed the change in inputs that would result from equal increases of one million FCFA of

IVA in the domestic production of exportable and importable activities.[41] Data given in table 6.11 were used for the estimates. The results using both trade and production weights are given in table 6.12.[42]

The Ivory Coast was a net exporter of unskilled labor and a net importer of management and skilled labor in 1972. In fact, when all activities (including NRB production) are considered, it was a net importer of all modern sector labor under the trade weights, meaning that it was artisanal labor that accounted for net exports. This conclusion is not surprising, given the predominance of artisanal production in NRB exportables. For the modern sector, however, the Ivory Coast was a net exporter of unskilled labor and a net importer of skilled labor. The Ivory Coast's comparative advantage in modern manufacturing is most clearly pinpointed in the calculations for HOS exportables and HOS importables requiring protection. There the net factor coefficient was negative for management and skilled labor and positive for unskilled labor.

6.6   Employment Effects of Ivorian Commercial and Factor Market Policies

A variety of questions come to mind when we consider the ramifications of Ivorian policies upon the labor coefficient estimates of the last section. Earlier, I described Ivorian commercial policy as being moderately less restrictive than those of many LDCs; import-competing production received more preferential treatment than exportables and,

Table 6.12   The Net Labor Content of Trade

	Modern Sector[a]				Artisanal	Grand Total
	Man	Sk	Unsk	Total		
All Activities						
Production weights	− 8	− 40	201	152	1,108	1,261
Trade weights	−37	−241	−509	−787	4,673	3,886
Modern HOS[b]						
Production weights	−12	− 8	1,075	1,055	15	1,070
Trade weights	−13	− 34	1,002	955	5	960
Modern HOS exports and importables requiring protection[c]						
Production weights	−43	−223	615	348	9	357
Trade weights	−32	−173	707	503	10	513

Note: Net labor content of trade = net man-hours employed per million FCFA of IVA of balanced trade expansion. Computed from table 6.11.
[a]Man = management; Sk = skilled; Unsk = unskilled.
[b]Including naturally protected importables.
[c]Excluding naturally protected importables.

within the category of exportables, HOS production was treated more preferentially than NRB production. In factor markets, the only significant distortions were the investment code and minimum wage legislation. These policies contributed to an increase in the share of HOS commodities in exports and the displacement of some finished consumer goods imports by domestic production.

This section examines issues related to the employment effects of these policies. Among other things, we will seek to determine (1) if employment has been discouraged by the greater protection on importables than on exportables and the consequent shift in production patterns; (2) if, and how, incentives to capital under the investment code have affected capital and labor utilization; and (3) if the minimum wage system has discouraged labor utilization.

6.6.1   Effects of the Trade Regime upon Factor Utilization

Theory predicts that, within commodity categories, less protected activities should more closely embody Ivorian comparative advantage relative to the destination of exports or source of import competition. That is, for exportables and DC importables, less protected activities ought to be more labor-intensive than more protected activities. The reverse should be true for LDC importables if the Ivorian capital labor endowment is greater than those of other LDCs.

I focused only upon modern sector HOS activities[43] to analyze these issues (largely because of data problems). My approach was twofold. First, I estimated Pearson correlation coefficients between my measures of protection (nominal and effective) and estimates of the capital/labor ratio for activities within a commodity category to determine if significant relationships existed. In general this procedure did not provide meaningful results (see below).[44] For the second procedure, I classified activities within a commodity category as receiving above or below average protection within the category. Then I calculated average ERPs and labor requirements for each subgroup. This procedure provided somewhat more meaningful results that tended to support the contentions mentioned above and that suggested an overall capital-using bias in the Ivorian trade regime.[45]

The Pearson correlation analysis was performed separately for DC and LDC importables only, since exportables included only five activities. The results for these two categories were not robust. The only statistically significant correlation coefficient in one-tailed tests at a 95 percent confidence level was that between the capital/labor ratio and nominal protection on output ($-.526$) for the LDC importable category. Nonetheless, the estimated coefficients offer partial corroboration of biases caused by protection on importables, since the signs were invariably correct and some coefficients were fairly large (e.g., $-.366$ and

.216 between the capital/labor ratios and ERPs of LDC and DC importables, respectively).

Table 6.13 gives the results of my estimates of ERPs and labor requirements for more and less protected activities within a commodity category. The strongest results are found in the exportable and DC importable categories. In both cases, less protected activities used more labor (about 25 percent) than protected activities, as expected. A second result is the almost uniform relative shares of unskilled labor used by more and less protected activities *within* a commodity category (there are differences among commodity categories, as was observed in section 6.5). For example, unskilled labor constitutes 80 to 85 percent of the exportable labor requirement whether or not the activity is highly protected. This uniformity suggests either that commercial policy exerted an influence through changing the composition of output or that factor market policies were uniformly applied across commodity categories. That is, policies distorting factor prices for one or more activities in a category should produce different estimates for unskilled labor components for more and less protected activities in that category.

Refer now to the results for LDC importables. These are ambiguous, and their interpretation depends upon whether petroleum refining is treated as an HOS good in the analysis.[46] Two sets of calculations are given, one including and the other excluding refining. When refining is included, less protected LDC importables have lower average labor requirements than more protected activities, as expected. When refining is excluded, the opposite result is obtained.

While the results of these two exercises are far from conclusive, they generally support the contention that Ivorian commercial policy was biased toward capital-using industries at least in exportables and DC importables. In both cases, more protected activities tended to use less labor than less protected activities. For LDC importables the evidence is less clear. As expected, LDC importables were more labor-intensive than DC importables, but the ambiguity provided by petroleum refining makes it unclear if protection encouraged the production of more or less labor-intensive commodities.

6.6.2   Changes in the Composition of Production

My objective here is to present some fragmentary evidence suggesting the direction by which changes in output composition affected factor utilization. If protection is not "made to measure,"[47] more protected industries should be better able to compete with imports than less protected industries. If so, the production of more protected industries will be encouraged, and evidence of this encouragement should be found in comparisons of the relative role of domestic production in total supply (imports plus production) of more and less protected activities within

Table 6.13   Total Labor Requirements for Activities Receiving Below-Average and Above-Average Protection in a Commodity Category

	Number of Activities	Average ERP (Percentage)	Labor Requirements[a] (Man-Hours per Million FCFA of DVA)				Percentage Unskilled[b]
			Man	Sk	Unsk Plus Artisans	Total	
Exportables							
Below average	3	1	43	455	2,197	2,695	81.5
Above average	2	140	67	270	1,823	2,160	84.4
Average[c]	5	35	53	383	2,051	2,488	82.5
Importables requiring protection							
Below average	8	21	63	356	1,115	1,534	73.7
Above average	9	154	60	412	1,237	1,709	72.4
Average[c]	17	84	61	394	1,197	1,652	72.4
DC importables							
Below average	5	17	65	436	1,206	1,707	70.7
Above average	5	85	56	348	966	1,370	70.5
Average[c]	10	45	60	387	1,073	1,520	70.6
LDC importables							
Below average	3	48	68	337	1,198	1,603	74.8
(Excluding petroleum)	(2)	(12)	(83)	(386)	(1,912)	(2,382)	(80.3)
Above average	4	208	57	433	1,329	1,819	73.9
Average[c]	7	139	61	399	1,283	1,743	73.6
(Excluding petroleum)	(6)	(152)	(63)	(421)	(1,468)	(1,951)	(75.3)

Note: Weighted averages using DVA of domestic production as weights except for the ERP column, which uses IVA weights.

[a]Man = management; Sk = skilled; Unsk = unskilled.

[b]Includes artisanal labor.

[c]Averages taken or calculated from tables 6.10 and appendix table 6.A.1.

a commodity category. Alternatively, the statistic T_i should vary inversely with the level of protection. As T_i increases, domestic production falls relative to domestic consumption, and imports supply proportionately more of consumption.

We calculated average T_i statistics for below and above average protected activities in each category, using DVA as weights. These calculations are particularly revealing. For DC importables, the average is 0.448: below and above average protected activities have averages of 0.529 and 0.383, respectively. For LDC importables, the average is 0.178; below and above average protected activities have averages of 0.289 and 0.118, respectively. In each category, more protected importables were more likely to be produced domestically than less protected importables. These results, coupled with the analysis above, lead to the conclusion that Ivorian trade policy exerted a sizable influence upon labor utilization through changing the composition of output.

6.6.3 Priority Firm Status and Capital Market Distortions

Recall that there are two classes of privately owned firms in the Ivory Coast (priority and common-law firms). While both receive concessions under the investment code, those granted to priority firms are larger than those given to common-law firms. Additionally, the negotiations for priority status usually include both tax and tariff (or nontariff) concessions. My purpose here is to examine differences in protection for these two categories of firms to determine if priority firms received greater protection than common-law firms. A second objective is to estimate returns to capital to see if differences exist across commodity categories and between priority and nonpriority firms.

Protection of Priority Firms

In table 6.14 I have assembled a series of data on protection, factor intensities, capacity utilization, and the relative importance of priority-firm production for our three commodity categories.[48] Observe first that priority status was applied equally between exportables and importables (see last line of item 6). However, within the importable category, LDC importables were much more likely to receive priority status than DC importables, reflecting the emphasis of Ivorian import substitution efforts upon finished consumer goods.

Priority firms received greater protection and had higher capital/labor ratios (items 1 to 4) than common-law firms in exportable and LDC importable production.[49] The difference between protection and capital/labor ratios of the two classes of firms was most pronounced within the LDC importable category. In that category there were two competing influences upon labor utilization. Protection encouraged the production of relatively labor-intensive goods (see earlier discussion),

Table 6.14   Comparison of Priority and Nonpriority Firms by Commodity
Category, 1972

	Export-ables	Importables Requiring Protection		
		DC	LDC	All
1. Effective protection (percentage)				
Priority firms	58	40	142	105
Common-law firms	9	51	78	62
2. Nominal protection on output (percentage)				
Priority firms	85	15	22	20
Common-law firms	— 3	21	35	24
3. Nominal protection on traded inputs (percentage)				
Priority firms	— 6	7	6	7
Common-law firms	—11	4	18	10
4. Capital/labor ratios (FCFA/man-hour)				
Priority firms	1,846	1,522	3,824	3,050
Common-law firms	868	1,900	442	1,447
5. Capacity utilization (percentage)				
Priority firms	72	68	85	79
Common-law firms	78	73	82	76
6. Ratio: DVA of priority firm production to DVA of total production (percentage)				
Less protected activities	65	66	76	71
More protected activities	100[a]	64	96	84
All activities	78	65	89	79

Source: Calculated from data in Monson (1978, tables II–D, IV–D, VI–E, VI–F).
Note: Weights for the protection estimates are IVA of domestic production; weights for the capital/labor ratios and capacity utilization estimates are DVA of domestic production.
[a]Rounded to 100 percent; the actual value is 99.7 percent.

while the concessions to capital under the investment code encouraged the utilization of capital-intensive production techniques. The net result appears to be absolute inefficiency, with LDC importables requiring more of both capital and labor than DC importables.

For the DC importable category, common-law firms had higher capital/labor ratios and received greater protection than priority firms. I suspect a certain degree of "made to measure" protection here. Some DC importable activities received forms of natural protection because of transport costs (e.g., cement) or because there were domestic sources of inputs (e.g., rubber). Thus domestic production did not require high levels of protection to compete effectively with imports. When these two industries (cement and rubber) are eliminated from the estimates, priority firms are more protected and have higher capital/labor ratios than common-law firms.

Returns to Capital

Unfortunately, I did not have adequate data for 1972 to determine if returns to capital differed between priority and common-law firms and to determine if returns to capital differed across activities. Data to investigate these problems were available for 1974 only (RCI Ministère de l'Economie 1976). As a proxy for returns to capital, I calculated the ratio of interest payments plus depreciation plus net profits to equity plus debt. As indicators of differential treatment of taxes and credit facilities, I calculated ratios of (1) profits taxes plus property taxes to gross profits,[50] and (2) interest charges to total debt. The commodity categorization of this data source was more aggregated than that used in my study. I was able to separate HOS activities only into exportables and importables. However, the data allowed me to calculate these ratios for all modern activities, mixed public-private firms with majority governmental control (*sociétés d'économie mixte*), priority firms, and all HOS firms.

My calculations are summarized in table 6.15. The results contradict notions that incentives to capital were equally distributed and returns to capital were equalized among activities in 1974. (An alternative explanation is that capital was not mobile enough to equalize rates of return.)

Table 6.15   Returns to Capital, Taxes, and Interest Rates, Various Activity Categorizations, 1974

	Returns to Capital[a]	(Profits Tax + Property Tax)/Gross Profits	Interest[b]/ Debt
HOS exportables	33.7%	5.9%	4.9%
HOS importables requiring protection	13.2	19.7	6.7
All modern activities (NRB, HOS, home goods)	12.2	30.5	3.8
Sociétés d'état[c]	9.6	56.0	3.8
Sociétés d'économie mixte[d]	20.6	5.3	3.3
Priority firms	13.5	17.9	3.8
All manufacturing firms	15.1	30.7	3.3

Source: Various tables in RCI Ministère de l'Economie (1976).
[a](Interest + depreciation + net profits)/(equity + debt).
[b]Interest charges/short- and long-term debt.
[c]Totally publicly owned corporations.
[d]Mixed-ownership firms with majority government equity.

HOS exportables and priority firms paid significantly lower profits and property taxes than all other categories of firms except mixed public-private firms, and returns to capital were highest in exportable activities. Interestingly, returns to capital in priority firms were lower than the average for all manufacturing firms. In part this result reflects the higher overall capital/labor ratio of priority firms (see discussion above).

6.6.4 Other Influences on Protection

Besides priority-firm status and preferential tax treatment, there were a variety of other influences upon protection and factor utilization in 1972. Most important was the extent of foreign and government ownership. The calculations summarized in table 6.16 indicate that foreign equity either received or moved into lines of production receiving greater protection than government or private Ivorian equity (with the exception of exportables). Thus, in addition to the tax provisions of the investment code, greater protection was given foreign equity in an effort to attract foreign direct investment. No pattern was observable between protection and government equity. In some cases it was high because of the "essential" nature of the industry (e.g., fertilizer); in other cases it was low because inputs were heavily taxed (e.g., tobacco). It was only in exportables that government equity systematically raised protection through the subsidization of inputs.

To isolate other less obvious factors influencing protection, I estimated Pearson correlation coefficients between all variables and my indicators of protection (ERP, nominal protection on output and inputs). There

Table 6.16   Weighted Average Protection by Source of Equity, 1972

	Exportables	DC Importables	LDC Importables
Effective protection			
Foreign equity	45%	43%	144%
Government equity	53	22	115
Private Ivorian equity	20	36	133
Nominal protection on output			
Foreign equity	2	16	24
Government equity	2	7	21
Private Ivorian equity	3	16	21
Nominal protection on traded inputs			
Foreign equity	−8	7	5
Government equity	−9	4	11
Private Ivorian equity	−6	3	20

Source: Monson (1978, tables IV–B and VI–D).
Note: Weights are IVA of domestic production multiplied by the relative shares of each equity source in production.

were positive relationships of varying degrees of significance between variables representing the percentage of management personnel in an activity's labor force, the percentage of foreign equity in total equity, the scale index and the concentration ratio, on the one hand, and variables representing protection, on the other.[51] The general conclusion from this analysis is that an industry was more likely to enjoy (or require) higher levels of protection: (1) the greater the extent of foreign ownership; (2) the larger the size of the firm; (3) the more concentrated the activity; and (4) the larger the relative role of management in the labor force.

6.6.5   Labor Market Distortions

The principal labor market distortion was the system of minimum wages established for all categories of labor.[52] In 1972 minimum wage legislation appeared to be effective only at the unskilled level. That is, the minimum wage was set above the shadow wage of unskilled labor. In that year, the industrial minimum wage for unskilled labor was FCFA 58.7 per hour. This wage was less than the average for all non-NRB informal activities (FCFA 66.5).[53] However, informal activities were not subject to labor overhead charges such as social insurance (*charges sociales*), which were estimated to be 40 percent of the base wage.[54] When added to the minimum wage, a differential of about 23 percent was introduced between unskilled wages in the modern and informal urban sectors. Table 6.17 gives the applicable minimum wages in 1971 and median wages received in each skill category from the 1971 labor force survey (RCI Ministère du Plan 1973). For all but unskilled labor, the minimum wage appears to be inoperative, since wages actually received were in the upper extremes of the minimum wage range. Note, however, that the average wage for unskilled labor (*manoeuvres*) in general, and migrant Africans in particular, was below the minimum, suggesting some noncompliance with the statutes for migrant Africans. Another explanation of the low average wage is that the minimum wage in the table refers to the industrial sector, while the median wage information includes workers in both modern NRB and industrial activities throughout the country. The agricultural minimum wage was less than that of industry, and other Africans working in agricultural activities depressed their average.

Thus minimum wage legislation apparently distorted employment patterns of unskilled labor and might have had secondary effects upon other labor categories by encouraging substitution of skilled for unskilled labor or through complementarities between skilled labor and capital as capital utilization was encouraged.

If we assume that the minimum wage was 20 percent above the shadow wage for the lowest category (*manoeuvres*) of unskilled labor in 1972,

Table 6.17   Wages by Skill Level and Nationality, 1971 (Thousand FCFA per Month)

Skill Category	Median Wage[a]				Minimum Wage[b]
	Ivor	MA	NA	Average	
Management					
Direction	104.5	61.8	191.2	174.6	n.a.
Cadres	105.3	114.9	185.5	165.3	61.4–144.5
Skilled Labor					
Supervisors	57.5	60.1	143.6	73.0	38.8–64.2
White-collar	34.8	34.8	90.1	38.8	22.8–38.9
Blue-collar	26.6	26.0	71.9	26.5	18.0–39.7
Unskilled Labor[c]					
Semiskilled white-collar	19.2	15.3	—	17.0	10.1–17.5
Semiskilled blue-collar	17.8	15.9	—	17.1	12.6–15.8
Unskilled	12.8	8.7	—	9.7	10.1–11.5

Sources: RCI Ministère du Plan (1973), vol. 2, various tables; RCI Ministère du Plan (1972).

[a]Ivor = Ivorians; MA = migrant Africans; NA = non-Africans.

[b]The range given is for the various skill categories within each occupational level for a person with less than three years experience. For cadres, the work week is forty-eight hours. There is no minimum wage for the direction category in the private sector.

[c]Data for apprentices were not available.

that the demand for labor had a unitary price elasticity, and that the supply of labor was perfectly elastic, then removal of the minimum wage requirement would have increased modern unskilled employment in all activities by about twenty thousand, or 20 percent over its 1972 level (10 percent increase in total modern employment).

The presumed effect of minimum wages would be largest in exportable production because of its high unskilled labor component. In other activities, the impact would be less significant but still important, since unskilled labor dominated employment in all commodity categories. If we assume the same elasticities as above, unskilled employment would have risen by 10 percent in exportables and by 5.5 percent in importables after a 20 percent decrease in the minimum wage.

6.6.6   Evidence of the Overall Capital-Using Bias of Ivorian Policies

Overall, we have found that Ivorian policy exerted a capital-using bias in 1972. As a final exercise of this section, I attempt to measure crudely the extent of resource misallocation caused by protection of HOS activities. To do this, I asked the following questions: (1) If all resources employed in producing importables in 1972 were transferred frictionlessly to exportable production and employed at the exportable capital/labor ratio, how much additional employment could be generated while maintaining an unchanged exportable capital/labor ratio? and (2) As a measure of the absolute inefficiency of LDC importable production, how large would be the increase in IVA if resources employed in LDC importables were transferred frictionlessly to DC importable production and employed at the DC importable capital/labor ratio?

Table 6.18 summarizes the data necessary to respond to these questions. Notice that importables employed about twice as much capital as exportables, used 25 percent more labor, and produced 50 percent more IVA. Also notice that LDC importables were absolutely inefficient; they used 70 percent more capital and 50 percent more labor than DC importables, yet produced about 10 percent less IVA.

The transfer of resources from importables to exportables could have released about twice as much capital as needed to absorb the labor released at the exportable capital/labor ratio. About 32.5 million man-hours could have been transferred. These man-hours would have required about FCFA 36.2 million of capital to be employed at the exportable capital/labor ratio of FCFA 1,115 per man-hour. Capital valued at FCFA 17.8 million would have become unemployed. The IVA in exportable production could have risen by 133 percent (FCFA 8,891 million).[55] Alternatively, 50 percent more labor than that released from importable production would have been required to fully employ the capital released from importable production in exportables. If this labor

Table 6.18   **Capital/Labor Ratios, IVA, and Capital and Labor Employed in Production by Commodity Category, 1972**

	Exportables	Importables Requiring Protection		
		DC	LDC	All
1. Capital/labor ratio[a] (FCFA/man-hour)	1,115	1,665	1,661	1,662
2. IVA of production (millions FCFA)	6,687	5,279	4,665	9,944
3. Employment (man-years)	13,528	6,860	10,259	17,119
4. Replacement value of gross investment (millions FCFA)	27,225	20,098	33,862	53,960
5. Capital/labor ratio[b] (millions FCFA per man-year)	2.01	2.93	3.30	3.15

Source: Monson (1978, tables II–B, V–A, VI–A1).

Note: Figures are for modern sector, including HOS exportables and importables requiring protection; NRBs are excluded.

[a]Man-years from row 5 were converted to man-hours by average hours worked per year in each category.

[b]Row 5 = row 4/row 3.

had been forthcoming, the IVA of exportables would have increased by 200 percent. The latter figure represents a one-third increase over the 1972 IVA in importables.

The effects of transferring resources from LDC to DC importables would have been a large increase in IVA and, depending upon which capital/labor ratio (from table 6.18) was used, slightly more or less capital would have been released to maintain the DC importable capital/labor ratio. Using the capital per man-year estimate, FCFA 30,056 million of the FCFA 33,862 million of LDC capital would have been required to employ the LDC labor force of 10,259 in DC importables at the capital per man-year ratio of 2.93. Using the capital per man-hour estimate, FCFA 33,940 million of capital would have been required to absorb the 20.4 million man-hours ($10,259 \times 1,987$ man-hours per year) released from LDC importable production. The capital deficiency would have been 0.2 percent in that case, and 10,235 man-hours would have been absorbed along with the FCFA 33,862 million of capital. These resources would have increased the IVA of DC importable production by 168 percent, or FCFA 8,894 million (about 90 percent more than that generated in LDC production [FCFA 4,465 million] in 1972). Clearly, resources were misallocated to LDC importable production.[56]

These calculations provide rough orders of magnitude to illustrate the capital-using bias in the Ivorian trade regime in 1972 and the relative inefficiency of LDC importable production. At the very least, changes in Ivorian commercial policy that provided equal treatment of all importables would have substantially increased economic well-being in the Ivory Coast.[57] But a more ambitious policy that placed greater emphasis upon exportable production would have helped absorb the growing numbers of unemployed at a much lower cost than policies aimed at increasing importable production. Trends since 1972 suggest that Ivorian policy is moving in the opposite direction (at least with respect to importables). Not only has there been an increase in tariff protection (with the elimination of reciprocity on EEC imports), but there has been increase in the utilization of quantitative restrictions, with the possible effect of a slower rate of employment growth.

6.7 Summary and Conclusions

Probably the most significant conclusion about the Ivorian trade pattern is that it can be largely explained in the context of the standard trade model. Ivorian export-oriented policies have generally encouraged employment because Ivorian comparative advantage lies in the export of labor-intensive commodities to DCs.

However, some aspects of policy have fostered a certain degree of economic inefficiency and discouraged labor utilization. First, more labor-intensive exportables were discriminated against by receiving somewhat lower protection than less labor-intensive importables. Second, within the category of importables, greater protection of LDC importables encouraged economic inefficiency, since they required more of both labor and capital per unit of IVA. Third, incentives to capital under the investment code probably favored the utilization of capital-intensive production techniques. Fourth, minimum wage legislation discouraged utilization of unskilled labor but not necessarily other labor skill categories.

The labor coefficients calculated in section 6.5 indicated that all Ivorian exportables used unskilled and artisanal labor more intensively than importables. For modern sector activities, importables were more capital-intensive and skilled-labor-intensive than exportables. The importable capital/labor ratio was about 50 percent greater than that of exportables.

Ivorian commercial policy provided significant protection for all HOS production, with effective protection rates of 35 and 84 percent, respectively, for exportables and importables requiring protection. LDC importables enjoyed higher effective protection (139 percent) than DC importables (45 percent). This pattern of protection generally encouraged resources to move into more protected and less efficient importable lines of production, for, as we saw, domestic production of more protected activities contributed more to total supply than that of less protected activities in each commodity category, and the highly protected LDC importable category appeared to use more of both capital and labor than other trade categories.

Factor market distortions (the investment code and minimum wage statutes) favored capital utilization. In general, I found that priority firms receiving concessions under the investment code had higher levels of protection and larger capital-labor ratios than common-law firms. Priority status was also related to the extent of foreign equity, the size of the firm, and the concentration of the industry. The heavily protected activities were dominated by a small number of large, foreign-owned priority firms that tended to have higher capital and labor requirements than less protected activities.

The minimum wage statutes distorted prices of unskilled labor and may have levered the entire wage structure upward, thus discouraging utilization of all labor categories. This distortion at the unskilled level was significant, since the lowest category of unskilled labor (*manoeuvres*) constituted close to 50 percent of total modern employment in 1972. Under stipulated assumptions, I estimated a total unskilled employment increase of about twenty thousand, or 10 percent of total modern employment (20 percent of unskilled employment) in 1972 if the minimum wage were lowered by 20 percent.

Although Ivorian policies largely exploited the country's comparative advantage in labor-intensive NRB and HOS exports to DCs until 1972, policies appear to have altered since then. Further research, using current data, is now needed to determine if the basis of Ivorian comparative advantage has changed and to analyze the employment effects of the general tightening of Ivorian policies in the mid-1970s. For, if Ivorian comparative advantage remains in labor-intensive production today, as it was in 1972, then current trade and factor market policies will not enhance economic welfare, nor will they provide maximum employment growth. I hope that this study will provide a stimulus for continued research along these lines.

Appendix

Table 6.A.1 Total Labor Requirements by Activity Within Major Trade Categories (Man Hours per Million FCFA of Value Added)

	Per Unit of DVA						Grand Total per Unit of IVA
	Modern Sector[a]						
Trade Category and Sector	Man	Sk	Unsk	All Modern	All Artisanal	Grand Total	
NRB exportables							
Coffee	9	38	99	147	22,197	22,343	12,195
Cocoa	7	33	86	125	16,243	16,368	9,430
Other export agriculture—artisan	5	26	53	83	92,908	92,991	78,456
Other export agriculture—modern	117	613	7,038	7,768	7	7,775	6,560
Other export agriculture—average	70	366	4,104	4,540	39,025	43,565	36,755
Logs—artisan	1	9	21	31	17,088	17,118	17,118
Logs—modern	49	330	2,066	2,445	36	2,481	1,556
Logs—average	43	287	1,790	2,120	2,338	4,458	2,870
NRB importables							
Traditional agriculture—artisan	2	9	22	33	13,097	13,130	13,313
Traditional agriculture—modern	335	643	8,809	9,788	3	9,791	9,928
Traditional agriculture—average	5	17	128	150	12,940	13,090	13,273
Fishing—artisan	1	9	13	23	12,808	12,831	18,681
Fishing—modern	70	229	1,776	2,075	153	2,228	3,244
Fishing—average	46	152	1,159	1,357	4,582	5,939	8,647
HOS exportables							
Canned fruit	55	238	2,879	3,172	7	3,179	3,098
Canned coffee	52	221	350	623	4	627	23,859

Table 6.A.1—*continued*

Trade Category and Sector	Per Unit of DVA						Grand Total per Unit of IVA
	Modern Sector[a]				All Artisanal	Grand Total	
	Man	Sk	Unsk	All Modern			
Processed cocoa	15	73	277	365	6	371	996
Edible oils—artisan	1	2	5	8	14,667	14,675	23,159
Edible oils—modern	71	281	2,103	2,455	63	2,518	4,008
Edible oils—average	66	264	1,973	2,303	969	3,272	5,205
Lumber	53	730	2,875	3,658	9	3,667	4,052
HOS competitive importables							
Bakeries—artisan	1	4	8	13	7,251	7,264	5,959
Bakeries—modern	92	552	2,098	2,742	22	2,764	2,267
Bakeries—average	73	437	1,662	2,172	1,533	3,705	3,038
Wood products	108	719	3,653	4,480	11	4,491	9,657
Paper	60	212	1,762	2,034	6	2,040	1,517
Milled products—artisan	15	38	77	130	3,958	4,088	3,508
Milled products—modern	17	92	218	326	—	326	279
Milled products—average	15	41	85	141	3,732	3,873	3,321
Processed food—artisan	2	11	28	41	8,011	8,052	6,599
Processed food—modern	54	14	3,245	3,313	93	3,406	2,785
Processed food—average	16	12	906	934	5,850	6,784	5,556
Beverages	58	390	920	1,368	13	1,381	607
HOS importables competing with DC imports							
Paint	61	284	551	896	8	904	2,315
Soap	51	265	668	984	29	1,013	1,871

Table 6.A.1—*continued*

Trade Category and Sector	Per Unit of DVA						Grand Total per Unit of IVA
	Modern Sector[a]			All Modern	All Artisanal	Grand Total	
	Man	Sk	Unsk				
Plastics	90	317	1,659	2,066	9	2,075	3,681
Other chemicals	54	302	994	1,350	13	1,363	2,565
Rubber	59	383	4,181	4,623	8	4,631	4,043
Cement	64	263	1,187	1,514	14	1,528	1,633
Automobiles	39	426	665	1,130	8	1,138	1,425
Other vehicles	42	558	878	1,478	18	1,496	1,784
Metalwork—artisan	7	17	36	60	25,923	25,983	29,758
Metalwork—modern	44	444	838	1,376	6	1,382	3,157
Metalwork—average	31	302	603	936	8,662	9,598	20,708
Printing, miscellaneous—artisan	5	18	39	62	6,040	6,102	8,736
Printing, miscellaneous—modern	109	605	925	1,639	83	1,722	2,467
Printing, miscellaneous—average	43	235	366	644	3,842	4,486	6,423
HOS importables competing with LDC imports							
Flour	29	136	423	588	1	589	28,440
Tobacco	48	186	789	1,023	9	1,032	1,001
Textiles	55	472	1,368	1,896	13	1,908	4,776
Clothing	107	522	2,665	3,294	8	3,302	40,608
Shoes—artisan	9	27	55	91	8,863	8,954	30,392
Shoes—modern	122	459	1,979	2,560	9	2,568	8,675
Shoes—average	88	328	1,395	1,812	2,691	4,503	15,231
Petroleum	47	271	238	556	7	563	1,071
Fertilizer	54	369	1,241	1,664	9	1,673	6,148

Table 6.A.1—continued

	Per Unit of DVA						
	Modern Sector[a]				All Artisanal	Grand Total	Grand Total per Unit of IVA
Trade Category and Sector	Man	Sk	Unsk	All Modern			
Noncompeting importables							
Minerals	50	459	1,243	1,753	41	1,794	1,542
Basic chemicals	68	74	1,518	1,660	24	1,684	2,245
Machinery	108	567	891	1,556	10	1,576	5,283
Home goods							
Artisanal wood	—	2	5	7	19,845	19,852	28,984
Artisanal textiles	1	12	26	39	14,952	14,991	14,991
Auto repair	100	558	770	1,428	1,943	3,371	3,085
Water/energy	68	576	294	937	20	957	899
Construction	44	436	1,395	1,875	4,732	6,601	5,941
Transportation	57	463	1,095	1,615	22	1,637	1,573
Postal system	75	512	817	1,404	24	1,429	1,412
Rentals	11	62	122	195	60	256	254
Services	173	424	1,300	1,898	167	2,065	2,011
Traditional commerce	13	83	191	287	3,713	4,000	3,954
Local commerce	202	522	1,061	1,785	30	1,815	1,772
Export commerce	89	327	902	1,318	7	1,325	1,284

Source: Monson (1978, data appendix).
Note: Labor requirements include direct plus indirect labor in home goods.
[a]Man = management; Sk = skilled; Unsk = unskilled.

Notes

1. For a discussion of the flow of African migrants, see Stryker (1974, pp. 16–21). The undeveloped educational structure is illustrated by the following data. In 1961 there were only 11,000 secondary school students and 850 university students (studying abroad) in an age 15–24 cohort of about 700,000. In 1961 only 270 students received the equivalent of the American high school diploma (*baccalaurèat*). Moreover, in the decade before independence, only 965 students graduated from secondary school (République de France 1970).

2. The author contributed to a World Bank research project on incentives in West Africa directed by Bela Balassa. Some of the protection estimates used in this study are borrowed directly or adapted from that project. See Pursell and Monson (n.d.) for details of the project and its estimates.

3. See Bastiaan A. den Tuinder (1978) for a complete review of the Ivorian growth experience.

4. Use of the consumer price index for African families as a deflator (as noted in table 6.1) may overstate the real rise in GDP if prices of services rise more rapidly than other prices, and if services weigh more heavily in consumer expenditures than in GDP.

5. The relatively high population growth rate of 4 percent implied by the difference between GDP and GDP per capita is due to a high reproduction rate coupled with high rates of migration from neighboring countries. See discussion in section 6.2 for details.

6. "In the Ivory Coast, as in all developing countries, many economic activities are carried on outside the scope of laws and regulations governing such matters as the establishment of shops and workshops, labor-management relations, taxation and supervision of technical skills and of product quality. In general, these economic activities are included in what is commonly known as the 'traditional' sector, but which in current ILO practice is called the 'informal' sector" (Joshi, Lubell, and Mouly 1975, p. 49). I follow the Ivorian practice of calling these activities "artisanal."

7. Taxation of NRB exports is mainly for revenue purposes. Taxes on the three major exports (coffee, cocoa, logs) account for about 20 percent of total direct and indirect tax revenue.

8. In 1972, nontariff barriers protected about 20–25 percent of modern manufacturing output. More recently there appears to be greater use of quotas, especially in the textile industry. See section 6.3 for details.

9. Other members are Benin (formerly Dahomey), Niger, Senegal, Togo, and Upper Volta.

10. The two most important are the newly formed (1974) West African Economic Community (CEAO) consisting of the Ivory Coast, Senegal, Mali, Upper Volta, and Niger, and the broader Economic Community of West African States (ECOWAS), which encompasses all West African countries.

11. As examples of these changes in the composition of imports, note that in the period 1972 to 1976 import volumes of rice, fruit, vegetables, clothing, and sugar fell, while volumes of canned food, tobacco, textiles, fertilizer, and beverages rose by less than 50 percent, much less than 160 percent growth in total import volume for the same period. It should also be noted that the large increase and high growth rate in the "other imports" category in table 6.2 is a statistical discrepancy caused by difficulty in comparing the 1960 data with those of other years. Growth rates of imports in categories besides "other" are probably under-

stated, since some imports categorized as "other" in 1972 and 1976 were categorized incorrectly in other categories of table 6.2 in 1960.

12. Crude oil imports (not included in table 6.2) rose from 5.6 to 11.5 percent of import expenditures from 1972 to 1976. The volume of crude oil imports rose by 37 percent, while price rose by 310 percent.

13. Imports and import duties as given in the text include crude oil and clinker, both of which are subject to special taxation. The percentages mentioned refer to averages for the period 1968–71.

14. The two duties are the *droit fiscal d'entrée* and the *droit de douane*. EEC source imports were subject to only the *droit de douane* before June 1975, effectively lowering their entry duty to one-half or less of that borne by imports from other sources.

15. When first implemented, this regulation caused some bottlenecks in the provision of imported inputs needed for domestic production. It has since been relaxed and now applies generally only to noncompeting imports.

16. Author's estimate, based upon data in A. Achio (1970) and Bangoura Moktar (1973).

17. A national census was conducted in 1975. Unfortunately, a detailed nationality breakdown was not available at the time this chapter was written.

18. The management category is the sum of the Ivorian classifications *direction* (management) and *cadres-techniciens* (occupations requiring postsecondary specialized training, for example, computer programmers, accountants, engineers). The skilled category consists of shop supervisors (*maîtrises*), skilled blue- and white-collar workers (*ouvriers qualifiés* and *employés qualifiés*). The unskilled category includes all other workers—semiskilled white- and blue-collar labor (*employés non-qualifiés* and *ouvriers specialisés*), unskilled labor (*manoeuvres*), and apprentices (*apprentis*).

19. For example, in 1976 the nominal unskilled industrial wage (SMIG, or *salaire minimum industriel garanti*) was FCFA 115 in the Ivory Coast, FCFA 47 in Upper Volta, FCFA 48 in Niger, and FCFA 70 in Mali.

20. There are wide differences in wages received by the different nationality groups in the Ivory Coast. However, skill differences are the principal causes of these differentials. For 1972 I estimated average yearly earnings per worker in the modern sector to be FCFA 3.1 million for expatriates, FCFA 294 thousand for Ivorians, and FCFA 232 thousand for migrant Africans. Given each group's predominance in a particular skill category, it is probable that the differences in average wages primarily reflect skill differences.

21. Namely, deflating annual gross investment by the building materials price index and annual increases in production by the consumer price index.

22. Detailed data and a description of the categorization are included in the data appendix to this chapter (Monson 1978), available for the cost of reproduction from the National Bureau of Economic Research.

23. Two HOS activities (petroleum refining and flour milling) had negative T_is but were classified as importables. Both had high levels of protection (see discussion, section 6.4, for details) and probably would not be exported given less protection.

24. This point is arguable for canned fruits and edible oils. Fresh pineapples exported for immediate consumption are of a higher quality than pineapples used for canning. It is possible that the canning pineapples are exportable only if canned. If so, the activity should be treated as NRB production. I reject this view. For the edible oils category, exports are predominantly semirefined palm oil. The

degree of processing is limited. However, since the unprocessed palm kernels could be exported, the processing is properly regarded as an HOS activity.

25. In separating DC and LDC importables, I first calculated the average percentage of imports in these classifications from DC and LDC sources (87.6 and 12.4 percent, respectively), then considered LDC imports to be significant wherever they were greater than 12.4 percent. Otherwise they were classified as DC-competing importables.

26. Current protection is somewhat higher, since EEC imports became subject to both entry duties in 1975.

27. One additional aspect of the tariff code is the existence of officially fixed prices (*valeurs mercuriales*) upon which the tariff may be calculated. Their original use was to avoid underinvoicing and to attack supposed cases of dumping. They can be used to supply additional protection if set above the border price. In 1973 they applied to approximately 10 to 15 percent of all imports and to about 30 percent of textile and clothing imports.

28. Special agreements were in effect in 1973 that provided for duty exemption of certain products from Niger, Senegal, and Upper Volta. Since the dissolution of the UDEAO and formation of the customs union (CEAO) in 1974, preferences for imports from member West African states have been negotiated product by product. There no longer is an across-the-board uniform reduction on all imports from these countries.

29. Products are prohibited because of health reasons or state security or because productive capacity exists at home (e.g., cement, flour, flashlight batteries). The restricted and liberated lists include products for which domestic productive capacity either does not exist or is insufficient to supply domestic needs; items on these two lists change depending upon needs of the economy and availability of domestic substitutes. See Olopoenia (1975) for further discussion.

30. In early 1976 the taxes on coffee and cocoa were increased but, at the higher prices then prevailing, were equivalent to about 14 percent of their 1976 average f.o.b. price.

31. Converted at the exchange rate FCFA 250 = U.S. $1. The accounting year is from mid-October to mid-October; 1973–74 refers to October 1973 to October 1974.

32. The estimates also include any additional protection provided, as described in note 27, through the use of officially fixed prices as opposed to actual border prices for purposes of calculating import duties on certain goods. Direct price comparisons of imports with local production were used to estimate nominal protection for most categories of HOS goods. IVA weights were used to calculate averages by commodity category. DVA weights are inappropriate, since they would tend to inflate the average ERP estimates. That is, whenever the ERP coefficients for all activities within a category are low, the differences between DVA and IVA are small and use of DVA weights will not change the weighted averages appreciably. However, if one or more activities have high ERPs their DVAs are large relative to their IVAs, and using DVA weights will inflate the average for the category. For example, the IVA and DVA production-weighted averages for HOS exportables are 35 and 458 percent, respectively. The extreme ERP for canned coffee (6,111 percent) dominates the DVA weighted average; when IVA weights are used, the canned coffee contribution to the category's IVA weights are used, the canned coffee contribution to the category's IVA is only 0.3 percent. For details of the estimates for each activity see the data appendix to this study (Monson 1978).

33. By way of comparison with other LDCs, Balassa (1971, p. 54) reports ERPs for Brazil, Chile, and Pakistan of at least 100 percent for most commodity categories. The average ERP for all HOS activities in the Ivory Coast is about 30 percent.

34. Canned coffee producers obtain green coffee beans at the world market price minus the full exit tax and sell a large portion of their output domestically or in CEAO countries providing Ivorian production with high levels of protection (e.g., the Ivory Coast supplies 98 percent of the market in Senegal, for which the tariff is 30 percent). Subsidizing of the coffee input reduces IVA to a small value relative to DVA and causes the extreme ERP estimate. Lumber and processed cocoa receive indirect subsidies, since lumber exports are subject to only a small portion of the exit tax paid on log exports, and processed cocoa is subject to the exit tax only on cocoa pod inputs considered to be of an exportable quality (about 50 percent of its cocoa pod inputs).

35. In general, priority firms are more protected than nonpriority firms (see discussion in section 6.4). By way of comparison, priority firms produce 86 percent of production in HOS importable activities requiring protection.

36. I multiplied employment data for the available year by the ratio of 1972 wages to those of that year (adjusted for wage increases) to obtain my estimate of 1972 employment. The implicit assumption was that the skill composition of the labor force was unchanged over the period. See Monson (1978, pp. 68–70) for details.

37. Traditional foodstuffs (yams, manioc) for self-consumption are usually interplanted on cocoa and coffee plantations. Stryker (1974, p. 44) estimates that, on average, 32 percent of the year is spent on cocoa and coffee production by heads of families and family workers. The rest of the year they are either unemployed or tending crops for self-consumption or engaged in seasonal wage employment elsewhere.

38. From 1965 to 1972, 200,000 hectares were added to cocoa and coffee production while about 250,000 hectares were added to oil palm, rubber, cotton, coconut, pineapple and other plantation agriculture. Note also that exploitable forest acreage fell from about 9 million hectares in 1960 to 5.5 million hectares in 1973.

39. Estimates using trade weights were similar to those using production weights. Most estimates did not change markedly, because the level of protection was low and because there were few factor market distortions. When differences occurred, the change generally was in the expected direction: trade-weighted labor coefficients increased for exportables and LDC importables and decreased for DC importables. The only changes greater than 10 percent were in the coefficients for competitive importables and LDCs importables. For the former, imports are more heavily weighted toward less labor-intensive activities than is domestic production. For LDC importables, weighting by imports indicated higher labor coefficients than weighting by current production.

40. It was thought that including flour and clothing, both of which have high ERPs and therefore high capital and labor requirements per unit of IVA, might make the averages for LDC importables unrepresentative for the industries concerned. However, similar calculations excluding these activities yielded approximately the same results.

41. For example, the production-weighted net labor content for all activities is 11,533 (table 6.11 exportable production) minus 10,272 (table 6.11, importable production).

42. Generally the trade weights (as compared with production weights) increased the net labor content of trade, since most trade is with DCs whose com-

parative advantage is in more capital-intensive goods. The lower net labor content of trade using production weights indicates that domestic production was more heavily weighted with LDC importables than was trade.

43. Actually, only HOS exportables and DC and LDC importables were considered. Competitive HOS importables were excluded because their natural protection did not make them easily susceptible to analysis. I should also note in passing that NRB exportables had higher labor requirements than NRB importables. This was true on average (19,993 versus 12,687 man-hours per million FCFA of DVA) and for each industry except logging, where most production was carried out by the modern sector.

44. The lack of significant results in the correlation analysis probably is due to faults in estimating capital stocks used to obtain capital/labor ratios. To obtain values of the capital stock, I adjusted gross investment estimates for a sample of firms in each activity, using the Abidjan building materials price index to deflate construction costs and the industrial equipment price index for France to deflate equipment costs. For details see Monson (1978, section 6).

45. There are problems related to degrees of freedom associated with both procedures. We are dealing with a limited number of activities in each category (five exportables, ten DC importables, and seven LDC importables). It is unrealistic to expect much by way of systematic behavior with these small samples. Furthermore, I could not combine categories, since I expected the relationships among labor and capital coefficients, capital/labor ratios, and protection for LDC importables to be different from those for exportables and DC importables. For example, for LDC and DC importables, I anticipated a negative and a positive correlation, respectively, between the capital/labor ratio and effective protection.

46. Factor proportions in refining may not have any relationship to the location of a refinery in the Ivory Coast that serves the domestic market and Upper Volta and Mali. Availability of NRB inputs and high costs of transportation may be the determining factors. Production is highly skilled labor- and capital-intensive (FCFA 4.8 million of capital per million FCFA of DVA, while only 44 percent of its labor force is unskilled labor).

47. For a discussion of the "made-to-measure" concept, see Corden (1974, chap. 5).

48. The capacity-utilization data are poor. They refer to the ratio of actual to potential output per shift. They do not account for variations in the number of shifts worked per day. The definition of potential output is also ambiguous. The capital data used in the capital/labor ratios are also open to question. They refer to the replacement value (1972 prices) of gross investment for a sample of firms in the various activities. Replacement value was obtained by separating gross investment into its components (construction and equipment), then identifying the year in which investment occurred. Finally, these values were deflated by appropriate construction and equipment price indexes. These estimates are questionable for a variety of reasons. They should be interpreted as giving relative, not absolute, magnitudes.

49. Priority firms in the competitive importable category also had higher capital/labor ratios and received greater protection than common-law firms.

50. Profits taxes and property taxes are the major subjects of tax concessions under the investment code.

51. For example, the Pearson correlation coefficient between the management personnel variable and ERP was .526, that between the scale index and ERP was .267, that between the concentration index and ERP was .345, and that between the foreign equity variable and nominal protection on output was .344.

52. The Ivory Coast's heavy reliance upon foreign labor introduces the possibility of a second distortion, namely wage discrimination between expatriates and Africans. Using regression analysis, it was found that human and physical capital characteristics explained about 70 percent of the variation in each nationality's wage. These results suggest that economic factors were the primary cause of the wide wage differentials observed between Africans and expatriates and that labor markets were not heavily distorted. However, I take an iconoclastic view and suggest that further research on this topic is warranted. Our data are not strong enough to permit a definitive conclusion.

53. Calculated from Monson (1978, table V-A2), using employment weights.

54. RCI, Bureau de Développement Industriel (1974). More recent estimates place these charges at about 45 percent (Ministère du Plan, 1976).

55. Using the capital per man-year estimates, IVA in exportables would rise by 126 percent (FCFA 82,462 million), and 40 percent of capital formerly employed in importables would become unemployed.

56. Using the capital per man-year estimate, FCFA 30,056 million of capital would be required to employ the 10,259 men. The IVA of DC importable production would rise by 150 percent (FCFA 7,895), which represents about a 70 percent increase over the IVA of LDC production.

57. This analysis is intended primarily to illustrate the absolute inefficiency of LDC importable production. Hal B. Lary has suggested (correctly, in my opinion) that caution be exercised in extending my results to mean that the Ivory Coast should indiscriminately encourage resources to shift from LDC to DC importable production. Ivorian production of DC importables probably differs in nature from actual DC imports to a greater extent than is apparent in this study because of the level of aggregation used here. For example, auto production in the Ivory Coast consists of relatively labor-intensive assembly operations that differ from the capital-intensive production of autos (including components) in DCs. Our analysis indicates that the Ivory Coast could benefit by shifting resources into the production of DC importables that are relatively labor-intensive. It is not to be interpreted as meaning that the Ivory Coast should encourage capital-intensive DC importable production.

References

Achio, A. 1970. Le problème du chomage en Côte d'Ivoire. Ministère du Plan. Mimeographed.

Balassa, Bela. 1971. *The structure of protection in developing countries.* Baltimore: Johns Hopkins University Press.

Banque Centrale des Etats de l'Afrique de l'Ouest (BCEAO). Various years. Indicateurs économiques—Côte d'Ivoire. In *Notes d'Information et statistiques.* Paris: BCEAO.

———. 1973. Le bois en Côte d'Ivoire. *L'Economie Ouest Africaine,* no. 206 (May). Paris: BCEAO.

Berg, Elliot J. 1971. Structural transformation versus gradualism: Recent economic development in Ghana and the Ivory Coast. In *Ghana and the Ivory Coast: Perspectives on modernization,* ed. Philip Foster and Aristide R. Zolberg, pp. 117–230. Chicago: University of Chicago Press.

Chambre d'Industrie de Côte d'Ivoire. Various years. *Principales industries installées en Côte d'Ivoire au 1ᵉʳ janvier.* Abidjan.

Corden, W. M. 1974. *Trade policy and economic welfare.* New York: Oxford University Press.

den Tuinder, Bastiaan A. 1978. *Ivory Coast: The challenge of success.* Baltimore: Johns Hopkins University Press.

Elliott, Howard J. C. 1974. Animation rurale and encadrement technique in the Ivory Coast. CRED Discussion Paper no. 40, Center for Research on Economic Development, University of Michigan, Ann Arbor. Mimeographed.

International Bank for Reconstruction and Development. 1977. *World debt tables—supplements: External public debt of LDCs.* September. Washington, D.C.: IBRD.

International Monetary Fund. Various years. *International financial statistics.* Washington, D.C.: IMF.

————. 1970. *Surveys of African economies.* Vol. 3. Washington, D.C.: IMF.

Joshi, Heather; Lubell, Harold; and Mouly, Jean. 1976. *Abidjan: Urban development and employment in the Ivory Coast.* Geneva: International Labour Office.

Krueger, Anne O. 1977. *Growth, distortions and patterns of trade among many countries.* Princeton Studies in International Finance no. 40: Princeton: Princeton University.

Moktar, Bangoura. 1973. Population et développement économique: Un exemple—La Côte d'Ivoire. Paris: OECD Development Center. Mimeographed.

Monson, Terry D. 1978. Ivory Coast—Data appendix. NBER project on trade regimes and employment in LDCs (available upon request from the NBER for cost of reproduction). New York: National Bureau of Economic Research.

Olopoenia, R. A. 1975. The domestic resource cost of foreign exchange in the manufacturing sectors of the Ivory Coast: 1960–1970. Ph.D. diss., University of Michigan.

Pursell, Garry, and Monson, Terry D. N.d. Incentives in the Ivory Coast. In *Incentives in West Africa,* ed. Bela Balassa. Baltimore: Johns Hopkins University Press. Forthcoming.

République de Côte d'Ivoire. Bureau de Développement Industriel. 1974. Couts des facteurs en Côte d'Ivoire. Abidjan.

République de Côte d'Ivoire. Ministère de l'Economie et des Finances. Various years. *Statistiques du commerce exterieur de la Côte d'Ivoire en* [various years]. Abidjan.

————. 1976. *Centrale de bilans, 1974.* Abidjan.

République de Côte d'Ivoire. Ministère du Plan. 1972. *Rémunerations: Traitements et salaires en Côte d'Ivoire.* Abidjan.

————. 1973. *Le secteur privé et para-public en Côte d'Ivoire 1971, resultats de l'enquête main d'oeuvre.* 4 vols. Abidjan.

————. 1976. *La Côte d'Ivoire en chiffres.* Abidjan.

République de France. Secretariat d'Etat pour les Affaires Etrangères. 1970. *Structures et statistiques de l'ensignement pour 14 états africaines et malagaches.* Vol. 1. *Tableaux d'ensemble par état, 1951–1970.* Paris.

Stryker, J. Dirck. 1974. Exports and growth in the Ivory Coast. In *Commodity exports and African economic development,* ed. Scott R. Pearson and John Cownie. Lexington, Mass.: Lexington Books.

7 Trade Policies and Employment: The Case of Pakistan

Stephen Guisinger, with the assistance
of Mohammad Irfan

Introduction

Pakistan's trade with the rest of the world has, from the beginning of the country's existence, played a crucial role in its development.[1] It is axiomatic that international trade is important for all developing countries because they lack capital and intermediate manufactured goods and must earn foreign exchange to import them. But in Pakistan the foreign trade sector has made an unusually important contribution to economic growth, largely because of the historical circumstances of the country's creation and the international economic conditions during the early years of its existence. In 1947 Pakistan was created by a partition of the subcontinent into three regions: India, West Pakistan, and East Pakistan. The latter two regions were united in one national government until 1972, when East Pakistan seceded and became Bangladesh. Both East and West Pakistan were principally agricultural areas before 1947, and, when trade with India was severed in the wake of the partition there emerged extremely severe shortages of manufactured goods, previously purchased from the manufacturing centers of Bombay and Calcutta. The shock of such a sudden cessation of trade and the large latent domestic demand for manufactured products launched Pakistan on a program of rapid domestic industrialization.

The international economic environment in the early 1950s pushed Pakistan toward reliance on import substitution as a means of promoting domestic industrialization. The collapse of the Korean War commodity boom cut Pakistan's foreign exchange earnings sharply, and the government responded by erecting an elaborate exchange control system

Stephen Guisinger is associated with the University of Texas at Dallas. Mohammad Irfan is associated with Cornell University and the Pakistan Institute of Development Economics.

that provided lavish profits for domestic entrepreneurs (see Papanek 1967; Lewis 1969). Import substitution fueled industrial growth until the early 1960s, when the strong and steady growth of world demand for manufactured goods prompted Pakistan's planners to raise substantially the effective exchange rates (EERs) for exports of manufactured goods. A surge in Pakistan's manufactured exports gave support to Pakistan's continued rapid expansion of the manufacturing sector. Even the rapid growth of agriculture during the 1960s can be attributed in part to Pakistan's trade policies. Export taxes on a number of commodities were reduced, and import restrictions on fertilizers, insecticides, and other farm inputs were liberalized.

   Another significant development in Pakistan, as we mentioned above, was the secession of East Pakistan from what was then known as Pakistan in 1972, when West Pakistan became the Pakistan of today. Since then Pakistan has experienced much political turmoil, culminating in the military coup of 1977 that deposed Prime Minister Bhutto. During this period of political unrest, economic policy was neglected, and the well-established economic administrative structure of the 1960s deteriorated somewhat.

   The importance of Pakistan's trade sector has been analyzed in a number of studies (Lewis 1969, 1970; White 1974; Guisinger 1976), but the analysis has focused on the relationship of trade policies to the rate of economic expansion. This focus on growth stems in part from the widespread belief of economic planners and theorists alike during the 1960s that growth, employment, and equity in the distribution of income were complementary, not competitive, social goals. Rapid expansion of national income, they believed, would percolate through the economic structure, raising employment in all sectors and redressing income inequalities. The rise of urban unemployment in many developing countries, coupled with a sharp public outcry in Pakistan over the excessive wealth concentrated in the hands of a few industrialists, led the government to reassess its emphasis on rapid economic growth. Since the early 1970s the government has adopted a number of antipoverty measures that have sought to ensure increased real wages and increased employment opportunities for the poorest segment of society. For various reasons, some of which were completely beyond the control of government—adverse weather conditions, the oil price increase, and the world recession—these antipoverty measures have had little apparent effect.

   In considering what policies can be used effectively to raise the level of employment in Pakistan, it is important to examine the following questions: first, What has been the effect in the past of trade policies on both the rate and the structure of employment? and, second, What modifications of existing trade policies would expand employment opportunities and reinforce the government's efforts to reduce the overall levels of unemployment and underemployment in the economy? In the following two sections we will briefly review the main features of Pakistan's economic growth and describe the structure of foreign trade and protection. We will explore the contribution of export and import-competing industries to employment by examining the labor content of imports and exports, and subsequent sections will indicate the degree to which the labor content of imports and exports has been influenced by distortions in factor markets.

Two important aspects of the scope of this study should be noted at the outset. First, the geographical coverage is limited to present-day Pakistan or what was, before 1972, West Pakistan. "Pakistan" is used to refer both to the geographical region contained within the boundaries of only present-day Pakistan and to the original boundaries that included what is now Bangladesh. Where some confusion might arise in the use of this simplifying convention, the words "All" (i.e., West Pakistan plus East Pakistan) and "West" are inserted in parentheses to clarify which geographical region is being described. While this ambiguous use of the word "Pakistan" is far from satisfactory, it is less cumbersome than repeated references to "pre-1972" Pakistan and similar terms.

Second, the principal benchmark year of analysis for this study is the Pakistani fiscal year 1969/70—that is, July 1969 to June 1970. The selection of this year was based on several considerations. As we pointed out above, the period since 1970 has been extremely tumultuous from both political and economic points of view. It would be difficult to argue that any year during this period was representative or typical. Although no year is ever free from random and nonrecurring events, 1969/70 is perhaps more nearly typical than any of the more recent years. Most important, the most complete source of value-added and employment data for this study was the *Census of Manufacturing Industries, 1969–70.* In some cases data on industry are available for 1970/71, and these are incorporated in the study where appropriate. Certain data series—on wages and effective export exchange rates, for example—are available for more recent years, and these are also included to relate this study as closely as possible to current economic issues.[2]

7.1 Growth and Structural Change: An Overview

7.1.1 Growth: 1950–70

One of the poorest countries of the world at the time of its creation— "an economic wreck," according to a *Time* magazine story in 1947— Pakistan managed to increase its real per capita income over the decade of the 1950s by only 10 percent. But over the 1960s, real per capita income rose by 50 percent. During the latter decade, economic performance was quite respectable by comparison with countries in the same per capita income bracket and gave the lie to predictions of the previous decade that Pakistan—resource poor and people rich—was caught inextricably in a low-income equilibrium trap.

Perhaps the most dramatic and unexpected change was in the pace of agricultural growth. As table 7.1 shows, the annual rate of agricultural growth in Pakistan averaged 5 percent during the 1960s, a figure thought unattainable on a sustained basis by any developing country, especially Pakistan. The movement from virtual stagnation to a 5 percent rate of expansion was the result of two "revolutions": a tubewell-chemical revolution in the first half of the decade, and the Green Revolution in the second half. Technological innovation and adaptation were at the core of both revolutions, but the primary force behind the acceptance and spread of the new technologies was the government's price policies. In contrast to the previous decade, when the internal terms of trade were tilted in favor of the manufacturing sector, the government permitted agricultural prices to rise relative to industrial prices. The commodity-fertilizer price ratio became so attractive that use of chemical fertilizers increased, agricultural productivity rose, and the real income of farmers expanded significantly.

While agriculture stagnated in the 1950s, industry flourished because of the high protection afforded by the exchange control system and because of the pent-up demand for consumer goods no longer available from traditional sources. Import substitution in cotton and synthetic textiles, leather goods, soaps, matches, bicycles, and other simple-technology consumer goods occurred rapidly during the 1950s. One important factor shaping the pattern of industrial growth during this period

Table 7.1	Sectoral Rates of Growth, 1950–70 (Average Annual Percentage Rates at Constant 1959–60 Prices)	
Sector	1950–60	1960–70
Agriculture	1.7	5.0
Manufacturing	18.2	9.8
Other	3.8	7.3
Total GNP	3.5	6.8
Population	2.3	2.7
Per capita GNP	1.2	4.1

Source: 1950–60, Papanek (1967, p. 20); 1960–70, Government of Pakistan, *Economic Survey 1975–76* (1976), App. p. 10.
Note: "Manufacturing" excludes small-scale industries, which are included in "other."

was the availability of domestic raw materials. Products requiring imported inputs to any large extent were not prime candidates for import substitution in spite of high protection. Rather, those goods made with locally produced raw materials, such as textiles and leather products, grew most rapidly because producers did not have to undergo the costly and time-consuming procedure of attaining import licenses for the principal inputs. The restrictions on imported inputs slowed the growth of the investment goods industries because of the higher import component. By 1963 more than three-quarters of consumer goods were produced at home, compared with only one-third of investment goods.

The pace of manufacturing growth slowed in the 1960s. In part this was inevitable because high rates of growth from an extremely small base are not difficult, but it becomes more difficult to maintain these rates as the base expands. But several real economic factors did dampen the rate of manufacturing expansion. The elimination of easy opportunities for import replacement caused investors to search outside the manufacturing sector for new business ventures. Moreover, rates of protection diminished during the first few years of the decade, adding to investors' reluctance to build new manufacturing plants. The rate of growth in manufacturing was still extremely rapid by international standards—almost 10 percent per annum for large- and small-scale units combined.[3] Success in maintaining the momentum in industry during this period can be traced, to a very great degree, to a de facto devaluation of the export exchange rate brought about by the introduction of the export bonus voucher scheme. This scheme, described more fully in a subsequent section, in effect gave exporters an opportunity to sell their foreign exchange earnings at a very favorable rate. Although the bonus voucher's value fluctuated, it nevertheless augmented the official exchange rate, and Pakistan avoided to some extent the trap that import substitution set for many developing countries: a stagnant export sector languishing behind a heavily overvalued local currency.

In summary, the 1960s represented a quantum jump in Pakistan's economic performance as compared with the previous decade. Not all of Pakistan's success can be attributed to her own policies. The willingness of donors to supply foreign aid in the first half of the 1960s was undoubtedly a major factor in the acceleration of growth. The steady growth of the world market for labor-intensive, agriculturally based products during the decade was, if not a necessary condition, a major element in the expansion of manufacturing exports. Yet none of these external factors would have had a measurable effect on the overall rate of economic growth if Pakistan had not undertaken a major reform of her economic policies after 1958. These reforms, for the most part, took the form of rationalization and liberalization of the direct controls of the previous decade. Many distortions remained, but the overall tendency was to bring about more, rather than less, uniformity in the degree of distortions among sectors and subsectors of the economy.

7.1.2   The Structure and Pattern of Trade

Since 1947 the pattern of Pakistan's trade has changed dramatically. Exporting almost solely agricultural goods and minerals in the early 1950s, Pakistan rapidly became an exporter of manufactured goods. Although these largely involved the first stages of processing of agricultural goods—converting raw cotton into yarn and hides into tanned leather, for example—the rapid rise of manufactured goods as a share of total exports is rather remarkable given Pakistan's relatively low level of development. In 1969/70, manufactured goods accounted for two-thirds of all exports. The structure of imports has also undergone substantial change, but in a different form. The division of total imports between natural resource based goods (agricultural products and minerals) and manufactured goods has remained approximately the same over two decades of Pakistan's development (1950–70). But the composition of each of these two categories has altered. Within the manufactured goods group, for example, imports of consumer goods have been replaced by imports of intermediate and investment goods. The composition of imports and exports in 1969/70 is shown in table 7.2, which also shows product classification according to its trade orientation (see section 7.3 for the discussion on the allocation of trade by commodity category).

Trade in Natural Resource Based Goods

Pakistan's imports of natural resource based (NRB) goods in 1969/70 consisted basically of three products: wheat, crude oil, and wood. Imports of wheat have varied greatly depending on the availability of PL 480 financing and Pakistan's own agricultural production. By comparison with imports both before and after 1969/70, wheat imports in this year were below normal. Pakistan produces crude oil, but only enough to supply about 10 percent of domestic needs. Pakistan imported almost no other minerals in unprocessed form because of the lack of domestic processing capacity.

Pakistan's exports of NRB goods in 1969/70 consisted primarily of raw cotton, rice, fish, hides, and wool. Raw cotton was by far the major export product, accounting for more than two-fifths of all NRB exports.

Manufactured Goods

The distribution of both imports and exports of manufactured goods across the three principal product categories—consumer, intermediate, and investment goods—is shown in table 7.2. Each manufactured commodity is further classified into one of three categories: export, import-competing or noncompeting import. The T statistic described in the in-

Table 7.2   Trade Flows, 1969/70

Commodity Group	Value of Exports (Rs 000s)	Total Exports (%)	Value of Imports (Rs 000s)	Total Imports (%)	T Statistics[a]	Trade Category[b]
Manufactures						
Consumer goods						
Sugar and confectionery	11,170	.7	1,150	0	.01	C
Tea and coffee	0	.0	13	0	.01	C
Edible oils and fats	2.270	.1	13,900	.4	.01	C
Food processing	92,900	6.1	32,100	1.0	.01	C
Beverages	1,530	.1	3,720	.1	.10	C
Tobacco	1,690	.1	1,090	0	−.05	C
Cotton textiles	511,600	33.8	530	0	−1.30	X
Other textiles	1,690	.1	16,070	.5	.01	C
Footwear	87,600	5.8	1,500	0	−.70	X
Wood, cork, and furniture	600	0	32,400	1.0	.50	C
Drugs and pharmaceuticals	15,350	1.0	72,450	2.2	.08	C
Printing and publishing	2,300	.2	10,700	.3	.00	C
Sporting goods	30,400	2.0	4,600	.1	−1.13	X
Total consumer goods	758,240	50.0	190,223	5.6		
Intermediate goods						
Paper and paper products	1,100	.1	30,800	.9	.22	NC
Leather and leather products	117,100	7.7	1,000	0	−6.38	X
Rubber and rubber products	4,100	.3	64,250	1.9	.50	NC
Chemicals	12,000	.8	526,400	15.6	.56	NC
Petroleum and petroleum products	39,800	2.6	32,100	1.0	.56	NC
Railroad ties	100	0	13,600	.4	.9	NC
Total intermediate goods	174,200	11.5	668,150	19.8		

Table 7.2—*continued*

Commodity Group	Value of Exports (Rs 000s)	Total Exports (%)	Value of Imports (Rs 000s)	Total Imports (%)	T Statistics[a]	Trade Category[b]
Investment goods						
Nonmetallic minerals	20,100	1.3	45,500	1.4	− .07	C
Basic metals	200	0	365,100	10.8	.64	NC
Fabricated metal products	7,300	.5	115,500	3.4	.42	NC
Nonelectrical machinery	6,550	.4	709,000	21.0	.87	NC
Transportation equipment (except motor vehicles)	1,200	.1	183,000	5.4	.71	NC
Instruments	17,500	1.2	50,700	1.5	.05	C
Motor vehicles	530	0	157,100	4.7	.71	NC
Electrical machinery	4,800	.3	218,850	6.5	.53	NC
Total investment goods	58,180	3.8	1,844,750	54.7		
Total manufactures	990,620	65.3	2,703,123	80.1		
NRB goods						
Rice	93,683	6.2	—	—		
Wheat	—	—	98,484	2.9		
Cotton	223,800	14.8	—	—		
Other	155,667	10.3	315,316	9.4		
Mining	24,500	1.6	220,400	6.5		
Miscellaneous industries	25,000	1.7	27,600	.8		
Total NRB goods	522,650	34.7	661,800	19.9		
Total trade flows	1,513,270	100.0	3,364,923	100.0		

troductory chapter (see section 7.3 for more discussion) is shown in column 5 of the table.

Export industries. More than three-quarters of Pakistan's manufactured exports are concentrated in just four industries: cotton textiles, leather products, footwear, and sporting goods. The remaining one-quarter are dispersed fairly evenly over the other industry categories. Two of the four major export industries accounting for more than 60 percent of total manufactured exports—cotton textiles and leather products—rely to a great extent on domestic raw materials and, depending on how close that link is, could be classified as processed NRB or as manufactured exports. The other two leading industries—footwear and sporting goods—appear to derive their comparative advantage strictly from relative factor costs. In both industries, a principal intermediate input—rubber for footwear production and wood for sporting goods (cricket bats, tennis rackets)—is imported.

In two of the export industries, small-scale producers—defined as those with fewer than twenty workers—have a significant share of the market. Since export data are not compiled separately by size of firm, the actual contribution of small producers to exports is unknown. Informal estimates have been made that as much as half of all exports of gray cloth originates in the small-scale sector. It is interesting that since the late 1960s the fastest-growing export industries have been dominated by small-scale firms—carpets, surgical instruments, and sporting goods. As will be shown below, the rapid growth of exports from small-scale producers came at a time when the overall employment of the small-scale sector was declining, suggesting, on the one hand, a major restructuring of this sector as it adapted to changing consumer tastes and competition from the large-scale sector but, on the other hand, a strong export potential, possibly based on its labor intensity. Little is known about the small-scale sector because it falls outside normal data collection channels, since small producers are not subject to compulsory registration. As a result, the data on factor intensities presented in a subsequent section do not include small-scale producers.

Import-competing industries. In eleven industries, domestic consumption is roughly equal to domestic production, and by the three-way di-

---

Notes to Table 7.2

Source: Government of Pakistan, *Pakistan Trade Statistics: 1969/70.*

[a]T statistics are averages of 1969/70 and 1970/71 data. T_i statistics were not calculated for NRB goods, since this study focuses upon manufacturing activity only. Rice and cotton are exportables, other NRB is an importable, and wheat and mining are noncompeting importables.

[b]C = import-competing industry; X = export industry; NC = noncompeting industry.

vision introduced earlier they are therefore considered import-competing. Not surprisingly, only 10 percent of all manufactured imports compete with these industries because import substitution in these industries is almost complete. Nine of the eleven industries in this category are in the consumer goods sector, the remaining two being nonmetallic minerals (cement) and scientific instruments. It is somewhat misleading to state unequivocally that import substitution possibilities in consumer goods have been exhausted, because the level of aggregation employed in this analysis masks a number of remaining opportunities. For instance, consumer durables (refrigerators, air conditioners, etc.) are still largely imported but are classified in table 7.2 as investment goods.

Noncompeting industries. Almost all of the intermediate and investment goods industries fall under the heading "noncompeting." The only exceptions are one export industry—leather products—and the two import-competing industries noted above, nonmetallic minerals and scientific instruments. The degree of "noncompetitiveness" of industries under this heading varies widely. Some, like basic metals, have since become, or will soon become, import-competing because of investment projects now nearing completion. In other industries, such as motor vehicles, scale factors make widespread import substitution an unlikely prospect for the short run because Pakistan's internal market is too small to accommodate plants of efficient size.

7.1.3 The Pattern of Trade

Perhaps the most important feature of the origin and destination of Pakistan's trade during the late 1960s was the economic union with what was then East Pakistan. A third of Pakistan's exports in 1969/70 went to East Pakistan, and 15 percent of her imports originated there. The cotton group (raw cotton, yarn, textiles) and rice accounted for almost half the exports to the eastern wing, with the rest spread over many different product groups. The principal imports from East Pakistan included tea, jute manufactures, paper, and matches. These together accounted for more than half of East Pakistan's exports to Pakistan.

The actual gains from trade accruing to each of the two wings of the country are the subject of considerable controversy. It is important to recognize, however, that changes in trade with East Pakistan made a relatively small contribution to Pakistan's industrial growth. It has been estimated that less than 5 percent of the growth of industrial output could be attributed to the expansion of exports to East Pakistan or to the domestic replacement of imports coming from East Pakistan (Guisinger 1976). Moreover, after the severance of ties with East Pakistan, Pakistan had relatively little difficulty marketing the items abroad that were formerly shipped to East Pakistan or finding alternative sources of imports. While the composition of both exports and imports changed between the pre- and postseparation periods, there is no evidence that these changes arose because of the separation itself.

Insofar as trade with other countries is concerned, by far the bulk of imports came from developed countries. In 1969–70 more than three-quarters of all imports came from Europe (38 percent), North America (28 percent), Japan (10 percent), and Hong Kong (1 percent). The centrally planned economies supplied 8 percent of imports, and the rest was divided among other developing countries. No trade took place with India in 1969/70 because of a ban that was in effect from the early 1950s until 1976.

Pakistan's exports to developed countries amounted to almost half of all exports. Exports to North America came to 7 percent, Europe to 24 percent, and Hong Kong and Japan combined to 18 percent. The centrally planned economies absorbed 15 percent of the export total. In comparing import and export shares by region, one should bear in mind that imports in 1969/70 were roughly double the value of exports, so that, for example, the deficit in trade with North America was, in dollar terms, far greater than the respective shares of imports and exports would suggest.

7.1.4 Patterns of Industrial Growth

The major influence on Pakistan's pattern of trade over the period 1950–70 was the growth of large-scale manufacturing. In sheer quan-

Table 7.3   Annual Rates of Growth of Manufacturing and Its Principal Sectors

	All Pakistan			West Pakistan	
Sector	1951/52– 1954/55 (Current Prices)	1954/55– 1959/60 (Current Prices)	1959/60– 1963/64 (Current Prices)	1963/64– 1970/71 (Current Prices)	1963/64– 1970/71 (Constant Prices)[a]
Large-scale manufacturing					
Consumer goods	43%	16%	13%	14.5%	11.0%
Intermediate goods	28	27	14	11.2	5.7
Investment goods	16	28	26	7.2	1.7
Total large-scale	38	20	16	12.9	9.0
Large- and small-scale manufacturing, total (West Pakistan only)	34	12	16	—	

Source: See Guisinger (1976, table 2).
[a]Prices of 1963/64.

titative terms, import substitution was successful in eliminating almost all consumer goods imports. The rapid rise of manufacturing enabled Pakistan to diversify its export base and to expand imports of intermediate and investment goods. Table 7.3 presents rates of growth of output for the major commodity groups for four separate time periods.

The pattern of growth rates bears out a number of the familiar features of Pakistan's early industrialization. Growth rates for the manufacturing sector fell off sharply after 1955, remained more or less constant at a fairly high level between 1955 and 1963, then declined again.

Sources of Industrial Growth

The changes in the nature of Pakistan's industrialization can be seen from an analysis of the "sources" of growth. Growth can be attributed to three sources: import substitution, export expansion, and the increase in domestic demand. The contributions of these three sources to manufacturing growth in Pakistan for four different subperiods covering roughly the first two decades of Pakistan's industrialization are shown in table 7.4.

The pattern of sources clearly shows the deflection of manufacturing from an almost exclusive strategy of import substitution toward a more even pattern of expansion. Perhaps the most striking feature of these sources is that import substitution, which was practically the only source of growth in the initial period, accounted for no more than one-quarter of the increases in manufacturing output as a whole and in its main subsectors in subsequent periods. It is interesting that, even before the introduction of the export bonus voucher scheme, exports were an important source of manufacturing growth, largely due to the comparative cost advantage that jute and cotton textiles had even at a highly overvalued exchange rate (see section 7.4).

Industrial structure. The cumulative effects of Pakistan's pattern of industrialization can be seen in the data on sector and trade shares contained in table 7.5. In 1970, consumer goods accounted for four-fifths of manufacturing value added. Since Pakistan's premier manufacturing industry—textiles—is included in this study as part of consumer goods, it is perhaps not surprising that this sector commands such a high percentage of total industrial output. The preponderant position of consumer goods has very important implications for the future rate and patterns of growth in the manufacturing sector.

The other interesting pattern evident in table 7.5 is the differential effect that past import substitution has had on the shares of imports in the total supplies of the three sectors. Import substitution is almost exhausted in consumer goods, where only 6 percent of the total supplies of these goods is obtained from abroad. In the intermediate and investment

Table 7.4   Sources of Manufacturing Growth: Percentage of Increased Output

Sector	All Pakistan 1951–54			All Pakistan 1954–59			All Pakistan 1959–63			West Pakistan 1963–70		
	Domestic Demand	Export Expansion	Import Substitution	Domestic Demand	Export Expansion	Import Substitution	Domestic Demand	Export Expansion	Import Substitution	Domestic Demand	Export Expansion	Import Substitution
Consumer goods	3	1	96	56	16	28	110	−1	−9	59	26	15
Intermediate goods	7	5	87	34	58	8	48	22	30	77	23	0
Investment goods	−7	1	106	72	1	27	109	1	−10	71	3	26
All industries	2	2	96	53	24	23	96	5	−1	70	17	13

Source: Guisinger (1976).

Table 7.5   Structure of Manufacturing in Pakistan, 1970

Sector	Share in Value Added	Share of Imports in Total Supplies[a]	Share of Exports in Total Supplies[a]
Consumer goods	80%	6%	29%
Intermediate goods	7	58	15
Investment goods	13	63	4

Source: Guisinger (1976).
[a]Total supply is gross value of output plus imports.

goods sectors, imports account for 58 and 63 percent, respectively, of the goods supplied, and thus in a technical sense ample opportunities for import substitution remain, though the scope for economically sound import replacement in these sectors cannot be determined from these data. On the export side, the consumer goods sector, led by textiles, has the highest export share, 29 percent, with the intermediate goods and investment goods sectors substantially below that level with 15 and 4 percent, respectively.

7.1.5   Structure of Employment

Pakistan's concerns with employment are perhaps as pressing as those of any developing country covered by this project. On the one hand, population growth has been very rapid, averaging 2.8 percent annually from 1950 to 1970 and 3 percent from 1970 to 1975. Almost 60 percent of the labor force was in agriculture in 1975, and so population pressures will intensify the need to create nonagricultural employment opportunities.

Open unemployment has not been a major factor in Pakistan until recently: real incomes simply are too low. However, there have been measures that have raised the real wage in the formal sector, and the formal/informal labor market distinction is growing in importance. As will be seen in section 7.4, the growing differential is, in part, one of the factors causing total employment in manufacturing to grow very slowly.

The levels of open unemployment, in both rural and urban areas, are low compared with many developing countries. No national survey, apart from the 1972 housing, economic, and demographic (HED) survey, has recorded an unemployment rate greater than 5 percent. The 13 percent figure reported in the HED survey is the only exception and appears to be due to differences in the definition of unemployed persons, since the 1971/72 and 1974/75 labor force surveys both record unemployment rates below 5 percent. The low level of open unemployment may seem paradoxical in view of Pakistan's extreme poverty and high rate of population growth. Yet the absence of open unemployment makes sense if, as later sections of this chapter make clear, few barriers exist to the movement of labor among sectors, especially between the formal and informal sectors. Underemployment is a far greater problem. Few workers replied to survey interviewers that they were unable to find any work, even though the work they did find often left them below the poverty line (on the incidence of poverty, see Naseem 1973 and Guisinger 1977*b*).

The pattern of growth during 1950–70 led to changes in the structure of employment, as is evident from table 7.6. Between the two census years, 1951 and 1961, the share of the labor force engaged in agriculture fell while the shares of manufacturing and the various service industries rose. The largest gainer, in absolute terms, was manufacturing, reflecting the particularly rapid rate of expansion of this sector.

During 1961–72, roughly the decade of the 1960s, the share of agricultural employment in total employment remained almost the same, implying a relatively fast rate of growth for agricultural employment. There are a number of possible causes for this, but certainly one impor-

Table 7.6   **Labor Force, Employment, and Distribution of Employment by Industry in (West) Pakistan, 1951–72**

				Net Percentage Change	
Labor force	1951	1961	1972	1951–61	1961–72
Total (thousands)	9,812.0	12,763.0	19,016.0	+30.1	+49.0
Employed (thousands)	9,331.0	12,469.0	16,373.0	+33.6	+31.3
Unemployed (%)	3.2	1.5	13.0	− 1.7	+11.5
Not classifiable (%)	.7	.8	.9	+ .1	+ .1
Employment distribution (%)					
Agriculture	67.5	59.9	59.3	− 7.6	− .6
Mining	.1	.2	1.0	+ .1	+ .8
Manufacturing	10.0	14.1	8.3	+ 4.1	− 5.8
Electricity, gas, and water }	1.9	.2	.1 }	+ .5	− .1
Construction }		2.2	4.6 }		+ 2.4
Wholesale and retail trade	7.1	7.3	9.3	+ .4	+ 2.0
Transportation	1.8	3.0	3.9	+ 1.2	+ .9
Finance	—ᵃ	.2	.7	—ᵃ	+ .5
Services	11.6	12.9	12.8	+ 1.3	− .1
Total	100.0	100.0	100.0	—	—

Source: 1951, Farooq (1976) p. 88; 1961, Farooq (1976) p. 56; 1972, Government of Pakistan (1972), Housing, economic and demographic survey, table 20.
Note: Includes males and females.
ᵃIncluded with wholesale and retail trade in 1951 census.

tant factor was the rapid growth in agricultural output. In spite of the technological changes that occurred in this sector after 1960, the rate of expansion was so great that the demand for agricultural labor kept pace with the growth of the labor force.

The most difficult shift to explain during 1961–72 is the decline in manufacturing's share of total employment, from 14.1 percent to 8.3 percent. This decline was not only relative; the number of persons employed in manufacturing fell, as can readily be seen from comparing the group share with total employment. Errors or redefinitions in sector classification in the census are possible, but the decline is also apparent in the data collected through the annual labor force surveys.

Manufacturing employment in both large-scale and small-scale establishments for 1961 and 1972 are shown in table 7.7. Because the data on total employment and large-scale employment are derived from two different surveys, the levels of small-scale employment, calculated as the difference between total and large-scale employment, must be considered as only orders of magnitude. This is particularly true of employment changes for a particular industry group but is still true when

Table 7.7   Manufacturing Employment by Industrial Category, in (West) Pakistan, 1961 and 1972 (Thousands of Workers)

	1961			1972		
Industry	Total Employment	Large-Scale	Small-Scale	Total Employment	Large-Scale	Small-Scale
Food, beverages, and tobacco	131	30	101	99	57	42
Leather products, textiles, and clothing	842	178	664	856	254	602
Wood products	162	2	160	82	4	78
Paper products and printing	22	11	11	29	12	17
Iron and steel products, fabricated metal products, transportation equipment, electrical goods, and non-electrical machinery and equipment	281	64	217	108	82	26
Nonmetallic mineral products	161	12	149	143	17	126
Products of petroleum and coal, rubber products, and chemical products	25	18	7	40	36	4
Miscellaneous	82	22	60	76	18	58
Total	1,706	337	1,369	1,433	480	953

Source: Guisinger (1978).
Note: See text for reservations regarding the data, especially for small-scale establishments.

aggregate employment of all industry groups is considered. Nonetheless, the overall drop in employment in the small-scale sector is striking and probably too great to be solely the product of erroneous data. On the basis of these data, employment in the small-scale sector declined roughly 30 percent over the eleven-year period. This apparent decline runs counter to the common assumption among planners in Pakistan that small-scale sector employment expanded during the 1960s. Indirect evidence on employment growth in this sector is mixed. Certainly, in some industries—notably carpets, surgical instruments, and sporting goods—the rapid growth in exports must have been accompanied by an expansion of employment. For the largest of the small-scale industries, cotton textile weaving, Anwar (1975) suggests that employment may have grown by as much as 5 percent over 1961–72. However, Anwar (1975) and Malik (1975) concluded that there are such great ambiguities in the data on textile production and use that little can be said with confidence about the growth of either employment or output in this sector. For many rural small-scale industries, such as pottery and ironworking, Eckert (1972) found abundant indirect evidence of a sharp decrease in employment.

The employment picture in manufacturing is thus somewhat clouded by inadequacies of the data. However, it is true that employment in large-scale manufacturing grew over the 1961–72 period at an annual rate of 3.2 percent, while large-scale manufacturing output was increasing by more than 10 percent per annum. According to available data, this expansion of large-scale employment was not sufficient to offset the decline in small-scale employment, with the result that total manufacturing employment actually declined over the period. The probable cause of the low expansion of employment in the large-scale sector is a relatively low output elasticity of employment (about 0.2). In 1959/60 prices, output grew by 220 percent from 1961 to 1972 while employment rose by just 42 percent.

7.1.6   Income Distribution

Pakistan is unusual for a developing country not only because the degree of income disparity is relatively low, but also because it has shown a tendency to fall rather than rise during a period of rapid economic growth. The data in table 7.8 show a slight downward trend in the Gini coefficient for both the total population and the rural sector. The change in income distribution involved more than a reshuffling of income among the upper income brackets, as can be seen from the increases in the shares of income received by the bottom 20 and 40 percentiles shown in columns 3 and 4. Although the change in income distribution between 1963 and 1971 may not be statistically significant, the important implication of these data is that income inequalities did not widen. These data, like all similar data on self-reported income, ought

Table 7.8   Measures of Income Distribution Based on Household
              Income, 1963–72

	Gini Coefficient		Income Shares (Urban + Rural)	
Year	Total	Rural	Lowest 20%	Lowest 40%
1963/64	.347	.339	7.1	19.2
1966/67	.342	.313	8.1	19.3
1968/69	.326	.261	8.5	20.1
1969/70	.323	.292	8.7	20.6
1970/71	.315	.284	8.8	21.1
1971/72	.332	.293	8.2	20.4

Source: Naseem (1973).

not to be regarded as unfailingly accurate. Yet, when various aspects of the income-employment picture are viewed together—the growth of employment in all sectors,[4] the rise in real wages reported in a subsequent section, the slow rate of rural to urban migration—stability in the measures of income inequality is at least plausible.

7.1.7 Inflation

During the period covered by this study, inflation was not a major issue. Between 1960 and 1970, consumer prices rose 43 percent, or at an annually compounded rate of less than 4 percent. More than half of the 43 percent increase occurred between 1964 and 1967, a period that included a major military confrontation with India and two disastrous harvests for lack of adequate rainfall. After 1970 the rate of inflation soared, and the price level doubled in just five years. Many factors contributed to the price rise, including the devaluation of 1972, the oil price increase and the general increase in the prices of Pakistan's imports, domestic fiscal policy that perennially produced budget deficits, and the adverse weather conditions that drove up the prices of food grains.

7.2 The Trade Regime

Pakistan has undergone three phases in its trade regime history (for a complete discussion, see Lewis 1969, 1970 and Papanek 1967). The first phase, roughly covering the period 1950–60, was characterized by a very restrictive and pervasive system of controls to protect import substitution activities. In the second phase (1960–72) these restrictions were liberalized (although not eliminated), and exports were promoted through an export bonus voucher system. The final phase began in May 1972 when the licensing system was scrapped, tariffs were lowered, and the degree of cascading contained in the tariff was reduced.[5]

7.2.1   The Trade Regime: 1950–60

The major instrument of protection to import-substituting industries during the 1950–60 period was the system of import licensing. The value of import licenses issued and the distribution of these licenses across import categories were determined by the chief comptroller of imports and exports. Both the level and the product composition of import licenses changed from year to year, but in all years demand for imports exceeded the controlled supply, creating a gap between importers' costs (c.i.f. prices plus duties and sales taxes) and market prices. The margin above importers' costs represented a windfall profit for those fortunate enough to have the import licenses. Also, domestic manufacturing firms were able to sell their products at prices well above importers' costs because of the scarcity markups created by restrictive licensing. Tariff protection was, in most product lines, a far less significant factor in overall protection than the licensing of imports. The structure of nominal and effective *tariff* protection, therefore, provides little indication of the production incentives created by the trade-control system during this period. A study by Lewis (1970, p. 69) suggests that the scarcity markup—the percentage increase of the wholesale price above the importer's cost—was 67 percent. Lewis also found that, for his sample, nominal rates of protection across the three major subcategories of manufacturing—consumer, intermediate, and investment goods—appeared to be uniform.

7.2.2   The Trade Regime: 1960–72

The reorientation of economic policy undertaken by the Ayub government after its accession in 1958 had important ramifications on the structure of protection. A new philosophy of planning and government control was enshrined in the second five-year plan (1960–65).

The Plan proposes a decisive move towards a more liberal economy and a bold switch over from direct controls to a policy of regulation of the economy through suitable fiscal and monetary controls.

Direct controls have so far been the chief instrument of economic planning. There is a multiplicity of such controls on capital issues, prices, profits, imports, exports and distribution of certain goods and commodities. These controls were not only inefficient in many cases; they have also placed an additional burden on the scarce administrative talent of the country, which could be better employed on development. . . . Such controls cannot be continued for long without hampering private investment and production, reducing capital formation in the economy and aggravating the imbalance between demand and supply. [Government of Pakistan, *Second Five-Year Plan*, pp. 78–80]

The major forms liberalization took were the export bonus voucher scheme and the introduction of liberalized licensing, especially the creation of the "free list," though several other policy changes were also implemented.

The Export Bonus Voucher Scheme

During the 1950s it became clear that exporters were caught in a continually worsening cost-price squeeze. The maintenance of an overvalued exchange rate through restrictive import controls implied (1) a constant rupee return per dollar of goods exported; but (2) production costs that had a tendency to escalate when foreign exchange became scarce and the scarcity premium on imported raw materials rose. To offset this disadvantage, the export bonus voucher scheme was introduced in 1959. For every Rs 100 of foreign exchange earned, the exporter received a voucher for either Rs 20 or Rs 40, depending on the type of product, that effectively became a license to import goods up to the face value of the voucher. The bonus vouchers were licenses to import only goods from a list of importable items, but the list was quite broad and encompassed consumer, intermediate, and investment goods.

Exporters had considerable freedom in deploying their vouchers. They could be used to import raw materials for processing into export or import-competing goods. They could be used for personal imports of luxury items, such as automobiles. Or they could be sold on the open market, commanding a price well in excess of their face value. This latter alternative was extremely popular, and bonus vouchers were traded on the Karachi stock exchange with the premium—that is, the price expressed as a percentage of its face value—quoted daily. Importers purchasing the vouchers could then import any item on the bonus list. If the premium was 150 percent and the c.i.f. value of the imported item was $1, or Rs 4.76 at the official rate of exchange, and the duty 50 percent, the total cost to the importer was: Rs 4.76 + 1.5 (Rs 4.76) + 0.5 (Rs. 4.76) = Rs 14.28. Since many items were purchased with bonus voucher premiums and customs duties of these same levels, it is clear that the marginal EER for exports exceeded the official exchange rate by a substantial amount.

For the exporter, the bonus voucher scheme offered a differentiated and variable EER. Agricultural goods carried a bonus rate—the share of foreign exchange earned returned in the form of vouchers—of zero while manufactured goods carried rates of 20 or 40 percent initially. The bonus rate structure, the number of rate categories, and the commodities assigned to the various categories were changed from time to time. Also, the premium fluctuated between 100 and 200 percent, though an attempt was made to stabilize the bonus premium at about 150 percent. The EER for exports ranged, therefore, from Rs 4.76 to Rs 7.61 (Rs 4.76 + 1.5 × 0.4 × Rs 4.76).

The Free List

The introduction of the free list into Pakistan's import control system represented a major step toward relaxing the direct control mechanism. Before January 1964, when the free list was announced, all importers had to be registered, and licenses were issued only to certified importers up to a limit that was based on the importer's level of purchases during a base period. The system stood as a barrier to new entrants into import trade and, because of the compartmentalization of import quotas, resulted in obvious inefficiencies when some importers had excess demands for importable goods while others had an excess supply of licenses. In principle, licenses were not transferable; in practice they were, but at considerable cost to the integrity of government civil service.

The free list essentially enumerated those commodities that could be imported without licensing procedures. Because the pent-up demand for imports was so enormous, the free list was never truly free (see the comments on the free list by Thomas, summarized by Lewis 1970, p. 28). Nevertheless, the free list represented a step toward the market mechanism.

After 1964 all imports came into Pakistan under one of four categories: free list; license; cash-cum-bonus; or bonus. In some cases the domestic prices of importable goods were below the landed cost of imports (c.i.f. prices plus duties and taxes) because import substitution had proceeded so far that local production was able to satisfy demand, and competition among local producers made tariffs partially redundant. But for most industrial categories, scarcity margins above landed cost were the rule. As in the previous decade, measures of tariff protection did not adequately convey the degree or direction of the protection afforded by the trade control system.

No major reforms of the trade policy system were undertaken between 1964 and 1972, but there were still important modifications in various trade control instruments. The export bonus scheme, for example, was altered in several ways. The number of bonus rate categories—two initially—was raised to six, and commodities were shuffled among these categories on several occasions. The list of products that could be imported on bonus was changed from time to time, and other limits were placed on the amounts of certain items—automobiles, for example—that could be imported by any one party under the bonus scheme. The free list never played the vital role in the latter half of the decade that it did in 1964 and 1965, though it still performed a useful "safety valve" function that released pressures inherent in any direct control system.

Tariff and sales tax rates for some product groups increased over the period, but because of the scarcity margins due to the system of restrictive licensing, this upward movement did not represent a change in the structure of protection. After the 1965 war with India, aid donors' enthusiasm about the prospects for tranquil economic growth on the subcontinent waned, and the availability of foreign exchange shrank. Two poor harvests in 1966 and 1968 aggravated both the general economic picture and import demand, and interest in liberalization slackened.

7.2.3   The Trade Regime: 1972 to the Present

The entire structure of Pakistan's trade-control system underwent a complete revision at the time of devaluation in May 1972. The export bonus scheme was dropped, tariffs were lowered, and the degree of cascading in the tariff system was reduced. Most important, the licensing system was scrapped. "An import license would now (post-1972) be issued freely to any Pakistani on registration" (*Pakistan Economic Survey 1971–72*, p. 16).

Data are not available to analyze completely the effects of these changes. However, the volume of exports rose from their 1969 level by about 40 percent and then leveled off in the early 1970s. The incentives for import substitution, on a net basis, probably did not change radically, but more uniformity in protection afforded by the tariff system may have been achieved.

7.2.4   Levels and Structure of Protection

The trend in protection over the period 1963/64–1970/71 is evident from the data in table 7.9. The nominal rates of protection for a post-devaluation year—1972/73—are shown for comparison. A cascaded structure of protection can be observed in each of the three time periods. Consumer goods have a higher average level of protection than either intermediate or investment goods. This is true whether nominal or effective rates[6] are taken as the measure of protection.

While the structure of nominal and effective rates of protection at two points in time provides some idea of variations in the level of incentive over time, these measures fail to take fully into account trends in domestic inflation and, especially for export incentives, trends in prices abroad. Changes in trade policies are sometimes needed to offset the effects of domestic and foreign price movements in order to maintain a constant real incentive; or, put another way, the absence of any changes in the face of price movements at home and abroad may alter the incentive structure and affect domestic production and trade.

Guisinger (1977a) found that the real EER[7] for exports actually rose between 1968 and 1971, as the result of both changes in trade policies and factors in the international economic environment. While no direct comparison with the real incentive for producing import sub-

Table 7.9   Comparison of Rates of Protection, Manufacturing Activities 1963/64, 1970/71, and 1972/73

Sector	1963/64		1970/71		1972–73
	Nominal Pro-tection	Effective Pro-tection	Nominal Pro-tection	Effective Pro-tection	Nominal Pro-tection
Consumer goods					
Sugar	215	nva	266%	585%	57%
Edible oils	106	nva	54	130	62
Cotton textiles	56	733%	76	172	0
Other textiles	350	nva	141	317	88
Printing and publishing	28	22	43	36	57
Soaps	94	178	43	106	34
Motor vehicles	249	nva	270	595	61
Simple average	157	nc	128	277	63
Intermediate goods					
Wood and lumber	73	1,150	85	197	108
Leather tanning	56	567	76	177	0
Rubber products	153	nva	55	132	48
Fertilizers	15	nva	25	64	n.a.
Paints and varnishes	102	257	56	134	34
Chemicals	81	300	56	106	34
Petroleum products	107	−6	121	274	65
Paper products	94	376	57	177	69
Simple average	85	nc	66	158	43
Investment and related goods					
Nonmetallic mineral products	154	335	76	182	70
Cement	75	64	76	182	70
Basic metals	66	525	96	220	32
Metal products	95	nva	102	235	64
Nonelectrical machinery	89	355	81	188	44
Electrical machinery	60	138	83	192	47
Simple average	90	nc	86	200	50
All industries					
Simple average	110	nc	92	207	52

Source: Guisinger (1978).

Note: Nva = negative value added at international prices; nc = not calculable because of presence of negative value-added industries.

stitutes is possible, it appears that export production became substantially more attractive than production to replace imports. Since we will observe that exports are labor intensive (section 7.3), trade policies during this period assisted employment growth.

After 1972, however, the real EER declined, especially since 1974/75. The decline was due to inadequate government response to domestic inflation: measures were taken to increase the nominal EERs—the elimination of certain export taxes—but these efforts were not sufficient to offset the rise in domestic prices. If the erosion in real EERs continues indefinitely, it will plainly hamper employment growth in export manufacturing because of the labor intensity of that sector.

7.3 Labor Content of Tradable Goods

7.3.1 Labor Intensity of Production

Given the simultaneous emphasis on the processing of traditional agricultural goods and the rapid rise of the intermediate and investment goods sectors, it is perhaps not surprising to find highly labor-intensive and capital-intensive manufacturing activities coexisting in Pakistan's manufacturing sector. The data on labor per unit of value added for the different branches of the economy, shown in table 7.10, bear out this point. Four different measures of labor intensity are included in the table: labor per unit of value added for both direct labor and direct plus indirect home goods employment; and labor per unit of international value added, again for both direct labor and for direct plus indirect home goods employment. The last column of table 7.10 shows the ratio of domestic to international value added, which measures the degree of protection afforded each activity by the tariff and trade-control system.

On any of the four measures, the range in labor intensities among industries is extremely broad, especially when the agricultural activities are included in the comparison. Within manufacturing, there are five industries (sugar, edible oils, cigarettes, fertilizers, and petroleum products) that require fewer than 40 workers, directly employed in the industry, to produce a million rupees of value added, while eight industries (among them cotton textiles) require more than 120 workers to produce the same amount of value added. Note that this threefold gap in labor intensity is considerably narrowed if the direct plus indirect home goods measure is used: the "total" labor coefficients increase by roughly 50 percent.[8] This change is due to the sizable indirect home goods used in production and the fact that home goods are very labor-intensive. Several aspects of these labor coefficients deserve mention. First, the direct labor coefficients shown in table 7.10 are industrywide averages

Table 7.10 Direct and Total Labor Requirements in Man-Years per Unit of Domestic or International Value Added, 1969–70

	Per Million Rupees of DVA		Per Million Rupees of IVA		
Industry	Direct Employment	Direct and Indirect Employment[a]	Direct Employment	Direct and Indirect Employment[a]	Ratio of DVA to IVA
NRB					
Rice growing and processing	289	284	—	—	—
Wheat growing and processing	362	353	—	—	—
Cotton growing and ginning	277	275	—	—	—
All other agriculture	269	268	—	—	—
Mining	6	83	—	—	—
HOS					
Sugar refining	40	90	274	324	6.85
Edible oils	39	109	88	160	2.30
Cigarettes and tobacco	28	75	205	252	7.31
Food and beverages	62	129	104	171	1.68
Cotton textiles	122	151	338	367	2.77
Other textiles	149	176	621	648	4.17
Footwear	113	133	313	337	2.77
Paper and paper products	101	150	240	289	2.38
Printing and publishing	124	147	169	192	1.36
Leather and leather products	79	98	219	238	2.77
Rubber and rubber products	62	125	184	247	2.97
Fertilizers	34	96	56	118	1.64
Industrial chemicals	63	82	147	166	2.34
Nonindustrial chemicals and pharmaceuticals	52	91	107	146	2.06

Table 7.10—*continued*

Industry	Per Million Rupees of DVA		Per Million Rupees of IVA		
	Direct Employment	Direct and Indirect Employment[a]	Direct Employment	Direct and Indirect Employment[a]	Ratio of DVA to IVA
Cement	46	79	130	163	2.82
Basic metals	119	164	381	426	3.20
Metal products	207	219	689	701	3.33
Electrical machinery	101	119	295	313	2.92
Nonelectrical machinery	222	227	639	644	2.88
Motor vehicles	151	165	1,049	1,063	6.95
Other transportation equipment	190	292	969	971	3.34
Wood, cork, and furniture	230	231	683	684	2.97
Miscellaneous manufacturing	77	107	213	243	2.77
Coal and petroleum products	6	83	22	99	3.74

Source: Guisinger (1978).

[a]Number of persons employed (man-years) per unit of direct plus home goods indirect value added.

of the coefficients for subcategories that show, in some cases, an extremely high degree of dispersion. As an indication of the range of dispersion among the constituent subcategories of these industry groups, the highest and lowest labor coefficients among the subcategories are shown in table 7.11, next to the industry average. The employment contribution of some of these subcategories is extremely small, but it is important to underscore the fact that shifts in the composition of employment among the subcategories can affect the industry average without a change in the factor intensity of any given activity.

Second, the labor intensity of production varies by size of firm. Small establishments (10–50 workers) generally have a higher labor intensity than larger establishments. However, the decline in labor intensity is not monotonic. In several of the industry groups, the largest size category is *not* the least labor-using. In some industries—leather goods and transportation equipment, for example—firms in the largest size category use much more labor per unit of value added than medium-size firms.

7.3.2   Labor Contents by Commodity Category

The data on individual requirements can be combined with the trade and production data to generate estimates of the labor embodied in various "bundles" of tradable goods. For Pakistan, a relatively poor country with a large, unskilled labor force, one would expect that exports would be more labor-intensive than importable goods, whether produced at home or imported. One would also expect that the reverse would hold true for the capital and human skills embodied in tradable goods. Because of data inadequacies, it was not possible to determine the capital and skill content, but the data on labor content are consistent with the expectations that Pakistan's exports are labor-intensive.

The individual activities were allocated to trade categories on the basis of their T_i statistics. A T value well below zero indicates an export item; values near zero suggest that an industry is principally import-competing; and values well above zero suggest that domestic production does not effectively compete with imports, even though that condition may eventually be eliminated through subsequent import substitution. With −0.1 and 0.1 as cutoff points,[9] there are four export, twelve import-competing, and eleven noncompeting industries. Of the latter group, however, only paper and fabricated metal products show a T value less than 0.5. Paper is a borderline case ($T_i = 0.22$) and is assigned to the noncompeting category, since all its raw material needs (pulp) are imported. In the absence of protection, it probably would not be produced domestically.

One property of these estimates of average labor content by commodity category should be made clear at the outset. As previously

Table 7.11 Variation in Direct Labor Requirements within Industry Groups and by Firm Size, 1969/70 (Direct Employment per Million Rupees of Domestic Value Added)

Industry	Mean	Range within Group		Size of Establishment		
		High	Low	Small	Medium	Large
Rice growing and processing	289	—	—	—	—	—
Wheat growing and processing	862	—	—	—	—	—
Cotton growing and ginning	277	—	—	—	—	—
All other agriculture	269	—	—	—	—	—
Mining	6	—	—	—	—	—
Sugar refining	40	—	—	—	—	—
Edible oils	39	—	—	—	—	—
Cigarettes and tobacco	28	—	—	—	—	—
Food and beverages	62	91	29	127	57	54
Cotton textiles	122	274	122	184	171	111
Other textiles	149	—	—	—	—	—
Footwear	113	244	85	307	236	91
Paper and paper products	101	102	100	248	170	82
Printing and publishing	124	271	119	198	131	109
Leather and leather products	79	84	30	126	25	58
Rubber and rubber products	62	299	20	434	168	39
Fertilizers	34	—	15	—	—	—
Industrial chemicals	63	95	15	229	64	31
Nonindustrial chemicals and pharmaceuticals	52	136	36	—	—	—
Cement	46	—	—	—	—	—

Table 7.11—*continued*

Industry	Range within Group			Size of Establishment		
	Mean	High	Low	Small	Medium	Large
Basic metals	119	240	117	124	17	126
Metal products	207	538	115	296	157	205
Electrical machinery	101	242	45	286	86	98
Nonelectrical machinery	222	473	189	279	208	209
Motor vehicles	151	—	—	273	84	269
Other transportation equipment	290	—	—	—	—	—
Wood, cork, and furniture	230	—	—	—	—	—
Miscellaneous manufacturing	77	—	—	—	—	—
Coal and petroleum products	6	—	—	—	—	—

Source: Guisinger (1978).

discussed, only four industries qualify as "export industries" on the basis of the T statistic. It has also been noted that two of them—cotton textiles and leather products—could be considered natural resource based (NRB) manufacturing industries because of their reliance on domestically produced raw materials. Application of this criterion (though perhaps unduly restrictive) would leave only two export industries—footwear and sporting goods—clearly marked as Heckscher-Ohlin-Samuelson (HOS). However, exports originating in these two industries are less than half the value of HOS exports originating in industries classified as importable and non-competing. A serious bias would be introduced if no account were taken of the labor embodied in these "nonexport industries." Therefore, in the following discussion, estimates of the labor content of Pakistan's exports will refer to all exports of manufactures excluding, except as noted, PCB goods. Calculations of the labor content of Pakistan's imports will, on the other hand, relate only to those classified as importables since, for purposes of this comparison, there is no need to include goods of which there is no competing production in Pakistan.

Direct Employment per Unit of Domestic Value Added

In table 7.12, the average direct labor coefficients for various classifications of imports and exports are shown in column 1. In general, HOS exports use 42 percent more labor, on a direct basis, than is required to produce import-competing manufactures. If NRB manufactured exports are excluded—namely, cotton textiles and leather products—the margin of labor intensity falls to 24 percent (row 2c). This occurs because several industries that exported in 1969/70 (though not considered export industries by the procedures described in the previous section) are extremely capital-intensive. These are petroleum products, sugar, edible oil, and food and beverages. The export of petroleum is the result of the export of bunker oil that Pakistan refines but cannot absorb in its own market.

With regard to the direction of trade, manufactured exports exclusive of processed NRB goods to developed countries are 29 percent more labor-intensive than HOS imports from these countries. For trade with developing countries, the reverse is true, probably because Pakistan is relatively more industrialized than its LDC trading partners. However, note that imports from developing countries form a small part of total imports (about 2 percent).

Consequently, they have little effect upon the average labor intensity of all importables. It may also be noted that, if HOS exports were limited to the two export industries that fall unequivocally into this category—namely, footwear and sporting goods—the average labor content of exports to developing countries would be 160 instead of 88 as reported in

Table 7.12   Labor Content of Pakistan's Trade in HOS Manufactures by Major Trade Flows, 1969/70 (Number of Workers per Million Rupees of Value Added)

	Direct Employment per Unit of DVA[a]	Direct Plus Indirect Employment		Trade Flow as Percentage of Pakistan's Total Exports or Imports
		Per unit of DVA[a]	Per unit of IVA[a]	
1. Trade with all countries				
a. Exports, including PCB goods[b]	101	135	310	65.8
b. Exports, excluding PCB goods[b]	88	125	258	24.3
c. Imports[c]	71	96	202	21.7
d. 1a ÷ 1c	1.42	1.41	1.53	
e. 1b ÷ 1c	1.24	1.30	1.28	
2. Trade with developed countries				
a. Exports, excluding PBC goods[b]	90	132	255	10.1
b. Imports[c]	70	91	186	19.3
c. 2a ÷ 2b	1.29	1.45	1.37	
3. Trade with developing countries				
a. Exports, excluding PCB goods[b]	88	120	260	14.2
b. Imports[c]	120	150	364	2.4
c. 3a ÷ 3b	.73	.80	.71	

Note: Trade values have been used as weights in obtaining average coefficients. Small-scale producers are not included in the estimates.

[a]DVA = domestic value added; IVA = international value added.

[b]PCB = primary commodity based (see text).

[c]Including only products classified as import-competing.

table 7.12. But, since these two industries account for less than a quarter of all HOS goods exported to developing countries, the omission of the other, more capital-intensive exporting industries would give a misleading estimate of the true factor content of Pakistan's export trade.

Direct Plus Indirect Home Goods Employment

None of the findings on relative labor intensity of the various combinations of imports and exports discussed in the previous section are reversed when the employment generated indirectly in the home goods industries is added to the direct employment. In fact, the margin in labor-use between imports and exports excluding PCB goods widens when the direct plus indirect effects are considered. A comparison of columns 1 and 2 of table 7.12 shows that adding indirect home goods employment raises the labor content of manufactured exports slightly more when PCB goods are excluded than when they are included. Since there are no important differences in labor utilization ratios in home goods industries, this suggests that the traditional processing industries, cotton textiles and leather, do not require home goods inputs in as great a quantity as the other industries.

It is interesting that consumer goods exports are more labor-intensive (146 workers per unit of DVA) than intermediate goods (94 workers), though only slightly more labor-intensive than investment goods exports (129 workers). One implication of these data is that, for any given level of exports, the higher the share of intermediate and investment goods, the lower the average labor coefficients for all exports. Although some investment goods are produced with labor-using techniques, it will be seen below that investment goods industries are afforded high absolute levels of protection (though not as high as consumer goods) and the labor intensity may be a result of inefficient overmanning instead of efficient use of relatively cheap manpower.

Labor Content at International Prices

The principal effect of recalculating the labor content coefficients at international prices is to roughly double the labor coefficients while leaving their relative position unchanged. When value added at international prices is used as the denominator of the labor coefficients, exports remain between 25 and 50 percent more labor-using than imports. This result suggests that exportables and importables are subject to roughly the same level of protection in commodity markets.

7.3.3   Summary

Labor requirements in Pakistan's manufacturing sector vary considerably between and within activities. However, it is generally true that export activities have higher labor requirements than importable activities.

Consequently, we can conclude that the trade policies followed during the 1960s, namely promoting export activities while simultaneously protecting import substitutes, did not lead to as much employment growth as other more export-leaning policies might have done. That overall employment fell in manufacturing in the 1960s (though not in large-scale manufacturing) probably is due partially to these policies.

7.4   Factor Market Distortions and the Labor Content of Trade

Distortions in factor prices can affect employment levels in a variety of ways. The most obvious of these is through shifts in relative factor prices that alter the capital/labor ratios in production. In developing countries, factor price distortions such as minimum wage legislation have often pushed the market wage above its equilibrium level and lowered the market price of capital to some investors via subsidized interest on loans to industrial investors, tax holidays, and accelerated depreciation. Distortions not only alter relative prices but are also symptomatic of blockages in the free flow of capital and labor among sectors. It is important then to identify distortions in the markets for both labor and capital. This is a particularly difficult exercise, since the data on wages and rentals are fragmented and not very reliable.

7.4.1   Wage Trends and Wage Distortions

In the early 1960s, Pakistan was still widely regarded as the archetypical labor surplus economy. Employment growth in agriculture during the previous decade failed to keep pace with population growth. The fastest growing employer, large-scale manufacturing, was still too small to make more than a small contribution to solving the growing unemployment problem. It is fair to say that the common expectation for the wages of unskilled workers in all sectors of the economy was continued stagnation at near-subsistence levels, and even deterioration in real terms if population growth could not be curtailed.

Wages in Large-Scale Manufacturing

Wage data for production workers in the large-scale manufacturing sector shown in table 7.13 provide a rather clear indication that the expectation of stagnant real wages has not been realized. Real wages have fluctuated over the period 1960–75, but a definite upward trend can be observed.[10]

Three distinct periods can be discerned in the series on real wages (col. 5). In the first period (1955–63), real wages conform to the prediction of the labor surplus model as they remain more or less constant. In the second period (1964–67), real wages break out of their stagnant trend, first rising, then falling back in the wake of the inflation following

Table 7.13   Money and Real Wages of Production Workers in Large-Scale Manufacturing (Rupees per Worker per Year)

Year	Money Wages[a]		Cost of Living Index[b] (3)	Real Wages	
	Current Rupees (1)	Index[b] (2)		1959 Rupees (4)	Index[b] (5)
1954	981	90	87	1,122	103
1955	896	82	85	1,058	97
1957	994	91	93	1,059	97
1958	1,045	96	96	1,094	100
1959/60	1,091	100	100	1,091	100
1960/61	1,135	104	104	1,091	100
1961/62	1,156	106	108	1,070	98
1962/63	1,189	109	107	1,110	102
1963/64	1,195	110	110	1,088	100
1964/65	1,340	123	114	1,180	108
1965/66	1,464	134	117	1,245	114
1966/67	1,510	138	127	1,189	109
1967/68	1,536	141	137	1,116	102
1968/69	1,735	159	138	1,257	115
1969/70	1,931	177	143	1,351	124
1970/71	2,094	192	151	1,384	127
1971/72	2,389	219	159	1,504	138
1972/73	2,914	267	174	1,679	143
1973/74	4,012	368	226	1,775	163
1974/75	4,953	454	286	1,730	159

Source: Guisinger (1978, table 4-1).

[a]Money wages from 1970/71 onward are not directly available and, reversing the usual sequence, have been derived from the real wage series by application of the cost of living index.

[b]1959/60 = 100.

the 1965 war with India. Finally, in the third period (1968–75), real wages show a definite break with the past, rising steadily (except for 1974/75) and gaining more than 50 percent by the end of the period.

The take-off of real wages can be traced to various factors. Part of the increase is due to the changing skill composition of employment. The wage data shown in table 7.13 are for production workers, a broad category that includes both skilled and unskilled workers. During the 1960s production in the large-scale manufacturing sector shifted from the simple processing of consumer goods to more sophisticated and technically complex production of intermediate and capital goods. Since it is likely that the average skill required of manufacturing workers rose, this shift in skill composition probably contributed to the increase in the average wage in manufacturing without any changes in the real wages of each skill category.

Another part of the increase is the result of shifts in the supply and demand for industrial labor. As described below, there is some evidence that the wages of hired agricultural workers rose during this period, and, since unskilled workers are fairly mobile between industrial and agricultural labor markets, the increase in agricultural wages put upward pressure on urban wages. The supply schedule of industrial workers may also have been affected by the emigration of unskilled and semiskilled labor to the Middle East. On the demand side, employers may have increased wages to reduce labor turnover as a way of improving profit margins that began to narrow with the liberalization of trade controls in the early 1960s.

However, the major part of the increase in real wages occurred in the 1970s and appears to be due to nonmarket factors, particularly the wage policies introduced during the period. Trade unions, the other major nonmarket influence on wages in developing countries, had little direct effect on wage levels in Pakistan because of the constraints placed on their activity by legislation adopted in the late 1950s. The first government intervention in wage determination was, however, not intended. It was in 1963 when the government revised its own pay scales, and this pay increase spilled over into the private sector. The decline in real wages after 1965 provoked considerable labor unrest, which in turn contributed to the change in government in 1968. The new government was committed to improving labor conditions and instituted a number of reforms in labor policy. The government issued an Industrial Relations Ordinance in 1969, the objective of which was to improve the standards of living of workers. This included a new minimum wage that was rigorously enforced. The effects of the minimum wage on the average wage of all production workers can be seen in table 7.13 by the 26 percent increase in money wages between 1967/68 and 1969/70. Money wages continued to rise through the early 1970s as the coverage and enforcement of the minimum wage legislation was extended.

The change in government in 1971 produced a new set of labor policies that boosted industrial wages still further. Reforms in February 1972 extended workers' participation in management, made compulsory the payment of annual bonuses at stipulated rates, and set minimum standards for education, life insurance, and separation and medical benefits. Workers' entitlement to a share in profits was doubled from 2.5 to 5 percent. These fringe benefits, coupled with the residual effects of the 1969 minimum wage legislation, added more than 22 percent to the earnings of workers.

In August 1973 the government adopted the Employee Cost of Living (Relief) Ordinance requiring employers in both the private sector and the public sector to award cost of living adjustments at a rate fixed by government. There have been three such adjustments under the 1973 ordinance: Rs 35 monthly in August 1973; Rs 50 in June 1974; and Rs 25 in April 1975. Thus, a worker in an industrial area outside Karachi, earning the statutory minimum wage of Rs 125 in June 1973, was earning Rs 235 by June 1975—an increase of 88 percent in two years. Since consumer prices rose by approximately 65 percent during the same period, real wages of the workers at the low end of the pay scale rose substantially. The wage of the average worker rose by a smaller percentage than the increase in the minimum wage, but it too showed an increase in real terms, as can be seen in column 5 of table 7.13.

In summary, over the period 1960–75 real wages in large-scale manufacturing rose by almost 60 percent. In just seven of those years— 1967/68 to 1974/75—real wages rose by 55 percent, or by 6.5 percent per annum. Few developing countries have experienced more rapid increases in real wages for that length of time.

An analysis of wage dispersion in the large-scale manufacturing sector by Guisinger and Irfan (1975) did not reveal any widespread differences in average earnings per worker among industries. In fact, when account was taken of market influences on interindustry wage differences—the skill mix, for example—the residual differences that could then be termed "interindustry" distortions were almost insignificant compared with the wage dispersion observed in other developing countries. However, there was a growing tendency for nonmarket factors to widen wage differences among industries. Nonmarket factors included trade union influence and the share of the industry controlled by foreign investors. The implication of these findings is that, though interindustry wage distortions were not a serious problem in 1969/70, evidence was mounting that serious distortions could emerge in the future.

Public Sector Wages

Government workers, together with workers in the large-scale manufacturing sector, constitute the bulk of formal-sector employment in Pakistan. Not counting defense personnel, who are excluded from the labor force statistics, workers in central, provincial, and local government positions account for approximately 6 percent of the total labor force, of which one-third are teachers and educational administrators.

The most interesting feature of government wages over the period 1960–75 was the decline in real wages for workers in each of the twenty-two grade levels. Moreover, since the real wages of the most highly skilled workers declined faster than those of the least skilled, skill differentials narrowed. The decline in public sector wages, particularly at the higher grades, actually reduced the distortion between public and private sector wages that was a legacy of the country's colonial history. The degree to which public sector wage scales influence private sector wage scales is unknown, but there is circumstantial evidence that. the two are related (Guisinger, Henderson, and Scully 1978). Public policy in this area has thus had the effect of moderating skill differentials in both the private and the public components of the formal labor market as well as between these two sectors.

Urban Informal Sector Wages

While workers in large-scale manufacturing and government constitute more than half the formal sector employment in urban areas, the vast majority of urban workers are employed in the informal sector. Wages in the informal sector are determined by forces of supply and demand and do not come under the direct influence of trade unions or labor legislation.

Wage data for informal sector workers are only infrequently reported in censuses and surveys, and when reported they are often difficult to interpret. The informal sector is far more heterogeneous than the formal sector in terms of the age, education, and occupation of workers. The average wage of all workers in the informal sector has little meaning, since the characteristics of the workers may be changing over time. Also, many informal sector workers—such as hawkers and peddlers—work for profit rather than wages, and their reported earnings frequently include an implicit return to the capital that they use in their work.

While the available evidence on wage trends in the urban informal sector is clearly preliminary, there is no basis for concluding that the gap between formal and informal sector wages widened between 1960 and 1975. Data compiled by Guisinger (1978) suggest that the real wages of some of the least-skilled informal sector occupations experienced an increase over this period. Moreover, regression analysis of the determinants of personal earnings, taking into account such factors as education, age, and other socioeconomic characteristics, showed that including a dummy variable for informal sector workers did not add significantly to the explanation of interpersonal earnings differentials.

Agricultural Wages

The real wages of both permanent and casual agricultural workers did not increase during 1960–66, but between 1966 and 1973 real wages of these workers increased by more than 2 percent per annum (see Guisinger 1978 for details). Moreover, the low rates of rural-to-urban migration reported by Eckert (1972) tend to confirm the strong labor demand implied by rising real wages. Fewer than one hundred thousand workers a year moved from rural to urban areas, a surprisingly small figure for a total labor force of more than twenty million.

7.4.2   The Price of Capital and Relative Factor Costs

The Price of Capital, 1960–75

The price of capital in Pakistan, as in most developing countries, is shaped as much by the investment and trade policies of the government as by market forces. Throughout Pakistan's development, capital has been regarded as the essential ingredient in the growth process, and therefore it has been carefully controlled to be channeled into priority areas. Large-scale manufacturing, a priority sector in Pakistan's past development plans, has always been the beneficiary of various forms of investment incentives, including: subsidized interest rates; accelerated depreciation allowances; tax holidays; and, perhaps most important, licenses for the import of capital goods, whose scarcity value was several times their face value. These and other less direct incentives have combined to reduce the actual (market) price of capital below its opportunity cost—the price that would have prevailed if a neutral set of government policies had been in effect and if all markets had functioned smoothly.

To understand the full effect of Pakistan's investment incentive measures, it is essential to know the degree of subsidy implicit in the package of incentive policies and how it has varied over time. The price of capital is, unfortunately, an elusive concept both theoretically and practically: theoretically because no single measure fully reflects the complete general equilibrium ramifications of investment incentive policies; practically because data are available from official sources on only a few of the elements that make up the price of capital. Moreover, during the 1960s access of a firm to the various investment incentives offered by government depended on its size, its geographic location, and the economic sector in which it operated. It is unlikely that any two investments received the same package of incentives. Without detailed data on investment incentives disaggregated by industry, firm size, and geographic location, an average price of capital cannot be determined.

In what follows we shall nevertheless attempt to estimate the price of capital, taking into consideration all factors that may have influenced its deviation from the opportunity cost.

The appropriate partial equilibrium concept for measuring the price of capital is the annual rental value of a unit of capital, also referred to as the user cost of capital. Just as a firm rents labor services it does not own, the rental value of capital is the amount the firm would be charged by a competitive asset-leasing firm to rent the use of capital for one year. Even though most firms own the majority of their assets, the hypothetical rental cost is the relevant price of capital to be compared with the price of labor in determining optimal factor proportions.

It can be shown that, under certain specific conditions described below, the rental cost of capital, P_k, is:[11]

(1)
$$P_k = \frac{K_w f(1+m)\left[r + d_t - \dfrac{u}{S^n_1} \sum_{h+1}^{n} \dfrac{d'_t}{(1+i)^t}\right]}{1 - u\left(\dfrac{S^n_{h+1}}{S^n_1}\right)},$$

where:

> d_t is the economic rate of depreciation in year t;
>
> d'_t is the depreciation allowance in year t permitted by the tax laws;
>
> f is the exchange rate of local currency per unit of foreign exchange;
>
> h is the number of years for which complete exemption from corporate taxes is granted under a tax holiday scheme;
>
> i is the discount factor;
>
> k_w is the foreign exchange price of the capital asset;
>
> m is the tariff on capital goods;
>
> n is the economic life of the asset;
>
> P_k is the annual rental value of capital;
>
> r is the annual interest rate on the financial capital required to purchase the capital asset;
>
> $S^y_x = \sum_{t=x}^{y} \dfrac{1}{(1+i)^t}$; and
>
> u is the rate of corporate profits tax.

The conditions under which this equation is valid are the following. First, the value of the asset is restored at the end of each year to its original cost by an investment equal to the economic depreciation incurred during the year. In other words, the asset remains intact and its book value does not diminish. Therefore rental costs remain constant, since the value of the asset is not affected by depreciation. The second condition implicit in this expression is that the asset is financed completely by equity, whose costs to the firm are not deductible from income for tax purposes. If the asset is leveraged and interest is deductible, then a more complex formula is required to incorporate the tax advantages of interest deductions. In the extreme case of a totally leveraged asset (100 percent financed by debt), no profits would exist in a competitive leasing industry, since tax deductible costs—interest plus depreciation—would equal income.[12] Finally, it is assumed that the corporate income tax liability is passed on in the form of a higher rental cost rather than absorbed by the suppliers of equity capital. This is a reasonable assumption given the observed mobility of financial capital among various branches of the economy.

From equation (1) it is evident that the price of capital is influenced by three types of factors. The first category of factors comprises the terms in the numerator outside the brackets—the cost of the capital asset (K_w), the exchange rate (f), and the tariff on capital goods (m). These three variables determine the domestic price of the capital asset. The higher any of these factors are, the higher will be, all other things being equal, the rental cost of capital. The second category consists of the factors within the brackets—r, d, u, and d'. These establish the annual costs of owning capital assets. The higher the costs of financing (r) and the higher the economic depreciation (d), the greater the annual cost. On the other hand, if accelerated depreciation is permitted, the larger the permissible rate (d') and the tax savings represented by the rate of corporate tax (u), the *lower* is the annual cost of owning capital assets. The final category includes the factors in the denominator. The higher the rate of taxation, the higher the rental cost. But the longer the tax holiday period (h), the *lower* will be the rental cost. The term $u(S^n_{h+1}/S^n_1)$ represents the effective tax rate incorporating the discounted benefits from the tax holiday scheme.

This concept can be used to measure the divergence between the market and equilibrium (shadow) prices of capital. Table 7.14 shows the

Table 7.14   Annual Rental Value of a $21 Machine under Various Incentive Policies: Pakistan, 1959/60

Policy Type		User Cost (Rs)	Incremental Reduction in User Cost (%)
Case A	Neutral policies[a]	58	—
Case B	Subsidized exchange rate—case A and imports at official rather than equilibrium rate of exchange ($f = 4.76$ instead of Rs 7.6)	36	38
Case C	Subsidized financial cost of capital—case B with $r = 5.74\%$ instead of 15%.	20	44
Case D	Accelerated depreciation—case C with half the original cost written off in three years	16	20
Case E	Tax holiday—case D and no income tax liability for first eight years.	14	12.5

[a]Equilibrium financial cost of capital ($r = 15\%$); tax and economic rates of depreciation equal ($d = d' = 0.063$); corporate tax rate applied to all investments without tax holiday privileges ($u = 50\%$); and capital equipment imported at equilibrium rather than official exchange rate ($f = $ Rs 7.6/$).

estimated incremental effects on the price of capital of the four major investment incentives prevailing in Pakistan in fiscal year 1960. Case A represents the equilibrium price of capital for a machine with an original c.i.f. cost of $21 or Rs 100 ($21 at 4.76 Rs/$). Case B represents the situation where an overvalued exchange rate constitutes the only source of implicit subsidy. For example, if investors are permitted to import machinery at the official exchange rate of Rs. 4.76 instead of the estimated equilibrium exchange rate for 1959/60 of Rs 7.6, the rental value of capital will be Rs 36. Case C shows what happens if, in addition to purchasing capital at an overvalued exchange rate, investors obtain funds at less than the true opportunity cost of financial capital. Under these conditions, investors would be able to use the $21 machine for an average implicit rental of only Rs 20. Accelerated depreciation (case D) and an eight-year tax holiday (case E) would reduce the rental cost still further by 4 and 2 rupees, respectively. The 12.5 percent incremental reduction in the cost of capital owing to the tax holiday itself has little practical significance because, unlike the effects of the other incentive policies, the tax holiday and accelerated depreciation incentives are almost mutually exclusive substitutes—the benefits of accelerated depreciation are not felt during a tax holiday, so that the major part simply replaces accelerated depreciation. The tax holiday reduces the price of capital from 20 to 14, while accelerated depreciation reduces it from 20 to 16.

The comparison of case A (neutral policies) with case E (all four incentives operating) is striking. The market rental cost of capital is only one-fourth the equilibrium cost of capital; or, viewed from the opposite perspective, eliminating all incentive policies would raise the cost of capital 300 percent! The example, however, exaggerates the effect of incentives in several important ways. First, all firms are leveraged to some extent, and interest is deductible from income for tax purposes; thus the tax holiday and accelerated depreciation policies would have a less significant influence. Second, it has been assumed that government policies can effect a reduction in the cost of equity analogous to the way government can subsidize the costs of debt to firms by rationing credit at artificially low interest rates. Finally, the neutral case assumes a 50 percent corporate tax burden. If all incentive policies were stripped away, such a high corporate tax rate might not be necessary. One can always question whether the appropriate benchmark for comparison is a set of policies with some form of taxation, such as a corporate tax, but no incentive policies, or a completely distortionless environment—the classic laissez-faire paradigm.

For these reasons, the rental cost calculations in table 7.14 are only illustrative. Nevertheless, the percentage reductions in the rental cost of capital gave an indication of the quantitative effect of investment incentive policies on the cost of capital, and there can be little doubt that those policies provided a significant incentive to adopt capital-intensive techniques of production.

Trends in the Rental Cost of Capital: 1960–75

During 1960–75, important changes occurred in both the (controlled) market and the equilibrium rental values of capital. The government altered the tax holiday scheme on two occasions, changed the lending rate on bank credit to industry, and varied the tariff levied on capital goods. Both the market and the equilibrium cost of capital were affected by changes in the c.i.f. price index for machinery. Values for the variables in equation (1) have been computed for 1960–75, and market and equilibrium rental values have been calculated for each year as if a new investment were being made in that year. Changes in incentive policies would, of course, affect the rental cost on existing capital assets, but the time series in table 7.15 show only the rental cost of new investments.

From the two time series of rental costs of capital it is clear that, until the devaluation of 1972, the distortion in the price of capital remained considerable: the equilibrium rental cost was never less than three

Table 7.15   Rental Cost of Capital, 1959/60 to 1974/75

Years	Market Prices[a] (Rupees) (1)	Equilibrium (Shadow) Prices (Rupees) (2)	Ratio of Equilibrium Rental to Market Rental (%) (2)/(1) = (3)
1959/60	16	58	3.62
1963/64	22	85	3.86
1960/61	17	55	3.24
1961/62	21	69	3.29
1962/63	22	88	4.00
1964/65	19	81	4.26
1965/66	24	73	3.04
1966/67	29	126	4.34
1967/68	30	100	3.33
1968/69	34	109	3.21
1969/70	32	95	2.97
1970/71	30	118	3.93
1971/72	38	140	3.68
1972/73	86	109	1.27
1973/74	93	118	1.27
1974/75	108	137	1.27

[a]Market cost of capital is the annual rental cost in rupees for a machine costing $21 (Rs 100) in 1959/60. Since not all firms had access to tax holidays, only cases A and D in table 7.14 are compared in this table.

times the market rental cost. With devaluation the overvaluation of the rupee was largely eliminated and the tax holiday scheme abandoned. The gap between market and equilibrium rental costs closed dramatically.

The Rental Cost of Capital for Large and Small Firms

The rental cost formula also offers insight into the differential cost of capital between small and large firms. In the early 1960s, few small-scale manufacturing firms in Pakistan had access to import licenses, and when they purchased foreign equipment it was through import agents who appropriated the scarcity value of the import licenses for themselves. Even when small firms purchased machinery made locally, the prices generally reflected the full scarcity margins and tariff duties of the imported intermediate inputs used in their production. The prices paid by small investors for capital equipment were thus approximately those of the equilibrium situation. Small entrepreneurs also lacked access to bank credit, and the interest rates on the funds they borrowed in the informal market were substantially above the rates paid by individuals investing in large-scale projects in the same industry, and not dissimilar from the opportunity cost of capital. On the other hand, small-scale firms were usually unincorporated and thus exempt from the corporate income tax. On these assumptions, the user cost of a $21 machine for a small manufacturing establishment in 1959/60 would have been of the order of Rs 35. Its trend over time would have been very similar to that of the equilibrium cost of capital. Thus, until 1972 small investors faced capital costs more than twice those of their large-scale competitors. This, coupled with the fact that wages are lower for workers in small-scale firms than in large-scale firms, provided a very strong economic rationale for the observed tendency for small-scale firms to be more labor-using than comparable large-scale firms.

Relative Factor Prices: Market and Equilibrium

Factor proportion decisions by investors are not made on the basis of either the price of capital or the price of labor alone, but rather on their ratio. The central issue in exploring the employment effect of movements in both price series is thus the trend in relative factor prices. In table 7.16, column 3, the ratio of relative factor prices in market terms has been computed. Between 1959/60 and 1970/71, the wage/rental ratio fluctuated between 50 and 70 with no clear trend in either direction. However, between 1970/71 and 1972/73 the ratio dropped by more than 50 percent as a result of the steep increase in the price of capital following the 1972 devaluation that largely eliminated the overvaluation of the rupee. After 1972/73, the declining trend was reversed and the relative price of labor rose more than 30 percent.

Table 7.16   Factor Prices (in Rupees) and Factor Price Ratios, 1959/60–1974/75

	Market Prices			Equilibrium Prices			Distortion Indicator (3) ÷ (6) (7)
	Wages (1)	Capital (2)	Ratio (1) ÷ (2) (3)	Wages (4)	Capital (5)	Ratio (4) ÷ (5) (6)	
1959/60	1,091	16	68.2	687	58	11.8	5.8
1960/61	1,135	17	66.8	709	55	12.9	5.2
1961/62	1,156	21	55.0	720	69	10.4	5.3
1962/63	1,189	22	54.0	742	88	8.4	6.4
1963/64	1,195	22	54.3	764	85	9.0	6.0
1964/65	1,340	19	70.5	786	81	9.7	7.3
1965/66	1,464	24	61.0	796	73	10.9	5.6
1966/67	1,510	29	52.1	818	126	6.5	8.0
1967/68	1,536	30	51.2	840	100	8.4	6.1
1968/69	1,735	34	51.0	873	109	8.0	6.4
1969/70	1,931	32	60.3	971	95	10.2	5.9
1970/71	2,094	30	69.8	1,047	118	8.9	7.8
1971/72	2,389	38	62.9	1,200	140	8.6	7.3
1972/73	2,914	86	33.9	1,462	109	13.4	2.5
1973/74	4,012	93	43.1	2,007	118	17.0	2.5
1974/75	4,953	108	45.9	2,477	137	18.0	2.5

Sources: Col. 1, table 7.13; cols. 2 and 5, table 7.15; col. 4, implied equilibrium wages from Guisinger (1978, table 4–12).

It is interesting to compare changes in the wage/rental ratio at market prices with changes in the ratio at equilibrium prices, the latter being shown in column 6 of table 7.16. Apart from a few exceptional years, the equilibrium factor price ratio did not behave very differently from the market factor price ratio until 1971/72. Then, however, while the market factor price ratio declined with devaluation, the equilibrium ratio rose and continued to rise until 1974/75 because of the continued inflation in the world prices of machinery.

To show the degree of distortion, a "distortion indicator" has been constructed expressing the market factor price ratio in each year as a percentage of the equilibrium factor price ratio. Thus, if the market price of labor were fifty times the market price of capital, but the equilibrium price of labor were only ten times the equilibrium cost of capital, the distortion would be fivefold. This represents a "distortion gap" owing to an excess in the market price of labor over the equilibrium price or a subsidy to the market price of capital or both. If these distortions were eliminated, the distortion measure in this example indicates that the relative cost of using labor would fall by four-fifths.

The distortion series for the period 1959/60 to 1974/75 is shown in column 7 of table 7.16. Although the distortion gap fluctuated during the 1960s, the most dramatic change occurred after the 1972 devaluation, with the gap narrowing by almost two-thirds in one year. There is nevertheless still a considerable degree of absolute distortion favoring the use of capital.

Perhaps the most striking feature of the factor price trends shown in table 7.16 is the size of the gap that persisted until the 1972 devaluation. The wage/rental ratio at market prices was roughly five times the equilibrium ratio. No comparable data exist for other developing countries with which to contrast the magnitude or effects of Pakistan's factor market distortion. A measure of the significance of this distortion, however, can be obtained by estimating the effects that changes in the factor price ratio would have had on employment in the large-scale manufacturing sector.

One study has estimated that a 25 percent reduction in relative factor prices of labor and capital in Ghana would have increased total employment in manufacturing by 20 percent more than would otherwise have occurred over a decade during which the industrial sector expanded at an annual rate of 10 percent (Roemer 1972). This study was limited to the case where changes in factor prices affected factor proportions in new investments only, leaving unchanged the factor proportions associated with the initial stock of fixed assets. The employment effects of factor price changes were examined under several assumptions about the elasticity of substitution between capital and labor and labor's initial share of value added.

A similar estimate can be made for Pakistan's large-scale manufacturing sector. The elasticity of substitution and labor's share are assumed equal to 1.0 and 0.25, respectively, while the growth rate of manufacturing output is taken as 10 percent. If the factor price ratio remains constant and no technological change occurs, employment would of course grow at 10 percent per annum. If, however, the wage/rental ratio had been reduced by 50 percent and maintained over the eleven-year period ending in 1970/71, employment would have grown at an annual rate of 13.8 percent. Thus it is possible that instead of a large-scale manufacturing labor force of 500,000 in 1970/71, this sector might have employed as many as 700,000 workers if the factor price ratio had been reduced as indicated. That 200,000 additional jobs might result from a 50 percent decline in the wage/rental ratio may be an underestimate for at least three reasons. First, in the large-scale sector, some alteration of factor proportions in the existing capital stock is possible with a change in the factor price ratio, particularly when it declines by as much as 50 percent. Capital/labor ratios in materials handling processes are extremely sensitive to factor price ratios, and new jobs would probably have emerged in existing plants if factor prices had been less distorted. Second, increasing the cost of capital in the large-scale sector would have made small-scale establishments more cost-competitive and expanded employment growth in this sector. This would have lowered the rate of output expansion in the large-scale sector, causing employment to grow at something less than 13.8 percent per year. But the expansion of the small-scale sector, which employs twice as many workers as the large-scale sector, might have more than made up for this shortfall. It is not known in what degree firms in the large- and small-scale sectors are competitors, but it is clear that in some of the important small-scale industrial categories—particularly food processing and textiles—the two manufacturing sectors are more competitive than complementary. Finally, in this exercise, output is held constant. Changes in factor prices would also change patterns of domestic demand, perhaps making exports grow faster once they were more competitive.

7.5 Summary and Conclusions

In many ways Pakistan's pattern of trade is singularly conventional and consistent with what one would expect from its factor endowment. More labor is employed to produce a unit of value added in export industries than is employed to produce the same amount of value added in industries that compete with imports. This holds true whether only direct employment is considered or whether a broader concept of direct plus indirect employment is used. When labor intensities are calculated on the basis of units of international value added, the same pattern holds. The only aspect of trade patterns where exports do not appear to be more labor-intensive than importable goods is in the regional direction. Imports of goods from developing countries show a higher labor intensity than Pakistan's exports of similar goods to these countries. This result is not unexpected, given that Pakistan's level of industrial development is probably greater than that of its LDC trading partners.

Distortions in the prices of commodities introduced by the trade control system obviously did not distort trade patterns to the point of creating perverse reversals in labor content. Trade policies did, however, help shape the structure and growth of employment. Initially, Pakistan relied on high protection to promote import-substituting industrialization. But at a relatively early stage in the import substitution program, incentives for the export of manufactured goods were adopted that served to counteract the disincentive of a highly overvalued local currency. Moreover, the structure of protection gave a greater incentive to produce consumer goods than to produce either intermediate or investment goods. Since the last two industries are more capital-intensive, the unevenness in protection levels did favor the more labor-using industries.

The ability of trade policies to affect employment in industry has weakened since 1970. Opportunities for efficient import substitution in the most labor-using industries have almost been exhausted, and continued tariff protection will have little effect on employment. Further import substitution, particularly in the intermediate and investment goods industries, will not generate nearly as much labor per unit of value added as investments in consumer goods industries did during the 1960s. The most serious detriment to employment growth in recent years has been the deterioration of the real EER for manufactured exports. Unless the real incentives for exporters of manufactured goods are allowed to rise, the large employment potential of these industries will not be realized.

Distortions in factor prices have historically favored the use of capital and provided a penalty on the use of labor. The fact that employment grew in large-scale manufacturing despite these strong disincentives should not be construed as evidence that distorted factor prices are meaningless. Very important structural changes in the economy occurred during the 1960s, particularly the remarkable growth of agriculture, and the employment effects of these structural changes overcame the negative effect on employment of factor market distortions. If the same strong demand for agricultural labor could be expected in the 1970s that was observed during the 1960s, far less concern could be attached to distortions in factor prices. But from 1970 to 1975 agriculture grew at only a 2 percent annual rate. Perhaps most important, mechanization of agriculture has continued at a rapid pace.

The greatest distortion in the price of capital was eliminated with the devaluation of the rupee in 1972. The major danger to the structure of relative factor prices now comes from the acceleration in wage increases. Between 1968 and 1975, *real* market wages increased at more than 5 percent per annum, and money wages increased at a much higher rate. There seems to be little economic justification, on the basis of allocative efficiency, for a continued 5 percent rise per annum in real wages.

If Pakistan manages to bring the increase of wages under control and to restore adequate incentives for manufactured exports, their expansion could contribute significantly to the growth of employment opportunities in Pakistan.

Notes

1. The reader interested in a general survey of economic development in Pakistan is referred to Papanek (1967) and Lewis (1970).
2. The underlying data used for this study may be found in Guisinger (1978), available for the cost of reproduction from the National Bureau of Economic Research.
3. Small-scale industry includes all manufacturing units with fewer than ten workers if power is used and twenty workers if power is not used.
4. This is with the exception of manufacturing employment during 1961–72. Growth of employment in all sectors combined can be easily inferred from table 7.6.
5. Only the last subperiod sources relate to West Pakistan, but all-Pakistan data provide fairly good approximation of trends in West Pakistan.
6. The effective rates of protection are based upon price comparisons and thus incorporate the premium on import licenses.
7. This is the PPP-PLD-EER of chapter 1.
8. For the definition of home goods, see chapter 1.
9. The relatively low cutoff point for the noncompeting imports is primarily due to the level of aggregation.
10. Throughout, "wages" and "earnings" are used interchangeably to designate the total compensation of workers, including—where data exist—the imputed value of noncash benefits such as food and lodging.
11. For a derivation of this specific formula see Guisinger (1978) and, for the general case, Shafa (1978).
12. The simplifying assumption made in all such analyses is that the returns to management and risk-taking are zero.

References

Anwar, S. 1975. Output, value added and employment in the small scale textile industry. *Pakistan Development Review* 14:120–34.

Eckert, J. 1972. *Rural labour in the Punjab: A survey report.* Lahore; Planning and Development Department, Government of the Punjab.

Farooq, G. M. 1976. *Dimensions and structure of labour force in relation to economic development: A comparative study of Pakistan and Bangladesh.* Islamabad: PIDE.

Government of Pakistan. 1960. *Second five-year plan.*

———. 1970a. *Census of manufacturing industries, 1969–70.*

———. 1970b. *Pakistan trade statistics.*

———. 1972. Housing, economic, and demographic survey. unpublished data.

———. 1976. *Economic survey 1975–76.*

Guisinger, S. E. 1976. Patterns of industrial growth in Pakistan. *Pakistan Development Review* 15:8–27.

———. 1977a. A note on the effective exchange rate for Pakistan's manufactured exports. *Pakistan Development Review* 16:101–11.

———. 1977b. Urban poverty and income distribution: Data from Rawalpindi. Mimeographed.

———. 1978. Trade policies and employment: The case of Pakistan. In manuscript.

Guisinger, S. E.; Henderson, J. R.; and Scully, G. 1978. Earnings, rates of return to education and the earnings distribution in Pakistan. Mimeographed.

Guisinger, S. E., and Irfan, M. 1975. Inter-industry differentials in wages and earnings in Pakistan's manufacturing sector. *Pakistan Development Review* 14:274–95.

Lewis, S. R., Jr. 1969. *Economic policy and industrial growth in Pakistan.* London: Allen and Unwin.

———. 1970. *Pakistan: Industrialization and trade policies.* London: Oxford University Press.

———. 1974. *Economic policy and industrial growth in Pakistan.* Princeton: Princeton University Press.

Malik, M. I. 1975. Some comments on cotton cloth consumption in Pakistan. *Pakistan Development Review* 14:238–44.

Naseem, S. M. 1973. Mass poverty in Pakistan: Some preliminary findings. *Pakistan Development Review* 12:317–60.

Papanek, G. 1967. *Pakistan's development: Social goals and private incentives.* Cambridge: Harvard University Press.

Roemer, M. 1972. Relative factor prices in Ghanaian manufacturing 1969–70. *Economic Bulletin of Ghana* (Accra), pp. 3–24.

Shafa, H. S. 1978. An analysis of the impact of investment incentives on the rental cost of capital: The case of Iran. Ph.D. diss., University of Texas, Dallas.

White, Lawrence J. 1974. *Industrial concentration and economic power in Pakistan*. Princeton: Princeton University Press.

8 Export Promotion and Employment Growth in South Korea

Wontack Hong

Introduction

The phenomenal growth Korea has achieved over the past two decades is by now well known.[1] Korea's growth rate has exceeded that of any other country in the world. Growth was based upon an export promotion strategy that resulted in an average annual growth rate of the dollar value of exports of more than 40 percent annually even before the worldwide inflation of the mid-1970s. Exports have continued to grow rapidly in real terms even since that time.

The rapid growth of real GNP has transformed the Korean economy, and many other policies were changed in addition to trade policy. Among the results of the transformation has been the virtual elimination of open unemployment and a rapid rise in the real wage.

Korea's success has stimulated a great deal of interest on the part of other countries in the policies she followed and their results. Although the rapid growth of trade and its effects on GNP have been closely studied (see Frank, Kim, and Westphal 1975; Westphal and Kim 1977), less attention has been devoted to an assessment of the relationship between Korea's choice of an export-oriented trade strategy and the rapid rate of growth of urban employment and real wages. Because of that gap, this examination of Korea's commodity composition of trade and its relationship with employment should be of great interest.

Focus in this study is upon 1970, a year for which data are readily available. By 1970 the export-oriented growth strategy had been in effect for ten years. Real wages were rising rapidly, and the rapid accumulation of capital implied that Korean factor endowments were beginning to change. I therefore examine not only the pattern of trade in 1970, but also the way it evolved over time. During the 1970s, Korean policy

Wontack Hong is associated with Seoul University.

341

began to shift toward the encouragement of capital-intensive industries. A final focus of this paper is upon those policies, and upon their compatability with the continued success of an export-oriented growth strategy in Korea.

8.1   Major Characteristics of the Korean Economy

8.1.1   Growth and Structure

Table 8.1 gives salient data on the growth and structure of the Korean economy. In the early 1950s Korea was one of the poorest countries in the world, with a very high population density and a per capita income of only $240 measured in 1977 prices. There was little manufacturing activity, reflecting both the underdeveloped state of the economy and the aftereffects of the Korean War. Exports were almost nonexistent and consisted primarily of agricultural commodities (see table 8.2).

After the devastation of the war, Korea pursued inward-looking policies. Throughout the 1950s it had most of the characteristics of an import substitution, relatively slow growth economy. The exchange rate was overvalued, and numerous direct controls were applied to international transactions. Aid inflows were sizable, since foreign-exchange earnings failed to cover more than a small part of the import bill.

By the late 1950s it was evident to all that aid flows would not be sustained and that Korea, dependent on imports for most raw materials, could not grow satisfactorily through further import substitution. In the early 1960s, policy signals were reversed, starting with a large devaluation in 1960, followed by a program of export incentives that maintained the real exchange rate for exports despite fairly rapid domestic inflation (see section 8.1.2). The switch to an export promotion strategy was followed by rapid increases in exports: from 1962 to 1972, exports rose from 2 to 18 percent of GNP, while per capita income rose from $275 to $541 in 1977 prices. Per capita income growth has continued to be rapid and is estimated to have been $864 in 1977. Over the period 1962 to 1977, per capita GNP rose at an average annual rate of nearly 8 percent. Government development programs and investment and credit policies were largely concentrated on export promotion, although that concentration necessarily implied attention to infrastructure for ports, transport, communications, and other facilities necessary for the success of the export promotion drive.

The switch in incentives in the trade sector was accompanied in 1964–65 by a very significant set of monetary and fiscal reforms, which raised the nominal interest rate and lowered the inflation rate significantly. For this and other reasons, the domestic savings rate rose rapidly. This was absolutely essential, since the inflow of United States aid,

Table 8.1   Growth and Changes in Industrial Structure, 1953–77

	1953	1957	1962	1967	1972	1977a
Industries (percentage distribution of value added)						
Agriculture and forestry	46	42	39	32	23	16
Fishery	2	2	2	2	2	3
Mining and quarrying	1	1	2	1	1	1
Manufacturing	6	9	12	17	25	35
Electricity, water and sanitation	0	0	1	1	2	2
Transportation and communications	2	2	3	5	6	7
Construction	2	2	3	4	5	6
Wholesale and retail trade	11	13	15	15	18	17
Banking and other services	8	8	9	8	8	6
Education and public administration	17	14	12	10	8	5
Ownership of dwellings	5	4	4	3	2	2
GNP (in billions of 1977 $)	5.0	6.1	7.3	11.2	18.0	31.5
Per capita GNP (in 1977 $)	240	266	275	368	541	864
Commodity exports/GNPb	1	1	2	7	18	33
Commodity imports/GNPb	10	11	16	21	25	35
Trade (in billions of current $)						
Commodity imports	0.35	0.44	0.42	1.00	2.52	10.81
Service importsc	0.01	0.01	0.03	0.08	0.19	1.68
Commodity exports	0.04	0.02	0.06	0.32	1.62	10.05
Service exportsc	0.12	0.04	0.10	0.30	0.49	2.69
Official aidd	0.19	0.37	0.22	0.15	0.07	0.00
Foreign loans	—	—	0.00	0.17	0.63	1.02

Source: Bank of Korea, National Income in Korea and Economic Statistics Yearbook
aPreliminary data.
bIncludes freight and insurance.
cTotal invisible payments or receipts minus investment income and donations.
dIncluding imports financed by properties and claims funds from Japan.

which had peaked in 1957 at nearly $400 million, had already begun to decline. The government not only increased taxation and raised interest rates to encourage domestic savings, but also enacted measures designed to encourage an inflow of foreign loans. Borrowing from abroad turned out to be a major source of capital formation in Korea in the late 1960s and early 1970s.

As can be seen in table 8.1, the acceleration in the growth rate was accompanied by a very rapid shift in the structure of production. Agri-

Table 8.2   Composition of Korean Exports by Major Sectors, Selected
                  Years 1953 to 1975 (Percentage Distribution)

SITC Code Year	Food and Beverages (0 and 1)	Crude Materials (2 and 4)	Mineral Fuels (3)	Chemicals (5)	Manufactured Goods (6 and 8)	Machinery and Transportation Equipment (7)
1953	5.6	89.6	2.6	—	2.3	—
1955	6.2	81.8	2.7	.5	7.3	1.3
1957	15.2	65.9	.0	.0	18.2	.3
1960	30.9	48.8	3.5	1.2	12.3	.3
1963	20.8	30.5	3.0	1.0	39.8	4.7
1965	16.6	21.2	1.1	.2	57.6	3.1
1968	11.7	13.5	.5	.7	68.2	5.4
1970	9.6	12.0	1.1	1.4	68.7	7.4
1972	7.5	7.4	1.1	2.2	71.2	10.6
1975	13.2	3.0	2.0	1.3	66.3	13.8

Source: Bank of Korea, Economic Statistics Yearbook, various years.
Note: Figures do not add to 100 owing both to rounding and to a small "unclassified" category in Korean imports.

culture, forestry, and fishing, which had accounted for 44 percent of GNP in 1957, constituted less than 20 percent by 1977. Manufacturing rose from 9 to 35 percent of GNP over the same period. Accompanying these changes, the share of agricultural employment fell from 61 percent of total employed persons in 1963 to 40 percent in 1977.

The high rate of economic growth in Korea has been accompanied by a high rate of population growth, although it has fallen significantly in recent years. During the period 1963–76, the population aged fourteen years and over increased at an average annual rate of about 3 percent. Despite this, recorded urban unemployment has fallen sharply (see section 8.1.4).

8.1.2   International Trade

The Pattern and Composition of Trade

Reflecting the transformation of the entire economy, the commodity composition of Korea's trade has changed markedly from that of the 1950s. Until the early sixties, the major export items were such primary products as metals, ores, and concentrates, raw materials of vegetable or animal origin, fish, swine, and raw silk. By the mid-sixties, plywood, textiles, clothing, and miscellaneous manufactures emerged as the principal export commodities. In the early 1970s, electronic products, footwear, steel plates and sheets, and woven synthetic fabrics joined the list of major exports. In addition, the rapid expansion in Korean shipping, tourist services, remittances from Korean workers abroad, and revenues from overseas construction projects made large contributions to a remarkable increase in noncommodity exports.

The rapid shift in the commodity composition of exports can be seen from the data in table 8.2. Starting from a NRB-dependent/export structure (albeit with exports equaling only a small fraction of GNP), manufactured goods—from SITC sectors 5 through 8—rose from less than 5 percent of exports in 1953 to about 14 percent in 1960, 77 percent in 1970, and 81 percent in 1975. Table 8.3 enumerates the fifteen largest four-digit export categories for 1971. As can be seen, textile and apparel items were dominant, although iron and steel products, plywood, footwear, and fishery products were also important.

Table 8.4 gives data on the origin and destination of exports and imports. The United States was the largest single market for Korean exports, with Japan second. Exports to LDCs were relatively unimportant until the mid-1970s, accounting for 13 percent of exports in 1970, the year I focus on. A higher share of imports—17 percent—originated in LDCs, but these were mostly raw materials. Because of data difficulties and the relatively small size of Korea's trade with developing countries in 1970, no separate estimates are given below for the factor proportions of trade with DCs contrasted with LDCs.

Table 8.3   **Major Four-Digit Commodities Exported, 1971**

SITC Code	Commodity	Value (Millions of U.S. Dollars)
8414	Clothes and accessories, knitted or crocheted	132.9
8411	Clothing of textile fabrics	129.2
6312	Plywood	126.8
8999	Miscellaneous manufacturing n.e.c.	70.6
7293	Valves and tubes	48.5
2613	Raw silk	39.3
8510	Footwear	37.4
8412	Clothing and accessories made of fabric	36.2
6521	Cotton fabrics (unbleached)	20.7
0311	Fish (fresh, chilled, and frozen)	20.0
6516	Yarn and thread of synthetic fibers	19.2
6743	Iron and steel plates and sheets	19.2
6556	Twine, cord, and rope	17.2
6535	Fabrics made of synthetic fibers	14.4
0313	Crustaceans and mollusks	14.1

Source: Bank of Korea, *Economic Statistics Yearbook*, various years.

Table 8.4   Pattern of Trade among Countries, Selected Years
                 1953 to 1975

	Exports			Imports		
	United States	Japan	Other Developed Countries	United States	Japan	Other Developed Countries
1953	77%	15%	1%	23%	16%	2%
1955	41	40	7	23	6	11
1960	11	61	13	39	20	27
1965	35	25	14	39	36	10
1970	47	28	12	29	41	13
1975	30	25	24	26	33	13

Sources: Korean Traders Association, Trade Yearbook: 1953; Bank of Korea, Annual Economic Review, 1957; Economic Planning Board, Statistical Yearbook, 1966 and 1977.

The Trade Regime

In the 1950s the Korean currency was highly overvalued because of destruction caused by the war, the resultant shortages of various essential goods, and the associated inflation. The government nonetheless resisted devaluation as long as possible. Export promotion was not given serious consideration.

Trade and industrialization policies were designed essentially to overcome the various side effects of currency overvaluation, which had resulted in inefficiencies of resource allocation. The government bureaucracies, especially the Ministry of Commerce and Industry (MCI) and the Ministry of Finance (MOF), gained powerful controls over the private economy by maintaining a disequilibrium system associated with the currency overvaluation. It was only in the sixties that a movement toward import liberalization and a vigorous export promotion began, although some early measures, as for example export incentives, were begun in the late 1950s.

Not only were the range and variety of export incentives smaller in the fifties than later, but the scale and intensity of each incentive scheme were much weaker. For instance, although an export credit system existed in this period, the automatically synchronized short-term export credit system (awarding a specified number of won per dollar exported) via unlimited rediscounts at the Bank of Korea and the allocation of large amounts of long-term loans for direct investment in export production became possible only in the sixties. Tariff exemptions on equipment and raw materials imported for export production, together with generous wastage allowances, were also introduced in the sixties.

The policymakers of the fifties simply could not imagine the possibility of Korea's exporting large amounts of rice, as it did in the colonial period, or exporting, on the basis of its very limited experience, significant quantities of manufactured goods. Their major concern was to maximize aid inflows, save foreign exchange, and promote import substitution. This is not meant to imply that the policymakers of the sixties started export promotion policies because they could perceive all the advantages of export-oriented growth as later revealed. The adoption of an export promotion policy was a natural response to the declining grants-in-aid and expanding demand for foreign exchange. The officials promoted exports, saw the benefits, and consequently adopted an export-oriented growth strategy. Several instruments were used for the purpose, including tax incentives, tariff exemptions, and financial and other inducements.[2]

It seems clear that most of the export promotion policies of the sixties did not systematically favor specific export industries selected with a view to their factor intensity. As demonstrated by the First Five-Year Plan document, in the early sixties the government did not envision a major role for labor-intensive manufactured exports. However, as export expansion developed along the lines of classical comparative advantage theory, the government quickly started to encourage investments into such emerging export sectors as textiles, clothing, plywood, electronics, and wigs. While the authorities maintained a high effective exchange rate for exports, it was private entrepreneurs who played the major role in determining sectoral resource allocation for exports. Of course some policies, such as the subsidized financing of capital goods imports, could have indirectly affected the factor intensity of exports as well as import substitution.

In preparing the Fourth Five-Year Plan (1977–81), the Korean government appears to have adopted policies that may directly affect the factor intensity of exports. It has started to plan investment schedules for such industries as shipbuilding, electronics, machinery, steel and metal products, and petrochemicals, anticipating that Korea will soon have comparative advantage in these industries and will be in a position to export their products. Thus, by selecting specific industries to be promoted as major export sectors, government decisions have started to affect directly the factor intensity of exports and employment growth.

After the sixties, Korean entrepreneurs soon learned that generous subsidies and other promotional schemes would be provided for production activities the government wished to support, while various disincentives would be applied to nonfavored activities. As a result, in the seventies most of the large firms that could successfully accumulate wealth from light manufacturing, including textiles and footwear production, have willingly started to invest in manufacture of steel and other metal products, electrical and nonelectrical machinery, electronic products, shipbuilding, other transportation equipment, and petrochemical products.

In Korea a successful entrepreneur usually owns, possibly as a result of economies of scale in financial operations, a group of firms involved in various activities extending from import substituting production for the domestic market to exclusively export-oriented production. As the emphasis of the government shifts from simple labor-intensive manufactures to more skill- and capital-intensive manufactures, the entrepreneur begins to adapt to this shift by investing in a new set of projects, adjusting the relative scale of existing production activities, and reshuffling workers accordingly. This ability of Korean entrepreneurs to adapt to changing economic variables and venture into new activities, combined with government policies that encourage continual shifts in production activities, seem to constitute the necessary ingredients for rapid economic growth.

In weighing the policies underlying successful export expansion in Korea since 1962, one should not fail to note that the most important factor has been the commitment of the government to promoting exports. This effort has involved the government at all levels from the president down to officials responsible for export administration work, together with the entire private sector related to exports, through the monthly sessions of the "Expanded Meeting for Export Promotion." It is at these meetings that various problems in export expansion are identified and activities coordinated. Furthermore, successful exporters are highly honored and encouraged. This has an immense psychological impact in a society that still carries remnants of traditional Confucianism. This honor and encouragement bestowed on exporters has undoubtedly helped channel the best of the entrepreneurial class in Korea into export activities.

With such a strong national commitment to export promotion, the relevant ministers, especially the minister of commerce and industry, are expected to show no less enthusiasm for the cause. The MCI announces the annual export target at the beginning of each year. If there develops a risk that the target will not be met, the staff of the MCI and other officials concerned with export administration work seven days a week and overtime to expedite administrative processes, to strengthen existing export support schemes, to institute new subsidies, and to exert irresistible pressures on businessmen to accelerate exports even though it may entail losses. If all such efforts fail to achieve the target amount, MCI officials may even try to adulterate export statistics—for example, by counting receipts in advance of exports or exports without drafts in bonded processing as actual exports. This is why there have been significant differences between the MCI export figures and the Bank of Korea's (BOK) export figures, which are based on customs clearances, and why MCI has sometimes reported a sharp drop in exports in January. Such overenthusiasm for export expansion has apparently caused some losses (Hong 1976), but it has kept fueling the export oriented growth process in Korea.

As I mentioned already, quantitative restrictions and import licensing were important components of the trade regime in the 1950s. Their importance diminished substantially in the 1960s. Quantitative controls were lessened after the 1964 devaluation. They were further relaxed in 1967 when a switch was made in the MCI system from a positive list of items that could be imported, with or without authorization, to a negative list of items that could not be imported without specific government authorization. Import licenses were automatically approved for all commodities (AA items) unless they were on the list of restricted or prohibited items.

Under the negative list system, more than half of the 1,312 basic (five-digit SITC) import items became AA commodities. There were about seventy prohibited import items during 1967–76, but the number of quota items has decreased steadily from more than one hundred in 1967–68 to zero in 1976. On the other hand, the number of items that, though not subject to quotas, require recommendations from MCI or other appropriate ministries has steadily increased from more than 300 items in 1967 to 550 in 1975 (see table 8.5) and more than 600 in 1976. Importers of these items must acquire approval to import and frequently must also get approval for the quantity of imports from MCI or other appropriate authorities. Although this system is more flexible than a quota or a system linking imports to export performance, the government can still effectively control the amount of imports of each commodity group by imposing annual import ceilings on the basis of estimated import needs and the overall balance of payments situation. More than half the items that require approval have been subject to such ceilings, resulting in an effect similar to quantitative restrictions.[3]

In principle, imports of finished consumer goods have not been allowed. Imports of raw materials for exports were normally approved automatically, irrespective of their classification. However, quantitative restrictions were sometimes applied when there were influential domestic suppliers of these raw material. This generated conflicts between export producers who wanted to use low-priced (and high-quality) imported raw materials and domestic producers of high-priced (and allegedly poor-quality) raw materials.

To accelerate investment, capital goods imports received preferential treatment and, to raise the utilization rate of existing capacity, intermediate goods imports also received preferential treatment. Since the

Table 8.5   Sectoral Pattern of Import Restrictions, Based on 1,312 Basic (Five-Digit) SITC Items

Sector	1967 (Second Half)		1970 (Second Half)		1975 (Second Half)	
	Prohibited, Linked, and Quota Items	Recommendation Required	Prohibited, Linked, and Quota Items	Recommendation Required	Prohibited, Linked, and Quota Items	Recommendation Required
Total restricted imports	220 (100%)	337 (100%)	157 (100%)	437 (100%)	110 (100%)	553 (100%)
Agriculture and fishery	2 (1%)	41 (12%)	2 (1%)	49 (11%)	1 (1%)	53 (10%)
Mining	2 (1%)	1 (0%)	2 (1%)	9 (2%)	0 (0%)	20 (4%)
Manufacturing	216 (98%)	295 (88%)	153 (97%)	379 (87%)	109 (99%)	480 (87%)
Food products	8 (4%)	48 (14%)	7 (5%)	60 (16%)	6 (6%)	74 (15%)
Textile products	83 (38%)	16 (5%)	41 (27%)	51 (14%)	39 (36%)	53 (11%)
Wood products	9 (4%)	11 (3%)	4 (3%)	13 (3%)	3 (3%)	12 (3%)
Paper products	15 (7%)	8 (2%)	11 (7%)	10 (3%)	6 (6%)	21 (4%)
Rubber products	10 (5%)	2 (1%)	10 (7%)	1 (0%)	6 (6%)	2 (0%)
Chemicals	16 (7%)	52 (15%)	10 (7%)	61 (16%)	4 (4%)	73 (15%)
Nonmetallic products	9 (4%)	8 (2%)	4 (3%)	7 (2%)	0 (0%)	18 (4%)
Basic metals	3 (1%)	22 (7%)	10 (7%)	23 (6%)	0 (0%)	31 (7%)
Metal products	14 (6%)	26 (8%)	11 (7%)	26 (7%)	7 (6%)	26 (5%)
Machinery	0 (0%)	13 (4%)	5 (3%)	17 (5%)	6 (6%)	42 (9%)
Electrical machinery	2 (1%)	21 (6%)	4 (3%)	22 (6%)	12 (11%)	15 (3%)
Transportation equipment	0 (0%)	12 (4%)	0 (0%)	19 (5%)	0 (0%)	21 (4%)
Miscellaneous manufactures	47 (21%)	56 (17%)	36 (24%)	69 (18%)	20 (18%)	92 (19%)
Amount of import ($ million)	70	220	128	842	590	3,190
Share in total imports	(7%)	(23%)	(6%)	(42%)	(9%)	(44%)

Source: Hong (1977).

intermediate and capital goods imports were subject to fewer quantitative controls, import substitution for these goods could not be as profitable as for consumption goods. Korea's relative failure to promote intermediate and capital goods industries in the fifties and sixties positively contributed to the rapid export expansion in the late sixties and seventies, because manufacturers of export goods were relatively free to use low-cost imported intermediate and capital goods instead of high-cost domestic products. While there was some earlier import substitution, as for example in fertilizers, it was largely in commodities that exporters did not use as inputs.

In the mid-seventies, however, the government's emphasis has clearly shifted to active development of various intermediate and capital goods industries both for domestic consumption and for export. Should these industries fail to achieve efficiency in terms of international competitiveness because of abuse of tariff and nontariff protection measures, the adverse effects may spread over the entire field of production in Korea whether for domestic consumption or for export. The effect of high-cost intermediate and capital goods may be more serious than that of high-cost consumer goods, although this could occur only if exporters were constrained to buy from domestic sources.

Balance of Payments

As was seen in table 8.1, imports of commodities and services exceeded exports until the mid-1970s. Korea achieved a current account surplus for the first time in 1977. As I already mentioned, the deficits of the 1950s were financed almost entirely by foreign aid: with an overvalued exchange rate and almost no exports, Korea was not creditworthy for foreign loans, and prospects for repatriation of profits were not attractive to foreign investors. As aid flows diminished in the late 1950s, the Korean government began taking measures to attract foreign capital, primarily in the form of loans. As can be seen from table 8.1, these loans increased in size and importance. In recent years, foreign direct investment has assumed some importance in Korea, although it has remained much smaller than foreign borrowing.

Exchange Rate Policies

Table 8.6 gives data on nominal, effective, and price level adjusted exchange rates for exports and imports. The price level deflated EER for exports, with or without adjustments for trading partners' price levels, rose significantly from the mid-1950s to the early 1960s. After sizable fluctuations in the early 1960s (not all shown in table 8.6), the real exchange rate has fluctuated much less since that time. This reflects the government's policy of relying much more on the exchange rate to promote exports and import substitutes.

Table 8.6 Nominal, Effective, and Price-Adjusted Exchange Rates for Exports and Imports, Selected Years, 1955–75 (Won per Dollar)

Rate	1955	1958	1961	1964	1967	1970	1973	1975
A. Official exchange rate	37	50	128	214	271	311	398	485
Export rates								
B. Export dollar premiums	n.a.	64	15	40	—	—	—	—
C. Export subsidies	n.a.	1	9	27	62	88	94	81
D. Effective exchange rate (EER) for exports (A + B + C)[a]	72	115	151	281	333	399	493	566
E. Price level deflated EER for exports	n.a.	289	294	310	286	273	255	163
F. Purchasing power parity EER for exports[b]	224	281	289	305	299	308	396	321
Import rates								
G. Tariffs and tariff equivalents	n.a.	14	20	33	26	26	19	25
H. Effective exchange rate (EER) for imports (A + G)[a]	42	64	147	247	296	336	418	510
I. Price level deflated EER for imports[a]	n.a.	160	287	272	256	231	216	147
J. Purchasing power parity EER for imports[b]	131	156	282	268	266	260	332	287

Sources: Frank, Kim, and Westphal (1975); Westphal and Kim (1977).

[b]Immediately preceding item multiplied by average price level of trading partners.

[b]Immediately preceding item multipled by average price level of trading partners.

8.1.3   Structure of Protection

Table 8.1 depicts the rapid growth of manufacturing's importance in the South Korean production structure and the steady decrease in the importance of NRB sectors. By 1977 the modernized manufacturing sector contributed about 35 percent of GNP, while the social overhead sectors contributed nearly 10 percent. The once-dominant agricultural sector had declined to a mere 16 percent of GNP, and even the share of the service sectors was reduced to about 35 percent, from 43 percent in 1962. Paralleling these trends in output, the composition of employment also altered: the share of agricultural employment fell from 61 percent of total employed persons in 1963 to 40 percent in 1977.

8.1.4   The Labor Market

A consistent series of employment data for Korea is available only for the period after 1962. Korea's labor force has grown at an average annual rate of 3 percent since 1963. Before 1963, nearly two-thirds of employed persons were engaged in agriculture, and unemployment in nonfarm areas was estimated to have been more than 16 percent.

Industrial employment began rising sharply in the sixties. As can be seen from table 8.7, the real wage began rising after 1964. Simultaneously, the share of employment in agriculture fell and the overall unemployment rate was reduced. In 1977 the urban unemployment rate was estimated to have fallen to 5.8 percent.

Although there is reason to believe that capital was implicitly subsidized through a variety of credit-rationing devices, the Korean labor market seems to have been fairly distortion-free by the late 1960s: unions were nonexistent or had relatively little power, and government regulations did not result in a wage above market-clearing levels. It appears that the Korean labor market was transformed from one fairly typical for LDCs, with open unemployment and slow urban employment growth, to a neoclassical, full-employment labor market by the 1970s.[4]

8.1.5   Inflation

Inflation has been a significant factor in Korea throughout the period since 1953, although inflation rates have varied substantially in different subintervals. On a 1970 base, wholesale prices in 1953 were only 8.2, and they rose to 31.0 in 1960. This represented an average annual rate of increase of 19 percent. As already discussed, this contributed to the overvaluation of the exchange rate and the severity of exchange controls during the 1950s.

The period from 1960 to 1964 was one during which the switch in policies away from import substitution was made. This was followed, in 1964–65, by a series of budgetary and financial reforms, including, as

Table 8.7   Korean Labor Force and Employment: 1963–77

	Population Fourteen and over (Thousand Persons)	Total Employment (Thousand Persons)	Manufacturing Employment (Thousand Persons)	Unemployment Rate		Manufacturing Real Wage (1975 = 100)
				Farm Household (%)	Nonfarm Household (%)	
1963	15,085	6,933	610	2.9	16.4	55.1
1964	15,502	7,799	637	3.5	14.4	51.8
1965	15,937	8,206	772	3.1	13.5	57.7
1966	16,367	8,423	833	3.1	12.8	59.6
1967	16,764	8,717	1,021	2.3	11.1	63.0
1968	17,166	9,155	1,170	1.9	9.0	68.8
1969	17,639	9,414	1,232	2.2	7.8	80.5
1970	18,253	9,745	1,284	1.6	7.4	89.9
1971	18,984	10,066	1,336	1.5	7.4	95.3
1972	19,724	10,559	1,445	1.3	7.5	95.6
1973	20,438	11,139	1,774	1.0	6.8	93.7
1974	21,148	11,586	2,012	1.2	6.8	97.4
1975	21,833	11,830	2,205	1.3	6.6	100.0
1976	22,549	12,556	2,678	1.0	6.3	113.7
1977	23,336	12,929	2,798	1.1	5.8	131.7

Source: Economic Planning Board, *Annual Report on the Economically Active Population,* various issues, and Bank of Korea, *Economics Statistics Yearbook,* various issues. GNP deflator was used to compute real wage rates.

I already mentioned, an increase in nominal interest rates. One result of this was that wholesale prices, whose index stood at 62.3 in 1964, rose much more slowly during the 1960s, averaging a 7.9 percent increase per year. As in most countries, inflation has accelerated in the 1970s, with rates of increase of 42 and 21 percent in 1974 and 1975 respectively.

In addition to monetary reforms, however, the Korean government began in about 1964 maintaining the real exchange rate at a fairly constant level, as already seen. Since the early 1960s, therefore, the Korean trade and payments regime has been fairly well shielded from the effects of the inflation.

8.1.6   Summary

The salient features of Korea's growth have been the emphasis upon export promotion and the transformation of the economy under those policies. Growth has been so rapid that a snapshot of the economy at any one point in time fails to capture the phenomenon: exports and the domestic production structure shifted from a heavy emphasis on rural, primary-commodity activities toward a modern, industrial sector orientation. Per capita incomes have risen sharply in this process, and urban employment and real wages also increased rapidly. A central question is the extent to which the export promotion policies accounted for the turnaround in the labor market and in employment. Closely related is the question whether recent policies, with somewhat greater emphasis upon heavy industry, will permit a continuation of past trends in employment and real wages.

8.2   The Trade Regime and the Structure of Protection

8.2.1   Tariffs

In the fifties and early sixties, the government relied on various quantitative import restrictions to offset the adverse effects of the overvaluation of the domestic currency on the balance of payments. A complex structure of multiple exchange rates also developed; nonetheless, on balance the structure of incentives during this period was biased against exports. Import liberalization in the 1960s consisted primarily of reduced reliance on quantitative controls and the shift already mentioned from a positive list to a negative list system. Tariff rates were not altered significantly during 1963–75. Data for 1968–72 can therefore be regarded as broadly representative of the rates in effect throughout the export promotion years.

According to the Major Taxation Statistics data of the Bureau of Taxation, available for years after 1968, the average legal tariff rate (including special tariffs) for all commodity imports was about 26 percent during 1968–72. The average legal tariff rate was reduced to 24 percent in 1973 and to between 12 and 15 percent during 1974–75. However, because of tariff exemptions on materials for export production and for key industries and foreign investment projects (whose imports were rapidly increasing), the average rate of tariffs actually collected was only 8 or 9 percent from 1966 to 1970 and declined further to about 6 percent during 1971–72. This was due partly to generally lowered legal tariff rates and partly to a sudden increase in tariff-exempt imports of crude oil, which had been subject to a 5 percent tariff during 1968–74. The average rate of tariffs actually collected has amounted to only about 5 percent since 1973.

To ascertain the extent to which tariff data are sensitive to the choice of weights, I computed weighted average legal tariff rates using actual individual import volumes as weights. The average legal tariff rate so computed on all commodity imports was raised from 17 percent in 1963–67 to 26 percent in 1968–72 but was lowered to 20 percent in 1973–74 and to 12 percent in 1975 (see table 8.8). The 1967 tariff reform appears to have slightly lowered the simple arithmetic average tariff rate on all imports, but substantial shifts in the import pattern tended to raise the weighted average legal tariff rate. The legal tariff rates were very low on minerals, relatively low on agricultural products, and very high on most manufactures. Lower rates were preserved for essential raw materials than for finished goods and for noncompeting capital goods than for competing consumption goods.

8.2.2 Effective Rates of Protection

According to the sectoral effective rates of protection estimated by Westphal and Kim for 1968, the average ERP for agriculture, as shown in table 8.9, was about 18 percent and that for mining was about 3 percent, while the average ERP for manufacturing as a whole was a minus 1 percent (Westphal and Kim 1977). The average level of protection, especially that in manufacturing, was very low in Korea compared with other developing countries, which may reflect the fact that the exchange rate in 1968 was not greatly overvalued. However, the average ERP on import-competing manufacturing industries was estimated to be as high as 92 percent in 1968, while that on export industries and noncompeting industries was estimated to be below minus 10 percent. Furthermore, while the effective protection rates for domestic sales of import-competing and export-import industries were fairly high, the rates for export sales were either near zero or negative for all categories of industries. As Westphal and Kim suggest, ERPs may be indicators either of relative profitability or of relative inefficiency. Hence the negative rates on export industries and export sales of other industries

may indicate no room for either excess profitability or substantial inefficiency, while the extremely high rate on import-competing industries
may indicate the opposite. The results might be interpreted as indicating that Korea's export promotion policies were relatively more efficient
than its import substitution policies.

Table 8.8   Weighted Average Sectoral Tariff Rates (Basic Rates)

Sector	1963–67	1968–72	1973–74	1975
Rice, barley, and wheat	14%	18%	16%	0%
Other agriculture	11	17	13	5
Forestry	10	10	10	7
Fisheries	28	39	37	36
Coal	10	10	10	0
Other minerals	1	6	5	3
Processed foods	37	35	12	11
Beverages	180	150	150	150
Tobacco	224	95	126	150
Fiber spinning	30	64	52	47
Textile fabrics	75	98	81	80
Textile products	49	89	75	77
Lumber and plywood	12	16	30/25	25
Wood and furniture	80	91	76	75
Paper and products	10	10	11	15
Printing	0	0	0	0
Leather and products	75	68	61	60
Rubber products	41	51	44	38
Basic chemicals	23	24	24	21
Other chemicals	26	47	45	27
Chemical fertilizer	5	0	0	0
Petroleum products	18	20	20	20
Coal products	20	5	5	5
Nonmetallic minerals	17	29	26	22
Iron and steel	10	12	11	18
Steel products	16	28	28	19
Nonferrous metals	12	25	22	16
Metal products	33	45	40	40
Machinery	16	20	15	18
Electrical machinery	21	29	28	33
Transportation equipment	32	38	15	17
Miscellaneous manufacturing	19	55	55	52
Scrap	21	7	6	6
Agricultural products	13	15	13	3
Minerals	2	6	5	3
Manufacturing	20	34	26	23
All commodities	17	26	20	12

Source: Hong (1977).

Table 8.9   Average Effective Protection Rates by Major Industrial Groups: 1968

	Legal Protection[a]	Nominal Protection[a]	Effective Protection		
			Export	Domestic	Average
Agriculture	36%	17%	−16%	19%	18%
Mining	10	7	−1	4	3
Manufacturing	59	11	3	−1	−1
Export industries[b]	54	5	5	−18	−11
Import-competing[c]	55	32	−9	93	92
Exports-imports[d]	46	23	−2	73	45
Noncompeting[e]	64	5	−1	−16	−16
All tradables	49	13	—	—	10

Source: Westphal and Kim (1977).
Notes: Based on Balassa method.
[a]Legal protection is tariff protection. Nominal protection is actual, or realized, protection on prices. Legal tariff rates sometimes exceed nominal rates owing to tariff redundancy and duty exemptions as exporters import their raw material and intermediate imports duty-free.
[b]Manufacturing industries exporting more than 10 percent of total production.
[c]Manufacturing sectors in which imports provide more than 10 percent of total supply.
[d]Exports greater than 10 percent of total production and imports greater than 10 percent of total domestic supply.
[e]All other sectors. This classification system is not the same as the one used in other studies in this volume. For comparison, "export industries" and "export-import" here would include some of both "import competing" and "noncompeting imports" used in other studies.

8.3   Factor Supply and Factor Intensity of Trade

8.3.1   Factory Intensity of Trade

Table 8.10 shows factor requirements of trade in Korea in 1970, computed using domestic production as weights. Note that factor requirements are measured here by the amount of capital and the amount of labor per unit of value of output, and that factor intensity is measured by the ratio of capital requirements to labor requirements.[5] The total amount of labor required to produce $100 million worth of exports was 67,000 persons, while the capital required amounted to about $99 million. On the other hand, the labor required to produce $100 million worth of import-competing goods was 74,000 persons, and capital requirements amounted to about $115 million.[6] Import-competing replacements thus appear to have been slightly more capital-intensive than exports.

The most remarkable fact emerging from table 8.10, however, seems to be that the capital-intensity of Korea's noncompeting non-NRB im-

Table 8.10   Factor Requirements per $100 Million of Tradable Goods
                  by Trade Category, 1970

Category	Capital (K) (Million 1970 Dollars)	Labor (N) (Thousand Persons)	Factor Intensity (K/N)
Exports (HOS and NRB)	99.0	67.0	1,478
Import-comepting products (HOS and NRB)	115.0	74.0	1,554
Noncompeting imports, applying			
1947 United States coefficients	182.9	8.9	20,551
1958 United States coefficients	165.2	7.3	22,630
1965 Japanese coefficients	135.7	33.3	4,075
1970 Japanese coefficients	130.9	27.3	4,795

Source: Hong (1977).

Note: The amount of capital directly and indirectly required for exports was computed with $k [I - A^d]^{-1}$ and that for import-competing products with $k[I - A]^{-1}$, where k represents the direct capital-output ratio, A^d the matrix of domestic input coefficients, and A the matrix of domestic and imported input coefficients for import-competing products. Labor requirements were computed in the same fashion. Both matrixes include indirect requirements of tradables. The justification for the different treatment of exports and import-competing products is that export industries can import raw materials and intermediate inputs, whereas import-substituting industries usually have to use domestic inputs. See text for the list of excluded NRB items.

ports, estimated by using the United States and Japanese sectoral factor coefficients, was much higher than that of either the export or the import-competing sectors. Crude oil, timber, raw cotton, raw sugar, crude rubber, and wool were excluded from the computation, being regarded as noncompeting NRB tradable goods.

Westphal and Kim (1977) have also estimated the factor intensity of trade, again using production (not value added) as weights. Their results for 1968 correspond with those reported in table 8.9: they estimated total labor requirements of all exporting sectors to be 7.53 man-years of labor per million 1965 won of output compared with 6.62 man-years for a comparable value of import-competing production (which probably had a higher ratio of value added to output). Westphal and Kim were also able to estimate factor intensities separately for manufacturers. For manufactured exports, they estimated labor requirements at 7.9 man-years, with a corresponding figure of import-competing production of 5.56. The labor-capital ratio in manufactured exports was 4.29, and that of import-competing production was 2.74 (Westphal and Kim 1977, pp. 4–47).

Therefore Korea's trade appears to have been consistent with the HOS comparative advantage doctrine, especially with respect to exports versus noncompeting, non-NRB imports, and manufactured exports versus manufactured import-competing production.

The largest difference in factor intensities lies not between exports and import-competing goods but between both of these categories and noncompeting imports.

8.3.2   Capital Accumulation and Changes in Factor Intensity of Trade

The factor intensity of trade has been changing over time. According to the trade statistics in BOK's input-output tables, commodity exports increased about thirty-five times (in 1970 prices), while the estimated number of persons employed directly and indirectly in export production increased about 8.5 times (from 0.15 million to 1.24 million) during 1963–75. This implies average annual growth rates of about 35 percent and 20 percent, respectively, and an export expansion elasticity of employment of about 0.6. The fixed capital stock directly and indirectly employed for export production increased about thirty-seven times (from $0.10 billion to $3.90 billion) over the same period, implying an average annual growth rate of 35 percent and an export expansion elasticity of capital absorption of about 1.0.

Production of competitive imports increased about 6.4 times while the estimated number of persons required directly and indirectly to replace these competing imports increased about 2.5 times (from 0.41 million to 1.02 million) during 1963–75. This implies average annual growth rates of about 16.5 percent and 8.0 percent, respectively, and an import replacement elasticity of employment of about 0.5. The fixed capital stock directly and indirectly required for import replacements increased about 7.2 times (from $0.39 billion to $2.80 billion) over the same period, implying an average annual growth rate of 18 percent and an import replacement elasticity of capital requirement of about 1.1.

Han (1970) has computed the amount of fixed capital stock employed in Korean industries on the basis of the 1968 National Wealth Survey. To estimate the fixed capital stock by years for the period after 1953, I used Han's estimate for 1968 as a benchmark and subtracted or added the BOK's fixed capital formation figures for successive years. The results, starting with 1962, are shown on a per capita basis in constant 1970 prices in table 8.11.

Total net real fixed capital stock in Korea, excluding household wealth in the form of dwellings, increased at an average annual rate of 3.5 percent during 1953–61, at 6.7 percent per annum during 1962–66, and at a remarkable 13 percent per annum during 1967–76. Per capita, however, the net capital stock increased by only about 30 percent during the thirteen-year period from 1953 to 1966, and it was only after 1966 that it began to increase rapidly. From then until 1976, capital stock per capita increased by about 170 percent. Owing to rapidly in-

Table 8.11   Changes in Factor Endowment

Year	All Industry Net Capital Stock (1970 Dollars)		Total Employed Persons (Millions)	Manufacturing Net Capital Stock per Worker (1970 Dollars)		Total Number of Workers (Millions)
	Per Capita	Per Employed Person		M and M Census	Han–BOK Data	
1963	175	624	7.66	—	1,534	0.61
1964	179	641	7.80	—	1,549	0.64
1965	185	649	8.21	—	1,388	0.77
1966	201	702	8.42	1,723	1,528	0.83
1967	220	761	8.72	1,637	1,426	1.02
1968	249	837	9.16	1,610	1,437	1.17
1969	287	962	9.41	1,831	1,557	1.23
1970	322	1,065	9.75	1,983	1,665	1.28
1971	356	1,163	10.07	2,302	1,759	1.34
1972	383	1,214	10.56	2,326	1,701	1.45
1973	418	1,280	11.14	2,748	1,583	1.77
1974	453	1,358	11.59	2,806	1,488	2.01
1975	495	1,477	11.83	3,119	1,447	2.21
1976	545	1,557	12.56	3,220	1,310	2.68

Source: Hong (1977).

creasing employment, capital stock per employed person increased by only about 120 percent. However, this still implies a significant overall capital deepening during 1966–76.

For the manufacturing sector alone, data from the Census of Manufactures indicate that the capital stock per worker has steadily and significantly increased since 1966, rising from $1,723 per worker in that year to $2,302 in 1971 and to $3,220 in 1976.[7]

According to the Farm Household Survey data, capital stock per man-year input in agriculture was estimated at about $240 before 1967 but increased significantly during 1967–73 to reach $560 in 1973. The capital stock per farmer (without taking account of underemployment) estimated on the basis of the Han–BOK capital stock data also doubled during 1966–74.

Annual wages of farm employees increased rapidly after 1967 (from about $200 in that year to $410 in 1975 in 1970 prices), as did the wages of employees in manufacturing (from about $410 in 1967 to about $680 in 1975). On the other hand, the weighted average real interest rates on all types of loans supplied by both banking institutions and curb markets reached their peak in 1967 and thereafter declined steadily and substantially. Hence we can conclude that, since 1967, there has been a rapid and significant capital accumulation and capital deepening in Korea accompanied by a fast-rising wage/rental ratio (see tables 8.14 and 8.20).

As capital accumulates and the wage/rental ratio rises, one can expect more capital-intensive production techniques to become profitable both for domestic consumption and for exports, and production of more capital-intensive commodities will increase. Hence there should be a shift in factor intensity of both output and export production.

The capital intensity (i.e., capital/labor ratio) of Korea's export bundle grew steadily during 1960–75. The ratio of capital to labor required directly and indirectly for export production (excluding imported inputs) was about 0.6 in 1960 and increased to about 3.1 in 1975 (defined as in table 8.12). However, the capital intensity of import-competing products did not increase as rapidly as that of exports during this time. Consequently, although import-competing production was much more capital-intensive than production of exports during 1963–68 (e.g., 1.6 versus 1.0 in 1966), the difference subsequently became smaller. After 1970 there seem to have been only moderate differences in their factor intensities. In 1975 the capital intensity of exports was above that of import-competing products. In theory, there is no reason why the capital intensity of exports from Korea should be lower than that of its import-competing products.

The total amount of labor required per unit of exports (at constant prices) steadily decreased from 1960 to 1975. That is, the (direct plus

Table 8.12   Changes in Factor Intensity of Trade (Millions of 1970 Dollars and Thousands of Persons)

I-O Trade Data	1960	1963	1966	1968	1970	1973	1975
A. Production for export							
1. Direct factor intensity	(0.47)	(0.58)	(0.78)	(0.86)	(1.08)	(1.73)	(2.86)
a. Capital content	49	45	42	37	43	38	60
b. Labor content	105	78	54	43	40	22	21
2. Factor intensity of domestic inputs	(0.83)	(0.85)	(1.25)	(1.49)	(2.07)	(2.69)	(3.47)
a. Capital content	49	64	55	55	56	43	59
b. Labor content	59	75	44	37	27	16	17
3. Factor intensity of imported inputs	(—)	(—)	(1.63)	(1.88)	(2.75)	(3.50)	(3.38)
a. Capital content	(—)	(—)	13	15	22	35	27
b. Labor content	(—)	(—)	8	8	8	10	8
4. Aggregate Factor Intensity	(0.59)	(0.71)	(1.00)	(1.15)	(1.48)	(2.13)	(3.13)
a. Total capital employed (A1a + A2a)	97	109	97	91	99	81	119
b. Total labor employed (A1b + A2b)	164	153	97	79	67	38	38
B. Import-competing production							
1. Direct factor intensity	(0.34)	(0.70)	(1.40)	(0.98)	(1.05)	(1.57)	(1.72)
a. Capital content	36	57	60	42	46	44	43
b. Labor content	105	82	43	43	44	28	25
2. Factor intensity of domestic inputs	(1.05)	(1.45)	(1.83)	(2.08)	(2.27)	(4.00)	(4.17)
a. Capital content	44	61	53	52	50	44	57
b. Labor content	42	42	29	25	22	11	14
3. Factor intensity of imported inputs	(—)	(—)	(1.75)	(1.77)	(2.11)	(3.91)	(3.67)
a. Capital content	(—)	(—)	21	23	19	43	33
b. Labor content	(—)	(—)	12	13	9	11	9
4. Aggregate factor intensity	(0.54)	(0.94)	(1.58)	(1.46)	(1.55)	(2.60)	(2.75)
a. Total capital required (B1a + B2a + B3a)	79	117	134	117	115	130	132
b. Total labor required (B1b + B2b + B3b)	147	124	85	80	74	50	48

Source: Hong (1977).

Note: Factor intensity (figures in parentheses) is the amount of capital required divided by the amount of labor required per $100 million worth of exports or import-competing production. Note that, for reasons explained in the note to table 8.10, the aggregates for exports do not include, and the aggregates for import-competing production do include, the factor content of imported inputs.

indirect) labor/output ratios in export production as a whole decreased at an average annual rate of about 10 percent over the period. This trend seems to reflect the rapidly increasing labor productivity in export production owing to technical progress, factor substitution, and increasing returns to scale, on the one hand, and to shifts in the composition of the export bundle toward less labor-intensive products on the other. But in the case of capital requirements there was no rapid or sustained decline in the amount used per unit of exports. From the analysis in table 8.13, we can see that the substantial increase in capital intensity of Korea's exports during 1966–73 was predominantly due to labor-saving factor substitutions in production processes and only slightly due to shifts in the composition of exports.

8.4   Export Promotion and Subsidies on Capital Use

Along with the significant increase in capital intensity of exports and import-competing products, there has been a sharp rise in the wage/rental ratio in Korea since 1966. Although some of the capital-labor substitution in Korean industries may be attributed to the increase in capital stock per capita and the associated rise in the wage/rental ratio (that is, to a shift in the basic comparative advantage position), a substantial portion, especially that which occurred in export industries, may have to be attributed to the subsidy on capital use.

One of the most familiar themes in development economics is that wages paid by the modern manufacturing industry are higher than the marginal social cost of labor, while capital tends to be underpriced; together these circumstances tend to make the private profitability of capital-intensive projects exceed their social profitability. Most literature on labor markets in developing countries suggests that labor legislation and trade union activities are the major sources of the excess of wage rates above opportunity costs. In Korea there are no powerful labor unions or government legislation to affect wages. No thorough study of the Korean wage structure has been undertaken, but the apparent differences between rural and urban wages seem to reflect either or both of two things: (1) an imperfectly functioning labor market coupled with structural distortions; (2) the greater skill of the urban work force and the higher costs associated with urban living in such areas as housing, transportation, and public service fees.

To the extent, therefore, that there is an identifiable factor market distortion, it originates in government policies to encourage capital formation, and my focus is thus upon those policies. I will first examine the implicit subsidies on capital use in the form of accelerated depreciation allowances and low prices for imported capital goods. Then I will esti-

Table 8.13   Change in Factor Intensity of Commodity Exports Due to Factor Substitution and Shifts in Composition of Exports: 1966–73

	Average	1966	1968	1970	1973	Due to Changes in Export Composition		
						1966-68	1968-70	1970-73
Direct factor intensity of exports (capital/labor ratios)								
Applying 1966 coefficients		0.78	0.84	0.81	0.88	2.5%	−1.1%	7.1%
Applying 1968 coefficients		0.87	0.86	0.87	0.90	7.7%	−3.6%	8.6%
Applying 1970 coefficients		1.11	1.11	1.08	1.17	−1.1%	1.2%	3.4%
Applying 1973 coefficients		1.54	1.59	1.60	1.73	0.0%	−2.7%	8.3%
						3.2%	0.6%	8.1%
Due to factor substitution 1966–68	5.9%	11.5%	2.4%	7.4%	2.3%	10.3%	—	—
1968–70	27.7%	27.6%	29.1%	24.1%	30.0%	—	25.6%	—
1970–73	44.5%	38.7%	43.2%	48.1%	47.9%	—	—	60.2%
Direct plus indirect factor intensity of exports (capital/labor ratios)								
Applying 1966 coefficients		1.00	1.06	1.05	1.09	2.3%	1.2%	5.0%
Applying 1968 coefficients		1.12	1.15	1.16	1.21	6.0%	−0.9%	3.8%
Applying 1970 coefficients		1.51	1.54	1.48	1.56	2.7%	0.9%	4.3%
Applying 1973 coefficients		2.05	2.02	2.00	2.13	2.0%	−3.9%	5.4%
						−1.5%	−1.0%	6.5%
Due to factor substitution 1966–68	10.5%	12.0%	8.5%	10.5%	11.0%	15.0%	—	—
1968–70	31.3%	34.8%	33.9%	27.6%	28.9%	—	28.7%	—
1970–73	34.7%	35.8%	31.2%	35.1%	36.5%	—	—	43.9%

Source: Hong (1977).

mate the magnitude of, and interest rates on, domestic and foreign loans and the associated subsidies on capital use by estimating the real opportunity cost of capital use in Korea.

8.4.1 Accelerated Depreciation Allowances and Import Duty Exemptions on Capital Goods

Since 1967, corporations in mining, fishing, or manufacturing that get more than half their total revenue from foreign exchange earning activities have been allowed an extra depreciation allowance equal to 30 percent of the ordinary depreciation specified in the corporation tax law. The extra allowance is 15 percent of the basic allowance in the case of corporations whose foreign exchange earnings constituted 20 to 50 percent of total revenue. An extra 20 percent depreciation allowance was extended, in 1970, to firms operating in specified industrial estates such as the Gu-Mi Electronics Industrial Estate, the Ulsan Petrochemical Industrial Estate, and the Chang-Won Machinery Industrial Estate.

According to the Presidential Emergency Decree on Economic Stabilization and Growth issued on 3 August 1972, firms in specified key industries were entitled to a special depreciation allowance of 40 to 80 percent of the ordinary allowance during the five-year period starting in 1972 and ending in 1976. The industries that received an 80 percent rate were petrochemicals, steel, nonelectrical machines, electronics, shipbuilding, and tourist hotels. Electrical machinery, nonmetallic mineral products, textiles, ceramics, deep-sea fishing, mining, and electricity received a 60 percent rate, and the chemical industry received 40 percent. Since 1972, those mining, fishing, construction, and manufacturing industries not listed above have been entitled to an 80 percent special depreciation allowance for the portion of capital invested in domestically produced equipment. This provision was to be effective, even after 1976, for all industries.

In the aggregate, the ratio of provisions for the consumption of fixed capital to gross fixed capital formation in manufacturing jumped from about 40 percent during 1962–71 to nearly 70 percent in 1972–76. The expansion of accelerated depreciation allowances in the early seventies in terms of degree and industry coverage must have had a very biased effect on investment toward the capital-intensive sectors and techniques.

Turning to the cost of capital goods, we see that the tariff law has allowed duty-free imports of basic plant facilities and equipment for important industries since 1949. On the basis of this law, imports of machinery for export production received a tariff exemption from 1964 until 1974, when the tariff exemption system was changed into a deferred payment system on an installment basis. Capital goods imported for foreign investment projects in Korea have also been exempted from tariffs since 1960.

During 1953–66, about one-third of gross fixed capital formation was in the form of electrical and nonelectrical machinery and transportation equipment, compared with about 40 percent for 1967 to 1975. Of this machinery component, according to the BOK's input-output tables, the import content was as high as 73 percent in 1963 and 71 percent in 1973.

In the fifties, imports of capital goods were mostly financed by United States project assistance and partly by nonproject assistance. Official exchange rates were applied to project assistance imports, and hence imported capital goods were underpriced to the extent that the domestic currency was overvalued. In the sixties, however, an increasing proportion of imports was financed with nonaid funds. In addition, repeated devaluations eliminated the excessive overvaluation of domestic currency. Hence the subsidy on imported capital goods during this period consisted mainly of tariff exemption and subsidized financing of the imports by domestic or foreign loans.

Since a large part of capital goods was imported duty-free for either export production (until 1974), key industries, or foreign investments, the amount of duties actually collected on machinery imports amounted to only about 4 or 5 percent of the aggregate c.i.f. value during 1966–74, while that on electrical machinery was 8–12 percent before 1971 and between 3 and 4 percent after 1973. Duties actually collected on transport equipment amounted to about 7–11 percent before 1971 and 4–5 percent after 1972.

The absolute value of tariff exemptions per annum on capital goods imports was some $30 to $50 million during 1966–67, about $100 to $135 million during 1968–72, and about $140 to $150 million during 1973–74 (in 1970 prices). These exemptions were equivalent to approximately 5 percent of annual gross fixed capital formation in Korea.

8.4.2   Allocation of Domestic Bank Credit

During 1953–76, interest rates on bank loans (and savings) were usually kept extremely low compared with those on curb market loans. Although low interest rates raise the present value of the yield from real investments relative to their costs, the volume of such investments was necessarily restricted by credit rationing. It was this credit rationing that provided a financial subsidy to export production.

Credit rationing took the form of low-interest loans, both short-term and long-term, given by ten specialized government-operated banks and five nationwide commercial banks.[8] Short-term loans for export financing were provided within the limit specified by the BOK per dollar of exports at an interest rate of 13.8 to 9.13 percent per annum during 1960–63, 8.03 to 6.5 percent during 1963–67, 6 percent during 1967–73, and 7 to 9 percent since May 1973. The financial institutions could obtain rediscounts from the BOK on export loans they provided for foreign-exchange-earning activities at an interest rate of 10.22 to 5.48 percent during 1960–63, 4.38 to 4.5 percent during 1963–64, and 3.5 percent since June 1964.

Because exports have increased rapidly and steadily and because short-term export credit is provided automatically as a fixed proportion of the export value, the net annual increase in export credit has also expanded rapidly. The average annual increase in export credit was equivalent to 16 percent of the increase in the money supply and 34 percent of that in bank notes issued during 1962–69. During 1970–76, however, these percentages rose to about 40 percent and 90 percent, respectively.

According to BOK data on loans for exports, the share of such short-term loans in total loans provided by the Deposit Money Banks (DMB) and the Korea Development Bank (KDB) increased from about 3 percent in 1961–66 to about 6 or 7 percent in 1967–72 and to between 12 and 13 percent in 1973–76. At the same time the share of long-term loans for export production increased from about 1 to 3 percent in 1965–70, to between 8 and 9 percent in 1973–76. According to these data, loans for exports were mostly short-term in the sixties, but long-term loans for investment in export production began to increase rapidly in the early seventies, so that nearly 40 percent of loans for exports were long-term by the mid-seventies. The BOK data on long-term loans for exports consisted mostly of loans by Medium Industry Bank (based on medium industry export promotion fund) and foreign currency loans by foreign exchange banks.[9] However, since all DMB and KDB loans have been allocated among industries according to the "Regulations on Loan Funds," which gave preferential treatment to export businesses, the BOK data do not seem to adequately approximate the "long-term" financial support for export production in Korea.

8.4.3   Encouragement of Foreign Loans and Investments

Faced with the prospect of declining United States grants-in-aid, the first serious efforts to attract foreign loans and investments were made in 1960. The Foreign Capital Inducement Law of 1966 allowed foreign, or joint, direct investment, capital and technology inducement, and foreign cash borrowing. Foreign investment earnings (as well as royalty earnings from technology inducement) were entitled to complete exemption from income and corporation tax for the first five years, a two-thirds exemption for the following two years, and a one-third exemption for the next year. Capital equipment imported for foreign-investment businesses was also exempted from tariffs. Furthermore, the law granted a complete income tax exemption on interest earnings arising from foreign loans since 1963, and no limits were placed on conversion and remittance of legitimate profits and dividends. The government has also provided guarantees of repayment and repatriation to foreign lenders and investors since 1962.

Although the volume of bank loans increased greatly after the interest rate reform in 1965, the banks still could not meet the full demand for loan funds. The main long-term lending institution was the Korean Reconstruction Bank, which depended on limited government fiscal funds and repayments of past loans. Private enterprises, in the absence of well-developed institutional arrangements for equity financing and in light of the shortage of funds for long-term loans and high interest rates on short-term funds, were very much inclined to look abroad to finance their capital expansion needs. The government met their demand by opening doors to external credit from private sources and by continuing to encourage private borrowing from abroad (Cole and Lyman 1971, p. 81).

According to the Foreign Capital Inducement Law, the Economic Planning Board (EPB) minister could approve foreign loans to business if they would contribute significantly to improving the balance of payments position and the development of key industries, public enterprises, and projects specified in the economic development plan. The Korea Development Bank actually guaranteed the repayment in won, and the Bank of Korea assured convertibility of the won into foreign exchange. All such guarantees required the formal approval of the National Assembly until 1966.

Approval of private loans increased rapidly after the government introduced a system of repayment guarantees by the commercial banks in 1966 that bypassed the need for review and approval by the National Assembly. Government repayment guarantees are limited to loans to large-scale key national industries, which are regarded as difficult for a commercial bank to guarantee. Since very little foreign borrowing could be arranged without a repayment guarantee, the foreign loan guarantees gave the government, and particularly the EPB, which assumed the main responsibility for approval, a means of controlling the kinds of investment and loans being undertaken.

The total inflow of foreign investment (on an arrival basis) to the end of 1976 was $0.7 billion, contrasted with cumulative foreign loans to that time of about $6.4 billion. As these numbers make clear, foreign investment was small relative to foreign borrowing.

8.4.4   Interest Rate Subsidies on Capital Use

Table 8.14 provides information on loans and real interest rates for 1957–76. The major sources of loans in Korea were DMB loans, KDB loans, private and government foreign borrowing, and curb loans. The DMB loans constituted about 40–50 percent of total loans (as measured by year-end balances) during 1964–75. The share of KDB loans

Table 8.14   Loans and (Weighted Average) Real Interest Rates

	DMB Loans[a]		KDB Loans[a]		Curb Loans		Private Foreign Borrowing		Government Foreign Borrowing	
	Amount[b] (Billion Won)	Interest Rate (%)	Amount[b] (Billion Won)	Interest Rate (%)	Amount[b] (Billion Won)	Interest Rate (%)	Amount[b] (Million Dollars)	Interest Rate (%)	Amount[b] (Million Dollars)	Interest Rate (%)
1957	10.9		9.2				—			
1958	15.9		10.5				—	2.7		
1959	18.3		14.1				2.1	22.1		
1960	24.3		15.9				2.0	92.1	1.1	19.9
1961	32.7	0.1	20.3				1.7	92.1	2.1	90.0
1962	44.8	4.0	24.3	−1.0	—	—	1.5	−1.8	8.1	−2.4
1963	49.4	−7.5	27.6	−12.3	11.7	31.9	19.8	−15.0	32.1	−18.1
1964	49.9	−21.3	31.7	−26.2	20.4	27.2	36.0	35.6	43.0	32.6
1965	67.1	6.2	36.8	−0.8	22.6	48.9	60.3	19.8	53.8	16.4
1966	95.6	12.5	46.6	2.9	38.9	49.8	161.7	−1.3	114.5	−4.5
1967	168.4	15.4	52.4	6.1	78.2	50.1	288.7	−0.5	188.1	−3.9
1968	315.9	13.4	66.4	4.6	112.1	47.9	517.1	−0.8	292.8	−4.3
1969	540.4	13.9	96.1	5.4	181.6	44.5	829.3	3.1	433.7	−0.4
1970	682.1	8.4	129.0	3.3	218.4	40.6	1,039.6	5.4	576.7	1.7
1971	865.0	7.8	157.5	3.8		37.8	1,256.2	9.5	886.6	6.0
1972	1,125.6	3.7	239.1	−4.1	204.2	25.0	1,412.5	5.8	1,335.1	2.5
1973	1,492.8	7.0	318.5	2.8	246.4	26.4	1,720.5	2.3	1,790.2	−1.6
1974	2,303.9	−28.1	425.7	−32.4	323.6	−1.5	2,125.9	−32.0	2,112.0	−36.3
1975	2,751.6	−12.9	577.8	−15.3	408.4	14.8	2,766.9	0.0	2,548.2	−2.9
1976	3,552.1	1.6	739.0	−0.8	—	28.4	3,180.3	−5.1	3,168.4	−7.3

Source: Hong (1977).

Note: Real interest rates on domestic loans were computed by subtracting the rates of increase in the wholesale price index from nominal interest rates. Real interest rates on (private or government) foreign borrowing were computed by taking account of the rate of devaluation in Korea as well as the rate of change in the domestic wholesale price index.

amounted to about 20–30 percent of total loans during 1964–66, but their share was reduced to about 10 percent thereafter. The share of foreign loans was negligible until 1962, but it has rapidly increased to about 30–40 percent of total outstanding loans in Korea since 1966. The share of curb loans, admittedly underestimated, amounted to about 11 percent of total loans during 1964–71 and about 7 percent during 1972–75.[10]

The weighted average real interest rate on DMB loans reached its peak of 15 percent in 1967, then steadily declined to become negative in 1974. The real rate on KDB loans was almost always negative except during 1966–71. Taking account of the devaluation effect, the real interest rate on private foreign borrowing was about 8 percent during 1962–66, 3 percent during 1967–71, and −6 percent in 1972–75. The interest rate on foreign borrowing by the government was estimated to have averaged about 5 percent during 1962–66, about zero percent during 1967–71, and about −10 percent during 1972–75.

To estimate the magnitude of subsidies on capital use, we need to have some idea of the real opportunity cost of capital use. For this purpose, I have attempted to estimate the aggregate as well as sectoral rates of return on capital in Korea by dividing the aggregate or incremental amount of national income that can be attributed to capital by the total or incremental stock of capital. The return on nonlabor factors in the business-accounting sense can indicate how much a unit of capital can earn in Korea under the existing pace of technical progress and scale economies, the average quality of entrepreneurship, the existing power structure among factor owners and institutional arrangements, the natural resource endowment, and the general business climate. Since the returns on nonlabor include returns on physical capital, technical progress, economies of scale, market imperfection, and entrepreneurship, what we will call the "rate of return on capital" represents the rate of return on all factors but labor. We presume indivisibility among these nonlabor factors of production. The value added may or may not include the depreciation allowance or indirect taxes or both depending on the selected estimate of the value-added/fixed-capital ratio.

From the estimates shown in table 8.15, and using (per footnote a to the table) the results for the primary sector when land is included in total fixed capital stock, we can observe that the real rate of return on capital has been very high in manufacturing, relatively low in agriculture and services, and lowest in the social overhead sector. Artificially low prices in this last sector seem to have enhanced rates of return in other sectors, especially in manufacturing. In any case, such marked differences in the rate of return on capital among sectors may explain the rapid expansion of manufacturing, the moderate decline in the service sector, and the drastic decrease in the share of GNP contributed by

Table 8.15   **Estimates of Sectoral Rates of Return on Capital: 1954–75 (Percentage)**

Annual Average	Ratio of Net Nonlabor Value Added to Net Capital				Ratio of Gross Nonlabor Value Added to Gross Capital			
	Primary[a] Sector	Manu-facturing	Social Overhead Sector	Service Sector	Primary[a] Sector	Manu-facturing	Social Overhead Sector	Service Sector
	Applying Net Incremental VA/I Ratios at Market Price				*Applying Gross Incremental VA/I Ratios at Market Price —Type IV*			
1954–61	291	37	9	63	161	25	10	15
1962–66	292	47	10	31	172	38	12	14
1967–71	43	62	7	28	31	47	8	21
1972–75	27	108	6	14	20	54	8	10
	Applying Net-VA/Net-K-Stock Ratios at Market Price				*Applying Gross-VA/Gross-C-Stock Ratios at Market Price —Type III*			
1954–61	170	24	5	10	118	18	5	9
1962–66	153	31	7	13	102	23	6	10
1967–71	115	41	7	17	77	31	7	13
1972–75	82	60	6	18	56	39	7	13
	Applying Net Incremental VA/I Ratios at Factor Cost				*Applying Gross Incremental VA/I Ratios at Factor Cost —Type II*			
1954–61	291	23	6	41	160	17	8	10
1962–66	292	26	6	23	172	26	10	11
1967–71	43	38	5	19	31	32	6	15
1972–75	27	64	5	8	20	36	6	7

Table 8.15—*continued*

	Ratio of Net Nonlabor Value Added to Net Capital				Ratio of Gross Nonlabor Value Added to Gross Capital			
Annual Average	Primary[a] Sector	Manu-facturing	Social Overhead Sector	Service Sector	Primary[a] Sector	Manu-facturing	Social Overhead Sector	Sector Service
	Applying Net-VA/Net-K-Stock Ratios at Market Price				*Applying Gross-VA/Gross-C-Stock Ratios at Factor Cost —Type I*			
1954–61	1,701	15	4	7	118	12	3	7
1962–66	152	19	5	9	102	15	5	7
1967–71	115	25	5	12	77	20	6	9
1972–75	82	26	5	12	55	26	6	9

Source: Hong (1977).

Note: VA stands for value added, *I* for investment, *K* for net capital, and *C* for gross capital. The computations are made by applying non-labor shares in value added in 1970. See text for further details.

[a]The estimated average annual real rates of return on capital in the primary sector as shown in the table are extremely high because the value of land is excluded from total fixed capital stock. If land is included in total fixed capital stock, based on the Farm Household Economy Survey data, the rate of return on capital in the primary sector would be, at most, 17 to 20 percent during 1966–73. This range in the rates of return is more realistic.

agriculture. It may also explain the need for government direct investment in the social overhead sector.

The estimated rates of return to capital based on net value added versus net capital (left-hand side of table 8.15) are much higher than those based on a nondepreciating capital assumption. Since the so-called allowance for consumption of fixed capital stock is a legal concept that does not accurately reflect the actual depreciation, the "net" investment figure may have grossly underestimated the real amount of capital. To be on the conservative side, I decided to use the estimates based on gross-value-added/gross-capital ratios (right-hand side of table 8.15) to approximate the rate of return on capital. There are four such sets of estimates, two including indirect taxes and two excluding them. In the case of manufacturing, I took the set estimated at market prices (i.e., including indirect taxes) and incremental ratios as a possible upper limit (type IV) and the set estimated at factor cost and stock ratios as a possible lower limit (type I) for the real opportunity cost of capital in the manufacturing sector. The other two sets (types II and III) are fairly similar to each other and may be regarded as medium-level estimates for the rate of return on capital.

Taking type II estimates in table 8.15 for manufacturing and type III estimates for the service and social overhead sectors, I also estimated the weighted average rate of return on capital in all nonprimary sectors combined. I took the gross sectoral fixed capital stock as weights. Since there are many different sets of estimates for sectoral rates of return, the specific set selected for the computation was based on my subjective judgment of what may be regarded as reasonable estimates. So computed, the rate of return in Korean industries as a whole increased from about 11 percent in 1954–62 to about 15 percent in 1967–75. Considering the estimated rate of return on capital in agriculture including land, it does not seem likely that the rate of return in the primary sector could deviate wildly from these weighted average rates of return in the nonprimary sectors.

Next, I estimated the average real rates of return on fixed capital in manufacturing, using various methods depending upon the treatment of net working capital and capital loss. The results are shown in table 8.16. Using the type II estimate and taking account of capital loss, the estimated real rate of return was 12 percent in 1954–61, about 17 percent during the First Five-Year Plan period, 26 percent during the Second Five-Year Plan period, and about 27 percent during the Third Five-Year Plan period. This striking increase implies that the use of large amounts of domestic and foreign borrowed capital at low interest rates has yielded extremely high rates of return on equity investment in Korean industries. On the basis of the above estimates we can approximate the total amount of interest rate subsidies associated with bank loans and foreign borrowings in Korea by subtracting the real (weighted average) interest rates on these loans from the real (average) rate of return on capital.

To get some idea of the aggregate magnitude of interest subsidies, I estimated the ratio of the total interest subsidy associated with domestic and foreign loans in the manufacturing sector to the total (gross or net) fixed capital stock in the manufacturing sector. The results are shown in table 8.17. The ratio of the subsidy to net stock was about 4 percent on the average during 1957–61 and about 6 percent during 1962–66. Between 1967 and 1971 it reached approximately 14 percent, and since 1972 it has exceeded 25 percent. The most remarkable fact is that, although the absolute amount of interest subsidies associated with foreign loans was negligible before 1966, after that it was equivalent to more than half the total amount of interest subsidies associated with KDB and DMB loans together. Moreover, the ratio of the interest subsidy to

Table 8.16   **Estimated Real Rates of Return on (Opportunity Cost) Capital Use in Manufacturing (Percentage)**

	Excluding Indirect Taxes		Including Indirect Taxes	
	Based on VA/C-Stock (Type I)	Incremental VA/I (Type II)	Based on VA/C-Stock (Type III)	Incremental VA/I (Type IV)
Annual Average	Possible Lower Limit	Possible Medium Range		Possible Upper Limit
Without Taking Account of Net Working Capital				
1954–61	13	17	17	25
1962–66	16	26	22	37
1967–71	20	32	31	47
1972–75	30	42	42	57
Taking Account of Net Working Capital				
1954–61	10	13	13	19
1962–66	12	20	17	29
1967–71	17	27	26	39
1972–75	25	35	35	48
Taking Account of Capital Loss				
1954–61	9	12	12	18
1962–66	9	17	14	26
1967–71	16	26	25	38
1972–75	17	27	27	40

Source: Hong (1977).

Note: Gross value added to gross capital ratios were used assuming nondepreciating capital stock. The type II estimate might be interpreted as representing marginal rate of return on reproducible (but nondepreciating) capital, and the type III estimate the average rate of return in manufacturing.

Table 8.17   Estimated Rate of Interest Subsidy Associated with Domestic and Foreign Loans to the Manufacturing Sector (Millions of 1970 Dollars and Percentage)

Year	Total Fixed Capital Stock		DMB and KDB Loans				Total Foreign Borrowing			
	Gross (C)	Net (K)	Total Loans	Subsidy Rate (%)	S/C (%)	S/K (%)	Total Loans	Subsidy Rate (%)	S/C (%)	S/K (%)
1957	972	647	124	12	2	2	—	—	—	—
1958	1,047	697	193	13	2	4	—	—	—	—
1959	1,110	735	236	13	3	4	3	9	0	0
1960	1,177	772	250	13	3	4	2	−10	0	0
1961	1,243	813	259	13	3	4	2	−80	0	0
1962	1,331	869	307	15	3	5	5	19	0	0
1963	1,447	936	257	27	5	7	27	32	1	1
1964	1,560	987	216	40	6	9	44	−18	−1	−1
1965	1,718	1,072	291	14	2	4	55	−2	0	0
1966	1,985	1,273	365	7	1	2	156	19	2	2
1967	2,251	1,456	501	13	3	4	273	27	3	5
1968	2,608	1,682	819	14	4	7	419	27	4	7
1969	3,013	1,918	1,168	13	5	8	514	23	4	6
1970	3,428	2,138	1,242	19	7	11	659	21	4	6
1971	3,852	2,351	1,437	19	7	12	624	16	3	6
1972	4,269	2,458	1,693	24	10	17	963	21	5	8
1973	5,036	2,809	2,234	21	9	17	977	26	5	9
1974	5,663	2,994	2,843	55	28	53	1,037	59	11	20
1975	6,361	3,190	2,743	40	17	35	1,286	27	5	11

Source: Hong (1977).
Note: S represents the amount of loans multiplied by subsidy rate; that is, the amount of interest subsidy.

(gross) capital stock has been steadily increasing from a moderate 3–4 percent before 1962 to more than 14 percent during the Third Five-Year Plan period (1972–76). The ratio of the interest subsidy to gross fixed capital formation in manufacturing increased from about 40 percent during 1962–66 to about 75 percent during 1967–71 and to more than 100 percent after 1972.[11]

8.5 Employment Implications of Trade and Subsidy Policies

8.5.1 Employment Growth in Korea

As I mentioned in section 8.1, the population fourteen years old and over, which represents Korea's potential labor force, increased by nearly 50 percent from 1963 to 1976 (i.e., from 15.7 million to 22.6 million). During the same period, the total number of employed persons in Korea increased by nearly 64 percent, implying an average annual growth rate of about 4 percent. The total number of employed males increased by about 3.5 percent per annum, while the number of employed females increased by nearly 5 percent per annum on the average. As a result, the labor force participation rate of males stayed at about 74–76 percent throughout the period 1963–76, while that of females steadily increased from about 36 percent in 1963 to about 42 percent in 1976. Although the annual growth rate of total employment was only about 1 percent higher than that of the total potential labor force from 1963 to 1976, there was a rapid transfer of labor from relatively less productive to more productive forms of employment. Moreover, there was a significant rise in the absolute level of productivity in the former.

The number of employed persons in manufacturing increased from 0.6 million in 1963 to 2.7 million in 1976, implying an average annual growth rate of about 12 percent (see table 8.7). Total male employment in manufacturing increased by about 11 percent per annum (from 0.43 million to 1.66 million), while female employment increased by about 14 percent per annum (from 0.18 million to 1.02 million). The number of employed persons in the service and social overhead sectors increased by about 5.5 percent per annum (about 5 percent for males and 6 percent for females). On the other hand, employed persons in the primary sectors increased by only about 1.2 percent per annum (about 0.5 percent per annum for males and 2.0 percent for females).[12]

The most noteworthy trend in employment was therefore an extremely rapid increase in the number of employed persons in manufacturing accompanied by a very slow increase in the primary sectors. Another important trend was the more rapid expansion in female employment than in male employment in every industrial sector in Korea.

According to data from the census of manufactures, the annual real wage rate in manufacturing (in 1970 United States dollars) increased from $373 in 1966 to $569 in 1971 (an average growth rate of 9 percent per annum) and to $683 in 1975 (an average growth rate of 5 percent per annum) (see table 8.18). On the other hand, possibly owing to rapid capital accumulation and technical progress in the agricultural sector, farm income per worker increased from about $224 in 1966 to $352 in 1971 (average growth rate of 10 percent per annum) and to $447 in 1975 (average growth rate of 6 percent per annum). Hence one may attribute the rapid increase in the wage rate in manufacturing to capital accumulation in manufacturing and the associated increase in labor productivity that was sustained by a rising minimum wage floor (such as Lewis proposes) via the rising average product of farm workers. Furthermore, there was a significant decrease, especially after 1972, in the ratio of urban to rural earnings in Korea, as may be seen in table 8.18.

8.5.2 Subsidies and Composition of Output and Trade

During 1957–75, the share of loans allocated to the agricultural and service sectors in total loans (total KDB, DMB, and foreign loans) was much smaller than the share of these sectors in GNP, while the reverse was true of the manufacturing and social overhead sectors. On the other hand, the relative contributions of agriculture and the service sector to GNP declined, while the proportion of GNP arising from manufacturing increased from 9 percent in 1957 to 32 percent in 1975 and that from the social overhead sector rose from 3 percent in 1957 to 9 percent in 1975 (see table 8.19). Hence one can easily detect what seems to be a close association between the pattern of loan allocations and shifts in the industrial structure.

Among the manufacturing industries (as may also be seen in table 8.19), the food products sector received very small loans in relation to its share in total manufacturing output, while the chemical sector (including petroleum refining and fertilizer) received a very large share of loans over the period 1957–75. The share of the food products sector in total manufacturing output declined from about 40 percent in 1957 to about 20 percent in 1975, while that of chemicals expanded from about 4 percent in 1957 to about 14 percent in 1975.

On the whole, one may conclude that there was a positive association between the pattern of loan allocations and the shifts in the industrial structure, with the exceptions of the mining sector and, to a lesser extent, the paper, nonmetallic mineral, basic metals, and metal products manufacturing sectors. These exceptional cases are explained in terms of Korea's limited mineral endowments and the extremely capital-intensive production techniques of these sectors.

For exports there is a drastic fall in the share of agricultural and mining products and a rapid increase in the share of manufactures in

Table 8.18   Differences in Urban-Rural Earnings (1970 Dollars and Percentage)

Year	Farm Income per Worker A (dA/A)	Wage Rate for Farm Employee B (dB/B)	Wage Rate in Manufacturing		Ratio of Urban to Rural Earnings	
			Census Data C (dC/C)	Office of Labor Data D (dD/D)	C/A	C/B
1962	225 (—)	220 (—)				
1963	256 (14%)	210 (−4%)		334 (—)		
1964	255 (0%)	250 (19%)		308 (−8%)		
1965	218 (−15%)	190 (−24%)		338 (10%)		
1966	224 (3%)	170 (−10%)	373 (—)	348 (3%)	1.7	2.2
1962–66 average	(1%)	(−5%)		(2%)		
1967	225 (0%)	200 (18%)	405 (9%)	375 (7%)	1.8	1.9
1968	251 (12%)	230 (15%)	449 (11%)	424 (13%)	1.8	1.9
1969	273 (9%)	260 (13%)	495 (10%)	502 (19%)	1.8	1.9
1970	283 (4%)	270 (4%)	532 (7%)	563 (12%)	1.9	2.1
1971	352 (24%)	300 (11%)	569 (7%)	601 (7%)	1.6	2.0
1967–71 average	(10%)	(12%)	(9%)	(12%)		
1972	363 (3%)	300 (0%)	563 (−1%)	608 (1%)	1.6	2.0
1973	378 (4%)	350 (17%)	635 (13%)	617 (1%)	1.7	1.8
1974	429 (13%)	380 (9%)	632 (0%)	659 (7%)	1.5	1.7
1975	447 (4%)	412 (9%)	683 (8%)	674 (2%)	1.5	1.6
1976	513 (15%)	451 (10%)		785 (16%)		
1972–76 average	(8%)	(9%)	(5%)	(5%)		

Source: Ministry of Agriculture and Fisheries, *Report on the Results of Farm Household Economy Survey*; Economic Planning Board, *Report on Mining and Manufacturing Census (or Survey)*; Bank of Korea, *Economic Statistics Yearbook.*
Note: GNP deflator for all industries and the exchange rate of 310.6 won per dollar were applied to get 1970 dollar values.

Table 8.19 Sectoral Share in Value Added, Loans, and Exports

Sector	Share in Total Value Added 1957 (1)	Share in Total Value Added 1975 (2)	Share in Total Loans 1957–75 (3)	Loan Share vs. Value-Added Share 1957–75 (4) (3)/(1)	Share in Total Exports 1960 (5)	Share in Total Exports 1970 (6)	Share in Total Exports 1975 (7)
GNP[a]	3,266[d]	13,295[d]					
Total loans[b]			2,665[d]				
Total exports[c]					91.1[d]	1,208.7[d]	3,932.3[d]
Agriculture	42.4%	18.6%	7.5%	0.18%	12.1%	2.4%	1.8%
Fisheries	1.9	3.0	2.6	1.37	4.1	4.2	4.2
Mining	1.0	1.0	2.0	2.00	10.9	3.2	0.9
Social overhead sector	2.9	9.0	17.7	6.10	24.1	12.0	9.1
Service sector	42.4	36.3	14.9	0.35	22.5	9.9	9.5
Manufacturing	9.3	32.1	47.7	5.13	23.8	61.9	74.5
Total	100.0%	100.0%	100.0%		100.0%	100.0%	100.0%
Food products	39.6%	20.8%	8.7%	0.22%	24.2%	7.3%	7.4%
Textiles	25.1	13.4	⎫ 23.5	⎫ 0.70	23.7	26.4	12.5
Wearing apparel	7.1	15.3	⎬	⎬	1.6	16.7	22.7
Leather	1.2	3.3	⎭	⎭	1.1	0.4	3.8
Wood products	3.3	1.6	4.6	1.39	3.8	12.0	5.0
Paper and products	0.7	1.8	3.9	5.57	1.1	0.5	0.6
Rubber products	1.5	1.3	⎫ 24.4		8.1	2.7	4.7
Fertilizer	—	1.7	⎬	4.78		0.8	0.0
Other chemicals	2.7	6.2	⎬		5.4	1.2	1.9
Petroleum and coal	0.9	5.7	⎭				2.7

Table 8.19—*continued*

Sector	Share in Total Value Added 1957 (1)	Share in Total Value Added 1975 (2)	Share in Total Loans 1957-75 (3)	Loan Share vs. Value-Added Share 1957-75 (4) (3)/(1)	Share in Total Exports 1960 (5)	Share in Total Exports 1970 (6)	Share in Total Exports 1975 (7)
Nonmetallic minerals	2.5	3.7	7.4	2.96	3.2	1.3	2.2
Basic metals	1.0	2.7	8.3	8.30	4.3	2.4	5.4
Metal products	1.3	1.2			0.5	1.8	2.5
Machinery	2.0	1.1	13.7	1.90	2.7[d]	0.4	0.9
Electrical machinery	1.0	8.9			5.9[d]	6.2	12.3
Transportation equipment	2.9	5.9			5.4[d]	0.7	4.0
Miscellaneous manufacturing	7.3	5.4	5.6	0.77	10.2	16.3	11.3
Total	100.0%	100.0%	100.0%		100.0%	100.0%	100.0%

Source: Bank of Korea, *National Income in Korea*; Bank of Korea, *Input-Output Tables of Korea*; Hong (1977).

[a]Includes foreign sector.

[b]Annual average of total KDB, DMB, and foreign loans.

[c]Includes unclassifiable exports.

[d]Millions of dollars.

[e]Mostly reexports.

total exports during 1957–75. Among manufactured exports, the share of food products declined most rapidly, while that of electrical machinery (mostly electronic products) and wearing apparel expanded most rapidly. There was a significant expansion in exports of metal products, but there was no matching expansion of their share in total manufacturing output, which may reflect the fact that their exports were heavily dependent on imported intermediate input materials such as hot coils for steel sheets and pipes.

The shares of textiles and miscellaneous manufactures in total manufactured exports increased significantly in the sixties. However, loans to these industries were not commensurate with their shares in total output. Their share in total exports started to decline in the seventies. The expansion of exports of textiles, wearing apparel, and miscellaneous manufactures can be attributed more to the basic comparative advantage of Korea (i.e., low wages) than to subsidized interest rates associated with bank loans.

The share of basic metals, metal products, and electrical machinery sectors in total loans was relatively large, and their exports expanded rapidly in the early seventies. Since Korea mostly took care of the very labor-intensive "final-touch" (or assembling) processes, their export expansion may be attributed to both the low wage level and the availability of subsidized loans.

Although, as I noted above, the rapid expansion of the chemical sector's output in the sixties may be attributed to the allocation of a large amount of subsidized loans, there was no matching expansion of the sector's share in total exports. There was also a relatively large loan allocation to the nonmetallic mineral products sector, and its share in exports even declined. Hence the allocation of subsidized long-term loans to these extremely capital-intensive and inefficient sectors has contributed mostly to import substitution rather than to export expansion, as indicated by the rising proportion of value added in these industries as shown in table 8.19.

Other industries which received a large proportion of loans are steel sheets and plates, chemical fibers, and ships. They are moderately capital-intensive products. In these industries there was not only a substantial output expansion, but also significant increases in their export/output ratios. This may be attributed to the pattern of loan allocations in Korea during 1957–75. Most of these sectors could not be regarded as major export sectors of Korea in the early seventies, and yet the absolute amount of exports of these products has significantly increased over the period, which surely accelerated the rising trend in capital intensity of Korea's export commodity bundle.

8.5.3   Interest Rate Subsidies and Allocation of Capital

The data summarized in table 8.20 provide a basis for examining the association between changes in the wage/rental ratio and changes in the capital/labor ratio in manufacturing as well as in the entire industrial sector. Associative relationships of this type cannot, of course, be used as proof of causality, but the empirical relationships between changes in factor supplies, factor prices, and employment, in the aggregate, over time, are highly suggestive.

During 1967–73 the real wage rate increased by about 13 percent per annum on the average, while the weighted average interest rates on total KDB, DMB, curb, and foreign loans for all industries decreased by about 12 percent per annum.[13] This implies an average annual increase in the wage/rental ratio for all industries of approximately 25 percent.[14]

On the other hand, fixed capital stock for all industries increased by about 13 percent annually during 1967–73 on the average, while the total number of employed persons increased by about 4 percent annually. This implies an average annual increase in the capital/labor ratio for all industries of about 9 or 10 percent and an "elasticity of factor substitution" of about 0.4.[15]

According to the manufacturing census data, the average annual growth rate of fixed capital stock in manufacturing was about 19 percent between 1967 and 1973. Since the total number of workers in manufacturing increased by about 9 percent per annum, the capital/labor ratio increased by about 10 percent per annum, implying an elasticity of substitution of approximately 0.4.[16]

The numerical results outlined above clearly demonstrate that the wage/rental ratio rose during the period of export-oriented growth in Korea. A basic question, however, is whether the wage/rental ratio rose in response to increasing demand for labor or whether, instead, the rise in the wage/rental ratio precluded additional employment and prevented its growth.[17] That the former was more likely can be seen from the following demonstration. Suppose that the interest rate had not fallen after 1967 and instead had remained at the 12.5 percent level for all industries during the period. Assuming that both the fixed capital stock for all industries and the wage rate increased by about 13 percent annually during this period (as they actually did) the elasticity of substitution of 0.4 implies that employment would have had to increase by nearly 9 percent per annum instead of the actual 4 percent per annum. This implies that total employment in Korea would have increased by nearly 70 percent rather than 30 percent over this period, implying at least an additional 3.0 million extra persons employed. With this line of reasoning, one can go on to argue that, if the Korean government had

Table 8.20 Rate of Change in Wage and Rental, 1967–73

Real Annual Wage Rate in Manufacturing

	Office of Labor Data		M and M Census Data		Average Real Interest Rate on Loans		Wholesale Price Index	
	GNP Deflator (1970 $)	Manu-facturing Deflator (1970 $)	GNP Deflator (1970 $)	Manu-facturing Deflator (1970 $)	All Industry (%)	Manu-facturing (%)	All Commodities (1975 = 100)	Capital Goods (1975 = 100)
1967	$375	$329	$405	$335	12.5%	16.2%	33.4	44.6
1973	$617	$668	$635	$687	5.5%	8.4%	55.6	70.2
Average annual percentage change in 1967–73	9%	13%	8%	12%	−12%	−10%	9%	8%

Fixed Capital Stock (Million 1970 Dollars)

	(Han-BOK Data)				M and M Census Data		Number of Workers (Thousand Persons)	
	All Industries		Manufacturing		Manufacturing		All Industries	Manu-facturing
	Gross	Net	Gross	Net	Gross	Net		
1967	10,217	6,637	2,251	1,456	1,634	1,062	8,717	1,021 (649)*
1973	21,315	14,253	5,036	2,809	4,579	3,167	11,139	1,774 (1,153)*
Average annual percentage change in 1969–75	13% (12%)	14% (12%)	15% (14%)	12% (9%)	19% (19%)	20% (20%)	4% (4%)	10% (10%) 10% (10%)

Source: Hong (1977).

Note: Figures with asterisks were obtained from the mining and manufacturing census data, which cover establishments with more than tried to raise the weighted average interest rates on total loans to the manufacturing sector from 16.2 percent in 1967 to the estimated real rate of return on capital of about 26 percent by 1973, the real interest rate could have increased by about 8 percent instead of falling by 10 percent during 1967–73. This would imply only an approximate 4 percent increase in the wage/rental ratio per annum instead of 22 percent (applying census data). The annual rate of employment growth would then have been roughly 7 percent greater than the actual rate in manufacturing, using the 0.4 elasticity, implying about 50 percent more employment in manufacturing during 1967–73.

That this could not have happened is evident from the facts on labor force participation rates and unemployment in Korea. Even the differential in urban/rural earnings has been declining since 1970. Estimated unemployment rates in the early 1970s were very low—generally less than 5 percent of the labor force. Thus, employment has been relatively full in Korea since the early 1970s, and government policies that have affected the interest rate on loans cannot have affected the level of employment as significantly as demonstrated in the above numerical exercises.

What, then, have been the principal effects of interest rate subsidies in Korea? First, Korea could have achieved "full employment" instead of "relatively full employment" by the early seventies if there were no interest subsidies. The second point is related to the optimum utilization of capital. My results show that Korea has oversubsidized the use of capital since the late 1960s (as may be seen from tables 8.15, 8.16, and 8.20), when the real rates of return on capital began to exceed the real interest rates on loans. It seems evident that, during the early period of the export promotion drive, new investments were primarily in the labor-intensive export industries and the efficiency of allocation of resources was rapidly increasing. However, with the interest rate subsidies, some capital-intensive investments were undertaken that probably were not yet economical, given Korea's factor endowment at that time. Thus, although Korea's resource allocation in the mid-1970s was undoubtedly more economical than it had been before the export drive started, the subsidies to capital encouraged the development of some industries and the use of some processes that were too capital-intensive. Insofar as that was the case, the demand for labor might have shifted upward even more, with a higher real wage, had the subsidies to capital been eliminated. In terms of employment, however, the narrowing wage differentials between industry and agriculture, combined with the rapid decline in the unemployment rate, both suggest that Korea was at, and remained at, relatively full employment during the early 1970s.

8.5.4   Conclusion

Section 8.3.2 examined changes in the factor intensities of Korea's exports. Their direct plus indirect capital intensity was seen in table 8.13 to have increased during 1966–68 by 2.3 percent owing to shifts in export composition but also by as much as 11 percent owing to sectoral factor substitutions. Moving on to 1970–73, there is a further increase of about 5 percent in the capital intensity of exports owing to shifts in export composition, but a much greater change of about 35 percent owing to factor substitution in production processes. Some of the sectoral capital/labor substitution, as well as shifts in export composition, may be attributed to the increase in per capita capital stock in Korea and the associated rise in the wage/rental ratio. However, a substantial portion of the factor substitution should be attributed to the subsidy on capital use.

A notable fact seems to be that in the 1960s the capital intensity of Korea's exports was much lower than that of the manufacturing sector as a whole, but the difference between the two became smaller thereafter, and by 1975 the former exceeded the latter. This might imply that factor market distortions caused by the export promotion policy were significantly stronger than those caused by the general industrialization policy characterized by extensive subsidized capital financing. We have already seen that employment implications of export promotion and import substitution became approximately equal since the late sixties.

My conclusions on the employment implications of the export-led growth in Korea are as follows. First, there has been a continuous shift in employment from the farm sector to the manufacturing sector, as a direct result of the rapid export-led growth of manufacturing production. In the farm sector this has resulted in a rising real wage rate since about 1967 and a lessening of the difference between urban and rural earnings since about 1970. Second, within the manufacturing sector, capital intensity has been increasing since the early 1960s, with the rate of increase at first higher in import-competing industries than in export industries until the early 1970s, when capital intensity began to rise faster in exports. This has been attributed to the higher rate of capital subsidization in export industries, resulting in the differential increase in the wage/rental ratios. Thus, with this extensive capital subsidization, manufactured exports have not been creating as much employment as they otherwise would have.

A similar conclusion is drawn with respect to the manufacturing sector as a whole vis-à-vis other sectors. But, overall, my results show that Korea began to have relatively full employment about 1970, implying that the growth in total employment could not have been substantially higher even had the wage/rental ratios not increased as much as they did. Therefore the effect of export promotion on employment in Korea was a rapid growth in total employment in the 1960s, a relatively full employment since about 1970, a change in the sectoral distribution of employment, and higher real wages than would otherwise have been possible.

It should also be noted that deducing the employment effects of trade and subsidy policies in terms of employment growth does not provide an adequate basis for judging the overall efficiency of such policies. For instance, Korea's exports might have been less capital-intensive if there had been no subsidy on capital use, but one might question whether Korea could have expanded its exports (and GNP) so rapidly if it had insisted upon using less capital-intensive production techniques. Slower growth in export earnings might also have resulted in slower growth of the Korean economy as a whole, thus reducing overall employment growth rates.

Appendix

Table 8.A.1   Persons Employed by Industry (Thousands)

Year	Primary Sector	Manu-facturing	Social Overhead Sector and Services	Total Employed Persons	Labor Force Participation Rate		Unemploy-ment Rate
					Male	Female	
1963	4,894 (—)	610 (—)	2,158 (—)	7,662 (—)	76.4%	36.2%	8.2%
1964	4,878 (0%)	637 (4%)	2,284 (6%)	7,799 (2%)	75.6%	35.4%	7.7%
1965	4,887 (0%)	772 (21%)	2,547 (12%)	8,206 (5%)	76.6%	36.5%	7.4%
1966	4,956 (1%)	833 (8%)	2,634 (3%)	8,423 (3%)	76.5%	36.2%	7.1%
1967	4,905 (−1%)	1,021 (23%)	2,791 (6%)	8,717 (3%)	76.0%	36.8%	6.2%
1968	4,913 (0%)	1,170 (15%)	3,072 (10%)	9,155 (5%)	76.1%	38.2%	5.1%
1969	4,939 (1%)	1,232 (5%)	3,243 (6%)	9,414 (3%)	76.6%	37.5%	4.8%
1970	5,027 (2%)	1,284 (4%)	3,434 (6%)	9,745 (4%)	75.1%	38.5%	4.5%
1971	4,968 (−1%)	1,336 (4%)	3,762 (10%)	10,066 (3%)	74.2%	38.5%	4.5%
1972	5,400 (9%)	1,445 (8%)	3,714 (−1%)	10,559 (5%)	74.7%	38.9%	4.5%
1973	5,616 (4%)	1,774 (23%)	3,749 (1%)	11,139 (5%)	73.9%	40.8%	4.0%
1974	5,634 (0%)	2,012 (13%)	3,940 (5%)	11,586 (4%)	74.8%	40.6%	4.1%
1975	5,485 (−3%)	2,205 (10%)	4,140 (5%)	11,830 (2%)	74.5%	39.6%	4.1%
1976	5,666 (3%)	2,678 (21%)	4,212 (2%)	12,556 (6%)	74.6%	42.3%	3.9%
1977	5,508 (−3%)	2,798 (4%)	4,623 (10%)	12,929 (3%)	75.9%	40.7%	3.8%

Source: Economic Planning Board, *Annual Report on the Economically Active Population Survey.*

Note: Figures in parentheses show percentage increase over preceding year.

Notes

1. This paper summarizes my study *Trade, Distortion and Employment Growth in Korea*, undertaken while I was at the Korea Development Institute (Hong 1977). The study was partly financed by the Council for Asian Manpower Studies.

2. See Hong (1977) for a detailed list of these incentives. It is remarkable that during the Second Five-Year Plan, a time of unprecedented expansion of exports of labor-intensive light manufactures, the government established a legal foundation to promote the so-called heavy and chemical industries. The government introduced several laws that specified various tax-cum-financial supports for these industries. However, these promotion schemes were not completely implemented until the beginning of the Third Five-Year Plan period (1972–76).

3. The trade program for imports financed with government-held foreign exchange (KFX) has been prepared by the MCI. Imports financed by foreign grants and loans have been programmed separately by the Economic Planning Board (EPB) in consultation with the MCI. The foreign exchange budget has been based on the principles of increasing capacity to repay foreign debts, expanding export industries, and restricting imports of nonessential goods without obstructing the efficient supply of raw materials and goods required for stable economic growth.

4. See section 8.5 for further discussion of the behavior of the wage/rental ratio.

5. This measurement of factor requirements in relation to value of output differs from the methodology followed in most other country studies in this volume, where requirements are expressed per unit of value added.

6. Requirements of both labor and capital in exports were smaller than those in import-competing goods because estimates of the former include, as indirect inputs, only domestically produced intermediates, whereas estimates of the latter also include inputs of (competing) imported goods (see notes to table 8.10 and table 8.12).

7. According to the Han-BOK capital stock data, net capital stock per worker in manufacturing increased only about 15 percent during 1966–71, then fell by 5 percent during 1972–76, and gross capital stock per worker increased about 21 percent over the period 1966–71 but again fell by 25 percent during 1972–76. According to the manufacturing census data, however, both the gross and the net capital stock per worker increased by about 35 percent during 1966–71 and further increased by 30 to 40 percent during 1972–76. The enormous differences between these two sets of data seem to be due to serious problems associated with price conversions and allowance for the consumption of capital. It seems that the Han-BOK data substantially underestimate the magnitude of real capital formation in Korean manufacturing sector throughout the period.

8. The government is the majority stockholder in these banks.

9. The government began to provide foreign currency loans through foreign exchange banks in 1967 in order to finance the importation of capital equipment and raw material to be used in export industries recommended by the MCI. These loans were also provided for import-substituting industries and for government-planned investment projects on the basis of the recommendation of the competent minister. Foreign currency loans were provided mostly with government-held foreign exchange, but the branches of foreign banks stationed in Korea have also provided loans since 1969.

10. In compliance with the August 3 (1972) Presidential Emergency Decree, 40,677 enterprises reported their debts in the form of curb loans, which totaled 345.6 billion won.

11. I also estimated the ratio of the total interest subsidy associated with domestic and foreign loans to total (gross or net) fixed capital stock in all industries in Korea (excluding ownership of dwellings). The ratio to gross or net capital stock increased from about 1–2 percent during 1957–66 to more than 4–5 percent during the Third Five-Year Plan period. The ratio of the interest subsidy to gross fixed capital formation increased from about 20 percent during 1962–71 to more than 35 percent after 1972.

12. For further details, see appendix table 8.A.1.

13. Since our concern is with the costs confronting manufacturers rather than with the real purchasing power of wage earners, I applied the implicit price deflator for manufacturing output to estimate wages in 1970 prices.

14. The wholesale price index for all commodities rose at an average annual rate of about 9 percent during 1967–73, and that of capital goods rose at about 8 percent, implying a decrease in the relative price of capital goods of approximately 1 percent per annum. Since this magnitude was rather small, I decided to ignore it in order to simplify the exercise. The relative price of capital goods fell substantially only from 1974 to 1976.

15. The so-called elasticity of substitution I computed represents a historical association under the given (but unidentified) pace of technological change. It may be regarded as a "stylized fact" that can be observed but that has yet to be explained by an appropriate analysis.

16. To allow for time lags in factor substitution, I also computed the average annual rate of change in fixed capital stock and employment for the period 1969–75. The results were very close to those for the period 1967–73.

17. Of course, the wage/rental ratio and employment are simultaneously determined. In econometric terms, the problem posed here is one of "identification"— whether the demand for labor (and capital) shifted in such a way as to alter the wage/rental ratio or whether the wage/rental ratio was altered, thereby inducing movements along the demand curve for factors of production. In reality, there must have been some aspects of both, and the argument here goes simply to the relative importance of each.

References

Bank of Korea. Various years. *Economic statistics yearbook*. Seoul.

———. Various years. *Input-output table of Korea*. Seoul.

———. Various years. *Monthly economic statistics*. Seoul.

———. Various years. *National income in Korea*. Seoul.

Bureau of Taxation. Various years. *Major taxation statistics*. Seoul.

Cole, D. C., and Lyman, P. N. 1971. *Korean development*. Cambridge: Harvard University Press.

Economic Planning Board. Various years. *Annual report on the economically active population*. Seoul.

———. Various years. *Report on mining and manufacturing census (or survey)*. Seoul.

———. Various years. *Population and housing census of Korea*. Seoul.

————. 1972. *Report on national wealth survey* (as of 31 December 1968). Seoul.

Frank, C. R., Jr.; Kim, K. S.; and Westphal, L. E. 1975. *Foreign trade regimes and economic development: South Korea.* New York: NBER.

Han, K. C. 1970. *Estimates of Korean capital and inventory coefficients in 1968.* Seoul: Yonsei University.

Hong, Wontack. 1976. Distortions and static negative marginal gains from trade. *Journal of International Economics* 6 (August): 299–308.

————. 1977. Trade, distortion and employment growth in Korea. Working Paper 7711. Duplicated. Seoul: Korea Development Institute.

Ministry of Agriculture and Fisheries. Various years. *Report on the results of farm household economy survey.* Seoul.

Westphal, L. E., and Kim, K. S. 1977. *Industrial policy and development in Korea.* World Bank Staff Working Paper no. 263.

9 Trade Strategy for Employment Growth in Thailand

Narongchai Akrasanee

Introduction

In the past two decades, Thailand has had one of the more rapidly growing economies in Southeast Asia.[1] Since 1960, gross domestic product (GDP) has increased at an annual rate of about 7 percent. Manufacturing activity has become more important in this period; its share of GDP rose from 13 to 18 percent while manufacturing employment increased from 3.4 to 8.3 percent of total employment between 1960 and 1976. Nonetheless, the economy remains principally dependent upon the primary sector: agriculture absorbs 79 percent of the labor force and generates about one-third of GDP.

The rapid growth of the manufacturing sector can be attributed in part to Thailand's promotion of import substitution activities. However, its policies have not been overly restrictive. Tariff protection is relatively moderate, quantitative restrictions are not extensively used, and the currency has been only slightly overvalued. In recent years, policies have shifted to place more emphasis upon promoting exports.

This study has the important objective of analyzing the relationship between trade policies and employment growth in Thailand. Employment creation is a pressing problem. The country has relatively high growth rates of total population (3 percent annually) and urban population (5 percent); urban unemployment is close to 10 percent, according to official figures. Thus, in spite of impressive gains in manufactur-

Narongchai Akrasanee was associated with the Faculty of Economics, Thammasat University, Bangkok. He is now with the Asian and Pacific Development Institute, Bangkok.

Report of Council for Asian Manpower Studies, Project no. 76-3-06. I would like to thank Anne O. Krueger and Hal B. Lary for their advice and most valuable comments on the earlier drafts of this paper.

393

ing output and employment, it is important to determine if Thailand's import substitution policies have been able to generate as much employment as alternative (export promotion) policies might have done. This analysis centers upon 1973, primarily because of data availability. The year 1973 falls into the period when policies were shifting to place more emphasis upon exports. However, not all aspects of the export promotion scheme had then occurred (e.g., there was a change in tariff rates in 1974). The data should therefore be broadly representative of the latter phase of the import substitution period.

9.1 Major Characteristics of Thailand's Economy

9.1.1 Growth and Structure

Thailand is a relatively prosperous developing country. In 1976 its per capita GNP was baht 7,541, or about U.S. $370 at that year's exchange rate (baht 20.4 per U.S. $1). Real GDP growth from 1972 to 1976 averaged 6.6 percent annually, down slightly from the 7.1 percent rate in the period 1960 to 1972 (see table 9.1). This rapid growth was due mainly to a relatively high rate of fixed capital formation, which increased as a percentage of GDP from 14.9 in 1960 to 21.0 in 1972 and 23.5 in 1976.

Primary-sector activities (agriculture, mining, and quarrying) dominate Thailand's economy, although their importance has fallen over time. In 1976 they accounted for 31 percent of GDP, compared with 40 percent in 1960. In the first half of the 1970s, primary sector exports, some raw and some in semiprocessed form (SITC sections 0–4),[2] generated about 80 percent of total exports. The most important were rice, maize, rubber, tin, tapioca products, and sugar.

The importance of manufacturing activities has increased rapidly since 1960. As I mentioned above, its shares in GDP and total employment rose from 13 and 3.4 percent to 18 and 8.3 percent, respectively, from 1960 to 1976. The bulk of manufacturing output is produced by import substitution industries. However, the recent emphasis upon manufactured exports (see discussion, section 9.1.2) has had some effect. In 1976 they were either 17 or 37 percent of total exports (depending upon whether an SITC or an ISIC classification is used to categorize activities).[3]

9.1.2 International Trade

The Pattern and Composition of Trade

Thailand is heavily dependent upon trade. Together exports and imports averaged about 36 percent of GDP in 1972–76. Its trading part-

Table 9.1   Some Salient Features of the Thai Economy

	1960		1972		1976
Population (million)	27		39		43
Annual growth rate (percentage)		3.0		2.7	
GNP per capita (baht, current prices)	2,056		4,257		7,541
GNP per capita (baht, 1962 prices)	2,198		3,495		4,051
GDP (million baht, current prices)	55,816		164,626		325,112
GDP (million baht, 1962 prices)	59,400		135,169		174,866
Annual growth rate (percentage)		7.1		6.6	
Gross fixed capital formation as percentage of GDP	14.9		21.0		23.5
Primary value added as percentage of GDP	40.2		32.1		31.1
Manufacturing value added as percentage of GDP (ISIC 3)	13.1		17.0		18.4
Utilities, construction, services, etc., as percentage of GDP	46.7		50.9		50.5
Imports as percentage of GDP	17.2		18.8		22.1
Manufacturing imports (SITC 5–8) as percentage of total imports	74.6		74.2		64.2
Exports as percentage of GDP	15.4		13.7		18.4
Manufacturing exports (SITC 5–8 less tin[a]) as percentage of total exports	1.4		10.1		16.6
Manufacturing exports (ISIC 3) as percentage[a] of total exports	n.a.		28.0		36.5
Manufacturing employment as percentage of total employment	3.4		8.8		8.3
Share of manufacturing output in the Central region[b]	73.2		73.9		82.7

Sources: National Economic and Social Development Board (NESDB) and the Bank of Thailand (1976).

[a]See notes 2 and 3 for the differences in manufacturing definitions in ISIC and ISTC codes.

[b]There are four regions in the country: Central, North, South, and Northeast. The Bangkok metropolis is in the Central region.

ners, especially as a source for imports, are developed countries. About 60 to 70 percent of its imports and 50 percent of its exports originated in or were destined for developed nations in the 1970s. Member countries of the Association of Southeast Asian Nations (ASEAN) took about 20 percent of Thai exports but accounted for a very small share of Thai imports.

As I mentioned above, most exports are NRB goods or processed NRB goods. Only 17 percent of exports in 1976 are classified as manufactured under the SITC nomenclature (SITC 5–8). However, this represents a dramatic increase over the 1.4 percent value in 1960. Most manufactured exports go to developed countries. Data on some major HOS exportables are given in table 9.2.

On the other hand, imports consist primarily of manufactured goods, although their share in total imports fell from 74 to 64 percent from 1972 to 1976 owing to the higher prices of crude oil. The composition of imports has changed markedly since 1960, when consumer goods constituted 32 percent of imports and when intermediate products (including raw materials) and capital goods accounted for 18 percent and 27 percent, respectively.[4] The proportion of consumer goods imports has declined continuously since then. It was 13 percent in 1977, with most of the reduction taking place in nondurable consumer goods. In the meantime, the shares of intermediate products and capital goods imports have increased, reaching 25 percent and 35 percent, respectively, in 1976. These changes reflect the import substitution bias of the trade regime. The rapid growth in the domestic production of consumer goods has entailed increased imports of intermediate products and capital goods. Data on imports of the main import-competing industries are given in table 9.3.

The Trade Regime

Since World War II, Thailand's trade policies have evolved from being very restrictive to being fairly liberal.[5] In the 1960s they emphasized import substitution industries; only recently have exports been promoted in a systematic fashion. In general, though, Thailand has not had a clear-cut trade policy. Responsibility for trade matters extends over a wide range of ministries and therefore there has been no specific objective except to earn income through exports, to meet development

Table 9.2   Characteristics of Major Exportable Industries

| | Exports, 1973 (Thousands of Baht) | | | Factor Intensities |
| | | | | Workers per |
Product	Developed Countries	Developing Countries	Total	Million Baht of DVA
Sugar	250.7	1,214.0	1,464.7	18.1
Shaved wood	383.8	76.3	460.1	25.5
Leather	51.0	53.1	104.1	80.2
Wood manufactures	246.5	9.8	256.3	23.4
Textiles	846.7	399.0	1,245.7	29.4
Clothing	683.0	13.4	696.4	72.3

Sources: For exports, U.N. Statistics of Foreign Trade, Thailand, 1973; for factor intensities, table 9.12.

Table 9.3   **Characteristics of Thailand's Main Import-Competing Industries**

Product	Imports (Thousands of Baht)			Factor Intensities
	Developed Countries	Developing Countries	Total	Workers per Million Baht of DVA
Dairy products	517.0	0.1	517.1	14.8
Chemical materials	2,014.9	237.2	2,252.1	25.2
Pharmaceuticals	833.4	9.9	943.3	24.1
Chemical products	1,556.9	129.5	1,686.4	19.5
Rubber tires and tubes	54.9	2.7	57.6	13.8
Paper and paperboard	544.7	97.3	642.0	20.1
Metal manufactures	942.4	130.0	1,072.4	42.0
Radio, television, and household appliances	632.3	55.4	687.7	37.4
Passenger cars	1,041.8	1.9	1,043.7	9.5
Buses and trucks	99.0	0.1	99.1	11.5
Motorcycles and nonmotorized road vehicles	336.0	52.5	388.5	22.7

Sources: For imports, U.N. Statistics of Foreign Trade, Thailand, 1973; for factor intensities, table 9.12.

requirements through imports, and to generate tax revenue (import duties form about 25 percent of government revenue).

Subject to these provisos concerning the lack of a clear policy focus, we can identify four phases of varying degrees of trade restrictiveness since World War II. The first period (1944–55) was the only one with very restrictive trade and exchange controls, particularly in rice trade (Corden 1967). Licenses were required for exports and imports, and all export proceeds had to be sold to—and foreign exchange to pay for imports bought from—the Bank of Thailand at the official rate. Foreign exchange controls were replaced by a multiple exchange rate system in 1947 (Yang 1957; Marzouk 1972), and trade controls were gradually relaxed through the period. In 1955, after an improvement in the balance of trade, the multiple exchange rate system was abolished and trade was liberalized.

The end of trade control and the multiple exchange rate system marked the beginning of a liberal phase in trade policy (1955–61). The only significant measure retained from the previous period was the taxation of rice exports. The government did not interfere in trade, though it was involved in the establishment of public industrial enterprises.

When Field Marshall Sarit came to power in 1957, the policy of direct government participation in industrial production was also dropped. No more industrial state enterprises were created, and some of the existing ones were leased to the private sector. The government, with assistance from the World Bank, designed a new strategy for economic development, which later became the first National Economic and Social Development Plan.

The First Six-Year Plan, inaugurated in 1961 and implemented by the newly established National Economic Development Board, marked the beginning of the import substitution phase (1961–71). This plan and the ensuing one covering 1967–71 essentially dealt with sector programming, the organization of government revenue, the planning of government expenditures on infrastructure, and project evaluation over a longer period of time (National Economic and Social Development Board 1963, 1968).[6]

The plans imposed no general policy restrictions or guidelines on foreign trade, implying that imports were allowed and exports were not actively encouraged. However, they directly affected trade through their encouragement of industrial development, which was to be left to the private sector. This encouragement took the form of protecting domestic production that competed with imports and was reflected in the system of taxation of foreign trade and tax exemptions for domestic production, and in the promotion of industrial investment under various investment promotion acts.[7] While the structure of taxes provided a certain degree of protection, most incentives to domestic production were found in various provisions (tax exemption, etc.) in these promotion acts. Toward the end of the period these investment incentives were reduced, but tariff protection was increased.[8] The government also used a number of other measures to help import substitution industries. These included industrial controls (which regulated entry and expansion), import and export controls, and credit assistance. Throughout the period, exports were discouraged or neglected. Some primary exports were taxed, and there was no effective promotion scheme for manufactured exports.

After 1971 the trade regime began to promote exports, especially manufactured goods, while simultaneously continuing to encourage import substitutes. This policy increased tariff protection through a revision of the tariff schedule in 1970, which was actually intended to correct the deficit in the balance of payments. Then in 1972 the Investment Promotion Act was revised to include incentives for manufactured exports. In addition, the Export Promotion Act (1972) provided a number of other measures to encourage exports.[9] In the meantime there was more frequent resort to direct controls on trade, industry, and prices. The outcome of all these changes was a reduction in the bias against exports. In addition to the promotion of manufactured exports, the new Investment Promotion Act was aimed at stimulating employment. That is, priority in promotion was to be given to firms that would create a large amount of employment.

In summary, there were three areas of policy that affected domestic sales and exports sales during the 1972–76 period: taxation and subsidization, promotion of industry and exports, and restrictions and controls on trade and industry. All three are discussed in greater detail in section 9.2.

Balance of Payments

Since World War II, Thailand has almost continuously experienced relatively large current account deficits, offset to a major degree by large capital inflows, mainly direct investment inflows (see table 9.4). Changes in current account balances have often caused adjustments in trade policies. For example, as I mentioned above, the loosening of trade controls in 1955 was a direct result of an improvement in the current account. Similarly, the shift to the simultaneous encouragement of exports and import substitutes after 1971 was due, in part, to worsening merchandise balance (from 1965 to 1970, the merchandise balance fell from −U.S. $117 million to −U.S. $584 million).

Exchange Rate Policies

Thailand has adjusted its exchange rate only infrequently, probably becaues inflation has not been a major problem and because the general consensus in Thailand is that currency overvaluation is not important. To correct balance of payment problems, policymakers have instead adjusted tariffs or imposed controls. After the elimination of multiple exchange rates in 1955, Thailand maintained a rate in the neighborhood of baht 20.5–baht 20.8 per United States dollar until 1974, when it was lowered slightly to baht 20.25–baht 20.45 per dollar.[10] During this period, inflation averaged about 2–3 percent per year except for 1972–74, when it rose to double-digit figures. Since 1974, prices have risen by about 5–6 percent annually.

Table 9.4   Thailand's Balance of Payments, Selected Periods 1960–74
(Millions of U.S. Dollars)

	Averages 1960–64	Averages 1965–69	Averages 1970–74
Goods and services balance	−52.4	−126.6	−208.2
Current account balance	−13.3	− 72.0	107.4
Capital inflows	60.8	110.4	236.4

Source: International Monetary Fund, International Financial Statistics, various years.

The currency has been slightly overvalued. According to a study of the Bank of Thailand (Wibulswadi et al. 1979), the baht was found to be overvalued by 17 percent in 1970–71, 7 percent in 1972, ±2 percent in 1973, 3–6 percent in 1974–76, and ±2 percent in 1977. When adjusted for purchasing power parity, the over (under) valuation ranged from 20 percent (1970) to −9 percent (1977). My own calculations using the Bacha and Taylor (1971) approach, which includes tariffs and export taxes (not considered by Wibulswadi et al.), place the overvaluation at about 20 percent. Considering capital flows in response to real interest differentials, currency overvaluation is probably not significant relative to that found in many developing countries.

9.1.3   The Structure of Production

Table 9.5 shows in detail the structure of trade and domestic production of manufactures in 1973, using the product classification followed in my analysis of protection and of factor proportions in the following sections. Instead of using value added, the value of total output is here used to measure production, so that the figures can be compared directly with the value of exports and imports. Products have been divided into seven subgroups: processed foods, beverages and tobacco, construction materials, intermediate products, consumer nondurables, consumer durables, and machinery and transportation equipment. The column on the far right gives the trade classifications of these activities.

The bulk (56 percent) of manufacturing output is produced by import substitution industries, most of which (83 percent) are located in Bangkok. About 40 percent of manufacturing output is produced by exportable industries, and the rest (4 percent) is produced in industries classified as not competing with imports.

While imports consist mainly of intermediate products, machinery, and transportation equipment, domestic production is more widely spread over all product categories. Since we are using gross value here, not value added, it should be noted that the concentration in the value of some products may be due to the high value of their inputs. If we were using value added, we would see larger shares of domestic production in beverages and tobacco, processed food, and construction materials and a smaller share in machinery and transportation equipment.

About 50 percent of production of importable activities consisted of processed foods, beverages, and consumer goods in 1973; the remainder was roughly evenly divided between intermediate and capital goods production. Those activities that faced greater import competition belong largely to the intermediate products and consumer nondurable groups. Some of these products are rubber tires and tubes, glass products, yarn and thread, chemical products, chemical materials, paper products, plastic materials and products, metal products, pharmaceuticals, and foot-

Table 9.5   Domestic Production, Imports and Exports of Manufactures, 1973 (Million Baht and Percentage)

Product	SITC	Output	Percentage of Total	Imports	Percentage of Total	Exports	Percentage of Total	Trade Category[b]
Processed foods		6,129	8.2	662	2.3	1,621	15.3	—
Dairy products	02	1,575	2.1	521	1.8	41	0.4	M
Cereal preparations	048	663	0.9	135	0.5	14	0.1	M
Tapioca flour	055.465	1,146	1.5	—	—	397	3.8	X
Sugar	061	2,272	3.0	5	—	1,161	11.0	X
Confectionery	062	122	0.2	—	—	4	—	M
Monosodium glutamate	099.0(4)	351	0.5	—	—	3	—	X
Beverages and tobacco		8,357	11.2	37	0.1	19	0.2	—
Nonalcoholic beverages	111	199	0.3	—	—	—	—	X
Alcoholic beverages	112	4,249	5.7	28	0.1	10	0.1	M
Cigars and cigarettes	122	3,909	5.2	9	—	9	0.1	M
Construction materials		4,169	5.6	103	0.4	351	3.3	—
Cement and concrete	661	2,619	3.5	29	0.1	336	3.2	X
Nonmetallic construction materials	662, 226	1,549	2.1	74	0.3	15	0.1	M
Intermediate products		32,205	43.0	13,255	46.2	6,978	66.0	—
Shaved wood	243	4,974	6.6	95	0.3	644	6.1	X
Vegetable oils and fats	42	392	0.5	14	—	31	0.3	X
Chemical materials	51–53	2,563	3.4	2,184	7.6	56	0.5	M
Leather	611	1,554	2.1	2	—	105	1.0	M
Yarn and thread	651	2,691	3.6	683	2.4	161	1.5	M
Cordage and rope	655.6	633	0.8	52	0.2	96	0.9	X
Glass products	664–65	780	1.0	57	0.2	3	—	M
Iron and steel	67	1,680	2.2	3,928	13.7	135	1.3	NC

Table 9.5—continued

Product	SITC	Output	Percentage of Total	Imports	Percentage of Total	Exports	Percentage of Total	Trade Category[b]
Nonferrous metals	68	50	0.1	1,052	3.7	11	0.1	NC
Chemical products	56, 57, 59	2,097	2.8	2,500	8.7	91	0.9	M
Plastic products	58	595	0.8	139	0.5	48	0.5	M
Materials of rubber[a]	621	4,944	6.6	122	0.4	4,578	43.3	X
Articles of rubber	629	59	0.1	130	0.4	19	0.2	M
Rubber tires and tubes	629.1	433	0.6	58	0.2	22	0.2	M
Wood manufactures	632	284	0.4	29	0.1	259	2.4	X
Paper and paperboard	641	329	0.4	597	2.1	29	0.3	M
Paper products	642	178	0.2	125	0.4	30	0.3	M
Textiles	652–55	6,478	8.6	339	1.2	507	4.8	X
Textile articles	656–57	437	0.6	47	0.2	42	0.4	M
Metal manufactures	69	1,056	1.4	1,104	3.8	112	1.1	M
Consumer nondurables		11,648	15.5	2,242	7.8	1,411	13.3	—
Pharmaceuticals	54	2,061	2.7	950	3.3	64	0.6	M
Essential oils, perfume, and toiletries	55	1,717	2.3	332	1.2	18	0.2	M
Leather products	612–13	262	0.3	5	—	105	1.0	X
Pottery and china	666	73	0.1	14	—	4	—	M
Batteries and electric bulbs	729.1–.2	611	0.8	135	0.5	7	0.1	M
Clothing	84	2,466	3.3	73	0.3	703	6.6	X
Footwear	85	576	0.8	8	—	4	—	M
Miscellaneous manufacturing necessities	89	2,530	3.4	626	2.2	202	1.9	M
Printed matter	892	1,186	1.6	101	0.4	302	2.9	X
Matches	899.3(2)	166	0.2	—	—	2	—	M

Table 9.5—*continued*

Product	SITC	Output	Percentage of Total	Imports	Percentage of Total	Exports	Percentage of Total	Trade Category[b]
Consumer durables		1,860	2.5	740	2.5	47	0.5	—
Radio, television, and household appliances	724–25	1,023	1.4	731	2.5	17	0.2	M
Furniture	82	837	1.1	8	—	30	0.3	X
Machinery and transportation equipment		10,595	14.1	11,675	40.7	149	1.4	—
Nonelectrical machinery	71	765	1.0	5,941	20.7	68	0.6	NC
Agricultural machinery	721.5	1,362	1.8	255	0.9	16	0.2	M
Electric wires, cables, and machinery	723.1	822	1.1	1,819	6.3	22	0.2	M
Passenger car assembly	732.1	2,484	3.3	544	1.9	8	0.1	M
Bus and truck assembly	732.2–.4	3,607	4.8	1,080	3.8	5	—	M
Vehicle parts	732.8	392	0.5	1,656	5.8	22	0.2	NC
Motorcycle and nonmotorized vehicles	732.9, 733	1,162	1.6	381	1.3	8	0.1	M
Total		74,962	100.0	28,713	100.0	10,584	100.0	

Source: Exports and imports are from Customs Department, *Statement of Foreign Trade of Thailand*, 1973, Bangkok; Output data are from the NESDB.

[a]This item consists almost entirely of processed natural rubber. It was included here because it is classified under SITC 621.

[b]Code: X, exportable; M, importable; NC, noncompeting production (see section 9.2 for a description of the categories).

wear. In other product groups there were also some import-competing items such as passenger cars, buses and trucks, electric wires and cables, and agricultural machinery in the machinery and transportation equipment category, and radio, television, and household appliances in consumer durables. Products in the processed foods, beverages and tobacco, and construction materials groups had little import competition. Thus most of them may be considered to be "competitive" with imports in the sense that they did not need protection to survive in the market. Some of these products, however, were exported to such an extent that they are classified as export industries.

Manufactured exports are a recent phenomenon in Thailand. Most of the export products developed from being import substitution industries in the 1960s or earlier, and some consist of the processing of domestic primary products to higher levels of production. Thus, manufactured exports are found in the processed foods, construction materials, intermediate products, and consumer nondurables groups. The more important manufactured exports are sugar, tapioca flour, cement, shaved wood and wood products, textile fabrics and products (including clothing), and leather products (see table 9.2).

9.1.4 The Labor Market

Table 9.6 gives some data on population and the labor force. Thailand's population growth rate is high, even for a developing country. It has averaged at least 3 percent annually since 1950. Reflecting this high rate, the fraction of the population under fifteen years of age has been rising and in 1970 stood at 45 percent.

Population growth at such a high rate would itself indicate the need for rapid creation of new jobs. But the situation in Thailand is further confounded by the fact that the country has a large rural population (79 percent in 1970), a high (5 percent) rate of urban population growth, and a high urban unemployment rate (currently placed at 9.4 percent in official documents).

Thus, employment opportunities in Thailand must grow both to provide for expansion of the labor force and to permit some part of the expanding rural population to shift into nonagricultural activities. In view of these needs, Thailand's performance has not been satisfactory. Despite an annual average growth rate of 10 percent for manufacturing output, manufacturing employment has grown at an average annual rate of only 4 percent.

There is, unfortunately, very little reliable information on workers and their characteristics; so inferences about the functioning of the labor market and distortions in incentives that affect the choice of technique are hard to draw. The minimum wage in Thailand does not appear to have been set high enough to affect firms' employment decisions: the

Table 9.6   Labor Force and Employment in Thailand, 1960–77

Year (1)	Population, Midyear (Millions of Persons) (1)	Manufacturing Employment (Thousands of Persons) (2)	Total Employment (Millions of Persons) (3)	Unemployment Rate (Percentage of Labor Force) (4)	Manufacturing Real Wage (1970 = 100) (5)
1960	26.40	n.a.ᵃ	n.a.	0.6	
1961	27.20	n.a.	n.a.	n.a.	104.1
1962	28.05	n.a.	n.a.	n.a.	92.4
1963	28.92	n.a.	n.a.	n.a.	111.9
1964	29.82	n.a.	n.a.	n.a.	127.8
1965	30.74	n.a.	n.a.	n.a.	123.9
1966	30.96	n.a.	n.a.	n.a.	94.7
1967	31.79	n.a.	n.a.	n.a.	92.1
1968	34.04	n.a.	n.a.	n.a.	99.4
1969	35.11	n.a.	n.a.	n.a.	101.2
1970	36.4	n.a.	n.a.	1.1	100.0
1971	37.5	n.a.	n.a.	n.a.	121.8
1972	38.6	1,411.4	16.06	n.a.	98.5
1973	39.7	1,353.8	16.75	6.7	108.6
1974	40.8	1,909.5	15.40	8.7	68.3
1975	41.9	1,958.9	14.17	n.a.	66.3
1976	43.0	1,514.0	18.19	5.3	72.2
1977	44.0	n.a.	19.7	5.7	n.a.

Source: (1) East Asia and Pacific Regional Office, Thailand, *Toward a Development Strategy of Full Participation: A Basic Economic Report*, report no. 2059–TH, 1 September 1978, table 1.1, p. 137.
(2) (5) ILO.
(3) ILO for 1972–75 and the Bank of Thailand for 1976–77.
(4) The same source as (1) for 1960, 1970, and the Bank of Thailand for 1973, 1974, 1976, and 1977.
ᵃn.a. = not available.

legal minimum has been well below the wage paid to unskilled workers in all industries. There do not appear to be any other significant government interventions with employment in the private sector. Real wages have tended to fall in recent years (see table 9.6). However, the government has subsidized credit, placed legal ceilings on interest rates, and permitted the importation of machinery at implicitly overvalued exchange rates. All these policies have undoubtedly encouraged the use of more capital-intensive techniques and the introduction of more capital-intensive industries than would have occurred in their absence.

Wage data by occupation or other category are lacking except for 1971 and 1973. Even for those years, few data are available. As will be seen in section 9.4, there are no reliable indicators of the training, experience, and skill of labor force members. As a consequence, sex is the only characteristic against which wage differentials could be examined. Although wage differentials seem wide, the male/female dichotomy seems highly significant, and it is difficult to draw any firm conclusions about the nature of the labor market in Thailand without further evidence. Nonetheless, the small fraction of the population that is now urbanized, the increasing number of young persons who will enter the labor force, and the pressure on urban areas all suggest that pressures will arise in the future, either upon the level of real wages or on unemployment, unless the rate at which industrial jobs are created increases.

9.1.5 Summary

Thailand has had an impressive record of growth since 1960. GDP grew at an annual average rate of about 7 percent, while manufacturing output grew at an even faster rate of about 10 percent. However, the economy remains rural-based, with NRB production representing one-third of GDP and the rural population constituting 79 percent of total population. Growth in the manufacturing sector was due in part to policies promoting import substitutes. These policies included tariff protection, implicit subsidization of capital goods, and various other direct interventions. However, despite these high rates of growth, employment creation continues to be a major problem. The rate of rural-urban migration has been high, and urban unemployment is increasing.

9.2 The Trade Regime and the Structure of Protection in the Early 1970s

9.2.1 The Trade Regime in the Early 1970s

Thailand has had no clear-cut focus to its trade policies. Responsibility for trade matters is scattered over a range of agencies, and changes in policies are more often than not a response to changing balance of payments situations.

In principle, the Ministry of Commerce administers all foreign trade matters. In practice, responsibility is widely diffused. For NRB exports, policies are formulated under the jurisdiction of the Ministry of Agriculture and Cooperatives and the Ministry of Industry; the Ministry of Commerce has only partial control on rice and sugar exports through the rice premium and sugar export surcharge;[11] export taxation is under the authority of the Ministry of Finance. For manufactured exports, both the Ministry of Commerce and the Ministry of Finance promote exports directly, while the Bank of Thailand has a credit facility to assist exporting.

For imports, the Ministry of Commerce exercises control through quantitative restrictions, and the Ministry of Finance administers control through import duties and other forms of taxation. But, since imports are mostly investment goods, their importation depends upon decisions to invest, which in turn depend partly upon the policy of the Board of Investment. Furthermore, the Bank of Thailand may regulate credit to finance imports and, together with the Ministry of Finance, may change the exchange rate.

In the early 1970s, the three major trade policy instruments affecting manufacturing activities were tariffs and domestic taxation, tax incentives, and a variety of other measures affecting specific industries (e.g., price controls and legal barriers to entry). The various tariff, tax, and "subsidization"[12] policies of the Ministry of Finance appeared to have the largest effect upon trade in manufactured goods. The next most important were the various promotional activities of the Board of Investment and the Ministry of Finance. Activities of the Ministry of Commerce, the supposed administrator of foreign trade matters, were relatively unimportant, since its major policy instrument (quantitative restrictions) was not extensively used during the period under review.[13] The various policy instruments are discussed below.

Tariffs and Taxation

The 1960 tariff schedule, based upon the four-digit BTN and consisting of 1,097 items, is in use today, although rates have been changed to make it more escalated. Tariffs were initially imposed to raise revenue. Hence rates were not high in the early 1960s except for a few luxury consumer goods. Nonetheless, they did provide some protection for domestic production. Throughout the 1960s a number of upward adjustments were made, and there were major revisions in 1964 and 1970.[14] However, protection of domestic production was not the main objective assigned to tariff policy in Thailand. The stated purpose of these adjustments was to check the balance of payments deficit.[15] Finally, a tariff revision in 1974 responded to demands for greater tariff protection after the reduction in tax incentives under the investment promotion scheme.

Thus Thailand's tariff structure has evolved to be more of a protective device than it was in the 1960s. Although the highest rates have been on processed food, alcoholic beverage, and tobacco imports, these rates do not really reflect Thailand's tariff policies, since domestic production in these industries usually does not compete with imports—that is, domestic production is different in nature from imports.

The escalation is seen by analyzing the evolution of tariff protection in other commodity groups. In 1964 rates were about 25–30 percent for intermediate products and 15–20 percent for machinery and transportation equipment. In 1970 rates for durable and nondurable consumer goods were increased to range between 30 and 55 percent, but rates for intermediate products and machinery and equipment were unchanged. Finally, in 1974 rates on imports of consumer goods that did not compete with domestic production were cut to as little as one-tenth of the old rate. Likewise, rates for a large number of raw materials and intermediate products were reduced to one-tenth of the old level, while those for machinery and mechanical appliances, both for agricultural and for industrial uses, were reduced from 15–20 percent to 10 percent. The rates for other consumer goods remained the same (Akrasanee 1973, 1975). The net result is an escalated tariff structure providing greatest protection to activities producing finished products.

In addition to tariffs, several other taxes provide some protection. One, the business tax, is imposed on both imports and domestic production. On imports, business tax rates are a percentage of the estimated market value, which is equal to the c.i.f. price plus tariff plus a (predetermined) standard profit rate, and the tax is collected by the Customs Department. On domestic products the manufacturer pays the tax if the goods are destined for the domestic market.[16] Before 1961, business tax rates were very low, most items being subject to a rate of 2 percent. The general rate for finished products has increased gradually, rising to 5 percent in 1961 and to 7 percent in 1970, while the rate for raw material and intermediate products has remained at 1.5 percent. The rates for goods considered luxuries have always been high, ranging from 10 or 15 percent to 30 or 40 percent. The rates were the same for both domestically produced goods and imports until 1973 and had no nominal protective effect. In December 1973 the business tax rates on many domestically produced goods were reduced as a move to check inflation (Akrasanee 1975). Those on imports remained unchanged. For example, rates on several items of domestic raw materials and food fell to zero, and for others the rates were reduced if they used purchased inputs. Thus the new business tax now has a protective effect.

Besides the business tax, an excise tax has been imposed on a few domestic products and imports. Goods liable to the tax, whether domestically produced or imported, are alcoholic and nonalcoholic beverages, tobacco products, playing cards, and snuff. For these products the excise tax has a protective effect, since the rates on imports and those on domestic products differ slightly. On the other hand, domestic production (and not imports) of cement, petroleum products, matches, and mechanical lighters is subject to the tax; in this case the tax has negative protective effect (Akrasanee 1975).

Finally, Thailand's traditional exports are subject to an export duty, namely (in 1973): rice (5 percent), rubber (7.3 percent), logs and wood (18.7 percent), and raw hides of bovine animals (22.3 percent). Other exports are not subject to export duty, but before 1973 most of them were subject to the business tax of 2 percent. In addition, a special export tax called "premium" has been imposed on rice (0–30 percent, depending on the year) and sugar, the latter since 1974. On the other hand, there have been subsidies on the export of cement, sugar (during 1961–66), and, since 1972, many other manufactured products.

Tax Incentives and Other Promotional Measures

In 1954 the first Act on Promotion of Industries was passed, and the Board of Investment was established to render assistance to would-be entrepreneurs and investors under the provisions of the 1954 act (Board of Investment 1959). This act was revised in 1962 and again in 1972. Encouragement is provided through both tax and nontax incentives. In addition, the Board of Investment is to coordinate policy measures under the jurisdiction of other government agencies that affect industrial incentives.[17]

The most important provision in the original promotion act was tax concessions on imported machinery, equipment, raw materials, and intermediate inputs needed directly for production. Tax concessions on these inputs depended upon the classification of promoted industries. Initially, industries were classified into three groups according to their "importance" to the national economy (Silcock 1967; Akrasanee 1973). Group A received full exemption from tariffs and business taxes, and groups B and C received one-half and one-third exemption, respectively. Toward the mid-1960s most industries under group A were reclassified into groups B and C, and since 1967 only group C has been left. In 1972 tax incentives were given in relation to location and orientation.[18] Firms granted tax concessions earlier but not meeting the new criteria continued to be entitled to them until their expiration. As these tax incentives were being phased out, they were replaced by tariff increases on some finished products and tariff reductions on some inputs.

Most firms obtaining these concessions until the early 1970s were involved in import substitution production. Export promotion measures were not effective despite official statements and policies to encourage manufactured exports. For example, since the late 1950s exports have been eligible for the partial refund of duties and business taxes on imported inputs. Probably the administrative fragmentation (and lack of an overriding trade policy orientation) caused the ineffectiveness of this policy measure.

Since 1972 manufactured exports have been actively promoted. Measures used include full exemption from tariffs and business taxes on imported inputs, refunds of all taxes assessed in the production process, discounts on short-term loans at the Bank of Thailand, and exemption from business taxes on the products. These incentives are in addition to those provided under the general investment promotion scheme.

Restrictions and Controls on Trade and Industry

Apart from the tariffs, taxes, and concessions listed above, the government intervenes through controls on prices, imports, and exports and through restrictions on various kinds of industries. Although not extensively used previously, these restrictions and controls have been increasing since the latter part of the 1960s. They have been used primarily to protect existing firms or else to stabilize domestic prices.

Price controls were applied on only a few commodities before 1970—rice, meat, rice meal, and ice. In 1971 gunnysacks, condensed and evaporated milk, gasoline, diesel fuel, and kerosene, and in 1972 white sugar were added to the list. The export prices of many commodities increased rapidly in 1973 and pulled domestic prices along with them. The government accordingly imposed price controls on cotton, synthetic thread, and most types of textiles. In 1974 price control over most textiles was lifted, but many other kinds of commodities were put on the list; among them were monosodium glutamate, cement, vegetable oil, detergent, iron rods, and printing and writing paper.[19]

Most of the commodities under price control were exportables whose domestic prices had increased as a result of an increase in foreign prices. Price control, which is usually applied to the producer as well as to consumer prices, is thus a measure intended to stabilize the domestic price level. It is not an integral part of protection policy, but it has the effect of reducing the overall level of incentives for the products concerned. However, price control has not significantly affected exportable production. Probably it is most important in the case of thread and yarn, both of which have small ratios of exports to total sales.

There are quantitative restrictions on some imported commodities. Imports of some commodities for which it is believed there is sufficient domestic production are banned. Most items under control are subject to "approval" that, in practice, is usually not granted. However, these controls are not very pervasive. Often they are imposed on a short-run, ad hoc basis. In 1962 controls were imposed on sugar, old newspaper, paper umbrellas, silk textiles, tinfoil, paper files, and gold, and they are still in effect. During 1966–69, imports of garlic, glass tumblers, truck and bus tires, cotton yarn, corn, sorghum, salt, canvas shoes, and swallows' nests were controlled, but the control lasted only a short time. In 1970 and 1971 many items were added to the list of goods under control—iron gas containers, all kinds of paper, fuel oil, used cars, white cement and clinker, used motorcycles, monosodium glutamate, iron bars and rods, used trucks, and polyester fibers; these controls were in effect in 1973, the year on which this study focuses.

Export controls are also applied ad hoc and are intended to assure an adequate supply for the domestic market and to stabilize domestic prices. Commodities under control are mostly NRB products such as rice, livestock, sugar, maize, and mineral ores. It was not until 1974 that controls were placed on manufactured products such as gunnysacks, thread and yarn, pig iron, detergent, vegetable oil, polyester fibers, monosodium glutamate, pulp and wood-free paper, insecticides, plastic granules, and oils for mixing paint, including thinners, most of which had only recently begun to be exported. The export of most of these items requires "approval," which is usually granted. Quotas are applied in the case of cattle and buffalo, cement, gunnysacks, maize, aluminum scrap, and pig iron.

Given the objective of promoting manufactured exports, export control is seen by the government as only a temporary device to check domestic prices of the products concerned when export prices are higher. By doing so, however, it automatically discourages production.

There is another measure the government has used to control the export of rice. Known as the reserve requirement, it requires exporters to sell a certain amount of rice to the government at a nominal price when they export rice. This is in addition to the rice premium and the export duty on rice. Since the price set by the government is usually much lower than the f.o.b. price, the measure can be regarded as an additional export tax (Akrasanee and Wattananukit 1976).

The Ministry of Industry can control industries in many ways. It is empowered to permit or to ban new entries and the expansion of existing firms and to establish conditions for new entry. The ban on entry and expansion is applied when the Ministry of Industry thinks that domestic demand for a product can be satisfied by the existing firms or when the producers are in difficulty and ask the ministry to prevent greater competition. Before 1970 there was a ban on entry and expansion in milk products, plastic bags, other plastic products, and ice factories. Later, about ten other industries were added to the list. The controls are designed to be temporary, but in fact have usually remained in effect for as long as four or five years; exceptions were controls on chloric acid, textile fabrics, nails, newsprint and writing paper, and fishing nets, which lasted for only one or two years.

Conditions have been imposed on entry into some industries; namely, fertilizer, ceramics, glass products, motorcycle assembly, and car assembly. Conditions pertain to promotion, equity share, type of product market, size of investment, capacity, and so forth. Another control on industry is local content requirements; that is, some industries are required to obtain a certain percentage of inputs or specified parts from domestic sources. This control of their imports has been applied to milk products, steel wire, electric wire, motorcycles, and automobiles.

The Ministry of Industry is empowered to control even the types and quality of products and the time of production. For example, it can regulate the models of cars to be produced; it requires new glass-product firms to produce mostly bottles for medicine; it stipulates that sugar mills are to produce 50 percent white sugar and 50 percent raw sugar; and it can decree the time the mills start producing each year.

Summary

Table 9.7 summarizes the incentives to import substitution and export industries in the early 1970s, as well as the various agencies involved in their administration. In general, trade policy in this period favored import substitutes while also attempting to reduce disincentives for exports. The structure of tariffs and taxes favored import substitutes, while exports were encouraged through the various concessions of the promotion acts. A variety of other controls existed. However, my assessment is that these other controls were quantitatively unimportant compared with the other aspects of trade policy.

9.2.2   The Structure of Protection in the Manufacturing Sector

Data and Methodology

I used production coefficients for 1971 obtained from the Manufacturing Survey of that year (National Statistical Office 1971) to calculate

Table 9.7   Comparison of Incentives for Import Substitution and for Exports, by Government Agency, 1972–76

	Incentives	
Government Agency	Import Substitution	Exports
Board of Investment	1. Full exemption from import taxes and local taxes on machinery and equipment.	1. Full exemption from import taxes on machinery and equipment.
	2. No exemption from taxes on imported or local raw materials, parts and components, except firms in promoted areas, which received up to 50 percent deduction on import taxes.	2. Full exemption from taxes on imported and local raw materials, parts, and components.
	3. No exemption from business tax on sales, except firms in promoted areas, which received up to 90 percent deduction for 5 years.	3. Full exemption from export duty and business tax on exports, for promoted exports.
	4. Income tax holiday for 3–8 years.	4. Income tax holiday for 3–8 years.

Table 9.7—*continued*

	Incentives	
Government Agency	Import Substitution	Exports
	5. Other nontax incentives for promoted firms. 6. Temporary import surcharge and import ban (not used very much).	5. Other nontax incentives for promoted firms.
Ministry of Finance Customs Department	1. Escalated tariff structure. 2. Lower business tax rates for domestic production than for imports for some products (since 1973).	1. Full exemption from import taxes on raw materials, parts, and components. 2. Full exemption from export and business taxes on some products.
Fiscal Policy Office	—	1. Tax refund for the total amount of taxes in the cost of production.
Ministry of Commerce	1. Import control for about 40 manufactured items (disaggregated at the seven-digit level) 2. Price control for about 20 manufactured items (disincentives).	1. Export control for about 20 manufactured items (disincentives). 2. Export Service Center (to provide miscellaneous service to exporters).
Ministry of Industry	1. Control on entry, expansion, and local contents for about 25 industries.[a] 2. National committees to promote basic industries.[b]	—
Industrial Estate Authority	1. One industrial estate.	1. Export processing zone (to be built).
Bank of Thailand	1. Rediscount facility at 5% interest rate for 180-day promissory notes issued by commercial banks.[c]	1. Rediscount facility at 5% interest rate for 180-day promissory notes issued by commercial banks.[c]

Source: Information from agencies indicated in the table.

[a]Control on entry creates incentives for existing firms; effect of control on expansion is unclear; requirement of local contents creates disincentives.

[b]Committees were mostly set up in 1974–76, but only a few have been active.

[c]Commercial banks charge 7 percent interest on these notes.

ERPs by the Corden method.[20] International value added (IVA) was calculated by deflating the value of output and material inputs by appropriate NRPs, taking into consideration tax rebates under the investment promotion scheme.[21] Two different sets of NRPs are given in the tables below. "Potential" protection refers to protection implied by the tariff and tax rates. "Realized" protection is derived from price comparisons and measures the actual protection used by domestic producers.[22] The presentation of these two NRP estimates is interesting in its own right for, as we see, protection actually "realized" is typically less than that implied by the tariff and tax rates.

Activities are classified into trade categories following the T_i statistic method outlined in chapter 1. Exportables had a T_i statistic less than zero; importables had T_i statistics between zero and 0.6 to 0.9. The variable value to separate importable from noncompetitive production was due to the level of aggregation in each activity. The cutoff point was 0.6, 0.7, 0.8, or 0.9 depending on whether the activity was classified at a two-, three-, four-, or five-digit SITC level.

Importables were next classified into protected and competitive subgroups, depending on whether their estimated ERPs were relatively high or low. Exports of manufactures were further broken down between those processing NRB goods and those processing other goods. Note, however, that the latter distinction is not without problems. Some of the products in the processed NRB group (e.g., cement) might have been excluded altogether as essentially natural resource based (NRB) products rather than HOS manufactures. Others in the group—especially shaved wood, wood products, and cordage and rope—might have been assigned to the non-NRB manufactures category on the ground that their inputs are internationally traded so that production is not bound to local availability of materials.

The Structure of Protection

Nominal rates and effective rates as of 1973, both potential and realized in each case, are shown in tables 9.6 to 9.8, classified according to the trade orientation of each industry. Table 9.9 summarizes ERPs by trade category. For export industries, rates are shown separately for domestic and export sales. Primary interest focuses on the last column of table 9.6 and table 9.7 and the last two columns of table 9.8 that show realized effective rates.

For importables, noncompeting importables, and domestic sales of exportables, the nominal potential rates were all positive with the exception of petroleum refining and tapioca flour, for which the rates were zero and minus 2 percent, respectively. Generally the potential nominal rates were quite high, especially for consumer products.

For export sales of export industries, nominal rates were zero, unless there was an export tax on the product, in which case the nominal rates were negative (e.g., shaved wood and tapioca flour). Many of the non-processed NRB export industries sold a large proportion of their products in the domestic market, where they were protected by generally very high tariff rates (though, as noted below, realized rates were usually much lower).

From tables 9.6 to 9.8, we see that the difference between potential and realized nominal rates depends on the trade category of the industry. In protected importable and noncompeting importable industries, the difference is usually not large. In fact, in most cases the rates are similar. Exceptions where the realized rates are lower include alcoholic beverages, sheet glass, sweetened condensed milk, pharmaceuticals, footwear, rubber products, and radio, television, and electrical household appliances. In such cases, the lower realized rates indicate tariff redundancy caused by number of firms producing a growing proportion of total domestic demand. Alternative explanations are preferences for imported products and price control. The factor of preference is particularly true for radio, television, and electrical household appliances. In these cases imports sell at prices above those of domestic production. Price control was imposed on condensed milk, and prices of sheet glass were agreed upon with the Board of Investment as a condition for promotion privileges.

For importable industries that are competitive without needing protection, and industries that are able to export but still rely largely on the domestic market, realized nominal rates in 1973 (for the latter, of domestic sales) were much lower than the potential rates. In fact, in most cases the rates were zero, either because the difference in prices was negligible if quality differences are considered or because the domestic and imported products were different in nature.

Effective rates of protection ranged from minus 42.6 percent for wood shavings to very high levels for alcoholic beverages, passenger cars, sweetened condensed milk, cigars and cigarettes, and domestic sales of many exportables. As expected, products with very high potential effective protection belong to the importable group.

For products in the exportable group, their high potential effective rates on domestic sales were the result of high tariff rates on imports of like products. But when the products were exported, the potential effective rates were zero in most cases because of the tax refund and tax exemptions on their inputs.[23] This was the case except for a few traditional exports, such as tapioca flour and shaved wood, that were not entitled to such benefits.

When realized effective protection is considered for the importable category, the rates for some products were lower than potential rates,

Table 9.8   Nominal and Effective Rates of Protection: Importable Industries, 1973

Products	Nominal Rates		Effective Rates	
	Potential	Realized	Potential	Realized
Protected				
Alcoholic beverages[a]				
Beer	272.8%	35.7%	9,803.2%	35.6%
Whiskey	309.2	79.1	3,204.8	147.4
Passenger cars	91.2	91.2	236.4	236.4
Buses and trucks	40.0	40.0	95.3	95.6
Electric wires and cables	20.9	20.9	21.0	21.0
Rubber tires and tubes	26.9	26.9	25.2	25.2
Glass and glass products				
Glass products	40.7	n.a.	54.1	n.a.
Glass sheet	48.0	16.2	101.0	18.2
Dairy products (sweetened condensed milk)	40.0	13.4	273.2	2.4
Textile yarn and thread				
Synthetic	20.0	20.0	25.5	25.5
Cotton	24.6	24.6	39.3	39.3
Essential oils and perfume materials	95.0	n.a.	209.5	n.a.
Chemical products	28.0	28.0	25.0	25.0
Paper and paperboard	20.3	20.3	33.3	33.3
Paper products	39.4	39.4	55.4	55.4
Motorcycles and nonmotorized vehicles				
Motorcycles	37.8	37.8	56.7	56.3
Bicycles	30.0	30.0	6.8	16.6
Pharmaceuticals	53.4	36.8	101.2	48.8
Chemical materials	31.4	31.4	31.4	31.4
Agricultural machinery (tractors)	4.5	4.5	5.3	5.3
Plastic materials	50.0	n.a.	88.6	n.a.
Metal products				
Finished structural	23.4	23.4	24.9	24.9
Household equipment	32.8	n.a.	103.5	n.a.
Furniture	50.0	n.a.	104.5	n.a.
Footwear	57.0	48.0	85.0	60.1
Iron rods	15.0	15.0	21.5	21.5
Textile articles	37.0	37.0	44.1	44.1
Pottery, china, and earthenware	47.8	47.8	71.8	71.8
Radio, television, and electrical household appliances		25.0	52.3	22.8
Radio assembly and parts	39.8	25.0	52.3	22.8
Television and household appliances	52.9	41.7	166.7	58.6
Competitive				
Cigars and cigarettes[a]	86.0	n.a.	378.9	n.a.
Petroleum refinery	0	0	−0.8	−0.8
Nonmetallic construction materials	33.0	n.a.	41.4	n.a.
Rubber products	49.4	0	107.5	−12.4

Table 9.8—*continued*

Products	Nominal Rates Potential	Nominal Rates Realized	Effective Rates Potential	Effective Rates Realized
Cereal preparations	60.7	0	1,044.0	−5.5
Confectionery	81.1	0	—b	−13.3
Soap, detergent	50.1	25.4	65.5	20.7

Source: Tariff and taxes are from Customs Department; For the computation, see text.

aAlcoholic beverages and cigars and cigarettes are included under import-competing because their T statistics, although very small, are positive. For both products the recorded value of trade is small, but the availability of foreign alcoholic beverages in Thailand is obvious. It is also well known that without protection domestic alcoholic beverages cannot compete with foreign ones. Foreign brands of cigarettes are sold at prices competitive with local brands.

bNegative value added at world prices.

but products classified as "protected" remained the more protected products. For this group the realized rates were close to, or the same as, the potential rates, implying that protection was fully utilized. This was also true for products in the noncompeting importable group. For these industries, high realized effective rates mean that they were either making excessive profits or were very inefficient. However, there was no industry in this group with negative value added at world prices. On the whole, we may say that substantial inefficiency or excessive profits are indicated in about fifteen or sixteen industries for which the calculation was made (i.e., those with realized effective rates exceeding 35 percent). These include beer, whiskey, passenger cars, buses and trucks, cotton yarn and thread, paper products, motorcycles, pharmaceuticals, footwear, textile articles, pottery, china, and earthenware, and four products for domestic sales in the group of export industries—parquet flooring, veneer and plywood, textiles (noncotton), and leather products. Most

Table 9.9 **Nominal and Effective Rates of Protection: Noncompeting Importables, 1973**

Products	Nominal Rates Potential	Nominal Rates Realized	Effective Rates Potential	Effective Rates Realized
Iron and steel	13.5	13.5	18.4	18.4
Nonferrous metals	10.5	10.5	4.1	4.1
Vehicle parts	38.4	38.4	68.7	68.7
Nonelectrical machinery	15.9	15.9	4.2	4.2
Sewing machines	20.0	n.a.	4.3	n.a.

Source: See table 9.8.

Table 9.10   Nominal and Effective Rates of Protection: Export Industries, 1973

	Nominal Rates			Effective Rates[a]		
	Domestic Sales		Export	Domestic Sales		Export
Products	Potential	Realized	Sales	Potential	Realized	Sales
Primary-commodity based						
Cement, concrete products						
Cement	17.5	0	0	10.6	−16.3	0
Concrete products	26.1	n.a.	0	40.7	n.a.	0
Vegetable oils and fats	44.2	n.a.	0	274.7	n.a.	0
Materials of rubber	33.0	0	0	*	−0.5	0
Sugar	115.5	0	0	*	2.9	0
Tapioca flour	−2.0	−2.0	−2.0	−29.8	−29.8	−29.8
Wood products						
Parquet flooring	30.0	0	0	*	68.90	0
Veneer and plywood	60.0	0	0	*	43.2	0
Shaved wood	—	−18.7	−18.7	—	−42.6	−42.6
Cordage and rope	27.7	27.7	0	26.3	26.3	0
Non-primary-commodity based						
Nonalcoholic beverages	69.6	0	0	47.2	−20.9	0
Monosodium glutamate	101.6	0	0	537.5	−17.5	0
Textiles, noncotton	44.2	44.2	0	64.0	64.0	0
Cotton fabrics	41.5	19.65	0	59.4	7.6	0
Printed matter	5.3	0	0	−13.2	−20.3	0
Furniture	50.0	0	0	152.3	−2.1	0
Matches	66.0	0	0	23.3	−9.5	0
Clothing	54.3	20.0	0	86.2	−7.1	0
Leather products	44.2	44.2	0	48.6	48.6	0

Source: See table 9.8.
[a]An asterisk means negative value added at world prices.

of them are important industries in terms of their output value, as can be seen from table 9.6.

In the exportable group, except for products produced specifically for exports, the realized effective rates were calculated mostly for domestic sales, since these industries still sold a large part of their products in the domestic market. As may be seen from table 9.10, and also for competitive industries in the importable group in table 9.8, the calculated realized effective rates were much lower than the potential rates. In fact, they are mostly negative. The results are due to the relatively low realized nominal protection together with the use of import-competing inputs, prices of which were inflated by the extent of tariff and taxes.[24] But when the products were exported they were entitled to the tax refund and tax exemptions on their inputs. Thus the effective rates in the latter case are estimated to be zero.

Table 9.11 gives a summary of the structure of protection in existence in the early 1970s. The system provided greatest incentives to protected importable industries and to domestic production similar to the noncompeting imports, whereas industries in the exportable group were clearly discriminated against, having low or negative ERPs. In general, though, protection was relatively moderate in comparison with many other LDCs.

9.3 Factor Proportions of Trade and Domestic Production

In this analysis I measure factor proportions by labor requirements (in number of workers) per unit of value added. Two measures are used—direct labor requirements and direct plus indirect in home goods labor requirements.[25] Nonmaterial inputs, such as electricity and water, maintenance costs, and other services are treated as home goods. Data on number of workers, value added (net of indirect taxes), and the value of home goods used are from the Manufacturing Survey of 1973. Indirect labor and value added in home goods are estimated from the NESDB 1971 input-output table, the national income accounts statistics, and information from the electricity and water authorities.[26]

The results are presented first for each activity and then according to the trade categories defined above and employed in tables 9.8 to 9.11. I also computed labor intensities according to the direction of

Table 9.11   Average ERPs by Trade Category, 1973

Category	Realized ERPs
Importables	53%
Protected	69
Competitive	28
Noncompeting importables	42
Exportables[a]	2 (-10)
Processed NRBs	-18 (-18)
Other	26 (0)
Total	35

Note: ERPs are weighted by DVA of domestic production.

[a]Values in parentheses refer to protection on export sales.

trade. But since Thailand's trade in manufactures is overwhelmingly with developed countries, the labor coefficients on trade with LDCs are ambiguous and thus are not reported here.

9.3.1   Factor Proportions of Different Activities

The direct and direct plus indirect labor requirements, shown in table 9.12, have a wide range of values for direct requirements (col. 2). The ten least labor-intensive industries in 1973 were alcoholic beverages, cigars and cigarettes, cement and concrete products, passenger car assembly, iron and steel, bus and truck assembly, electric wires and cables, rubber tires and tubes, glass products, and vegetable oils and fats. The ten most labor-intensive were the pottery, china, and earthenware group, confectionery, cordage and rope, textile articles, footwear, leather products, clothing, cereal preparations, nonelectrical machinery (small), and rubber products.

The most and the least labor-intensive industries had labor requirements differing by a factor of about 25; compare the direct labor requirement of 118.2 workers (confectionery) to 4.9 workers (alcoholic beverages) per one million baht of value added in current domestic prices. However, the majority of industries clustered within the range of 14 to 30 workers per one million baht of value added.

The variation in labor requirements among industries can also be seen from the direct plus indirect requirements (col. 4), which provide a similar picture with some small changes in the ranking. This measure, which indicates total employment effects, indicates that the labor intensity of the less labor-intensive industries is sharply increased when home goods are included, whereas that of the more labor-intensive industries shows little change. This change occurs because home goods are relatively labor-intensive, though not as much as the most labor-intensive industries. When this indirect effect is taken into consideration, therefore, differences in labor coefficients among industries are reduced but still remain significant.

9.3.2   Factor Proportions by Commodity Category

We next calculated weighted averages of factor requirements for the exportable and importable categories, using domestic value added in production as weights and subdividing exportables and importables as was done earlier (section 9.2). These calculations are given in table 9.13.

Including alcoholic beverages and cigars and cigarettes in the computations has a significant effect upon the results, since they have large weights in production (see table 9.6) and value added. Treating them as home goods and excluding them completely would, however, be a questionable practice because imports compete with domestic products

Table 9.12 Direct and Direct Plus Indirect in Home Goods Labor Requirements, by Industries According to Trade Categories, 1973 (Number of Workers per One Million Baht of Domestic Value Added)

Industry	Trade Categories[a] (1)	L/VA[b] (2)	Rank[c] (3)	L/VAT[b] (4)	Rank[c] (5)
Alcoholic beverages	ICP	4.9	1	12.2	2
Cigars and cigarettes	ICC	5.3	2	6.4	1
Cement and concrete	EP	8.8	3	20.4	4
Passenger car assembly	ICP	9.5	4	22.5	7
Iron and steel	NCI	10.7	5	23.2	9
Bus and truck assembly	ICP	11.5	6	23.0	8
Electric wires and cables	ICP	11.7	7	19.5	3
Rubber tires and tubes	ICP	13.8	8	26.5	17
Glass and glass products	ICP	14.3	9	24.5	12
Vegetable oils and fats	EP	14.3	10	20.5	5
Nonalcoholic beverages	ENP	14.4	11	34.0	30
Dairy products	ICP	14.8	12	25.8	15
Textile yarn and thread	ICP	16.1	13	21.6	6
Essential oils, perfume, and toiletries	ICP	16.2	14	26.8	19
Materials of rubber	EP	18.0	15	24.3	11
Sugar	EP	18.1	16	24.2	10
Chemical products	ICP	19.5	17	39.7	35
Tapioca flour	EP	20.0	18	26.5	18
Paper and paperboard	ICP	20.1	19	27.4	20
Paper products	ICP	21.6	20	25.9	16
Motorcycle and nonmotorized vehicles	ICP	22.7	21	28.7	22
Wood products	EP	23.4	22	25.6	13
Pharmaceuticals	ICP	24.1	23	29.3	23
Miscellaneous manufacturing necessities	ICC	24.5	24	32.1	26
Monosodium glutamate	ENP	24.9	25	25.8	14
Chemical materials	ICP	25.2	26	28.4	21
Agricultural machinery	ICP	28.1	27	36.6	32
Shaved wood	EP	25.5	28	30.6	24
Textiles	ENP	29.4	29	32.3	28
Printed matter	ENP	30.1	30	31.1	25
Plastic materials	ICP	31.4	31	32.3	27
Nonferrous metals	NCI	33.2	32	33.2	28
Furniture	ENP	34.4	33	35.9	31
Nonmetallic construction materials	ICC	34.6	34	37.6	33
Vehicle parts	NCI	36.7	35	38.4	34

Table 9.12—continued

Industry	Trade Categories[a] (1)	L/VA[b] (2)	Rank[c] (3)	L/VAT[b] (4)	Rank[c] (5)
Radio, television, and electrical household appliances	ICP	37.4	36	40.1	36
Metal products	ICP	42.0	37	42.5	37
Matches	ENP	45.5	38	45.7	38
Rubber products	ICC	49.2	39	47.9	39
Nonelectrical machinery	NCI	61.8	40	58.4	41
Cereal preparations	ICC	61.9	41	57.7	40
Clothing	ENP	72.3	42	66.1	43
Leather products	ENP	80.2	43	58.8	42
Footwear	ICP	84.4	44	74.3	46
Textile articles	ICP	84.4	45	71.8	44
Cordage and rope	EP	86.5	46	71.9	45
Pottery, china, and earthenware	ICP	89.3	47	74.9	47
Confectionery	ICC	118.2	48	101.3	48

Source: Akrasanee and Chintayarangsan (1976).
[a]ICP = import-competing, protected; ICC = import-competing, competitive; EP = exports, primary-commodity based (PCB); ENP = exports, non-primary-commodity based; NCI = noncompeting imports.
[b]L/VA = workers per one million baht of value added, direct; L/VAT = workers per one million baht of value added, direct plus indirect of home goods.
[c]Ranking from the least labor-intensive industries.

everywhere in the country, even though import statistics show a relatively small value. I therefore computed Thai coefficients both including and excluding these products.

Obviously, these results show that exportables are significantly more labor-using than importables. This is true for direct labor requirements only and also for direct plus indirect requirements. Including indirect requirements in home goods results in only a slightly smaller difference between the degrees of labor intensity of the two categories. According to the latter measure, products belonging to the group of exportable industries are still about 50 percent more labor-intensive than importable industries.

With regard to employment implications, the most meaningful comparison is between the coefficients for the "protected" importables (col. 5), which indicate the employment effects of import substitution, and the coefficients for non-NRB exportables (col. 3), which indicate the employment effect of export expansion. This comparison suggests that employment creation would be much greater through export expansion than through import substitution for the same amount of value added.

This conclusion is true whether we look at different labor requirements only or at direct plus indirect requirements, and whether we include or exclude alcoholic beverages in estimating requirements for "protected" importables. Moreover, the conclusion would be unchanged, though the margin in favor of exports would be slightly reduced, if shaved wood, wood products, and cordage and rope were shifted to the non-NRB manufactures group in line with what was said earlier about the uncertainty attaching to the NRB classifications of these products.

With regard to noncompeting importables, given the limited size and the probable noncomparability of imports and domestic production, the value added and employment data entering into table 9.12 cannot be taken as relevant for imports. I have accordingly not attempted to calculate labor coefficients for the noncompeting import sector.

9.4 Factor Market Policies

Besides the pattern of protection, policies affecting factor prices also affect factor utilization and therefore may have significant employment implications.[27] My purpose in this section is to examine these potential effects in Thailand.

Table 9.13   Labor Coefficients in Manufacturing Industries, Exports and Import-Competing Goods, 1973 (Number of Workers per One Million Baht of Domestic Value Added—Weighted Averages)

Measures of Labor Coefficients	Export Industries			Import-Competing Industries[a]		
	Total (1)	NRB Manufacturing (2)	Non-NRB Manufacturing (3)	Total (4)	Protected (5)	Competitive (6)
Labor per direct value added	21.87	16.68	33.72	10.53 (20.53)	10.45 (18.58)	10.72 (29.11)
Direct plus indirect labor per direct plus indirect value added[b]	29.55	25.37	36.28	19.21 (29.51)	21.43 (27.84)	15.21 (35.35)

Source: Labor coefficients for each industry are from table 9.9. Domestic value added weights are from Akrasanee and Chintayarangsan (1976). For computation, see text.

[a]Figures in parentheses show averages excluding alcoholic beverages (from the "protected" group) and cigars and cigarettes (from the "competitive" group).

[b]"Indirect" refers only to home goods as defined in text.

9.4.1   Wage Differentials in Manufacturing

Wage differentials may be caused by a variety of economic and non-economic factors. In Thailand one might expect the labor market to be relatively undistorted, since minimum-wage legislation was introduced only in 1973 and since the government has not otherwise intervened heavily in wage determination.

Data to adequately analyze wage differentials in Thailand are sparse. A limited amount of information was available for twenty-seven industries in 1973. I performed a variety of exercises with these data (for details, see Akrasanee and Chutikul 1977). First, average wages for skilled and unskilled labor were calculated for large and small firms. It was found that there was a large variation in the wages paid by industry and that larger firms tended to pay higher wages. Next, cross-sectional regression analysis was carried out, regressing the average skilled and unskilled wage rates of each industry on various independent variables such as firm sizes (AFS), the male/female worker ratio (MF), profitability (π), foreign share in ownership (FS), and unionization (U). Both linear and log-linear forms were tried. The results, shown in table 9.14, should be interpreted with caution, since no data on the skill characteristics of the labor force were available.

An important feature of these results is that a large portion of the wage variation in 1973 could be explained by a small number of variables. The most important were the male/female ratio, average firm size, and unionization; wages tended to be higher in industries with higher ratios of male-to-female workers, in industries composed of larger firms, and in industries with higher levels of unionization.

To further investigate the significance of the male/female ratio, another regression analysis was made, this time for wages paid in firms of similar size, in order to exclude the influence of the latter variable. The results presented in table 9.15 show clearly, especially for unskilled workers, that firms of a given size with more male workers tend to pay higher wages.

One may argue that wage differentials between male and female workers could be accounted for by skill or physical differentials. That is, male workers may tend to have higher skills or be physically stronger. There may also be other reasons that women are less productive than men. If that is the case, then it cannot be said with certainty that sex discrimination causes distortions in the labor market. However, the evidence suggests that the presence of unions does tend to distort wages.

The question of sex discrimination cannot be answered because of lack of data on skill characteristics. While further research is warranted on this issue, I do feel at this time that only part of male/female variable represents skill differences. This belief stems from the frequent observation in Thailand that unskilled female workers are paid less than unskilled male workers for similar work to an extent that cannot be fully justified by skill differences.

If, for whatever reasons, this discrimination exists, then there are implications for employment creation. Female-dominated firms, paying lower wages, dominate the exportable category. For example, the male/female ratio (MF) in spinning and weaving is 0.3, in knitting, 0.27, and in garments, 0.18. On the other hand, the male/female ratio in major importable categories is very high. For example, it is 2.39 in rubber products, 6.76 in motor vehicles, and 2.08 in paper products. Thus, the import substitution bias of the trade regime not only has encouraged the production of relatively less labor-intensive industries, it possibly has also discriminated against employment creation for women.

9.4.2 Differentials in the Price of Capital

Compared with the labor market, there are many more policy measures and other forces that may distort the price of capital. We may divide such influences into three groups: those affecting tax liability, those affecting financial capital, and those directly affecting the price of physical capital.

The differing income tax treatment of various activities under the various promotion acts distorts the price of capital to the extent that the tax is borne by capital. Tax holidays lower the average tax rate over the life of the investment, thus lowering the price of capital to promoted firms. The textile industry has been the most important recipient of promotion privileges. Other industries taking considerable advantage of these privileges in the early 1970s were chemical products, iron and steel, motor vehicles, thread and yarn, metal products, rubber tires and tubes, and household electrical goods and appliances. The extent to which promotion is selective may have resulted in differential cost advantages to these industries.

Besides tax holidays, promoted firms do receive a clear-cut subsidy through duty-free import of capital goods, thus reducing the original cost of capital goods. In general, duties on capital goods have been much lower than those imposed on consumer goods and intermediate imports at higher levels of fabrication. Therefore, in relative terms, tariff rates increase the price of capital goods less than that of other goods. On the other hand, I believe that the currency was mildly overvalued in 1973 (see discussion in section 9.1). If this is true, the price of capital goods would have been lower because of this overvaluation, and capital-intensive industries would have been generally favored.

Finally, there is really no effective subsidization of financial capital in Thailand except the rediscount facility at the Bank of Thailand. The most important sources of financial capital are the commercial banks.

Table 9.14   Determination of Wages of Unskilled and Skilled Workers: Regression Results, 1973

Dependent Variable	Form of Equation	Intercept	Market Power (MP)	Foreign Share (FS)	Wage Share (WS)	Profitability (π)
W_u	linear	1770.3	−68.598 (−1.33)	2.397 (.079)	249.713 (2.792)*	.036 (.769)
W_s	linear	12074.1	−161.312 (−1.713)***	15.317 (.276)	228.721 (1.397)	.154 (1.784)
W_u	linear	4271.1				−.015 (−.281)
W_u	linear	4638.1				.059 (1.136)
W_s	linear	14298.0				.074 (.837)
W_u	log-linear	4.192	−.293 (−1.603)	.028 (.735)	.209 (1.731)***	−.272 (−2.677)**
W_s	log-linear	6.066	−.318 (−1.876)***	.061 (1.711)***	.046 (.414)	−.189 (−2.014)***
W_s	log-linear	8.187				−.105 (−1.098)
W_u	log-linear	8.130				.003 (.025)
W_s	log-linear	8.862				−.058 (−.647)

Source: Akrasanee and Chutikul (1977).

Note: W_u = unskilled wages; W_s = skilled wages; MP = the share of gross output originating from the largest producer in the industry; FS = percentage of the industry equity contributed by nonresidents; WS = wage share in total cost; π = profit per employee; VA = value added per employee; LT = number of employees who left employment in percentage of total employees; AFS = average sale volume; MF = ratio of male to female unskilled workers; $NLVA$ = nonwage value added per employee; U = percentage of total employees that are union members.

*$p < .01$.
**$p < .05$.
***$p < .10$.

The interest rates charged vary from about 10.5 percent for "big regular customers" to about 14 percent for small-scale firms. No clear differential exists along industry lines; differential access to finance most likely exists between firms of different sizes, although quantitative evidence cannot be presented because there are problems of disclosure. Small firms whose credit-worthiness is in question resort either to finance companies or to sources outside the organized sector, both of which usually charge considerably higher rates.

Productivity (VA)	Labor Turnover (LT)	Average Firm Size (AFS, or AFS^2)	Male-Female Ratio (MF)	Capital Intensity (NLVA)	Unionization (U)	R^2
.046 (1.285)	369.289 (1.032)	6.558 (.432)	210.744 (4.480)*			.822
.021 (−.263)	1724.95 (1.104)	.944 (.101)	442.119 (5.136)*			.756
		9.33 (1.906)***	212.54 (4.918)*	.067 (1.251)	94.091 (2.315)**	.762
		10.243 (1.838)***	208.893 (4.285)*	.007 (.132)		.698
		1.913 (.244)	389.343 (5.640)*	.001 (.012)	135.443 (2.086)**	.739
.703 (3.105)*	.021 (.129)	.104 (1.115)	.188 (2.567)**			.764
.531 (2.529)**	.226 (1.471)	.133 (1.522)	.217 (3.199)*			.766
		.155 (1.779)***	.301 (5.697)*	.088 (.866)	.140 (8.046)*	.723
		.185 (1.799)***	.316 (5.062)*	.004 (−.032)		.591
		.126 (1.538)	.269 (5.409)*	.065 (.679)	.128 (2.937)*	.715

All the forces described above indicate that the price of capital tends to be lower than the "market equilibrium" price, although I have not found it possible to measure the difference. But, if this distortion exists, it is probably not very large, for funds are allowed to move rather freely in and out of the country, and trade is not restricted, as I explained earlier. My assessment is therefore that small firms pay the scarcity price of capital, whereas larger firms and promoted firms pay somewhat lower prices.

Table 9.15   Regression Results of Wage Determination by Firm Size, 1973

Dependent Variable	Intercept	Male Female Ratio	Nonwage Value Added (per Employee)	R^2
W^1_s	7,741.3	205.874 (2.071)***	.047 (.071)	.251
W^2_s	10,720.9	554.115 (1.535)	.026 (.586)	.152
W^3_s	11,816.8	361.728 (.615)	.047 (2.17)**	.233
W^4_s	8,927.2	614.833 (6.991)*	.137 (3.407)*	.729
W^5_s	20,034	1060.82 (1.764)***	.039 (1.251)	.291
W^1_u	3,251.38	118.373 (2.495)**	.045 (1.332)	.361
W^2_u	3,931.08	559.404 (2.625)**	−.011 (.025)	.269
W^3_u	4,796.09	313.816 (1.862)***	.024 (3.790)*	.523
W^4_u	3,910.92	313.631 (8.511)*	.067 (4.019)*	.797
W^5_u	10,143.9	797.207 (2.941)*	−.002 (−1.668)	.406

Source: Akrasanee and Chutikul (1977).
Note: W^i_s, W^i_u: average wage by industry for skilled and unskilled workers respectively in firms size i, where i is in terms of number of employees as follows: $i = 1$: 10 employees and less; $i = 2$: 11–19 employees; $i = 3$: 20–49 employees.
*$p < .01$.
**$p < .05$.
***$p < .10$.

9.4.3   Factor Prices, Labor Intensities, and Effective Protection

From the analysis above, we can tentatively conclude that there is a small degree of distortion in both labor and capital markets. In general, larger, male-intensive firms tend to pay higher wages than smaller, female-dominated firms. Benefits due to various capital market distortions have accrued to larger promoted firms. Thus the rental rate of capital probably is lower for these activities than for small-scale industries. Both sets of distortions seem to favor capital utilization in larger, male-dominated, and promoted firms, most of which produce importables. On the other hand, smaller, female-dominated, exportable firms probably tend to minimize the use of capital and use even more labor than if labor markets were not distorted.

One would also expect a positive relationship between levels of protection and capital utilization. As a crude test of this hypothesis, I regressed value added per employee, both direct and total (as a measure of capital intensity) upon the rate of effective protection. The results, given below, indicate that this relationship exists for the direct value added equation but not when home goods are included. Therefore, on the whole, the results suggest, at least weakly, that trade policy is biased toward capital-intensive industries and to that extent has hindered employment creation in Thailand.

(1) $\qquad VA/L = 39.81 + 2.782ERP \qquad R^2 = .136$
$$(.112) \qquad\qquad t = 2.47,$$

(2) $\qquad VAT/L = 30.26 + .06782ERP \qquad R^2 = .059$
$$(.0453) \qquad\qquad t = 1.50.$$

To summarize, my analysis tends to support the notion that factor market distortions are antiemployment for large-scale, capital-intensive, male-intensive industries and proemployment for small-scale, female-intensive industries. Second, the trade regime has a tendency to be anti-employment, since the ERP varies directly with the value added per worker ratio. Probably the latter effect is more important than factor market distortion.

9.5 Conclusion

Based on the foregoing analysis, the effects of trade policies on employment in Thailand may be summed up as follows: First, the policy of promoting manufactured exports, especially exports that are non-NRB related, is generally favorable to employment. Second, the employment pattern of production and trade is consistent with the known factor endowment. Third, there is a positive, though not strong, relationship between the degree of capital intensity of production and effective rates of protection. Protection tends to protect importables with higher capital intensity, whereas labor-intensive exportables receive lower or negative protection.

Since the strategy of export promotion has been found to be more employment-creating, the continued practice of import substitution has meant that employment is being created at higher cost, ceteris paribus, and that more employment could have been generated with an export oriented strategy. However, the bias in the incentive system has not been strong enough to reverse the pattern of factor intensity of production and trade from that predicted on the basis of factor endowments.

Two areas of policy implications regarding trade strategy for employment growth may be distinguished: the overall trade strategy and the incentives policy. If employment creation is one of the major development objectives, then the strategy of export promotion would create employment at lower cost. An export promotion strategy also means that less protection would be given to importable production. These goods would have to be more competitive and, as I have shown, "competitive" importables are more labor-intensive than "protected" importables; they also would create more employment than a policy of continued adherence to protecting capital-intensive importables.

Factor market policies aimed at employment promotion should seek to reduce wage/rental ratios facing capital-intensive, large-scale industries. This could be done by eliminating duty-free imports of capital, eliminating tax holidays, and subsidizing wages. This, in effect, would mean a change in the promotional activities of the Board of Investment. For labor-intensive industries, especially small-scale industries and firms, the wage/rental ratios facing them are already proemployment. But these ratios have been found to be too low in the sense that small entrepreneurs tend to pay lower wages, while they themselves are exposed to high capital charges (Sa-nguanruang and Tamboonlertchai 1976). If this is the case, higher mobility in the labor and capital markets would raise the wage rate of these workers and lower the price of capital for small-scale industries. Such changes might reduce employment per firm but increase the number of viable firms more than enough to compensate the lower labor intensity effect.

Trade policies have to be directed toward encouraging labor-intensive activities. This could be done by eliminating high protection afforded "protected" importables and by setting protection at uniform rates for all activities. Furthermore, exports might be directly encouraged through subsidization, or at least the elimination of controls on prices and production. The net result of these policies would be an increase in the employment generation capabilities of Thailand's manufacturing sector. This result is vital, given the increasingly difficult problems of finding employment for its rapidly growing urban labor force.

Notes

1. See Ingram (1971) and Sondysuvan (1975) for more detailed descriptions of Thailand's economic development.
2. SITC refers to Standard International Trade Classification, and ISIC refers to International Standard Industrial Classification.
3. The ISIC treats processed food, beverages and tobacco as manufactures; the SITC does not.
4. The remaining imports are classified as "other," which in fact is a very important group because it includes major items such as passenger cars, buses and trucks, and crude oil.
5. This section and the more detailed discussion in section 9.2 are adapted from Akrasanee (1977).

6. The name was later changed to National Economic and Social Development Board.

7. See Akrasanee (1973) for a discussion of that period. The system of taxation in use in the 1970s, which is basically similar to that of the 1960s, is discussed in section 9.2.

8. Tariff rates were increased both to provide additional protection and for revenue and balance of payments reasons; see Akrasanee (1975).

9. National Executive Council Decrees nos. 227 and 329, Bangkok, 1972.

10. After March 1978, the value of the baht was linked to a basket of currencies replacing the earlier fixed parity with the United States dollar.

11. The rice premium, an export surcharge on rice, is used to stabilize the domestic price of rice. Therefore the premium rate is adjusted according to the changing world price of rice. For the most comprehensive history of the rice premium, see Siamwalla (1975). The sugar export surcharge was introduced in 1974, when the world price of sugar was very high, to tax the profits of exporters. The rates are based on a sliding scale with a minimum level below which the rate is zero. In 1977, when the world price of sugar became very low, the surcharge was therefore zero.

12. The term "subsidize" here means only the tax-refund or tax-exemption measures of the ministry.

13. The ministry maintains an ad hoc list of goods under export and import controls, and the list is changed from time to time. In 1973 the import control list and export control list included thirty-five and seventeen items, respectively. In most cases the control is for the purpose of inspecting the goods. See discussion below for details on these controls.

14. Usually changes in tariff rates are made for a few items each year. These changes are announced by the Ministry of Finance and are published in the Bank of Thailand *Monthly Bulletin.*

15. Another interpretation is that the balance of payments deficit was used as a pretext for tariff adjustments that were demanded by domestic producers before the deficit.

16. Most exports are exempt from the business tax. For more detail on the computation of taxes, see Akrasanee (1973).

17. For example, to request tariff protection from the Ministry of Finance, to request restriction on entry of new firms from the Ministry of Industry, and so forth.

18. National Executive Council Decree no. 227, Bangkok, 1972.

19. Information from the Ministry of Commerce.

20. The 1973 coefficients became available later, but I did not recalculate the ERPs.

21. The general formula for the calculation of ERP is given in the introductory chapter. The formula used in this study is from Akrasanee (1973).

22. See Balassa et al. (1971) for more discussion of potential and realized protection. See also Akrasanee (1973) for more detail on the method of calculation for Thailand.

23. With tax exemption and tax refund, output and inputs are valued at their border prices, resulting in domestic value added in the industry approximately equaling the IVA. Note also that in export industries, assuming that producers entitled to tax exemption and tax refund in their export sales claim their privileges, potential rates and realized rates are equal.

24. This was also true for promoted firms, because they were entitled to only one-third of rebates.

25. These requirements were also calculated per unit of nonwage value added. But since the results lead to the same conclusion, they are not reported here.

26. The 1971 I-O table of the National Economic and Social Development Board (NESDB) is still in preliminary stage. I have therefore not used it for other calculations in this study. The national income account statistics are from the NESDB. The electricity and water supply authorities are the Electricity Generating Authority of Thailand, the Metropolitan Electricity Authority, the Provincial Electricity Authority, and the Metropolitan Water Supply Authority. For more detail on the data used, see Akrasanee and Chintayarangsan (1976).

27. See Krueger (1977a, b) and the introductory chapter for details on this argument.

References

Akrasanee, Narongchai. 1973. The structure of industrial protection in Thailand during the 1960s. *Economic Bulletin for Asia and the Far East* 24, no. 2/3:36–56.

———. 1975. *The structure of effective protection in Thailand: A study of industrial and trade policies in the early 1970s.* Report prepared for the World Bank. Washington, D.C.: World Bank.

———. 1977. Industrialization and trade policies and employment effects in Thailand. In *Trade and employment in Asia and the Pacific*, ed. Narongchai Akrasanee et al. Honolulu: University of Hawaii Press.

Akrasanee, Narongchai, and Chintayarangsan, Rachain. 1976. *Factor proportions in trade.* CAMS Discussion Papers. Manila: Council for Asian Manpower Studies.

Akrasanee, Narongchai, and Chutikul, Siri-laksana. 1977. Wage differentials in manufacturing industries. Mimeographed. Bangkok: Thammasat University.

Akrasanee, Narongchai, and Wattananukit, Atchana. 1976. Comparative advantage in rice production in Thailand. *Food Research Institute Studies* 15:177–212.

Bacha, Edmar, and Taylor, Lance. 1971. Foreign exchange shadow prices: A critical review of current theories. *Quarterly Journal of Economics* 85:197–224.

Balassa, Bela, et al. 1971. *The structure of protection in developing countries.* Baltimore: Johns Hopkins University Press.

Bank of Thailand. 1976. *Annual report, 1976.* Bangkok.

———. Various years. *Monthly bulletin.* Bangkok.

Board of Investment. 1959. *Brief information concerning investment in Thailand.* Bangkok: State Lottery Printing Press.

———. 1971. *Investors manual.* Bangkok: Board of Investment.

Corden, W. M. 1967. The exchange rate system and the taxation of trade. In *Thailand: Social and economic studies in development*, ed. T. H. Silcook. Canberra: Australian National University Press.

Customs Department. Various years. *Customs tariff and business tax.* Bangkok: Ministry of Finance.

Ingram, James C. 1971. *Economic change in Thailand, 1850–1970.* Stanford: Stanford University Press.

Krueger, Anne O. 1977a. *Alternative trade strategies and employment— Plan of research for country studies.* NBER Working Paper no. 164. New York: NBER.

———. 1977b. *Growth, distortions, and patterns of trade among many countries.* Princeton Studies in International Finance no. 40. Princeton: Princeton University.

Marzouk, Girgis A. 1972. *Economic development policy: Case study of Thailand.* Amsterdam: Rotterdam University Press.

National Economic and Social Development Board. 1963. *First national economic and social development plan, 1961–1966.* Bangkok.

———. 1968. *Second national economic and social development plan.* Bangkok.

National Statistical Office. 1971. Manufacturing survey of greater Bangkok area, 1971. Worksheet.

Sa-nguanruang, Sang, and Tamboonlertchai, Samsak. 1976. *Small and medium scale industries in Thailand.* Report. Bangkok: Industrial Finance Corporation of Thailand.

Siamwalla, Ammar. 1975. A history of rice policies in Thailand. *Food Research Institute Studies* 14:233–48.

Silcock, T. H. 1967. *Thailand: Social and economic studies in development.* Canberra: Australian National University Press.

Sondysuvan, Prateep, ed. 1975. *Finance, trade and economic development in Thailand.* Bangkok: Sompong Press.

Wibulswasdi, C., et al. 1979. Effective exchange rates and equilibrium exchange rates for baht. Mimeographed. Bangkok.

Yang, Shu-chin. 1957. *A multiple exchange rate system: An appraisal of Thailand's experience, 1946–1955.* Madison: University of Wisconsin Press.

10 Alternative Trade Policies and Employment in Tunisia

Mustapha K. Nabli

Tunisia is a relatively small North African country that gained independence from France in 1956.[1] Since independence, it has had two distinct phases in its trade policies. In the 1960s it followed a clear import substitution policy that, while resulting in a significant degree of industrial development, contributed little to employment generation. In the 1970s it has reversed its policy direction, liberalizing trade and providing some support for exports with the explicit goal of increasing employment opportunities. These two phases of trade policies, coupled with a trade pattern oriented almost exclusively toward Europe, make Tunisia a relatively uncomplicated and interesting case study of the relationships between trade strategies and employment.

The focal year for my analysis is 1972. The reasons for this choice are two. The first is data availability, especially the existence of an input-output (I-O) table and a census of manufactures allowing us to estimate factor requirements of trade.[2] The second is that 1972 is a transition year between the import substitution and export promotion policies. As described below, the trade regime begins to change in 1969, and by mid-1972 policies promoting exports were instituted. However, at the time this study was undertaken, relevant data for a careful appraisal of the export promotion policies were not available. My results must there-

Mustapha K. Nabli is associated with the Faculté de Droit et des Sciences Politiques et Economiques, Tunis.

This work has greatly benefited from the advice, encouragement, and many comments of Anne O. Krueger, director of the project. Hal Lary's reviews and comments were also of great help in improving the style and content of this study. I am also indebted to Dr. Mondher Gargouri for help and encouragement in carrying out this research. Part of the work was done while I was visiting at the Centrum voor Economische Studien, Katholieke Universiteit, at Louvain, Belgium, and I am grateful for their support.

fore be viewed as providing a picture of factor proportions under an import substitution regime, with only a glimpse at the sort of potential that export promotion may have.

10.1 Overview of the Tunisian Economy

10.1.1 Growth and Structure

At independence, Tunisia had all the characteristics of a colonial, less developed country. Gross domestic product (GDP) per capita was 70 dinars (1957 prices), or U.S. $170.[3] Agriculture was the predominant activity, employing the bulk (57 percent) of the labor force and generating one-third of GDP. Agriculture had a dualistic structure: modern, highly productive agriculture remained in the hands of the colonials, while traditional agriculture, carried out on less fertile land, occupied most of the Tunisian population. Manufacturing (mainly food processing) was relatively unimportant. It employed about 8 percent of the labor force and generated less than 2 percent of GDP. The economy was open, with the ratio of imports to GDP varying around 30 percent. Trade was centered upon France, the former colonial power, which provided three-fourths of its imports and absorbed slightly more than half of its exports. The major exports were minerals (of which phosphates made up half), wines, and olive oil.

Economic policy in the early years of independence (1956–61) was characterized by a laissez-faire, noninterventionist approach. Real GDP increased at an irregular and moderate rate, with an annual average of 3.7 percent or 1.6 percent per capita. This slow rate of growth, coupled with a rapid deceleration of capital accumulation and an acceleration in population growth,[4] motivated a policy shift in 1961. Centralized economic planning was adopted as a basic framework for conducting economic policy, and a ten-year perspective plan and a three-year medium-term plan[5] were introduced. A major aim of economic policy became the reduction of Tunisia's economic dependence upon foreign conditions; this was to be accomplished primarily by promoting import substitution activities. Accompanying these changes was an increase in the government's role in the economy. Most economic activities became, directly or indirectly, regulated by the government. These policies were in turn abruptly abandoned in September 1969 after the emergence of strong resistance to the extension of the cooperative system of agriculture. The new policy that has evolved since 1970 places more reliance upon the market system and attempts to minimize the direct role of government, which remains, however, the main economic agent and still controls most economic activity.

Table 10.1 gives values for total and per capita GNP and industrial output for selected years since 1961. For the periods 1962–65, 1966–69

Table 10.1   Selected Economic Indicators, 1961–75

Year	Real GNP (Millions of Dinars)[a]	Real Industrial Output[b] (Millions of Dinars)[a]	Population (Thousands)	Real GNP per Capita (Dinars)[a]
1961	425.9	67.7	3,970	107.3
1965	521.5	86.4	4,438	117.5
1969	610.5	116.0	4,867	125.4
1972	883.4	151.6	5,216	169.4
1975	1,079.0	199.8	5,577	193.5

Sources: Real GNP and real industrial output: Ministry of Planning, unpublished sources; population: author's estimates based upon interpolation of results of 1956, 1966, and 1975 censuses.
[a]In 1966 dinars.
[b]Industry includes food processing (except olive oil, wines, and several other small activities), utilities, manufacturing (except petroleum refinery), mining (except crude oil), and construction.

and 1970–75, the growth rates of real GNP averaged 5.2, 4.1 and 10.1 percent. The slowdown in the growth rate from 1961 to 1969 and its acceleration again after 1970 are explained to a large extent by the behavior of agricultural output, which was affected by a series of drought years in 1966–68 and good rainfall afterward. Industrial output grew more steadily, with average rates of 6.3, 7.8, and 9.6 percent for the respective three periods. Annual per capita GNP growth rates for the same periods were 3.0, 1.7, and 7.6 percent. From 1961 to 1975, real GNP per capita increased by about 80 percent and reached 194 dinars, or about U.S. $460, in 1975.

Significant changes in the structure of economic activity accompanied this growth. The average share of agriculture and food processing in GDP decreased from 27.5 percent in 1962–65 to 22.2 percent in 1966–69 and 23.0 percent in 1970–75. The share of manufacturing in GNP rose from 3.4 percent to 5.3 and 6.2 percent, respectively. The new industries of tourism and petroleum became significant, with shares about 3.5 percent each in the early 1970s.

These structural changes in the Tunisian economy were due in part to the major role played by the government in increasing the rate of capital accumulation. Direct investment by government, including social overhead and other direct investment in agriculture, transportation, and services, constituted about 36–40 percent of total investment during 1961–69 but declined after the policy shift of 1970 to 19 percent in 1973 and 1975. In addition to direct government investment, investment by public firms, which in 1961 accounted for 22 percent of total gross fixed capital formation, rose to 46 percent in 1965 but declined afterward. The share of investment undertaken by private firms and households declined from 37 percent in 1961 to 17 percent in 1965 but has been increasing since and reached 50 percent in 1973 and 47 percent in 1975. This direct control by the government allowed it to determine, to a large extent, the sectoral allocation of investment. Emphasis was placed during the 1960s on the development of infrastructure and social overhead. Investment in manufacturing also increased considerably, reaching more than 19 percent of total investment in 1965 when some major projects were being carried out in the metallurgy and mechanical industries.

Money stock growth was moderate in Tunisia by other developing countries' standards. Money stock M1 increased at a compound annual rate of 7.5 percent between 1960 and 1970 and accelerated to 21.3 percent for 1970–75, while the figures for M2 were 9.7 percent and 21.6 percent, respectively. Major reasons for the acceleration of money growth after 1970 are an acceleration of real GNP growth on the demand side and substantial increases in foreign reserves on the supply side. The Central Bank has almost complete control over the money stock, essentially through the discount window and quantitative regulation of credit. There is practically no money market, and monetary authorities regulate to a large extent the portfolio of the banks as well as all interest rates.

With respect to fiscal policy, the ratio of taxes to GNP has remained almost constant at about 20 percent during 1960–75. Indirect taxes make up about three-fourths of total taxes (excluding petroleum royalties). Major taxes are a production tax retained by the producer, a consumption tax on "luxury goods," and import taxes. Various taxes on imports including duties were about 50 percent of total indirect taxes in 1975.

The only reliable information on income distribution is on the distribution of expenditure from household surveys. From surveys for 1965–68 and 1975 it appears that the proportion of total expenditure accruing to the poorest 20 percent of the households was 6.3 percent and did not change. However, the proportion accruing to the richest 20 percent was 49.5 percent in 1965–68 and about 43 percent in 1975 (35 percent and 28 percent for the richest decile). These figures show a fairly unequal distribution of expenditure in spite of some improvement during the decade 1965–75. The poorest segment of the population has a very low income compared with the richest: for instance, the expenditure per year per person of the 25 percent poorest is lower than 66 dinars, while that of the 25 percent richest is higher than 210 dinars in 1975 and the average is 147 dinars.

10.1.2   The Trade Regime

During the early independence years, 1956 to 1958, Tunisia remained aligned with the French franc zone, and the colonial system remained almost entirely in effect, with a formal customs union agreement with France and Algeria. The first step in the emergence of a Tunisian foreign exchange regime was taken in September 1958 with the creation of a Tunisian Central Bank and a national currency (the dinar) pegged to the French franc. Soon after, the French franc was devalued. Tunisia decided not to devalue the dinar for considerations of political sovereignty and in the naive belief that the exceptionally good performance of exports in 1958 would continue. Exchange control was extended to relations with France, and a new tariff code was promulgated with a structure designed to discourage imports of finished and "nonessential" consumer goods. Tariff rates were generally low, averaging less than 10 percent for intermediate goods and equipment, 28 percent for food products, and 20 percent for other consumer goods.

The balance of payments situation worsened after 1958 (see table 10.2). Quantitative restrictions (QRs) were introduced to limit imports while maintaining a fixed exchange rate. The administrative control system depended on the category of the import and its origin.[6]

The trade deficits in the early 1960s resulted from several factors: the de facto revaluation of the dinar with respect to the franc in 1958, a series of bad harvests, and increased imports of capital goods resulting from the ambitious industrialization program that was adopted when planning began in 1961–62. The balance of payments difficulties led naturally to the following reinforcements of foreign exchange control within the existing framework: imposition (in November 1961) of guarantee deposits on imports[7] and of quotas on imports of some products

Table 10.2   **Balance of Payments, 1958–75 (Values in Millions of Current Dinars)**

	1958	1961	1965	1969	1972	1975
Imports	64.9	108.2	168.0	180.3	282.9	629.7
(as percentage of GNP)	(23.3)	(30.6)	(32.5)	(27.2)	(26.4)	(36.2)
Exports of goods and services	64.4	73.2	99.1	149.9	270.6	545.6
Net transfers	8.5	2.3	−10.8	−19.8	− 8.5	− 5.9
Current account balance	37.2	−32.7	−79.7	−50.2	−20.2	−90.0
Long- and medium-term capital flows	−.4	22.0	77.5	59.6	66.5	78.7
Changes in reserves	8.0	− 7.9	− 4.4	9.8	37.7	−11.1
Net gold and foreign exchange reserve holdings	39.0	30.7	− 6.7	− 2.1	92.9	146.2

Source: 1961–75, Ministry of Planning, unpublished national accounts; 1958, IMF *International Financial Statistics*.

from France (in 1962); introduction of a requirement to repatriate exchange receipts from service exports; and reinforcement of administrative restrictions on almost all imports. Despite these measures, balance of payments difficulties persisted, and in 1964 the dinar was devalued by 25 percent,[8] with some measures of liberalization. But liberalization did not proceed very far.

The period 1965–69 was characterized by the development of very tight and comprehensive exchange control. The import controls were part of an increasingly centralized economic system where licensing was the dominant feature along with price controls. The approval of import licenses was also centralized, as all had to be approved by the Direction de Commerce and the Central Bank. This phase ended in 1969–70 with the fall of the government that pursued the increasingly interventionist policies.

The present government economic policy is characterized by greater reliance on markets. New procedures were introduced to encourage imports, and a new tariff code was introduced in 1973.[9] The relaxation of administrative controls led to decreasing quantitative restrictions and elimination of most shortages. It appears that premiums on import licenses have fallen sharply since 1970, especially for food products and consumer manufactures.[10] This liberalization policy, however, did not completely do away with QRs. Imports still have to be licensed, the exchange rate is thought to be overvalued, and balance of payment deficits are chronic.[11]

Until 1972 there were no systematic policies to encourage exports, and currency overvaluation served as a deterrent. A number of ad hoc measures existed in the 1960s to promote exports such as a reduction of one percentage point in the discount rate for export-related commercial paper. The only consistent feature of export policy was the decision to increase domestic processing of primary products previously exported as raw materials (phosphate, lead, and alfa).[12] In 1972 new legislation was enacted to promote exports and to attract direct foreign investment. These new measures provide a number of benefits to export-oriented industries, such as duty-free entry of intermediate and capital goods and various other tax exemptions.

Tunisian authorities have made little use of the exchange rate instrument. With the exception of the 1964 devaluation, changes in the exchange rate came about mostly through effective revaluation of the dinar when foreign currencies were devalued, such as the franc in 1970 and the dollar in 1971. Inflation was relatively mild over the period studied, averaging about 3.8 percent annually from 1961 to 1973 and 11.3 percent from 1974 to 1977. Thus, given the relative stability of the official nominal rate, the price level deflated rate decreased by about 26 percent between 1965 and 1971 and 46 percent between 1965 and 1974. The purchasing power parity nominal exchange rate (PPP-NER) decreased by 10.7 percent between 1965 and 1971. It increased afterward and in 1974 was slightly higher than the 1965 rate (see table 10.3). During the intensive development of the import control system and the import substitution policy, therefore, the exchange rate increasingly favored importers and penalized exporters.

Moreover, during this period tariff rates and taxes remained stable. Minor changes occurred only in 1973. Therefore, effective exchange rates (EERs) exclusive of premiums on imports essentially reflect changes in the nominal exchange rate. The evolution of EERs for import commodity categories is shown in table 10.3, where no account is taken of QRs in their calculation. For exports, there was little difference between nominal and effective rates, so the PPP-NER can be taken as the export PPP-EER. It is clear that imports fall into two major categories: consumer goods, which have high EERs, and intermediate and capital goods. Effective exchange rates were not calculated for exports, since they have been very close to the official rate.

Table 10.3   Nominal and Effective Exchange Rates, 1961–75

	1961	1965	1969	1972	1975
Official rates					
Dinars per 10 francs	.850	1.063	1.010	.946	.943
Dinars per U.S. dollar	.420	.525	.525	.420	.423
PLD-NER[a]					
Dinar/franc rate	1.024	1.073	.931	.779	.584
PPP-NER[b]					
Dinar/franc rate	.912	1.049	1.005	.965	1.011
EERs[c] (dinars per 10 francs)					
Foodstuffs	1.229	1.537	1.460	1.368	1.345[d]
Consumer manufactures	1.125	1.407	1.337	1.253	1.236[d]
Industrial equipment	.957	1.197	1.137	1.065	1.029[d]
Agricultural equipment	.915	1.144	1.087	1.018	.973[d]
Intermediate products	.962	1.203	1.143	1.071	1.039[d]
Energy products	.952	1.191	1.131	1.060	1.031[d]

Source: Nabli (1978).
[a]Official rate divided by GDP deflator.
[b]PLD-NER multiplied by the wholesale price index of industrial products in France (1966 = 100).
[c]Calculated as $EER_j = OR \ (1 + t_j + t_j \cdot T_j)$, where $OR =$ the official exchange rate; $t_j =$ tariff rate on import category j; $T_j =$ indirect tax rate of import category j. (Indirect taxes are levied on imports valued inclusive of tariffs, and the term $t_j \cdot T$ accounts for differential taxation on imports relative to domestic production.)
[d]Refers to 1974.

10.1.3   International Trade and the Tunisian Economy

As described above, a major aim of economic policy in the 1960s was to reduce the dependence of the Tunisian economy on foreign conditions. This explains the choice of the import substitution policy as a means of reducing imports in the face of uncertain foreign exchange receipts from exports of primary products. However, the massive effort at industrialization and development of infrastructure resulted in a rapid increase of imports, particularly capital and intermediate goods. The economy remained highly open, with imports averaging about 30 percent of GNP, and the current account deficit remained high until 1967, ranging between 10 and 15 percent of GNP. During 1968–73, the import substitution policy and foreign exchange controls had the effect ot reducing the ratio of imports to GNP to about 26 percent, but this ratio rose very fast again in 1974 and 1975. The ratio of the current account deficit to GNP, however, dropped significantly—and it seems permanently—to less than 7 percent after 1967.

A sizable part of the investment effort was financed through external borrowing and foreign aid. The foreign capital inflow also served to offset partially the increasing trade deficit, as is evident in table 10.2. Foreign capital inflows were mainly grants and long-to-medium-term official aid loans. Private commercial loans and direct foreign investment were small during most of the period. Despite these capital receipts, the net gold and foreign exchange position deteriorated dramatically from 1961 to 1967, reaching a negative position of 21 million dinars. The reserve situation has improved since then, and export revenue, tourism, and workers' remittances from abroad have increased.

The direction of Tunisia's trade has not changed significantly since independence. About 80 percent of exports are destined for developed countries, mainly France and the EEC, while 85 percent of imports originate in developed countries, again mainly the EEC.

On the other hand, the structure of Tunisia's trade has changed since the introduction of import substitution policies in the early 1960s. As one would expect, the share of manufactured consumer goods and foodstuffs in total imports fell from 50 to 35 percent from 1961 to 1969. Since then, they have stabilized at about 30–32 percent. The relative share of intermediate capital goods rose from 40 to 56 percent of total imports in the same period and has stayed at that level. On the export side, from 1961 to 1975 the share of foodstuffs and minerals (excluding crude oil) fell from about 80 percent to less than 35 percent as industries were developed to process materials previously exported raw. Oil exports became a major foreign-exchange earner in the late sixties and now generate more than one-third of Tunisia's export earnings. The share of manufactured exports increased steadily throughout the period, with most growth occurring in processed minerals. From 1961 to 1975, the share of manufactured exports including processed minerals in total exports rose from 17 to 21 percent; excluding processed minerals, the share rose from about 4 percent to 11 percent in the same period. However, most of the increase in the share of manufactured exports came after 1971 (in 1971, their share was only 6 percent).

A comparison of export growth rates from 1961 to 1969 and 1970 to 1975 highlights the different emphases of the trade policies in each period. From 1961 to 1969, all exports grew at an annual rate of about 9 percent. If crude oil is excluded, the annual average was about 5 percent; manufactured exports rose from a small base at an annual rate of about 20 percent. Comparable average annual growth rates of exports from 1970 to 1975 were 35 percent (all exports), 28 percent (excluding oil), and 32 percent (manufactures).

Table 10.4 shows the structure of merchandise trade by trade category (discussed below in section 10.3) for 1972, my reference year.[13] Observe that HOS goods constituted 75 percent of total imports, of which

Table 10.4   **Structure of Foreign Trade by Trade Category, 1972
(Thousands of Dinars)**

	Imports, c.i.f.		Exports, f.o.b.	
Trade Category	Value	%	Value	%
Exports	16,792	7.6	139,684	91.6
HOS (excluding refined oil)	3,867	1.7	37,026	24.3
NRB mining (including crude oil)	7,917	3.6	53,976	35.4
NRB agriculture and related food processing	682	0.3	46,743	30.7
Refined oil	4,326	2.0	1,939	1.2
HOS imports	66,455	30.0	4,888	3.2
Foods[a]	9,335	4.2	158	0.1
Manufactured consumer goods	16,517	7.4	3,454	2.3
Intermediate goods[b]	24,115	10.8	1,108	0.7
Capital goods	16,488	7.4	168	0.1
NRB imports (agriculture and marble)	19,483	8.7	2,375	1.5
Noncompeting imports	116,885	52.0	—	—
HOS[c]	101,175	45.0	—	—
NRB	15,710	7.0	—	—
Other sectors (sectors classified as home goods, handicrafts, miscellaneous)	2,665	1.2	5,449	3.6
Total	222,280	100.0	152,397	100.0

Source: Nabli (1978).
[a]Includes soybean oil.
[b]Includes linseed oil.
[c]Including sectors listed in the input-output table but having no domestic production; i.e., codes 40, 114, 140, and 164.

imports directly competing with Tunisian production were 30 percent and noncompeting imports were 45 percent. NRB imports formed 16 percent of total imports, and the remaining imports came from activities classified as export sectors. Competing imports were dominated by manufactured consumer goods and intermediate products, but capital goods were also significant. On the export side, NRB products made up two-thirds of total exports versus 24 percent for HOS products (the remaining exports came from import-competing activities). HOS exports were, for the most part, related to NRB production—for example, phosphoric acid and fertilizers (based on phosphates) and steel and lead (based on iron ore and lead mining).

10.1.4   Factor Markets

As I mentioned above, Tunisia is one of the many developing countries that, at the time of gaining independence, had a very sizable proportion of the economically active population engaged in agriculture and a fairly rapid rate of population growth. In 1956, 57 percent were in the agricultural sector, and the rate of population growth was over 2 percent and rising. It averaged 2.8 percent over the decade 1956–66 and 2.3 percent from 1966 to 1975. During that period there was significant out-migration of Tunisians to Europe and Libya in search of employment. Since these persons are not counted in the Tunisian population, the growth rate (and rate of growth of the labor force) is understated. Thus, Tunisia must foster rapid growth of employment opportunities in nonagricultural sectors if the growing numbers in the labor force are to be employed. The urban population has been growing at an average annual rate of about 3.5 percent.

A lack of data on wages and characteristics of the labor force makes detailed analysis of the labor market in Tunisia difficult. Nonetheless, available statistics suggest that, in spite of a fairly rapid rate of growth of manufacturing employment and sizable out-migration of workers (estimated to be 5 to 10 percent of the labor force), the problem of urban unemployment is fairly severe. The official statistics put the total rate at about 14 percent in 1975, and the urban rate was even higher with respect to the male population.

Manufacturing employment grew from 33,400 in 1961 to 106,300 in 1975. This represented an employment elasticity with respect to value added in manufacturing of 0.8 as manufacturing value added rose at an average rate of 10.4 percent annually.[14]

There appear to have been distortions in the labor market between manufacturing sectors in Tunisia, which are analyzed in section 10.4.1 of this chapter. However, an overall minimum wage does not appear to have been binding in Tunisia, and the significant distortion appears to have been between the public and the private sectors. Table 10.5 gives data on the labor force, manufacturing employment, urban and rural minimum real wages, and the average real wage over the period 1960 to 1975. As can be seen, average real wages, based on 1966 = 100, did not rise even 5 percent over the entire period 1963 to 1973. The ratio of the urban to the rural wage fell from 1 to 0.8 over the same period, which is consistent with the notion that migration from rural to urban areas reduced the wage differential and simultaneously prevented significant increases in the real wage in an undistorted (unskilled) labor market. Thus, it does not appear that high and rising wages have been a major factor in private labor markets in Tunisia, and observed labor coefficients in the private sector were probably the outcome of cost minimization on the part of firms facing market-determined wage rates. To

Table 10.5   **Labor Market Indicators in Tunisia**

	Labor Force (Thousands) (1)	Manufacturing Employment (Thousands) (2)	Real Minimum Wage (1966 = 100)		Average Real Industrial Wage (1966 = 100) (4)
			Industry (3a)	Agriculture (3b)	
1960	—	—	102	92	—
1961	—	33.4	105	91	88
1962	—	34.7	107	92	101
1963	—	38.6	105	105	103
1964	—	44.8	100	100	96
1965	—	50.6 (100.3)	94	104	96
1966	1,093	55.5	100	100	100
1967	—	61.0	97	97	100
1968	—	65.6	95	123	99
1969	—	69.5	91	130	95
1970	—	73.8	90	128	99
1971	—	76.1	98	132	101
1972	—	80.2	103	130	101
1973	—	91.1	99	124	104
1974	—	98.9	118	159	115
1975	1,560	106.3 (244.2)	114	163	129

Sources: Column 1: Active population age fifteen or more from Census of Population data.

Column 2: Manufacturing includes food processing (except olive oil and wine) and rugs. Data are based on census of manufactures but are adjusted to include rugs and to account for limited coverage of food processing and are smoothed by taking averages of end-of-year data. These adjustments make the data comparable with National Accounts value-added data.

For 1966 and 1975 figures in parentheses indicate employment according to census of population data. They are larger than other estimates, which do not cover unorganized sector and less than fully employed.

Columns 3 and 4: Nabli (1978), table V-1.

the extent that individual processes were more capital-intensive than they might have been within the private sector, the driving force was probably implicit subsidization of machinery and equipment rather than labor market interventions.

There is reason to believe that there was underpricing of capital goods, principally owing to an overvalued exchange rate and low interest rates on bank loans. As I mentioned above, the exchange rate has probably been significantly overvalued since 1961. (For instance, Blake 1974 estimates the overvaluation in 1969 to range between 19 and 40 percent.) This implicit subsidy to imports of capital goods probably affected all sectors equally because of the limited substitution possibilities between domestic and imported equipment and the liberalized import procedures for the latter. As seen in table 10.3, EERs for industrial and agricultural equipment were fairly close to the official exchange rate. Credit was also strictly rationed, and the subsidy rate varied considerably, since access to credit was determined by personal relationships and nonmarket phenomena. It is likely that publicly owned firms, which had priority access to credit, benefited more than private firms.

10.2 The Structure of Protection

Tunisia followed a restrictive import substitution policy during the 1960s, began to relax these policies after 1969, and in 1972 adopted an export oriented policy. In this section, I provide ERP estimates that describe the protective system as it existed in the transitional period 1969–72. The discussion ignores the tariff reform of 1973 and the new export policy largely because we lack the relevant data to appraise their effects upon employment.

The main elements of protection in Tunisia are the tariff system, differential indirect tax treatment of imports and domestic production, QRs, and subsidies.[15] QRs were probably the most significant form of protection from 1969 to 1972. Import licenses were given if domestic production did not exist or if need for the import could be demonstrated. As I mentioned above, QRs were most restrictive in foodstuffs and consumer goods. The other forms of protection had varying degrees of effectiveness. Tariffs were low, with a ratio of tariff collections to the value of imports varying from 6 to 10 percent over 1961 to 1975. Some protection also originated in a higher indirect tax rate applied to imports than to domestic production. Finally, subsidies of various forms (differential pricing of utilities, preferential credit facilities, etc.) applied in an ad hoc fashion to various activities.

There are two studies of effective protection available for Tunisia (Ministry of Planning 1975; Blake 1974). The Ministry of Planning

(MP) study relates to 1972 and covers a wider range of industries than Blake's study, which relates to 1969. Both studies assume that elasticities of substitution between primary factors and intermediate inputs are zero and use the Balassa method, which assumes that the ERP on home goods is zero.[16] The two studies differ markedly in their method of estimating nominal protection. In the MP study, nominal protection estimates are based upon the tariff, with account taken of differential indirect tax treatment and subsidies. Blake uses direct price comparisons that should capture the effects of QRs and avoid redundant tariffs. The Blake study is theoretically superior and yields more reasonable estimates than the MP study.[17] However, though I use both sets of estimates in my analysis, I will tend to rely more upon the MP estimates because of their broader coverage. My results are generally insensitive to the set of ERPs chosen.

In addition to ERPs, I also present estimates of domestic resource costs (DRCs) from the MP study. These estimates are deficient in that they use market prices rather than shadow prices for factors of production. However, they complement the ERP estimates by providing indications of the variation in returns to domestic factors of production.

Table 10.6 summarizes these estimates by trade category (see discussion in section 10.3 for a description of these categories). The main conclusions to be drawn from this table are that protection is relatively high in Tunisia and that import substitution activities are favored relative to export activities. The unweighted average ERP[18] is 251 percent in the MP study (or 81 percent if ERPs greater than 400 are excluded from the estimates). The corresponding figures from Blake's study are 85 and 52 percent. ERPs on export activities are significantly lower than those for import-competing activities in both studies. In fact, many export sectors had negative ERPs. This pattern is a natural consequence of the absence of policies promoting exports in the period studied. Exporters sold their production at world prices and bought inputs at prices above the world level.

There is no clear pattern of protection among types of exports. However, a pattern emerges within the importable category. Those activities stressed under the import substitution program (food and consumer goods) received significantly greater protection than intermediate and capital goods.[19]

In addition to the obviously better treatment of import substitution activities, there is evidence that protection was not applied evenly within categories. The coefficient of variation among industries within categories always exceeds unity, reflecting a wide dispersion of protection rates within categories. For example, in the importable consumer goods category, ERP estimates ranged from −40,161 percent (footwear) to

Table 10.6   The Structure of Protection and Domestic Resource Costs by Trade Categories

| | Ministry of Planning Estimates (1972) | | | | Blake Estimates (1969) | |
| | Effective Rates of Protection % | | Domestic Resource Costs (Dinar/Dollar) | | Effective Rates of Protection % | |
Trade Category[a]	Mean	Standard Deviation	Mean	Standard Deviation	Mean	Standard Deviation
All HOS tradables	250.6 (81.0)	713.5 (90.7)	1.107 (1.029)	0.422 (0.346)	85.2 (52.2)	125.8 (59.9)
HOS exports	23.0	44.6	.868	0.202	−1.0[b]	22.2
Traditional	39.9	30.5	1.135	0.243	37.2	0.0[c]
Primary commodity based	1.1	37.2	0.768	0.160	−12.9	10.7
Manufactured products	42.0	54.8	.858	.133	−8.0	2.7
HOS import-competing goods	300.7 (95.9)	772.4 (92.7)	1.159 (1.070)	.436 (.359)	90.3 (67.9)	110.8 (58.7)
Foods	737.4 (188.4)	1230.6 (99.4)	1.557 (1.437)	.293 (.134)	471.4 (—)	0.0 (—)
Manufactured consumer goods	547.2 (151.2)	1148.4 (113.6)	1.465 (1.346)	.465 (.393)	74.0 (—)	54.6 (—)
Intermediate goods	92.6 (59.4)	177.1 (63.9)	.901 (.885)	.243 (.233)	29.1 (—)	10.2 (—)
Capital goods	70.3	70.4	1.058 (—)	.411 (—)	104.2 (—)	83.0 (—)

Note: Means are unweighted averages of sectoral rates. The classification is that of table 10.A.3. The first figure in each category is for all sectors with $ERP > -100\%$, and the second figure (in parentheses) is for sectors with $-100\% < ERP < 400$ percent.

[a]For composition of trade categories see tables 10.A.1 and 10.A.3. Note, however, that tobacco (code 51) is excluded throughout.

[b]Excludes the steel mill sector (52), which has a high ERP.

[c]The standard deviation of zero is due to the fact that only one activity (canning) was included in Blake's estimates for this commodity category.

4,760 percent (perfumes). In the importable intermediate goods category, ERPs ranged from −605 percent (tanneries) to 888 percent (explosives).

Therefore protection created a highly differentiated incentive structure that was the result of the nonsystematic, piecemeal approach to trade policy. Within the general framework of import controls, specific advantages were accorded to public enterprises as well as to private firms. Pressure groups at the industry level and private individuals with personal influence were able to obtain differential treatment. In many cases monopoly positions and import limitations were obtained simply through administrative licensing of investment and imports. This structure must have had significant effects on resource allocation and efficiency, as well as on the commodity composition of trade.

The DRC estimates in table 10.6 follow the same pattern as the ERP estimates. DRCs are lower in exportable than in importable activities, indicating that more foreign exchange could be earned by transferring resources to export production. Within the importable category, the highest DRCs are found in food and manufactured consumer goods—those categories generally most favored by the import substitution regime. Again, there is a certain degree of dispersion within commodity categories, although not as large as that for ERPs. This dispersion is further evidence of the resource misallocation caused by the nonsystematic approach of the trade regime.

10.3 Factor Proportions in Tunisian Trade

10.3.1 Data

Data to obtain estimates of value-added and factor inputs were available at a highly disaggregated level (150 activities) in the 1972 input-output table and in the census of manufactures (101 activities). The census of manufactures provided a breakdown of workers into seven categories: management and engineers, white-collar employees, supervisory personnel, skilled and semiskilled labor, unskilled labor, apprentices, and seasonal workers.[20] Consistent domestic value added (DVA) and employment data were obtained from the two sources. International value added (IVA) data were obtained by combining the MP study of ERPs described in section 10.2 with the domestic value added data of the I-O table. IVA was calculated by dividing DVA by 1 + ERP.

I calculated three variations of direct and total (direct plus indirect in home goods) labor per unit of value added. The first is total man-years per unit of value added, either domestic or international (L/DVA or L/IVA). The second is man-years of unskilled labor per unit of value added (UL/DVA or UL/IVA). Unskilled labor includes all seasonal employees, apprentices, unskilled labor, and a fraction of the skilled and semiskilled category.[21] Finally, an index of the skill content of the labor force, SK, was calculated which measures "pure skill" relative to total man-years.

SK is defined as $(LS - L)/L$, where $LS = \Sigma\, w_i\, S_i$, L is total man-years, S_i is man-years of skill category i, and w_i is a weight derived by dividing the average wage in skill category i by the average unskilled wage. The range of w_i was 0.36 (apprentices) to 6.77 (management and engineers).[22]

10.3.2   Trade Categories

The next step is to aggregate these individual requirements by commodity category. Following the procedure outlined in chapter 1 of this volume, I separated the 150 domestic production activities into HOS exportables and importables, NRB exportables and importables, home goods, and noncompeting production. In general, exportable activities had a negative T_i statistic, importables had T_i values between 0.0 and 0.8, and noncompeting production had a T_i in excess of 0.8. Several additional distinctions were made in the HOS categories: HOS exportables were separated into traditional production (mainly food processing), NRB production (industries such as fertilizer that transform raw materials), and manufactures (mainly new exports that do not correspond to the other two categories); HOS importables were divided into the four categories of food products, manufactured consumer goods, intermediate goods, and capital goods.

The distinction between trade with developed countries and trade with less developed countries is of no importance in Tunisia and will not be pursued here. For HOS exports, the share of trade with developed countries is greater than 75 percent for all but four activities.[23] These exports are olive oil related activities and construction materials (cement, ceramics, sanitary fixtures). All are mainly destined to Algeria and Libya. For HOS importables, competition is mainly with developed countries. The ratio of imports from developed nations to total imports in an activity is greater than 70 percent except for sugar, glazed tiles, and morocco leather.

The sheer number of activities would make a complete listing by commodity category very tedious. The interested reader can find a list of the activities and their SITC codes in appendix table 10.A.1 and a breakdown by category in appendix table 10.A.3. Text tables 10.7 and 10.8 give details on major HOS exportable and importable activities. The discussion below briefly describes the composition of the various categories.

There are 33 exportable activities, of which 22 are HOS and 11 are NRB commodities. In the HOS category, the three traditional export-

Table 10.7   **Characteristics of Major HOS Exportable Activities, 1972**

| | | | | | Exports in 1972 (Thousands of U.S. Dollars) | | |
I-O Code	ISIC Number	Industry	Commodity Category	T_i	Developed Countries	Developing Countries	Total
22	3113	Canning and preserving of fruit and vegetables	Traditional	$-.43$	6,337	224	6,561
23	3114	Canning, preserving and processing of fish	Traditional	$-.93$	2,000	73	2,073
52	3710	Iron and steel	NRB based[a]	$-.03$	5,665	1,760	7,425
53	3720	Nonferrous metal smelting	NRB based	$-.89$	2,746	1,794	4,540
63	3692	Cement, lime	Manufactures	$-.08$	40	619	649
70	3691	Ceramics	Manufactures	$-.59$	—	2,101	2,101
71	3610	Sanitary fixtures	Manufactures	$-.29$	33	590	623
77	3319	Cork and products	NRB based	$-.94$	1,278	25	1,303
78	3512	Fertilizers	NRB based	-1.06	16,483	6,479	22,962
138	3511	Phosphoric acid	NRB based	-8.17	7,289	—	7,289
89	3523	Household soaps	Traditional	$-.20$	2,007	28	2,035
99	3411	Paper pulp	NRB based	-1.93	3,585	233	3,818

Source: Nabli (1978), appendix tables I-A-1972-2 and III-4.
[a]NRB is used here in the sense of PCB-HOS as described in the Introduction.

Table 10.8   **Characteristics of Major HOS Importable Activities, 1972**

I-O Code	ISIC Number	Industry	Commodity Category	T_i	Imports in 1972 (Thousands of U.S. Dollars)		
					Developed Countries	Developing Countries	Total
29	3118	Sugar refining	Foods	.51	7,757	6,194	13,951
51	3140	Tobacco and products	Foods	.02	1,159	4	1,161
56	3710	Foundries	Intermediate goods	.67	9,531	34	9,565
57	3813	Scaffolding, containers, etc.	Capital goods	.43	3,064	65	3,129
59	3819	Iron and metal products	Capital goods	.47	14,901	340	15,241
61	3843	Motor vehicle assembly	Capital goods	.56	13,394	232	13,626
97	3551	Rubber products	Consumer goods	.34	4,172	115	4,287
101	3419	Articles of paper and cartons	Intermediate goods	.17	1,255	26	1,281
102	3420	Printing, except newspaper	Intermediate goods	.29	2,083	745	2,828
104	3211	Spinning yarn, except jute	Intermediate goods	.51	11,897	2,314	14,211
105	3211	Weaving, except jute	Consumer goods	.14	7,210	156	7,366
108	3212	Wearing apparel	Consumer goods	.07	1,477	6	1,483

Source: Nabli (1978), appendix tables I-A-1972-2 and III-1.
Note: Industries listed had 1972 value added of more than 1,000 dinars (2,380 U.S. dollars) in 1972.

ables are canned foods, canned fish, and household soap. The HOS activities processing raw materials include among others refined petroleum, steel, cork, phosphoric acid, and fertilizer. Manufactures include cement and ceramics. NRB processing industries are the most important HOS exportable activities. NRB exportables include traditional olive oil and wine production plus minerals (phosphates) and crude oil.

There are 66 HOS and 4 NRB importable activities. The predominant categories among HOS importables are food and consumer goods, which together generate 80 percent of value added. Major HOS importable products are sugar, tobacco, rubber products, clothing, paper, textiles, and motor vehicles. The NRB importable category includes most traditional agricultural activity. It will be ignored in the remainder of this study.

The remaining categories consist of 29 home goods (including construction, utilities, and nontraded products such as bread) and 10 noncompeting activities, for which domestic production exists in 6. Additionally, there are two other categories that will not be considered here. One is handicrafts; the other is services that generate foreign exchange (mainly tourism and transportation).

10.3.3   Estimates of Labor Requirements by Activity

Appendix table 10.A.2 gives a complete listing of labor requirements for all activities. Text tables 10.9 and 10.10 give direct estimates for selected important activities in HOS categories. Inspection of appendix table 10.A.2 indicates first that direct and total estimates of L/DVA and UL/DVA and SK are nearly identical. Correlation coefficients between the direct and total measures were greater than 0.98 for L/DVA and UL/DVA and about 0.90 for SK. Therefore I base my discussion in the remainder of this section upon the direct coefficients. Incidentally, correlation analysis also found a strong positive relationship between L/DVA and UL/DVA and a negative correlation between those indexes and the skill level.[24]

A second conclusion from table 10.A.2 is the wide range of variation of the labor coefficients. Total labor coefficients range from 0.016 (man-years per 1,000 dinars of domestic value added [DVA]) for crude petroleum to 5.00 for toy manufacturing. Other activities with labor coefficients lower than 0.30 are tobacco, sugar processing and refining, oil pipeline and oil refining, coffee preparation, iron and steel, sulfur refining, rubber products, paper and paper carton products, and air and sea transportation. For all these sectors, the unskilled labor coefficient is smaller than 0.20. In addition, the following activities have an unskilled labor coefficient smaller than 0.15: utilities, vanilla, lead transformation, sewing-machine manufacturing, industrial gases, chemicals of dyes, paints, inks, insecticides, toilet products, and phosphoric acid. It is clear

Table 10.9   Factor Intensities of Major HOS Exportable
         Activities, 1972 (Man-Years/Thousand
         Dinars)

Industry	L/DVA	UL/DVA	SK
Canning of fruit and vegetables	1.848	1.656	.181
Canning of fish	.513	.440	.274
Iron and steel	.263	.134	.749
Nonferrous metal smelting	.819	.583	.395
Cement	.923	.615	.412
Ceramics	1.313	1.033	.345
Sanitary fixtures	1.935	1.146	.479
Cork products	1.113	.734	.374
Fertilizers	.537	.300	.687
Phosphoric acid	.382	.096	1.479
Household soap	3.855	2.765	.469
Paper pulp	Negative DVA		

Source: Appendix table 10.A.2.
Note: Direct requirements only.

Table 10.10   Factor Intensities of Major HOS Importable
         Activities (Man-Years/Thousand Dinars)

Industry	L/DVA	UL/DVA	SK
Sugar refining	.299	.188	.541
Tobacco and products	.055	.029	.636
Foundries[a]	1.096	.691	.498
Scaffolding, containers[a]	1.096	.691	.498
Iron and metal products	.808	.464	.548
Motor vehicle assembly	.977	.392	.959
Rubber products	.235	.097	1.021
Articles of paper and cartons	.283	.163	.657
Printing, except newspaper	1.161	.594	.699
Spinning yarn, except jute[b]	.869	.451	.586
Weaving, except jute[b]	.869	.451	.586
Wearing apparel	2.279	1.295	.512

Source: Appendix table 10.A.2.

Note: Direct requirements only.

[a]The census of manufactures aggregated these two industries
into one activity. We applied aggregated labor requirements to
each industry.

[b]Spinning and weaving were aggregated in the census data. The
same procedure was followed as for foundries and scaffolding.

that most chemicals, oil, rubber, and paper products use relatively little labor. On the other hand, these activities have high skill content coefficients (greater than 0.80 in most cases).

Activities that have high labor coefficients (greater than 1.5 for total labor and greater than 1.00 for unskilled labor) are mining, canning of fruits and vegetables, bakeries, electrical and electronic machinery, mechanical and electrical repairs, wood mills, furniture, cement, tiles and sanitary fixtures, hosiery, wearing apparel, toys, chalk, and jewelry. The skill index is lower than 0.8 for all these activities and lower than 0.6 for most of them.

10.3.4   Estimates of Factor Requirements by Commodity Category

Table 10.11 presents weighted average labor coefficients for the trade categories outlined above. Only direct coefficients are presented, since, as with the estimates by individual activity, the differences between direct and total coefficients were minor. The weights are: exports—the value added content of actual exports; and imports—the value added

Table 10.11   **Indexes of Relative Factor Proportions in Exportable and Importable Activities (HOS Import-Competing Sectors Excluding Those with Negative IVA = 1.0)**

Trade Category	Direct Requirements		
	L/DVA	UL/DVA	SK
I. All exports[a]	0.66	0.76	0.78
A. HOS exports (excluding refined oil)	1.28	1.58	0.81
1. NRB exports	0.79	0.76	1.23
2. Traditional exports	2.41	3.58	0.45
3. Manufactured products	2.08	2.69	0.65
B. NRB exports			
1. Excluding crude oil	3.31	3.82	0.69
2. Including crude oil	0.56	0.63	0.77
II. HOS importables			
A. All activities	1.24	1.20	1.05
B. Excluding activities with negative IVA	*1.00*	*1.00*	*1.00*
1. Food products	0.18	0.18	0.96
2. Food products, excluding tobacco	0.55	0.61	0.90
3. Manufactured consumer goods	1.42	1.35	1.06
4. Intermediate goods	1.22	1.22	1.08
5. Capital goods	1.70	1.76	0.81

Source: Nabli (1978).

[a]For composition of trade categories, see tables 10.A.1 and 10.A.3.

content of domestic production and competing imports.[25] For ease of interpretation, the table is presented in index form, the base being the category HOS importables excluding those with negative IVA. That is, a value less than (more than) one means that the labor coefficients for that commodity category is less than (more than) that in the HOS importable category excluding negative IVAs.

The most important conclusion to be drawn from this table is that HOS exports have higher total labor requirements (L/DVA) and unskilled labor requirements (UL/DVA), but lower skill contents (SK) than HOS importables. This is the general result one would expect from HOS model. However, when NRB exports, particularly crude oil, are added to HOS exports, the pattern reverses, at least as regards L/DVA and UL/DVA.

Within the HOS exportable category, traditional and manufactured exports have higher total and unskilled labor requirements than those in NRB-based exports that actually have a lower labor requirement than most importables. It is also important to distinguish among subcategories of the import-competing group. Including tobacco (which has an extremely low labor coefficient with a value of 0.05 for L/DVA) tends to lower the average considerably. When we compare the factor intensities of the manufactured consumer goods, intermediate products, and capital goods (lines II.B.3, 4, and 5), with HOS export sectors (line I.A), we observe that on the average, exports are not more labor-intensive than imports.[26] On the other hand, if we compare the traditional exports and manufactured exports (lines I.A.2 and 3) with the last three subgroups of HOS importables, the evidence is strong that exports are more total and unskilled labor-intensive than importable activities. Moreover, the category "HOS NRB exports" (line I.A.1) yields labor coefficients lower than those for the import-competing group and a skill index that is higher. These activities are mostly the processing of primary products previously exported in raw forms: iron ore, phosphate, lead, alfa, and cork. These activities are borderline cases between NRB and HOS activities, and it is not obvious how their labor coefficients should be interpreted.

The existence of some industries with a negative IVA among importable activity poses some difficulties. Estimates are given for import-competing sectors including and excluding such sectors. Even though including such activities tends to yield higher L/DVA estimates, the general pattern of differences between exports and importables is not greatly affected. Notice, in this regard, that the skill content index, which does not depend for its interpretation on differences in DVA, is much less sensitive to the inclusion or exclusion of such sectors.[27]

Thus far I have not mentioned labor requirements for noncompeting imports. These cannot be estimated from the country's observed data but must be inferred from some partner country's data. Since France is Tunisia's main trading partner, estimates of labor requirements are based on a 1972 French input-output table.[28] The data for output and value added are available with a ninety-one-sector breakdown, and those for total employment at a forty-four-sector breakdown. Noncompeting imports were allocated to the corresponding categories of the French I-O table; then the value-added content of those imports was calculated.[29] Then I calculated the labor content of one unit of value added of noncompeting imports, using the sectoral labor coefficients, for total imports and for commodity categories. It should be noted here that I am considering the labor input that would be used per unit of value added if such noncompeting imports were produced domestically, but only up to a first round of substitution for such imports. I do not consider the production of noncompeting goods indirectly imported in other noncompeting imports.

Another problem is whether factor intensity in the domestic production of such goods would be the same as that observed in France. Presumably, owing to the overall differentials in factor prices and factor endowments, the domestic labor intensity in such industries would be higher than that observed in France. I assume here that labor intensity would be x times higher in Tunisia than in France, where x is the ratio of labor coefficients in Tunisia and France for a given commodity produced in both countries. I estimated x by comparing labor coefficients in textiles and footwear in the two countries. It was found that the Tunisian coefficient was 2.6 times higher for both sectors. Thus the calculated labor requirements using French labor coefficients are all adjusted by this factor.[30]

In table 10.12 the coefficients are compared with those of exportables and import-competing activities. The calculations were carried out for the baskets of noncompeting imports both from France and from all developed countries, and the results were very similar in all respects.

The results show clearly that noncompeting imports are significantly less labor-intensive than either exportables or competing imports. HOS exports are about 55 percent more labor intensive than noncompeting imports, while import-competing goods are 20 percent more labor-intensive. The latter figure is low because of the low labor intensity of foodstuffs, and the differential in labor intensity is much higher (50–100 percent) for manufactured consumer goods and intermediate and capital goods.

The labor intensity differential for intermediate and capital goods is, however, probably underestimated. In fact, to obtain the adjusted figures for noncompeting imports I used the same adjustment factor for all industries. As I noted above, that factor was based on the differential in textiles and footwear, which are manufactured consumer goods. Apply-

Table 10.12   Factor Proportions in HOS Export and Importable Activities
Compared with Factor Proportions in Noncompeting Imports
(Index Values with Noncompeting Imports = 1.00)

	Direct Requirements—L/DVA—in Trade	
Trade Category[a]	France	All Developed Countries
HOS exports (excluding refined oil)	1.55	1.57
HOS Importables (using Tunisian data)		
All	1.21	1.22
Foods (excluding tobacco)	0.88	0.91
Manufactured consumer goods	1.60	1.54
Intermediate products	1.44	1.54
Capital goods	1.88	2.02
Noncompeting imports	1.00	1.00

Source: Nabli (1978).
[a]For composition of trade categories see tables 10.A.1 and 10.A.3.

ing the same adjustment factor to all industries implies an assumption of identical elasticities of substitution. But if there are greater factor substitution possibilities in consumer manufactures than in capital and intermediate goods production, the adjustment factor should be smaller for the latter industries, implying a lower labor intensity for noncompeting imports.

10.3.5   Net Labor Content of Trade

Given Tunisia's level of development, one would expect it to be a net exporter of labor. I have already mentioned that there was net out-migration of labor in the 1960s. However, my first net labor content estimates were somewhat ambiguous (see table 10.13). Lines 1 and 2 give the case of equal expansions of exports and imports in sectors classified either as exportables or importables. A comparison of the export and import labor requirements computed this way indicates that, on average, the net labor content of Tunisian trade is negative. I suspect that this is probably a spurious result due to the inadequacy of the MP ERP estimates used to calculate IVA. In fact, note that the labor coefficients increase as the ERP increases, which would indicate either that IVA is undervalued owing to the use of unduly high ERPs or that there are economically inefficient import-competing activities using more labor as well as more capital per unit of IVA.

As an alternative approach to measuring the net labor content, I considered a uniform expansion of all exports of HOS goods (line 3) and of all imports of HOS goods (line 4) regardless of whether classified in

Table 10.13   Labor Requirements per Unit of International Value Added and Skill Content by Trade Categories (Man-Years/Thousand Dinars)

Trade Category	Direct Requirements			Direct Plus Home Goods Indirect Requirements		
	L/IVA	UL/IVA	SK	L/IVA	UL/IVA	SK
1. HOS exports	0.793	0.556	0.472	0.848	0.534	0.552
2. HOS Importables	1.194	0.675	0.579	1.120	0.606	0.637
Activities with $ERP \leq 50$ percent	0.578	0.330	0.599	0.632	0.355	0.616
Activities with $50 < ERP \leq 125$	1.585	0.916	0.555	1.309	0.707	0.642
Activities with $125 < ERP \leq 200$	2.364	1.394	0.533	1.830	1.037	0.585
Activities with $ERP > 200$	5.225	2.799	0.598	2.225	1.149	0.660
3. Bundle of all HOS exports	0.918	0.601	0.481	0.933	0.561	0.550
4. Bundle of all HOS importables (Tunisian data)	1.012	0.576	0.574	1.001	0.547	0.627
5. Bundle of HOS importables (French data)	0.575	—	—	—	—	—
6. Bundle of HOS noncompeting imports	0.528	—	—	—	—	—
7. Bundle of all HOS imports	0.541	—	—	—	—	—

Source: Nabli (1978).
Note: These are not index values, as in table 10.12, but rather refer to actual man-years, except for SK, which is itself an index.

the exportable or the importable category. With this broader composition of export and import flows, the results still indicated that Tunisia is a net importer of labor, although not as much as in the first case. Furthermore, with this exercise, exports now became more unskilled labor-intensive.

One way to avoid the problem presented by faulty ERP estimates in deriving IVA coefficients is to rely on French data not only, as one must, for noncompeting imports but also for import-competing products. This practice was adopted with the French data adjusted as discussed earlier. Lines 5 to 7 give these adjusted direct requirements[31] for HOS importables, noncompeting imports, and all HOS imports. These values now show clearly that Tunisia is a net exporter of labor, with exports (line 3) about 70 percent more labor-intensive than imports (line 7).

10.3.6   Factor Intensities and Effective Protection

To conclude this section, I will analyze the relationship between the height of protection and labor intensities. Krueger (1977) suggests that they should be negatively correlated in a labor-abundant country. This hypothesis follows from the HOS model, which predicts that, to induce domestic production of a commodity that would not be produced with no protection, protection must be higher the further away the production of this commodity would be from its comparative advantage. I tested this hypothesis in several ways. The results suggested that there was a weak (negative) relationship between protection and total labor requirements and a stronger (negative) relationship between protection and unskilled labor requirements.

The first test involved computing simple (Pearson) correlation coefficients between the various indicators of factor intensity and effective rates of protection, using both MP and Blake estimates. Activities with negative IVAs and those with extremely high ERPs (more than 400 percent) were excluded from the calculations. The resulting correlation coefficients showed no significant relationship between total labor intensities and ERPs, but there was some evidence of negative correlation between unskilled labor intensity and ERPs.

A weakness of this analysis is that it is based on the assumption that ERPs and labor requirements are measured correctly and precisely on an interval scale. However, this assumption may not be warranted given all the measurement problems that are encountered in measuring ERPs. So, rather than using point estimates of ERPs, I classified activities into seven groups according to their level of protection.[32] (That is, I assume that the point estimate is only roughly indicative of the level of protection.)

For each group, I computed the weighted average labor requirements per unit of DVA. A close examination of these group averages suggests results about the same as those obtained from the correlation analysis. There is weak evidence of a negative relationship between the height of effective protection and total labor requirements but stronger evidence of a negative correlation between the height of effective protection and unskilled labor content.[33] For example, the average unskilled labor requirement in the two least protected groups is 37 percent greater than that of the two most protected groups.

Summary

The analysis performed in this section indicates first that Tunisia's export production is more labor-intensive than its importable production. This is especially true for traditional and manufactured exports, but it is not true for those HOS export activities processing raw materials. Second, my results imply that Tunisia is a net exporter of labor, especially unskilled labor. Finally, there is evidence, although weak, that suggests that protection is negatively correlated with labor requirements. This result implies that the trade regime has been biased against labor. That is, those activities receiving high protection tend to have low labor requirements.

10.4   Factor Market Distortions and Their Effects upon Factor Proportions

I mentioned in the overview that there was reason to believe that distortions existed in both labor and capital markets. In this section I will provide more detail on the nature of these distortions, then analyze their effects upon factor utilization in Tunisia.

10.4.1   Labor Market Distortions

One needs detailed data on wage rates, by activity, for homogeneous units of labor to determine if labor market distortions exist. Unfortunately, the only wage data available in Tunisia are average wage payments per man year for sixty-eight HOS tradable activities in the 1972 census of manufactures.

I have calculated average wages for several different categorizations of these sixty-eight activities (see table 10.14) that seem important in Tunisia. These categorizations are: (1) public versus private—the public group includes activities consisting of only public firms or where public firms predominate in terms of employment; (2) monopolistic versus nonmonopolistic—the monopolistic group includes activities that do not have more than three establishments (given the level of disaggregation of my analysis this may not be too gross an approximation, though it is true that some activities classified as nonmonopolistic may be made up of monopolistic firms producing relatively nonhomogeneous products); and (3) large versus small firms—the first group includes activities with firms having fifty employees or more, and "small firms" are activities with firms having fewer than fifty employees; activities with firms in both size groups are omitted.

From table 10.14, it is immediately apparent that the public, monopolistic, and large-firm groups pay significantly higher average wages than the private, nonmonopolistic, and small-firm groups. There is a differential of about 45 percent for the public-private and for the monopolistic-nonmonopolistic dichotomies. The differential between large and small firms is about 25 percent, but it is obscured by the fact that both groups include mostly monopolistic sectors. Column 3 of table 10.14 also indicates that wage differentials are sizable within each group (coefficients of variation range between 32 and 49 percent). A comparison of coefficients of variation between public and private firms, monopolistic and nonmonopolistic firms, and large and small firms shows that wages vary more in private, nonmonopolistic, or smaller firms than in public, monopolistic, or larger firms. This suggests that the labor market can be dichotomized into large, public, monopolistic nucleus paying higher wages with a smaller degree of variability than the small, private, nonmonopolistic group.

The average wage data can be combined with other information to investigate the extent by which wage differentials can be explained by nondistortionary and distortionary factors. We first estimate the following regression equation for all activities and for the various groups mentioned above.

Table 10.14   Wage Structure in Industry, 1972 (HOS Tradables)

Groups	Number of Activities (1)	Mean Wage (Thousand Dinars/Man-Year) (2)	Coefficient of Variation % (3)	Residual Coefficient of Variation[a] % (4)
Total	68	0.794	47.9	37.0
Public	28	0.973	42.0	32.6
Private	40	0.669	45.0	38.7
Nonmonopolistic	37	0.664	48.6	31.2
Private	28	0.574	31.8	23.3
Monopolistic	31	0.950	40.5	34.7
Public	19	0.987	38.8	29.1
Private	12	0.891	46.5	45.8
Large firms	19	0.960	38.9	29.8
Small firms	12	0.798	44.0	48.0

Source: Nabli (1978).

[a]Column 4 is obtained by dividing the standard error of regression of appropriate equations in table 10.15 by the mean of the dependent variable.

$$\text{WAGE}_i = a_o + a_1 \text{SSK1}_i + a_2 \text{SSK2}_i$$
$$+ \, b \, \text{SEX}_i + u_i,$$

where i is an activity index, and

$$\text{WAGE} = \frac{W}{L}$$

L is total man-years,

W is total wage bill paid by firms in the ith activity and includes:
gross wages inclusive of taxes,
payments in kind,
charges, which include social security payments, insurance premiums, family allowances, and other social benefits. These benefits are included in wage rate calculations because they are additional costs to employers that significantly affect real wage payments. For most activities they make up between 15 and 25 percent of total wage payments, and they even exceed 30 percent in a few cases.

SSK1 is the proportion of white-collar employees[34] in total employment,

SSK2 is the proportion of skilled and semiskilled workers,

SEX is the proportion of female labor, and

u_i is the error term.

We do not have any information on educational levels, age, and experience of workers, but presumably a major part of these effects is reflected in the occupational groupings. If so, then in addition to errors in measurement, the error term would capture mostly distortionary effects related to union strength and to size and ownership of firms, while the independent terms should capture the nondistortionary effects.

The regression results are given in table 10.15. From equation (1) it is seen that a significant part of the interindustry wage differentials can be explained by skill and sex-composition differentials. The residual coefficient of variation is 37 percent compared with the total coefficient of 48 percent. A significant part of the differential is explained by the white-collar composition of the labor force. The sex-composition variable is also significant.[35] However, a large share of interindustry wage differentials is not explained by either skill or sex differences. Other factors, mostly distortionary, also contribute to the variance of the wage structure in industry.

Next, we investigate whether there are significant differences in wage structures between different components of the labor market.

A dummy variable for public sector was incorporated in regression equation (2). It had a significant effect. But, according to this specifica-

Table 10.15   Factors Influencing Wage Differentials in Industry—Regression Results (Dependent Variable: WAGE = Total Wage Payments per Man-Year)

Regression Equation	Groups	Number of Sectors	Constant	SSK1	SSK2	SEX	PUBLIC	MONO	R^2	S	Mean	F	SSR
1	All	68	0.398* (3.63)	1.685** (6.62)	0.156 (0.76)	−0.591** (2.55)			0.43	0.294	0.794	16.46	5.560
2	All	68	0.342* (3.17)	1.557* (6.21)	0.140 (0.71)	−0.428*** (1.84)	0.182** (2.45)		0.48	0.283	0.794	14.82	5.075
3	All	68	0.298*** (2.64)	1.527* (6.02)	0.297 (1.44)	−0.586** (2.62)		0.184** (2.45)	0.48	0.283	0.794	14.82	5.075
4	Public	28	0.312 (1.58)	2.010* (4.39)	0.581 (1.53)	−1.759 (1.07)			0.48	0.317	0.973	7.55	2.412
5	Public	28	0.281 (1.15)	2.006* (4.29)	0.610 (1.49)	−1.750 (1.04)		0.032 (0.23)	0.48	0.323	0.973	5.45	2.407
6	Private	40	0.453* (3.67)	1.345* (3.81)	−0.048 (0.21)	−0.380*** (1.75)			0.33	0.259	0.669	6.04	2.420
7	Private	40	0.388** (3.35)	0.975* (2.78)	0.158 (0.71)	−0.474** (2.34)		0.261* (2.76)	0.45	0.238	0.669	7.28	1.985
8	Monopolistic	31	0.543* (3.22)	1.183* (3.33)	0.481 (1.45)	−0.797*** (1.83)			0.36	0.330	0.950	5.04	2.950
9	Monopolistic	31	0.551* (2.83)	1.185* (3.27)	0.481 (1.42)	−0.815 (1.69)	−0.012 (0.09)		0.36	0.336	0.950	3.64	2.949
10	Monopolistic public	19	0.256 (1.28)	1.866* (3.63)	1.057** (2.50)	−2.685 (1.40)			0.53	0.287	0.987	5.69	1.236
11	Monopolistic private	12	0.840** (2.54)	0.678 (0.92)	0.042 (0.07)	−0.924 (1.50)			0.29	0.408	0.891	1.12	1.331

Table 10.15—*continued*

Regression Equation	Groups	Number of Sectors	Constant	SSK1	SSK2	SEX	PUBLIC	MONO	R^2	S	Mean	F	SSR
12	Non-monopolistic	37	0.248** (2.09)	2.482* (7.29)	-0.125 (0.53)	-0.236 (1.07)			0.63	0.207	0.663	18.81	1.424
13	Non-monopolistic	37	0.269** (2.58)	2.245* (7.31)	-0.244 (1.17)	-0.81 (0.40)	0.244* (3.28)		0.72	0.182	0.663	21.01	1.064
14	Private	28	0.315* (3.64)	1.640* (4.69)	-0.053 (0.29)	-0.184 (1.19)			0.52	0.134	0.574	8.66	0.431
15	Large	19	0.307 (1.00)	1.524* (3.30)	0.807 (1.66)	-0.786 (1.65)			0.53	0.286	0.960	5.72	1.234
16	Small	12	0.519*** (2.25)	1.097 (0.99)	0.182 (0.15)	-0.887 (0.61)			0.20	0.383	0.798	0.70	1.174

Notes: Explanatory variables:
SSK1, SSK2: proportion of white-collar workers and of skilled and semiskilled workers, respectively.
SEX: proportion of female labor.
PUBLIC: dummy = 1 if sector is public or predominantly public,
= 0 otherwise

MONO: dummy = 1 if sector includes no more than 3 establishments,
= 0 otherwise

Numbers in parentheses are Student's t-ratios.
*$p < .01$ for a two-tailed test;
**$p < .05$ for a two-tailed test;
***$p < .10$ for a two-tailed test.
Summary statistics are:
R^2: coefficient of determination unadjusted for degrees of freedom;
S: standard error of the regression;
Mean: Mean of dependent variable;
F: F-statistic;
SSR: Sum of squared residuals.

tion, only unskilled workers would be paid differently in public and private sectors. A Chow test for homogeneity of wage structure between public and private sector, based on the results of equations (1), (4), and (6), yielded results suggesting that, though the public sector may be paying higher wages for unskilled labor, there is no significant difference for skilled labor wage payments.

Comparison of regression equations (4) and (6) shows that skill and sex composition explain a larger share of the wage variance in the public sector than in the private sector. In fact, the residual coefficient of variation is higher for the private than for the public sector by 20 percent, while for the total coefficient of variation it is higher by 7 percent only.

A dummy variable for monopolistic activities was significant in regression equation (3). A Chow test rejected the null hypothesis of structural homogeneity at the .01 level of significance. Therefore it seems that the wage structure is significantly different between the monopolistic and nonmonopolistic sectors. Moreover, from regression equations (8) and (12) we see that skill and sex differentials explained a much larger share of the wage variance in the nonmonopolistic sector.

These results indicate that distortionary effects are much stronger in the labor market within the monopolistic groups. This is further supported by comparing the results for large-firm and small-firm groups in regression equations (15) and (16). Most of the sectors in these two groups also belong to the monopolistic set. The results are significantly different, and the small-firm group differentials are not explainable to any significant degree by skill and sex-composition differences. The poor results of the small group may, however, be due to serious errors in measurement, since we are dealing with single small firms, and their reported data may be unreliable.[36]

Regression equations (9) and (13) in table 10.15 also indicate that the dummy variable PUBLIC is highly significant for the nonmonopolistic group, although not for the monopolistic group. This suggests the need to separate the nonmonopolistic private and public sets. In fact, the nonmonopolistic private group exhibits the lowest degree of wage variation. On the other hand, the monopolistic private group (11) exhibits a much higher degree of variation that is not explainable by skill differentials.

My analysis suggests the following tentative conclusions regarding the labor market in Tunisia:

1. The skill composition of the labor force explains a significant part of interindustry wage differentials.

2. There is some evidence, though not very strong, that female labor is paid less than male labor, but it cannot be determined whether this is

due to sex discrimination or to male/female productivity and skill differences.

3. The labor market may be categorized in three ways.

   a. The nonmonopolistic private component, exhibiting the smallest degree of distortions in the labor market, with the largest share of interindustry wage differentials explained by skill differentials.

   b. The public sector, which exhibits a higher degree of wage variation that is not explainable by skills. The evidence is also that the public sector pays higher wages for unskilled labor.[37]

   c. The monopolistic private component, which exhibits a highly variable wage structure that is not explainable by skill differentials and that pays very high average wage rates.

I introduced size and labor intensity of firms as two additional explanatory variables in the final stage of the analysis (Nabli 1978).[38] The results confirm all the conclusions obtained above, with the following additional findings:

1. Size of firm and labor intensity explain a significant part of interindustry wage differentials.

2. Labor intensity is associated significantly with lower wages in the public sector, but not in the private nonmonopolistic groups.

3. Larger firm size is significantly associated with higher wages in the private nonmonopolistic group but not in the public sector.

To sum up this analysis of interindustrial wage structure, the evidence suggests the existence of significant distortions in the labor market, which exhibit the regular patterns described above.

10.4.2   Capital Market Distortions

In addition to labor market distortions, there were significant capital market distortions, caused either by the underpricing of capital goods owing to an overvalued exchange rate or by low interest rates on bank loans. It is believed that the exchange rate was significantly overvalued throughout the period. For instance, Blake (1974) estimates that the overvaluation for 1969 ranges between 19 and 40 percent. I observed earlier that QRs were prevalent and that tariff rates ranged from 10 to 28 percent according to import categories. From table 10.3 it appeared that EERs were higher for foodstuffs and consumer manufactures than for industrial equipment by 28 percent and 18 percent, respectively. The estimation of these EERs did not account for QRs, which were less restrictive for capital goods. I estimate the premium on QRs for foodstuffs and manufactures at about 25 percent (Nabli 1978). With these values the EER differentials between consumer and capital goods would be about 50 percent. This percentage is an upper bound to exchange rate overvaluation.

If the demand for the liberally imported capital goods is price-elastic, the overvaluation would be smaller. It follows that imports of capital goods were underpriced to the extent of overvaluation, probably by about 30 percent. Owing to limited substitution possibilities between domestic and imported equipment and the liberalized import procedures for the latter, this subsidy affected the costs of capital in all sectors equally, except possibly for special exemptions and treatment. However, credit was strictly rationed, and the total subsidy must have varied considerably among sectors and firms depending on access to credit, which was determined by personal relations, nonmarket phenomena, and government policy. It is probably true that public firms, which had priority access to credit, benefited almost uniformly from subsidized credit on medium- and long-term loans.

The net result of my review of distortions in the labor and capital markets is that the public sector pays higher wages than the private sector and benefits from large subsidies on imported capital and credit. Therefore the public-sector wage/rental ratio is higher than that of the private sector. From analysis of the labor market it appears that unskilled labor wage rates are on the average about 20 percent higher in the public sector. If we assume a conservative rate of 10 percent for the real opportunity cost on capital, the rate of subsidy on capital use in the public sector is 6 percent, assuming a 4 percent maximum real interest rate on credit. If we assume that all public investment is credit financed, that a private firm's investment is half financed through credit, and, in addition, that only the public firm has access to imported capital equipment, the wage/rental ratios in the public sector will be 2.4 times higher than in the private sector.[39]

Within groups, there is a more homogeneous wage/rental ratio in the public sector, while for the private nonmonopolistic group I conjecture that the degree of variability is much higher, with the larger firms facing higher wage/rental ratios.

10.4.3   Effects upon Factor Proportions

The pattern of distortions described above implies that the public sector should use more capital-intensive techniques than private monopolistic or nonmonopolistic sectors at any given level of protection. One way to test this hypothesis is to calculate average labor intensities within each group for the seven levels of protection introduced in section 10.3. These calculations, shown in table 10.16, tend to confirm this hypothesis. The public sector has lower labor requirements than the nonmonopolistic private sector in all but two categories of protection (1 and 4). Likewise, the public sector has lower labor requirements than the monopolistic private sector for any level of protection except the first and sixth.[40]

Table 10.16 Factor Proportions in Importable Activities Grouped by Level of Protection and Type of Factor Market (Direct Requirements in Man-Years per Thousand Dinars of DVA)

Level-of-Protection Group	Nonmonopolistic Private		Monopolistic Private		Public	
	L/DVA (1)	UL/DVA (2)	L/DVA (3)	UL/DVA (4)	L/DVA (5)	UL/DVA (6)
1	0.455	0.223	0.500	0.178	0.802	0.358
2	1.264	0.755	0.789	0.466	0.468	0.296
3	1.130	0.734	0.413	0.141	0.316	0.186
4	0.831	0.509	—	—	0.875	0.465
5	1.208	0.696	—	—	0.817	0.479
6	1.020	0.599	0.528	0.255	0.600	0.321
7	2.156	1.149	2.194	1.548	0.945	0.406

Source: Nabli (1978).

Note: Groups are defined in terms of their range of *ERP*s as follows:

    Group 1, −75%–0%
    Group 2, 0%–50%
    Group 3, 50%–75%
    Group 4, 75%–125%
    Group 5, 125%–200%
    Group 6, larger than 200%
    Group 7, negative IVA.

In turn, the nonmonopolistic private labor intensities are higher, or approximately the same as, those of the monopolistic private sector for any level of effective protection.[41]

Another approach to this issue is to repeat the correlation analysis between the ERP and my indicators of labor intensity (L/DVA and SK) separately for public and private activities. (Recall that this approach was applied in section 10.3 with results generally supporting the notion that protection was biased against employment.) This was done using both MP and Blake ERPs. The results are given in table 10.17. The most striking result to be observed from the table is the consistently highly significant relationship (with expected signs) for the public sector, but not the private sector. This implies that there was a very strong association between the import substitution thrust of the trade regime and public sector industrial development. Public sector firms were mainly involved in import substitution activities; the participation of public firms in exports was largely confined to those industries processing natural resources, which, as I observed earlier, had low labor coefficients. The same was true for the monopolistic private sector. However, the nonmonopolistic sector was more involved in exports. Thus, the trade regime favored the development of the capital-intensive public (and to a lesser degree private monopolistic) sectors.

The absence of any negative relationship for the private sector estimates is puzzling. I suspect it is due to an uneven application of factor market distortions in the private sector. Recall that we saw earlier that factor prices were more distorted but less variable in the public than in the private sector. This is particularly true in view of capital market fragmentation and the significant effect of firm size on wage rate differentials in the private sector. Thus, more variable factor price differentials may have had a significant effect upon factor intensities and therefore washed out any association between factor intensities and protection.

Distortions in the factor markets appear to have generally hindered employment creation. These distortions were partly of domestic origin and partly due to the trade regime. The import substitution strategy was implemented to a large extent through the expansion of the public sector. This fact, together with the higher wage/rental ratio in the public sector, led to the development of relatively capital-intensive industries and/or the adoption of capital-intensive production techniques. In the absence of such distortions the average labor intensity of HOS activities probably would have been higher.

10.5   Alternative Trade Policies and Employment

The policies pursued during the 1960s did not reverse the optimal pattern of trade (as evidenced by my net labor content estimates). How-

Table 10.17   **Correlation Coefficients between Factor Intensity Indicators and Effective Rates of Protection in Public and Private Sectors**

	Number of Sectors	L/DVA	UL/DVA	SK
Ministry of Planning ERPs				
Public sectors only	13	−0.037	−0.381*	0.662**
		−0.025	−0.386*	0.642**
Public and predominantly public sectors	16	−0.084	−0.431**	0.652**
		−0.082	−0.432**	0.615**
Private sectors only	14	0.060	0.083	0.054
		0.041	0.043	0.220
Private and predominantly private sectors	27	0.038	0.039	0.061
		0.011	−0.000	0.195
Blake ERPs				
Public and predominantly public sectors	7	−0.637*	−0.570*	0.093
		−0.627*	−0.588*	0.003
Private and predominantly private sectors	13	0.727**	0.501**	−0.044
		0.643**	0.402*	−0.018

Note: For each group the first line is relative to direct requirements coefficients, and the second to direct plus indirect requirements. Only sectors with ERP ≤ 400% and no negative IVA are included in the calculations.
*$p < .10$, one-tailed test.
**$p < .05$, one-tailed test.

ever, neither did they expand employment as rapidly as alternative policies might have done. Labor absorption in manufacturing was quite low. The elasticity of employment with respect to output was about unity in 1961–65, then fell dramatically to 0.8 in 1965–69 and 0.5 in 1969–72. It increased afterward to more than unity between 1972 and 1975.[42] This is consistent with my findings that import substitution industries were less labor-intensive than exportable industries, and that, within the import substitution group, the industries that received more protection were less labor-intensive (especially unskilled labor) than the other. This was particularly true within the public sector.

To see some of the biases of the trade regime, I have calculated the distribution of value added and employment for the public and private sectors by level of effective protection (table 10.18).[43] Note first that groups 5 and 6 (the highly protected industries)[44] contributed 40 percent of total value added in all importable industries. Most value added and employment (about two-thirds) in the public sector originated in these groups. In contrast, only 13 percent of value added and employment in the private sector originated in these groups. Second, the public

Table 10.18　Value Added and Employment in Importable Activities in Public and Private Sectors by Level of Protection

Group	Nonmonopolistic Private Value Added (1)	Nonmonopolistic Private Direct Requirements L (2)	Nonmonopolistic Private Direct Requirements UL (3)	Monopolistic Private Value Added (4)	Monopolistic Private Direct Requirements L (5)	Monopolistic Private Direct Requirements UL (6)	Public Sector Value Added (7)	Public Sector Direct Requirements L (8)	Public Sector Direct Requirements UL (9)	Total Value Added (10)	Total Direct Requirements L (11)	Total Direct Requirements UL (12)
1	371	169	83	28	14	5	972	780	348	1,371	963	436
2	3,992	5,046	3,014	221	174	103	1,183	554	350	5,396	5,774	3,467
3	2,126	2,402	1,560	335	138	47	1,173	371	218	3,634	2,911	1,825
4	3,760	3,125	1,914	—	—	—	1,777	1,555	0,826	5,537	4,680	2,740
5	1,898	2,293	1,321	—	—	—	3,629	2,965	1,738	5,527	5,258	3,059
6	801	817	480	206	109	053	8,639	5,183	2,773	9,646	6,109	3,306
7	5,779	12,460	6,640	36	79	56	1,481	1,400	601	7,296	13,939	7,297
Total	18,727	26,312	15,012	826	514	264	18,854	12,808	6,854	38,407	39,634	22,130

Source: Nabli (1978).

Note: Value added: thousand dinars; employment: man-years. Labor requirements, both L and UL, were obtained by multiplying the appropriate value added column by the corresponding labor column in table 10.16.

and nonmonopolistic private sectors each accounted for about 49 percent of total value added in importable activities. However, the public sector accounted for only one-third of total man-years (and even less for unskilled man-years), while the private sector accounted for two-thirds of employment. Finally, public sector firms falling in groups 5 and 6 accounted for one-third of total importable value added yet provided only one-fifth of total importable employment.

The development of the public sector was the major instrument of the import substitution strategy. It is obvious that its growth has clearly been associated with (if it did not cause) the development of capital-intensive industries and high protection.

This section provides estimates of the likely order of magnitude of two hypothetical policy alternatives. The first policy limits Tunisia to an import substitution strategy but investigates the employment effects of a different choice of import substitution industries. The second investigates the employment effects of an export oriented policy.

10.5.1 Alternative Import Substitution Policies

My findings indicate that an import substitution strategy aimed at labor-intensive industries would have generated more employment growth during the sixties. I analyze the employment effects of the following three strategies: an expansion of existing labor-intensive industries, the use of more labor-intensive techniques, and the development of new industries that are labor-intensive.

Expansion of Labor-Intensive, Low-ERP Industries

I have identified seven importable industries to expand and fifteen importable industries to contract (so as to leave total value added unchanged) under a more efficient import substitution policy (see table 10.19). Each of the industries to expand satisfies the following conditions: (1) it is labor-intensive; (2) its ERP is less than 125 percent; and (3) expansion could increase value added by more than 100,000 dinars and be sold in the domestic market. All these activities are in the private nonmonopolistic group. The industries to contract are not classified as labor-intensive according to at least two of the three criteria.[45] Most fall in groups 6 and 7 in the ERP levels, and most are public firms.

I assume that each industry expands to the point where its production completely satisfies domestic demand at unchanged domestic prices (i.e., imports are eliminated). This expansion would increase importable value added by 7,241 thousand dinars (19 percent of value added in all importable industries) and increase employment by 9,429 man-years, of which 5,647 would be unskilled (see table 10.19).

Table 10.19   Effects of a Reallocation of Resources in the Importable Industries (Based on Value Added and Employment Data for 1972)

I. Labor-Intensive, Low-Protection Activities to Expand

Sector (I-O Code)	Imports (Thousand Dinars)	Value-Added Content of Imports[a] (Thousand Dinars)	Percentage Increase in DVA	Employment Created[b] (Man-Years) L	UL
56 Foundries	4,253	2,411	180	2,628	1,630
57 Steel structures and containers	1,789	1,014	98	1,102	674
66 Glazed tiles	240	103	41	154	109
72 Glass and products	1,970	989	140	918	563
76 Fishing vessels	2,511	2,041	356	3,624	2,155
102 Printing except newspaper	1,272	567	42	657	341
116 Merceries and jewelry	924	116	102	346	185
Total	12,959	7,241	135	9,429	5,647

Table 10.19—continued

II. Non-labor-Intensive, High-Protection Activities to Contract

Sector (I-O Code)	Value Added (Thousand Dinars)	Employment (Man-Years)	
		L	UL
29 Sugar refining	1,474	564	343
32, 33 Vanilla, yeast, bakery products	11	9	2
35 Margarine	19	14	7
41 Alcoholic beverages	55	65	30
55 Lead processing	194	106	58
61 Electrical and electronic machinery	1,075	1,073	490
83 Explosives	233	197	143
86 Paints and varnishes	834	378	183
88 Glues	141	83	45
92 Toilet articles	114	70	29
94 Perfumes	283	179	90
97 Rubber products	1,724	643	290
137 Paper	1,099	438	228
Total	7,256	3,819	1,938

[a]Assuming the same value-added/output ratio as for existing domestic production.
[b]Using direct plus indirect in home goods requirements coefficients.

The elimination of the fifteen nonlabor intensive, higher-ERP activities would almost exactly offset the gain in value added (7,256 versus 7,241). Employment would fall by 3,819 man-years, of which 1,938 are unskilled. The net employment effect of this reallocation is employment growth of 5,610 man-years (9,429–3,819), of which 3,719 are unskilled (5,647–1,938). This growth represents increases of 14 percent and 17 percent,[46] respectively in total and unskilled employment in the importable category as a whole.

Use of More Labor-Intensive Techniques and Expanded Production

As a second alternative, I consider the possibility of using more labor-intensive techniques. I identified eleven industries that are classified as labor-intensive by either Lary (1968) or Banerji (1975) but whose labor coefficients are lower than the average of the importable group in Tunisia. In 1972 these industries (see table 10.20) produced about 37 percent of total value added in import-competing industries.[47] About three-fourths of their value added originated in activities classified as being public or monopolistic private. Most of these industries were highly protected.

Assume that the labor coefficient increases by 25 percent for each activity. Under competitive conditions and assuming a Cobb-Douglas production function, this increase would require a 36 percent decrease of the wage/rental ratio, entailing a decrease of that magnitude in the wage rate, or a 56 percent increase in the rental rate or some combination of the two.[48] Alternatively, this could be achieved through the use of appropriate shadow prices in project evaluation, particularly for the public sector.

The effect of the increase in labor intensity is illustrated in table 10.20. The actual labor coefficients are increased by 25 percent for all sectors[49] to obtain those indicated in column 8 for total labor. I assume, furthermore, that all employment gains per unit of value added are unskilled labor. The coefficients of column 10 are computed accordingly.[50] Altogether, employment in these industries would rise by about 2,690 man-years. This growth represents a 25 percent increase in employment in these industries and a 48 percent increase in their unskilled labor forces.

In addition, for a given capital stock used in the subset of industries, total value added could be increased; that is, there would be scope for more import substitution. In fact, under the above assumptions and a Cobb-Douglas production function, the possible increase in value added is 25 percent. If additional import substitution is undertaken in sectors 59, 104, and 105,[51] for the amount of 3,512 thousand dinars of value added the additional gain in employment would be 3,860 man-years, of which 2,353 would be unskilled.[52]

Table 10.20 Effects of Use of More Labor-Intensive Techniques

Sector (I-O Code)	Value Added in Domestic Production (Thousand Dinars) (1)	Competing Imports		Actual Labor Coefficients and Employment[a]				Assumed Labor Coefficients and Employment[a]			
		Value (Thousand Dinars) (2)	Value Added Content (Thousand Dinars) (3)	Total Labor		Unskilled Labor		Total Labor		Unskilled Labor	
				L/DVA (4)	L (5)	UL/DVA (6)	UL (7)	L/DVA (8)	L (9)	UL/DVA (10)	UL (11)
58 Sewing machines	194	111	60	0.488	95	0.134	26	0.610	118	0.256	50
59 Iron and metal products	3,351	7,389	2,397	0.830	2,781	0.461	1,545	1.038	3,477	0.669	2,242
73 Wood sawing	523	14	9	0.680	356	0.430	225	0.850	445	0.600	314
93 Floral essence oils	371	10	4	0.541	201	0.266	99	0.676	251	0.401	149
96 Candles	30	—	—	0.695	21	0.552	17	0.869	26	0.726	22
98 Plastics	991	1,184	516	0.625	619	0.385	381	0.781	774	0.541	536
101 Paper and carton products	1,856	645	399	0.382	709	0.212	393	0.478	886	0.308	572
104 Cotton and wool spinning	1,670	6,946	2,000	0.876	1,463	0.426	711	1.095	1,829	0.645	1,077
105 Weaving	4,738	4,133	1,199	0.894	4,236	0.444	2,104	1.118	5,295	0.668	3,165
106 Jute spinning and weaving	265	14	4	0.901	239	0.460	122	1.126	298	0.685	181
115 Lighting fixtures	62	—	—	0.576	36	0.265	16	0.720	45	0.409	25
Total	14,051	20,446	6,588	0.765	10,756	0.401	5,639	0.957	13,444	0.593	8,333

Sources:

Cols. 1, 2: From I-O table, 1972.

Col. 3: Col. 2 times ratio of value added to production.

Cols. 4, 6: Appendix table 10.A.2.

Cols. 5, 7: Col. 1 times col. 4 and 6 respectively.

Cols. 8, 10: See text.

Cols. 9, 11: Col. 1 times col. 8 and 10 respectively.

[a]Direct plus home goods indirect requirements.

The total increase in employment from both changes would be 6,550 man-years, of which 5,043 would be unskilled. These increases represent gains of 17 and 23 percent, respectively, of the labor force employed in importable activities.

A Program for Additional Import Substitution

As a final alternative, I consider the possibility of encouraging new labor-intensive import substitution manufacturing activities. This program would not pose major capital financing problems, as is shown below.

First, scrutiny of the level of actual imports[53] indicates that there is further scope for substitution[54] in seven activities, particularly in the electrical and electronic industry (see table 10.21). These activities fall in the groups of highly protected industries, especially group 7 or industries with negative IVA. This seemed to indicate that it would be undesirable to expand their output. However, all these industries are those usually considered labor-intensive, for which an LDC would have a comparative advantage.[55]

French value added to output ratios were used to compute the potential value-added gain from substituting domestic production for imports. The Tunisian value added figures are likely to be low, because of inefficiency in these industries. Likewise, the observed labor coefficients are likely to be too high. So the employment effect was measured by applying the average labor coefficients in all importable industries. The employment gain from eliminating these imports would be 3,778 total man-years, of which 2,166 are unskilled.

Next, there is scope for substitution in noncompeting imports. We identified a number of products of which there was no domestic com-

Table 10.21   Additional Substitution for Competing Imports, 1972
(Thousand Dinars)

Input-Output Code and Product	Value of Imports (c.i.f.) (1)	Value-Added Content of Imports (2)	Domestic Production (3)
62 Electrical and electronic machines	7,199.6	3,240.0	4,184
75 Furniture and pleasure boats	355.0	148.7	1,981
107 Hosiery	186.0	81.1	5,306
108 Wearing apparel	623.0	271.6	6,680
109 Tanneries and leather	104.3	22.5	2,116
110 Footwear (leather)	179.1	84.4	2,310
117 Morocco leather	209.6	82.8	597
Total	8,856.7	3,931.1	23,174

peting production in 1972 but which are classified as labor-intensive by Lary (1968) and Banerji (1975). These products are shown at the three-digit SITC classification in table 10.22. To obtain this list I con-

Table 10.22   Substitution for Noncompeting Imports (Thousand Dinars)

SITC Code	Product (1)	Value of Imports (2)	Substitutable Imports (3)	Value-Added Content (4)
611	Leather	148.0	148.0	31.4
642	Paper and paperboard	175.8	105.5	31.5
651	Textile yarn	156.5	123.4	45.5
657	Special textile fabrics and related products	2,564.7	2,457.5	926.5
663	Mineral manufactures	672.3	443.2	231.7
664	Glass	266.2	132.0	85.4
666	Pottery	251.5	251.5	96.5
693	Wires	171.1	167.9	91.5
695	Tools for use in the hand or machines	664.8	558.6	304.6
697	Household equipment of base metals	130.8	—	—
699	Manufactures of base metals	337.2	—	—
741	Heating and cooling apparatus	2,597.7	2,333.5	1,343.2
742	Pumps for liquids	1,832.0	1,765.1	1,016.0
743	Other pumps and compressors	2,236.9	2,236.9	1,287.6
745	Other nonmetallic machinery, etc.	921.2	769.0	442.6
751	Office machines	947.8	882.1	591.4
764	Telecommunications equipment	3,588.5	3,349.1	2,075.2
775	Household equipment	178.6	113.3	69.4
778	Electrical machinery and apparatus n.e.c.	2,035.3	1,770.5	779.9
784	Parts and accessories of motor vehicles	3,538.3	3,537.8	1,477.8
785	Motorcycles, etc.	577.2	527.5	222.1
791	Railway vehicles	605.7	455.1	190.7
884	Optical goods	117.0	—	—
885	Watches and clocks	197.6	—	—
894	Baby carriages, toys, games	159.0	—	—
895	Office and stationery supplies	127.1	—	—
899	Miscellaneous manufactures	194.1	—	—
Total		25,392.8	22,157.7	11,340.5

Note: Col. 2: c.i.f. values.

Col. 3: part of relevant col. 2 for which the six-digit trade nomenclature element is larger than 100,000 dinars.

Col. 4: obtained by applying French 1972 VA/output ratios to col. 3, after correcting import values for freight-insurance charges to make them comparable with the French production figures.

sidered items at the six-digit level whose value of imports was larger than 100,000 dinars.[56] This limitation requires new industries to be significantly large enough to allow them to take advantage of minimal economies of scale. The relevant figures are given in column 3 of table 10.22. This import substitution program would result in about 22 million dinars of output and 11 million of value added, and the employment effect is 11,100 total man-years, of which 6,500 would be unskilled.[57]

Assuming a capital/value-added ratio of 3.0,[58] this program would have required capital expenditure of about 46 million dinars in 1966 prices. The contraction of a number of sectors considered in table 10.19 would have released a significant amount of capital for the expansion of new industries. More capital could have been obtained by refraining from the development of two major projects, the steel mill, and the pulp and paper plant.[59] Therefore the financing of the additional import substitution program would have required merely a reallocation of resources to these more labor-intensive industries.

The total employment effects of the three import substitution programs are summarized in table 10.23. If all three had been implemented, total employment would have increased by 27,000 man-years, or by 68 percent of the 1972 importable employment, or alternatively, by 17 percent of total HOS employment. Unskilled employment would have increased even more, by 82 percent. Finally, total output would have been 49 percent larger. These impressive output and employment gains would

Table 10.23   Employment Effects of an Alternative Import Substitution Program

Component of Program	Value Added (Thousand Dinars)	Employment Gain Man-Years	
		L	UL
Expansion of labor-intensive and low effective protection industries, and contraction of capital-intensive, highly protected industries	—	5,610	3,719
Use of more labor-intensive techniques and expanded production			
Change in labor intensity	—	2,690	2,690
Expansion of production	3,512	3,860	2,353
Additional import substitution			
For competing imports	3,931	3,778	2,166
For noncompeting imports	11,340	11,100	6,500
Total	18,783	27,038	17,428
Increase as percentage of 1972 total for import-competing industries	49	68	82

have required only a reallocation of resources in favor of the more labor-intensive industries, with no additional capital. The estimated employment gains would have been much larger if account were taken of indirect employment effects. In my calculations, I assumed that all intermediate inputs (except home goods) in the expanded industries would be imported. To the extent that such inputs could be domestically produced, the employment implications would be larger. Income multiplier effects would have generated additional indirect employment.

While the employment gains from such an alternative import substitution program are impressive and significant, it is also quite clear that no import substitution program would be able to significantly relieve the employment problem. It is sufficient to compare the 27,000 man-years gained to 95,000 persons less than fully employed[60] in the total nonagricultural labor force of 850,000 (1975 census) and to the 140,000 persons estimated to have migrated to other countries in recent years. Therefore it is clear that industrialization aimed at absorbing urban unemployment must be based on a policy of encouraging exports of labor-intensive manufactures.

10.5.2 Export Promotion Policies

The import substitution policies of the 1960s were clearly biased against employment. Overall, and for individual activities, employment elasticities with respect to value added (see table 10.24) fell, manufactured exports grew slowly, and employment created through exports was negligible throughout the period. I estimate that fewer than 5,000 man-years were employed in manufacturing for export in 1972 by producers classified as export industries.[61] In addition, there were about 2,000 man-years involved in export production by activities classified as importables. These 7,000 man-years are a small amount representing less than 10 percent of total employment in manufacturing in 1972. Moreover, the major part of export employment was created in processing raw materials that have low labor intensities.

The poor employment performances of both manufactured exports and import substitutes, coupled with a change in government, led to the export promotion scheme of 1972. In April 1972, new legislation provided incentives to encourage export-oriented industries and to attract direct foreign investment. These incentives included duty-free entry of intermediate and capital goods, tax benefits, and foreign exchange facilities.

I do not have data to fully appraise this policy change. However, the existing data indicate that Tunisia has not yet been able to benefit substantially from exports to absorb its growing labor force. Beginning from a small base, the value of manufactured exports increased more than fourfold from 1971 to 1975; the share of manufactured exports (exclud-

Table 10.24 Employment Elasticities with respect to Value Added, and Incremental Employment/Value Added Ratios, 1961–76

Activity	Employment Elasticities with Respect to Value-Added[a]				Incremental Employment/ Value Added[a] Ratios 1972–76	Increase in Employment (Man-Years), 1972–76
	1961–65	1965–69	1969–72	1972–75		
Manufacturing exclusive of food processing and rugs	1.121	0.785	0.455	1.087	1.056	35,894
Electrical and mechanical industries	1.549	0.629	0.398	2.036	0.939	6,200
Construction materials—glass	2.296	0.455	0.327	1.095	1.113	5,900
Chemicals—rubber	0.701	0.620	0.453	0.675[b]	—[e]	2,050
Wood, cork, paper, miscellaneous	1.207	0.792	0.395	1.141	1.140	5,700
Textiles, clothing, leather	1.187[c]	0.652[c]	0.738[c]	0.603[c]	1.321	26,284
Spinning and weaving	—	—	—	—	0.681	2,044
Apparel	—	—	—	—	0.872	10,380
Hosiery	—	—	—	—	1.156	2,080
Leather	—	—	—	—	1.540	1,540
Rugs	—	—	—	—	4.655	10,240

[a]Employment elasticities are based on compound annual growth rates for the various subperiods, as reported in Nabli (1978), table VI.2. Employment data are from Institut National de la Statistique, and real value added (at 1966 prices for 1961–69 and 1972 prices for 1969–75) are from Ministry of Planning national accounts.

[b]For the period up to 1974 only. In 1975 output was very low, owing to slack international demand.

[c]Excluding rugs.

[d]Based on change in value added (million dinars) and changes in employment (thousand man-years). (See Nabli 1978, table VII.5.)

[e]Negative change in value added.

ing processed minerals) in total exports rose from 6 to 10 percent in the same period. Growth was heavily concentrated in textiles, particularly apparel, which provided over 60 percent of the increase; their share in total manufactured exports[62] increased from about 9 percent in 1970–71 to 25 percent in 1974–75. Other major exports were paper products, foodstuffs, and products from the mechanical industries.

Total manufacturing employment[63] rose by about 36,000 from 1972 to 1976, with about 45 percent (16,000) caused by expansion of textile production. Export-related direct employment increased by only 5,500 workers,[64] which is small relative to the country's employment problem but large relative to initial exportable employment. This small increase is due to the continued decrease in textile's employment elasticity and the small incremental labor/value added ratio in the fastest growing textile industries (spinning-weaving and apparel). In all other manufacturing activities, employment elasticities improved (rose) after 1972; that for textiles fell (see table 10.24). Thus, while there were significant employment gains, these gains would have been larger had output or export growth or both been concentrated in other industries.

The low incremental L/DVA in textiles after 1972 was due either to the use of fairly capital-intensive techniques or to high rates of profit in the industry. It cannot be attributed to improvements in the rate of capacity utilization. Most of the increased output and employment in textiles was due to increased capacity. Until 1972, capital formation was practically stagnant, and the existing capital stock was located principally in the spinning and weaving industries. Capital formation increased rapidly after 1972, with new capacity created mainly in the apparel and hosiery industries.

A final problem was that export growth was heavily concentrated in one activity—wearing apparel—and oriented toward France and other European countries. This factor made the new export activity highly vulnerable to possible restrictions by the importing countries, as is shown by recent experience.

To summarize, Tunisia's limited experience with export promotion has not yet been as successful as anticipated. Employment growth has been concentrated largely in a limited number of activities, which makes it vulnerable to market conditions. These activities use capital-intensive techniques, enjoy high levels of profits, or both.

10.6 Conclusions

This study has evaluated the implications of trade policies for employment of skilled and unskilled labor in Tunisia. It has focused largely upon the import substitution policies of the 1960s, although some effort was made to analyze the export promotion policies recently enacted.

Its results were broadly consistent with the HOS explanation of trade. Despite commodity markets distortions caused by protection, Tunisia was a net exporter of labor; that is, the labor content of its exports was larger than that of its imports—both competing and noncompeting. When manufactured exports and manufactured imports only were compared, however, the evidence was ambiguous, with results generally indicating that the country was a net exporter of unskilled labor and a net importer of skills. Also, I found evidence of a negative association between unskilled labor intensity and height of effective protection.

The factor market analysis showed that significant distortions existed in the labor and capital markets. The major dichotomy was between the public and private nonmonopolistic sectors, with the public sector facing a higher wage/rental ratio and having smaller variability within groups. This result suggested that distortions are larger and more evenly applied in the public sector than in the private sector. Labor intensities in the public sector were found to be significantly lower than those in the private sector at most levels of protection.

I also found that advantages associated with capital goods imports and credit policies tended to bias the choice of production techniques against labor creation. However, I was not able to quantify the employment effects of this bias with precision.

These findings have major employment implications. The low labor absorption performance of Tunisian manufacturing during the 1960s can be explained to a large extent by its import substitution policy. This policy tended to protect the development of more capital-intensive activities to produce for the domestic market. Moreover, the development of the public sector was a major instrument of the import substitution policy and was associated with the development of capital-intensive industries, industries using capital-intensive techniques of production, and industries benefiting from high effective protection.

The system of incentives did not promote faster growth of the more labor-intensive sectors. Rather, it favored the creation of less labor-intensive industries, which had a negative effect on employment. I estimated that an alternative import substitution program, implemented through a different system of incentives, could have generated a more efficient allocation of resources and about 27,000 more man-years of employment in 1972. This would have represented a 68 percent gain over total employment in import substitution industries.

Even though alternative import substitution policies would have generated relatively large increases in employment, I found that such policies would not have significantly helped to reduce the unemployment problem. Tunisia would have had to follow more export-oriented policies in order to have a significant amount of employment creation through trade.

During the 1960s the Tunisian trade policy provided very few incentives for promotion of exports and even discriminated against them, thereby preventing any significant employment creation through that avenue. A more efficient resource allocation could probably have induced the development of a significant export sector that would have generated more employment in labor-intensive industries.

Since 1972 the Tunisian trade policy has been aimed at expanding exports to create more jobs. To date its results have been modest, especially because exports have been concentrated in a few goods, particularly wearing apparel. However, I was not able to fully evaluate the consequences of this recent policy in this study. Further research, based along lines followed here, is warranted.

Appendix

Table 10.A.1   I-O Table Sectors, SITC Correspondence, and Trade Category

I-O Code Number (150 × 150)	SITC Code (1975)[a]	Name of Sector	Classification[b]
1	041, 043, 044, 045, 0542, 05482, 121, 263	Cereals, industrial crops	NRB–IC
2	0541, 0544, 0545, 05798	Vegetables	NRB–IC
3	0571, 0572, 0574, 0575, 0576, 05774, 0579, 2238, 292	Horticultural crops (including olives and grapes)	NRB–Export
4	0811	Animal feed	NRB–Export
5	244, 245, 246, 247, 248	Forestry	NRB–Export
6	001, 0223, 025, 0616, 268	Livestock	NRB–IC
7	0341, 0360, 29197	Fishing	NRB–Export
8	*	Irrigation	H
9	2713	Phosphate rock mining	NRB–Export
10	281	Iron-ore mining	NRB–Export
11	287, 52216	Nonferrous metals mining	NRB–Export
12	27312	Marble extraction	NRB–IC
13	27311, 27313, 27323, 2733, 2734, 27821, 6613	Quarrying, except marble	H
14	2783	Salt	NRB–Export
15	333, 341	Crude petroleum and natural gas	NRB–Export

Table 10.A.1—*continued*

I-O Code Number (150 × 150)	SITC Code (1975)[a]	Name of Sector	Classification[b]
16	334	Oil refining	HOS–Export
17	351	Autoproduction of electricity	H
18	351	Electricity	H
19	*	Gas manufacture and distribution	H
20	*	Water supply, except for irrigation	H
21	011, 211	Slaughtering of meat	H
22	056, 058	Canning: fruits and vegetables	HOS–Export
23	0342, 035, 0360, 037	Canning: fish	HOS–Export
24	046, 047	Cereal-grain milling	H
25	04841	Bakery	H
26	04842	Pastry, biscuits	H
27	062, 072, 073	Chocolates, sugar confectionery	H
28	0481, 0483	Cereal-food preparation	H
29	061	Sugar factories, refining	HOS–IC
30	061	Sugar pressing	HOS–Export
31	061	Vanilla sugar	HOS–IC
32	09806	Yeast	HOS–IC
33	09806	Baking powder	HOS–IC
34	022, 023, 034	Milk and products	HOS–IC
35	09141	Margarine	HOS–IC
36	1123	Breweries	H
37	1110	Mineral water and soda drinks	H
38	*	Manufactured ice	H
39	1121	Wineries	NRB–Export
40	5121	Pure alcohol	NCI
41	1124	Liquors and spirits	HOS–IC
42	*	Boukha (dried fig alcohol)	H
43	09807	Vinegar	H
44	071	Coffee preparation	H
45	4235, 08135	Crude olive oil	NRB–Export
46	4235	Olive oil refining	HOS–Export
47	08134, 4241	Linseed oil refining	HOS–IC
48	4232	Soya oil refining	HOS–IC
49	08139	Other vegetable oil refining	HOS–Export
50	0813, 0814,	Feed preparations for animals	HOS–IC
51	122, 57211, 64241, 89932	Tobacco and products	HOS–IC
52	671, 672, 673, 677	Iron and steel	HOS–Export
53	52241, 52247,	Nonferrous metals smelting	HOS–Export

Table 10.A.1—*continued*

I-O Code Number (150 × 150)	SITC Code (1975)[a]	Name of Sector	Classi- fication[b]
	6811, 6821, 6851		
54	69401	First transformation of iron	HOS–IC
55	6852	First transformation of non-ferrous metals (lead)	HOS–IC
56	678, 679, 6842	Foundries	HOS–IC
57	691, 69211, 69243, 7415, 7868, 8121	Scaffolding, containers, radiators, etc.	HOS–IC
58	7243, 7245	Sewing machines	HOS–IC
59	693, 6940, except 69401, 695, 696, 69731, 69732[c]	Ferrous metal products	HOS–IC
60	69213, 69735, 69743, 684, 69913	Aluminum products	HOS–IC
61	713, 781, 782, 783, 77831	Motor vehicle assembly	HOS–IC
62	761, 762, 763, 764, 771, 772, 778, 7754, 873	Electrical and electronic machinery	HOS–IC
63	6611, 6612	Cement, lime	HOS–Export
64	27324	Plaster	HOS–IC
65	66182	Cement and mosaic tiles	HOS–IC
66	66245	Glazed tiles	HOS–IC
67	66332	Pipes and canals of cement	H
68	66183	Articles of absesco cement	HOS–IC
69	66332	Other cement products	HOS–IC
70	66241	Ceramics	HOS–Export
71	8122	Sanitary fixtures	HOS–Export
72	664, 665	Glass and products	HOS–IC
73	247, 248, 6351	Sawmills and wood mills, local wood	HOS–IC
74	63441, 6353, 63542, 8211, 82192, 85103	Wood mills, foreign wood	HOS–IC
75	79321, 8211, 82192	Furniture and pleasure boats	HOS–IC
76	79324	Fishing vessels, construction, repairs	HOS–IC
139	63442	Panels of marquetry and inlaid wood	HOS–IC
77	633	Cork and products	HOS–Export
78	52222, 562	Fertilizers	HOS–Export
138	52224	Phosphoric acid	HOS–Export
140	52214, 52311	Fluor products	NCI
79	27892, 52324, 52393, 52394	Barium sulfate and calcium carbonate	NCI

Table 10.A.1—*continued*

I-O Code Number (150 × 150)	SITC Code (1975)[a]	Name of Sector	Classification[b]
80	52327	Soda silicates	HOS–IC
81	52215	Sulfur refining	HOS–IC
82	52211, 52218, 52399	Industrial gases	HOS–IC
83	57212, 5722	Explosives	HOS–IC
84	5723	Pyrotechnic products	NCI
85	531, 532	Dyes, colorants	HOS–IC
86	533, except 5332	Paints, varnishes	HOS–IC
87	5332	Printing inks	HOS–IC
88	592	Glues	HOS–IC
89	431	Household soap	HOS–Export
90	5542, 5543	Detergents	HOS–IC
91	591	Insecticides, disinfectants, deodorants	HOS–IC
92	553, 5541	Toilet products	HOS–IC
93	551	Floral essential oils	HOS–IC
94	553	Perfumes	HOS–IC
95	541	Pharmaceuticals	HOS–IC
96	89931	Candles	HOS–IC
97	625	Rubber products	HOS–IC
98	82122, 893	Plastics	HOS–IC
99	2519	Paper pulp (alfa)	HOS–Export
137	6412	Paper	HOS–IC
100	6413	Packing paper	HOS–IC
101	642	Articles of paper and carton	HOS–IC
102	8921, 8924, 8928	Printing, except newspaper	HOS–IC
103	8922	Newspaper printing	H
104	2633, 651	Spinning except jute	HOS–IC
105	652, 653, 654, except 6545, 658, 847	Weaving, except jute	HOS–IC
106	65198, 6545	Spinning, weaving of jute	HOS–IC
107	655, 844, except 8441, 8451, 846	Hosiery	HOS–IC
108	842, 843, 8441, 845, except 8451	Wearing apparel	HOS–IC
109	611	Tanneries and leather finishing	HOS–IC
110	85101, 85102	Footwear, leather	HOS–IC
111	89972	Brushes, brooms	HOS–IC
112	8942, except 89421	Toys	NCI
113	27891	Chalk	NCI
114	883	Movie films	NCI
115	8124	Lighting fixtures, lusters	HOS–IC

Table 10.A.1—*continued*

I-O Code Number (150 × 150)	SITC Code (1975)[a]	Name of Sector	Classification[b]
116	8998, 8933, 897	Merceries, jewelry, ornamental articles	HOS–IC
117	831	Morocco leather	HOS–IC
118	Hand 6512	Hand spinning of wool	NC
119	Hand 652, 65433	Handicraft weaving	NC
120	Hand 6592	Carpets	HOS–Export
121	Hand 6576	Chechias (hats)	HOS–Export
122	Hand 851	Handicraft shoemaking	NC
123	Hand 821	Handicraft furniture	NC
124	Hand 6597	Mats and mattings	NC
125	Hand 6595	Scourtins	NC
126	Hand 666	Pottery	NC
127	*	Construction	H
128	*	Hotels	HOS–Export
129	*	Tourist nonhotel restaurants	HOS–Export
130	*	Air transportation	HOS–Export
131	*	Pipeline	HOS–Export
132	*	Port services	H
133	*	Wholesale, retail trade	H
134	*	Mechanical, electrical repairs	H
135	*	Telecommunications	H
136	*	Other services	H
161	*	Financial services	H
164	6623	Refractory bricks	NCI
165	*	Rail transport	H
166	*	Sea transport	HOS–IC
167	*	Road transport	H
169	82122	Bed products	HOS–IC
171	*	Miscellaneous products	H
181	89584	Typewriter ribbons	NCI
182	885	Watches	HOS–IC
183	*	Dummy variables	

[a]Standard International Trade Classification, Revision 2, Series M, no. 34/Rev. 2, United Nations, 1975.

[b]The symbols are:
H: home goods
IC: import competing
NCI: non-import-competing goods
HOS: Heckscher-Ohlin-Samuelson goods
NRB: Natural resource based goods
NC: not classified
*: no corresponding SITC.

[c]Includes also: 69241, 69242, 69734, 6975, 6978, 699, 8219, 89421.

Table 10.A.2   Labor Requirements per Unit of Domestic Value Added
(Man-Years per Thousand Dinars) and Skill Content

	L/DVA		UL/DVA		SK	
I-O Code[a]	D	D + I	D	D + 1	D	D + I
9	2.389	1.850	1.589	1.182	.418	.464
10	2.193	1.463	1.628	1.008	.280	.359
11	1.780	1.539	1.053	.894	.387	.404
12	1.254	1.163	.794	.709	.691	.662
13	.795	.807	.551	.551	.450	.463
14	.678	.701	.336	.346	.824	.797
15	.016	.137	.005	.080	1.562	.605
16	.117	.216	.039	.096	1.162	.888
18	.300	.381	.090	.142	1.396	1.175
19	.300	.401	.090	.154	1.396	1.132
20	.373	.415	.205	.228	.608	.612
22	1.848	1.555	1.656	1.254	.181	.308
23	.513	.603	.440	.466	.274	.374
24	.852	.877	.532	.511	.602	.647
25	1.809	1.598	.922	.818	.684	.685
26	.873	.904	.564	.544	.580	.628
27	.597	.700	.372	.408	.665	.687
28	.892	.939	.489	.501	.815	.781
29	.299	.383	.188	.233	.541	.561
30	.030	.237	.058	.129	.412	.662
31	.818	.818	.181	.181	2.000	2.000
32	.818	.950	.181	.331	2.000	1.490
33	.818	.818	.181	.181	2.000	2.000
34	.462	.587	.307	.355	.469	.563
35	.631	.730	.315	.374	.966	.864
36	.436	.624	.270	.363	.545	.588
37	1.199	1.155	.800	.742	.617	.623
38	.436	.567	.270	.335	.545	.580
41	1.254	1.185	.536	.549	1.061	.919
42	1.254	1.229	.536	.591	1.061	.877
44	.268	.386	.171	.217	.839	.836
50	.803	.890	.647	.573	.368	.523
51	.055	.064	.029	.033	.636	.640
52	.263	.399	.134	.198	.749	.759
53	.819	.804	.583	.512	.395	.517
54	1.200	1.173	.900	.840	.516	.543
55	.335	.547	.194	.298	.895	.771
56	1.096	1.090	.691	.676	.498	.516
57	1.096	1.087	.691	.665	.498	.532
58	.427	.488	.095	.134	.927	.903
59	.808	.830	.464	.461	.548	.592

Table 10.A.2—*continued*

I-O Code[a]	L/DVA		UL/DVA		SK	
	D	D + I	D	D + 1	D	D + I
60	.808	.895	.464	.495	.548	.604
61	.977	.998	.392	.456	.959	.830
62	2.965	1.952	1.418	.945	.798	.779
63	.923	.852	.615	.522	.412	.535
64	1.000	.959	.852	.690	.405	.490
65	1.777	1.470	1.350	1.051	.329	.397
66	1.777	1.493	1.350	1.063	.329	.399
67	.452	.553	.288	.350	.440	.473
68	1.003	.972	.794	.660	.283	.461
69	1.008	1.007	.794	.742	.283	.358
70	1.313	1.196	1.033	.869	.345	.432
71	1.935	1.394	1.146	.771	.479	.583
72	.906	.928	.003	.570	.611	.650
73	.637	.680	.426	.430	.583	.622
74	1.649	1.503	1.038	.916	.496	.532
75	2.026	1.789	1.102	.956	.597	.623
76	1.870	1.776	1.126	1.056	.372	.384
77	1.113	1.083	.734	.678	.374	.447
78	.537	.699	.300	.376	.687	.675
80	.821	.830	.688	.655	.332	.374
81	.290	.420	.168	.235	.879	.780
82	.493	.699	.187	.340	.890	.718
83	.821	.847	.688	.613	.332	.449
85	.355	.409	.169	.205	1.053	.955
86	.355	.454	.169	.219	1.053	.949
87	.355	.479	.169	.237	1.053	.910
88	.390	.588	.212	.316	.761	.710
89	3.855	3.019	2.765	2.104	.469	.492
90	.656	.787	.430	.480	.623	.630
91	.500	.822	.178	.393	2.320	1.110
92	.500	.614	.178	.253	2.320	1.747
93	.455	.541	.223	.266	1.175	1.049
94	.455	.633	.223	.319	1.175	.939
95	.802	.860	.354	.399	.824	.780
96	.666	.695	.600	.552	.379	.500
97	.235	.373	.097	.168	1.021	.837
98	.547	.625	.368	.385	.440	.540
		Negative Domestic Value Added				
100	.778	.843	.394	.444	.605	.609
101	.283	.382	.163	.212	.657	.670
102	1.161	1.159	.594	.601	.699	.688

Table 10.A.2—*continued*

I-O Code[a]	L/DVA		UL/DVA		SK	
	D	D + I	D	D + 1	D	D + I
103	.583	.680	.227	.296	1.178	1.013
104	.869	.876	.451	.426	.586	.702
105	.869	.894	.451	.444	.586	.677
106	.869	.901	.451	.460	.586	.638
107	2.793	2.124	1.515	1.131	.532	.573
108	2.279	1.888	1.295	1.042	.512	.559
109	1.190	1.110	.767	.656	.551	.626
110	1.126	1.079	.636	.581	.463	.553
111	1.310	1.259	.565	.544	.725	.736
112	5.000	5.000	4.000	4.000	.900	.900
113	4.500	4.500	3.000	3.000	.811	.811
115	.516	.576	.241	.265	1.199	1.116
116	3.853	2.983	2.073	1.598	.525	.544
117	.996	.984	.567	.541	.625	.663
127	1.444	1.304	1.200	.992	.256	.354
130	.214	.582	.061	.292	1.140	.719
131	.028	.246	.006	.146	1.250	.532
132	.902	.904	.734	.733	.264	.269
133[b]	.922	.919	.341	.352	1.034	.995
134	2.289	2.168	1.527	1.432	.402	.415
135[b]	.761	.810	.236	.287	1.038	.960
136[b]	1.129	1.149	.609	.627	.638	.626
137	.273	.399	.151	.203	.802	.701
138	.382	.614	.096	.263	1.479	.897
139	.637	.631	.426	.432	.583	.616
161[b]	.922	.927	.341	.354	1.034	1.003
165	.964	.973	.464	.474	.594	.605
166	.125	.189	.042	.075	1.576	1.253
167	.695	.730	.385	.400	.510	.536
169	.640	.712	.263	.304	.892	.866
182	3.176	2.085	2.323	1.400	.460	.534

Note: The variables are:
L/DVA: total man-years per thousand dinars of DVA
UL/DVA: unskilled man-years per thousand dinars of DVA
SK: index of "pure skill" content relative to total man-years
D: indicates direct requirements and D + I direct-plus-indirect in home goods requirements.

[a]For manufacturing sectors not appearing in this table the census of manufactures does not provide information, and such sectors are ignored in the analysis. They are not, however, quantitatively significant.

[b]For these home goods producing sectors factor requirements estimates have been derived independently, since the census of manufactures does not provide information on them.

Table 10.A.3   Partition of Activities among Commodity Categories

Commodity Category	I-O Code Numbers of Sectors Included[a]
All exportables	9, 10, 11, 14, 15, 16, 22, 23, 30, 52, 53, 63, 70, 71, 77, 78, 89, 99,* 138
HOS exportables (excluding refined oil)	22, 23, 30, 52, 53, 63, 70, 71, 77, 78, 89, 99,* 138
Traditional exportables	22, 23, 89
NRB exportables (excluding refined oil)	52, 53, 77, 78, 99,* 138
Manufactured exportables	30, 63, 70, 71
NRB	
Excluding crude oil	9, 10, 11, 14
Including crude oil	9, 10, 11, 14, 15
HOS importable activities[b]	*12*, 29, 31, 32, 33, 34, *35, 41*, 50, 51, 54, 55, 56, 57, 58, *59, 60, 61, 62,* 64, 65, 66, 68, 69, 72, 73, 74, 75, 76, 80, 81, 83, 85, 86, 87, 88, *90, 91,* 92, 93, 94, 95, 96, 97, 98, 100, 101, 102, 104, 105, 106, *107, 108, 109,* *110, 111, 115, 116, 117, 137, 139, 169, 182*
Foods	29, 31, 32, 33, 34, *35, 41*, 51
Manufactured consumer goods	62, 66, 74, 75, 90, 91, 92, 93, 94, 96, 97, 98, 105, 106, *107, 108, 110,* 111, 115, 116, 117, *169, 182*
Intermediate products	50, 54, 55, 56, 64, 65, 68, 69, 72, 73, 80, 81, 82, 83, 85, 86, 87, 88, 95, 100, 101, 102, 104, *109*, 137, 139
Capital goods	57, 58, 59, *60, 61, 76*

[a]Italic numbers indicate sectors having negative IVA according to Ministry of Planning estimates. Sector 99, which is starred (*), has negative DVA and is not included in computations.

[b]Sector 12, marble, even though it is based on a natural resource, is included here because the resource is domestically available, and because the sector covers finishing of both domestic and imported raw marble. It is, however, excluded from the commodity group classification in the lower part of the table.

Notes

1. There is no recent complete survey of the Tunisian economy. Blake (1974) gives a detailed discussion of the trade regime; Duwaji (1967) gives an account of Tunisian development through the mid-sixties. The complete study upon which this chapter is based may also be useful to the general reader. It is available for the cost of reproduction from the National Bureau of Economic Research.

2. The input-output table is from Institut d'Economie Quantitative Ali Bach-Hamba, Tunis, and the census of manufactures is from the Institut National de la Statistique, Tunis.

3. The exchange rate in 1957 was 1,000 old French francs to the dinar (making one dinar equal to approximately 2.4 dollars).

4. It is estimated that the ratio of gross capital formation to GDP fell from about 20 percent in 1950–51 to 10 percent in 1956–58 and that the average rate of population growth increased from 2.1 percent in 1946–56 to 2.8 percent in 1956–66, then declined to 2.3 percent in 1966–75.

5. Secrétariat d'Etat au Plan et Finances, "Perspectives Décennales de Développement, 1962–71," and "Plan Triennal, 1962–64."

6. Imports were divided into four categories: the liberalized regime without QRs mostly for raw materials and capital goods, the quota regime for consumer goods, relative prohibition for goods that could be imported only if domestic supply was deficient, and total prohibition for some goods. Import licenses were required for all imports, but the procedure depended on whether the import originated in France.

7. Their values ranged from 25 to 100 percent of the value of imports to be held for up to three months.

8. The exchange rate changed from 0.420 dinars to 0.525 dinars to the dollar.

9. Law of 23 July JORT, 13 September 1973.

10. This can be seen by comparing rates of change in c.i.f. and wholesale prices of restricted and unrestricted imports. From 1970 to 1973, both sets of prices for unrestricted goods generally changed at the same rate. However, for restricted goods, a different pattern emerged. In 1970–71, both sets of prices moved at the same rate; in 1972–73, c.i.f. prices rose more rapidly than wholesale prices. These changes in price behavior indicate importers began to absorb c.i.f. price increases as restrictions were being relaxed.

11. In 1974 both the current account balance and merchandise balance were positive because there was a large increase in the price of oil and phosphates. However large deficits reappeared in 1975 (see table 10.2).

12. Alfa is a plant used to make paper pulp.

13. Note that the values given in table 10.4 refer to merchandise trade only. They therefore differ from the values of table 10.2, which include trade in goods and services. Service trade is important to Tunisia. In 1972 service exports (mainly tourism and transportation) were 41 percent of total exports of goods and services. Likewise, service imports were 17 percent of total imports of goods and services in 1972.

14. For these estimates, food processing (except for olive oil and wines) and rugs were treated as manufacturing activities. Excluding food processing and rugs gives an elasticity of 0.9.

15. A detailed presentation of these is given in the Ministry of Planning (1975) study of effective protection.

16. The Corden procedure, which should be used, cannot be used from these studies.

17. A detailed comparison of the two studies is found in Nabli (1978).

18. In all calculations, sectors with ERP < -100 percent are excluded.

19. The large figure for capital goods in the Blake estimates is due to the inclusion of mechanical and electrical industries (sectors 61 and 62), which have large ERPs.

20. The number of seasonal employees was converted from man-days to man-years, assuming 1 man-year $= 250$ man-days. Also, all estimates of employment are averages of the number of workers as of 2 January 1972 and 2 January 1973. This helps reduce the sampling error of estimates.

21. It was assumed that half the workers in this category were semiskilled and the rest were unskilled. This division was inferred from other survey data and is thought to be reasonable.

22. The weights, w_i, were 6.77, 2.23, 2.95, 1.41, 1.00, 0.36, and 1.00 for the seven labor categories in the text. Two other indexes for unskilled labor and two for skill content were calculated with results generally the same. Results with other indexes are given in Nabli (1978).

23. Sector 30, pressed sugar, had zero exports in 1972 but is classified as an export sector. Traditionally, output from this sector has been exported to Algeria.

24. The correlation coefficients are as follows: 0.95 for L/DVA and UL/DVA, -0.342 for L/DVA and SK, and -0.514 for UL/DVA and SK.

25. For details of calculations see Nabli (1978).

26. It should be noted in this respect that inclusion or exclusion of sectors with negative IVA does not affect the results.

27. If one were willing to assume that physical capital and skills were complementary, the skill content indicator would be a good indicator of capital intensity. In this regard, note in table 10.11 that exportables are less skill-intensive and therefore perhaps less capital-intensive than importables.

28. The data are unpublished and were obtained from the Institut National de la Statistique et des Etudes Economiques, Paris. No skill breakdown of the labor force or wage bill was available, so skill indexes could not be calculated.

29. I also made a gross adjustment for the value of imports in order to make the figures comparable with those of the I-O table for production, which are at producer's values. I subtracted freight and insurance charges on imports at a uniform rate (8 percent), and also domestic (in France) trade margins.

30. Direct plus indirect home goods requirements were not calculated but would not be very different from the direct only estimates, since the labor coefficients in home goods are close to the average of all sectors in France.

31. Again here I am considering only the labor content of noncompeting imports that are directly imported and ignoring indirectly imported noncompeting goods. A more appropriate procedure would be to calculate the labor content of "direct plus indirect in noncompeting" noncompeting imports, but this would be a difficult empirical task.

32. Most sectors are in the interval of -25 to $+100$ percent, but a large number of sectors are highly protected: 15 have ERPs of 200 percent or more, and 16 have negative IVA. The ranges of ERPs are as follows for groups 1–6, respectively: -75 to 0; 0 to 50; 50 to 75; 75 to 125; 125 to 200; and ≥ 200. The seventh group includes sectors for which IVA is negative according to the Ministry of Planning study. The results of the analysis are not changed when using the effective protection estimates of Blake and are not reported here.

33. The evidence is even stronger using other unskilled labor indexes with a narrower definition of unskilled labor.

34. This category includes managers, engineers, salaried employees, and supervisory personnel.

35. The coefficient of SEX could be interpreted as the premium (negative) of a female unskilled worker relative to a male unskilled if the differential affects only unskilled female labor. But the large coefficient of SEX is evidence that this interpretation is not valid and that differentials are present at all skill levels.

36. There is a high degree of data variability for these firms. It is well known that the accounting practices are weak, and they are often unable to provide accurate information.

37. Comparing the constant terms of regression equations (4) and (14) of table 10.15 suggests that such a differential does not exist. But this comparison is misleading, since the constant term a_o includes also the average effect of the omitted elements in the determination of wages; that is, $a^*_o = a_o + E(u)$, when $E(u) \neq 0$.

38. Size is the proportion of employment in firms of fifty employees or more in the sectoral totals, and labor intensity is measured by the labor/domestic value added ratio.

39. I also assume a 30 percent currency overvaluation, no tariffs or taxes on capital goods, and a 40 percent import content of investment. Note that the ratio of wage/rental ratios in the public and private sectors is $1.2/[(1 - .3 \times .4)4/7] = 1.2/.5 = 2.4$. The ratio of wage/rental ratios is $1.2/x$ where the ratio of rental rates is $x = \dfrac{(1 - 0.3 \times 0.4)4}{7}$.

40. The first group of the public sector includes two labor-intensive activities: pharmaceuticals and animal feed.

41. Results based on UL/DVA are only slightly different from the ones outlined here (see table 10.16).

42. See table 10.24.

43. The level-of-protection groups were defined in the preceding section. See table 10.16 and note 32.

44. Account is not taken of group 7 in these comments.

45. The labor intensity criteria were: (1) L/DVA higher than 0.961 for direct plus home goods indirect, or UL/DVA higher than 0.551; (2) the activity was included in Lary's (1968, table C–1) list of labor-intensive manufactures; or (3) the activity was on Banerji's (1975, table A–11) list of labor-intensive manufactures.

46. Here and throughout the rest of this section, employment figures cited refer to direct plus indirect labor.

47. They accounted for only 27 percent of total man-years and 25 percent of unskilled man-years.

48. With a Cobb-Douglas production function $Y = AK^{\alpha}L^{1-\alpha}$, and a change in the wage/rental ratio from

$$\frac{w_o}{r_o} \text{ to } \frac{w_1}{r_1} = (1 + \rho)\, \frac{w_o}{r_o}, \text{ we have } \frac{K_1}{L_1} = (1 + \rho)\, \frac{K_o}{L_o} \text{ and }$$

$$\frac{L_1}{Y_1} = \left(\frac{1}{1 + \rho}\right)^{\alpha} \frac{L_o}{Y_o},$$

with $w_1 = w_o$, $r_1 = 1.56\, r_o$, $\rho = -0.36$, $\alpha = 0.5$, and $\left(\dfrac{1}{1 + \rho}\right)^{\alpha} = 1.25$.

49. Strictly speaking, the argument above applies to direct requirements. Since in almost all the sectors considered the direct plus indirect coefficients are larger than the direct-only coefficient, the required increase in the direct coefficients should be larger than 25 percent, but the difference should be small, because the indirect requirements are generally small.

50. That is, column 10 = column 6 + (column 8 — column 4). This would imply, in fact, an average increase in unskilled labor-intensity of 48 percent.

51. Mechanical industries and textiles.

52. Applying average total and unskilled labor ratios of 1.100 and 0.670, respectively.

53. Total imports of the activity are larger than 100,000 dinars (c.i.f.). The large amount of imports in each activity may be due to aggregation problems; that is, the imports may be qualitatively different from domestic production. For sector 62 there are fifteen import categories from the six-digit Trade Nomenclature. Six of them make up 77 percent of the total, and eleven have value added greater than 100,000 dinars and account for 98 percent of imports in the sector. The pattern is similar in other sectors. Generally, two or three import categories predominate. Exceptions are sectors 109 and 117.

54. That is, in addition to the actual import substitution and to that considered above.

55. It is likely that the high rates of effective protection for those industries (according to Ministry of Planning estimates) are due to measurement errors and to existing inefficiencies. And these industries did not in fact expand because priority in investment was given to other capital-intensive projects.

56. Some SITC groups were not considered even when satisfying this condition, because they involve mostly machinery production where the 100,000 dinar minimum may not be strict enough, since taking advantage of economies of scale would require a much larger value of output; those SITC groups are 721, 723, 724, 725, 727, 728, 736, 737, 774, 793, 874, 881, and 882.

57. The labor coefficients were calculated using the average labor coefficients of the most similar domestic industry or the average coefficients of the import-competing industry.

58. The marginal capital value added ratio for manufacturing for the period 1961–72 was about 2.8.

59. The pulp and paper plant had negative DVA.

60. That is, who worked one to four days during the week before the census.

61. This estimate includes direct employment plus direct and indirect requirements in home goods production; see Nabli (1978).

62. Excluding olive oil and wine.

63. Excluding the artisanal carpet-weaving activity.

64. Calculated on the basis of incremental export-output ratios and employment created: construction materials (none), electrical, mechanical (584), chemicals-rubber (about 500 from new projects), wood, paper, miscellaneous (244), textiles (4,000 excluding carpets).

References

Banerji, R. 1975. *Exports of manufacture from India.* Tübingen: J. C. B. Möhr.

Banque Centrale de Tunisie (BCT). Various years. *Statistiques financières.*

Blake, Robert, Jr. 1974. Import controls in Tunisia. Ph.D. diss., Department of Economics, University of Michigan, Ann Arbor.

Duwaji, A. 1967. *Economic development in Tunisia.* New York: Praeger.

Institut National de la Statistique. Various years. *Recensement des activités industrielles.*

International Monetary Fund. Various years. *International financial statistics.*

Krueger, Anne O. 1977. *Growth, distortions and patterns of trade among many countries.* Princeton Series in International Finance, no. 40. Princeton: Princeton University.

————. 1978. *Foreign trade regimes and economic development: Liberalization attempts and consequences.* Cambridge, Mass.: Ballinger, for NBER.

Lary, Hal. 1968. *Imports of manufactures from developing countries.* New York: NBER.

Ministry of Planning. Various years. *National accounts.* Various documents, unpublished, including Rapports sur le budget économique.

————. 1975. La protection effective des branches d'activité de l'économie tunisienne: Mesure et analyse. July. Unpublished.

Nabli, Mustapha K. 1978. Trade strategies, patterns of trade and employment in a developing country: The case of Tunisia. August. Mimeographed.

11 Uruguay: Alternative Trade Strategies and Employment Implications

Alberto Bension and Jorge Caumont

Introduction

Among the countries covered in this volume Uruguay is unique in several regards. First, and most important in terms of the study, Uruguay is the country where the least prior research has been done and where data availability poses the severest constraint upon analysis. Second, Uruguay is by far the most affluent country in the study, with a per capita GDP of $1,190 in 1974 (World Bank 1976, p. 5). Many social indicators reflect this: 91 percent of the population over seven years old is literate, life expectancy at birth is sixty-eight years, and population growth since 1908 has been about 1.2 percent per annum (Banco Central del Uruguay 1976a).

However, from the mid-1950s until the early 1970s, Uruguay's economic growth performance was almost as dismal as her initial standard of living was favorable. Uruguay was a very rich agricultural exporter in the 1920s and shifted policies toward import substitution after the Great Depression and World War II. This shift resulted in an annual growth rate of real GDP of only 1.6 percent over the decade 1935–45, 4.8 percent over the next ten years, and 0.7 percent per annum from 1955 to 1974 (Banco Central del Uruguay 1976b, p. 22—hereafter cited as BCU). Thus, per capita income in 1974 was probably slightly below its level twenty years earlier and probably no higher than it was in the 1920s.

Alberto Bension and Jorge Caumont are associated with the Universidad de la Republica, Montevideo.

The authors would like to thank Anne O. Krueger and Hal B. Lary for their very helpful comments and guidance throughout the entire work. Financial support was received from the National Bureau of Economic Research through a grant provided by the United States Agency for International Development.

499

In this paper we will analyze the employment implications of Uruguay's trade strategies. Focus is upon the year 1968, in the midst of the period when Uruguayan policies were directed heavily toward import substitution. The reason for this choice is, of course, data availability. In 1972 Uruguay did begin altering her policies toward a more systematic effort at export promotion. However, not enough time has elapsed since the change in orientation for us to interpret the results, and, in any event, data are not available beyond 1975. Indeed, for purposes of analysis, the terminal date for this study is 1974. When evidence does exist for later years that either strongly supports or tends to contradict the results based on an earlier period, that is indicated in the text or in the notes, as seems appropriate. However, by and large, experience with the altered trade and payments regime is far too limited to permit many inferences from it at this stage.

11.1 Overview of the Uruguayan Economy

11.1.1 Growth

Like those of most Latin American countries, Uruguayan policies shifted heavily toward protection of the home market and the encouragement of new industries during the Great Depression. Although, as already noted, growth was very slow during the depression and war years, the initial decade after World War II saw more rapid growth, spurred by output increases in the nontraditional industries. The so-called protected industries—those sheltered behind stringent exchange control, high tariffs, and the usual range of other protective devices—had contributed only 28.5 percent of total industrial production in 1930; by 1955 their share had risen to 40.5 percent (Facultad de Ciencias Económicas 1969). Also by 1955, half of industrial production represented consumption goods, while imports were more heavily oriented toward capital goods, fuels, and raw materials (23, 16, and 42 percent of total imports, respectively) (BCU 1955).

From 1955 to 1974 growth was sufficiently slow so that one can discuss the structure of the economy without regard to a specific date. For example, agriculture's contribution to GDP was 16.6 percent in 1955 and 15.3 in 1974 (BCU 1976b, pp. 4, 5). Crops and cattle retained their relative importance within agriculture: cattle accounted for 62 percent of agricultural product in 1955 and averaged the same over 1970–74. There were fluctuations in that proportion in the intervening years, but they were attributable to relative price changes rather than to underlying production shifts. As will be seen below, agriculture's contribution is even greater to exports than to GDP.

The composition of Uruguay's GDP reflects one of the factors accounting for slow growth: gross fixed capital formation fell from 15 or 16 percent of GDP in the early 1960s to an average of only 10 percent in 1973–75 (BCU 1976b, p. 1). Government consumption expenditure rose from about 10 to 13 percent of GDP over that period, while private consumption expenditure remained fairly constant at about 75 percent. Exports of goods and services have averaged about 14 percent of GDP in recent years, a significant drop from the 21 percent level in 1949–52, although these were the years of the Korean War. Part of the economic difficulties experienced over the next two decades stemmed from the need to curtail imports commensurately with the decline in export earnings. From 20 percent of GDP in 1960, imports of goods and services declined to an average of 14 percent in 1970–74.

That Uruguay's attempt at inner-oriented development did not succeed is reflected clearly in the behavior of industrial production and its various sectoral components over 1955–74. These data are given in table 11.1. As can be seen, only two relatively small sectors (rubber products and paper products) experienced growth rates over 5 percent, and the growth of industrial production as a whole averaged only 1.1 percent per annum over the two decades. Industrial output constituted about 23 percent of GDP during the 1960s, compared with about a 15 percent contribution for agriculture. Both these numbers are relatively low be-

Table 11.1   Structure and Growth Rates of Uruguayan Industry, 1955–74

Sector	Average Annual Rate of Growth	Percentage of Industrial Production		
		1955	1965	1974
20 Food products	0.6	23.3	21.4	21.5
21 Beverages	2.3	7.7	8.2	9.6
22 Tobacco products	3.6	2.5	3.7	4.0
23 Textiles	−1.3	15.7	14.2	10.0
24 Clothing and footwear	0.0	4.8	6.3	3.9
27 Paper and paper products	7.1	0.9	2.2	2.8
28 Printing and publishing	1.2	2.6	2.8	2.7
30 Rubber products	5.5	1.0	1.6	2.2
31 Chemicals	3.2	5.3	5.8	7.8
32 Fuel and fuel derivatives	0.8	5.1	5.5	4.9
33 Nonmetallic mineral products	4.2	5.5	5.5	9.8
35 Metal products	−4.5	4.2	3.0	1.4
37 Electrical machinery	−1.5	3.6	4.0	2.1
All others	0.9	17.8	15.8	17.3
Total	1.1	100.0	100.0	100.0

Source: Banco Central del Uruguay (BCU) 1970–76b (March 1976), p. 38.

cause of the large share of the service sector in Uruguay: in 1955 and again in 1974 housing and services together accounted for over 61 percent of GDP.

11.1.2   International Trade and Payments

Table 11.2 gives data on Uruguay's balance of payments for selected years over the period 1953–74. In general, import licenses have been issued to restrain imports to the available foreign exchange. When export earnings fell after 1953, imports were drastically reduced. Thereafter, the value of licenses issued was based upon export earnings. Capital flows and nonmerchandise trade items have been relatively unimportant in Uruguay's balance of payments most of the time. In 1974, however, capital inflows were a sizable offset to the negative balance on goods and services.

Uruguay's imports, reflecting the high degree of protection of the domestic market for manufactured goods, have consisted predominantly of fuels and raw materials. Capital equipment imports constituted 18 percent of the total over 1955–59 and fell to 13 percent in 1970–74, influenced by the low level of capital formation.[1] Imports in the years 1965–69 averaged $165 million, c.i.f., compared with an average of $203 million, c.i.f., in 1955–59. As with most Latin American countries, the fraction of imports originating with the Latin American Free Trade Area (LAFTA) trading partners increased, going from 19 percent in 1955 to 34 percent in 1974. The United States share of Uru-

Table 11.2   **Uruguay's Balance of Payments, Selected Years, 1953–74 (Millions of U.S. Dollars)**

	1953	1958	1963	1968	1974
Exports, f.o.b.	269	155	166	179	381
Imports, f.o.b.	274a	124	152	135	433
Trade balance	— 5	31	15	43	— 52
Services	n.a.b	— 17	— 19	— 27	— 83
Goods and services balance	n.a.	14	— 4	16	—135
Transfers	n.a.	1	4	7	17
Capital	n.a.	10	— 5	24	112
Deposit money banks	n.a.	9	4	15	— 6
Monetary authorities	n.a.	12	3	— 37	80
Net errors and omissions	n.a.	— 22	— 2	— 25	— 68

Sources: 1974, BCU 1970–76 (October 1976); 1968, BCU 1970–76 (1970); 1963, 1958, and 1963, BCU, Departamento de Investigaciones Economicas, *Balance of Payments Series*, various issues, especially 1970.

ac.i.f.

bn.a. = not available.

guay's imports fell from 18 to 7 percent over that period, while the EEC share dropped from 32 to 17 percent (Oficina de Planeamiento y Presupuesto 1973). In the later part of the period, Uruguay's imports of oil increased, thus increasing the share of imports originating from the rest of the world.

Table 11.3 gives some detail on the composition of exports from 1950 to 1974. As can be seen, nonagricultural exports were negligible until the late 1960s. Among agricultural commodities, animal products constituted the major portion. Meat and by-products have increased in relative and absolute importance over the years, while export earnings from wool and wool products have decreased in both respects since the early 1950s. These shifts, however, reflect the behavior of international prices: export volumes fluctuated over the twenty-year period with no clear trend.

Historically, the EEC countries were Uruguay's largest customers, taking more than half her exports. In 1960 that figure reached 60 percent. Thereafter, however, the EEC share fell steadily, reaching 28 percent in 1974.[2] The United States was never a large customer, with a maximum share of 17 percent in 1965. That share also fell thereafter, as exports to LAFTA increased from 2 percent of the total in 1960 to 36 percent in 1974.[3]

11.1.3 Labor Market

Uruguay is unusual among the countries in the project in that her demographic characteristics are much more like those of developed countries than like those of other LDCs. Only 28 percent of the population was under fifteen years of age in 1975 (compared with 45 percent in Thailand, for example), and 12.7 percent were over sixty. In like vein, 80.8 percent of the population resided in urban areas, and 20.2 percent of the labor force was employed in the manufacturing sector in 1975, down from 23 percent in 1963. Population growth averaged 0.6 percent per annum during 1960–70 and is estimated to have been only 1.3 percent annually from 1908 to 1960. The potential labor force (defined as persons fourteen years of age and older) actually fell between the 1963 and 1975 censuses. Educational standards are also high, and 91 percent of the population over seven years of age is classified as literate.

Thus, the "employment problem" in Uruguay is not one of a rapidly growing labor force. It is rather the productive and efficient utilization of the labor force. Unemployment in Montevideo has been fairly steady, officially estimated at about 8 percent of the labor force from 1968 to 1974, although the rate has risen since then. Value added per employee is estimated to have been $2,023 in 1972 United States dollars in 1973;

Table 11.3   Composition of Uruguay's Exports, 1950–74 (Millions of U.S. Dollars and Percentage of Total, Annual Average)

Product	1950–54	1955–59	1960–64	1965–69	1970–72	1973–74
Wool and wool textiles	135.1 (55)	99.5 (62)	86.6 (54)	85.3 (47)	69.6 (32)	101.9 (29)
Meat and by-products	44.0 (18)	18.9 (12)	40.8 (26)	55.3 (30)	86.6 (40)	135.4 (38)
Hides	24.3 (10)	12.3 (8)	17.0 (11)	17.6 (10)	23.0 (11)	24.8 (8)
Other agricultural products	36.1 (15)	29.1 (18)	13.4 (8)	17.4 (9)	24.9 (11)	39.2 (11)
Other exports	4.0 (2)	.2 (—)	2.2 (1)	7.5 (4)	13.4 (6)	50.0 (14)
Total exports	243.5	160.0	160.0	183.1	217.5	351.9

Source: Oficina de Planeamiento y Presupuesto 1973.

in 1960 it was $1,958 (in 1972 United States dollars) (World Bank 1976). This level was exceptionally high in 1960 and still well above that of most other Latin American countries in 1973. But the startling part of those numbers is the lack of growth of labor productivity and the lack of growth of manufacturing employment. Stagnation of employment and productivity have been Uruguay's chief problems in her labor markets and throughout the economy.

Very few data are available to analyze the functioning of the labor market in Uruguay. Like most other high-inflation countries, Uruguay has had a negative real interest rate and an overvalued currency, both of which have tended to make capital goods artificially cheap and to encourage the use of capital-intensive techniques. Although the real price of capital goods began rising after about 1968 as the exchange rate became more realistic, high social security taxes and other taxes on the employment of labor, combined with the influence of unions, probably prevented any increase in the relative price of capital that might otherwise have occurred. Taxes on wages rose from 12 percent in 1955 to 28.5 percent in 1967. Thus, although the real wage received by industrial workers probably remained about constant, the wage paid by employers rose in real terms and was probably high to begin with.

11.1.4 Inflation

Inflationary pressures have been experienced by Uruguay throughout the postwar period. Inflation rates were already high in the early postwar years, averaging about 12 percent annually between 1950 and 1954. Thereafter inflation accelerated. For 1955–60 the annual rate was just over 20 percent. By the second half of the 1960s it was 71 percent, and it remained almost that high in the first half of the 1970s (see table 11.4 below).

It is not the purpose of this study to analyze the causes of Uruguayan inflation.[4] What is important for understanding the environment within which the trade and payments regime operated is that the Uruguayan authorities first attempted to reduce or eliminate inflation through controls over the exchange rate, the interest rate, and prices of a limited number of commodities considered necessities, and afterward (June 1968) through a general freeze on prices and wages. Thereafter, until 1975 it was illegal to increase prices for any commodity or service without seeking prior approval of the Ministry of Finance. In addition to the misallocations of resources that resulted from this policy, there also ensued considerable excess demand for foreign exchange, as the price controls served, at least to some extent, to keep prices below the level they would have reached had market forces been permitted to operate freely.

11.2   The Uruguayan Trade and Payments Regime about 1968

11.2.1   Emphasis on Import Restriction

Starting with the balance of payments difficulties that were encountered at the beginning of the Great Depression, the Uruguayan trade and payments regime evolved into a highly restrictive, import substitution oriented control system. Initially, the controls were imposed as a direct response to balance of payments deficits. For this purpose, import licensing was instituted, and controls were exereised over both the commodity composition and the country of origin of imports. Multiple exchange rates were also instituted at that time, and tariffs were raised on those commodities for which import licenses were issued. Controls extended to the outright prohibition of imports of some commodities.

Gradually, the system evolved from its original purpose of restricting the flow of imports into one designed to foster domestic industrial production. In this process, export earnings stagnated, and the system became highly restrictive. As excess demand for imports intensified, additional instruments of control were employed. Tariffs were imposed on imports, along with a variety of additional charges. Complex methods of valuation were devised for establishing the base upon which import duties were to be levied. Prior deposits, special levies, and other charges were also applied. The end result was a system that was highly detailed and specific, and few generalizations can withstand close scrutiny. An additional consequence is that it is very difficult to gather data that accurately capture the nature of the system.

Nonetheless, it is against this background of more than thirty years of restrictive trade and payments practices that we must interpret the trade and payments regime of 1968, the year on which this analysis of the employment implications of alternative trade strategies focuses. At that time imports were regulated by various instruments applied by various public institutions. Quotas, in some cases prior guarantee deposits of long duration, and a complicated tariff system that included preferential margins for other LAFTA members served to restrict imports in general and imports of competing goods in particular. Export policy as of 1968 was simpler. Traditional natural resource based (NRB) exports —basically meat, wool, and hides—were taxed, while nontraditional exports were favored by a subsidy system that was started in the mid-1960s and gradually consolidated since then.

In this section, therefore, attention first turns to the behavior of the real exchange rate. Next, the surcharges and subsidies that distinguish the effective exchange from the nominal exchange rate are examined. We then briefly analyze the system of quantitative restrictions as it was in 1968. Thereafter, the effective rates of protection for a variety of goods are calculated. Finally, an assessment is made of the overall effect of the trade and payments regime on various categories of goods, and the implications of those findings for interpretation of the estimates of employment are examined.

Real Exchange Rates

We have already noted that Uruguay experienced rapid inflation throughout the postwar period. By 1950 the exchange rate was probably already overvalued, though it is difficult to estimate by how much in light of the relatively high prices received in world markets for Uruguay's exports at that time. Table 11.4 gives basic data on the official

Table 11.4   Inflation and the Real Nominal Exchange Rate, 1950–75

Year	Official Exchange Rate[a]	Price Index[b] (1961 = 100)	PLD-NER[c]
1950	1.9	17	11.18
1951	1.9	21	9.05
1952	1.9	23	8.26
1953	1.9	25	7.60
1954	1.9	27	7.04
1955	2.1	30	7.00
1956	2.9	32	9.22
1957	3.6	37	9.81
1958	3.5	45	7.91
1959	3.5	67	5.25
1960	11.0	91	12.12
1961	10.9	100	10.98
1962	10.9	111	9.89
1963	16.4	160	10.25
1964	18.7	216	8.66
1965	59.9	407	14.72
1966	75.8	607	12.50
1967	200.0	1,433	13.96
1968	250.0	2,383	10.49
1969	250.0	2,729	9.16
1970	250.0	3,300	7.58
1971	370.0	4,477	8.26
1972	718.0	8,716	8.24
1973	937.0	15,472	6.06
1974	1,586.0	32,065	4.95
1975	2,660.0	53,497	4.97
1976	4,000.0	74,896	5.34

Source: Banco Central del Uruguay 1970–76*b*.
Note: [a]selling price of the United States dollar in the commercial market at the end of each year.
[b]cost of living—Dec./Dec.
[c]PLD-NER = Price level deflated nominal (i.e., official) exchange rate.

(or nominal) exchange rate and the price index for the years since 1950. As can be seen, the official exchange rate was increased by only 85 percent between 1950 and 1959, while the price level quadrupled. The result was a drastic decline in the deflated nominal exchange rate from 11.18 pesos per dollar in 1950 to 5.25 in 1959. After that year, the greater frequency of devaluations prevented the real exchange rate from again reaching that level until the mid-1970s, but there were nonetheless large fluctuations in the real purchasing power of the peso. By 1968 the real purchasing power of the peso had almost reattained its 1950 level, although it is doubtful that the exchange rate played as much of a role in equilibrating supply and demand for pesos in 1968 as it did in 1950: it will be recalled that price controls resulted in some understatement of the rate of price increase during the 1960s, and also that the Uruguayan economy had grown at a moderate rate between 1950 and 1968, without any increase in export earnings. Finally, table 11.5 shows the evolution of the effective exchange rate in nominal and real terms from 1967 to 1976.

Additional Charges on Imports

The most important of the measures designed to contain the demand for imports was a system of "exchange surcharges" levied at rates ranging, in 1968, as high as 225 percent, depending on the nature of the commodity involved. The chief purpose was to protect domestic industries, and rates were generally highest when competing domestically produced goods were available. The exchange surcharge was generally levied on the c.i.f. value, but in some instances the authorities also set "minimum" prices for imports, and in these cases the surcharge was levied on either the c.i.f. value or the assessed "minimum" price, whichever was higher.

In addition to the exchange surcharges in 1968, imports were subject to a complex system of tariffs. The first component of the tariff system was a general duty on imports at a rate of 18 percent of the c.i.f. value, from which there were many partial or total exemptions. Thus, some commodities were subjected to an 18 percent rate, some to 10.8 percent, some to 2.7 percent, and some to no duty at all. In addition to the general duty, there was a variable levy on imports. The rates of this second component of the tariff system varied between 20 and 110 percent of the c.i.f. value of the goods. As in the case of the exchange surcharges, some products were taxed according to an assessed value at domestic prices. In such cases, given the rapid rate of Uruguayan inflation, the importance of these variable duties diminished over time. Something similar happened with the last component of the tariff system, the specific taxes that were applied in domestic currency on imports of particular commodities.

Table 11.5   Inflation and the Effective Exchange Rate, 1967–76

Official Exchange Rate (Ur.$/U.S.$) (1)	Imports			Traditional Exports			Nontraditional Exports		
	Taxes % (2)	EER (Ur.$/U.S.$) (3)	PLD-EER (1967 Ur.$) (4)	Taxes % (5)	EER (Ur.$/U.S.$) (6)	PLD-EER (1967 Ur.$) (7)	Subsidies % (8)	EER (Ur.$/U.S.$) (9)	PLD-EER (1967 Ur.$) (10)
200	18	236	236	22	156	156	1	202	202
250	17	293	175	38	155	93	2	255	152
250	18	295	155	25	188	99	7	268	141
250	21	302	131	21	198	86	9	273	188
370a	21	448	145	11	329	106	10	407	132
718	15	826	135	22	560	92	4	747	122
937	14	1,068	99	49	478	44	15	1,078	100
1,586	10	1,745	78	30	1,100	50	27	2,014	90
2,660	08	2,873	77	4	2,554	68	35	3,591	96
4,000	12	4,480	86	2	3,520	68	59	6,360	122

Sources: Col. 1: BCU 1970–76*b*; col. 2: Import duty collections divided by value of imports, c.i.f., from BCU 1970–76*a*. Pesos were converted into dollars using the annual average of the commercial rate of exchange. Columns 5 and 8 are from table 11.6.

aIn 1971 a short-term surcharge of Ur. $120 on the selling price of foreign currency was imposed.

EER = Effective exchange rate.

PLD-EER = Price-level-deflated effective exchange rate.

The EERs in cols. 3 and 4 pertain to commodities that were actually imported. Tariffs were prohibitive for some items, and premiums accrued on import licenses. These are not included. See text.

In addition to the exchange surcharges and the tariff system, port fees also acted as a tax on imports. The fees considerably exceeded any cost that could reasonably have been incurred by the port authorities, as they ranged from 13 to 19 percent of c.i.f. value.

Finally, in 1968 "consular fees" were paid at about 12 percent of the f.o.b. value of the goods. Although there were numerous exemptions (basic consumer goods, raw materials, agricultural inputs, and machinery and equipment), this tax was included as a part of the legal basis on which other taxes were collected.

As we have already mentioned, there were numerous exemptions and special treatments for particular categories of commodities. Notable among these was the preferential treatment accorded to goods traded within LAFTA. With all the special categories, exemptions, and regulations, the administration of the import regime was often chaotic. Tariff policy was applied by such different means for different commodities, and in such an incoherent manner, that many unintended outcomes resulted. For example, many final products ended up subject to import duties at rates lower than those imposed on the raw materials used in their production. Because of the reliance upon assessed values, which lost meaning as inflation continued, and the flexibility of the exchange surcharge system, the latter increased in importance over time. Whereas this tax accounted for 35 percent of total foreign trade taxes collected in 1955, by 1963 it accounted for 80 percent.

Quantitative Controls on Imports

As we have already mentioned, in 1968 there were physical controls along with surcharges and levies. In general, each importer was assigned a quota according to the amount he had imported in prior years. Imports were not permitted without a quota, and there was little flexibility in the assignment of quotas. Indeed, prior deposit requirements for import applications without licenses were in practice so high as to be prohibitive. The only exception to the rigid licensing system arose in instances where particular firms could demonstrate that they could not continue to produce, and that employment would thereby be harmed, if they did not receive larger imports. This practice provided some flexibility, especially for large firms that were better able to avail themselves of these provisions.

Export Taxes and Subsidies

The export regime as applied in 1968 distinguished in effect between two categories of exports: traditional commodities (chiefly meat and unprocessed wool and hides) and nontraditional exports. Taxes on traditional exports do not require any particular explanation: they amounted to between 12 and 26 percent of export receipts and were an important source of revenue for the government.

Nontraditional exports were increasingly encouraged by the government. The subsidy system applied to them started in the mid-1960s and was increased in scope and importance thereafter. It was set as a percentage of the f.o.b. value of exports, and the rates were determined for individual export industries. Table 11.6 gives data on the relative importance of taxes on traditional exports and subsidies on nontraditional ones. As can be seen, after 1970 and except for 1972 subsidies ranged from 16 to 20 percent of the value of nontraditional exports.

In addition to the subsidies established for nontraditional exports, exporters were accorded the right to import needed intermediate goods duty free, and also capital goods employed in exporting industries. Because the commodities exported received the higher effective exchange rate resulting from the export subsidy, these duty-free imports constituted yet another incentive for exports of nontraditional items.

Effective Rates of Protection

The foregoing discussion gives some idea of the levels of protection (or discrimination) but provides little idea of the variation among industries. To that end, we calculated weighted average rates of effective protection facing each two-digit industrial sector, according to whether the output was exported or sold in the internal market. The results are

Table 11.6   Tax Collections and Subsidy Payments on Exports, 1967–76 (Millions of U.S. Dollars)

	Traditional Exports			Nontraditional Exports		
	Value (1)	Taxes (2)	(2)/(1)	Value (3)	Subsidies (4)	(4)/(3)
1967	132	22	.17	27	1	.04
1968	147	38	.26	32	2	.05
1969	149	25	.17	51	7	.13
1970	174	21	.12	58	9	.16
1971	147	11	.07	58	10	.17
1972	163	22	.13	51	4	.08
1973	236	49	.21	86	15	.17
1974	238	30	.13	144	27	.19
1975	194	4	.02	190	35	.18
1976	251	2	.01	296	59	.20

Sources: Cols. 1 and 3: Dirección General de Comercio Exterior, 1975–76.
Col. 2: BCU (1970–76*a*). Pesos were converted to dollars at the annual average of the commercial rate of exchange.
Col. 4: Revista Búsqueda (1976), p. 51, converting pesos to dollars as in col. 2.

given in table 11.7.[5] In some instances the legal rates proved to be redundant, because domestic demand was satisfied by domestic production and few, if any, imports resulted. Indeed, the entire system of protection was designed to induce this result: once domestic production capability was established, the tariffs, other charges, and quotas imposed on imports were designed to protect domestic production and discourage imports completely. For export industries, the NRPs and ERPs were calculated using the actual subsidy rates, and there is every reason to believe that the rates reflect fairly accurately the actual rates of protection for exporters.

In many sectors the legal ERPs for the domestic market shown in table 11.7 at the two-digit level strikingly exceed those for export. Where the information was available for the component industries, an export subsidy rate was used to estimate effective protection for the internal market in order to calculate international value added (see the model in section 11.3.4). The spread between NRPs for domestic and export sales was taken as evidence of redundancy in the tariff for the protection of the internal market. Recent studies based upon direct price comparisons have confirmed that there is water in the nominal tariff structure despite high levels of effective protection.

Using the export rates as indicators of the true protection of the internal market, we find two types of industry for which ERPs are low: those with an important NRB content that produce for both the internal and external markets—numbers 23 (textiles), and 29 (leather and leather products)—and two capital goods sectors—numbers 36 (machinery) and 37 (electrical machinery). These rates, combined with high rates on other commodities and wide differences among industries in value added/output ratios, have resulted in a large coefficient of variation—74—in the ERP rates. In the case of export industries, the relative dispersion was not as large, the coefficient of variation being 58.

A final observation on the structure of ERPs pertains to their height. Given that they are all high when domestic production takes place, there seems to be no clear bias in resource allocation to a particular industry within the nontraditional sector. A priori, one might expect that, under an all-out import substitution regime, protection would be as high as necessary to stimulate domestic production. In Uruguay this would imply that ERPs and capital/labor ratios should be in a direct and strong relationship. However, correlation analysis showed a nonsignificant statistical result, suggesting that other factors were involved.

The data in table 11.7 show strikingly high levels of nominal and effective protection for the industries the government was trying to encourage. To test the hypothesis that these protective rates were prohibitive, we took a sample of 324 goods produced in the country in 1968. This represents about 75 percent of the value of manufacturing production in that year. The results obtained from the sample are given in table 11.8. The first column gives the value of production in the sample of commodities relative to the entire output of the sector in question. The second column gives the value of production. The third column indicates the number of different products in the sample, and the fourth shows

Table 11.7   Nominal and Effective Protection Rates, 1968

Industry	Production for Domestic Market		Production for Export	
	NRP	ERP	NRP	ERP
20 Food products	314%	150%	1%	25%
21 Beverages	370	1,014	20	92
22 Tobacco products	73	188	n.e.	n.e.
23 Textiles	341	303	10	61
24 Footwear	394	892	25	67
25 Wood and cork products	n.a.	n.a.	n.e.	n.e.
26 Furniture	n.a.	n.a.	n.e.	n.e.
27 Paper and paper products	467	535	n.e.	n.e.
28 Printing and publishing	13	17	n.e.	n.e.
29 Leather and leather products	10	20	1	24
30 Rubber products	257	602	25	62
31 Chemicals and chemical products	114	182	8	43
32 Petroleum and coal products	63	164	n.e.	n.e.
33 Nonmetallic mineral products	301	548	n.e.	n.e.
34 Primary metals	n.a.	n.a.	17	156
35 Metal products	167	463	30	37
36 Nonelectrical machinery	60	55	30	55
37 Electrical machinery	239	591	22	45
38 Transportation equipment	299	689	n.e.	n.e.
39 Miscellaneous manufacturing	263	568	20	99
Total	264	384	4	37

Note: n.e. = no exports; n.a. = not available; NRP = nominal rate of protection. NRP coefficients were calculated from tariff schedules and the following taxes: exchange surcharges and other tariffs for internal market industries, and subsidies for export industries. The NRPs at the two-digit level and the aggregate NRP for the industrial sector as a whole are weighted averages of the NRPs for the goods included in a sample (see table 11.8) used by the Banco Central to estimate periodically the level of industrial activity in the country (weights being the share of each good in the value of industrial output). To estimate the components of the ERP, a study was conducted of the input-output structure of the goods included in the sample. Cost declarations for these goods submitted to the Ministry of Finance in 1968 and to the Ministry of Industry in 1975 were the sources for the ERP estimates. The input structure was classified according to the origin of the inputs. For inputs reported to have been imported, only the c.i.f. values were taken; tariffs and other taxes were excluded. The value of internal inputs was divided into (1) domestic, (2) imported but purchased locally, and (3) nontradables. Domestic taxes were excluded.

Table 11.8   Principal Manufactures Produced in 1968 and Competing Imports

Industry	VP_S/VP_T % (1)	M/VP_S % (2)	Number of Products in Sample (3)	Number of Products in Sample also Imported (4)	Ratio of (4) to (3) % (5)
20 Food products	80.6	2.4	61	5	8.2
21 Beverages	70.1	0	15	0	0
22 Tobacco products	95.4	0	3	1	33.3
23 Textiles	94.4	0	27	6	22.2
24 Footwear	60.4	0	39	1	2.6
27 Paper and paper products	90.6	8.3	22	2	9.1
30 Rubber products	96.0	0	5	0	0
31 Chemicals and chemical products	46.1	0.6	36	2	5.6
32 Petroleum and coal products	95.1	8.6	5	4	80.0
33 Nonmetallic mineral products	83.5	0.2	24	2	8.3
35 Metal products	73.4	12.3	51	14	27.5
37 Electrical machinery	54.2	0.5	14	5	35.7
38 Transportation equipment	15.0	0	5	0	0
39 Miscellaneous manufacturing	43.1	0.5	17	4	23.5
Total	75.1	2.1	324	46	14.2

Source: The table was constructed by considering the components of the industrial sample of the Banco Central del Uruguay and their relative importance in manufacturing in 1968 and using import series for that year—classified by product—published by the Banco de la Republica.

Note: (1) VP_S = Value of production of the industrial products that compose the sample that the Banco Central del Uruguay uses to estimate the level of industrial activity every three months; VP_T = Value of production of the industrial sector. (2) M = Value of imports of goods similar to the ones domestically produced and included in the sample cited above.

the number of those products of which there were imports of a similar type. For each commodity listed we examined the import list to determine whether there was import competition for the particular good in question. As can be seen, only for forty-six of them were any similar imports found. The values of imports that competed at all with domestic production represented only 2.1 percent of domestic production. Even then, they may not have been strict substitutes. Although sample data can never be entirely convincing, it seems evident that imports were virtually ruled out when domestic production was available.

It thus seems clear that rates of protection were so high that whatever was domestically produced was not imported. Conversely, what was imported was not domestically produced. Imports consisted mainly of intermediate inputs, crude oil, and capital goods. They all had relatively low tariffs, which explains why import duty collections as a percentage of value of imports shown in table 11.5 were so small contrasted with the high nominal tariff rates shown in table 11.7.

11.2.2 Resource Allocation Resulting from the Trade Regime

Although one cannot pinpoint the precise pulls of resources within the modern manufacturing sector in Uruguay, it does seem possible to categorize Uruguayan industries into several meaningful groups. First, as exemplified by meat and leather, there are some traditional manufacturing activities that are based on domestic natural resources and enjoy costs of production sufficiently low to enable them to sell abroad even if they are not highly efficient. Second, there are some industries, such as textiles, clothing, and cement, that, though using outputs based on domestic natural resources, could not export, at prevailing official exchange rates, were it not for the subsidies they receive. Finally, a third group utilizes imported raw materials and parts behind high levels of protection. It is this group, producing only for the domestic market behind excessively high tariff walls, that is subject to the largest comparative disadvantage and is the chief beneficiary of the protection system.

It is the protection of this third group that prevents the emergence of either of the first two groups as exporters on a significant scale. The import barriers erected to protect the high-cost industries also permit maintenance of an overvalued currency that acts as an implicit tax on the exportation of the output of the other industries and diminishes the incentive to expand the production of exportables. The subsidies to nontraditional industrial exports compensate this second group of industries in part for the overvaluation of the currency. However, those subsidies, as we have already seen, constitute only about 15–20 percent of the nominal exchange rate, whose variation in real terms over the years has considerably exceeded that amount. Moreover, the subsidies to nontraditional exports, while offsetting to some extent the discrimination against them, enable still further discrimination against the traditional exporting activities in which comparative advantage is very large. This is because exports of nontraditional commodities are higher because of the subsidy than they would otherwise be, and so the pressure on the Uruguayan government to adjust the exchange rate is less than it would be in the absence of those exports.

There can be little doubt that the Uruguayan trade and payments regime has transferred income from consumers, importers, and traditional exporters to import substituting producers. In addition there is a net real cost of the system, since the social cost of domestic production of import substitutes is considerably higher than that abroad, and the marginal rate of transformation domestically exceeds considerably that on world markets. The precise outcome of the system for the producers of nontraditional exports is less clear, and it is not evident whether that group on balance benefits or loses from the protective system as contrasted with an efficient allocation of resources.

It is against this background of complex controls and a pattern of production vastly different from that which would obtain under optimal resource allocation that the data for 1968 must be viewed when examining the employment implications of alternative trade strategies.

11.3   Labor Intensity of Industries

11.3.1   Industry Classification

Our analysis of the labor intensity of Uruguayan trade is based on the 1968 industrial census and data available at the three-digit level of the International Standard Industrial Classification for a sample of 350 goods. Those goods represent more than 80 percent of total industrial output. These data were combined with cost data described in the notes to table 11.7. Data from the costs declarations lodged before COPRIN (the prices and wages controller) in 1974 and 1975 were used to obtain producer prices and a breakdown of costs, including the value of imported inputs, domestic inputs, and taxes. For exportable goods, we obtained additional data on sales prices abroad. Despite the difficulty of developing accurate and comparable data against the background of high rates of inflation and the inherent problems associated in melding 1968 and 1974–75 data, the sample is believed to be representative of the input-output cost structure of the Uruguayan industrial sector.

Commodity classifications among the three-digit industries were as follows. All agricultural and mining activities were classified as NRB, as were seven manufacturing branches: meat (201), alcoholic beverages (213), wool-washing (230), wool tops (231), other textiles (239), tanned hides (291), and the edible oil industry (312). All these sectors had exports primarily to the developed countries, except alcoholic beverages, which exports primarily to other developing countries.

All the remaining manufacturing sectors were classified as HOS industries, except for furniture (26), printing (281), and oil refining (321), which were judged to be home goods, as were all energy, transportation, and financial activities.

Among the HOS industries, six—dairy products (202), wool spinning and weaving (234), footwear (241), clothing (243), textiles (244), and leather products (292)—were classified as HOS exportables to developed countries, and five—fish-preserving (204), parquets (254), tires (301), glass products (332), and cement (334)—as HOS exportables to developing countries. Twenty three-digit sectors were classified as HOS importables: grain products (205), sugar (207), tobacco products (220), cordage (233), sawmilling (251), paper (270), paper products (274), other paper industries (279), molded rubber products (302), industrial chemicals (311), secondary chemical products (313), household chemical products (315), pharmaceuticals (316), cement products (335), nonmetallic mineral products (339), iron and steel (241), nonferrous metals (342), machinery and repair (362), motor vehicles (383), and bicycles (385). The same classification was applied to three entire two-digit sectors: metal products (35), electrical machinery (37), and miscellaneous manufacturing (39). Finally, several industries were classified as production not competing with imports. These included industries within the metal manufacturing, machinery, electrical appliances, and transportation equipment sectors.

The criterion for classification based on the T_i statistic defined in the introductory chapter (i.e., ratio of net imports to consumption in industry i) was as follows:

exportable if T_i less than 0;
import-competing if $0 < T_i < 0.7$;
noncompeting import if $0.7 < T_i$.

Table 11.9 indicates the relative importance in trade of the various categories. As can be seen, NRB exports were 93 percent of total exports in 1968, the greater part being destined for developed countries.

Table 11.9   **Composition and Direction of Uruguay's Trade in 1968 (Millions of U.S. Dollars)**

	Developing Countries	Developed Countries	Total
Exports			
NRB goods	21.1	146.2	167.3
HOS goods	7.2	4.7	11.3
Total	28.3	150.9	179.2
Imports			
NRB goods	30.5	11.0	41.5
Import-competing HOS goods	17.6	13.6	31.2
Noncompeting HOS imports	18.4	51.1	69.5
Total[a]	66.5	75.7	142.2

Source: Bension and Caumont (1977).

[a]Excluding 15.2 million of unclassified imports.

Since the reforms in the mid-1970s, of course, this concentration in NRB goods has diminished somewhat. On the import side, noncompeting imports and NRB goods predominated in trade, reflecting the degree of protection given to domestic import substitution industries. In 1977 petroleum, intermediate goods, and capital goods imports accounted for 93 percent of total Uruguayan imports.

Tables 11.10 and 11.11 give trade and factor intensities (discussed in section 11.3.3) of major HOS exportables and importable production. Note, as observed above, that most exportables are concentrated in NRB processing activities and importables are concentrated in foodstuffs and consumer goods.

11.3.2   Variables Indicating Factor Intensity

Three separate variables are used here to measure labor coefficients: total wage bill, number of workers, and hours worked. In addition, two separate indicators of skills are available, one being a classification of white-collar and blue-collar workers and the other a classification of skilled and unskilled workers. Both of these measures were deemed superior to attempting to use average wages per worker or per hour worked as an indicator of skills. This was primarily because, in the Uruguayan context, inflation is sufficiently rapid that the average wage variable may be a better indicator of the month in the year when wage-increases were granted than it is of the skill composition of the labor force: for the year under review, inflation was 60 percent.

In addition to measures of skill and labor intensity, there is available a measure of kilowatt consumption of various industries. As is well known, this measure is not entirely satisfactory because of the availability of other energy sources and because some forms of capital are not as intensive in energy use as others. Nonetheless, we deem it worthwhile to examine the "electricity coefficient" as at least a partial proxy for the capital intensity of various industries.

11.3.3   Factor Utilization in Uruguayan Industry

Tables 11.10 and 11.11 give factor intensities in major HOS exportables and importables, while table 11.12 gives estimates of direct factor utilization per unit of DVA by commodity category and, for wages only, also provides estimates of direct plus home goods indirect requirements. Weights used in the calculations were the domestic value added of production. The table distinguishes between NRB and HOS exports, as classified above, but even for those included in the HOS group other than tires the availability of domestically produced raw materials was of some influence in the location of production. It is nevertheless interesting that NRB and HOS exports seem to have fairly similar factor proportions on the average. Indeed, the more systematic distinctions

Table 11.10   **Characteristics of HOS Exportable Industries, 1968**

	Exports (Thousands of U.S. Dollars)			Factor Intensities		
	Developed Countries	Developing Countries	Total	Labor[a]	Capital[b]	Skill[c]
202 Dairy products	853	32	885	679	2,914	413
204 Fish-preserving	—	440	440	676	469	472
234 Wool-spinning and weaving	2,316	963	3,279	1,615	897	164
241 Footwear	94	—	94	570	437	247
243 Clothing	57	—	57	436	250	203
244 Textiles	7	1	8	489	279	276
254 Parquets	8	23	31	481	849	253
292 Leather products	659	—	659	530	563	251
301 Tires	—	289	289	218	1,133	15
332 Glass products	—	382	382	297	1,449	155
334 Cement	—	3,579	3,579	211	5,498	101
Total	3,994	5,709	9,703	366	1,483	163

Source: Bension and Caumont (1977).

[a]Number of persons employed per million dollars of DVA.
[b]Thousands of kilowatt-hours per million dollars of DVA.
[c]Number of unskilled workers per million dollars of DVA.

Table 11.11   Characteristics of Major Importable Industries

Sector	1968 Imports (Thousands of U.S. Dollars)	Factor Intensities[a]		
		Labor	Capital	Skill
205 Grain products	3,036	171	1,200	109
207 Sugar products	3,110	252	1,038	166
220 Tobacco products	2,567	34	86	19
302 Molded rubber products	172	265	1,245	52
311 Industrial chemicals	12,858	234	5,150	100
315 Household chemical products	351	287	571	121
316 Pharmaceuticals	9,389	187	224	78
35 Metal produtcs	1,816	373	1,303	176
37 Electrical machinery	5,973	336	1,032	166
39 Various	4,229	329	1,094	172
Total	43,501	238	1,163	116

Source: Bension and Caumont (1977).
[a]See table 11.10 for definitions of factor intensities.

appear to be (1) that exportables, both NRB and HOS, use more labor, particularly more unskilled labor, than import-competing goods, and (2) that exports to developed countries use more labor, particularly more unskilled labor, than exports to developing countries.[6] These observations are in line with what one would expect on theoretical grounds. It must be borne in mind, however, that import-competing goods are preponderantly produced at home rather than imported. Hence one could not conclude that Uruguay's pattern of production has not been seriously distorted.

A part of the explanation for the relatively low labor intensity of Uruguay's imports of HOS goods and of her exports of such goods to LDCs compared with those to DCs lies in the pattern of her trade with LAFTA and especially with her neighbors Argentina and Brazil. Because of preferential tariff systems, there are several domestic industries that import parts or semifinished unassembled goods from those countries and assemble the final product. That is the case, for example, with the automobile and household electric appliance industries. Since the factor endowments of Argentina, Brazil, and Uruguay are fairly similar, it is evident that the non-NRB trade between them owes its origins more to special factors such as tariff preferences than to any natural comparative advantage.

Note that table 11.12 (and also table 11.13) does not distinguish between DCs and LDCs in showing factor coefficients for import-competing goods, unlike the breakdown shown for exports. It is questionable

Table 11.12   Direct Factor Utilization per Million Dollars of DVA, 1968

	Wage Bill (Thousands of Dollars)[a]	Number of Workers				Hours Worked (Thousands)	Kilowatt-Hours (Thousands)
		Total	White-Collar	Blue-Collar	Unskilled Workers		
NRB exports							
Developed countries	664 (599)	365	45	320	252	551	1,339
Developing countries	438 (519)	179	2	177	128	370	1,731
Total	642 (571)	346	40	306	240	533	1,378
HOS exports							
Developed countries	771 (631)	441	48	393	215	932	915
Developing countries	506 (537)	239	43	196	76	352	2,573
Total	673 (586)	366	46	320	163	712	1,483
Import-competing HOS goods							
Total	453 (520)	238	49	189	116	344	1,163

Source: Bension and Caumont (1977).

Note: Conversions of value added and wage bill are made at official rate of exchange.

[a]Figures in parentheses are direct plus home goods indirect wages per million dollars at direct plus home goods indirect value added.

how meaningful such a distinction would be for Uruguay's imports. This is because, to repeat, Uruguayan protection of domestic production is so great that, once a good is domestically produced, imports are generally not permitted, and the only observed imports in the relevant sectors are presumably those of inputs for the domestic industry. It is probable, however, that most of these industries produce what would otherwise be imported from developed countries.

To estimate factor coefficients for noncompeting imports, the ratio of wages to value added in the industrial sectors was calculated both for the United States and for Uruguay at the three-digit level. For this category—including industries within the metal-manufacturing, machinery, electrical appliances, and transportation equipment sectors—the ratio of the wages share to that in other industries was calculated for the United States, and that ratio was then applied to the Uruguayan wage share in other industries. The resulting estimate, 534,000 dollars per million dollars of DVA, can be compared with the data in the first column of table 11.10. To the extent that the wage share is an accurate reflection of labor intensity (though it reflects human capital in the form of skills as well as the number of workers per unit of value added), it appears that the wage share in the noncompeting import categories, if these products were domestically produced, would lie somewhere between that for import-competing goods and that for exportables. Uruguayan exportables therefore appear to be labor-intensive relative to both import-competing and noncompeting imports.

Home goods indirect inputs can be brought into the calculations only for wages, the results (in terms of aggregate wages per million dollars of DVA) being shown in parentheses in the wages column of table 11.10. On this basis, Uruguayan exports still use more labor than import-competing goods, though the difference is smaller than for direct inputs only. The reason for this change is that, per unit of DVA, indirect labor incorporated in home goods is less than the direct labor in export production but greater than that in import-competing production. Similarly, the previously observed excess of labor requirements in HOS exports to developed countries compared with that in HOS exports to developing countries is narrowed, but not eliminated, when indirect inputs are included.

11.3.4   Factor Proportions and International Value Added

Two alternative courses are possible when passing from domestic to international value added in the case of industries that produce for the foreign as well as for the domestic market. The first is to work with the effective rate of protection as computed from tariffs and other charges on imports. The other is to consider the ERP that results from the subsidy to exports of the same commodity. In Uruguay, we will argue, the

ERP implicitly given by the nominal rate of the subsidy to exports is a more accurate way of handling the problem and gives a more meaningful result.

Starting with the competitive market case and making the small-country assumption, if a tariff is imposed on imports of a certain commodity, domestic market equilibrium without exports is achieved when Q_1 units of the commodity are produced and sold at a price P_D. In figure 11.1, D, S, P_w, t, and s are, respectively, domestic demand, domestic supply, the world price, the nominal rate of the tariff, and the nominal rate of the subsidy.

In this case, part of the tariff is redundant because P_D, which is below $P_w (1 + t)$, clears the domestic market. At the price $P_w (1 + t)$, the excess supply $(Q_3 - Q_2)$ would not be absorbed and the price would fall.

In order for exports to take place (and ignoring the c.i.f.–f.o.b. margin), domestic producers need a subsidy whose rate should be high enough to make P_D less than $P_w (1 + s)$. At that new price, producers are able to sell Q_5 units, Q_4 of which are sold to the domestic market and $(Q_5 - Q_4)$ to the rest of the world.

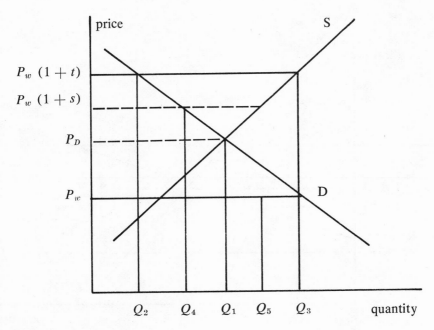

Fig. 1

The situation depicted above shows that, if the ERP given by the tariff is used in adjusting DVA to IVA, effective protection will be overestimated and IVA calculated from it will be underestimated. In contrast to that procedure, figure 11.1 indicates that a more accurate description of the real world is achieved when $P_w (1 + s)$ is considered as the domestic price and the price seen by domestic producers. Hence, the ERP given by the nominal rate s should be the one chosen to pass from DVA to IVA.

For the monopolistic case the situation is different. In figure 11.2, MC and MR are, respectively, marginal cost and marginal revenue. The profit-maximizing solution for the monopolist producing only for the domestic market is a scale of production of Q_1 units with a price of P_D. According to figure 11.2, the tariff is excessively high and therefore implies an overestimate of effective protection.

For exports to take place, the monopolist needs a subsidy whose rate should be higher than the one (i) that makes $MC = MR$ for Q_1 units.

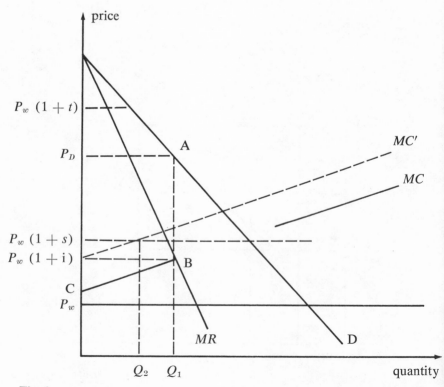

Fig. 2

However, s could be such that P_w $(1 + s)$ is less than P_D. With that rate of subsidy the monopolist is able to produce Q_2 units in addition to the Q_1 units he produces for the domestic market. MC' is the excess domestic supply.

For this case one would be tempted to pass from domestic to international value added using just an average of the effective rate given by the tariff and the one given by the subsidy weighted by the monopolist's sales to domestic and foreign markets. However, that is not quite right. In this special case the shaded area P_D ABC represents monopoly profits accruing to the monopolist when he produces for the domestic market. Even though these monopoly profits exist because of the tariff, they would disappear if the monopolist's rights were canceled or the franchise withdrawn.

Domestic value added including monopoly profits is not the appropriate measure because the franchise, and not the tariff, gives that implicit protection. The DVA that should be considered should not include extraordinary profits.

If the monopoly is exporting because of the subsidy, then the ERP resulting from that rate should be taken as the one pointing to a more accurate description of the industry protection. No franchise effect is present in this case that should count for some of the protection the industry receives.

Once the IVA is obtained, it is assumed that no variations exist either in the number of employed persons, in the hours worked, or in the wage bill, with respect to the figures considered for the case of the domestic value added.

The results are given in table 11.13. Direct capital and labor employment in terms of IVA shows that capital and labor requirements in import-competing industries are both larger than in the HOS export industries, and the same conclusion is reached whatever the index considered. This is clear evidence of the inefficiency of the import-competing industrial sector.

11.4 Conclusions

Uruguayan import-competing industries grew from the end of World War II until the end of the 1950s, after which a period of stagnation ensued. Protected by very high tariffs and other charges and by import prohibitions, these industries appear, on the basis of estimates for 1968, to have used much less labor per unit of DVA than did either HOS or NRB exportable industries. Expressed per unit of IVA, however, import-competing industries used both more labor and more capital, attesting to the overall inefficiency engendered by the import substitution policy. As Uruguayan policies have shifted toward encouraging exports in the

Table 11.13   Direct Factor Utilization per Million Dollars of IVA

| | Wages (Thousands of Dollars) | Number of Workers | | | | Hours Worked (Thousands) | Kilowatt-Hours (Thousands) |
		Total	White-Collar	Blue-Collar	Unskilled Workers		
NRB exports							
Developed countries	832	456	56	400	316	690	1,677
Developing countries	840	345	4	341	245	710	3,324
Total	832	449	52	397	311	690	1,786
HOS exports							
Developed countries	1,238	707	77	630	344	1,495	1,468
Developing countries	946	446	81	365	141	629	4,595
Total	1,140	620	78	542	277	1,206	2,511
Import-competing HOS goods							
Total	1,780	934	192	742	456	1,352	4,576

Source: Bension and Caumont (1977).

Note: Calculated as described in the text, using data in table 11.12.

1970s, it is quite possible that the demands for various categories of skilled and unskilled labor will grow in the future quite differently from their historical trends.

In that regard, it is important to note that one of the chief findings of this analysis is the very large and significant difference between factor proportions in HOS exportables to developed and to developing countries, the former being considerably more labor-intensive than the latter. Certainly the available data strongly indicate that the nature of Uruguay's trade with her neighbors in LAFTA is quite different from the nature of her trade with developed countries, even when attention focuses on HOS goods.

This study really represents a first step in the analysis of Uruguay's trade and payments regime and of her domestic factor markets, and there is considerable scope for future work. While the commodity market distortions inherent in the trade regime were quantified to some-extent in our estimates of effective rates of protection, we have not reported any results with respect to distortions in Uruguayan factor markets. Although a few pieces of data are available, it will require considerable further study before any conclusions can be reached about the extent to which Uruguayan factor markets and factor prices reflect underlying market forces. We did, for this study, attempt to analyze the wage structure as it existed in 1968, but data difficulties proved overwhelming: not only were data on skill and experience variables inadequate, but the 60 percent inflation that occurred in that year undoubtedly distorted the reported nominal wages, depending on the timing of wage adjustments as much as anything else. There are also significant differences in the observed labor intensity of large and small firms, with small firms employing fewer than ten workers in each two-digit industry having a higher share of wages in value added than the firms with a larger number of employees, and also that much remains to be done in analyzing the determinants of factor utilization in Uruguayan industries as well as in estimating the way they interact with the trade and payments regime and the observed commodity composition of trade. The available evidence, however, is all consistent with the hypothesis that the switch to a more export-oriented strategy should result in greater demand for labor.

Notes

1. Because of the balance of payments difficulties during that period, capital goods imports were subject to prior government authorization.

2. The share increased again in 1974–75, even though imports of meat by the EEC were drastically reduced, since nontraditional exports more than offset the drop.

3. The trend changed in 1975–76 as nontraditional exports to the United States rose sharply. In 1976 the share was 11 percent.

4. For a discussion of the nature of Uruguayan inflation, see Harberger (1974).

5. For the NRB industries, the ERPs are based on a rough estimate of the input-output relationship and are not strictly speaking consistent with the others. For machinery (36), no firm data giving an average nominal rate of protection were available, and we assumed that the nominal rate of protection was 60 percent.

6. Rather surprisingly at first sight, the amount of electricity used per unit of DVA appears to be substantially higher in export industries than in import-competing industries, seeming to suggest that the first are more capital-intensive than the second insofar as energy consumption reflects capital utilization. The explanation lies, however, in the exceptionally high energy requirements of cement manufactures exported to developing countries. If that industry were excluded from the computation—and it is, in any event, arguable whether cement should be classified as HOS or NRB—the total kilowatt-hours consumed per unit of DVA in HOS exports would be about 14 percent lower than that in import-competing production. Other factor coefficients for exports shown in table 11.10 are not greatly affected by the inclusion or exclusion of cement.

References

Anichini, Jose; Caumont, Jorge; and Sjaastad, Larry. 1977. *La politica comercial y la protección en Uruguay.* Montevideo: Banco Central del Uruguay.

Banco Central del Uruguay. 1955. *Estadísticas de comercio exterior.*

———. 1970–76a. *Boletín estadístico mensual.* Various issues.

———. 1970–76b. *Indicadores de la actividad económico-financiera.* Various issues.

———. 1976a. *Estadísticas básicas.*

———. 1976b. *National accounts statistics.*

Bension, Alberto, and Caumont, Jorge. 1977. Alternative strategies and employment implications. Mimeographed. New York: NBER.

Dirección General de Comercio Exterior. 1975–76. *Estadísticas de comercio exterior.* Various issues.

Dirección General de Estadísticas y Censos. 1970–76. *Indices de precios de consumo.* Various issues.

Facultad de Ciencias Económicas, Instituto de Economía. 1969. *Estadísticas básicas.*

Harberger, Arnold. 1974. El rol de los factores fiscales en la inflación Uruguaya. Mimeographed. Montevideo: Banco Central del Uruguay.

Oficina de Planeamiento y Presupuesto. 1973. *Plan nacional de desarrollo, 1973–1977.*

Revista Búsqueda . . . 1976. Los reintegros a la exportación: Una contribución al análisis económico de sus efectos. *Revista-Búsqueda* 52 (October): 48–51.

World Bank. 1976. *Atlas.* Washington, D.C.: World Bank.

Contributors

Narongchai Akrasanee
Asian and Pacific Develop-
    ment Institute
Sri Ayudhya Road
Bangkok, Thailand

Alberto Bension
Universidad de la Republica
Treinta y Tres 1420 Esc. 31
Montevideo, Uruguay

José L. Carvalho
Fundação Getúlio Vargas—EPGE
Caixa Postal 9052 ZC–02
Rio de Janeiro 20000 R.J.
Republic of Brazil

Jorge Caumont
Universidad de la Republica
Treinta y Tres 1420 Esc. 31
Montevideo, Uruguay

Vittorio Corbo
Concordia University
C.P./P.O. Box 460, Station H
Montreal, Quebec, Canada H3G 2L1

now at Departmento de Economía
    Universidad de Chile
    Casilla 3861
    Santiago, Chile

Stephen Guisinger, Program Head
International Management Studies
University of Texas at Dallas
Box 688
Richardson, Texas 75080

Cláudio L. S. Haddad
Fundação Getúlio Vargas—EPGE
Caixa Postal 9052 ZC–02
Rio de Janeiro 20000 R.J.
Republic of Brazil

Wontack Hong
Department of International
    Economics
College of Social Sciences,
    Office 7–417
Seoul University
Seoul 151, Korea

Anne O. Krueger
Department of Economics
University of Minnesota
Minneapolis, Minnesota 55455

Patricio Meller
CIEPLAN
Departamento de Economía
Universidad de Chile
Casilla 3861
Santiago, Chile

Terry Monson
School of Business
Michigan Technological University
Houghton, Michigan 49931

Mustapha K. Nabli
Faculté de Droit et des Sciences
   Politiques et Economiques
Campus Universitaire
Tunis

Mark M. Pitt
Professor of Economics
University of Minnesota
Minneapolis, Minnesota 55455

Francisco E. Thoumi
Chief, Section of Social Studies
Inter-American Development Bank
801 17th St., N.W.
Washington, D.C., 20577

Author Index

Subject Index

Administrative procedures, 94, 292, 409, 439–40

Africa. *See specific African countries*

Aggregates and aggregation, 13, 17, 24–25, 46, 166

Agriculture, 30, 48; in Chile, 84, 95; in Colombia, 137, 142, 149, 162; and commodities, 143, 503; employment in, 5, 305–7, 344, 353; expansion of, 260, 294; exports of, 16, 200; goods, 45–46, 296, 310, 314; in Indonesia, 186, 191–92, 204, 208, 218; in Ivory Coast, 248, 255, 273, 323; and labor input, 50, 510; mechanization of, 338, 402; peasant, 242, 252; plantation, 249, 255, 262; products and productivity, 91, 243, 252, 356; in South Korea, 356, 374, 378; in Thailand, 393–94, 436–37; in Tunisia, 444; in Uruguay, 500, 516; wages in, 327

Aid: and credit, 398; foreign, 205–6, 295, 351, 442; grants in, 368; inflows of, 343–47, 351; and loans, 442

Alcohol, 407, 415, 420, 423, 516

Andean Group, 139, 148, 164, 166

Artisanal activities, 242, 249, 255–56, 260–61, 265, 277

Assets: capital, 330, 332; fixed, 103, 335

Association of South-East Asian Nations (ASEAN), 213, 220, 395

Automotive industry, 91, 245, 258, 260

Balance of payments, 6; Brazil, 33; Chile, 92–94; Colombia, 141–43; Indonesia, 189; Ivory Coast, 245; South Korea, 349, 351, 355; Thailand, 399, 406–7; Tunisia, 439–40; Uruguay, 502, 506

Balance of trade, 218, 397

Banco Nacional de Desenvolvimento Econômico (BNDE), 60–62, 64

Bangladesh, 291, 293

Bank Indonesia, 196, 199

Bank of Korea (BOK), 346, 349, 360, 367–69

Bank of Thailand, 397, 400, 406–9, 425

Banks and savings institutions, 44, 60–62, 64, 137, 153, 158, 170; and credit, 332–33, 367–68; foreign exchange, 196; interest rates, 367; loans by, 367, 369, 382, 446, 467; medium industry, 368; notes by, 368

Barriers: import, 7; nontariff, 243; trade, 20, 47

Beverages, 89, 320, 400, 404; alcoholic, 407, 415, 420, 423, 516

Biro Pusat Statistik (BPS), 181, 186, 188, 192, 194, 211–12

Black market, 190, 202

Blue-collar workers, 103, 153, 155–57, 163, 166, 168, 212, 518

Board of Investment, 407, 409, 415, 430

Bogotá, Colombia, 144–45

Bonus Ekspor (export bonus), 195

Bonus export voucher schemes, 295, 302, 308–12, 325

Borrowing: domestic capital, 374–75; external, 442; foreign, 351, 371, 374–75; long-term, 245; private, 369